AMERICAN
INDEPENDENCE

AMERICAN INDEPENDENCE

From *Common Sense* to the *Declaration*

BENJAMIN PONDER

ESTATE FOUR PUBLISHERS
ESTATEFOUR.COM

© 2010 by Benjamin Ponder
All rights reserved

Printed in the United States of America

Visit our Web site: www.estatefour.com

Library of Congress Cataloging-in-Publication Data is available.

ISBN 978-0-615-35182-7

FOR AMY,
my beloved

Acknowledgments

The shortcomings of this book are of my own manufacture, but I cannot say the same of the study's strong suits. The robust support of the following individuals and organizations was instrumental to the development of this work:

David Zarefsky, Timothy Breen, Betsy Erkkila, Robert Hariman, Luke and Emily Anderson, John and Dana Kim, Dave and Rachel Hansen, Joe and Kari Lamancusa, Tom and Shana Christian, Dan and Barb Beitz, Tom and Jennifer Noble, David and Nary Houcque, Ken and Tammy Shull, Lee Huebner, Irv Rein, Dilip Gaonkar, Keith Topper, Angela Ray, the late Scott Deatherage, Tom Goodnight, the late Mike Leff, John Kirby, the late Tom Farrell, Tom Frentz and the late Janice Rushing, David Davidson, Andy Wehrman, James Coltrain, David Keenan, Vicki Brantly, Susan Bergman, Eugene Peterson, Paul Stevens, Elton Conrady, Kerim Zagra, David Wei, Andrew Wachtel, Simon Greenwold, Jenny Mann, Guy Ortolano, Rana Ozbal, John Pham, Kwame Onoma, Sean Murphy, Chris Campbell, Alan Brothers, Rhiannon Stephens, Kristen Syrett, Carmen Niekrasz, Paul Cadden-Zimansky, Ben Chen, Yaël Katz, Tomasz Strzalecki, Tobin Miller-Shearer, Lee Seymour, Dan Fitzmeier, Chris Lundberg, Brett Ommen, Randy Iden, Leslie Harris, Ebony Utley, Liz Benacka, Karin Lehnardt, Cindy Koenig, Karen Kelly, Rita Lutz, Mary Pat Doyle, Maggie Wildman, Pat Mann, Lesley Perry, James Ettema, Peter Miller, Henry Bienen, the Library Company of Philadelphia (especially Jim Green, Connie King, and Phil Lapsansky), the American Philosophical Society (especially Roy Goodman and J.J. Ahern), the Clements Library at the University of Michigan (especially Don Wilcox and Barbara DeWolfe), the University of Pennsylvania Archives (especially Director Mark F. Lloyd), the Northwestern University Library (especially Special Collections Librarian Scott Krafft, Special Collections Curator Russell Maylone, and Librarian Ronald Sims of the Galter Health Sciences Library), and the Fort Dearborn Chapter of the Daughters of the American Revolution.

And, finally, I offer my deepest gratitude to my family:

To my parents, Danny and Nell Ponder, and my parents-in-law, Robert and Adele Berry, for their boundless support, love, and understanding.

To my children, Ava, Elise, Lincoln, and Whit, who have placed my work and research in perspective time and time again. They bring unspeakable joy to their daddy's heart.

To my dearest Amy, who has endured much and has walked with me every step of this long journey. I marvel at you, value you above all others, and love you with my whole heart.

Table of Contents

A Chronology of Key Events   xv

Abbreviations   xxiii

Preface: From Reconciliation to Revolution   xxv
    The Difference of One Year
    Aims of the Study
    Theoretical Influences and the Trajectory of Method
    The Difference of Six Months

Chapter One: Natural Republicanism

    PART ONE: TAXATION AND PROTEST   2
        Stamped Out
        Distant Dissent

    PART TWO: FROM LONDON TO LEXINGTON   5
        Transatlantic Connection
        The Evolution of a Revolutionary

    PART THREE: PAMPHLET CULTURE   8
        The Distinctive Literature of the Revolution
        The Distinctive Rhetoric of the Revolution

    PART FOUR: THE PROBLEM WITH MONOREPUBLICANISM   13
        Republicanism in 1776
        The Least Worst Option
        Two Party System
        American Republicanisms

    PART FIVE: THE LOCKEAN MOMENT   20
        An Independent Whig
        An Appeal to Heaven
        The United States of Nature and War

    PART SIX: UNTANGLING THE ROOTS OF RADICALISM   25
        Radical Whigs
        Orthodox Radicalism

PART SEVEN: TOWARDS A REPRESENTATIVE DEMOCRACY 28
    Natural Representation
    Revolution in Style

Chapter Two: Kindling Controversy

PART ONE: A CATALYTIC COMPOSITION 37
    A Desperate Shortage
    Notes on the State of America
    Present Transactions

PART TWO: PAPER AND INK 44
    To the Press
    Media Res Publica
    Provincial Printing
    The Political Role of Print Culture

PART THREE: A PROMOTER OF PRINT 50
    Robert Bell, Bookseller
    Manufacture of Opinion
    A Material Scarcity
    Liberty of the Press
    The Reading Publics

PART FOUR: THE PUBLISHING SCANDAL 60
    The Price of Success
    Cause Célèbre
    Ink Wrestling
    A Matter of Shillings and Pence

PART FIVE: PROVEDORES 69
    Sentimental Reason

Chapter Three: Reformation and Regicide

PART ONE: UNIVERSAL REFORMATION 79
    Royal Culture
    A Protestant Revolution
    Reason and Demystification

PART TWO: POPERY OF GOVERNMENT 85
    Judging Monarchy
    The Pope of England

PART THREE: PREACHING INDEPENDENCE   88
    Scriptural Resemblance
    Colonial Unison
    Political Conversion

PART FOUR: HERETICAL QUAKERS   95
    The "Epistle" and Religious Toryism

PART FIVE: THE PERSISTENT WILKES & UNANSWERED PRAYERS
    Junius, Wilkes, and Liberty   99
    Wilkes Weary
    Political Supplications
    Petition and Proclamation

PART SIX: DETHRONING THE SOVEREIGN   109
    Royal Character
    The Speech of Separation
    Heredity and the Hessians
    Signing the Petition of Independence
    King of America
    Felling Monarchy

Chapter Four: Mechanics of a Revolution

PART ONE: NATURAL PHILOSOPHY   127
    Rational Mechanics
    Useful Knowledge
    Transit of Venus and Scientific Culture

PART TWO: A SCIENTIFIC TREATISE   132
    Paine's First Audience
    The Franklin Factor
    Paine and Science
    Baconian Induction and Newtonian Mechanics

PART THREE: LECTURES AND DEMONSTRATIONS   141
    Secondary Education
    Popular Newtonianism in England
    Machinery, Causation, and Motion
    The Radical Implications of Popular Science

PART FOUR: EXPERIMENTAL PROSODY   156
    Scientific Language
    Rhetorical Poetry
    Solving for Time

Chapter Five: Time and the Decision for Independence

PART ONE: THE CRAFTSMANSHIP OF TIME   171
    An American Newton
    A Rural Mechanic
    Causality and Temporality

PART TWO: *CHRONOS*   180
    Clock Time and the Potts-Pryor Astronomical Clock
    Dismantling and Reconstructing Time
    History and Expediency

PART THREE: *KAIROS*   187
    Seasonal Time and Father Abraham's Almanac
    Open Season
    Popular History

PART FOUR: *EPOS*   197
    Epic Time and the Norriton Observation of the Transit of Venus
    Lenses and Mirrors
    The Experience of Textual Time

PART FIVE: *KRISIS*   209
    Crisis Time and the Rittenhouse Orrery
    Space and Time Machine
    Textual Orrery
    Declaring Crisis

PART SIX: THE TIME IS NOW   222
    No Time Like the Present
    Temporal Virtue

Chapter Six: Declaration of Independents

PART ONE: DODGING BULLETS   238
    Divided by the Sword
    Massachusetts and *Common Sense*

PART TWO: COLONIAL READING   244
    American Literacy
    A Community of Readers

PART THREE: MARKETPLACE OF DISCOURSE   251
    Economies of Print
    Networked Printers
    Continental Congress: Gathering and Scattering

PART FOUR: FRONT LINES   264
    A General's Perspective
    Something Worth Fighting For
    The End of Britishness

Chapter Seven: *Common Sense* and Independence

PART ONE: TEXT AND MOVEMENT   281
    Reception and Progress
    An Uncommon Sensation

PART TWO: NEW YORK OR VIRGINIA   286
    New York and *Common Sense*
    Virginia and *Common Sense*
    New York and the Spirit of '87
    Virginia and Independence
    The Virginia Resolves and the Spirit of '76
    Richard Henry Lee and the Gauntlet of Independence

PART THREE: AMERICAN CONTROVERSY   304
    From Text to Discourse
    Finally, a Pamphlet Challenge
    The Circulation of Colonial Newspapers
    Philadelphia Flashpoint
    Propaganda and Critique
    Echoes of *Common Sense*
    Realizing Independence

Chapter Eight: Transatlantic Resistance

PART ONE: LOYALIST WHIGS AND PATRIOTIC TORIES   326
    The Gamble of Loyalism
    Maryland's Resistance
    Redefining Whig and Tory
    A Rational Choice

PART TWO: BRITISH COMMON SENSE   339
    A Useful Distraction
    A Gross Misunderstanding
    Almon's Hiatuses

PART THREE: FOG OF LOYALTY   356
    Reconciliation or Independence
    The Other Franklin and an Unwelcome Innuendo

Chapter Nine: A Conflict of Interest

PART ONE: DIVIDED LOYALTIES	365
Irreconcilable Differences	
PART TWO: SENTIMENTAL DEPENDENCE	367
Out of Edenton	
Henry Laurens and the Inner Conflict of Separation	
PART THREE: MERCANTILE INTEREST	372
Interest and Disinterest	
Class Consciousness	
Loyal Merchants	
PART FOUR: CONSTITUTIONAL OPPOSITION	379
An Excess of Moderation	
PART FIVE: CONFLICTED CLERGY	385
Ministers of the Administration	
Textual Sabotage	
No Man Can Serve Two Masters	
PART SIX: TREATING WITH BARBARIANS	393
Waiting for Commissioners, or: The Hessians are Coming	

Chapter Ten: A War of Words

PART ONE: DUELLING PENS	401
A Defining Debate	
A Man of Conflict	
PART TWO: SPEAKING FOR MONTGOMERY	404
Remembering the General	
William Smith's *Oration*	
Thomas Paine's *Dialogue*	
PART THREE: COMMISSIONERS AND COMMITTEES	410
Loyal Moderation	
Cassandra's First and Cato's Second	
The Constitutions of the People	
Cato versus Conventions and *Common Sense*	
Cassandra's Final Parry and Thrust	
PART FOUR: THE BATTLEGROUND OF PRINT	424
Cato on Alliances and Government	
The Forester Enters the Fray	
Identity, Causality, and Sentiment	

At the Point of the Pen
Cato's Grand Finale
Post Mortem on the Election
An Unfair Advantage
The Object of Attack
The Conclusion of Cato

Chapter 11: Bicameral Philadelphia

PART ONE: JOHN ADAMS'S TWO HOUSES 455
    John Adams and *Common Sense*
    John Adams and Bicameralism

PART TWO: PHILADELPHIA'S TWO HOUSES 461
    Pennsylvania State House and Government
    Coffee Houses in British Culture
    London Coffee House and Society
    Coffee House Argument

PART THREE: THE LOCUS OF SOVEREIGNTY 473
    Society and Government
    The Upheaval of Political Authority
    The Causes and Necessity of Taking up Sovereignty
    The People of America

PART FOUR: RECONCILIATION'S LAST GASP 483
    An Unpopular Assembly
    Electoral Compromise
    The First of May

PART FIVE: CIRCUMVENTING THE CONSTITUTION 490
    The Difference of Two Weeks
    Protest and Remonstrance
    Evacuating Philadelphia

PART SIX: DESTRUCTION OF THE INSTRUCTIONS 497
    Declaration of Indecision
    The Philadelphia Committee of Independence
    Battalion Resolutions
    Provincial Conference of Committees
    A House Undivided

Chapter Twelve: The American Mind

PART ONE: TEXTUALITY AND SOVEREIGNTY   516
    A Journey from Philadelphia
    A Journey to Philadelphia

PART TWO: CONTINENTAL CONGRESS AT THE HELM   520
    A New Source of Authority
    Appealing to the Constitution
    Inching into Independence
    Instructing the Instructors
    Resolution and Preamble

PART THREE: THE DRAMA UNFOLDS   531
    Casting the Die
    The Bustle of June
    Drafting Original Equality
    The Vote for Independence
    The Vote for the *Declaration*
    Subscribing their Lives

PART FOUR: PUBLIC OPINION AND *COMMON SENSE*   542
    About Face
    Problem Opinion
    Constitutional Criticism
    A Common Identity

Appendix   554
    The Text of *Common Sense*

Bibliography   611

Index   650

A Chronology of Key Events
Relating to *Common Sense* and Independence

June 13, 1774
Parliament passes the Quebec Act

June 22, 1774
Quebec Act receives the assent of King George III

September 5, 1774
First Continental Congress convenes in Philadelphia

September 30, 1774
Benjamin Franklin writes two "letters of introduction" for Thomas Paine, an Englishman about to set sail for America

October 26, 1774
Continental Congress sends "Appeal to the Inhabitants of Quebec"

November 30, 1774
Thomas Paine arrives in Philadelphia from England aboard the *London Packet*

December 1, 1774
American Non-importation Agreement takes effect

February 7, 1775
Parliament declares the Colonies in a state of rebellion

April 19, 1775
Battle of Lexington and Concord (Massachusetts)

May 1, 1775
Quebec Act takes effect

May 10, 1775
Second Continental Congress convenes in Philadelphia

May 29, 1775
News of Lexington and Concord reaches England

June 17, 1775
Battle of Bunker Hill outside of Boston

July 6, 1775
Declaration of the Causes and Necessity of Taking up Arms published by the Continental Congress

July 8, 1775
"Olive Branch" Petition approved, published, and sent by the Continental Congress to King George III

August 23, 1775
King George III proclaims the American colonies to be in open rebellion

September 1, 1775
Richard Penn presents the "Olive Branch" Petition to the Earl of Dartmouth on behalf of the Continental Congress

September 10, 1775
American Non-exportation Agreement takes effect

September–December 1775
Paine composes *Common Sense*

October 18, 1775
British siege and burning of Falmouth in New England [now Portland, Maine]

October 26, 1775
King George III opens parliamentary session with a speech highly critical of the American "rebellion"

October 31, 1775
News reaches Philadelphia of George III's proclamation of rebellion from August

November 7, 1775
Lord Dunmore, exiled governor of Virginia, issues proclamation freeing Virginia slaves who agree to fight the American rebels

November 9, 1775
George III's August proclamation published in Philadelphia

November 9, 1775
Pennsylvania Assembly instructs its delegates in Continental Congress to reject all measures tending toward independence

December 6, 1775
Continental Congress publishes a reply to the king's proclamation

December 22, 1775
Prohibitory Act, excluding all Americans from protection of the Crown and closing all American ports, passed in Parliament

December 31, 1775
Continental Army fails to seize Quebec City and General Richard Montgomery is killed in battle

January 1, 1776
British siege and burning of Norfolk, Virginia

January 8, 1776
King's speech opening Parliament arrives in Philadelphia via New York

January 9, 1776
Common Sense published by Robert Bell

January 9, 1776
King's October 26 speech published in Philadelphia

January 17, 1776
News of General Montgomery's death and defeat at Quebec reaches Philadelphia

January 27, 1776
Bell publishes a second edition of *Common Sense*

February 14, 1776
A new, expanded edition of *Common Sense* published in Philadelphia by William and Thomas Bradford

February 18, 1776
Continental Congress places an embargo on all exports to Britain and the British West Indies

February 19, 1776
William Smith, Provost of the College of Philadelphia, delivers an oration in memory of General Montgomery to Continental Congress

February 19, 1776
Paine leaves Philadelphia to visit New York

February 23, 1776
Gesunde Bernunft, the German edition of *Common Sense*, published in Philadelphia

February 27, 1776
Copies of the Prohibitory Act arrive in Philadelphia

February 27, 1776
Battle of Moore's Creek Bridge between loyalists and patriots in North Carolina

March 1, 1776
Prohibitory Act takes effect

March 2, 1776
Committee of Secret Correspondence instructs Silas Deane to negotiate for French aid

March 4, 1776
William Smith's *Oration in Memory of General Montgomery* published in Philadelphia by John Dunlap

March 9, 1776
First letter of "Cassandra" [James Cannon] appears in the *Pennsylvania Evening Post* (continued in multiple papers through May 1, 1776)

March 11, 1776
Royal proclamation authorizing the seizure of American "prizes" published in Philadelphia

March 11, 1776
First of eight letters "To the People of Pennsylvania" by "Cato" [William Smith] appears in the *Pennsylvania Packet* (continued in multiple papers through April 29, 1776)

March 13, 1776
Plain Truth by "Candidus" [James Chalmers] published in Philadelphia by Robert Bell

March 14, 1776
Continental Congress votes to disarm all loyalists

March 14, 1776
House of Lords debates and defeats a conciliatory motion introduced by the Duke of Grafton

March 17, 1776
British troops evacuate Boston

March 18, 1776
The Deceiver Unmasked by "A Loyal American" [Charles Inglis] published in New York by Samuel Loudon

March 19, 1776
New York Sons of Liberty destroy entire Loudon edition of *The Deceiver Unmasked*

March 22, 1776
The City of London submits a petition to the king supporting the Americans

March 26, 1776
South Carolina adopts a new constitution

April 1, 1776
First of four letters "To Cato" by "The Forester" [Thomas Paine] printed in the *Pennsylvania Packet* (continued in multiple papers through May 20, 1776)

April 6, 1776
Congress opens American ports to trade with all nations except Britain

April 8, 1776
Excerpts of *Common Sense* first reprinted in London newspapers

April 12, 1776
"Halifax Resolves" supporting independence passed by North Carolina Provincial Congress

April 22, 1776
Thoughts on Government [by John Adams] published in Philadelphia

May 1, 1776
Closely contested Philadelphia election carried by Moderate Party

May 8, 1776
Bell issues Second Edition of *Plain Truth*

May 10, 1776
Congress receives confirmation of intelligence that Hessian troops are coming to America

May 10, 1776
Congress passes a resolution instructing every colony to form new governments

May 15, 1776
Congress adds preamble to resolution of May 10

May 15, 1776
Virginia passes resolution calling on Congress to vote independence

May 15, 1776
Hessian troops embark for America

May 17, 1776
America observes Day of Fasting and Prayer

May 20, 1776
Philadelphia town meeting demands that the Pennsylvania Assembly cease functioning

May 27, 1776
"Virginia Resolves" and "Halifax Resolves" lain before Continental Congress

May 28, 1776
Long extracts of *Common Sense* printed in John Almon's *Evening Post* (continued in multiple London newspapers through June 13, 1776)

May 29, 1776
The True Interest of America Impartially Stated by "An American" [Charles Inglis] (edited reprint of *The Deceiver Unmasked*) published in Philadelphia

June 5, 1776
Reply of George III to a "Humble Address and Petition" of the Lord Mayor, Aldermen, and Common Council of the city of London (dated March 22, 1776) published in Philadelphia

June 5, 1776
Pennsylvania Assembly appoints committee to draw up new instructions concerning independence

June 7, 1776
Richard Henry Lee introduces a resolution on independence to the Continental Congress

June 8, 1776
Pennsylvania Assembly submits new instructions to delegates removing prior restriction but not providing positive instruction

June 11, 1776
Continental Congress appoints a draft committee to compose a declaration of independence

June 12, 1776
Continental Congress appoints a confederation committee and a treaty committee and adjourns until July 1

June 12, 1776
Virginia adopts a "Declaration of Rights" drafted by George Mason

June 14, 1776
Pennsylvania Assembly adjourns after a three week session

June 14, 1776
Connecticut Assembly approves positive instructions for its delegates

June 15, 1776
New Hampshire Assembly urges a vote for independence

June 19, 1776
Pennsylvania Provincial Conference begins

June 22, 1776
New Jersey Provincial Congress authorizes its delegates to vote for independence

June 24, 1776
Pennsylvania Provincial Conference submits new instructions for delegates in Continental Congress

June 25, 1776
Pennsylvania Provincial Conference ends

July 1, 1776
Continental Congress reconvenes and hears new instructions for Maryland delegates

July 1–4, 1776
Continental Congress debates the Jefferson's draft of a declaration of independence

July 4, 1776
Continental Congress "unanimously" approves declaration

July 7, 1776
Silas Deane arrives in Paris to negotiate with France

July 8, 1776
Declaration of Independence published and read publicly in Philadelphia

July 9, 1776
New York Assembly approves of independence

July–September 1776
Declaration of Independence published and proclaimed in other states

July 12, 1776
Continental Congress opens debate on draft of articles of confederation and perpetual union

July 15, 1776
Pennsylvania's Constitutional Convention convenes

August 2, 1776
Congressional delegates begin signing the *Declaration of Independence*

Abbreviations
Used in Notes and Bibliography

NYG	*The New York Gazette; and the Weekly Mercury*
NYJ	*The New-York Journal; or, The General Advertiser*
PEP	*The Pennsylvania Evening Post*
PM	*The Pennsylvania Magazine; or, American Monthly Museum*
PG	*The Pennsylvania Gazette*
PJ	*The Pennsylvania Journal; and the Weekly Advertiser*
PL	*The Pennsylvania Ledger; or the Virginia, Maryland, Pennsylvania, & New-Jersey Weekly Advertiser*
DPP	*Dunlap's Pennsylvania Packet, or, The General Advertiser*
PS	*Henrich Miller's Pennsylvanischer Staatsbote*
CW	*The Complete Writings of Thomas Paine*, 2 vols. (Philip S. Foner, ed.)
CS	*Common Sense*
AC	*American Crisis*
RM	*Rights of Man*
AR	*Age of Reason*
AA	Abigail Adams
AL	Arthur Lee
BF	Benjamin Franklin
BR	Benjamin Rush
CCC	Charles Carroll of Carrollton (son, Maryland delegate to Continental Congress)
CCA	Charles Carroll of Annapolis (father)
DR	David Rittenhouse
GM	George Mason
GW	George Washington
HL	Henry Laurens
JA	John Adams
KGIII	King George III
LN	Lord North
NG	Nathanael Greene
RHL	Richard Henry Lee
RS	Richard Smith
TJ	Thomas Jefferson
TP	Thomas Paine
SA	Samuel Adams

WL   William Lee
WS   William Smith

AAS   American Antiquarian Society
BL   British Library
APS   American Philosophical Society
HL   Houghton Library, Harvard University
HSP   Historical Society of Pennsylvania
LCP   Library Company of Philadelphia
MHS   Massachusetts Historical Society
NL   Newberry Library
NUL   Northwestern University Library
NYHS New York Historical Society
UPA   University of Pennsylvania Archives

LDC   *Letters of Delegates to Congress, 1774-1789* (Paul H. Smith, 1976-2000)
JCC(A) *Journals of the Continental Congress* (Robert Aitken, 1777)
JCC(F) *Journals of the Continental Congress* (Worthington Chauncey Ford, 1906)

Preface

From Reconciliation to Revolution

The minds of the inhabitants were overcast with fears, and tossed in a tumult of uncertainty. Their resolution was fixed never to submit to the claims of the British parliament, but how to extricate themselves from surrounding difficulties was a question that embarrassed their wisest politicians. While they were in this state of feverish anxiety, a pamphlet, under the signature of *Common Sense*, written by Mr. Thomas Paine, made its appearance. It proved the necessity, the advantages, and practicability of independence. It satisfied a great majority of the people that it was their true interest immediately to cut the Gordian knot which bound the American colonies to Great-Britain, and to open their commerce as an independent people, to all the nations of the world. Nothing could be better timed than this performance. It found the colonists greatly exasperated against the mother country, most thoroughly alarmed for their liberties, and disposed to do and suffer every thing that bid fairest for their establishment. In unison with the feelings and sentiments of the people, it produced astonishing effects. It was read by almost every American, and in conjunction with the cruel policy of Great-Britain, was by the direction of Providence, instrumental in effecting an unexampled unanimity in favor of independence. The decisive genius of Christopher Gadsden in the south, and of John Adams in the north, at a much earlier day, might have desired the complete separation of America from Great-Britain—but till the year 1776—the rejection of the second petition of congress—and the appearance of Mr. Paine's pamphlet—a reconciliation with the mother country was the unanimous wish of almost every other American.

David Ramsay
The History of South-Carolina (1809)

Let any man look at the position America was in at the time I first took up the subject, and published *Common Sense*, which was but a few months before the *Declaration of Independence*; an army of thirty thousand men coming out against her, besides those which were already here, and she without either an object or a system; fighting, she scarcely knew for what, and which, if she could have obtained, would have done her no good. She had not a day to spare in bringing about the only thing which could save her. A REVOLUTION, yet no one measure was taken to promote it, and many were used to prevent it; and had independence not been declared at the time it was, I cannot see any time in which it could have been declared, as the train of ill-successes which followed the affair of Long Island left no future opportunity.

Thomas Paine to Messrs. Deane, Jay, and Gérard
1779

The Difference of One Year

On July 8, 1775, the Second Continental Congress approved and published a petition, directed to King George III of Great Britain and referred to by the colonists as the "Olive Branch." The petition addressed the king with a deferential formality typical of royal culture and declared the American colonists to be "attached to your Majesty's person, family, and government, with all devotion that principle and affection can inspire."[1] Exactly one year later, on July 8, 1776, the Continental Congress's *Declaration of Independence* was first read publicly in Philadelphia and published in the *Pennsylvania Evening Post*. Thomas Jefferson's famed composition had much to say about the "present King of Great Britain" to whom the colonists had repeatedly declared their affection and attachment. But this new declaration, addressed "to a candid world," took a markedly different tone. Written by Jefferson in June and approved by the Continental Congress on July 4, the *Declaration of Independence* levied eighteen distinct charges, an itemized "long train of abuses and usurpations," perpetrated by the active agency of the king. The "United Colonies" had become "Free and Independent States," announced the Continental Congress, and the Americans, now "absolved from all allegiance to the British crown," were totally free from "all political connection" to Britain.

How was the longsuffering American affection for Great Britain and its king, still present in July 1775, transformed into the vehement disaffection evident in July 1776? This is a complicated question that admits of no simple answers. The multiplicitous causes stretched back decades and involved economic, political, religious, and military concerns on both sides of the Atlantic. We can acknowledge the longitudinal complexity and gradual degeneration of British-American relations, though, without forgetting that the glacial movement of imperial affairs was still subject to periodic avalanches. American protest against the Stamp Act, the Tea Act, and the Quebec Act were three of the most prominent periods of quickened resistance against what the colonists perceived to be schemes of parliamentary subjugation. American frustration with British rule spiked dozens of times in the thirteen years prior to 1776, but—Bostonians being the main exception—the colonists were remarkable for their rapid return to quiescence. When accused by parliament or the king of promoting nefarious schemes, colonial leaders fell over themselves to prove their unshakable allegiance to "the mother country." The American colonies prior to 1776 were not just dependent upon Britain in a political and economic sense; in their affairs they exhibited an emotional codependence on Britain, a pathetic, cyclical tug of war between adoration and mortification with no resolution in sight. Even after the Battle of Lexington and Concord on April 19, 1775, which signaled the start of open warfare, the American colonies scurried into provincial assemblies and to the Continental Congress to issue petitions and instructions reinforcing their unfailing loyalty to Britain. While the colonies waited for a favorable reply to their petitions, news reached America in November 1775 that the king had proclaimed them to be in a traitorous state of "open and avowed rebellion." Though the king indicated his commitment to "suppress such rebellion" at any cost, the vast majority of American colonists, in their private correspondence as well as in any public pronouncements, held fast to the hope of restored consanguinity.

As 1775 rolled into 1776, American politics remained stuck in the quagmire of rebellious affection. The British government absolutely refused to hear the grievances of hypocritical Americans who dared hold a petition in one hand and a musket in the other. The Americans, desperate to be treated as British subjects of equal rank with Englishmen, refused to submit to military coercion and, therefore, felt compelled to defend themselves. Pitched pleas for conciliation from the Americans sounded shrill to the British ministry and to a majority in parliament, whose unshakable perception of American disloyalty found conspiratorial evidence of treason in every affirmation of allegiance.

All of this political wheel-spinning would come to an end in July 1776 after six full months of public convulsions in every American colony. On November 9, 1775, the conservative Pennsylvania Assembly had "strictly" enjoined its delegates in Continental Congress to "dissent from and utterly reject any propositions" that might "cause or lead to a separation from our mother country," but by June 14, 1776, the same body was forced to rescind its restrictive instructions, because, as they put it, "The Situation of public Affairs is since so greatly altered."[2] The main thing that had changed between November 1775 and June 1776 was American public opinion.

Aims of the Study

This book is a study of the sea change in American public opinion during the first half of 1776. To claim that the Americans shifted from a dogged determination to be reconciled with Britain to a bold assertion of their political independence is nothing novel. What I am attempting to show here is precisely how it happened.

Between January and June of 1776, the most fundamental shift in the history of American public opinion propelled thirteen disaffected colonies, rebellious in their actions but loyal in their hearts, into a union of sovereign republican states at war with the British Empire. This decision was the culmination of a public controversy over independence that was ignited in January 1776 by Thomas Paine's pamphlet *Common Sense* and propelled throughout the spring and early summer of that year by the response of readers and writers to the agendas, vocabularies, and challenges of *Common Sense*. One cannot understand the Americans' decision to declare independence without first understanding the catalytic power of the independence controversy's touchstone text.

In this study, I have sought to answer the following interrelated questions:

1) How did Thomas Paine write, and how did colonial Americans read and respond to *Common Sense*?

2) How and why did the American colonies decide to declare their political independence?

The process of answering these questions has required my imaginative engagement with the cultures and discourses of the American colonies in early 1776 and, moreover, has demanded my entrance into the textual world of *Common Sense*. Thomas Paine is the subject of a wide-ranging, long-lived, and still-robust literature, and yet his first major pamphlet, *Common Sense*, remains a remarkably understudied text.[3]

I began my research with the objective of remedying this deficiency in text-centric scholarship on *Common Sense*, and so I set out to write a concise explication of Paine's pamphlet. I soon realized, however, that *Common Sense*, as a work of political rhetoric, could not be extricated from its historical context without losing its essential import. In other words, *Common Sense* cannot be fully understood apart from the movement it sparked, and the decision for independence cannot be fully understood without *Common Sense*. I have attempted, therefore, to perform a dialogical analysis of *Common Sense* and American independence that combines a careful attention to text, discourse, and history. By the end of the book, I hope to have demonstrated how *Common Sense* and the vigorous debate over independence during the first half of 1776 reseated political legitimacy and legal sovereignty in America, effectively replacing the "ancient" authority of the British Constitution with the newborn force of American public opinion.

Theoretical Influences and the Trajectory of Method

Rather than attempting to apply a single theoretical template to the text and context of *Common Sense*, I have cherry-picked elements from several different fields within the humanities. My goal in this hybridized model is to provide a comprehensive account of a complex political text through its full rhetorical lifecycle from private composition to public decision—in short, a textual biography. Though I have not attempted here to emulate any other scholar-writer, I consider Garry Wills's *Lincoln at Gettysburg: The Words that Remade America* (1992) and James Boulton's *The Language and Politics in the Age of Wilkes and Burke* (1963) to be the closest methodological cousins of this study. Wills's book is a study of *text* and *composition*, and Boulton's is an exposition of *discourse* and *controversy*. I have attempted in this book to weave these analytical foci—composition and controversy, text and discourse—into a seamless narrative tapestry.

Beyond what is evident from a scan of the bibliography, a handful of other individuals deserve special mention as influences upon the theoretical approach of this work. I first learned the ropes of exegesis and hermeneutics as a seminarian, but Michael Leff has been an able mentor for me in the practice of close reading as it applies to political texts. Ludwig Wittgenstein, John Austin, and John Searle, the pioneers of speech-act theory and ordinary language philosophy, have reminded me of the motive power of common speech, of the reality that words can *do*. Before the paint had dried on speech-act theory, Quentin Skinner and John Pocock began applying it to the political thought of the Renaissance and early modernity: their efforts at tracing upstream the ideological sources of discourse were an early inspiration for this study. Eric Havelock, Walter Ong, and Marshall McLuhan have been my guides in traversing the epochal shifts between orality and literacy (and back again). Additionally, the "persona" studies of Edwin Black, Philip Wander, Charles Morris, and others in the discipline of rhetorical studies have attuned me to the stratified archaeology of audiences. Finally, Benedict Anderson and Michael Warner germinated my views on the constitutive power of texts and the textual formation of publics.[4] I think of these distinguished scholars as the architects of the intellectual milieu within which this study operates, rather than as the engineers of my analytical instrumentation. Individually and collectively, their work has spurred, focused, and inspired my thoughts on method, even though I have avoided any direct cooptation of their theoretical formulae.

The interpretive mentality of this study, as distinct from its methodological framework, bears a close resemblance to an unlikely model: John McPhee's *Annals of the Former World* (1998), a survey of geological history and American culture through the lens of field geologists analyzing road cuts along Interstate 80 between New Jersey and San Francisco. At first glance, it would be difficult to imagine a research topic and methodology farther afield from a book on *Common Sense* and the American Revolution, but McPhee's descriptive framework was a formative influence upon this study. If McPhee could illustrate billions of years in the life of our planet by tracing the 40th parallel of latitude across the United States—I reasoned as I was formulating my initial research questions—then I was not out-of-line in my attempt to explain the essence of the American Revolution by tracing the path of *Common Sense* through the colonies in early 1776.

I have received immense benefit as a researcher from my exposure to diverse disciplinary approaches, and I have written this book with a view towards strengthening the methodological bridges that connect the humanistic disciplines. Rhetorical studies, the primary disciplinary perspective from which I write, posits that the methodologies of the literary critic and the historian are complementary. Each chapter of this study contains interwoven strands of interpretive and historical analysis, though I have tended to foreground the interpretive in the first half of the book and the historical in the second. The interpretive elements of the study reveal the interior dynamics of textual agency—the effect of a text upon readers—while the historical elements of the study reveal the exterior kinetics of textual causality—the effect of a text (through its readers) upon events. Thus, a major methodological goal of this study is the integration of interpretation and history, text and context, and agency and causality into a consonant analytical method.

The illusive familiarity of my research subject has also shaped my method. It is easy to forget that the values, language, and customs of early America were very different from our own, but during the course of my research and writing, I have often been reminded that I am engaged in an act of cross-cultural communication. A basic objective of my research, then, has been to dislodge my readers' presumption of familiarity with the world of the "founding fathers" and to replace that presumption with a more robust understanding of revolutionary political culture. To foster that enriched understanding, I have set out to replicate the *experience of* the American Revolution from the perspective of its first-hand participants rather than to win an *argument about* the American Revolution between second-hand critics. Because I am attempting to decode a culture over two centuries removed from my audience, my narrative task in this study—to communicate the textual and lived experience of American colonists during the first half of 1776—is fundamentally an act of translation. My success as a translator will be judged by how well a twenty-first century reader grasps, by the end of the study, the meanings of each of the following core concepts from an eighteenth-century perspective:

Chapter One: Representation
Chapter Two: Publication
Chapter Three: Religion
Chapter Four: Science
Chapter Five: Temporality
Chapter Six: Reading
Chapter Seven: Circulation
Chapter Eight: Loyalism
Chapter Nine: Interest
Chapter Ten: Discourse

Chapter Eleven: Sovereignty
Chapter Twelve: Constitution

Each of these concepts is a key to unlocking the effect of *Common Sense* upon late colonial political culture, but I must make clear that among these concepts, there is no master key. No serious engagement with the text of *Common Sense* and no earnest attempt to describe its rhetorical force can avoid the complexity and concurrence of events in colonial America during the first half of 1776. Paine's pamphlet worked on many different levels with many different readers in many different places—all at about the same time. The American colonists followed a winding path from *Common Sense* to the *Declaration of Independence*, and I have in this study eschewed the artificial straightening of their collective experience. From the first chapter to the last, I have highlighted the curious intersections of relationships, the recurring topographies of language, and the parallel logics of decision that coalesced into the nonlinear movement for American independence. *Common Sense* was a grab bag of pro-independence images, connotations, innuendoes, slanders, and rationales, and the text's phenomenal success in forging political unity was attributable, in part, to its calculated disarray. Paine's identificatory rhetorical style invited colonial readers to find *within* the text of *Common Sense* their own reasons for independence.

The Difference of Six Months

I began this preface with an account of the shift that happened in the Continental Congress in the span of a year. Before I commence in earnest my study of *Common Sense* and independence, it will be helpful to relay another, more localized and abbreviated instance of the same phenomenon. I cannot overstress at the outset of my analysis the unanimity with which the American colonies opposed independence at the end of 1775 and the beginning of 1776. For example, at a town meeting in Portsmouth, New Hampshire, on December 25, 1775, the assembled electors left no doubt concerning their support for independence. They unanimously approved instructions to their delegates in the New Hampshire Provincial Congress who were preparing to frame a new colonial government. The townsfolk urged "the greatest caution, calmness, and deliberation" in the measure, and they stressed the temporary nature of their government. According to the instructions,

> We are of opinion that the present times are too unsettled, to admit of perfecting a form stable and permanent, and that to attempt it *now*, would injure us, by furnishing our enemies in Great-Britain, with arguments to persuade the good people there that we are *aiming at independency*, which we *totally disavow*. We should therefore prefer the

government of the [Provincial] Congress, till God in his Providence, shall afford us quieter times.

The residents of Portsmouth fully expected "quieter times" to arrive soon. They enjoined their delegates to the provincial congress, "Should a *plan of accommodation* be proposed, the completion of which will terminate in an honorable settlement of the present dispute, *you give your assent* thereto."⁵

The New Hampshire Provincial Congress, meeting in Exeter on January 5, 1776, gathered because they had no other choice: there was no functioning government in the colony.⁶ Circumstances were dragging them by the wrist toward independence. The "sudden and abrupt departure" of the New Hampshire governor and his council had left the colony "destitute of legislation," and the closure of the criminal courts had made "the lives and properties of the honest people of this colony" suddenly "liable to the machinations and evil designs of wicked men." The New Hampshire Provincial Congress thus concluded that they had been "reduced to the necessity of establishing a Form of Government, to continue during the present unhappy and unnatural contest with Great-Britain." Even as they were setting up an independent form of government, they were simultaneously "protesting and declaring that we never sought to throw off our *dependence* upon Great-Britain, but felt ourselves happy under her *protection*, whilst we could enjoy our constitutional rights and privileges." The delegates promised, "We shall *rejoice* if such a *reconciliation* between us and our parent state can be effected, as shall be approved by the Continental Congress, in whose prudence and wisdom *we confide*."⁷

New Hampshire was strictly opposed to independence at the beginning of 1776. Six months later, though, the same colonists cheered the *Declaration of Independence* as "it was published by beat of drum in all the shire towns of New-Hampshire." According to the Reverend Jeremy Belknap of Dover, New Hampshire, the *Declaration* "relieved us from a state of embarrassment. We then knew the ground on which we stood, and from that time, every thing assumed a new appearance." He continued, "The jargon of distinctions between the limits of authority on the one side, and of liberty on the other, was done away. The single question was, whether we should be conquered provinces, or free and independent states." Belknap concluded, "On this question, every person was able to form his own judgment; and it was of such magnitude that no man could be at a loss to stake his life on its decision."⁸

I will now turn my attention toward the task of explaining what happened in the first half of 1776 to steer public opinion in New Hampshire and in the other American colonies away from reconciliation and toward independence.

Notes: Preface

[1] Quoted in Commager and Morris, *The Spirit of 'Seventy-Six*, 279-280.
[2] "The Pennsylvania Assembly's Instructions against Independence," 9 November 1775. Commager and Morris, 282; "The Pennsylvania Assembly: Instructions to Its Delegates in Congress," 14 June 1776. Willcox, *Papers of Benjamin Franklin*, 22:479-481.
[3] Although I am focused here on *Common Sense*, the text, rather than on Thomas Paine, the author, I do intend this study as a contribution to a fuller understanding of Paine as a writer, thinker, and person. In the development of my own understanding of Paine, I have found most useful the work of Clio Rickman, Moncure Conway, Harry Hayden Clark, Philip Foner, Richard Gimbel, Eric Foner, A. O. Aldridge, and John Keane.
[4] For a list of each author's works as they relate to the framework of this study, please see the Bibliography.
[5] "Instructions to Delegates from Portsmouth, New Hampshire, December 25, 1775." Quoted in "Seek Truth," "For the Pennsylvania Packet," DPP, April 22, 1776.
[6] According to Belknap, the New Hampshire convention of 1775 included 133 members representing 102 separate towns. Belknap, *History of New-Hampshire*, 361-362.
[7] "The following is the Form of Government lately assumed by the Colony of New-Hampshire.
In CONGRESS, at Exeter, January 5, 1776," reprinted in the PL, February 10, 1776; also quoted in "Seek Truth," "For the Pennsylvania Packet," DPP, April 22, 1776.
[8] Belknap, 366.

Chapter One

Natural Republicanism

You ought, my friend, to be little more upon your guard in declaring your republican sentiments to the Southern people. Virginians and Carolinians are not yet prepared for such doctrines.

> General Charles Lee to Benjamin Rush
> December 12, 1775

It is now toward the middle of February. Were I to take a turn into the country, the trees would present a leafless, wintry appearance. As people are apt to pluck twigs as they go along, I perhaps might do the same, and by chance might observe that a *single bud* on that twig has begun to swell. I should reason very unnaturally, or rather not reason at all, to suppose *this* was the *only bud* in England which had this appearance. Instead of deciding thus, I should instantly conclude that the same appearance was beginning, or about to begin, everywhere; and though the vegetable sleep will continue longer on some trees and plants than on others, and though some of them may not *blossom* for two or three years, all will be in leaf in the summer, except those which are *rotten*. What pace the political summer may keep with the natural, no human foresight can determine. It is, however, not difficult to perceive that the spring is begun.

> Thomas Paine
> *Rights of Man, Part the Second*
> 1792

PART ONE
TAXATION AND PROTEST

Stamped Out

The American battle cry of the late 1760s and early 1770s, "No taxation without representation," was a familiar topic to Thomas Paine. During many of those years, Paine was employed as a British excise officer, a circuit-riding tax collector, in Lewes, Sussex, and in several other towns around England.[1] The renowned British lexicographer and critic, Samuel Johnson, summed up in his *Dictionary of the English Language* (1776) the accepted English meaning of *Excise (n.s.)*: "A hateful tax levied upon commodities, and adjudged not by the common judges of property, but wretches hired by those to whom excise is paid."[2] Paine was one of those "wretches," and as he heard stories of the abuse suffered by British customs officers at the hands of the American colonists, he felt some empathy for the plight of the tarred, feathered, and carted collectors. Tax collection, whether in Britain or in America, balanced in its occupational scales the economic measure of low wages with the social weight of low repute.[3]

The Stamp Act of 1765 was the first in a series of tax duties passed by parliament in order to offset the expense of British troops stationed in North America. The American colonists resented the idea of a tax that neither required their consent nor permitted their oversight. Printers and lawyers, the two groups of colonists who had the most to lose by the passage of a law that required "stamps" on each document printed in the colonies, led the American resistance to the Stamp Act. The law was never well-enforced in America, because the colonists effectively intimidated the customs officers into "looking the other way."[4] As a tax collector, Paine was all-too-familiar with this kind of public coercion. He had been "sacked" from the Excise once for "stamping his ride," a common practice among excisemen who, in exchange for a bribe or to avoid retribution from hostile taxpayers, would bypass close inspections of merchants' inventories. The same dynamic was at work in America, where the glare of a pitchfork-wielding mob, roused by the pleas of printers in newspapers and broadsides, dissuaded most customs agents from collecting the stamp duty.

Mob violence was a powerful tool in the hands of average American townsfolk, but it was an embarrassment to most of the elites at the head of the colonial resistance movement. Elites preferred to protest the encroachment of parliamentary authority in America by means of economic noncooperation, appellate petitioning, and political pamphleteering. Formal resistance to the Stamp Act took all three forms of protest simultaneously: using conspicuously unstamped paper, American elites addressed petitions to King George III and the British

Parliament, and they began to write and publish political tracts like never before. The hand-pulled wooden presses of colonial America produced thousands of texts during the next few years: pamphlets, newspapers, broadsides, and petitions. The American colonists dusted off an ideal of the English Revolution, "the liberty of the press," and they made it a watchword for the vigilant protection of the liberty of the people.

The British Parliament, in order to save face, repealed the Stamp Act less than one year after initially passing it. The American colonists celebrated the repeal of the Stamp Act, and colonial elites congratulated themselves on the success of their loquacious objections. But the colonists' victory was short-lived; in 1767, parliament began to levy a series of new taxes on imported household goods. The jilted colonists responded by drafting and signing nonimportation and nonconsumption agreements. Consumer economics was an early battlefield of the revolutionary movement, but the gritty struggle to support public boycotts and to forego private indulgences resulted in spotty successes and ample failures.[5] As a matter of principle, the colonists shirked the taxation authority of a parliament in which they had no vote or voice, but the residents of "British North America" held fast to their general affection for, allegiance to, and deep psychological dependence upon "the mother country."

Distant Dissent

Instead of taking to the streets, American elites took up their quill pens to protest parliamentary "oppression." Why did colonial elites feel this overwhelming urge to write their grievances? The answer is simple: they *wrote*, because they could not *speak* their opinions to the British government across the Atlantic Ocean. Political power in Great Britain was centralized in London at St. James's and Westminster, where an oral culture of privy councils and face-to-face debates reinforced a decision-making structure that privileged proximity to the imperial center. Perched on the colonial periphery, even elite Americans found themselves excluded from the intimate conversation of imperial politics.

To write is to perceive and to speak across distance. Because writing, as a mode of communication, is less immediate than speaking, the presence of written discourse invariably signals some form of distance: geographical, temporal, or political.[6] Two individuals sitting next to one another in a room do not, under normal circumstances, communicate with pen and paper. They speak, and by speaking, they convey their thoughts with an oral immediacy impossible to achieve in a written exchange. The American colonial elite represented their dissent in written texts like pamphlets and petitions out of necessity, not choice.

These gentlemen did not *prefer* to write. As proof, one need only cite the scant records of the debates within the First and Second Continental Congresses: as John Adams recalled late in life, "The Oratory, while I was in Congress from 1774 to 1778, appeared to me very universally extemporaneous, and I have never heard of any committed to writing before or after delivery."[7]

The fretful inhabitants of British North America shipped their textual dissent directly to London, where their frustrated publications were received like rocks tossed over the castle walls. Since British political culture was dominated by oral communication, the colonists' reliance upon textual communication proved counterproductive to their goal of a redress of grievances. Rather than closing the distance that separated the two sides of the dispute, the Americans' written dissent only reinforced their outsider status and widened the breach of misunderstanding.

Thomas Paine had experienced this same backfiring of textual dissent prior to his arrival in America. Paine was an Englishman, but he was also a rambler and a perpetual outsider. During his time as an exciseman on horseback, Paine shifted from town to town, enduring on his journeys the ever-present risk of ambush by vengeful taxpayers or opportunistic outlaws. Paine understood that a solitary exciseman—an easy target for the wrath of overtaxed Englishmen—was just a petty personification of the Excise. The British system of mercantile taxation had real problems, Paine realized, but those problems were located not in the *persons* of the Officers of the Excise, but in the *system* of the Office of the Excise. As Paine discussed the endemic corruption and deplorable working conditions of his occupation with his fellow excisemen, he struck upon an idea: he would travel to London to register the collective dissent of his peer officers with the Board of Excise.

Paine wrote a short pamphlet, *The Case of the Officers of Excise* (1772), had it printed in Lewes, and then journeyed to London to distribute his text.[8] In the pamphlet, Paine confessed that an exciseman's meager wages practically forced him to accept bribes just to avoid impoverishment. If the government would pay the officers a living wage, Paine argued, then the Office of the Excise would more than recoup the added expense through substantial growth in collected revenue. Paine reasoned that a decent wage would naturally discourage excisemen from administering informal "tax breaks," an oblique form of employee theft that resulted in the depletion of government coffers. Paine was both candid and creative in his diagnosis of the local labor situation in the Excise, but his proposals did not budge the *status quo* policy. In fact, Paine's pamphlet had only one ascertainable effect: he was fired once again for dereliction of duty.

PART TWO
FROM LONDON TO LEXINGTON

Transatlantic Connection

But Paine's failure carried with it unexpected benefits. Through the introduction of two gentlemen whom Paine had met during the Excise agitation, the now-unemployed Englishman made the acquaintance of the most famous American then in Great Britain: Benjamin Franklin.[9] Paine and Franklin both shared a keen interest in Newtonian science, and the two became fast friends. By the early 1770s, Franklin had gained worldwide fame as an experimental scientist, and he moved with ease through all levels of London society. But even Franklin's unrivalled transatlantic social prowess could not gain him acceptance in the innermost circles of English politics. For much of his early life, Franklin had longed to be fully British, but after spending several years in London as Pennsylvania's official agent to the British government, he was beginning to accept and even embrace his American identity.[10]

The precise extent of the nascent relationship between Franklin and Paine in London is unclear, but we can be sure that the two enjoyed spirited discussions about taxation, education, and, especially, science. Franklin was impressed with his young friend's passionate curiosity about the natural world. As Franklin talked with fondness of his experiments and his life in Philadelphia, Paine soaked in every detail. The Englishman's personal life and professional outlook were in a shambles, and a fresh start in America sounded appealing.

In 1774, Paine introduced to Franklin his idea of sailing to America in order to set up a school on the model of the London dissenting academies. Franklin gladly agreed to write a letter of introduction on behalf of the "ingenious, worthy young man" who was, yet, "quite a stranger" in Philadelphia.[11] With Franklin's letter in hand and a recent divorce settlement to fund his trip, Paine set sail for Philadelphia in September 1774. He stood on the deck of the *London Packet* and watched as the English shore sunk below the eastern horizon. Paine was an unsuspecting passenger on a voyage toward independence: he was coming to America to start a new life, not a revolution.

The Evolution of a Revolutionary

During the period of Paine's arrival in America, he later recalled, he viewed the "dispute" between Great Britain and the colonies "as a kind of law-suit, in which I supposed the parties would find a way either to decide or settle it." As he settled into his new life in America, he had "no thoughts of independence or of arms." He added, "The world could not then have persuaded me that I should be either a soldier or an author. If I had any talents for either, they were buried in me." Paine arrived in America full of hope for the future, not malice toward the past: "I had formed my plan of life, and conceiving myself happy, wished everybody else so."[12]

The uneducated, unaccomplished, and unmotivated Paine must have been at the front of David Ramsay's mind when, in *The History of the American Revolution* (1789), the doctor wrote,

> It seemed as if the war not only required, but created talents. Men whose minds were warmed with the love of liberty, and whose abilities were improved by daily exercise, and sharpened with a laudable ambition to serve their distressed country, spoke, wrote, and acted, with an energy surpassing all expectations which could be reasonably founded on their previous acquirements.[13]

Paine would agree that the "the necessity of the times" had "dragged and driven" his buried talents into action. He described the colonial mindset when he arrived in America at the end of 1774:

> I found the disposition of the people such, that they might have been led by a thread and governed by a reed. Their suspicion was quick and penetrating, but their attachment to Britain was obstinate, and it was at that time a kind of treason to speak against it. They disliked the ministry, but they esteemed the nation. Their idea of grievance operated without resentment, and their single object was reconciliation.[14]

Like the rest of colonists, Paine believed the ministry to be "bad," but not "so rash and wicked" that they would commence "hostilities" against the colonies. And Paine never imagined that the policy would meet with the hearty encouragement of the British people. The shocking outbreak of war at Lexington and Concord in April 1775 shattered Paine's old beliefs about the dispute. In 1778, he reflected on the news of war three years earlier as the epiphany that changed his mind, changed his life, and changed history:

> But when the country, into which I had just set my foot, was set on fire about my ears, it was time to stir. It was time for every man to stir. Those who had been long settled had something to defend; those who had just come had something to pursue; and the call and the concern was equal and universal.[15]

It was the "necessity of the times" that transformed Paine, a twice-fired tax collector, a tailor of women's undergarments, an amateur pirate, and an unpropertied divorcé, into a man who "had something to pursue." He responded to the "equal and universal" call of war with a written text that metamorphosed his manifold failures into the defining agenda of the American Revolution.

Part Three
PAMPHLET CULTURE

The Distinctive Literature of the Revolution

Common Sense was the bestselling pamphlet of the American Revolution, and it was the first text to propose the establishment of an American Republic. Any thorough analysis of Paine's text, then, must account for the dynamic relationship between pamphlet culture and republicanism in early America. It will be helpful at the outset of this study, then, to grasp the interpretive framework used by most scholars to describe this relationship between a form of media and a form of government. Arguably the most influential work of early American historiography over the last half-century, Bernard Bailyn's *Ideological Origins of the American Revolution* (1967) is the perfect place to begin such an orientation. Bailyn's study was as innovative in its archive as it was ambitious in its scope. Bailyn's project began as a catalogue of eighteenth-century American political pamphlets and morphed into an interpretive *tour de force* of the causes and objectives of the American Revolution.

Bailyn famously described the American pamphlets as "the distinctive literature of the Revolution.[16] To be sure, colonial presses churned out unprecedented numbers of pamphlets during the revolutionary period, but, when compared to other forms of early American textual media like almanacs, broadsides, and newspapers, the sales volume and general readership of pamphlets were relatively modest attainments.[17] Upon what grounds, then, did Bailyn's assertion stand? One reason Bailyn could plausibly label pamphlets as "distinctive" is because they do not figure as prominently into other eras of American history. Pamphlets were a transitional medium, an early modern invention that economized production on equipment largely unchanged since the days of Johannes Gutenberg. The brevity and simple binding of pamphlets made them relatively affordable to produce and to purchase, at least compared to the leather-bound, gilt-lettered tomes of the day. Pamphlets were a hybrid innovation, the size of a book (usually octavo) and printed with the materials and techniques of a newspaper or broadside. The advent of wood pulp paper and mechanized printing during the early nineteenth century effectively commoditized book and newspaper publishing, pushing pamphlets into functional obsolescence.

The revolutionary pamphlets were distinctive, however, not just because of their flaring political prominence. To Bailyn, political pamphlets were the definitive medium of the American Revolution: "They reveal," he said, "more clearly than any other single group of documents, the contemporary meaning of that transforming event." Bailyn held that pamphlets remain our best source for understanding the rationale of "those who led and supported the Revolution."[18] And this is an important point: pamphlets were written by elites, as Bailyn puts it, "almost to a man lawyers, ministers, merchants, or planters."[19] This archive is tilted heavily toward a small cadre of genteel American men, a group much more likely to express deep concern for what Bailyn called the "ideological, constitutional, political struggle" of the era than were enlisted soldiers, leather-aproned artisans, housewives, indentured servants, or slaves.[20]

Because pamphlets were written by and for educated American elites, one would assume these texts to be early American literary masterpieces. As Bailyn acknowledged, however, the pamphlets were uniformly terrible compositions. They were "pallid, imitative, and crude," he said, and the harder their authors tried to match English standards of literary excellence, the worse they got.[21] London pamphlets from the late eighteenth century maintained a high standard of wit and elegance, while most American pamphlets from the same era came across as bug-eyed and stiff, like a modern high school production of a Broadway musical.

Bailyn dismissed this pathetic mediocrity with a reminder of American amateurism: the lawyers and ministers simply needed more practice, he argued. The error in this justification is that they *did* get plenty of practice in over two decades of sustained controversy, and they remained, almost to a man, terrible pamphleteers. Assuming Bailyn read or at least skimmed most of the near-2,000 pamphlets in his archive, he could find only three that were compelling and well-written, and these were the products of the most radical, if not volatile, minds of the Revolution: Thomas Paine, James Otis, and "that strange itinerant Baptist" John Allen.

These anomalous compositions, especially Paine's *Common Sense*, made an awkward fit into Bailyn's taxonomy of the period's pamphlets. He classed *Common Sense* among the "chain-reacting personal polemics," focusing—to the exclusion of the argument for independence or the vilification of monarchy—on Paine's constitutional ideas and the pamphlet responses these elicited from Tories and American patriots.[22] Because *Common Sense* did not fit Bailyn's classification system, he was forced to conclude that the "unique power" of the pamphlet was, like its author, an importation. Bailyn tagged *Common Sense* as an outlier and stripped it of any representative import. Because of its "alien quality," Bailyn disqualified from his theory the bestselling, most hotly-debated pamphlet of the American Revolution.

Without this strategic marginalization of *Common Sense*, a pamphlet so palpably subversive of the *status quo*, Bailyn would have been unable to conclude,

> For the primary goal of the American Revolution, which transformed American life and introduced a new era in human history, was not the overthrow or even the alteration of the existing social order but the preservation of political liberty threatened by the apparent corruption of the [British] constitution, and the establishment in principle of the existing conditions of liberty.[23]

This may have been true of the Federalists in 1787, but the Independents in 1776 harbored entirely different ambitions.

Common Sense, it turns out, was just as "alien" in England as it was in America. The London and Edinburgh editions were edited with a heavy hand, censured for their infelicitous style, and dangled before the public as a specimen of treasonous "American" thinking. Paine's writing did not fit the mold of Britain's mercenary publishing culture, where Grub Street scribblers and Court hacks spilled ink for pay. Paine's writing was so different, in fact, that his *Rights of Man* (1791-2)—a book Paine regarded as *Common Sense* adapted to British politics—became the bestselling and most controversial publication in British history. Immediately following the publication of *Rights of Man, Part the Second*, effigies of Paine were burnt at no fewer than 412 separate ceremonies around England in an overwhelming display of popular loyalism.[24] Calling William the Conqueror, progenitor of the monarchic line, a "French bastard landing with an armed banditti," as Paine did in *Common Sense*, was alien on both sides of the Atlantic Ocean.[25] Thomas Hutchinson, the former governor of Massachusetts, noted in his diary, upon reading extracts of *Common Sense* in the London press, "the book contains the most shocking abuses of the King—*Royal Brute, &c*. This a loyal subject, would not reprint."[26]

Bailyn later revisited *Common Sense* in an elegant short essay subtitled, "The Most Uncommon Pamphlet of the Revolution." He sought to isolate that "special quality" in *Common Sense* that set it off from the rest of the pamphlets of the American Revolution. He was unconcerned with the "unmeasurable" rhetorical contribution of *Common Sense* toward the movement for independence but was instead fascinated by this "extraordinary" literary quality, "something bizarre, outsized, unique." He acknowledged that Paine's pamphlet was set apart from the others by its "arresting prose" and by its argumentative focus on "reshaping the premises" of the debate, but he pronounced the text's inherent "rage" as its most distinctive feature. "The aim of almost every other notable pamphlet of the Revolution," Bailyn said, "was to probe difficult, urgent, and controversial questions and make appropriate recommendations. The aim of *Common Sense* was to tear the world apart—the world as it was known and as it was constituted."[27]

The Distinctive Rhetoric of the Revolution

Bailyn evaluated the American pamphlets on the basis of their literary sophistication, and, as a lot, he gave them a failing grade. But what of their rhetorical qualities, the primary textual function of the pamphlets in their own time and their *raison d'être*? "The pamphlets aim to persuade," said Bailyn.[28] Did, then, the pamphlets accomplish in potency what they lacked in sublimity?

Again, most of the pamphlets in Bailyn's archive failed to dislodge entrenched opinions or reformulate colonial policy in meaningful ways. Pamphlets written to address provincial controversies stood a better chance of being heard than pamphlets aimed at British colonial policy, which were met with polite applause in the colonies and deafening silence in London. Indeed, one of the most remarkable characteristics of these pamphlets is that the colonists kept publishing them in spite of their manifest political impotence. Reading the pamphlets and wading through their typically circuitous logic, onerous footnotes, and effete classicisms, the apparent objective of most eighteenth-century American pamphlets comes into focus: they were written with only a *secondary* intent to alter the political landscape; they were written *primarily* to impress their friends and to solidify their status as learned gentlemen.

Eighteenth-century British culture was obsessed with matters of style. The provincial elite worked very hard to be more English than the English, hoping that greater refinement would lead to full inclusion in British society. This compensatory impulse was not confined to the American colonies. The Scottish Enlightenment produced numerous treatises on rhetoric, taste, and cultural criticism. To Oxford-educated Adam Smith and to nobleman Henry Homes, Lord Kames, the Scottish provincial dialect was an embarrassment that stifled the cultural ascendancy of their homeland. Likewise, Edmund Burke, a parliamentarian of unmatched eloquence and also a celebrated aesthetic theorist, was born and educated in Ireland. Books and lectures on elocution proliferated throughout the Atlantic world, where the arts of public speaking and oral reading were considered to be reflections of a person's character and social standing.[29]

Historian Gordon Wood has claimed that the most salient feature of "the literature of the Revolutionary generation" was its "highly rhetorical character." Wood continued, "It was in fact the Revolutionaries' obsession with rhetoric and with its requirement of effectively relating to the audience in order to make a point that in the end helped contribute to the transformation of the American mind."[30]

As Wood made clear, however, the audience to which these gentlemen were relating was strictly limited to other gentlemen. "Despite their occasional condescension toward a larger public," said Wood, these amateur writers and amateur politicians were engaged "in either amusing men like themselves or in educating men to be or think like themselves."[31] To attain the status of a gentleman was itself a kind of rhetorical act, requiring a man to possess property—the public exhibition of personal independence—and to possess "good character"—the public performance of private virtue. This carefully-crafted gentlemanly persona and the concomitant circumscription of a pamphlet's audience reflected age-old assumptions about social and political order. The trickle-down logic of colonial politics rested upon the assumption that if an author, writing anonymously to convey disinterestedness, could convince the distinguished colonial gentry of a course of action, then the ignorant rabble would follow out of deference to their superiors. In short, elite pamphleteers believed that they had only to persuade other elite pamphleteers. Thus, the rhetorical arguments within pamphlet culture were designed for men who shared their conception of rationality, a deductive logic premised upon classical republican ideals and moderated by the excesses of the Cromwellian debacle a century earlier.

The revolutionary pamphleteers' self-congratulatory success in relating to their intended audience ironically sealed the failure of their pamphlets, for they had targeted the wrong audience. In matters of British imperial politics, the planters, merchants, and ministers of America held little sway. Prior to 1776, colonial governance did not require the assent of the colonial elite, as major decisions were made within a closed loop of royal governors, the ministry, and the king. Once royal authority had effectively dissolved, and especially after the colonies had declared their independence, American elected representatives realized that any political mandate came only from "the people out of doors," not from the musings of armchair political theorists. An elite pamphleteering strategy could only have succeeded in the uncertainty of late 1775, when the vacuum of political authority was at its height. Instead of seizing this opportunity, American elites waited with folded hands for a reply to their "Olive Branch" Petition. When these gentlemen awoke from months of expectant hibernation in late spring of 1776, revolutionary political culture had leapfrogged their traditional pamphlet culture, and a public they had once disregarded was now directing American affairs.

PART FOUR
THE PROBLEM WITH MONOREPUBLICANISM

Republicanism in 1776

Bailyn's *Ideological Origins* and Wood's *Creation of the American Republic* (1969) provide us with panoramic depictions of civic republican ideology in an American context. But to capture the sweep of events leading toward the climactic ratification of the *United States Constitution*, these venerable historians have sacrificed and blurred some important details. I take this elision to be simply a matter of the scope of their studies, not of the purity of their intentions. A panoramic photograph may capture a sense of the grandiosity of a scene, but it cannot depict a subject with the fine-grained detail and textural nuance of a high-resolution photograph.

When we point our telephoto lens toward 1776 and zoom into American politics of the first half of the year, we begin to see the crucial distinctions among republicans. The first observation we can make is that republican language was, prior to *Common Sense*, more of an implicit code than an explicit description of public policy. Colonial discourse was infused with allusions to republican ideals, but talk of actually establishing an American Republic was scandalous. In the fall of 1775, Paine first shared with his friend Benjamin Rush the idea he had of composing a series of essays on American affairs. Rush supported the idea but warned Paine that "there were two words which he should avoid by every means as necessary to his own safety and that of the public—*independence* and *republicanism*."[32] Though Paine disregarded his friend's advice, the political reality Rush described was essentially accurate: the ideas of independence and republicanism far outpaced the current state of popular opinion.

A second observation we can make by zooming into American political culture in early 1776 is the lack of clarity regarding what a republican government is or does. Paine's otherwise confident, fluid prose temporarily halted and stammered when, in the third section of *Common Sense*, he tried to describe a republican government structure.[33] This uncertainty about republicanism was not confined to Paine. The reason John Adams composed *Thoughts on Government* (1776) in the first place was because several of his peers in the Continental Congress had approached him asking for an idea of how to create a republican government. Richard Henry Lee of Virginia breathed a sigh of relief upon reading Adams's tract, because it showed "the business of framing government not to be so difficult a thing as most people imagine."[34]

A third observation we can make about republicanism during the American Revolution is the fluid boundaries of republican behavior. Close inspection demonstrates the difficulty of lumping all of the

American founders into the same republican camp, both within and beyond 1776. John Dickinson, republican *par excellence* and author of the most celebrated American pamphlets of the 1760s, *Letters from a Pennsylvania Farmer* (1767-1768), refused to sign the *Declaration of Independence* out of principle. Patrick Henry, firebrand orator and governor of Virginia, was a republican who championed independence in 1776 but staunchly opposed the Federalist Constitution of 1787, while John Jay, the republican coauthor of the pro-*Constitution The Federalist Papers* (1787-1788), disdained the idea of independence in 1776. Samuel Adams and his cousin, John Adams, were both republicans, but the former was known as a whiskey-swilling mobilizer of coercive mobs, and the latter was a buttoned-up, legalistic protector of the propertied. In 1776, no two delegates in the Continental Congress were more overtly republican than Thomas Jefferson and John Adams, but their underlying political principles would prove so divergent that the two later halted their communication for decades. Jefferson always suspected Alexander Hamilton, one of the key leaders in the drive for the *Constitution*, of a pervasive cryptoloyalism during the Revolution and even attributed *Plain Truth*, a loyalist pamphlet response to *Common Sense*, to Hamilton's pen. Scores more examples would belabor the point: republicanism was not as clearly defined during the revolutionary period as we have imagined.[35]

When an aged John Adams told his friend, the playwright and historian Mercy Otis Warren, that he had never known what the word "republican" meant, we must not dismiss his response as evidence of senility.[36] To understand what Adams intended by this reflection, one need only fast forward to our own times for a relevant analogy. The vast majority of Americans in the twenty-first century would declare their commitment to "democracy" as the best form of government, but "democracy" means very different things to different people, just as "republic" or "republican" did in the eighteenth century. Benjamin Rush had cautioned Paine about his vocabulary for good reason: for Paine's colonial audience, "independence" was a slippery slope to anarchy and "republic" entailed a Cromwellian dictatorship. If any signification of "republican" was accepted at the beginning of 1776, it was uniformly negative.[37]

The Least Worst Option

The politicians of the American resistance in 1776 suffered from a restricted descriptive vocabulary. In early modern political thought, there were only three pure forms of government imaginable: monarchy, aristocracy, and democracy. These divisions followed the accepted divisions of humanity into three unwavering classes: royalty, elites, and rabble. Democracy was wholly dismissed as "mobocracy" and a foolish transference of power to the uneducated, undisciplined, and immoral masses. So, although it was listed as a form of government, its inclusion was a theoretical formality, not a practical option. That left only two viable pure forms, both of which had proven in the laboratory of history to be fraught with corruption and tyrannical tendencies. The Crown-in-Parliament framework of the British Constitution, celebrated by Montesquieu and considered the pinnacle of English political innovation, was seen as a pathbreaking hybrid that took the best attributes of each component system and blocked the worst through a series of reciprocal checks on arbitrary power. In the English system, the interests of all three classes of humanity were represented in the Crown, the Lords, and the Commons. The constitution had authorized a compromise between the republicanism of the English Revolution and the restoration of the monarchy under William and Mary. Republicanism was itself a systemic hybrid of aristocracy and democracy, mediated by the vehicle of representation—making the English system, in fact, a compound hybrid.

American colonists had traditionally imported their political prejudices, along with their books, their household goods, and their tea, from England. To most Americans, then, the British Constitution was the only proper form of government. When royal authority in America began to unravel, colonial politicians found themselves stuck: they could not replicate the British Constitution—to them, the only government structure proven to secure liberty—without a king. There were no hereditary monarchs residing in the American colonies and awaiting a vacant throne, and the Hanoverian line that ruled much of Europe at the time had no interest in subverting the authority of their cousin, George III. Subtracting monarchy from the political equation meant that, in theoretical terms, the Americans were working with only two classes of humans: the elite and the rabble. But America had no official class of landed gentry as did England, where elite status was accompanied with concomitant titles and estates. Colonial elites were wealthier and better-connected than non-elites, but this matter-of-degrees distinction did not define a class upon which a government could be built. Therefore, the only manifest class in America, at least from the theoretical perspective of British politics, was the rabble. A self-governing rabble would be a pure democracy, a thought that made the self-appointed American elite gnash their teeth.[38] As colonial politicians learned of King George III's complicity in their oppression, they found themselves caught between a present tyranny of the Crown and a future tyranny of the mob. Elite American politicians scoured their history books for an escape from this dilemma, and they found their solution in the republicanism of the English Revolution.

In 1776, republicanism was the only option left on the American political menu, and it had an undesirable legacy. Rooted in the Ciceronian *res publica* of Ancient Rome—where it morphed into a dictatorial Empire—and filtered through the Machiavellian republics of Renaissance Italy—where it succumbed to frequent popular convulsions—historical republicanism had nevertheless enamored and emboldened the English resistance to Charles II in the mid-seventeenth century. The lofty ideals of Milton, Harrington, Sidney, and a litany of other republican writers had equipped the revolutionists to pry loose the Hobbesian justification of monarchy enough to result in the execution of the king. The republican triumph turned sour quickly, however, when Oliver Cromwell began to take advantage of his political *carte blanche* to exercise his own brand of tyranny. Constant convulsion and bloodshed marked the brief English republic, and after the accession of William and Mary, English politicians placed blame equally on the system of republicanism and the person of Cromwell. Republicanism's historical black eye left the Americans in a precarious situation: their only viable systemic alternative had proven a catastrophic failure in its most recent relevant experiment. Towards the end of March 1776, when his hopes of a reconciliation with Britain were fading, Joseph Hewes, a North Carolinian in the Continental Congress, confessed, "I hate republics and would almost prefer the Government of Turkey to live under," but Hewes sighed that he would soon be forced to "submit" to the system.[39]

Two Party System

What is now referred to by scholars as the political ideology of civic republicanism—as opposed chiefly to the frameworks of liberalism and communitarianism—carried several different labels in the eighteenth century. No one thought of himself in the eighteenth century as a "civic republican," but rather as a "republican," a "commonwealthman," a member of the "country party," an "independent whig," or a "radical whig." But these were the fine distinctions of English politics. In the 1770s, there were only two political camps in America, Whigs and Tories. These partisan affiliations were the enduring demarcations of English politics that had been imported from London along with the other accoutrements of the British Empire. In England and in America, Whigs were associated, to one degree or another, with republicanism, and Tories espoused, with less gradation, a calculated deference to monarchy. In America these stark categories endured until they were displaced by other homegrown partisan binaries: Federalists and Antifederalists in the Constitutional period, and in the early nineteenth century, Federalists and Democratic-Republicans.

In the spring of 1776, the debate initiated by *Common Sense* temporarily opened up three political classes: Independent Whigs, Moderate Whigs, and Loyalist Tories. Prior to the publication of

Common Sense, the moderate, pro-reconciliation position of the Moderate Whigs and the loyalist, pro-capitulation position of the Tories were the only viable public stances on Anglo-American affairs. The loyalist minority was dwindling, however, as increasing numbers of Tories shipped out for England to avoid public persecution at the hands of vigilante mobs. A major rhetorical aim of *Common Sense* was to upset the pro-reconciliation stasis of American politics. Paine identified the two existing options, Whig-reconciliation and Tory-appeasement. Paine separated party from policy, "Whig" from "reconciliation," and carved out a niche for his preferred position, Whig-independence, an option that had not been on the table prior to *Common Sense*. But, of course, he did not leave the matter there. He demonstrated that the Whig-reconciliation and the Tory-appeasement policies, in point of fact, produced the same undesirable result. The nominal distinction, therefore, between Whig-reconciliation and Tory-appeasement, Paine argued, proved to be a sophistic contrivance. That left only two policy clusters, at least according to the argument of *Common Sense*, Paine's new Whig-independence group and a Whig-reconciliation-Tory-appeasement coalition, a category that encompassed the overwhelming majority of Americans at the beginning of January 1776. Paine was attempting to siphon political sentiment away from the dominant reconciliation camp toward either independence or capitulation, in order to demonstrate the obviousness of independence. Paine thus made the entire complex of arguments turn on the single issue of independence. As he put it concisely the next year, "All we want to know in America is simply this, who is for independence, and who is not?"[40]

American Republicanisms

It was extremely rare for Americans to encounter the words "republican" or "republic" in political discourse during 1775 and 1776, and it is worth noting that one man, John Adams, talked about republicanism more than almost all other Americans combined. Adams had earlier stumbled upon the "great Writers" of English republicanism and had often faced "Sneer and Ridicule" whenever he mentioned their names. Adams contended that "any Man who has the Fortitude to read them" would be convinced that "all good Government is Republican." In his *Thoughts on Government* (1776), Adams presented a revealing logic: the "true Idea of a Republic, is 'An Empire of Laws and not of Men': and, therefore, as a Republic is the best of Governments, so that particular combination of Power, which is best continued for a faithful Execution of the Laws, is the best of Republics."[41] For Adams, then, the appeal of republican government was in its superior ability to maintain order.

Governments exist along a continuum from absolute liberty to absolute order, with anarchy at one extreme and totalitarianism at the other. Since both liberty and order are necessary for societal "happiness" (in its eighteenth century holistic sense), then the task of government formation and of political policy is to strike a proper balance between the two. Liberty is sacrificed to achieve greater order, and order is sacrificed to achieve great liberty.[42] Here we see the point of later divergence between Adams and Jefferson. The former preferred republicanism for its order, and the latter for its liberty.

Adams's advocacy for republican government was, in 1776, cavalier in the face of historical precedent. But, he argued, the failure of republican government was attributable to its execution, not to its principles. When Adams invoked the traditional definition of a republic as "An empire of Laws, and not of Men," his view bore a strong resemblance to Paine's phrase in *Common Sense*, "in America *the law is king*."[43]

If Adams's republicanism was, to some degree, contra-historical, Paine's republicanism was a-historical. In *Common Sense*, Paine used the word "republican" primarily in the sense of "not monarchical."[44] If we recall the partitioning of humanity discussed earlier (kings, nobles, masses) and the correlate government forms (monarchy, aristocracy, democracy), then Paine's examination of "the component parts of the English constitution" revealed an important distinction between his view of republicanism and Adams's. The constitution was composed of 1) "The remains of monarchical tyranny in the person of the king," 2) "The remains of aristocratical tyranny in the persons of the peers," and 3) "The new republican materials, in the persons of the commons, on whose virtue depends the freedom of England."[45] Paine's "new republican materials" were, in point of fact, the constitutional instantiation of democracy.

At the beginning of 1776, Paine could not yet refer to "democracy" as a viable political system; he was already pushing the envelope with his advocacy for an American "republic." But there was no material difference between the concepts of "democracy" and "republic" in Paine's mind. For him the words "republican" and "representative" were virtually interchangeable. The former meant no more and no less than the latter. This, of course, irked someone like John Adams, who wrote *Thoughts on Government* as a corrective to Paine's maverick and unschooled "hints" about representation in *Common Sense*. In Paine's basic system, the most republican government was that which was most representative of the totality of the people. Even at the end of his life, after decades of political reading and writing, Paine retained a simplistic notion of republican government. He reflected in 1808 that "the leading principle with me in writing" *Common Sense*, the *American Crisis* papers, and the *Rights of Man*, was "to bring forward and establish the representative system of Government," which he characterized as the antithesis of "the corrupt system of the English Government."[46]

Paine was able to equivocate between "republican," "representative," and "democratic" throughout his life because the terms were difficult to define. Samuel Johnson, a vigorous defender of the Crown and no friend of republicanism, defined *Republican (adj.)* as a neutral "placing the government in the people," while he defined the same word in its nominal form with a diabolical slant (to a Tory) "one who thinks a commonwealth without monarchy the best government." The word *Republic (n.s.)* likewise encompassed two definitions: "commonwealth; state in which the power is lodged in more than one" and "common interest; the public." What Johnson's entries demonstrate is the currency, even in the lexicographer's conservative elite circles, of specialist and non-specialist definitions, meanings freighted with ideological implications and, conversely, meanings not tethered to a partisan camp.

Even in *Common Sense*, Paine equated the most republican government with the most representative. Paine declared that there was "no political matter which more deserves our attention" than "the necessity of a large and equal representation," and he recommended James Burgh's *Political Disquisitions* (1775) as further reading on the subject.[47]

Part Five
THE LOCKEAN MOMENT

An Independent Whig

Burgh, in the General Preface to his *Political Disquisitions*, announced to his readers his own personal aspiration to live up to Thomas Gordon's description of a "true independent whig":

> An independent whig scorns all implicit faith in the state, as well as the church. The authority of names is nothing to him; he judges all men by their actions and behaviour, and hates a knave of his own party as much as he despises a fool of another. He contents not that any man or body of men shall do what they please. He claims a right of examining all public measures, and if they deserve it, of censuring them. As he never saw much power possessed without some abuse, he takes it upon him to watch those that have it; and to acquit, or expose them, according as they apply it to the good of their country, or their own crooked purposes.[48]

When colonial Americans encountered in a text the vocabularies of republicanism, the nature of the language itself triggered certain vague expectations. One of those expectations was the idea of independence. To be independent—economically, politically, morally—was a cornerstone of Whig political philosophy. It represented, as we shall see later in this study, a general freedom from encumbrance that enabled prudential decision-making. Independence took the forms of economic self-sufficiency, political disinterestedness, and religious conscientiousness, but it operated primarily as a micropolitical ethic. Paine in *Common Sense* was translating the principle, as an immutable scientific law, into a macropolitical rationale for national sovereignty.

Though it is rare to find explicit advocacy of "republican government" in the political writing of colonial America, it is easy to recognize a republican code vocabulary in the texts of the American resistance. In addition to the ideal of independence, concepts such as virtue, fortune, vigilance, corruptibility, representation, liberty, press freedom, and opposition to standing armies color nearly every page of late colonial political writing. After over twelve years of open resistance, though, the Americans were beginning to realize the limits of this implicit republican vocabulary.

One of the Americans' favorite sources, John Trenchard and Thomas Gordon's *Cato's Letters* from the 1720s, is a good illustration of this dawning incapacity.[49] The highest form of republican agency one finds in *Cato's Letters* is the watchman. In clever and incisive language across volume after volume, Trenchard and Gordon described a republicanism that was strong on defense and weak on offense. A republican could expose corruption, publish criticisms, and forecast pitfalls, but the model republican of *Cato's Letters* did not do much in a positive sense to steer change. Trenchard and Gordon, like Joseph Addison and Richard Steele's aptly-named *The Spectator* a decade earlier, were presenting a citizenship of judgment rather than of action.[50]

An Appeal to Heaven

Before 1776, the American colonists placed the blame for their troubles on a corrupt ministry and an unresponsive parliament. *Representation* had been such an important watchword for the colonists since 1765, because, they thought, the inclusion of Americans in parliamentary deliberation would fuse British and American interests, resulting in more reasonable colonial policies. Though this approach had not been particularly effective, it suited the Americans well for about a decade, until the eruption of open armed conflict at Lexington and Concord in the spring of 1775. In the months that followed this first battle between British soldiers and American militiamen, an awkward silence fell over American political discourse, reflecting the quandary of justifying civil resistance beyond formal objection. Classical republicanism proved empty of suggestions for the Americans' confusing situation.

The only English republican figure who provided any relevant advice for the Americans was the more radical John Locke. Previously, Locke had been less read and less cited by the American colonists than many other English political writers, but in 1776 he became the brightest star in the republican constellation. The Americans scoured the standard republic corpus for precedent, justification, and prescription, but none of the classical republican thinkers offered a rationale for their peculiar quandary. Only Locke seemed to describe their situation.

At the outbreak of the war with Britain, there was only one republican phrase that demonstrated a rationale for the American resistance, and it was lifted from the pages of Locke's *Second Treatise on Government* (1690): "an appeal to heaven." When all other methods of defensive resistance had been exhausted, the Americans dropped the ideological crutches of classical republicanism, grabbed their muskets, and marched for the battlefields. And even down to the level of the enlisted soldier, they understood that the rules of engagement had changed, or, as Paine put it in *Common Sense*, "By referring the matter from argument to arms, a new era for politics is struck; a new method of thinking hath arisen."[51] Only with the blessing of Providence would the American cause prevail. With the assurance that their cause was just—and with their fingers crossed that their lives were sufficiently virtuous—the Americans marched to war. One militia battalion in 1776 went to such lengths to demonstrate the grounds of their resistance that they headed off to battle behind a flag emblazoned with the phrase "An Appeal to Heaven."[52]

The early years of the revolutionary period and, to some extent, the later years of the American Revolution may have expressed a continuity with the Machiavellian strain of classical republicanism, but the first six months of 1776 was a Lockean moment.[53] The three most important texts from that period, George Mason's *Declaration of Rights*, Jefferson's *Declaration of Independence*, and Paine's *Common Sense*, all shared an affinity with, if not an outright cooptation of, Locke's *Second Treatise on Government*.

The United States of Nature and War

The first full section of *Common Sense*, "Of the origin and design of government in general," is at first blush the least remarkable section of the pamphlet. Paine's discussion of *origins* was, ironically, the least *original* argument in the text, and his readers knew it. In the rare case that a portion of *Common Sense* was omitted from republished excerpts, the editors always left out the early sections of the text. One pamphlet response even commented that the first section of *Common Sense* laid "a very indifferent Foundation for a very indifferent Building."[54]

Paine's fluency in the political language of John Locke and Jean-Jacques Rousseau during the months he was composing *Common Sense* is unclear. Whether his ideas were "borrowed from" or "rooted in" these theorists is, however, largely inconsequential, because Paine was not pretending to introduce anything original in the first section of the pamphlet. The concept that the earth's first inhabitants formed themselves first into a society and then into a government was patently Lockean, but it was also grossly fictitious. Paine did not believe that his introductory scenario had actually happened. In fact, in a temporal disorientation from the outset of the section, he presented this entire prehistoric narrative in the future tense. This group of people "settled in some sequestered part of the earth, unconnected with the rest," *represented* for Paine "the first peopling of any country, or of the world." These aboriginal people, existing in a "state of natural liberty," he said, "will" choose the positive benefits of society before implementing the negative restraints of government. Paine continued in this speculative mode: "Some convenient tree will afford them a State-House, under the branches of which, the whole colony may assemble to deliberate on public matters."[55] The reaction of a reader today is the same as it was in 1776: that Paine's story is a pleasant exercise in make-believe. And this is what Paine intended, for he wanted to demonstrate to his readers that ancient myths of origin were all fabricated. This is a theme he would return to again and again as he paraded the British Constitution around like the emperor's new clothes. Paine was showing that the embellished narratives of origins were no basis for a national government.

But Paine was also working a different angle in his foundational narrative, and he indicated his purpose by his use of the future tense. Paine was transporting his readers to a place of unspoiled beauty and promise, a place of infinite possibility untouched by European corruption. As Locke had put it a century earlier, "Thus in the beginning all the world was America."[56]

The hypothetical past was the actual present in America. When Paine described the first parliament where "every man, by natural right, will have a seat," he was not spinning a yarn; he was laying out a political agenda. Historical precedent and tradition became wholly superfluous because, as Paine would say later in the *Rights of Man*,

> The case and circumstances of America present themselves as in the beginning of a world; and our enquiry into the origin of government is shortened, by referring to the facts that have arisen in our own day. We have no occasion to roam for information into the obscure field of antiquity, nor hazard ourselves upon conjecture. We are brought at once to the point of seeing government begin, as if we had lived in the beginning of time. The real volume, not of history, but of facts, is directly before us, unmutilated by contrivance, or the errors of tradition.[57]

In the Lockean framework that Paine recapitulated in the first half of *Common Sense*—a framework which Paine had learned either by study or by osmosis—human communities found themselves in one of three states: a "politic society," a "state of war," or a "state of nature."[58] *Common Sense* stressed that "politic society" in America had been unraveling since 1763. Since the Battle of Lexington and Concord, Paine argued, the American colonies had been in a "state of war." Locke had described a "state of war" as a situation where "force or declared design of force" had been threatened and "where there is no common superior on earth to appeal to for relief."[59] Paine's critique of monarchy, as we shall see in Chapter Three, aimed precisely at those who thought they had not yet reached the desperation of this state of war "wherein there is no appeal but to Heaven."[60]

Many Americans did recognize that their land had been plunged into a "state of war," but very few perceived the colonies' unique opportunity to embrace a collective "state of nature." The American colonies had not yet united into a cohesive political society, and Paine realized that their situation amounted to a political "state of nature" unprecedented in recorded history. The Americans were, in Locke's language, "living together according to reason, without a common superior on earth" in a *de facto* state of nature. Locke's "state of nature" and "state of war"—though differentiated by the suasory presence of *reason* or *force*—both arose from a milieu defined by the absence of a "common superior on earth." The colonists, therefore, were at a perplexing crossroads between the two Lockean "states": they were both without government and under siege. The "one great reason," according to Locke, for humans to quit the state of nature was to "avoid this state of war." In order to prevent the saber-rattling British government from plunging America deeper into a "state of war," the colonists needed to find "an authority, a power on earth, from which relief can be had by appeal" or, if no judge could be found on earth, instructed Locke, "the appeal lies to God in heaven."[61]

Part Six
UNTANGLING THE ROOTS OF RADICALISM

Radical Whigs

Both Locke and Paine were regarded in the eighteenth century as "Radical Whigs," a distinct subset of British political culture that was often more conservative than the name implies. Samuel Johnson's dictionary defined *Radical (adj.)* as "primitive; original" or "implanted by nature." Johnson reserved some of his lexicographical cleverness for his definitions of Britain's two major political parties. His cheeky first definition of *Whig (n.s.)* was "whey," and his snide second definition was "the name of a faction." He began his definition of *Tory (n.s.)*, his own party, with an etymological apology: "a cant term, derived, I suppose, from an Irish word signifying a savage," and he continued with the actual definition, "one who adheres to the ancient constitution of the state, and the apostolical hierarchy of the church of England: opposed to a whig."[62] Johnson's definition of "Tory" revealed a basic fact of early modern life: the commingling of religious and political beliefs. As we shall see in Chapter Three, Paine exposed the incongruity between the general American antipathy toward apostolic succession in the form of an Episcopal bishop or of the creeping Catholicism of Quebec and the American affection for a quasi-apostolic hereditary monarchy. Following Johnson's definitions, during the eighteenth century, one could not be a "Radical Tory," because a *radical* found his principles in natural origins, while a *Tory* found his principles in tradition.[63]

In the eighteenth century and still today, the word "radical" tends to obfuscate crucial differences within discussions of politics. Though the word carries an etymological denotation of root-orientation (Latin, *radus*), in common usage it most often connotes bold or extreme political stances. "Radical Whig" described a wide swath of English republicans, including both Edmund Burke and Thomas Paine. Most Radical Whigs in early modernity were radical in the *denotative* ideological sense, but not in the *connotative* activist sense. In contrast, *Common Sense*—and all of Paine's political writing—was radical in both senses. Paine's was a radical republicanism, yes, but his "roots" were very different from the ideological republican camp. Instead of classical or Renaissance sources—which privileged, in fact, tradition rather than origin—Paine fixed his gaze primarily on first principles, in politics, science, theology, and economics, anchoring his writings in the logical structure of natural philosophy. Because of this attention to nature as the ultimate source for all knowledge, his politics could be described justly as "natural republicanism." Because nature is accessible to anyone, regardless of culture, ethnicity, education, or history, its central role in Paine's thought easily disguises itself as universal republicanism or vulgar republicanism, but these are extrinsic manifestations of an intrinsic logic. Paine's natural republicanism stood upon an inductive foundation and sparred with episcopal republicanism and any other system constructed upon a deductive or traditionary foundation.

Orthodox Radicalism

Toward the end of his *Creation of the American Republic*, Gordon Wood made an elegant and profound point that I will summarize for the sake of brevity: The Federalists of the 1780s couched their elitist assumptions about the nature of society and government in the language of radical democracy, essentially stealing the vocabulary of the Antifederalists and countermanding the Whig-republican political tradition. By employing the most democratic rhetoric available in defense of aristocracy, they repudiated the radical possibilities of 1776 in the very language of 1776 and, thereby, sealed off American political discourse from any genuine engagement between differing social interests. This was a monumental insight, yet no sooner had Wood made these striking observations about the entire American political tradition, than he returned to his Constitution-praising story, a story that began with radical Whig (*i.e.*, republican) ideology, transitioned to a "republican remedy," praised the republicanism of the radical state constitutions of 1776, and culminated in a profound transformation at the hands of the Federalists toward—you guessed it—a distinctively republican form of federal government. By calling everything republican, Wood, alongside Bailyn and others, managed to create an all-encompassing "ism" that is sapped of its descriptive power. These scholars incorrectly assumed that republicanism was manifestly *en vogue* even before 1776—which it was not—and, thereby, ignored the important transition from a latent whiggish conception of politics to an open avowal of republican government structure.

There is an uncanny tendency in this stream of scholarship to find republicanism behind every bush and under every rock, but another pattern in these writings bears heavier significance for American historiography. Wood and Bailyn employ the vocabularies of radicalism to describe aristocratic political developments. Even their book titles are revealing: *Ideological Origins* was originally titled *The Transforming Radicalism of the American Revolution*, and Wood's sequel to *Creation of the American Republic* was *The Radicalism of the American Revolution*. By labeling profoundly conservative developments as innately radical, these scholars have hamstrung other scholars who would prefer to talk about *actual* radicalism during the American Revolution without confusing their readers. The historical debate grinds to a halt when words like republicanism and radicalism are forced into a definitional monopoly.

We need to acknowledge that there were various species of republicanism alive in different places and different times during the revolutionary period. We cannot catch every political decision in the net of monorepublicanism, Even if we could, we should be wary of the endeavor, for a term that applies to every case invariably lacks the specificity requisite to forward historical understanding. Prior to 1776, the basic commonality between New York merchants, Massachusetts lawyers, Virginia planters, and Philadelphia artisans was that they lived on the same continent during the same period. The idea of a sanitized gentleman's revolution sweeps under the rug the politically-coercive colonial militias, the embarrassingly lascivious Continental Army, the forgotten Negroes, the bankrupt farmers, and the undereducated yet chaste women.[64] The American Revolution was not an era of republicanism, but of *republicanisms*, some of which were radical and some of which were not.

Part Seven
TOWARDS A REPRESENTATIVE DEMOCRACY

Natural Representation

Paine's view of republican government was remarkably consistent throughout his life, and he enunciated that view with the most specificity in the second part of the *Rights of Man*.[65] "It has always been the political craft of courtiers and court-governments, to abuse something which they called republicanism; but what republicanism was, or is; they never attempt to explain." He offered *four*, rather than three, possible forms of government: "the democratical, the aristocratical, the monarchical, and what is now called the representative." A republic, he clarified, is not indicative of a particular form of government but of the "whole and sole object" of government. *Republic* was, said Paine, "a word of a good original," and its etymology demonstrated a commitment to the "*res-publica*, the public affairs, or the public good," while the "base original signification" of *monarchy*, by contrast, revealed a system that held for its object the arbitrary exercise of power by an individual.[66]

Most governments that "style themselves a republic," Paine said, are actually aristocracies, while "the government of America, which is wholly on the system of representation, is the only real republic, in character and practice, that now exists."[67] Paine had left America prior to the ratification of the federal constitution, and he desired to see it succeed in principle, even if he took exception to some of its particulars. A nation's status as a republic, Paine said, pertained to the *business*, not the *form* of government. The form of the American government was "representation ingrafted upon democracy" constructed to scale with the population.[68]

Paine's idea of a republican system did not carry with it the theoretical complexity of James Madison's or John Adams's republican ideas. A republic was to Paine simply a democracy adapted to a scale where direct popular rule was impractical. Paine's idea of republican government had no irreducible requirements beyond a "common center" formed "by representation" in which "all the parts of society unite."[69] In Paine's conception of an American republic, the central point of contact for diverse and scattered constituencies was in a textual constitution.

In the British system of government, the central point of political contact was the unwritten "ancient" constitution and the trinitarian Crown-in-Parliament system. The nobles entered the government by the gateway of the House of Lords, the royalty by the gateway of the Crown, and the English people by gateway of the House of Commons (although the John Wilkes affair had called that into question). In

1776, the Americans, excluded from parliamentary representation, conceived of their only access to the center of British government as being through the gateway of the Crown. In *Common Sense*, Paine argued that this convoluted system was nonsense. He advocated "a republican government" because it was "formed on more natural principles."[70]

In point of fact, Paine would later say, there were only two modes of government that "prevail in the world": the first, "by election and representation" erected on the foundation of reason; and the second, "by hereditary succession" erected on the base of ignorance.[71] Hereditary succession, as will be discussed in Chapters Three and Four, follows a deductive logical path, while representation follows an inductive one.

Whereas John Adams's optimal governmental structure was the form best at maintaining legal order, Paine's rubric for evaluating government was how closely it approximated natural systems. Paine did not advocate governmental order because he had a particular desire to secure property, but because "Nature is orderly in all her works." For Paine, nature was a master template that applied equally to any decision, "a system of principles as universal as truth and the existence of man." Monarchy was wrong-headed, said Paine, because it was "a mode of government that counteracts nature," while the "representative system" on the other hand, was "always parallel with the order and immutable laws of nature."[72]

In both *Common Sense* and the *Rights of Man*, Paine shredded the traditional source of British civil liberties, the Constitution. Civil liberties emanating from the State were, for him, always subordinate to natural liberties that flowed from God via Nature.[73] Moreover, the fact that the British Constitution was unwritten and invisible, Paine constantly argued, meant that it did not really exist. Bare custom was an illegitimate foundation for a framework of national laws. When a right was violated or a procedure was disregarded, the affected citizens should be able to point to the specific section in the constitutional text pertaining to the question. The *Pennsylvania State Constitution of 1776*, Paine later remarked, had been "the political bible of the state," with a copy in every home and in the pocket of every politician.[74] The one element of the British Constitution that Paine did not wholly abandon in *Common Sense* was the *Magna Charta*. He viewed it as a relatively legitimate document, not because it aspired to broad political representation, but because its contents were written and accessible. Paine urged the colonies in *Common Sense* to "frame a CONTINENTAL CHARTER," what amounted to a constitution, on its model.[75]

Throughout Paine's political life, he always insisted on the necessity of a written constitution as the textual insurance of perpetual representation. Since a diffuse people can legitimately constitute a government only in writing, a government without a written constitution,

Paine said, "is power without a right."[76] Written constitutions bridge the distances of time and power to lay a systematic foundation for political power, while the oral agreements of leaders privilege proximity and access to power. Paine's emphasis on written constitutions, natural authority, and republican government were part and parcel of a larger unified fabric in his thought: to reorganize human civilization in alignment with the universal natural laws of early modern science.

Revolution in Style

In the context of the other pamphlets of the revolutionary period, *Common Sense* stands out first for its absence of classical references. This is attributable, on the one hand, to Paine's view of the illegitimacy of traditional forms of authority, and on the other hand, to Paine's disadvantaged childhood education. Irrespective of the reasons for Paine's avoidance of the classics, the fact that his readers did not have to wade through untranslated passages from Seneca the Elder and Plutarch carried staggering implications for modern politics. In the late eighteenth century, "literacy" still implied the ability to read and write Latin (and preferably Greek). Functional vernacular literacy—the partitioned ability to read or write English and to sign one's name—carried with it economic and religious advantages, but British political culture still assumed a classical education. By writing *Common Sense* in a style that waived all prerequisites, Paine opened up the contents of political judgment to a much broader audience than ever before. By writing in a vernacular style, Paine was redefining literacy in a way that mirrored the elimination of a mediatory authority in politics. Paine's audience did not have to know or cite Latin to make a valid argument, and they didn't have to defer to the aristocracy to make a valid political judgment. Through his new mode of direct textual representation, Paine was pushing the traditional modes of stylized address and cryptic authority into functional obsolescence.

Common Sense's initial colonial audience perceived the unusual accessibility of the pamphlet's prose, but few readers suspected that they were participating in a stylistic revolution of seismic political consequence. Once *Common Sense* explained the conflict with Britain in terms that made sense to common Americans, then the ancient shroud of complexity surrounding all politics began to fall away. If anyone could understand politics, then, it followed, anyone could make a wise decision as a participant in the political process. Moreover, if common folk were as capable as elites of making sound political judgments, then common folk were equally qualified to become politicians. As copies of *Common Sense* made it into the hands of colonists who had never before purchased a pamphlet, it became evident that the boundaries of the public were drawn by the style of political prose.

Thomas Jefferson, near the end of his life, reflected upon Paine's pioneering prose style. Jefferson noted that *Common Sense* had been initially attributed to Franklin because of the remarkable similarity of their unadorned styles. Jefferson contrasted Paine's style with that of the quintessential republican writer, Lord Bolingbroke, noting that each left "a model of what is most perfect in both extremes of the simple and the sublime." Bolingbroke had written, said Jefferson, with "the lofty, rhythmical, full-flowing eloquence of Cicero," a style characterized by sentences "of just measure, their members proportioned, their close full and round." Paine, on the other hand, had mastered the opposite pole of political prose. Jefferson explained, "No writer has exceeded Paine in ease and familiarity of style, in perspicuity of expression, happiness of elucidation, and in simple and unassuming language."[77] In the polarities of style, then, Jefferson had identified a crucial distinction between Bolingbroke and Paine. One wrote with the refined ornamentation of St. Paul's Cathedral, and the other with the radical simplicity of a Quaker meeting house. One described liberty with rhetorical elegance, and the other, equality with empirical thrift. One spoke the language of the classical republic, and the other of the modern democracy.

Notes: Chapter One

[1] Now "East Sussex."
[2] Johnson, *Dictionary of the English Language*. This entry in Johnson's *Dictionary* was quoted in the PJ, January 31, 1776, as a single-sentence refutation of Johnson's anti-American pamphlet, *Taxation No Tyranny*.
[3] For a thorough treatment of the role played by the Office of Excise in the formation of a consumer society in England, see Ashworth, *Customs and Excise*.
[4] See Morgan and Morgan, *Stamp Act Crisis*.
[5] The "consumer" resistance of colonial Americans during the early revolutionary period was an important step in the development of intracolonial and intercolonial associations and committees. Many of the economic organizations formed during this phase of the conflict became more focused on political and military resistance in the mid-1770s. For a thorough treatment of the central role of consumer economics in the American Revolution, see Breen, "Baubles of Britain" and *Marketplace of Revolution*.
[6] Elites in early modern Europe wrote for two main reasons: to speak to posterity (temporal distance) or to participate in the intellectual diaspora labeled the "republic of letters" (geographic distance).
[7] Cappon, *Adams-Jefferson Letters*, 451.
[8] As Moncure Conway points out in his *Life of Thomas Paine*, the pamphlet was "printed" but not technically "published"; nor was it available for sale until after Paine had become famous. It was printed in Lewes for circulation in parliament and among the Office of Excise; thus Conway explains Paine's later comment that *Common Sense* had been his first publication (beyond occasional pieces in newspapers and magazines).
[9] Oliver Goldsmith and George Lewis Scott, FRS.
[10] On the development of Franklin's distinctly American identity, see Brands, *The First American*; Isaacson, *Benjamin Franklin: An American Life*; Morgan, *Benjamin Franklin*; Schiff, *A Great Improvisation*; Wood, *The Americanization of Benjamin Franklin*.
[11] BF to Richard Bache, 30 September 1774. Willcox, *Papers of Benjamin Franklin*. 21:325-326; See also, CW 2:1161-1162.
[12] AC, No. 7, CW 1:143-144.
[13] Ramsay, *History of the American Revolution*, 1789.
[14] CW.1, pp. 143-144.
[15] CW.1, pp. 143-144.
[16] Bailyn, *Ideological Origins*, 8.
[17] Newspaper subscriptions were relatively expensive at the time, but a newspaper's actual readership dwarfed its official sales because many colonials read public copies kept at coffee houses and taverns. Broadsides were throwaway publications tacked up on doors and passed around by hand, usually containing excerpts from longer works or announcements of public events. Almanacs were the most ubiquitous of all colonial publications; these inexpensive texts contained a mish-mash of ephemeral information of interest and import to provincials from all walks of life.
[18] Bailyn, *Ideological Origins*, 8.
[19] Ibid., 13-14.
[20] Ibid., x.

[21] Ibid., 12.
[22] Ibid., 5.
[23] Ibid., 19.
[24] O'Gorman, "The Paine Burnings."
[25] CS 2.13.
[26] 8 April 1776. Hutchinson, *Diary and Letters of Thomas Hutchinson*, 2:32.
[27] Bailyn, "*Common Sense*," 38, 91-92.
[28] Bailyn, *Ideological Origins*, 19.
[29] See Campbell, *Philosophy of Rhetoric*; Kames, *Elements of Criticism*; Blair, *Lectures on Rhetoric and Belles Lettres*; Walzer, *George Campbell: Rhetoric in the Age of Enlightenment*; Howell, *Eighteenth-century British Logic and Rhetoric*; Adam Smith, *Lectures on Rhetoric and Belles Lettres*; Golden and Corbett, *The Rhetoric of Blair, Campbell, and Whately*; Priestley, *A Course of Lectures on Oratory and Criticism*; Sheridan, *A Course of Lectures on Elocution*; Fliegelman, *Declaring Independence*.
[30] Wood "Democratization of the Mind," 70; reformulated in Wood, *Revolutionary Characters*.
[31] Wood "Democratization of the Mind," 70.
[32] BR to James Cheetham, 17 July 1809. Butterfield, *Letters of Benjamin Rush*, 2:1008.
[33] CS 3.41-3.43.
[34] RHL to Patrick Henry, 20 April 1776. LDC, 3:564.
[35] Wood, *Creation of the American Republic*, 48.
[36] Ibid., 48.
[37] The nearest analogy to contemporary political economy would be if someone were today advocating a political system already proven bankrupt, like communism after 1991.
[38] This dilemma caused some Americans to toy with the idea of establishing an American monarchy or an official peership, two concepts that would endure in some form until George Washington's Farewell Address at the end of his second term as president and with the fading of the post-revolutionary Society of the Cincinnati.
[39] John Hancock to Samuel Johnston. 26 March 1776. LDC, 3:444.
[40] Paine, AC, No. 3. Abraham Lincoln employed this same rhetorical strategy during the American Civil War, which he construed to turn on the single issue of slavery.
[41] JA to John Penn, [19-27? March 1776]. LDC, 3:401-403.
[42] We see this in our own times in the contention between "civil liberty" and "security."
[43] Hyneman and Lutz, *American Political Writing*, 1:403; CS 3.47.
[44] CS 2.23.
[45] CS 1.10.
[46] TP to The Honorable Senate of the United States, 21 January 1808. CW 2:1490-1491.
[47] CS 4.23; CS 3.42.
[48] Gordon, *Tracts*, 1:311, from Burgh, *Political Disquisitions*, xvi-xvii.

[49] Trenchard and Gordon had also briefly published a serial, *The Independent Whig*, which was often included in their collected works and owned by many of the colonial leaders.
[50] Trenchard and Gordon, *Cato's Letters*; Addison and Steele, *Selections from the Spectator and the Tatler*.
[51] CS 3.5.
[52] Breen, *The Lockean Moment*.
[53] Pocock, *Maciavellian Moment*, and Breen, *Lockean Moment*.
[54] [Middleton,] *True Merits of a Late Treatise*.
[55] Cf. Paine's "Liberty Tree," published in the PM, March 1775. The last two stanzas of the poem:

> Beneath this fair tree, like the patriarchs of old,
> Their bread in contentment they ate,
> Unvexed with the troubles of silver or gold,
> The cares of the grand and the great.
> With timber and tar they Old England supplied,
> and supported her power on the sea:
> Her battles they fought, without getting a groat,
> For the honor of Liberty Tree.
>
> ——
>
> But hear, O ye swains ('tis a tale most profane),
> How all the tyrannical powers,
> Kings, Commons, and Lords, are uniting amain
> To cut down this guardian of ours.
> From the East to the West blow the trumpet to arms,
> Thro' the land let the sound of it flee:
> Let the far and the near all unite with a cheer,
> In defense of our Liberty Tree." (CW II, 1019-1092.)

[56] Locke, *Two Treatises*, 121.
[57] Chapter 4, "On Constitutions," RM 2, CW 1:376.
[58] Locke, *Two Treatises*, 106-108.
[59] Ibid., 108.
[60] Ibid., 109.
[61] Ibid., 109.
[62] Johnson, *Dictionary*.
[63] Jacobites were an extremist subset of Tories who desired to restore the Stuart monarchy, but they were not "radical" in the sense denoted by Johnson.
[64] See especially, Royster, *A Revolutionary People at War*; Shy, *A People Armed and Numerous*; Gross, *The Minutemen and their World*; Jordan, *White Over Black*; Breen, *Tobacco Culture*; Kerber, *Women of the Republic*.
[65] See Dedication to Lafayette, RM 2, CW 1:348.
[66] RM 2, CW 1:369. .
[67] Ibid., 370.
[68] Ibid., 371-372.
[69] Ibid., 372.
[70] CS 3.40.
[71] RM 2, CW 1:338.
[72] Ibid., 373-374.

[73] Benjamin Franklin used the term "parchment right" in a London newspaper article in 1773. See Willcox, *Papers of Benjamin Franklin*, 20:115a. Paine's emphasis on natural liberty is a significant forerunner to the wholesale adoption of "human rights" language in the twentieth century.
[74] RM 2, CW 1:278-279.
[75] CS 3.45.
[76] CW 1:375.
[77] TJ to Francis Eppes, 19 January 1821. Peterson, *Thomas Jefferson: Writings*, 1452.

Chapter Two

Kindling Controversy

It cannot... be forgotten that the politics, the opinions and the prejudices of the Country were in direct opposition to the principles contained in that work. And I well know that in Pennsylvania, and I suppose the same in other of the then Provinces, it would have been unsafe for a man to have espoused independence in any public company and after the appearance of that pamphlet it was as dangerous to speak against it. It was a point of time full of critical danger to America, and if her future well being depended on any one political circumstance more than another it was in changing the sentiments of the people from dependence to Independence and from the monarchial to the republican form of government; for had she unhappily split on the question, or entered coldly or hesitatingly into it, she most probably had been ruined.

Thomas Paine to a Committee of the Continental Congress
1783

Independence always appeared to me practicable and probable, provided the sentiment of the country could be formed and held to the object: and there is no instance in the world, where a people so extended, and wedded to former habits of thinking, and under such a variety of circumstances, were so instantly and effectually pervaded, by a turn in politics, as in the case of independence; and who supported their opinion, undiminished, through such a succession of good and ill fortune, till they crowned it with success.

Thomas Paine
American Crisis, No. 13
1783

PART ONE
A CATALYTIC COMPOSITION

A Desperate Shortage

In 1775 and 1776, the American colonies found themselves in a horrifying predicament. Every legislative body across the continent, from the Continental Congress down to county committees in every province shared the same anxiety. The colonists had been confident in the success of their resistance to Britain, but they suddenly realized a dramatic gap in their strategy. The colonists lacked something crucial, something embarrassing. The Americans needed saltpeter.

This may seem strange like a strange point of consensus, until we reflect upon the circumstances. Since April 1775, the American colonies had been involved in open war with the most formidable army and navy in the world. The colonies had also virtuously refused to trade with Great Britain, which they knew would roil British commerce and hopefully advance their cause. But what they didn't consider was where they would get saltpeter, which in the past they had always received from Britain. They needed saltpeter, potassium nitrate, because it was a crucial ingredient in gunpowder.

If the situation hadn't been so desperate, it would have been humorous. The politicians in white powdered wigs rose in the assembly rooms of every American colony and declaimed on their commitment to preserving the liberties of the people with the fullest measure of their of blood and treasure. These rhetorical flourishes sounded magnificent until reports from the field began to note depleting stores of black gunpowder. Gunpowder was made of three granular ingredients: sulfur, charcoal, and saltpeter, the last of which provided oxygen to the reaction. Without saltpeter, gunpowder doesn't explode.[1]

The shortage grew dire very quickly, and the American colonies found themselves in the unenviable position of fighting a war without ammunition. To make sure that the Continental Army rank and file understood the seriousness of the situation, General George Washington from his headquarters in Cambridge ordered that any soldier caught firing an unnecessary round would receive 39 lashes.[2]

Some delegates from the Continental Congress, especially Robert Treat Paine of Massachusetts, spent a tremendous amount of time organizing the American effort to produce saltpeter. In October 1775, Richard Henry Lee wrote from Philadelphia to the Virginia Committee of Safety,

> There is no powder here that can possibly be shared, and the wicked activity and power on the Sea of our enemies, render it an essential and indispensable duty on our Colony in particular to push the making of Salt Petre with unremitting diligence. We earnestly entreat you to

move the whole Colony most strongly on this point—All North America Expects it, and the safety of the whole does absolutely demand it; without this internal and essential security, the liberty & rights of America rest on doubtful ground.[3]

The Continental Congress published *Several Methods of Making Salt-Petre* (1775), which included "An Account of the manufactory of Salt Petre" by Benjamin Rush, who was then a professor of chemistry at the College of Philadelphia. Likewise the New York Committee of Safety published *Essays Upon the Making of Salt-Petre and Gun-Powder* (1775), which included "EXPERIMENTS made by Capt. [Thomas] Pryor and Mr. Thomas Paine, for the Purpose of fixing some easy, cheap and expeditious method of making Salt-Petre in private Families, in order to shew the practicability of a Plan proposed by Mr. Paine, of forming a Salt-petre Association, for voluntarily supplying the public Magazines with Gun-Powder."[4]

The Pennsylvania Committee of Safety met in Philadelphia nearly every day during the first six months of 1776, and an overwhelming percentage of their business pertained to the shortage of saltpeter.[5] Under the leadership of John Nixon, the Committee of Safety appointed Owen Biddle, a non-pacifist Quaker, to manage the provincial saltpeter works, while David Rittenhouse, the chief engineer for the Committee, oversaw the construction of a gunpowder mill outside of Philadelphia. Frequent newspaper advertisements and broadsides from the Committee of Safety and from the Continental Congress met with mixed results. The residents of Chester County in Pennsylvania responded to one plea by organizing "all those whose public virtue and patriotic spirit should excite them to so necessary an undertaking at this crisis of time" into a series of classes on "the art of making salt-petre."[6] In spite of their best efforts, the colonists couldn't seem to meet the demand. In May 1776 the Pennsylvania Saltpeter Works issued an urgent plea begging everyone in the province to start making saltpeter in their homes, or else, the proclamation implied, their homes were about to become British barracks.[7]

As Paine, Pryor, and Rush collaborated in the summer and fall of 1775 on saltpeter experiments, the three bemoaned the shortsightedness that had caused this problem in the first place. France and Germany had ample supplies of saltpeter, but the Americans were in no position to request supplies either from Britain's avowed enemy or from George III's extended Hanoverian family.[8] Paine and his friends could not help observing that America's future hinged on one missing ingredient, one simple catalyst. And so Paine began to write about independence.

Notes on the State of America

Paine had arrived in America planning to bide time until Franklin returned from England. He expected to find subsistence level employment as an assistant tutor for well-to-do children or as an assistant land surveyor until, with Franklin's patronage, he could set up an academy for young men and women on the model he had known in London. Franklin's letter of introduction, though, carried even more clout in Philadelphia than Paine had expected. In January he was offered the editor's position for *The Pennsylvania Magazine*, a new periodical published by Robert Aitken next door to Paine's lodgings. The Englishman was only marginally qualified for his new position, but his lively conversational demeanor and broad scientific knowledge had impressed Aitken. The seven or eight months that Paine spent working on the magazine functioned as an important literary apprenticeship for him, exposing him to a variety of ideas, allowing him to experiment with different generic forms, and affording him the opportunity for the first time to earn a living with his pen. Aitken had established the magazine as a vehicle for refined entertainment and intellectual stimulation and, with the financial backing of John Witherspoon, had managed to publish the first issue before Paine joined the enterprise. Aitken was eager to hand over the day-to-day responsibilities of generating and editing copy to the recent immigrant, and both were pleased with magazine's reception during the spring of 1775. Aitken was busy with his bookshop and other publishing projects, and he took a laissez-faire attitude toward the magazine. His only stipulation was that Paine steer the magazine clear of any overt engagement with politics. Contributors who felt compelled to comment on political affairs, Aitken thought, had ample opportunity to publish in newspapers. Some contributors managed, with Paine's wink, to treat political topics by metaphor and allegory, but most of the magazine's pages were filled with aesthetic, critical, and scientific pieces.[9]

We know that a salary dispute officially ended Paine's relationship with the *Pennsylvania Magazine* in the late summer of 1775, but it is unclear whether Paine's heightened politicization following April 19, 1775, added to the tension between the editor and his apolitical publisher. Paine had written a letter in May 1775 to George Lewis Scott, a distinguished member of the Board of Excise and Paine's initial connection to Franklin, saying, "Surely the ministry are all mad; they never will be able to conquer America."[10] Only a month after the Battle of Lexington and Concord, Paine's perspective on the conflict had begun to come into focus. The British government was not planning to make amends with the Americans; they were planning to annihilate them.

With the careful attention of an editor, Paine began in the summer of 1775 jotting notes about the American situation, the first faint sparks of *Common Sense*. Most of Paine's personal papers were lost in a fire during the nineteenth century, and no manuscript copy of *Common Sense* survives, but we can put together some of the details of its composition from other records.[11] Many years later, Robert Aitken told Massachusetts printer Isaiah Thomas, with a hint of bitterness, that Paine became a better writer after a glass of brandy.[12] This detail is not particularly surprising, because Paine had acquired an initial interest in politics through his membership in the Headstrong Club, an informal debating society that met in the White Hart Inn, a local tavern in Lewes. Paine and his comrades swilled beer and debated English politics in the wake of the John Wilkes affair. Paine's skills proved formidable in this setting, and his friends paid tribute to his knack for devastating arguments and witty repartee. Now in Philadelphia and beginning to grow weary of his employment situation, Paine took a sip of his brandy and imagined himself holding court back at the White Hart Inn.

Present Transactions

Benjamin Franklin, while still in England, had been glad to hear of Paine's engagement in the *Pennsylvania Magazine*, and after Philadelphia's elder statesman had returned home, he complimented Paine on the quality of the periodical. At Paine's request, Franklin had returned to Philadelphia with Oliver Goldsmith's eight-volume *An History of the Earth, and Animated Nature* (1774). Paine thanked his patron for going to the trouble of carting so many books across the Atlantic and asked to pay Franklin for them. Franklin, one of the wealthiest men in the colonies, refused Paine's money. Franklin leafed through the impressive work of Goldsmith, another of Franklin's and Paine's mutual friends in London, and commented that the American cause might best be advanced by publishing a definitive history of the conflict's progress. Paine carried the stack of books back to his room and began to read the first volume. Goldsmith described a world "furnished with advantages on one side, and inconveniences on the other" as "the proper abode of reason" and "the fittest to exercise the industry of a free and a thinking creature." As Paine neared the end of the first volume, he read words that seemed written directly for him:

> God beholds, with pleasure, that being which he has made, converting the wretchedness of his natural situation into a theatre of triumph; bringing all the headlong tribes of nature into subjection to his will; and producing that order and uniformity upon earth, of which his own heavenly fabric is so bright an example."[13]

Rush later recalled that Paine had "seized the idea," of writing such a history "with avidity." Utilizing materials given to him by Franklin, Paine began to write what he intended to become a multivolume "history of the present transactions," the first volume of which he thought Franklin would like to see published during the spring of 1776. In September 1775, the month prior to Franklin's oblique request, Paine had "formed the outlines of *Common Sense*, and finished nearly the first part," so Paine sped up his writing, hoping "to surprise him with a production on that subject, much earlier than he thought of." Paine had "supposed the doctor's design" in furnishing him with the materials to write a history "was to open the new year with a new system." In October and November, Paine immersed himself in the work of fleshing out the essays that would become *Common Sense*. He didn't tell Franklin about his plan or his progress but hoped to impress his mentor by bringing him a copy of the finished work.[14]

Though Paine chose not to involve Franklin directly in the project, he did not write *Common Sense* in isolation. Every time Paine completed another passage, he would carefully fold the paper, place it into his pocket, and begin walking toward the home of his friend Benjamin Rush. Rush, a practicing medical doctor as well as a chemist, had first met Paine in Robert Aitken's bookshop during the spring of 1775, and the two found an instant resonance in their opposition to African slavery.[15] Rush had been born in America, but he had been raised as a Scots-Presbyterian and trained as a physician in Edinburgh, so he had a natural affinity for Philadelphia's Scottish booksellers, Robert Aitken and Robert Bell, and he spent as much time as possible browsing their shelves. When in Aitken's shop, Rush made sure to say hello to Paine, and the two began to spend more time together. In April 1775 Paine and Rush became founding members of America's first anti-slavery society, and they continued to get together regularly to discuss morals and science, in particular.

Their scientific conversations often led to experiments, and when Captain Thomas Pryor overheard their animated exchanges at the London Coffee House, especially their discussions about saltpeter, he grew curious. Pryor was a wealthy Philadelphian whose love for science almost eclipsed his love for military affairs. An active member of the American Philosophical Society, Pryor had been an eager participant in several experiments of that scientific body. Pryor was a military man at heart, and he had been concerned about Pennsylvania's security since early in 1775. On April 13, 1775, six days before Lexington, Captain Thomas Pryor wrote to his senior officers in the Pennsylvania Militia that "matters have come to a serious period." He thought that Pennsylvania had been too negligent in its preparations for defense, and he wondered whether "we intend tamely to submit to the detestable claims of Parliament, or to oppose their measures." Pryor advocated an aggressive defensive posture and wanted to begin disciplining troops, "which you know has always been my mode, when we find the peaceable measures we have adopted do not succeed."[16] Pryor was overjoyed to hear the ideas of Paine and Rush on the subject of saltpeter production, and he eagerly volunteered to help with their efforts.

Pryor knew that Paine was working on a series of essays proposing a new course of action with Britain, but he remained uninvolved in the process of composition. Besides Paine, only Benjamin Rush took a substantive role in the composition of *Common Sense*. During the fall of 1775, Paine arrived at Rush's house on many evenings to read portions of the text aloud and to receive Rush's feedback. Decades later, Rush would still recall his amusement the first time he heard a line that Paine eventually decided to leave out of the final manuscript: "Nothing can be conceived of more absurd than three millions of people flocking to the American shore every time a vessel arrives from England, to know what portion of liberty they shall enjoy."[17]

Both Paine and Rush admitted to a degree of editorial collaboration, but they both knew that Paine was the sole author of *Common Sense*. Rush had cautioned against Paine's overt advocacy of independence and republicanism, but the doctor held only the power of suggestion and deferred to the author on matters of style and substance. As the drafts developed through November, both Paine and Rush realized that the text in front of them was not a proper history, but they still thought it a worthwhile endeavor. At this crossroads, they agreed to receive outside input from a man they both respected, David Rittenhouse. Rittenhouse was a master clockmaker, surveyor, mathematician, and engineer, who had lately moved to Philadelphia to pursue his chief passion, astronomy. Rittenhouse was not a trained critic or politician, but his scientific prowess made his opinion weighty with Paine and Rush. After reading through a draft of Paine's essays, Rittenhouse noted that they seemed like works of journalism rather than history. He thought they were quite good, and he encouraged Paine and Rush to forge ahead.

Rush took Rittenhouse's advice and began to talk with the printers of some of the Philadelphia newspapers. He never named Paine, and he avoided specifics, but he tried to get a sense of the possibility of inserting Paine's essays into consecutive issues of a single newspaper. Because of the nature of Paine's argument, which had already taken shape in its tone and content, Rush didn't bother calling on the more conservative printers of the *Pennsylvania Ledger* or the *Pennsylvania Gazette*. Rush spoke with Benjamin Towne of the *Pennsylvania Evening Post*, Thomas Bradford of the *Pennsylvania Journal*, and John Dunlap of the *Pennsylvania Packet*, but he couldn't get a firm commitment from any of them in advance. As political tensions continued to escalate at the end of 1775, the newspaper printers began to grow nervous that one wrong editorial decision could cause a great defection of subscribers. King George III's August proclamation of the Americans' open rebellion had caused almost universal gasps when it arrived in Philadelphia in early November. As Rush canvassed for a willing printer at the beginning of December, the newspaper publishers also noted that they would be receiving information on the current session of parliament any day, and that such information would automatically bump a trifling American opinion piece. Rush reported back to Paine of the "impossibility of getting them generally inserted" into the newspapers, and so the two decided that the best decision would be to reformat the serials into a single, four-part essay and to publish it as a pamphlet.

Paine made the necessary edits to restructure the work, while Rush, whose marriage to Julia Stockton was fast approaching, hastily tried to make arrangements to publish his friend's short treatise. Rush had sensed the skittish reactions of the newspaper printers whom he had called upon before, and he decided to approach them only as a last resort. Neither of Rush's closest friends among the printers, fellow Scotsmen Robert Aitken and Robert Bell, published a newspaper. Aitken's apolitical stance and the dissolution of his relationship with Paine left Rush with one obvious choice, if he hoped to publish the work quickly: Robert Bell.

Part Two
PAPER AND INK

To the Press

Robert Bell was one of the few printers in Philadelphia who published neither a newspaper nor an almanac. Almost every other Philadelphia printer published one or the other, and usually both. And this was for good reason: in the precarious and hardscrabble business of eighteenth century printing, advance-subscription newspapers and best-selling almanacs were rare guaranteed moneymakers. Publishing a newspaper did make a printer more susceptible to boycotts and other forms of social backlash, which tended to squelch any penchant for publishing more inflammatory pieces. Even if a newspaper printer agreed on a personal level with Paine's salacious positions, he couldn't have risked printing it. Because Bell published no newspaper, he was less exposed to rapid swings in popular opinion than most of his peers.

At the end of December, Paine realized that reports from the current parliamentary session would start rolling in soon, and he suspected that they would maintain the hostile tone of earlier messages. For that reason, and because of the fact that his sole intermediary, Rush, was about to get married, Paine pushed to have the pamphlet printed right away. The very fact that Bell's press was available at the first of the year, was something that could not be said for most colonial print shops. The colonial almanac industry operated on a similar schedule to today's calendar industry. Almanacs were time-sensitive goods, and December and January were the peak sales period of the best-selling publications in the colonies. If Rush had approached an almanac publisher during the last week of December or the first week of January, and asked him to stop his presses to print a pamphlet—which usually lost money—the printer would have chuckled. Almanacs were big business, and pamphlets were not.

Rush and Bell made a hasty agreement to print the pamphlet under conditions suggested by the anonymous author. Rush returned to share the good news with his friend and found Paine scrawling a title page for the piece that said "Plain Truth: Addressed to the Inhabitants of America." Paine thought the title emphasized the straightforward style of the pamphlet, but Rush thought it sounded too roast beef English. He persuaded Paine instead to use "Common Sense," which carried a more republican ring and, importantly, met with the approval of the pamphlet's new republican publisher.[18] Though naming the pamphlet was Rush's most visible contribution to *Common Sense*, the significance of the name change should not be inflated. The meanings of the two expressions did not diverge in a significant way. In fact, the terms were rather convertible: for instance, Joseph Addison had, in *The*

Spectator, No. 70 (1711), described a "Reader of plain common Sense" and that same practical equivalence carried through to Paine's day.[19] Neither term attempted to smuggle in philosophical subtlety, which was for the best, since such meanings would have been lost on Paine's American audience. Both terms meant no more and no less than Paine's readers expected them to mean, and that obviousness was precisely what Paine intended.[20]

Media Res Publica

Common Sense, like any text, was not simply a nebulous cluster of words floating in ether. It was published and circulated according to the material and economic dictates of its medium. We cannot proceed with our narrative of *Common Sense*'s publication, and we cannot understand *Common Sense* in its original context, without first grasping the details of late colonial print culture. Many surviving copies of *Common Sense* are only loosely bound with twine. It was typical, especially as the various editions of *Common Sense* added content, for readers to purchase stacks of print from a local bookseller and bind them with the original at home. Textual critics often refer to readers "constructing meaning." In the case of *Common Sense*, the readers did construct meaning, but many of them first constructed the text itself.

Bibliographer Charles Evans divided the political publications of the revolutionary period into five distinct forms: broadside, broadsheet, tract, pamphlet, and book. The broadside was a single unfolded sheet of varying sizes with printing only on one side. Broadsides typically were used for proclamations, handbills, advertisements, or sheet calendars. Broadsheets included printing on both the recto and verso, the front and back, and thus contained two pages in folio (a sheet folded in half), quarto (folded into quarters), or octavo (folded into eighths). Broadsheets were best fitted for circular letters and short political addresses. A tract was a single sheet folded and paginated with room for four pages of text in folio, eight pages in quarto, and sixteen pages in octavo.

A full sheet of printer's paper was large, like a newspaper today when completely unfolded, but usually of a much sturdier construction than newsprint made from wood pulp. If the printed text required between two and five of these full sheets folded and cut into pages, then it became a pamphlet. Any work that exceeded five sheets of paper was technically a book, regardless of its binding. A pamphlet, then, had a maximum capacity in octavo—the most common folded size because it was easy to hold and to carry—of eighty pages.[21]

Common Sense rode the line between being a pamphlet and a book, depending upon the typeface used and the inclusion of later appendices: some versions contained 36 pages and some almost 150.

Though regarded by most as a pamphlet, it was longer than a typical work of its kind. Bell's first edition of *Common Sense* ran to the maximum pamphlet size of 80 pages without any additional material. The significance of this from a publishing perspective is that the economics of pamphlet and book publishing were distinct. A normal pamphlet, like John Adams' pithy *Thoughts on Government* (1776), contained less than thirty pages and was printed in small quantities for a circumscribed audience. Authors would usually front the modest cost of the edition with little expectation of profit. The publication of a book, on the other hand, was initiated by printers and funded by advance subscription. Colonial Americans wrote so few books that in practical terms, there was no norm for the economic relationship between book and author. In America, book publishing was a printer-driven business, since most books printed in the colonies had been pirated from earlier European editions. If a printer miscalculated the demand for a particular work or if subscribers proved fickle or delinquent, then that printer would be exposed to a significant crunch in cash flow. Working in a context of decentralized currencies and steep inflation, provincial publishing was a difficult trade with long hours and thin margins, and a single economic misstep could precipitate the closing of a shop.[22]

The most important commonality, therefore, between the economics of colonial pamphlet and book publishing was the printer's vigilant attunement to minimizing his financial risk.[23] Someone else besides the printer *always* invested in a sizeable work prior to its publication: in the case of pamphlets, the *author* bore the financial burden, and in the case of books, the *audience* carried the risk by subscribing in advance. Printers were assemblers and purveyors of texts, and their investment was typically limited to providing labor and to forwarding the capital necessary to print numbers above their break-even subscription level.

Provincial Printing

The most prominent characteristic of American print culture before 1765 was its identity as a provincial extension of British print culture. The establishment of the first colonial press in Cambridge in the late seventeenth century amounted to a mere blip within the hegemony of London print culture. The American colonies lagged nearly a century behind the output of the London presses, stifled by relatively meager urban populations, a shortage of skilled labor, and a preponderance of dispersed rural communities connected by impossible wilderness roads. In print, as in all else, the colonies of the early eighteenth century were absolutely dependent upon the metropole. Paper, ink, labor, and wooden presses arrived only in crates shipped from London. Moreover, crates arriving from the mother country filled with books, pamphlets, and newspapers more than adequately satiated colonial demand for knowledge of politics and religion. Only after the 1720s did the colonies begin to see a steady rise in the number of working presses, and these were concentrated in the northern seaports.

Printing in America remained a feudal trade until the second decade of the nineteenth century. Technological innovations such as mechanized presses were still far distant, and at least until the 1790s, an American print shop remained, in its technologies, functions, and hierarchies, virtually indistinguishable from Gutenberg's shop.[24] Master printers and journeymen performed the tedious tasks surrounding the composition of plates from a very limited selection of typefaces. Indentured servants occupied their long workdays with the arduous tasks of cleaning, inking, beating, and pressing the large wooden levers that culminated in varying qualities of impressions. All of this was hard work, and yet the payoff was dubious. With very rare exceptions like Benjamin Franklin, even upper-echelon printers prior to the turn of the nineteenth century considered themselves of "the middling classes," artisan-entrepreneurs whose success depended on the whims of the market and a little luck. Printing was so labor- and time-intensive that a book could only be profitable under optimum conditions.[25] For this reason, only rarely did printers endeavor to publish large books, and even then they employed the most conservative marketing technique available: the advance subscription.

Only after the turn of the nineteenth century did population growth, technological advance, and the emergent popular novel enable consistently profitable book publishing in the young American states. Before then, in the colonial and revolutionary periods, printers turned to other types of publications that were more likely to turn a profit. Shorter publications such as broadsides, chapbooks, political pamphlets, and devotional tracts could be printed on inexpensive paper in large quantities and still be sold at an affordable price that would ensure their distribution. Until the political crisis with Britain came to a head in the latter half of the eighteenth century, the best bet for American printers remained religious materials like reprinted sermons and short educational books like the bestselling *New England Primer*. Books were commodities just like coffee, tea, and sugar, and were often sold in colonial bookshops alongside the miscellany procured by enterprising printer-merchants. Book advertisements often included additional items like rugs, boots, teapots, and saddles.

Print culture in the colonies began its ascension as major cities began to see the proliferation of local newspapers. These papers were compiled and published by the leading printers of the city, and they began as conveyors of transatlantic news and thinly-veiled advertising vehicles for the printer's bookshops and general stores. Most American newspapers were still printed on a weekly basis (still lagging behind the regular dailies of London), and these papers provided excellent publicity for their owners and also became a steady source of income to smooth the fluctuations of the print market. Over time, these newspapers began to acquire a distinctly local affiliation and included more and more colonial political commentary, becoming eventually flashpoints of colonial resistance.

The surest means to profitability for printers—and for most, this was their chief goal—was government printing. Benjamin Franklin, as mentioned earlier, made above-average money because of his creative franchising and his publication of popular almanacs, but he became a wealthy man primarily because of his government printing contracts with the royal and commonwealth governments of New Jersey and Pennsylvania. Printing the proceedings of provincial congresses and attendant legal documentation was a boon for any printer who could get his name written on a contract (and with only two exceptions it was "his," though some of the daughters and widows of revolutionary-era printers did become successful printers themselves in the early nineteenth century). The financial oasis provided by secure government contracts amidst the volatile paucity of the remainder of colonial printing became then the cultural backdrop for the frenzied response of the printers to the Grenville ministry's Stamp Act of 1765.

The Political Role of Print Culture

The Stamp Act controversy was a watershed for the role of print in the colonies. While printers by temperament tended to be rather flamboyant characters, their interest in governmental favor kept their eccentricities in check. The printers were aghast when they received word that parliament had passed the new stamp tax in order to fund the standing British Army in the American colonies—a very sore spot with colonists who recognized that lingering "protection" against the French and Indians was a guise for imposed imperial subordination. The Stamp Act taxed nearly every item coming into or going out of a colonial print shop. Newspapers were taxed as well as the paper on which they were printed. In an industry already beset by razor-thin profit margins, the printers took this as a personal affront. The printers were not alone, however, because the materials receiving the most severe taxing were legal documents, a strike against the lucrative government contracts of the printers but angering another significant profession of colonists just as much, the lawyers.

Though the Stamp Act was repealed less than a year after its passage, the printers and their presses had become inextricably entangled in the ebb and flow of continental resistance. Agitated colonial subjects began reading and discussing newspapers more frequently in taverns and coffeehouses, and printers met this increased demand by ramping up circulation and by publishing more and more politically-oriented broadsides and pamphlets.

Even in the piqued political climate in the decade following the Stamp Act, the numerous political pamphlets were usually only modest commercial successes. The contents of most of these pamphlets—despite their inexpensive production format—were geared toward a small "literate" audience. The tepid economics of colonial printing made pamphlet culture little more than vanity publishing, an extravagance allowed only to men of means who had the time and money to publish for publication's sake. The wealthy and learned classes of lawyers, ministers, merchants and planters dominated this elite discourse because they had the luxury of pursuing fame or controversy apart from the necessity of remuneration. Most of the "middling" classes and "lower sorts" could only eavesdrop on half-intelligible conversations punctuated with encrypted references to Horace and Tacitus. Some of the printers who issued pamphlets would have struggled to understand the freight of their arguments, but this was of little consequence, since the resource-full authors provided assurance of payment regardless of sales success.

PART THREE
A PROMOTER OF PRINT

Robert Bell, Bookseller

Robert Bell had finished in October 1775 the third and final volume of his edition of James Burgh's *Political Disquisitions*, and the end of the year was a pleasant respite from the frenzy that usually characterized his shop. His printing press was relatively free in late December and early January, a time when other presses around Philadelphia were glutted with almanacs. Besides Bell's personal relationship with Rush, there was another reason that recommended the colorful Scotsman as the right man for the job of publishing *Common Sense*. Bell had acquired a reputation as a publisher of risky ventures. While most other colonial printers were *minimizers* of personal risk, Bell could be described more aptly as an assiduous *manager* of risk. If he believed sufficiently in a principle or a project, he would undertake it without the same safeguards as other colonial printers, but he was by no means reckless in his decisions. He simply made sure that proper financial structures were in place to compensate him for his courage.

In the case of *Common Sense*, Bell had already signaled his openness to Paine's argument before Rush had approached him. The third volume of the Philadelphia publication of Burgh's *Political Disquisitions*, the edition that Rush and Paine had read, contained within its covers an advertisement by Bell for several books in his shop. Bell's entry for a book on architecture illustrated the congruence between the attitudes of Bell and Paine in late 1775:

> The first number of this useful and ornamental work, will be published on Wednesday the twentieth of September, 1775, at that very remarkable Epocha, when the Americans laid down external commerce, took up arms, and internal manufactures, to support their constitutional liberty against the despotic encroachments of royal, ministerial, and parliamentary Traitors; because false delicacy then vanished from royal names and royal things, as utterly insufficient to varnish over criminal actions, although attempted by men that once were, and might have continued majestic.[26]

When Bell believed in a principle, he pursued it into print, but he always had an economic fallback plan. Bell's primary means of managing the risk of publication was through his skill as a book auctioneer. In 1774, Bell had single-handedly pushed through legislation in the Pennsylvania Assembly reversing what he considered an anachronistic law prohibiting book auctions in the colony. Bell was a self-described "Professor of Book Auctioneering" who excelled in the cutthroat world of colonial publishing by the brash ingenuity with which he ran his business. Bell realized that stagnant book inventories were one of his greatest liabilities, so he advocated book auctions to liquidate old stock and to generate capital for new projects. Bell had come to Philadelphia in the mid-1760s to set up a press and a bookshop, and his peacock personality shone through right away in his editorial introductions and his newspaper advertisements. In a 1768 issue of Franklin's *Pennsylvania Gazette*, Bell advertised his bookselling services,

> If the Possessors choose to take the Chance of a public Sale, they may have them exhibited, with a regular catalogue, by Auction, at the Uppermost Vendue-House, in Second street, near Vine street, where the intrinsic merit and excellence of each book shall be rationally expiated upon, with Truth and Propriety; also the extrinsic or original Value Properly demonstrated for the satisfaction of Sellers and Buyers.[27]

Whenever the demand for Bell's books fell short, he always sold them at a discount or auctioned them off, even journeying to other colonies "to make things go." When Bell was reprimanded for unknowingly breaking the law prohibiting book auctions in Philadelphia, his initial response was to pack up his auctions like traveling shows. On one occasion, he conducted an auction "for eight or ten evenings successively" at the Royal Exchange Tavern in Boston beginning July 4, 1770.[28] Bell argued that selling books by auction was "a necessary Concomitant on the Increase of new Publications, and a grand Auxiliary to the Extension of Literature," a fact proven by its being a "daily Practice of the Booksellers of *London, Edinburgh, Glasgow, Dublin*, and by the Booksellers of all the Nations in *Europe*."

In addition to Bell's skill as a book auctioneer, he was also an exceptional bookbinder. On large projects, he did some of the printing work himself and farmed out portions to other shops. Bell's 1774 edition of Blackstone's *Commentaries*, the most ambitious work of its kind undertaken in the colonies to date, attracted over 1,500 subscribers. His press, next to St. Paul's Church on Third Street, was responsible for the publication of several other important works in the early 1770s, including Joseph Priestley's *Reply to Blackstone on Dissenters* (1772), Adam Ferguson's *Essay on the History of Civil Society* (1773), *A Dissent from the Church of England, Fully Justified* (1774), Nathan Ben-Saddi's *The Chronicle of the Kings of England* (1775), and James Burgh's *Political Disquisitions* (1775). In 1776, he published mainly pamphlets and military manuals. Besides publishing *Common Sense*, Bell would become the primary colonial publisher for James Chalmers's *Plain Truth* (1776), John Cartwright's *American Independence* (1776), and Henry Hugh Brackenridge's *Battle of Bunker's Hill* (1776).[29]

Bell understood the bookselling business as well as anyone in the colonies. He frequently gave an extra volume "Gratis" for those who subscribed for multiple copies, and he often allowed readers to exchange earlier editions of a work for an expanded or enlarged later edition "on paying the Difference between the Prices."³⁰ His ads sometimes included a one or two page "Specimen" to demonstrate the typesetting quality and to encourage subscribers. In one instance, he promised to sell a single volume of 300 pages octavo for 5 shillings "as soon as 500 subscribers approve the conditions."³¹ Bell was well connected to his peers in the other colonies, and his advertisements requested that potential subscribers send their names and residences to him "or to any of the Booksellers in America."³² Perhaps his most famous quotation, from a broadside advertisement he printed in January 1774 for an upcoming book auction, captures best the intersection of his sales technique and his economic philosophy:

> The more BOOKS are sold, the more will be sold, is an established Truth well known to every liberal Reader, and to every Bookseller of Experience; For the Sale of one BOOK propagateth the Sale of another, with as much certainty as the Possession of one Guinea helpeth to the Possession of another.³³

Without the privilege of attending Bell's riotous auctions in person, the best glimpse we can get of his outsized personality comes from his advertisements. As we have seen, any major publication in eighteenth century America required a list of advance subscribers before printing commenced. The third volume of Bell's edition of Burgh's *Disquistions* included a list of subscribers—standard procedure for the period—that devolved into one of Bell's quintessential tirades:

> Should any of Mr. Luke-warm's Family, who are always numerous among the timid, buy this Book, and unhappily think he hath too much for the Money—He may immediately apply the following remedy—Either tear the offensive leaf out—Or more effectually to punish the forward Editor—Burn the whole Book—That there may be immediate Occasion for a Second Edition—For some Minds are strangely squeamish, and think it a great Crime for a struggling Bookseller, to support or produce Opinions, although he charge nothing for them; but had he fortunately excised upon his Customers, so as to be esteemed rich, his Nonsense would soon be converted into sterling Sense, and his Obtrusions would then be very acceptable, for the Slaves of Riches, would then support him with a most infallible Reason—Hear him!—Hear him!—For he's very rich.³⁴

This excerpt reveals Bell's savvy approach to the business of public controversy and, at the same time, it foregrounds his economic self-consciousness and his quirky ability to express even antipathy in carnivalesque language. It is not surprising, in retrospect, that Bell's acerbic eccentricity and Paine's slashing wit would clash, causing the rapid degeneration of their nascent professional relationship. At the same time, it was this mutual repulsion and the crackling tabloid exchange between the two that piqued early interest in *Common Sense* and precipitated the dizzying proliferation of published editions over the next few months.

Manufacture of Opinion

In January 1773, three years before he printed *Common Sense*, Bell was agitating the Pennsylvania Assembly for a repeal of "one clause in an antiquated act" that prevented book auctions in the city of Philadelphia. He published a broadside, connecting the "success of the Paper Manufactory" with "the grand Art of Printing, which elevateth and refineth the human mind." He reasoned that the act was fitted for a time "before the consumption of Books was ever suspected to amount to a staple commodity in which thousands of pounds might be employed to the advantage of the community in general, and also to the benefit of many industrious individuals."[35]

Bell's argument continued with a description of the "state of the trade" of bookselling, beginning with a hypothetical case study of a printer desiring to publish a version of Chambers's *Universal Dictionary of Arts and Sciences* containing four volumes in folio. "To defray the very great expence of Paper, Printing, and Binding, and to be enabled to afford this valuable work at a moderate price to the purchasers," Bell said, "it is necessary that the bookseller should risk the cost of printing three thousand copies." But, Bell continued, the printer may have overestimated his market, and "after waiting for two or three years for the expected purchasers," would determine to sell them by auction, "the mode practiced in all other countries when an edition hath been overprinted." Selling the books by auction, "although at an under price, realizeth dead stock into live CASH, and will sooner enable him to repair with ready money to the Paper Manufacturers, in order to make another attempt upon some celebrated author, whose sublime works might diffuse universal knowledge to every corner of the American continent." By hindering the sale of books in the city, Bell wrote, the colony was enacting a virtual "embargo to prevent the adventuring booksellers" from printing books that would "both illuminate the minds, and illustrate the pockets of many members of the community."

Though he had "several times descanted on" the "formal" advantages his readers received from books, "their minds are either improv'd or delighted by these my daily labours," he focused his argument on the "material" advantages of the book trade. The public benefits "from these my speculations" as they consume "our paper manufacture, employ our artisans in printing, and find business for great numbers of indigent persons."

Bell's account of the lifecycle of colonial paper, contained in his 1773 broadside, sheds light on the economics and circulation of texts in eighteenth century America. Bell described "Those poor retailers, whom we see so busy in every street," collecting several "mean materials" and delivering "their respective gleanings to the merchant." The merchant carried these "gleanings" to the paper mill where they "give life to another trade" and "raise the rents" of those who have mills on their estates. As soon as the materials are "wrought into paper," they are distributed to the presses, where they are "stain'd with news or politicks" and then "fly thro' the town in *post men, post boys, daily-courants, reviews, medleys*, and *examiners*."

"Men, women, and children," Bell continued, "contend who shall be the first bearers of them, and get their daily sustenance by spreading them." As Bell reviewed the system through which "a bundle of rags" becomes "a quire of *spectators*" with "so many hands employ'd in every step," he concluded, "while I am writing a *spectator*, I fancy myself providing bread for a multitude."[36]

The paper even had a life after the press. Bell used it for lighting his pipe, and his landlady "desired some of my old spectators" to wrap her spices. They even, said Bell, "make a good foundation for a mutton pie, as I have more than once experienced, and were very much sought for last *Christmas* by the whole neighbourhood." Paper made from linen rags was reconstituted into fabric for clothes and furniture. "In a word, a piece of cloth, after having officiated for some years as a towel or a napkin, may by this means be raised from a dunghill, and become the most valuable piece of furniture in a prince's cabinet."[37]

A Material Scarcity

Bell's discourse on the role of print in the colonial economy proved prophetic in 1776. In addition to the dearth of saltpeter, the American colonies also experienced a startling lack of paper throughout 1776. Paper had most often been imported from Britain or Holland, but supplies grew scarcer because of American non-importation and British naval blockade. Ezra Stiles, a Congregational pastor in Rhode Island who would become president of Yale College in 1778, noted in his literary diary from 1776 that "The present Civil War has rendered Paper so scarce, that I could not get a Blank Book till the latter end of February. And now I transcribe the minutes I made on loose sheets of a very coarse paper: at least some of the principal ones. And I should have made more copious Extracts at the Time, but that I was daily expecting that I should find paper."[38]

Broadsides and broadsheets, though few of these ephemera survive today, came to be the prevailing form of communication as paper-intensive pamphlets became less economical. The only pamphlets that were published tended to deal directly with the conflict between America and Britain or with military preparedness, and diverse qualities and colors of papers were often used in the same work by desperate printers.[39] Newspaper publishers, who had to manage subscriber expectations, became frantic, and almanac makers, who relied on cheap paper to produce the most popular texts in the colonies, suffered most.

In the middle of the furor over independence, Benjamin Towne apologized to his readers that "Nothing less than a scarcity of paper" prevented his publishing a supplement to the *Pennsylvania Evening Post* "at this important juncture, in order to lay some things of consequence before the public."[40] In his *Pennsylvania Packet*, John Dunlap lamented that "the Paper-Mills about this city are almost idle for want of RAGS; and of consequence, the Presses, the important vehicles of *Instruction* and *Amusement*, must soon be reduced to the same unhappy station."[41] Dunlap was forced in June and July of 1776 to print the *Packet* on a rainbow of paper colors and textures, and newspapers across America were replete throughout 1776 with entreaties by printers for "clean linen rags."[42]

Whatever the textual form, the purveyors of print felt handcuffed during a period when their services seemed most necessary. When one third of Bell's *Additions to Plain Truth*, published in the late spring of 1776, had to be printed on coarse blue paper, Bell explained his predicament:

> To every purchaser. The impossibility of obtaining white, constituted the law of necessity, for part of these Additions to appear in blue. The philosopher reacheth beyond outward appearances.—The patriot surmounteth every difficulty. And the bookseller industriously attempteth business agreeable to the prescriptions and decrees of the British and American laws of freedom concerning the liberty of the press.[43]

Liberty of the Press

The "liberty of the press" was a republican watchword often employed by Bell and other colonial printers. In 1776, Bell found himself reminding newspaper readers about the liberty of the press in uncharacteristically nervous and defensive public pronouncements. By mid-March, the brash Scotsman had a serious problem on his hands. He had dared to publish a pamphlet that controverted the prevailing public opinion in Philadelphia. The pamphlet for sale in his book shop that made him so squeamish was not *Common Sense*. It was an attempted refutation of *Common Sense*, written by a pseudonymous "Candidus" and entitled *Plain Truth*. Bell was making money off of its sales, but at the same time he began to fear for his safety.

Press liberty had long been a fundamental right of English republicanism, and it was a favorite topic of Whig polemicists John

Trenchard and Thomas Gordon in their *Cato's Letters* from the 1720s. Traditionally, the concept referred to a press that was free from government coercion and influence. The press, in this model, was the principal mode of enacting republican vigilance to protect the public against the degrading corruption of power. This traditional model of a violation of press liberty had occurred in late 1775 when the exiled royal governor of Virginia, Lord Dunmore, countermanded a Williamsburg press and began printing royalist propaganda from his ship off the Virginia coast. There was, however, a new problem faced by American printers in late 1775 and in 1776. In the past, the press had been liberated from *government control* on behalf of the people, but now the press, argued some printers, needed to be liberated from the coercion of *the people themselves*. As we shall see in later chapters, the swing in popular opinion in the wake of *Common Sense* was so dramatic that printers risked personal injury at the hands of angry mobs if they printed arguments in favor of "dependence."

Bell, in particular, was in an odd situation. He had been saluted as a brave patriot when he placed his name on the title page of *Common Sense*. But later that spring he received sneers when he walked the streets of Philadelphia after he had been involved in printing some of the most notorious tracts in opposition to independence. It seems strange now that Bell would publish both pro-independence and anti-independence pamphlets, but this was a patently republican act in Bell's mind. He was laying out both sides of the argument, *pro et contra*, and allowing the public to weigh its options through careful deliberation. To many in the pro-independence camp, it seemed that he was stalling the decision or even defecting to the opposition. On his expensive three-shilling edition of *Common Sense* "with the Whole Appendix" (1776), he included before the title page a self-attributed quote: "Self-defence against unjust attacks needs no apology. Bell." In this same expanded edition, the last page contained a defense of the "Liberty of the Press" with supporting quotations by "Junius" and others. Bell himself addressed the public, claiming that he had "ushered into the hands of the public, certain speculations FOR AMERICAN INDEPENDENCY" upon the authority of "The Liberty of the PRESS," and he was now, "By the same Authority," printing for those capable of impartiality "certain speculations AGAINST AMERICAN INDEPENDENCY."[44] As Bell conceived it, the liberty of the press was a civil right, but he, ironically, hadn't anticipated the breakdown of the sources of that right that would occur in part as a result of his publication. Bell was so disoriented by this turn in events that as early as April 1776, his advertisements had taken on an uncharacteristic modesty. In an ad for *Plain Truth* in the *Pennsylvania Evening Post*, Bell said with relative meekness,

If to preserve any part of the works of valuable writers hath always been looked upon as doing good service to the public, the Editor hereof may hope that his present endeavours will prove acceptable, at least, to all the lovers of freedom who are so consistent as to acknowledge the press ought to be free for others as well as for themselves.[45]

The Reading Publics

As I have noted, the act of generating public discourse with a free press was an instantiation of the whiggish virtue of vigilance, but that was only half of the equation. In order to effectively keep the public eye fixed on the horizon for encroaching power, the press needed an audience of watchmen, individuals who would carefully follow public discourse. The major hurdle for a person of modest means—which was the vast majority of American colonists—to follow public discourse was affording the media of discourse. Books, pamphlets, and newspapers were all luxury goods to all but the wealthiest Englishmen and Americans. Broadsides, chapbooks, and almanacs were more affordable and therefore more widely circulated. Books and newspapers were circulated by advance subscription to cover the financial risk of production. Newspapers and pamphlets did find a wider audience in taverns and coffee houses, where a single newspaper might find dozens of readers per day surrounded by scores of quiet auditors and boisterous debaters tuning in for foreign and domestic news, along with a dollop of gossip.

The fact that books were designed for an elite audience did not bother Robert Bell. He was a bibliophile, and he took immense pleasure in the intricacies of print craftsmanship and of excellence in the book trade. On one occasion, Bell mused over the splendor of a British edition of Caesar's *Commentaries*, "the finest book that I have ever seen" because of "the beauty of the paper, of the character, and of the several cuts with which this noble work is illustrated." This book was a work peculiar to "the *English* genius, which, tho' it does not come the first into any art, generally carries it to greater heights than any other country in the world."[46] The quality of Bell's craft, then, was a reflection of national as well as personal character, and a slap-shod work of print spoke poorly of both. Books were not repositories, conveyors, or mediums of information exchange for Bell, they were *themselves* the message.

In the same reflection on book selling, Bell went on to use a fascinating expression, addressing "MY illiterate readers" who are "surprised to hear me talk of learning as the glory of a nation, and of printing as an art that gains reputation to a people among whom it flourishes." The idea of an "illiterate reader" seems like an oxymoron, until we remember the meaning of literacy in the eighteenth century. To be literate had nothing to do with reading or writing English; it described a person who had enjoyed a liberal education, marked especially by the ability to read or write Latin.

Bell continued his assessment of print culture by making patently clear that his handiworks were not intended for uncivilized readers. "But as I shall never sink this paper so far as to engage with Goths and Vandals," he said, referring to his "illiterate" audience with a literate reference to Ancient Rome, "I shall only regard such kind of reasoners with that pity which is due to so deplorable a degree of stupidity and ignorance."[47] There was, believed Bell, a politics inherent in the transaction between a printer and a reader. By printing fine books for individuals of refined taste, Bell made a statement about the domain of legitimate knowledge, and he carefully circumscribed the public sphere by trafficking in the most expensive printed commodity.

Bell's republicanism differed significantly from Paine's on the point of defining the boundaries of the public. In one of Bell's salacious rants about the author's character, Bell noted that he believed the original intention of *Common Sense* had been "to sound the depths of the multitude for a virtuous and glorious independency." Bell's idea of "the multitude," however, contrasted with Paine's, as he revealed with startling transparency in an advertisement for *Common Sense*. "The Provedore to the Sentimentalists," he crowed, "doth not PRINT decent EDITIONS for such ignoramus's as Lord Dunmore's NEGROES," referring to a last-ditch emancipation of slaves by the exiled governor of Virginia. At the end of his hybrid advertisement-essay, Bell reminded the public that he continued to sell his "large edition of *Common Sense*" to "all who are capable of making proper distinctions."[48] The quality of books and type mattered a great deal to Bell, because he made his living not just as a printer, but as a bookseller, bookbinder, and book auctioneer, Like other book publishers, he would print samples of new works so that prospective buyers could see his attention to publishing detail. He specialized in printing top shelf leather-bound books, not moderately-priced newspapers or cheap almanacs. Bell valued his fine textual craftsmanship so highly, indeed, that he regarded authorial ingenuity with the same blasé tone that a Hollywood producer might today speak of actors as "talent."

My reference to Hollywood is not a random analogue. It allows me to highlight two important aspects of the print culture surrounding *Common Sense*. The first was the question of textual ownership. Who controlled a text, its author or its publisher? This basic issue of copyright standards had not been settled in the late eighteenth century, and the uncertainty this caused in the case of *Common Sense* proved very significant for its subsequent circulation. Secondly, eighteenth century readers sometimes referred to *Common Sense* as a book, a treatise, or an essay, and more often they called it simply a pamphlet. But the most common categorical descriptor used by Paine's contemporaries in their correspondence was a word that seems peculiar to readers today: "performance." General Charles Lee wrote, for instance, to General George Washington that *Common Sense* was "a masterly, irresistible performance," which had convinced him that independence was a necessity.[49]

Common Sense was, indeed, a performance, not so different from a film or a theater production. It was both a composition and an action, something performed before an audience.[50] Bell, who was himself always on stage, definitely grasped this aspect of the text's function. But Paine had intended a different sort of performance than the kind to which Bell or Paine's eighteenth century audience was accustomed. Rather than dressing *up* in theatrical costumes, as Paine had seen so often in the Covent-Garden theater district in London, Paine's performance was more dressing *down* into a virtual state of nature. As Paine conveyed the concept in *Common Sense*, he imagined his reader as a person who had been polluted by prejudice in advance of the pamphlet's argument.[51] Unlike the elaborate performances of dress and decorum in genteel culture, Paine's readers need not "put *on*" their "true character"; like the image of God resting innately on each person, his readers simply need not "put *off*" that character which they already possessed by nature. A reader's reason and feelings will, if unhindered by the billowing robes of tradition, "determine for themselves" the proper course of action.[52] Thus, while *Common Sense* was a textual performance, an aspect of its identity that Bell understood and exploited, it also possessed a textual economy that Bell never could grasp. Josiah Bartlett, a delegate in the Continental Congress from New Hampshire, wrote home on January 13, 1776, and he spoke of *Common Sense*, a pamphlet "greedily bought up and read by all ranks of people." Bartlett enclosed a copy "to lend round to the people" of Portsmouth, New Hampshire, to alleviate their fears of independence.[53] Even in its earliest stages and at its highest price, there was something in *Common Sense* that made it attractive to "all ranks of people," and Paine's emphasis on the economics of publishing sought to align the intrinsic qualities of the text with the extrinsic qualities of acquisition and circulation. As we shall see, the Bell editions that published *Common Sense* as a *book* privileged textual *performance*, while the Bradford editions that published *Common Sense* as a *pamphlet* embraced textual *economy*.

PART FOUR
THE PUBLISHING SCANDAL

The Price of Success

On a cold, rainy Tuesday in Philadelphia, Robert Bell began to sell *Common Sense* in his book shop on Third Street.[54] As a hectic week of printing at Bell's shop came to a close, *Common Sense* was first advertised for sale that evening, January 9, 1776, in Benjamin Towne's *Pennsylvania Evening Post*, a newspaper in which Bell frequently purchased advertisements.[55] There was no ad in the Thursday edition, but beginning on Saturday, January 13, advertisements, commentaries, refutations, and reiterations of *Common Sense* absolutely dominated the Philadelphia press for the next four months. This was something entirely new for a colonial press that had been totally dependent on London for content. The American colonial press had existed primarily to parrot British news to those on the empire's fringe. Indeed, American colonial newspapers before 1776 had been little more than time-delayed, starched recitations of British political coverage focusing mainly on parliamentary debates and deferential petitions.

Bell had delivered the first completed proof of *Common Sense* to Rush, who then forwarded it to Paine who, in turn, took it straight to Franklin. Rush made sure that Paine had all of the contractual documentation in hand before Rush's wedding to young Julia Stockton on January 11, 1776.[56] Much of the miscommunication between Paine and Bell that led to the stormy controversy over the publication of *Common Sense* is actually attributable to Rush's unavoidable absence from the scene. Paine and Bell did not know each other, and Paine, closely guarding his authorial anonymity, meant to keep it that way. Paine asked his friend and collaborator on the saltpeter experiments, Thomas Pryor, to take Rush's place as mediator. When Paine learned that the pamphlet's first edition was selling at breakneck speed, he deduced that he had made a fast profit. In conversation with Pryor, a captain in the Pennsylvania Militia, Paine decided that the pamphlet's profits should be aligned with the pamphlet's arguments toward the public good. News of the Continental Army's defeat at Quebec reached Philadelphia on January 17. The Pennsylvania Militia determined to send an expedition to reinforce the beleaguered army, but their troops were ill-equipped for the harsh winter conditions that awaited them to the north. Paine and Pryor decided that the profits should go toward the purchase of mittens for the soldiers, and Pryor set out to inform Bell of their decision and to collect the profits. On his way, Pryor convinced his friend, Colonel Joseph Dean, to join him on their virtuous mission.[57]

The two officers assumed the transaction would go smoothly, and were stunned by Bell's dogmatic diminution of the amount Paine had informed them to collect. This was the first time Bell had heard of any charitable dispersion of the profits, and he was skeptical of the soldiers' intentions. He thought the author had sent the officers with an inflated bill to intimidate him out of the money he had justly earned. Pryor demanded the full amount, arguing that Bell's selfishness was depriving the army of necessary supplies. The difference between the two sides was only a few pounds, but a few pounds would buy a lot of mittens, and Pryor refused to budge as a matter of principle. Bell stood his ground, and the two officers stormed out of Bell's bookshop without any money at all. They returned to Paine and divulged the entire episode, emphasizing Bell's obstinacy and avarice, to the now-livid author. Paine looked over the contract, signed by both Bell and Rush, and thought the terms plain as day. Bell, he was convinced, had gone flush with greed when he saw what a gold mine he had stumbled upon. Paine fumed at Bell's attempt to swindle him out of his rightful share of the profits.

Because Rush's full attention was upon his new bride, and Pryor's mediatory errand had imploded, Paine felt his hands were tied. He wanted to preserve his anonymity, and he did not dare bother Benjamin Franklin with the menial task of profit collection, so Paine was at a loss as to how to proceed. In this state of dismay, Paine opened a copy of the *Pennsylvania Evening Post* of January 20, 1776, and almost fell out of his chair. In the newspaper, Bell was advertising a second edition of *Common Sense* to the public. Paine was irate. Bell had refused to settle his account from the first edition, and now the Scotsman dared to proceed with printing a second edition without informing or requesting permission from its author.[58]

Bell had sold out his first 1,000 pamphlet edition in eleven days, and on January 20 he published a "new edition."[59] Between Saturday, January 20, and Thursday, January 25, trouble brewed between Bell and Paine. Paine made hasty arrangements with Thomas Bradford, owner of the London Coffee House and publisher of the *Pennsylvania Journal*, to issue a new edition of *Common Sense*, sidestepping Bell entirely. On January 25, Paine ran a front page ad for the new edition in the *Pennsylvania Evening Post* with a special address "To the Public." In the ad, Paine claimed the new edition was "in the press" and would be "published as soon as possible," although the edition would not in fact come out for three full weeks. Paine claimed that Bell's new edition was lacking significant additions and was published expressly against Paine's "orders." Paine also added that the new expanded edition would sell for half the price of Bell's with further "allowance to those who take quantities." Paine's rationale for decreasing the price in spite of the increased size is hugely significant: "in order to accommodate it to the abilities of every man."⁶⁰

Cause Célèbre

Paine refused to hand over control of the text again. The forthcoming edition was directed to be sold "by appointment of the author," not of the new publisher. Paine boasted, "Several hundreds are already bespoke," including "one thousand for Virginia." This comment revealed Paine's intimacy by the end of January with members of the Virginia delegation in Congress, especially with Richard Henry Lee. Paine mentioned in the ad that a German edition was also "in the press." Bell's straightforward ad for a two-shilling new edition on the third page of the same paper, depicts the extent to which Paine's aggression caught the publisher off-guard.⁶¹ Bell responded in the next issue, on January 27, with a large ad for his "Second Edition" of *Common Sense*, this time with the tantalizing description "Written by an Englishman."⁶² If Bell had known Paine's name, he would have printed it as an exposé, but the author's nationality was the most specificity he could muster. The implication of Paine's Englishness—and the jab its disclosure represented—was the suspicion it aroused concerning the author's motives and intentions. Bell described, in a response letter "To the Public" the "absolute falsehoods" asserted by "an author, without a name." Without refuting Paine's claim that he had given Bell, "the printer and publisher," directions not to proceed with the publication of a second edition, Bell said that as soon as he "discovered the capricious disposition of the ostensible author, he disclaimed all future connection" and struck out on his own with a second edition. Bell "immediately declared his desirable independence from the trammels of catchpenny author-craft," and charged the anonymous author with a cunning strategy "to destroy the reputation of his own first edition" by advertising additions "before his earliest and best customers had time to read what they had so very lately purchased."⁶³

Bell then claimed never to have received oral or written instructions to refrain from printing, adding that even if he had, he would have treated them "with that contempt which such unreasonable, illegal, and tyrannic usurpations over his freedom and liberty in business deserved." Bell then addressed the author, "Mr. Anonymous," and his "imaginary triumph" and lack of equanimity. Bell claimed that Paine was reducing a price "which himself had a share in making." Bell reminded the public that he "scorneth duplicity in business or sentiment," and chastised the author for his improper attempt at "proving his attachment to generous principles" with "despicable ebullitions of dishonest malevolence." Bell closed his ad by mentioning the availability of Burgh's *Political Disquisitions* and also his plan to include "these intended additions" to his present second edition at a price "as cheap as possible."⁶⁴

The next edition of the *Pennsylvania Evening Post*, on Tuesday, January 30, included side-by-side advertisements for both competing editions of *Common Sense* that took up almost the entire back page of the newspaper. Bell's version was "OUT of the press, and now selling," while Paine's was "In the press, and will be published as soon as possible."⁶⁵ Bell's ad was identical to the prior issue, except for an addendum of great significance for the economics of circulation:

> But the public may be certain, that the new edition which is yet in the press, for smallness of print and scantiness of paper, when compared with Bell's second edition, which is out of the press, will resemble it in figure and utility as much as a British shilling in size and value resembleth a British half-crown.⁶⁶

Paine's ad for the Bradford publication followed the same format as that of the January 25 issue up to the announcement of a German edition. Then Paine added further background and perspective on the issue "for the sake of relieving the anxiety of his friends." He declared that his first intention was to publish the work as a series of letters in the newspapers, but he had been "dissuaded therefrom, on account of the impossibility of getting them generally inserted." He claimed to have known nothing of Bell, who had been "engaged to print it by a gentleman of the city" (referring to Benjamin Rush) who regretted the "unpleasant situation" in which he had inadvertently "involved his friend," the author. Paine reiterated that he had received no direct or indirect "profit or advantage whatsoever" from Bell's edition. Paine claimed that "the expence of printing" was to be paid "whether the work sold or not." Of everything "over and above" that expense, Paine had agreed to give "to this noisy man" one half of the profits, "amounting to upwards of thirty pounds, as a present for the trouble he might be at." The author had never intended to take any profit for himself, nor did he "mean to be known." When "the news of our repulse at Quebec arrived in this city," Paine gave "an order for the payment" of the other half of the profits, "together with said Bell's written promise for the same" to two gentlemen "for the purpose of purchasing mittens for the troops ordered on that cold campaign." The two gentlemen, Pryor and Dean, "whose names are left at the bar of the London Coffee-house" for the purpose of authenticating the author's assertions, "have not yet been able to settle with Robert Bell according to the conditions of his written engagement." Paine closed the address with a threat that Bell would be sued for the outstanding amount if he did not "perform within the course of the week." Paine effectively ended the conversation with the final sentence of the ad: "This is all the notice that will ever be taken of him in future."[67]

Bell did not abide the premature closure of the debate. In the Thursday, February 1, issue of the *Pennsylvania Evening Post*, Bell inserted a long, scathing letter addressed "To Mr. Anonymous." He called his adversary "weak," "wanton," "malicious," "imprudent," "shallow," "impolitic," "noisy," "self-conceited," "inglorious," "cowardly," "a rascally puppy," and "a wretched reptile." He accused Paine of freely giving away "other people's money" and boasting of his "imaginary importance" in "every beer-house." "Mr. Anonymous," said Bell, was an Englishmen encroaching upon the territory of the Irish, "a certain starved nation" who have always monopolized "Poverty and Pride." Or perhaps, he said, the author was a pupil of Lord Bute who had "come over to superintend the American treasury, upon his Scottish plan of public prodigality and extravagance," noting wryly that "Scotsmen have sometimes taught Englishmen."[68]

Among the most important remarks in Bell's harangue are those that pertain to the issue of authorship. Bell referred to "Mr. Anonymous" as the "Would-be-Author" in opposition to his identity as the "real Bookseller." Bell revealed his doubt regarding the pamphlet's authorship. "I do actually sympathise with the superior secret author, who had the misfortune to pitch upon so imprudent an ostensible author. Likewise Bell called his antagonist the foolish "foster-father author," and "with proper deference (to him, as yet unknown)" who had actually written *Common Sense*, Bell told the real author that he should have appointed "Robert Bell, bookseller, sole god-father of his pamphlet."[69]

Common Sense caused such a stir, in part, because everyone assumed it had been written by one of the leaders of the Congress, most likely by Benjamin Franklin, John Adams, or Samuel Adams. If Paine's actual identity had been discovered earlier in the pamphlet's history, it is likely that it would have met with a cooler initial reception. Every time Bell referred to "Mr. Anonymous," he stoked the flames of authorial speculation, and when he called the author "An Englishman," the public became even more curious, since that label disqualified Franklin and both Adamses.[70]

Ink Wrestling

Paine's "New Edition" (usually referred to as the "Bradford Edition") sold at shops all around Philadelphia, with advertisements listing retailers that included William and Thomas Bradford at the London Coffeehouse, John Sparhawk on Second Street near the Quaker Meeting House, William Woodhouse on Front Street, and Samuel Taylor at the corner of Market and Water Streets.[71]

Given the scarcity of colonial paper, the fact that Paine dared to increase the size of the new Bradford edition "upwards of one Third" over the earlier editions was a significant risk. The fact that Paine ordered 3,000 copies each from Benjamin Towne and from Melchior Steiner and Carl Cist was an even bigger gamble, considering that Paine's print order cost four times more than he had ever earned in a year.[72] The fact that Paine instructed Thomas Bradford "to sell them at the price of the printing and paper"—by simultaneously slicing the profit margin and the margin of error—may have been the biggest risk of all.[73]

Robert Bell possessed strong political views, but his primary economic credo, like that of most other colonial printers, was self-protection. In spite of his announcement that he would offer the "Additions" free, he concocted a scheme whereby he would assemble a political anthology along with Paine's new sections in order to justify selling his "Additions to *Common Sense*" for one shilling, the same price Paine and Bradford had placed on the entire pamphlet. Bell hastily purchased a copy of the "New Edition" on Wednesday and began resetting Paine's additions immediately to have them ready for the public the following Monday.[74]

Paine claimed that the dispute had begun when Bell refused to settle up according to their prearranged contract. Bell, on the other hand, attributed the dispute to Paine's conniving desire to control the terms of publication by underhandedly switching printers. More likely Paine grew frustrated by the inefficiencies of Bell's operation that led him to charge double what Paine was used to paying in London for a pamphlet of similar size. Paine saw clearly that the prohibitive price of Bell's edition was constricting the size of *Common Sense*'s audience. In short, Paine saw Bell's economics as a work of sabotage.

On February 20, the day after Bell's "Complete" edition was published, Paine inserted at the bottom of an ad for his "New Edition" in the *Pennsylvania Evening Post*, a special pointing-hand announcement: "The Pamphlet advertised by Robert Bell entitled ADDITIONS TO COMMON SENSE, or by any other Name he may hereafter call it, consist of Pieces taken out of News Papers, and not written by the Author of COMMON SENSE."[75] This curt reprimand sent Bell flying off the handle. In the next issue of the same paper, Bell published a two page letter of "self-defence against unjust attacks."[76]

Here Bell defended the "several excellent pieces" in his "Large Additions to *Common Sense*" on the basis of their encouragement by "some gentlemen, who are good judges of literary merit" and who thought the pieces "worthy of preservation" in a bound octavo volume. In an extraordinarily laissez-faire statement from Bell, he admitted that "those who think as [those gentlemen] do, will buy," while "those who do not think in that manner, will let them alone." This uncharacteristic relegation by Bell illustrates the principle, again, that printers always shifted economic risk to others. In this case, it appears, some wealthy patrons had capitalized the endeavor in advance.

Bell roused from his languor, though, again lashing out at "the envious Mr. Anonymous" whom he cast in a single sentence as a "murderer," a "ruffian," an "assassin," a "thief," a "predator," and a "devil" who had "crept into the field to ROB and DESTROY the reputation of authors" whose literary abilities outshone his as "the blaze of a torch" did the "glimmering of a candle."[77]

Bell reiterated his earlier accusations of his antagonist's feigned authorship, calling him again "the Foster-Father-Author," "the shadow of an author," "the ostensible author," and the "Amanuensis to a group of authors." Twice Bell called him a mere "go-between" who had "stolen applause" and borrowed "such usurped reputation."

Bell vowed that he would provide the public with the "true KEY" to the entire dispute. "When the work was at a stand for want of a courageous Typographer," Bell said, "I was then recommended by a gentleman nearly in the following words, 'There is Bell, who is a Republican Printer, give it to him, and I will answer for his courage to print IT.'" Bell then noted the "manly fortitude" required to emblazon his name "on the title of the flaming production." When the "Amanuensis" beheld "the success of the sale and of the sentiment," asserted Bell, he "formed the ungrateful design of jockeying the Printer." Bell had, "to please the authors" and to "serve the cause" performed fifty pounds worth of work for twenty, but as soon as he discovered "these shameful veerings" he decided, according to "the law of self defence," to "out-jockey if possible." It had been his own "knowledge in business" that made the pamphlet respectable, Bell argued, but the "ingrate GO BETWEEN," in his "capricious disposition" and "pretended generosity," had early designed to "circumvent the real bookseller." In a mocking jab at *Common Sense*, Bell said that "Mr. Anonymous" had decided "to be the MASSANELLO among authors and booksellers, at least for one DAY."[78]

A Matter of Shillings and Pence

Many historians and biographers have, because of the confusing claims of the debate, mistakenly thought that Bell claimed to have made no profit on the piece. In reality, Bell did claim to make a profit on the first print run of *Common Sense*; the dispute between him and Paine was simply over how much.

Paine expected a profit for himself of "upwards" 30 pounds, half of the total profit on the first 1,000-pamphlet edition. We don't know the exact amount that Bell offered Pryor and Dean, but we know that the amount was fourteen pounds less than Paine expected to receive, probably about 16 pounds. Bell, on the other hand, thought the "want of equity" between the two was a mere four pounds, since he expected a profit of only 20 pounds each or 40 pounds total on the edition. Their only point of dispute, said Bell, was over the cost of folding, cutting, collating, and stitching the 11,000 half-sheets, just a little over 4 pounds total.[79] Bell claimed this charge was "so very moderate that several booksellers declared the work done was worth double the money." As Bell recounted it, "for that very reasonable charge, one of said assignees would not settle the account," and Bell cheekily claimed that he had "not yet learned the necessity of forcing money upon those who are not willing to receive it." Closing his tirade, he promised the additions to all purchasers of the first and second editions "gratis." Then, in a pun on the pamphlet's title, he told his readers that he had "just as much common sense left as yet to spare a little to those who are volunteers in giving two shillings for the second edition."[80]

The month-long scintillating exchange between Bell and Paine, the publishing controversy that helped attract popular attention to the pamphlet and that, most significantly, ignited the decentralized distribution of *Common Sense*, was an argument over ten pounds. There are two simple explanations for this ten-pound difference: wholesale pricing and typeface size. Paine was a novice author and, therefore, may not have accounted for wholesale pricing in his profit estimate. Bell sold several of the first edition to other booksellers in Philadelphia and New York at a discounted wholesale rate, and therefore he made less profit on those copies. Bell sold bundles of two dozen copies of *Common Sense* to the printer Robert Aitken for one pound, 16 shillings, a wholesale discount of 25 percent or six pence less per pamphlet. At a price of two shillings each, the gross retail sales for one thousand pamphlets would have been 100 pounds. Those same thousand pamphlets, sold at Bell's wholesale rate, would have generated only 75 pounds worth of total revenue. News would have circulated fast among Philadelphia printers that Common Sense averaged sales of over 90 copies per day in its first week on the market, so we can be assured that Bell filled many wholesale orders. Ever eager to minimize his inventory liability, Bell obliged the other publishers, and thereby decreased—in the short run—his total revenue. Because he did not expect the rabid demand for *Common Sense*, Bell had brokered the deal with Rush under the assumption that he would sell the pamphlets at a slower pace but at the full retail price.

When we consider that Paine's bare-bones estimate of the production cost per pamphlet for his later edition, 8 ½ pence each, would amount to over 35 pounds for a 1000 pamphlet edition, we can see that the best case scenario, if every pamphlet had been sold at full retail price and if there had been no inefficiencies in the production process, was a total profit of under 65 pounds. The large typeface that

Bell used—because of his commitment to fine book craftsmanship—meant that his first editions of Common Sense consumed about eighty pages, compared to the later Bradford edition that had, in spite of additional material, about thirty *fewer* pages. When we factor in the expenses of stitching (a little over four pounds at "a penny per stitch"), newspaper advertising (about two pounds for eight advertisements before January 20), and Bell's inefficient use of paper (any publisher's largest category of expense), we can be assured that he was most likely telling the truth.[81]

It is not surprising that the contentious Paine and the hot-headed Bell would allow a simple financial misunderstanding to skyrocket into a vicious public controversy. In fact, if there was one consistent strand through Paine's rollercoaster life, it was his constant financial duress. When he had money, he gave it away, and when he lacked money—which was most of his life—he complained bitterly of the injustice and ingratitude of his more affluent associates. In the case of *Common Sense*, he literally gave away money he never had.

Paine's natural skill for mathematics never translated into the realm of finances, and his pathetic monetary record was a source of constant personal affliction. He had been fired from several jobs earlier in life and had managed to run the general store and tobacco shop of his second wife into the ground. As we have already seen, he parted ways with Robert Aitken, publisher of the *Pennsylvania Magazine*, after only a few months because of a salary dispute.[82] Paine's lifelong dream of building a single-span iron bridge over the Schuylkill or the Thames twice fizzled because of a lack of funding. He would spend decades decrying America's financial ingratitude for his services during the American Revolution, but after the State of New York granted him a sizable estate, he ended up selling off portions at a time to settle his debts. In Paine's mind, he was always underpaid and underappreciated, and so it was when he died in a Greenwich Village flat, penniless and forgotten.

Part Five
PROVEDORES

Sentimental Reason

For all of their differences, Paine and Bell did share one significant commonality: they both fixated upon the concept of *sentiment*. Bell constantly referred to himself as the "Provedore to the Sentimentalists."[83] In an advertisement "to the sons of SCIENCE in AMERICA," Bell described Adam Ferguson's *Essay on the History of Civil Society* (1767) as a "sentimental Banquet."[84] Bell's bookshop also contained a circulating library of over two thousand volumes, available by one or three month subscription, "or by agreement for a single Book." One of Bell's bookplates described his circulating library as a place "where SENTIMENTALISTS whether LADIES or GENTLEMEN, may become READERS."[85] In Bell's role as "Provedore to the Sentimentalists," he conceived of himself as a person who procured supplies for an army of thinking and feeling readers.[86]

The idea of sentiment in the eighteenth century did not carry the same sappy connotation as it does today. It was a synonym for thought, perception, or opinion, but it also carried an affective component. A sentiment was an opinion steeped in emotion. This seems hardly consistent with Paine's incessant espousal of reason as the vehicle of discourse, but here again we must make a distinction between the concept of reason in the eighteenth and twenty-first centuries, and more particularly for its use in Paine's writing. When Paine advocated "reason," he did not necessarily imply the dispassionate syllogisms of analytic philosophy; he was simply describing a process for arriving at right conclusions. Reason was not, for Paine and for most of his readers, opposed to feeling. One could be rational *and* emotional, or, more to the point, one could not be rational *without being* emotional. Reason was opposed to absurdity or unnaturalness, not to feeling.

Common Sense, according to its very first line, was a sentimental text. "PERHAPS the sentiments contained in the following pages," Paine began the pamphlet, "are not *yet* sufficiently fashionable to procure them general favor."[87] In *Common Sense*, Paine portrayed the possession of sentiment as the essence of humanity. King George III was an inhuman "wretch" and a "hardened, sullen tempered Pharaoh" because he could "unfeelingly hear" of his people's "slaughter, and composedly sleep with their blood upon his soul."[88] Deploying his argument from nature, Paine claimed that the affective motivation for retributive justice was constitutive of nature's very identity. As he put it, some injuries even "nature cannot forgive; she would cease to be nature if she did." Following the dictates of nature, the Americans could not "forgive the murders of Britain" any more than a lover could "forgive the ravisher of his mistress."[89] According to Paine, "The Almighty hath implanted in us these unextinguishable feelings for good and wise purposes. They are the guardians of his image in our hearts. They distinguish us from the herd of common animals." This was a significant twist on the ancient philosophical question of what distinguishes humans from other species of animals. Paine took the conventional answer of "rationality" and infused it with an emotive component. Likewise, the "unextinguishable feelings" were the fingerprint of God on humanity, and to erase those feelings would be tantamount to removing "his image" from human hearts. If people, Paine continued, were "callous to the touches of affection," the "social compact would dissolve, and justice be extirpated from the earth."[90] To Paine, the absence of sentiment was catastrophic for society.

Paine turned his attention to the particular situation of the American colonies. As the royal governments had begun to dissolve at the end of 1775, the Americans found themselves "without law, without government without any other mode of power than what is founded on, and granted by courtesy." Nothing more than "an unexampled concurrence of sentiment" held the individual colonial societies together, but they were still disunited in their objectives and measures "in the present unbraced system of things." Because the American people saw "no fixed object before them," their minds were "left at random" and pursued any idea that suited their "fancy."[91] Paine argued for independence as a first step to creating a legitimate foundation for government.

Paine realized that the disparate cultures and distant proximities of the American colonies led to radically different experiences of the conflict with Britain. Some residents of New England or Virginia, for instance, had faced British fire in person, while residents of other colonies experienced the conflict mainly through newspaper reports. Thinking especially of the residents of Philadelphia and New York, Paine said, "It is the good fortune of many to live distant from the scene of present sorrow; the evil is not sufficiently brought to *their* doors to make *them* feel the precariousness with which all American property is possessed." Paine continued, "But let our imaginations transport us for a few moments to Boston, that seat of wretchedness" and "that unfortunate city," whose inhabitants "but a few months ago" like Pennsylvanians and New Yorkers, "were in ease and affluence," but who were now under siege.[92] Paine reiterated, "Those men have other feelings than us who have nothing suffered."[93]

Paine saw that no one in the situation of the Bostonians could practically hope for reconciliation with the same power that was leveling their homes. Paine thus assumed an imaginative authorial empathy with the besieged. "I make the sufferer's case my own, and I protest, that were I driven from house and home, my property destroyed, and my circumstances ruined, that as a man, sensible of injuries, I could never relish the doctrine of reconciliation, or consider myself bound thereby."[94] Men who talked of reconciliation, said Paine, were ignorant of "all the various orders of men whose situation and circumstances, as well as their own" should be considered. He asked, "Do they put themselves in the place of the sufferer whose *all* is *already* gone, and of the soldier, who hath quitted *all* for the defence of his country?"[95] As we shall see unfolded in subsequent chapters, Paine's rhetorical task was to enact this empathy between distant Americans. The colonies, he realized, could not act in unison or think in unison until they *felt* in unison.

Paine was not alone in his emphasis on sentiment. At the end of November 1775, Thomas Jefferson used the language of sentiment to describe the American situation. "But by the god that made me I will cease to exist before I yield to a connection on such terms as the British parliament propose and in this I think I speak the sentiments of America." He continued, "We want neither inducement nor power to declare and assert a separation." Then, in a significant statement for this analysis, he declared, "It is will alone which is wanting, and that is growing apace under the fostering hand of our king."[96] The challenge that Jefferson identified was converting raw, loose *sentiment* into focused, propellant *will*.

Common Sense was not the only source of sentiment for those who began to desire independence. Some, like Jefferson, found it in what they interpreted as the malevolent intentions of the ministry or the king. Others, like the recent graduate of Yale College, Benjamin Tallmadge, were slowly awakened to the active pursuit of independence. Tallmadge recalled, "When first American blood was shed at Lexington by the British troops, and again repeated much more copiously at Bunker's Hill, near Boston, the whole country seemed to be electrified. Among others, I caught the flame which was thus spreading from breast to breast, and mounted my horse to go and see what was going on near Boston." There Tallmadge visited with his friends in the army, who encouraged him to quit his job superintending a Connecticut school and to join the service. Tallmadge was "sufficiently ardent to be pleased, and even elated with such a prospect, yet nothing was further from my intention at that time than to have entered upon a military life." His "military friends" did not relent and "continually importuned" him "to think of the oppression which was so abundantly exhibited by the British government towards the Colonies, until I finally became entirely devoted to the cause in which my country was compelled to engage." Even then, "full of zeal in the cause of my country," he returned to Connecticut and only "put on the uniform" when "the prospect of peace and reconciliation appeared almost hopeless." [97] Tallmadge, who would become a colonel in the Continental Army, was not sufficiently moved to become a soldier by his patriotic zeal, but by reflecting on "the oppression which was so abundantly exhibited by the British government towards the colonies" and by becoming convinced that "the prospect of peace and reconciliation" had evaporated. Tallmadge's decision-making process was accelerated in close *physical* proximity to the battle, and Paine's task in *Common Sense* was likewise to enact in textual form an *emotional* proximity to the battle that would speed up the decision-making processes of those colonists who were physically distant from the realities of war.

Tallmadge's account crystallized two fundamental conclusions that were shared by every American advocate of independence in 1776: the intentionality of British oppression and the implausibility of reconciliation. For many colonists, *Common Sense* created the flashpoint where they became convinced, like Tallmadge, that the war was neither accidental nor reversible. Everything about the text of *Common Sense*—the line-in-the-sand dichotomies, the arresting metaphors, and the clopping metricality of the prose—contributed to an emotional reading experience that transported Paine's audience to the frontlines of the battle. Standing transfixed and empty-handed at the virtual frontlines, these reader-soldiers *felt* a swell of pride as they imagined their fellow Continentals fighting with valiance in an epochal war against tyranny. But Paine's transported audience soon descended into swirling dismay as those same soldiers, carrying empty muskets and clutching growling stomachs, pleaded for rules of engagement fitted for brigades, not for brigands.

As Paine later put it, "Independence always appeared to me practicable and probable, provided the sentiment of the country could be formed and held to the object."[98] In order for American resistance to succeed, Paine was arguing in *Common Sense*, the colonies required the ammunition of independence. And the movement for independence could never catch fire in every colony until the Americans found in the recesses of their hearts an empathic connection for the thousands "already ruined by British barbarity," who had already sacrificed everything for the cause. "All they *now* possess is liberty," Paine reminded his readers, "and thousands more will probably suffer the same fate."[99] The colonists could either wait to share in that fate, or from a posture of affective compassion, act now to stop the course of destruction. Paine was harvesting the raw materials of sentiment to catalyze the explosive movement for independence.

Notes: Chapter 2

[1] The Americans had a relatively plentiful supply of sulfur ore ("brimstone") and charcoal, a source of carbon.
[2] Showman, *Papers of General Nathanael Greene*, 1:142. The famous statement attributed to General Israel Putnam at the Battle of Bunker Hill, "Don't fire until you see the whites of their eyes," would have been motivated by the same shortage.
[3] RHL to the Virginia Delegates to the Committee of Safety, 5 October 1775. Arthur Lee Papers, HL.
[4] Continental Congress, *Several Methods of Making Salt-Petre*; Committee of Safety of the Colony of New York, *Essays Upon the Making of Salt-Petre and Gun-Powder*. Paine and Pryor's "Experiments" had initially been published in the PJ on November 22 and December 6, 1775. In this essay, Paine's name is spelled "Pain." I have normalized it in the text of this dissertation, but it is worth noting that this was the last time his name would appear in print as "Pain" rather than "Paine." Rush had observed in his essay "that the climate and productions of the middle and northern colonies of North-America render them extremely proper for the manufactory of salt petre." Rush remarked upon the "success which has attended several experiments in that way," referring in particular to Paine and Pryor, who had gathered "about an inch and an half from the surface" of the ground underneath a barn "where fowls, hogs, &c. shelter" in order "to promote the public good."
[5] State of Pennsylvania. *Minutes of the Provincial Council of Pennsylvania*.
[6] Brannan and Finney. "To the Inhabitants of the County of Chester." PJ, March 20, 1776.
[7] DPP, May 27, 1776.
[8] See Showman, *Papers of General Nathanael Greene*. The colonists tried to procure saltpeter from France, but to little effect, as long as there was any possibility of "an accommodation." See, for example, Bayard Jackson & Co. of Philadelphia to Messrs. Montandouin & Frere at Nantz, 18 January 1776. Arthur Lee Papers, HL.
[9] For a helpful discussion of Paine's development as a writer during his editorship of the PM, see Larkin, *Literature of Revolution*, Chapter 1.
[10] TP to HL, 14 January 1779. CW 2:1160-1165.
[11] The Richard Gimbel Collection of Thomas Paine Papers at the APS contains a "manuscript" copy of *Common Sense*, but these are only manuscript extracts from the pamphlet by an unknown writer, possibly in preparation for a written response. In the eighteenth century, men and women sometimes would practice their penmanship by copying large extracts or even entire books, an example of which is a complete manuscript copy of *The Age of Reason* in the same collection at the APS.
[12] Besides the animosity generated from their parting of the ways, it should be remembered that Aitken, the first American Bible publisher, reported this detail to Isaiah Thomas *after* Paine had published the *Age of Reason*. Thomas, *History of Printing in America*, 2:152.
[13] Goldsmith. *History of the Earth, and Animated Nature*.

[14] AC, No. 3, CW 1:88-89. Larkin has written persuasively that Paine's continued ambition to write a history of the American Revolution was partly realized in his "Letter to the Abbè Raynal." See Larkin, *Literature of Revolution*.
[15] Rush. *An Address to the Inhabitants of the British Settlements in America, upon Slave-keeping;* "Justice and Humanity" [Thomas Paine], "African Slavery in America," PJ, March 8, 1775.
[16] Thomas Pryor to Thomas Mifflin and Edward Biddle. 13 April 1775. HSP. Pryor's name was spelled alternately as "Pryor" and "Prior." I have in this study normalized it as "Pryor."
[17] Corner, *Autobiography of Benjamin Rush*, 113-114. For the most likely original location of this sentence, see CS 3.28.
[18] BF had written a pamphlet called *Plain Truth* in the 1747, and of course, the first pamphlet rebuttal of *Common Sense* by James Chalmers chose its adversary's original working title. Neither potential title was particularly original. Franklin acknowledged in his *Autobiography* the authorship of *Plain Truth; or, Serious Considerations on the Present State of the City of Philadelphia, and Province of Pennsylvania, by "a Tradesman of Philadelphia."* Philadelphia: November 17, 1747. Three examples of eighteenth century political tracts bearing the name "Common Sense": *Common Sense: or, The Englishman's Journal. Being A Collection of Letters, Political, Humorous, and Moral; Publish'd Weekly under that Title, For the First Year.* London: J. Purser and G. Hawkins, 1738. UPL; *Common Sense a Common Delusion. Or, The generally-received Notions of Natural Causes, Deity, Religion, Virtue, &c. As exhibited in Mr. Pope's Essay on Man, Proved Ridiculous, impious, and the Effect of Infatuation; and the chief Cause of the present formidable Growth of Vice among Christians, and the great Stumbling-block in the Way of Infidels. Earnestly recommended to the Perusal of all Men of Good-Sense, and Lovers of Truth.* By Almonides a believing Heathen. London: printed for T. Reynolds, sold by R. Baldwin, W. Owen, R. Davis, etc., 1751. UPL. *Common Sense: in Nine Conferences between a British Merchant and a Candid Merchant of America, in Their Private Capacities as Friends.* London: J. Dodsley, 1775. NUL.
[19] Addison and Steele's *The Spectator* was still widely read and retained a cultural currency in late eighteenth century America. See *Selections from the Tatler and the Spectator*.
[20] Paine and Rush did not intend any technical meaning of "common sense," though it is tempting for scholars to play with such an idea, since *sensus communis* has had philosophical currency from Aristotle to Arendt. It is also important to note that the "common sense" philosophy of the Scottish Enlightenment, especially in Thomas Reid's *An Inquiry into the Human Mind on the Principles of Common Sense* (1764), was actually a highly specialized discourse responding to epistemological questions raised by John Locke and David Hume.
[21] Evans, *American Bibliography*, 5:xv.
[22] BF's financial success as America's first media mogul was a singular event during the colonial period. Only around the turn of the nineteenth century did American publishers begin to accumulate significant fortunes.
[23] I use the masculine pronoun here on purpose. The vast majority of American printers in 1776 were men, with only two women in principal charge of a minor press, one in Massachusetts and one in Maryland. Women would gradually

take on a more important role in American printing after the turn of the nineteenth century. See Hudak, *Early American Women Printers*.

[24] On the technological progress in printing at the turn of the nineteenth century, see Charvat, *Literary Publishing in America*.

[25] Silver, *American Printer*, 100.

[26] Burgh, *Political Disquisitions*.

[27] PG, April 14, 1768. Landis, "Robert Bell: Printer," 195-202.

[28] Bell, "A catalogue of new and old books, which will be exhibited by auction, by Robert Bell, bookseller and auctionier." Boston: 1770. LCP.

[29] These dates reflect the year of Bell's publication, not necessarily the first publication date for each work.

[30] Bell. Unattached advertisement. 1773. LCP.

[31] Bell, "PROPOSALS For Printing by Subscription, *A Dissent from the Church of England, Fully justified*." Philadelphia: Bell, 1774. LCP. It should be noted that at this rate—which included full binding rather than just stitching—that a work of 80 pages, like his first edition of *Common Sense*, should have, under the same circumstances, cost 1 shilling, 4 pence each, instead of the 2 shilling price of Paine's stitched pamphlet.

[32] Bell. Unattached advertisement. 1773. LCP.

[33] Bell, Broadside for a Book Auction. January 17, 1774. HSP.

[34] Philadelphia: Bell and Woodhouse, 1775. APS.

[35] Bell, "Observations relative to the Manufactures of Paper and Printed Books in the Province of *Pennsylvania*." January 25, 1773. LCP.

[36] A "quire" was a technical term for a set of printing leaves stitched together, and a "spectator" was another name for a newspaper or other printed sheet.

[37] Bell, "Observations."

[38] Stiles, *Literary Diary*, 1:648.

[39] Evans, *American Bibliography*, 5:xiv.

[40] PEP, February 29, 1776.

[41] DPP, May 13, 1776.

[42] DPP, June 17, July 1, July 15, 1776; See also, for example, PJ, July 3, 1776.

[43] Bell, *Additions to Plain Truth*. See also Evans, *American Bibliography*, p. xiv.

[44] The self-attributed quote first appeared in the PEP, February 22, 1776.

[45] PEP, April 11, 1776

[46] Bell, "Observations."

[47] Ibid.

[48] PEP, February 22, 1776.

[49] General Horatio Gates called it "an excellent performance" in a letter to Charles Lee. Horatio Gates to Charles Lee. 22 January 1776. Lee Papers, 1:252.

[50] See *Performance (n.s.)* in Johnson, *Dictionary*.

[51] See Hoffman, "Paine and Prejudice."

[52] CS 3.1.

[53] Josiah Bartlett to John Langdon. 13 January 1776. Mevers, *Papers of Josiah Bartlett*, 36-37. Bartlett also, of course, shared news about a shipment of saltpeter and gunpowder that had arrived in Philadelphia.

[54] On the weather in Philadelphia that day, see *Robert Treat Paine Diaries*, 9 January 1776. MHS.

[55] Jim Green of the LCP provided useful guidance in determining that Bell's first press run would have taken approximately five days to complete. See also, Pollak, "The Performance of the Wooden Printing Press."

[56] Later, Rush and his new father-in-law, Richard Stockton of New Jersey, both would sign the *Declaration of Independence*.

[57] This was not the first interaction between Bell and Paine's intermediaries, Colonel Joseph Dean and Captain Thomas Pryor. Both Pennsylvania militia officers had subscribed for a set of Bell's 1775 edition of James Burgh's *Political Disquisitions*. Also, the subscriber list at the back of the third volume indicates that Robert Aitken "encouraged" seven sets of the *Disquisitions*, and his "Wastebook" shows swift sales of the *Disquisitions* in 1775, including the sale of several copies back to Bell. See Aitken's "Wastebook," 260. Of dozens of subscribers in Bell's list, only two reserved more than a single set: Aitken and, interestingly, loyalist printer James Rivington of New York, who also subscribed for seven sets. See Burgh, *Political Disquisitions*, Vol. 3. John Adams's *Diary* indicates that he bought a set of the *Disquisitions* from Aitken in December 1775.

[58] For detail on the norms of author-publisher relations and for a helpful interpretation of the rift between Paine and Bell, see Green, "Author-Publisher Relations in America."

[59] Because there are two states of Bell's first edition, it is probable that Bell printed (at least) several hundred more to meet the demand, but I here lean on the conservative side of circulation estimates.

[60] PEP, January 25, 1776.

[61] Ibid.

[62] Bell also ran an ad in German and English in PS, January 26, 1776.

[63] PEP, January 27, 1776.

[64] Ibid.

[65] PEP, January 30, 1776.

[66] Ibid.

[67] Ibid.

[68] Bell, "To Mr. Anonymous," PEP, February 1, 1776.

[69] Ibid.

[70] An untitled poem by "A.B." published in the PEP on February 6, 1776, further attempted to identify the author. The mundane poem talked of "Bombast and Bedlam eloquence" and emphasized in all caps, "TOM" and "COMMON SENSE."

[71] Woodhouse had been a partner of Bell's on the *Political Disquisitions* project. PEP, February 15, 17, 1776.

[72] Based upon Paine's account, he paid £212/10/0 for 6,000 pamphlets at 8 1/2d. each. TP to HL, 14 January 1779. CW 2:1160-1165.

[73] TP to a Committee of the Continental Congress, [October 1783]. CW 2:1226-1242.

[74] PEP, February 17, 1776.

[75] PEP, February 20, 1776.

[76] PEP, February 22, 1776.

[77] Bell was alluding here to Biblical images of Satan from 1 Peter 5:8, "your adversary the devil, as a roaring lion, walketh about, seeking whom he may de-

vour" and also from John 10:10, "The thief cometh not, but for to steal, and to kill, and to destroy."

[78] Cf. CS 3.48.

[79] This account is reconstructed from advertisements for *Common Sense* in PEP, January 30 and February 1, 1776, and in DPP, February 5, 1776.

[80] Bell, "To Mr. Anonymous," PEP, February 1, 1776.

[81] See Aitken, "Wastebook," Jim Green of the Library Company of Philadelphia greatly assisted me in piecing together the story of this publishing controversy. Bell ran four ads in the PEP (Jan. 9-18), one in the PG (Jan. 10), one in the PJ (Jan. 10), one in the PP (Jan. 15), and one in the PL (Jan. 13). Assuming a cost of five shillings per ad, the standard charge among Philadelphia newspapers at the time, eight ads would have cost him two pounds total. It is possible that the newspaper publishers lessened their charges in exchange for extra discounts on copies of *Common Sense*.

[82] As Paine recounted the story, the Reverend Jacob Duché and Francis Hopkinson were called in by Aitken to arbitrate the dispute but, when Aitken learned that Duché favored Paine's claim, Aitken backed out of the agreement.

[83] Bell's bookplate in *Spectacle de la Nature*, Vol. 1. LCP. See also, PL, December 2, 1775.

[84] Bell, Unattached advertisement.,1773.

[85] Bell's bookplate in *Spectacle de la Nature*.

[86] Johnson's *Dictionary* defined *Provedore (n.s.)* as "One who undertakes to procure supplies for an army," and *Sentiment (n.s.)* as "1. Thought; notion; opinion. 2. The sense considered distinctly from the language or things; a striking sentence in a composition."

[87] CS F.1.

[88] CS 3.32.

[89] "Ravisher" here has the connotation of "seducer" or "rapist."

[90] CS 3.50.

[91] CS A.11.

[92] CS 3.22.

[93] CS 3.38.

[94] CS 3.38.

[95] CS A.13.

[96] TJ to John Randolph. 29 November 1775. Boyd, *Papers of Thomas Jefferson*, 1:268-270.

[97] Tallmadge, *Memoir of Colonel Benjamin Tallmadge*, 6-7.

[98] AC, No. 13. CW 1:235.

[99] CS 3.38.

Chapter Three

Reformation and Regicide

To *know* of any injury and to *redress* it are inseparable in the royal breast.

Sir William Blackstone
Commentaries on the Laws of England
1765-1769

The King is the author of all the measures carried on against America. The influence of bad ministers is no better apology for these measures, than the influence of bad company is for a murderer, who expiates his crimes under a gallows—You all complain of the corruption of the parliament, and of the venality of the nation, and yet you forget that the crown is the source of them both.—You shun the streams, and yet you are willing to sit down at the very fountain of corruption and venality.

Thomas Paine
"Dialogue between the Ghost of General Montgomery
and a Delegate in a Wood near Philadelphia"
February 1776

PART ONE
UNIVERSAL REFORMATION

Royal Culture

Since the restoration of the British monarchy in the seventeenth century, kings and queens no longer held absolute political power, but they retained massive symbolic and emotional power over their subjects. The American colonists considered themselves dutiful children of the king, "the Father of his People," and the British nation, "the Mother Country." Though the King of Britain never traveled to America, his symbolic presence was everywhere. Governors, assemblies, and military associations acted in "the name of the king." The king's coat of arms decorated every court house, every Anglican Church, and many storefronts around America. Many colonists of means kept pictures of the king up in their houses, and nearly everyone signed their personal correspondence with the rote deference of royal addresses, "Your most obedient, humble servant." The king's birthday in June was celebrated as a national holiday, and ministers and chaplains prayed for him as a basic part of their liturgies. The New York Assembly in 1770 erected an elaborate gilded lead statue of King George III riding on horseback. The imposing, four-thousand pound statue, fashioned with the magnificence of a Roman conqueror, announced the king's towering presence from its location in Bowling Green at the foot of Broadway.

The throbbing enmity between America and Britain had been a fact of imperial relations since the early days of George III's reign, but he was viewed, even in his youth, as a forlorn but distant father who always wished for and worked for the best interests of his subjects. In the 1760s, the Americans took issue primarily with a ruthless British Parliament that hoped to control its budget deficit by coercively tapping into the colonies' surplus. By the 1770s, the Americans' attention had begun to shift to Lord North's ministry, and not parliament in general, as the chief offenders against the colonies. Whether the Americans placed blame at the feet of parliament or the ministry, the king was always regarded as an innocent bystander, at best paralyzed with heartbreak and at worst, deceived into acquiescence. By 1775 a majority of Americans viewed the conflict as authored by the ministry who, by cunning design and strategic misinformation, had duped the king into passive complicity. Toward the end of Paine's editorship of the *Pennsylvania Magazine*, the publication published a eulogy for General Joseph Warren, who had been killed at the Battle of Bunker Hill. The eulogy summed up where the colonists placed blame in the summer of 1775: "Come hither, ye vindictive ministers, and behold the first fruits of your bloody edicts! What atonement can you make to his Children for the loss of such a Father?—To the King for the loss of such a Subject, and to your Country for the loss of such a Member of Society?"[1] In this writer's mind, the king and the British nation grieved alongside Warren's children, because of the misdeeds of "the ministerial army." They could not fathom that the king would take any active part in their subjugation.

The American colonists were blindsided by the argument in *Common Sense* that all blame for their suffering lay with the king. When, on the same day that *Common Sense* went on sale in Philadelphia, they read in the newspapers the king's aggressive speech at the opening of parliament, they felt utter dismay. To its initial readers, the most startling passages in *Common Sense* were those that disparage the King of Great Britain with a brashness unheard of in the eighteenth century. In our own day, we have grown accustomed to public figures who make their living by uttering uncouth remarks or by attempting shocking stunts, but eighteenth century audiences were not so desensitized and jaded as we are. Paine made some readers blush and others gasp when he called King George III "the hardened, sullen tempered Pharaoh of England," a "corrupt influence," and a "crowned ruffian" whose only job is "to make war and give away places; which in plain terms, is to impoverish the nation and set it together by the ears."[2] The most radical aspect of *Common Sense*, however, did not lie in scrappy insults to the person of the King but instead resided in the logic by which Paine was prying loose an abiding affection for monarchy from the minds of his colonial audience.

A Protestant Revolution

For Paine and for many of his contemporaries, the natural and the divine were two sides of the same coin. In *Common Sense*, he wrote, "Even the distance at which the Almighty hath placed England and America," here outlining a spatial rationale for independence, "is a strong and natural proof, that the authority of the one, over the other, was never the design of heaven." Then he transitioned to a temporal rationale, "The time likewise at which the continent was discovered, adds weight to the argument, and the manner in which it was peopled increased the force of it." He continued, squarely situating America as a preparation for and a culmination of the Protestant Reformation: "The reformation was preceded by the discovery of America, as if the Almighty graciously meant to open a sanctuary to the persecuted in future years, when home should afford neither friendship nor safety."[3]

Paine would later describe America as "the only spot in the political world, where the principles of universal reformation could begin."[4] What the Protestant Reformation had done for religion, and what Newtonian mechanics, as we shall see in the next chapter, had done for science, Paine desired to do for politics. The Reformation translated the Bible for the first time into the vernacular, and made the principles of scripture accessible to the laity. Modes of scriptural interpretation and church governance were flipped on their heads, creating a bottom-up approach to spirituality that emphasized, in response to the excesses of late medieval Catholicism, unmediated grace, the "priesthood of all believers," and personal holiness.

In England, the progress of the Protestant Reformation was stunted somewhat by Henry VIII's commandeering of the movement for his own purposes. The early Church of England was essentially the Roman Catholic Church where the rites were spoken in the vernacular and with the Archbishop of Canterbury as a quasi-papal authority. Seventeenth century England simmered with religious tension, as Catholics, Anglicans, and Dissenters—the most famous of which were the Puritans and the Quakers—all vied for a measure of liberty and control. Many of the early English settlers of America were from Dissenting sects that had grown frustrated with the exclusive and discriminatory religious environment of England or other European countries. The English Revolution of the late seventeenth century was as much a religious revolution as a political one. To support the Stuart monarchy was tantamount to declaring oneself a Catholic in many circles. To declare oneself a republican, likewise, suggested a strong affinity for Dissenting theologies. Early modern life was not partitioned into distinct "spheres" as we think of today; the provinces of religion, economics, politics, and science—among others—had as yet no fixed borders.

Reason and Demystification

It may be surprising to someone reading *Common Sense* today to observe the centrality of God and of biblical arguments in the work of one of the most famous deists in history (who has often been misrepresented as an atheist). Paine's *Age of Reason* (1794/1796) made him a few friends and a multitude of enemies for its raw attack on the Bible and Christianity. Much of Paine's historical marginalization, especially in America, is a product of the general rejection of his controversial religious doctrine in the *Age of Reason*, a book that, like most things Paine wrote, raised countless eyebrows and was gobbled up by the curious masses. The scorching content of the *Age of Reason* and the finger-wagging it provoked, have tended to invalidate the sincerity of Paine's earlier use of biblical arguments in *Common Sense* and *Rights of Man* especially. Paine had always been a religious searcher and skeptic, but he arrived gradually at the conclusions of the *Age of Reason*. In point of fact, he wrote most of the *Age of Reason*—a book containing scores of arguments from scriptural texts—from a prison cell in France where he had no access to a Bible. Paine was so adept at using the Bible and so passionate in his later repudiation of it because, earlier in his life, he had become so immersed in it. He came to the conclusion later in life that the whole of Christianity was systemically corrupt, not merely certain hierarchical expressions of it. *Common Sense* had attempted to replicate in the field of politics what the Reformation had wrought in the field of religion, but Paine later concluded that the Reformation had gone only part way in the process of demystifying spirituality and creation. The *Age of Reason*, then, sought to eradicate habitual superstition from religion in the same way that *Common Sense* had disrobed monarchy.

Returning to 1776, for every American colonist lacking a walnut-paneled study, classical history was both inaccessible and irrelevant. The efforts of Benjamin Franklin and others who organized subscription libraries beginning in 1731 helped alleviate the *inaccessibility* problem to an extent—a reader needn't purchase the book but must still afford the subscription—but the *irrelevance* problem remained. Only a very small set of Americans saw themselves as the intellectual heirs of Cicero and Aristotle, but an overwhelming majority of Americans saw themselves as the spiritual heirs of Abraham and Paul. The great figures of classical antiquity were by no means objects of derision; they were simply textbook echoes of virtue and vice with little personal or practical relevance for life in the wilds of America. The handful of colleges in colonial America were the only place where sufficient attention was paid to the Latin and Greek languages to enable more than a cursory reading of classical history.

A facility with the classics was one of the defining marks of early modern genteel culture. George Washington was always self-conscious about his lack of a formal education and his attendant difficulty with classical languages and literatures. To read or write Latin and Greek opened a vast library of privileged knowledge to a colonial gentleman and placed him on an intellectual and moral footing above his "illiterate" countrymen. A major differentiator between economic classes in early America, approaching in social significance the freehold of property, was an individual's fluency in the classics.

A typical eighteenth century pamphlet, written by and for the elite, contained copious Latin and some Greek quotations, often untranslated. This linguistic equivalent to a "No Trespassing" sign ensured that political knowledge remained cloistered in elite circles. One of the most basic differences between *Common Sense* and the bulk of the American pamphlet genre was Paine's disuse of classical references or quotations. He included two Italian sources but in translated form, and of the three Latin words in the pamphlet, "felo de se," "Appendix," and "FINIS," the first was a colloquial euphemism for suicide, while the second and third were standard printer's conventions. Certainly, we know that Paine had no choice but to avoid Latin quotations because he couldn't read Latin works. But the stylistic implications of Paine's apparent eschewing of classical authorities were nothing short of monumental.

The Protestant Reformation was a significant moment in Western history for many reasons, but one of the leading attributes of that complex religious movement was the translation of the Bible into the vernacular languages of Europe. Until reformers like John Wycliffe and William Tyndale in England made the Bible accessible to the common people in their home countries, parishioners were of necessity bound to the Catholic Church's teachings and authority. Placing the Bible in the hands of late Renaissance townsfolk who could read and write in their native tongues but who had never been afforded the opportunity to learn Latin was, concomitant with the invention of the printing press, the gateway to modernity. For the first time in centuries, parishioners could read and interpret the biblical text for themselves rather than receiving predigested morsels from priests and bishops. Religion and spirituality were transformed from a monologue to a dialogue, and the theological conversation now included blacksmiths and journeymen printers as well as cardinals and monastic scribes.

The American colonies, populated originally with communities of religious dissenters that had arisen out of the Protestant Reformation, retained in the eighteenth century a strong ideological affinity for Reformation values and modes of worship. Expository preaching was typically focused on one or two biblical passages, each usually a small number of verses within a single chapter, with frequent cross-references to other biblical books. Paine, who had read Methodist sermons as an itinerant lay minister back in England, replicated a typical sermonic structure in the second section of *Common Sense*.[5] To dispute the logic of monarchical government, he began by dismantling its accepted origins in the history most familiar and most relevant to the American colonists: "the scripture chronology" and specifically "the history of Jewish royalty" from the Old Testament.[6]

The United States of America has, throughout its national and proto-national history, or at least more often than not, understood itself to be a country specially called and sanctioned by God. This mode of thinking has sometimes enabled great feats of heroism and at other times has rationalized horrific defilements of human rights. This transhistorical constant, usually labeled "American exceptionalism," has never been stronger than it was during the late colonial and early national period. When American colonists, many of whom had fled religious persecution in one form or another, read in their Bibles about the chosen people of God entering into a promised land "flowing with milk and honey," they were not reading as spectators but as participants. Biblical revelation had direct relevance to their daily affairs, and biblical authority, for most early Americans, surmounted every competing claim. One critic of *Common Sense* put it this way: "As every Argument that has an Appearance of Scripture to support it, with many Persons, is decisive, the Author makes no small use of it against Kings and Kingly Government."[7]

The biblical narratives were to most colonists not simply morality tales like Aesop's fables; the scriptures were active texts that spoke truth to the Americans' hearts and revealed across millennia their deeper origins and identities. Most of the American colonists had, in fact, learned to read using a Bible as a textbook, and, in a closed loop of religious education, had learned to read in the first place with the principal goal of reading the Bible. From birth to death, the cadences and imagery of the biblical text were deeply ingrained in the minds of most colonial Americans. This did not mean that every American colonist was an upright churchgoer but that the surrounding culture deployed the moral vocabulary and theological imaginary of entrenched Protestantism.

Paine's writing possessed an audible "ring of truth" for eighteenth century Americans, and a major component of that "ring" consisted in the nuanced similitude of his prose style to the particular textures of biblical language. Paine built his audience upon a much more inclusive base than did those pamphleteers who expected their readers to be conversant with the erudite writers of antiquity and the late Renaissance. Most Americans did not know—nor did they care to know—about the laws of nations as espoused by Samuel von Pufendorf, Hugo Grotius, and Emerich de Vattel. What they *did* know was that to "the Almighty," the most common term for deity in the period, the nations of the earth were "as a drop of a bucket" and "counted to him less than nothing, and vanity."[8] The American popularity of John Locke's phrase "appeal to heaven" was less reflective of a wide circulation of the *Second Treatise on Government* than of the phrase's standalone resonance with biblical themes. The right of petition was, in essence, a right to pray for redress, and the right of appeal was, in essence, a right to pray to a higher authority. To "appeal to heaven" then, by a resort to arms, meant trusting Providence as the ultimate arbiter of justice and victory.

PART TWO
POPERY OF GOVERNMENT

Judging Monarchy

Common Sense argued that kingly government was a "Heathen" practice, the "most prosperous invention the Devil ever set on foot for the promotion of idolatry," yet "the children of Israel copied the custom" in stark faithlessness. Paine lamented the oxymoronic impiety in conflating the divine and the human, "the title of sacred majesty applied to a worm."[9] As he had argued before, "exalting one man so greatly above the rest" is unjustifiable "on the equal rights of nature" and also indefensible "on the authority of scripture." He highlighted two of the most famous "anti-monarchial parts of scripture" the narratives of Gideon and Samuel, to demonstrate scripture's express disapproval of government by kings.[10] The Israelites had lived in "a kind of republic administered by a judge and the elders of the tribes" for nearly three millennia "till the Jews under a national delusion requested a king."[11] Paine determined that "the idolatrous homage which is paid to the persons of kings" was clearly "ranked in scripture as one of the sins of the Jews," and, therefore, merited his further investigation into "the history of that transaction."[12]

He then recounted the narrative from Judges 8, of Gideon's military successes and the Israelites' elated plea to crown their general as a hereditary monarch, what Paine called "temptation in its fullest extent." Gideon did not simply deny the honor, as Paine put it, he "denieth their right to give it" and "in the positive style of a prophet charges them with disaffection to their proper sovereign, the King of Heaven."[13]

Paine then shifted his attention to a different passage, 1 Samuel 8, where the Israelites "fell again into the same error" of "hankering...for the idolatrous customs of the Heathens."[14] Paine claimed that Israel's main motive for asking the prophet Samuel to appoint a king to rule over them was "that they might be like unto other nations" when "their true glory lay in being as much unlike them as possible."[15] Then Paine pored over the text of Samuel's foreboding acquiescence to the people's request for a king, connecting Samuel's prophetic warnings about monarchical behavior with specific contemporary government practices such as "the present mode of impressing men" and "bribery, corruption, and favoritism," which were "the standing vices of kings."[16] The continuation of monarchy, Paine argued from the same passage, was an expression of God's resignation toward an obstinate people. Paine added that "the few good kings which have lived since" could not "sanctify the title, or blot out the sinfulness of the origin," noting that

Israel's greatest king, David, was honored as "a man after God's own heart" without respect to his official role of king.

Paine labeled these two passages of scripture as "direct and positive," admitting of "no equivocal construction." In a characteristic decisive antithesis, Paine concluded, "That the Almighty hath here entered his protest against monarchial government is true, or the scripture is false."[17] Since none of Paine's readers were prepared to affirm the latter conclusion, then the former conclusion stood as a valid premise for Paine's continuing argument.

The Pope of England

Because Catholicism was anathema to Paine's Protestant American audience, *Common Sense* is rife with instances of intertwining motives between kings and popes. The Bible was so clearly opposed to monarchy, said Paine, that he suspected "as much of kingcraft, as priestcraft in withholding the scripture from the public in Popish countries." In fact, monarchy and Catholicism were identical in their internal logic and only different in their respective fields of application. Paine cast monarchy in the worst possible light when he concluded his Old Testament exegesis with the searing statement, "For monarchy in every instance is the Popery of government."[18] Roman Catholicism had always privileged accumulated Church tradition over independent textual interpretation. The former, collected in papal bulls, creeds, and encyclicals over the centuries, was an amorphous patchwork record that resembled in its logic the accumulated British Constitution.

One of the basic analogies that governed Paine's argument in *Common Sense* was America's opportunity to accomplish in politics what the Protestant Reformation had accomplished in religion. Every reference to "popery," "superstition," and "jesuitical" reasoning carried with it flotsam and jetsam of Catholicism. The reason the Americans were suspicious of Canada and livid over Parliament's passage of the Quebec Act was the very same reason Britons hated Frenchmen and Jacobite rebels: because they were Catholic.

Catholicism represented everything corrupt, devious, debauched, and exploitative to the American mind, so much so, that calls for the necessity of treating with Catholic France and Catholic Spain were met with reluctant acquiescence. Colonists were aghast as rumors spread of Britain's plans to partition the colonies into thirds with France and Spain, primarily because of the prospect of coerced Catholicism.[19]

These were only momentary fears, though. For colonists who cherished their founding narratives as asylums of religious liberty, the real Catholic threat lay less in its literal expansion as an established religion than as a general tendency in all religious denominations to become hierarchical, persecuting, and false. Thus the Church of England could be just as "popish" as the Roman Catholic Church. The rumor circulating in the early 1770s of an Anglican bishopric being established in America was, to many colonists, tantamount to fortifying an "official" church in the colonies, many of which had been expressly created as havens for religious dissent against the Church of England.

It was also possible for a political system to take on the logic of Catholicism. Paine even asserted that kings, whose systems thrived on "ancient prejudices" and "superstition," benefited as much as priests from keeping their subjects ignorant of the Bible: "And a man hath good reason to believe that there is as much of kingcraft as priestcraft in withholding the scripture from the public in Popish countries." He added, "For monarchy in every instance is the Popery of government."[20] Though Paine didn't accept the premise that Britain was America's "parent country," he observed that "the phrase *parent* or *mother country* hath been jesuitically adopted by the king and his parasites with a low papistical design of gaining an unfair bias on the credulous weakness of our minds," evoking the image of medieval papal corruption.[21]

For all of Paine's vocal opposition to "prejudice," he used it to his own advantage in *Common Sense*. He preached pure reason and rationality but was far from a strict version of either. His was a political philosophy using common reasoning from common premises. Like the rest of common or vulgar life, the topics of Paine's arguments admitted a variety of prejudicial biases and logical slippages. He bent situations and texts to suit his arguments, such as the argument where he dismissed a scripture verse as inapplicable to monarchy because its historical context was imperial vassalage, a negligible distinction.[22] The most pervasive prejudice in *Common Sense*, one Paine had to sidestep on occasion, was its disgust for Catholic France. Paine, always aiming at origins, exhibited the Frankish roots of the British monarchy. He expected a remarkably low level of historical knowledge among his readers, as he told them parenthetically, "The first king of England, of the present line (William the Conqueror) was a Frenchman, and half the peers of England are descendants from that same country." Following the logic of the "parent country," then, "England ought to be governed by France."[23] Paine anticipated that his audience would scoff and huff at such a preposterous conclusion, but he was subtly redirecting their bias toward all things French into a bias toward all things English.

Part Three
PREACHING INDEPENDENCE

Scriptural Resemblance

One of the more obvious attributes of *Common Sense* is its reliance upon biblical forms and allusions. I mentioned earlier that the pamphlet's arguments and sentence structures often purposefully echoed the language of the King James Bible, the primary text for Paine's education as well as that of his audience. The only texts an English-literate, non-elite American was guaranteed to read were the Bible and a local almanac. If an average colonist were to branch out in his or her reading beyond these staples, a reprint of devotional material such as John Bunyan's *Pilgrim's Progress* or John Milton's *Paradise Lost* would be next in line, along with an occasional newspaper or pamphlet.[24]

History was divided into the "sacred" and the "profane," and in that context, biblical history and terminology always trumped the classical. For example, in *Common Sense*, Paine described ideal "National Manners" as reflective of biblical "chastity" rather than of classical "virtue."[25] Even when he made a nod to classical imagery, Paine was careful to couple it with its biblical equivalent, as when he referred to the British army as "that barbarous and hellish power."[26] Likewise, he even used classical vocabularies such as "the inability of moral virtue to govern the world" to describe religious concepts, in this case, natural depravity.[27]

Political theory, in its endless quest for the elusive sources of political legitimacy, has always been necessarily concerned with origins. In *Common Sense*, Paine treated classical history as largely irrelevant to the question of origins. For Paine's American audience, all legitimate "ancient" origins were to be found in the Bible. In *Common Sense*, therefore, he crashed into the British constitutional system using the Bible as wrecking ball. He would take this logic to its obvious conclusion in the *Rights of Man*, when his lengthy discussion of sovereignty focused on God's relationship with the first man, Adam.

In *Common Sense*, Paine capitalized on the inherent authority of the Bible in multiple ways. As we have seen, he constructed the second section on hereditary succession as a political sermon using two Old Testament passages as his exegetical text. A second method he utilized for identifying his argument with the biblical views of his audience was to focus on the issue of morality. Again, he was not dealing with classical "virtue" in the strict sense as much as he was speaking the language of moral pietism that had great traction with his American dissenting audiences. One example of Paine's advantageous deployment of his audience's moral framework was his question for advocates of reconciliation who wished for a return to colonial policy before the

Stamp Act: "Can ye give to prostitution its former innocence? Neither can ye reconcile Britain and America." Paine continued to use the imagery of sexual immorality, when he argued, "As well can the lover forgive the ravisher of his mistress, as the continent forgive the murders of Britain."[28]

Paine realized that two of the largest blocs of Pennsylvanians, the English Quakers and the German Mennonites, were staunch pacifists. With these groups in mind, he tried to build a quasi-theological case for just resistance in *Common Sense*:

> It is the violence which is done and threatened to our persons; the destruction of our property by an armed force; the invasion of our country by fire and sword, which conscientiously qualifies the use of arms.[29]

Some members of these and other denominations held tightly to the value of pacifism in any circumstance, while others viewed the use of force as acceptable in only a few instances, and acts of aggression against their loved ones was one of these exceptions to the general rule. By demonstrating the threat against wives and children as evidenced by the harm already done to others' families, Paine was attempting to activate the Americans' moral capacity for retributive justice. If "Men of passive tempers" could "shake hands with the murderers" who had killed their families, then they were "unworthy the name of husband, father, friend, or lover, and whatever may be your rank or title in life, you have the heart of a coward, and the spirit of a sycophant."[30] For those who could not be driven to shelve their pacifism by affective arguments, Paine's emphasis on biblical morality exploited the primacy of holiness above pacifism in the belief structures of his American audience. War, an act of aggression against humans, was bad, but immorality, an act of aggression against God, was worse.

Paine's most effective technique for channeling biblical authority toward his argument for independence was his use of biblical phraseology, diction, and syntax to make *Common Sense* sound like the Word of God. Paine's patron, Benjamin Franklin, had mastered the pithy secular proverb in his long-running *Poor Richard's Almanac*, and Paine followed suit, often closing paragraphs with an adage of his own crafting, such as "A firm bargain and a right reckoning make long friends," and "Though avarice will preserve a man from being necessitously poor, it generally makes him too timorous to be wealthy."[31] But Paine's engagement with biblical linguistic formations ran much deeper than did Franklin's. For example, in the third section of *Common Sense*, Paine placed the expedient present in opposition to the everlasting future, and he implied that unconscious or passive misjudgments—as opposed to intentional sabotage—by advocates of reconciliation would still lead to catastrophic consequences:

> Ye that oppose independence now,
> > ye know not what ye do:
> > ye are opening a door to eternal tyranny,
> > > by keeping vacant the seat of government.³²

The way Paine said this is almost as fascinating as what he said. The second clause, "ye know not what ye do," was a remarkable fusion of Jesus's rebuke of James and John's mother (who had demanded her sons' exaltation), "Ye know not what ye ask," and Jesus's haunting statement from the cross, "Father, forgive them; for they know not what they do."³³ Opponents to independence, in this formulation, partook of a naïve pride and an ignorant guilt that welcomed "eternal tyranny," otherwise known as hell, to America.

There are countless other examples of biblical language in *Common Sense*, of which I can only point to a few examples. When it appeared that the English people had turned their backs on America, Paine surmised, "The last cord now is broken," a grim inversion of the language of companionship in Ecclesiastes, "a threefold cord is not quickly broken."³⁴ Paine described the American consensus favoring the expulsion of the British army from the continent as an opinion held by "thousands and tens of thousands," an unassuming phrase used often in the Bible to describe both Hebrew clans, with whom the colonists identified themselves, and angel-armies ("hosts"), with whose assistance the Americans believed they fought.³⁵ Paine also wrote in the language of the prophet Isaiah that the king's speech had "prepared a way," for independence.³⁶ Paine was not simply mimicking biblical forms and phrases. When he used a particular biblical structure, it often carried with it connotative associations. For instance, Paine said, "Wherefore, laying aside all national pride and prejudice in favor of modes and forms," which was very structurally similar to Hebrews 12:1, "Wherefore...let us lay aside every weight, and the sin which doth so easily beset us." The syntactic similarity forges an analogical relationship between the two that makes "national pride and prejudice" both a "weight" and a "sin."³⁷ Paine also said the Crown-in-Parliament system of the British Constitution "hath all the distinctions of an house divided against itself," and his readers knew the conclusion and the context of that biblical clause. According to the Gospels, the "house divided against itself shall not stand," and the "house" was descriptive of Satan's kingdom, which would be "brought to desolation."³⁸

Though Paine employed words and images from the entire Bible, his strongest stylistic affinities were reserved for the Wisdom Books. Paine's audiences gave him the benefit of the doubt because what he was saying sounded so true. One example of many comes in a twist on Ecclesiastes 3, a passage declarative of "a time to every purpose under heaven." Paine instructed his audience about their connection to Britain:

> There was
> > a time when it was proper,
> and there is
> > a proper time
> > > for it to cease.³⁹

In the terminology of classical rhetoric, this is a chiasmus, a "crossing" of elements within a balanced statement in order to highlight a distinction between two positions. But the bulk of Paine's readers, and likely Paine himself, were unaware of the technical properties that made the statement work. They recognized his allusion to Ecclesiastes, but more importantly, they recognized a vague rhythm of the Hebrew poetry they had imbibed through sermons and personal reading. The poetic structure of the Wisdom Books, especially the Psalms and Proverbs, relied upon balanced phraseology and synonymic repetition to reveal truth by subtle turns.⁴⁰ Paine was simply mimicking the linguistic structures most familiar to him, and in so doing, he was molding rhetorical arguments into the form of ineffable truths. Monarchy, he argued, was "a form of government which the word of God bears testimony against," and Paine extended that testimony beyond content to a stylistic condemnation.⁴¹

Colonial Unison

Because of competing theological doctrines and denominational persuasions, the Bible, though omnipresent in early American culture, was not read with a good deal of unanimity. Two colonists may have vocalized the same text on the printed page, but what they were reading was separated by a heterodox chasm. Almanacs, the second most common textual form in the colonies, were highly localized publications, because the meteorological, astronomical, and agricultural forecasts were specific to particular geographies. For these reasons, *Common Sense* may have been the first publication that a majority of colonists read, heard, or were familiar with—and agreed upon. By virtue of Paine's accessible prose and his fierce resistance to equivocation, the pamphlet may have lived up to its name, and, for the first time, a single text had wrought or reflected a "common sense" among the colonists.

It is important to remember here the principle elucidated by Benedict Anderson in his book, *Imagined Communities* (1991): the act of simultaneous reading generated a sense of a trans-colonial or protonational public.⁴² In a political nation's shared experience of texts and images, their shared identity is forged. Most Americans read the Bible, it is true, but the multivocality of that text and clashing doctrines promulgated by denominational adherents tended to divide rather than unite. It was as if they read *Bibles* rather than *the Bible*. Though Paine implicitly bashed a small Catholic minority in the colonies, his writing was remarkably trans-denominational, helping the vast majority of his readers to see themselves as the political extension of the Protestant Reformation.[43]

One of the primary constitutive factors of a public is its act of engagement with a text, and *Common Sense* is a notable case study in this dynamic.[44] The pamphlet polarized its readership into a public and counter-public, Independents and Dependents; it circumscribed the debate by cordoning off a large number of topics as relevant (or irrelevant) to the issue at hand, and it formed a constellation of admissible vocabulary and associative meanings. Paine was placing—by his plebian language and emphasis on textual economy—the text of politics in the hands of the people, who were the political equivalent of the Reformation laity. This marked a fundamental shift toward a vulgar republicanism that was not so distinct from democracy.[45] In the same way that Luther, Calvin, and other reformers had reconstituted the hierarchy of the religious sphere by placing the onus of interpretation in the hands of the untrained individual believing reader, so Paine was placing the onus of representation in the hands of the individual electing reader. Unlike most of the American colonial pamphlets, Paine's text relied upon the symbolism and vocabularies of belief as much as it did on the lexicon of knowledge. Accumulated tradition governs interpretation in Catholic doctrine, a principle Paine saw at work in the British Constitution. In Protestant doctrine, on the other hand, tradition is always subordinated to textual interpretation and biblical exegesis. Paine's call for a *written* constitution was, in this framework, the political equivalent of the Reformation value of *sola scriptura*, "by scripture alone."

Though the written constitution would ensure political liberties, Paine thought it played an even more important role of preserving religious liberties. *Common Sense* described a continental charter as "a bond of solemn obligation" entered into "to support the right of every separate part" to "religion, professional freedom, or property."[46] Paine placed religion first in this list on purpose. When Paine threw out his "hints" about constitutional ingredients, he campaigned to make religious freedom the *sine qua non* of American liberty. Paine insisted that the new continental charter secure "freedom and property to all men," but demanded that it ensure "above all things, the free exercise of religion, according to the dictates of conscience."[47] Anticipating the doctrine of the separation of church and state, Paine argued that the government's only religious function was "to protect all conscientious professors thereof." Paine argued that "a diversity of religious opinions among us" prevented shallowness in "our religious dispositions" and afforded "a larger field for our Christian kindness." Paine viewed "the various denominations among us" as "children of the same family, differing only in what is called their Christian names."[48]

Political Conversion

Just as the preachers of the Great Awakening had in biblical language urged their hearers to the two-step process of conversion, repentance and baptism, so Paine was calling his audience to a similar two-step political conversion, what he called "the doctrine of separation and independence."[49] To *repent* was to turn away from one's former ways, and to be *baptized* was to declare one's new identity and membership in the religious community. Likewise, Paine called America to turn away from its superstitious and subservient colonial thinking and to declare itself an independent state, thereby taking rank with the states of Europe. Paine itemized this process in the two main points of his "Appendix." The first step involved the realization that it was in America's best interest "to be separated from Britain." The second step and "the easiest and most practicable plan" for America to pursue, was to assert her independence and to treat as a peer with European powers.[50]

Like the experience of religious conversion at one of the open air sermons of George Whitefield and other Great Awakening preachers, the ideological conversion to *Common Sense*'s offer of independent republicanism harbored implications for individuals as well as for communities. The process of religious conversion occurred first at the personal, internal level of a person's "soul," and so Paine's political sermon called for individual, internal assent before it urged communal response. *Common Sense* was not designed to be read before mass gatherings. Paine instead spoke to his potential "converts" one-to-one, author-to-reader, or in small groups bonded by kinship or friendship. *Common Sense* worked its political conversion not by mass broadcast, but through intimate social networks.

In Paine's view, the Americans had been mesmerized by the superstitious pomp of monarchy, and the sleepy language of petition would do nothing to arouse the people to action. What America needed was another Great Awakening. The religious awakening had elicited personal devotion from converts frustrated by the ceremoniousness, intellectualism, and hierarchy of the Church of England and, at the same time, disturbed by their own personal moral degeneracy. The blunt practical disconnect among laity, clergy, and scripture had, prior to the Great Awakening, precipitated a gnawing sense of communal alienation and moral complacency. The open air meetings and passionate, intelligible sermons of the Great Awakening quickened stagnant religious husks into vibrant spiritual beings by making a pietistic breed of Christianity relevant, immediate, and appealing to the American colonists.

The most controversial and ultimately the most radical aspect of the Great Awakening lay in the equalizing effect of sentimental experience. To be "filled" with God's spirit did not require *knowledge* but rather *feeling*. To be affected by religious experience usually involved some outward manifestation such as weeping, shaking, or singing, not the dry exposition of the original Greek texts. Most scandalous of all, a white man of social repute was no more likely a candidate for becoming a conduit of spiritual affectation than a teenage maidservant, an African slave, or a lowly tanner in attendance at the same church meeting.

The new religious communities and theologies birthed through the Great Awakening were markedly progressive and egalitarian. If God could speak directly to a woman or a slave as well as to a free white man, then patriarchal hierarchies within the church became meaningless. And if a woman or slave could stand up to address a congregation that included white gentlemen, then it became plausible that such marginal individuals might indeed have something of import to say outside the church service. This was, by no means, a rapid change or an irrepressible logic, but it did loosen the foundation stones of social hierarchies.

Part Four
HERETICAL QUAKERS

The "Epistle" and Religious Toryism

The Quakers, a religious sect that held a special place in Pennsylvania colonial politics and in Thomas Paine's life, possessed a flat social hierarchy that far predated the Great Awakening. Known for their egalitarian views on race and gender, their humble meeting houses, their inward devotion, and their principled pacifism, George Fox's Society of Friends—nicknamed "Quakers" for their characteristic convulsions during worship—had been in the seventeenth century a nonconformist thorn in the side of the English authorities. The Quakers' principled nonconformity attracted suspicion, exclusion, and persecution in Britain, and they sought, therefore, to create their own settlement in the New World. They had been the dominant religious group in the Pennsylvania colony since Charles II had granted it to William Penn in 1681. Following an influx of German Mennonites, Scotch Presbyterians, and other religious groups during the eighteenth century, by 1776, the Quakers' provincial primacy rested in their economic and political influence rather than their population. Quakers made up the core of the Proprietary Party in the Pennsylvania Assembly, and many of the wealthiest Philadelphia merchants were of the Quaker profession. Rather than embodying the quiet radicalism of their religious heritage, Philadelphia Quakers had become, by the late eighteenth century, staunchly conservative in their politics and economics in order to protect their high positions and substantial estates.

Thomas Paine's father was an English Quaker, and Paine's grammar school education had been conducted by Quakers. Paine attributed his lifelong ignorance of Latin to the Quaker distaste for the licentious works of Roman literature. Though Paine did not consider himself a Quaker as an adult, he nonetheless retained a lifelong affection for the sect, and, even after his invective against organized religion in the *Age of Reason*, he requested in his will to be buried in a Quaker graveyard.[51] In a *Pennsylvania Magazine* article, "Thoughts on Defensive War" from July 1775, Paine wrote, "I am thus far a Quaker, that I would gladly agree with all the world to lay aside the use of arms, and settle matters by negotiation," but his pacific Quakerism was interrupted by *real politick*, for "unless the whole will, the matter ends, and I take up my musket and thank heaven he has put it in my power."[52]

The "Epistle to the Quakers" seems initially a strange and tangential appendix to *Common Sense*, but when one considers the influence that the Quakers wielded in Pennsylvania politics and the influence that Pennsylvania politics had, in turn, on American politics, Paine's strategy becomes clearer. Paine only responded publicly to what he deemed the most serious attacks against *Common Sense*: Robert Bell's newspaper accusations of authorial duplicity, William Smith's newspaper letters under the signature of "Cato," and the publication of January 20, 1776, that elicited Paine's "Epistle," titled with typical eighteenth century loquacity *The Ancient Testimony and Principles of the People called Quakers Renewed, with Respect to the King and Government, and touching the Commotions now prevailing in these and other parts of America, addressed to the People in General.*

Paine addressed his letter, in order to constrain the representativeness of the *Ancient Testimony*'s authors, "To the Representatives of the Religious Society of the People called Quakers, or to so many of them as were concerned in publishing a late piece..." He continued to chastise the authors for "dabbling in matters" decidedly political in direct opposition to "the professed Quietude of your Principles."[53] Because the authors had "put yourselves in the place of the whole body of the Quakers," Paine confessed that he had been forced to put himself "in the place of all those who approve the very writings and principles against which your testimony is directed" in order to show that neither he nor they "have any claim or title to *Political Representation*."[54] Paine mocked the glaring inconsistency and laughable absurdity of their positions, claiming that such rationalization "could only have been made by those whose understandings were darkened by the narrow and crabbed spirit of a despairing political party; for ye are not to be considered as the whole body of the Quakers, but only as a factional and fractional part thereof."[55] This deliberate constriction of the *Ancient Testimony*'s authorial representativeness was calculated to prevent their opinions from spreading beyond a subset of Pennsylvania and New Jersey Quakers.

The logic the Quaker authors were using was, significantly, largely translatable to other pacifist dissenting sects such as the considerable German Mennonite population in Pennsylvania. Paine stressed the pacific rationale for independence, saying "*Our plan is peace for ever.* We are tired of contention with Britain, and can see no real end to it but in a final separation." Engaging in a defensive war, he argued, was consistent with this pacifist ethic because the Americans were bearing "the evils and burdens of the present day" in order to introduce "endless and uninterrupted peace."[56]

Paine then questioned the Quaker authors' sentimental "tenderness" to the plight of "the ruined and insulted sufferers in all and every part of the continent," and after disparaging their insensitivity, he skewered their euphemized motives: "But be ye sure that ye mistake not the cause and ground of your testimony. Call not coldness of soul, religion; nor put the bigot in the place of the Christian." He then recounted their denominational history for them, citing a Quaker address to Charles II on the eve of the English Revolution, "Had ye the honest soul of Barclay, ye would preach repentance to your king: ye would tell the royal wretch his sins, and warn him of eternal ruin." After laying out the historical ideals of authentic Quakerism, he concluded "that we do not complain against you because ye are *Quakers*, but because ye pretend to *be* and are not Quakers."

Paine's mention of the Quaker theologian Robert Barclay merits a further comment on Paine's Quaker upbringing. Paine attributed his "exceedingly good moral education" and "tolerable stock of useful learning" to his father's "Quaker profession." His longstanding distaste for politics made for a weak foundation of political knowledge whenever he first turned his thoughts toward issues of governance in the 1770s. The "system" he formed for himself "accorded with the moral and philosophic principles" in which he had been educated, and Quakerism was a crucial component of that education. Though Paine did not affiliate with the Society of Friends as an adult, he maintained a respect for their origins and principles.[57]

Robert Barclay, whom Paine quoted in the Epistle, was the greatest expositor of the Quaker belief in an "Inner Light." Barclay's *An Apology for the True Christian Divinity, Being an Explanation and Vindication of the Principles and Doctrines of the People Called Quakers* (1676/1678) was a theological defense of fifteen core Quaker beliefs. The second proposition in Barclay's list was regarded as the most distinctive element of Quaker belief: "The knowledge of God is given us by the Inner Light," said Barclay, adding, "This is first-hand knowledge and thus to be preferred to second-hand knowledge as obtained through Reason or the Scriptures."[58] The Quaker belief in an "Inner Light" was a significant forerunner to the concept of innate and unmediated human rights and also proved a compelling justification for democratic practice in the Quaker meeting house and beyond. Indeed, one cannot fully understand the origins of Paine's political thought and prose style apart from the influence of the Quaker values of spiritual egalitarianism, plainness, aversion to ritual, and disregard for titular authority.

Returning to Paine's Epistle, he was attacking the *Ancient Testimony* partly because of the potential damage it could do to the independent cause in Pennsylvania, but also because Paine held a special regard for Quakerism and despised seeing it used as a stalking horse for political loyalism. So, after gutting the *Ancient Testimony*'s authors of their representativeness and then proceeding to invalidate their very religious identity, Paine closed the Epistle by binding and gagging the Quaker authors with their own doctrine. The Quakers had argued for political abstinence upon the principle that "the setting up and putting down of kings and governments is God's peculiar prerogative," but, Paine countered, God "will not be robbed thereof by us." Following this quiescent principle "leads you to approve of every thing which ever happened, or may happen to kings, as being his work." With a smirk, Paine declared, "Oliver Cromwell thanks you," because "Charles, then, died not by the hands of man" according to the doctrine of the *Ancient Testimony*. If George III, "the present proud imitator" of Charles II should "come to the same untimely end," then, Paine said, the Quaker authors should "applaud the fact." Laying aside his playful sarcasm, Paine chided his opponents for their cloaked toryism and political naiveté, "Kings are not taken away by miracles, neither are changes in governments brought about by any other means than such as are common and human; and such as we now are using."[59]

Paine's invective against the Quakers' *Ancient Testimony* did not immediately silence the Proprietary interest in Pennsylvania politics, but it did compromise their moral credibility with other political groups. A number of leading figures in the Philadelphia independence movement that spring and in the framing of the Pennsylvania state constitution that summer were Quakers who had managed to reconcile the quietism of their faith with a doctrine of just resistance. Paine continued to contend with "ye fallen, cringing, priest-and-Pemberton-ridden people" throughout the American Revolution, and he held to the opinion "that a religious Quaker is a valuable character, and a political Quaker a real Jesuit."[60]

PART FIVE
THE PERSISTENT WILKES AND UNANSWERED PRAYERS

Junius, Wilkes, and Liberty

American writers had been unfailingly loyal and polite toward the King of Great Britain prior to *Common Sense*. The nearest precursor in style and tone to Paine's vicious attack on George III was not to be found west of the Atlantic. It came in an English essay from 1769, one of the famous *Letters of Junius*, addressed directly to the king. The anonymous author, writing under the signature of "Junius," published more than sixty essays in the London *Public Advertiser* from 1768 to 1771, many of which were related to the John Wilkes affair, a major political controversy that had called into question the notion of popular representation in England. Junius was credited with bringing down the Duke of Grafton's administration, which he regarded as dangerous in its subservience to the king's will.[61] Junius excoriated the parliament and the ministry in his early letters, and his language stoked the fires of the Wilkesite radical movement in England, an opposition that was aimed, in the king's view "at the very vitals of all government."[62]

John Wilkes and Junius carried on an extensive correspondence, but do not seem to have been personally acquainted.[63] Wilkes had been declared an outlaw as a result of his own scathing attack on the king in his publication, *North Briton, No. 45*. In March of 1768, Wilkes was elected to the House of Commons by a substantial majority, and the Grafton administration decided to fill his seat with a more palatable substitute. The same scenario was replayed in the next election, and Whigs across England were dismayed at the government's utter disregard for electoral representation and thus, for a core component of the British Constitution. In the midst of a constitutional crisis, Junius gave eloquent vent to the growing suspicion in England that popular representation was a ruse.

Junius's most famous piece, *Letter No. 35*, the infamous letter addressed to King George III, was published in London on December 19, 1769. While Junius reaffirmed the people's "most sanguine hopes" of the king's "natural benevolence," he declared that the original cause of "every reproach and distress" attending the government was the king's reactionary tendency to hear "the language of truth" only in "the complaints of your people." The people of England, said Junius, were "far from thinking you capable of a direct, deliberate purpose to invade those original rights of your subjects, on which all their civil and political liberties depend," because they were practiced in separating "your person from your government." Junius reiterated the commonplace doctrine of British constitutional law, "That the King can do no wrong," which allowed the king's subjects to "separate the amiable, good-natured prince from the folly and treachery of his servants, and the private virtues of the man from the vices of his government."⁶⁴ It was, significantly, this ability of the people to parse or separate the king's public actions from his private character that kept them from adopting "a style of remonstrance very distant from the humility of complaint."⁶⁵

Junius then introduced the disposition of the American colonies in 1769. "They were ready enough to distinguish between *you* and your ministers. They complained of an act of the legislature, but traced the origin of it no higher than to the servants of the Crown: They pleased themselves with the hope that their Sovereign, if not favourable to their cause, at least was impartial." Junius referenced the king's November 1768 speech where he had declared Boston to be in a "state of disobedience," "subversive of the constitution," and manifesting "a disposition to throw off their dependence on Great Britain. "The decisive, personal part you took against them," he said, "has effectually banished that first distinction" between "your government" and "your person." They distinguished now between "the Sovereign and a venal parliament on one side" and "the real sentiments of the English people on the other." He claimed the Colonies were "looking forward to independence," and in spite of their division "into a thousand forms of policy and religion," there was one point of unanimous agreement in the Colonies: "they equally detest the pageantry of a King, and the supercilious hypocrisy of a bishop."⁶⁶ Junius was falling into a commonplace mistake of British discourse on the American controversy. Britons, including the king, described America with the synecdoche of Massachusetts-Bay. They couldn't grasp the disparate cultures of the American colonies and assumed that Boston represented the rest of America, something that, before 1775, was patently untrue.

Returning to the people of England, Junius reminded the king that the people's loyalty to the house of Hanover had nothing to do with "nominal distinctions" but was rooted in the "solid and rational" principle that "the establishment of that family was necessary to the support of their civil and religious liberties." Referring to the Stuart monarchial line halted with Charles II's execution during the English Revolution, Junius cautioned George III: "The Prince, who imitates their conduct, should be warned by their example." In a scathing final sentence, Junius told King George III that, "while he plumes himself upon the security of his title to the crown, [he] should remember that, as it was acquired by one revolution, it may be lost by another."⁶⁷

Junius was conscious that his letter was offensive both in its "sentiments" and in "the style they are conveyed in." The king was "accustomed to the language of courtiers" whose affections were measured by "the vehemence of their expressions." In the decorous world of court politics, oblique discourse prevailed, so that the king admired the sincerity of indirect praise but grated at the novel directness of Junius's address.[68]

Junius had been an intermittent pest to the British government, but John Wilkes was a constant engine of angst. Wilkes had been a member of parliament in 1763 when he was jailed for publishing criticisms of the king's self-congratulatory speech given to Parliament at the end of the Seven Years' War, or what was referred to in America as the French and Indian War. After his release from prison, Wilkes was expelled from parliament and went into exile until 1768, when he returned to run for a seat in parliament from Middlesex. Wilkes won the election, but he was forbidden from assuming his seat in the House of Commons. He quickly became a popular symbol for the defense of constitutional liberties against royal encroachment. Wilkes's cause served to popularize what had formerly been theoretical concerns over royal accountability and the right of petition. The seventeenth century arguments about legitimate resistance to oppressive authority by Algernon Sidney and other republican writers gained tremendous currency in the furor over Wilkes.[69]

Because the Wilkes affair proved to the British public that parliament was corrupt to the core, British subjects directed incessant petitions toward the throne over the course of the controversy. The language of the Wilkesite petitions was more direct and less deferential than was typical of petitionary address at the time. The public's actions were becoming less deferential as well. With Wilkes again in prison in 1769, his supporters protested with their pens and with sticks. A group of loyalist merchants attempted to bring a congratulatory address to St. James's lauding the king for his resolute opposition to Wilkes, but they were ambushed en route to the palace. The crowd routed both the merchants' procession and a royal cavalry troops sent to protect them. The king and his ministers, locked inside the palace, feared for their lives, and one Tory observer noted that "many of the mob cried, 'Wilkes and no King,' which is shocking to think on."[70]

The peak of Wilkes's movement was the same period as Paine's initial political activation, when Paine began to affiliate with the Whig cause.[71] Wilkes's biographers indicate the likelihood the two met briefly as Wilkes passed through Lewes, a meeting that only possessed significance in retrospect.[72] Paine was, of course, familiar with the writings of Junius, whose "brilliant pen," Paine later said, "enraptured without convincing."[73] But as Paine's comment indicates, there was no linear connection between Paine and the Wilkesite opposition. Wilkes and Junius were extremely radical in their British context, but they were both fighting for civil liberties under the British Constitution. Paine, in America and later in Britain and in France, was mainly interested in fighting for natural liberties under God. Historians have generally concluded that Wilkes was a political opportunist who did not capitalize on the potential of his movement to effect positive change in British politics. His political ascendancy resulted in his election as Lord Mayor of London, a post from which he generally expressed support for the American cause. Although his tenure as Lord Mayor was not productive of great political change in Britain, an unintended effect of his presence in office proved crucial for the American independence movement.

Wilkes Weary

Much of George III's obstinacy toward the Americans during 1775 and 1776 was the direct result of his battle weariness after a long fight with supporters of John Wilkes. The king's inattentiveness to the supplications of Wilkes and his supporters had fueled popular discontent over the issue of representation and royal redress. The king's open contempt for the Wilkesite movement and his categorical refusal to hear their side of the issue spawned the formation of the Society of Supporters of the Bill of Rights, a pioneering group that specialized in extra-parliamentary campaigns in defense of the British Constitution. By the end of 1771, George III and his ministers endured a new level of opposition. The ministers were shoved, shaken, and insulted as they made their way to the House of Commons for the opening of the second parliamentary session of the year. The king's coach met with loud hissing from the crowds, and one bystander threw an apple at the king as he approached the House of Lords. Another man was arrested for shouting "No Lord Mayor, no King!" in reference to Wilkes's recent election as the Lord Mayor of London. The king's haughty disregard for public grievances was depicted in cartoons like "The Effects of Petitions and Remonstrances" and "The Fate of City Remonstrances" (1770) as the outworking of his foolish obedience to designing ministers.[74]

By 1775 the king's ministers had established what was snidely referred to by the public as a "committee of oblivion" to dispense with petitions protesting the "civil war" with America. Between 1775 and 1778, some 50,000 Britons signed petitions or addresses either in support of or opposition to the war with America, but most of these hopeful presentations fell into a chasm of royal inattention.[75]

The people of England began openly in 1775 to suspect that the king's silence masked malevolent intentions. When at the beginning of February 1775, an edition of the opposition serial *The Crisis* appeared in London, the situation grew still graver. The essay addressed "To the King" threatened that no one could protect George III "from the People's Rage, when drove by your Oppressions, and till now unheard of cruelties, to a State of Desperation." The anonymous author warned, "Whenever the State is convulsed by civil Commotions, and the Constitution totters to its Centre, the Throne of *England* must shake with it; a Crown will then be no SECURITY, and at one Stroke, all the gaudy Trappings of Royalty may be laid in the Dust." The author continued with his republican rationale, "The Rights of mankind will be the only Objects in View," adding a subversive statement reminiscent of the republican "Levellers" of the seventeenth century, "while the King and the Peasant must share one and the same Fate, and perhaps fall undistinguished together." The House of Lords convicted the paper's publisher of sedition and treasonous libel and had the paper burned publicly, but unwavering radical crowds tried to extinguish the flames.[76]

In a related event, Stephen Sayre, a wealthy American and a friend of Wilkes who had been recently elected a sheriff in London, was arrested and jailed in 1775 as an accomplice in an alleged plot to kill the king. The prosecution's principal witness, an American loyalist named Francis Richardson, claimed that Sayre had told him that George III was the only real obstacle to peace between Britain and America, since even the ministers had lost faith in their American policy. The plan, according to Richardson, was to kidnap George III on his way to open parliament, to send him into exile in his German dominions, and to establish a British republic led by Lord Mayor Wilkes and his sheriffs. "Tearing Lord Mansfield, Lord North, and Lord Bute to pieces would be of no material consequence," Sayre was accused of saying, "We must strike at the fountainhead."[77]

Beginning in April 1775, London radicals began a concerted effort to agitate the American question via petition. Lord Mayor Wilkes, along with some of the alderman and liverymen of London prepared a "Humble Address, Remonstrance, and Petition" to George III protesting the coercive measures against America. The petition found previous colonial legislation "oppressive" and raised the specter that the "real purpose" behind parliament's actions had been "to establish arbitrary power over all America." The petition called for the dismissal of conniving ministers whose "secret advice" violated the principles of the constitution. On April 10, 1775, the king received the London petition while on his throne, but his reply foreshadowed the course of future events, "It is with the utmost astonishment that I find any of my subjects capable of encouraging the rebellious disposition which unhappily exists in some of my colonies in North America." The king expressed his deference to the decisions of parliament, but his equation of a frankly-worded petition with the encouragement of colonial rebellion revealed a position of great consequence in the coming months.[78]

The king's consternation at receiving this petition precipitated the next day a letter from the Lord Chamberlain to the Lord Mayor informing Wilkes that "The King has directed me to give notice that for the future His Majesty will not receive on the throne any Address, Remonstrance, and Petition, but from the Body Corporate of the City." George III had received petitions in the past from the London Livery that were no less radical, but this time he made a distinction that he would only receive on the throne petitions from the City of London in Common Council assembled. This was an attempt on the king's part to control the more radical elements of the London Livery who had, in the king's opinion, crossed a line with their inflammatory tone. Even in the Middlesex election affair that had made Wilkes famous, though the king always denied petitions from the London radicals, he had never dismissed them without a hearing.[79]

Wilkes outlined the constitutional and practical implications of the king's decision in his response to the Lord Chamberlain on May 2, 1775. This was a remarkable break with precedent, Wilkes said, but the chief ramification of the king's policy would be increased suspicion that all petitions would now be unread, unheard, and unanswered. By placing the decision regarding what the king hears or doesn't hear in the hands of ministers "versed in the supple, insinuating arts" and "practiced in the magic circle of a court," Wilkes warned that crucial information would be withheld from the king to prevent him from hearing "disagreeable and disgusting, however important and wholesome truths." Thus said Wilkes, the cunning minister "will strangle in its birth the fair offspring of liberty, because its cries might awaken and alarm the parent, and thus the common father of all his people may remain equally ignorant and unhappy in his most weighty concerns."[80]

Wilkes's letter was prescient. The only petitions to which the king responded after this date were those from the City of London in Common Council assembled. The overwhelming majority of petitions were "graciously received" at the levee and conveniently dropped out of sight.

Political Supplications

On July 3, 1766, Thomas Paine wrote a letter to the Board of Excise requesting to be reinstated to his post after being fired the year prior. In a very short letter, Paine used the word "humble" five times. Paine did get his old job back (for the time being), but to do so, he had to take on a posture of humiliation. His letter was written in the language of petition.[81]

Today we think of petitions as street-level lists of citizen signatures, but this secularized notion of petitions did not arise until the nineteenth century. During the revolutionary period, petitions were what they had always been, *prayers*, and they were submitted as such, with bowed knee and humbled address. Invoking the aid of the sovereign as a matter of final recourse, royal petitions were addressed with the same laborious deference and self-flagellation that one would expect from a prayer spoken in the Church of England. And this was precisely the point: there was no material difference between the King of England and the Church of England with regard to sovereignty. Both were one step removed from the Almighty in the eyes of subjects and parishioners.

In an attempt to protect the monarch from being mobbed by an "overwhelming" accumulation of signatures, the Stuart statutes of 1661 had made the "tumultuous petitioning" of "lewd persons" an act of sedition.[82] The English Bill of Rights (1689) that followed the "Glorious Revolution" of 1688 had reinstituted the constitutional legality of petitioning the Crown, but theory and practice were often out of step. Trenchard and Gordon had argued in the 1720s that the right of petition was valid only if reciprocated by a duty of redress, but practical Hanoverian contractualism, especially during the reign of George III, was prone to the systematic marginalization of petitions.[83]

The idea of petition was, in fact, an adaptation necessitated by the reorganization of the British Constitution during the era of the English Revolution. Stuart monarchs had promoted the royal "touch" as a magical cure for disease, but the Bill of Rights, argued historian Steve Poole, "replaced the superstitious intercession of the touch with the 'rational' intercession of the *petition*. In its popularly understood form as a right to approach the body of the king in person, the petition, and the readiness of the king to respond, became the royal touch of the secular early modern state."[84]

British subjects were free to petition parliament, but the perceived selfishness and factionalism of the legislature and the sticky issue of virtual representation made the effort seem futile. Also, parliament's technical status as a petitioning body, meant that subjects would be petitioning petitioners. Nonetheless, reformers of all stripes petitioned parliament vigorously during the 1770s, in which case the clerk would often read the petition in a "barely audible voice" amidst "coughing and clamour." By petitioning the Crown directly, Britons thought that they were rising above factional politics and addressing one who genuinely cared for the welfare of his people.[85]

Petitions bridged, said Poole, "an imagined distance between monarch and subject" within the broader contractual system. The king, it was believed, welcomed from his subjects petitions of right or petitions of grievance, and his care and intercession were understood as part of the contractual exchange in return for his subjects' allegiance.[86]

King George III, "His Most Gracious Majesty," was not known for his infinite grace, and he wearied of his subjects' incessant intercession, first over the Wilkes affair and then over the American controversy. The king viewed most royal petitions as subversive of parliament's supreme legislative authority, and he thought that tamping popular enthusiasm for petitioning would win him the goodwill of parliament. On July 26, 1775, just prior to the arrival in England of the American "Olive Branch" Petition, George III wrote a letter to Lord North informing the first minister that he would no longer receive petitions concerning America while seated upon the throne (meaning, in his royal capacity).[87] The king then set up an intermediary system whereby he would accept petitions at the levee instead of on the throne and, even then, usually only after careful screening by the ministry. As he distanced himself from the reception of petitions, he also instituted a new practice that absolved him of any pressure to respond to his subjects' "prayers." Those subjects gradually began to notice the king's distance and unresponsiveness. Since they considered an appeal to their sovereign king the final and ultimate source of political agency, they were deeply disturbed and doubly humiliated. Many petitioners had turned to the Crown specifically because their petitions had already been turned away by parliament.[88]

Parliament had taken a clear stance earlier in 1775 when it refused to hear any petitions from merchants protesting the stoppage of trade between the colonies and Britain. To debate the issues of trade, taxation, or anything else, the legislators argued, was simply a red herring; they had determined to narrow the conflict to the single question of colonial submission. After parliament on February 7, 1775, had declared the colonies to be in a state of rebellion, all petitions regarding America were sent to the Crown. Because the king could not respond favorably to such petitions without contradicting parliament, he refused to consider them at all. The slow trickle of petitions became a flood when news of Lexington and Concord reached England, and the people of England began to realize that the government intended to achieve its objectives using force. Petitions rolled in, some supporting arms and others peace, but most arrived at a point when all branches of the British government had already determined that the colonists were in a state of rebellion.[89]

On both sides of the Atlantic, the rationale for the conflict was fluid. What began as a question of taxes and trade became, after the Commons refused to hear any more merchant petitions, an explicit question over parliamentary supremacy in the colonies. In point of fact, nothing short of an American declaration of parliamentary supremacy would have reconciled the colonies to the mother country. When the issue at hand was commercial policy and schemes of taxation, there was room for negotiation between the two sides, but when the issue was distilled to parliamentary supremacy, all ground for compromise had eroded. Parliament and the North administration held fast to this stance, and King George III followed their lead in his approach to negotiations and also in his treatment of petitions.[90]

Petitions were the mechanism by which bills were introduced in parliament. The petition was signed by the interested parties and presented to the House of Commons by a sponsoring member along with a bill that it was hoped would snake its way through both houses of parliament. Petitions, likewise, were the mechanism for rescinding legislation deemed ineffective or harmful. Edmund Burke advised his Bristol constituents concerned with the administration's coercive tactics in America that petitions were "the only peaceable and constitutional mode of commencing any procedure for the redress of public grievances." Presenting a petition was the beginning, not the whole of the process, and Burke advised those who contemplated drawing up a petition "to follow up their Petition by a regular solicitation, pursued through all the modes of civil resistance, and legal opposition," without which, he said, "they should not present it at all."[91] Petitions to parliament were thus ordinary measures of the British political process, but petitions to the Crown were extraordinary expressions of political will reserved for instances when all other means had proven futile.[92]

There was a direct correlation between the agitation surrounding petitioning and addressing and the intensity of pamphlet production in both England and America. The American controversy stimulated 14 British political pamphlets in 1773, 88 in 1774, 160 in 1775, and 169 in 1776. After 1776, the number of pamphlets fell off dramatically.[93] During this same period, the more than two hundred appeals to the Crown concerning America followed a remarkably similar trajectory, reaching a peak volume in late 1775 and early 1776.[94] Pamphlets were, as we saw in Chapter One, a form of political agency fitted to the same hierarchical conditions under which petitioning flourished. The abrupt drop-off in both pamphlets and petitions reflected how quickly these procedural exchanges became outmoded in the topsy-turvy political climate and pitched tension of open war.[95]

Petition and Proclamation

The Second Continental Congress's "Olive Branch" Petition, sent on July 8, 1775, addressed "To the KING's Most Excellent MAJESTY" and the colonies' "Most gracious Sovereign," reiterated that the king's "faithful subjects" in America were "Attached to your Majesty's person, family, and government, with all devotion that principle and affection can inspire." The Congress, "with all humility submitting to your Majesty's wise consideration," hoped that "your royal authority and influence may be graciously interposed to procure us relief from our afflicting fears and jealousies." The Continental Congress wished for "a happy and permanent reconciliation," but knew it would take time to work out mutually agreeable terms and asked that "in the meantime, measures may be taken for preventing the further destruction of the lives of your Majesty's subjects; and that such statutes as more immediately distress any of your Majesty's Colonies may be repealed."[96]

That same summer, while the Congress was combing through every word of their address, the king was preparing an address of his own. He regretted, in a letter to Lord North, that there had been "much delay" in composing a "Proclamation declaring the conduct of the Americans Rebellious." After many revisions, he thought it had finally "got into a good train" and was almost ready to be "read and ordered to be published." The king saw his proclamation as a "most necessary" step to "put people on their guard" and also to show "the determination of prosecuting with vigour every measure that may tend to force those deluded People to Submission."[97]

On August 23, the king's Privy Council published his Royal Proclamation concerning the American situation. Utilizing the first person plural of royal address, the king expressed his regret that "many of our subjects in diverse parts of our Colonies and Plantations in North America," had been "misled by dangerous and ill designing men," had forgotten "the allegiance which they owe to the power that has protected and supported them," and had "at length proceeded to open and avowed rebellion." He urged his civil and military officers "to exert their utmost endeavours to suppress such rebellion," and he then proceeded to make all correspondence with the American "rebels" an act of treason "against us, our crown and dignity."[98]

The Americans, it should be remembered, did not think of themselves as petitioning the *man*, George III, but the instead were approaching the sacred *office* and *title* of the Crown. As we saw in Chapter One, the Americans' only connection to the British constitutional framework was through their subjecthood to the king. The old adage, "The king can do no wrong," was interpreted by most Whigs as a confirmation of the king's accountability under the law, and "radical" Whigs viewed it as a justification to blame the king's ministers for every problem. Tories, on the other hand, interpreted it to be a statement of royal infallibility.[99] In fact, appealing to the king against parliament, as the Americans were doing, was consistent with a Tory view of the British Constitution. In the fall of 1775, Charles James Fox publicly accused Lord North of Toryism, and North's response demonstrated the constitutional complexity of colonial resistance. North argued that the Americans would be more justly called Tories than himself, since they appealed to the king's prerogative, while the ministry was plainly upholding parliamentary authority.[100]

PART SIX
DETHRONING THE SOVEREIGN

Royal Character

One of Paine's most revealing reflections on the composition of *Common Sense* came in his *American Crisis, No. 3* (1777). When the "Olive Branch" Petition from the Continental Congress "produced no answer," recalled Paine, the king's "indignity gave a new spring to independence." Paine said that many of his acquaintances had "predicted the fate of the petition" in advance, because they recognized "the savage obstinacy of the king" and "the jobbing, gambling spirit of the court." Paine described his line of reasoning: "For the men being known, their measures were easily foreseen." He elaborated on the principle of commensurability between character and action, advising his audience to ground their hopes not on "the reasonableness of the thing we ask" and instead on "the reasonableness of the person of whom we ask it." Because character predetermines action, no rational person would expect "discretion from a fool, candor from a tyrant, or justice from a villain," implying the applicability of all three labels to George III.[101]

Paine had good reason to ignore the conventional separation between the person and the office of the king. In the fall of 1775, while he was writing *Common Sense*, Paine believed he had an inside track on the king's public actions because of his privileged knowledge of the king's personal character. George Lewis Scott, Paine's distinguished friend in England and the man who had introduced him to Franklin, was born in Hanover, Germany, and was accordingly well connected in the Hanoverian monarchial system. Scott, who had been employed as a tutor for the young George III, entertained Paine with appalling stories about the prince's slovenly habits and insular existence. Scott was thoroughly unimpressed with George III and had transmitted that distaste to the impressionable Paine. In reality, Paine couldn't have predicted what would happen with certainty, but his intuitions, on this and other matters in the run-up to independence, proved to be staggeringly accurate.

The private correspondence between King George III and Lord North during the fall of 1775 reveals the centrifugal forces of misunderstanding and discursive silencing that continued to drive apart Britain and America. On October 15, the king encouraged North, "Every means of distressing America must meet with my concurrence as it tends to bringing them to feel the necessity of returning to their Duty."[102] On October 23, just three days before the opening of parliament, George III told North to refuse to admit a petition from the Georgia Provincial Congress "as coming from a body I cannot acknowledge," and the king added that "treating all Provincial and General Congresses in that manner for the future will be proper."[103] In November, he admitted to North that he had "always feared a Commission not likely to meet with Success," but he acquiesced in sending Commissioners "whilst every Act of Vigour is unremittingly carrying on."[104] In December, the king expressed "much satisfaction" with the "Bill for preventing intercourse with the Provinces in Rebellion" and was eager to sign it into law.[105]

George III despised the minority in parliament who opposed the use of coercive force against America, calling Charles James Fox "as contemptible as he is odious," Lord Chatham a "trumpet of sedition," and Edmund Burke "a pest."[106]

The Speech of Separation

There were literally dozens of *causes* that led to the *effect* of American independence, but we can identify a relatively small set of major causes or, at least, constituent justifications for launching a new and separate American nation. Besides *Common Sense*, the major causes were all external to America: the king's speech of October 26, 1775; the Prohibitory Act of December 22, 1775; and the announcement of Hessian troops embarking for America in the spring of 1776.[107] King George III was intimately involved in each of these catalysts for independence, though he, of course, had opposite intentions. I will not deal here with the Prohibitory Act in great detail besides pointing out that it was the impetus for the Continental Congress's Resolution of May 10 and 15, 1776, a crucial step toward independence because it encouraged each colony to set up its own government completely separate from the authority of the Crown. The Prohibitory Act officially excluded the Americans from the protection of the Crown and thus snapped one of the last remaining sinews of colonialism, the reciprocal duty of allegiance. Finally, the Prohibitory Act seemed to validate Paine's comment in *Common Sense*, "Our present condition, is, Legislation without law; wisdom without a plan; a constitution without a name; and, what is strangely astonishing, perfect Independence contending for dependence."[108]

No study of the political effect of *Common Sense* would be complete without accounting for King George III's October 26 speech at the opening of the new parliamentary session. The very same day that Robert Bell first advertised *Common Sense* for sale, the king's speech was published in the Philadelphia press.[109] Paine later claimed to have planned the coincidence, but he, in fact, had little direct control over the timing of *Common Sense*'s first printing. The synchronous publication of the king's speech and *Common Sense* did leave a deep impression on Paine, and he thereafter always dwelt upon the significance of dates and calculated the timing of his publications. His thirteen *Ameri-*

can Crisis papers, a series of essays written during the Revolutionary War, mirrored in number the original states. Paine published his final essay in the series, *American Crisis No. 13*, on April 19, 1783, the eighth anniversary of the Battle of Lexington and Concord that had opened the war.

The February "Appendix" to *Common Sense* addressed the almost divine convergence of events that happened on January 9, 1776, in Philadelphia. Paine implied a divine sanction for his argument when he noted, "Had the spirit of prophecy directed the birth of this production, it could not have brought it forth at a more seasonable juncture, or at a more necessary time."[110]

In the king's speech "His Majesty was pleased to say" that he was not at all pleased with the American colonies. He blamed the "Authors and Promoters of this desperate Conspiracy" who had "too successfully laboured to inflame My People in *America*" with "a System of Opinions repugnant to the true Constitution of the colonies" and "their subordinate Relation to *Great Britain*." These conspirators "now openly avow their Revolt, Hostility, and Rebellion" by their actions, while their "vague Expressions of Attachment to the Parent State" and their "strongest Protestations of Loyalty to Me" were "meant only to amuse" while "they were preparing for a general Revolt." The king declared, "It is now become the Part of Wisdom and (in its Effects) of Clemency, to put a speedy End to these Disorders by the most decisive Exertions." George III went on to describe those Americans resisting British arms as "the unhappy and deluded Multitude, against whom this Force will be directed." The king expressed his readiness "to receive the Misled with Tenderness and Mercy" and he apologized for the "extraordinary Burden" which the situation "must create to My faithful Subjects."[111]

Paine never admitted an unscrutinized word within the bar of his arguments. He qualified the king's speech—"if it may be called one"—as "willful audacious libel against the truth, the common good, and the existence of mankind." Intimating the rites of pagan worship, Paine called the speech "a formal and pompous method of offering up human sacrifices to the pride of tyrants." Paine recapitulated the idolatry inherent in monarchy, stressing that kings were unnatural fabrications, "beings of our *own* creating" who "know not *us*, and are become the gods of their creators."[112] The one good part of the king's speech, said Paine, was that it didn't pretend to be good. It was "not calculated to deceive" and its meaning was plain even to those who *wished* to "be deceived by it."[113] Paine saw in the "bloody mindedness" of the king's speech, the further "necessity of pursuing the doctrine" of *Common Sense*, and since the speech had aroused a spirit of vengeance in the hearts of the Americans, it had "instead of terrifying" paved the way "for the manly principles of Independence."[114] In the Appendix to *Common Sense*, Paine was enacting a "public execution" of the speech, as an act of judgment against its "general massacre of mankind." The king's speech itself, and not just his army, was an active agent in the persecution of America, since "every line convinces, even in the moment of reading" of the king's unparalleled savagery.[115]

Paine's reaction to the speech was consistent with that of Samuel Adams, whose acquaintance Paine had made by February and who was most certainly one of the conspirators singled out in the king's speech. On January 12, Adams wrote that the speech "which is falsely & shamefully called most gracious" had determined his "Opinion of the Author of it as a Man of a wicked Heart." Adams continued, "What a pity it is, that Men are become so degenerate and servile, as to bestow Epithets which can be appropriated to the Supreme Being alone" upon "Speeches & Actions" that deserved "the utmost Contempt and Detestation." He asked, "What have we to expect from Britain, but Chains & Slavery?" and he expressed his opinion that it was "high time" that America assume an independent "Character."[116] A little more than a week later Adams commented in another letter that the speech perverted "the plain Meaning of Words" with "the Tools of a Tyrant." The speech, he said, expressed the king's "most benevolent & humane Feelings" as well as the "Dictates of his own Heart." In that case, Adams asked, "why should we cast the odium of distressing Mankind upon his Minions & Flatterers only. Guilt must lie at his Door."[117] What is remarkable about Adams's comments is not that they were somehow dictated by *Common Sense*, but that they were spot-on consistent with *Common Sense*. Samuel Adams had raced well ahead of general American opinion for most of the controversy with Britain, but Paine was running in stride with him. And more significantly, what Adams said only in smoky rooms or in private letters, Paine published in the open and through persuasion accelerated American opinion to run with them both. The king's speech had crystallized the British position down to a single issue: unconditional submission, and *Common Sense* crystallized the American alternative: independence. These two texts made the events of 1776 a zero-sum game.

After dispensing with the king's speech, Paine shifted his attention to a "whining jesuitical piece" by Sir John Dalrymple that had recently arrived in America. Dalrymple's *The Address of the People of Great-Britain to the Inhabitants of America* (1775), a court-sanctioned attempt at diplomatic intimidation, had promised the Americans, "Your destruction is inevitable."[118] Dalrymple had itemized American disadvantages while swaggering with Britain's superiority. Paine, who never admitted the ethos of his opposition, referred to Dalrymple as the pamphlet's "putative father, and he called even its title "fallacious." Paine mocked Dalrymple's "vain supposition" that Americans were "frightened at the pomp and description of a king," even when "the real character of the present one" was known all too well. Dalrymple claimed that the King's "NOD ALONE" permitted the administration *"to do any thing."* Paine used this admission to equate Dalrymple's "toryism with a witness" and "idolatry even without a mask."[119]

In a summary statement on the role of the Crown in America, Paine considered the king's authority, words, and actions to be thereafter impotent and void, because George III had grossly violated both the natural and religious order of the universe, having "wickedly broken through every moral and human obligation" and, in a tragic inversion of a biblical metaphor depicting God's justice, Paine declared that the king had "trampled nature and conscience beneath his feet."[120] Neutrality to the king's debased demands, Paine argued, was morally indefensible. Anyone who could "calmly hear and digest such doctrine" had "forfeited his claim to rationality," had become "an apostate from the order of manhood," and had "sunk himself beneath the rank of animals."[121]

Heredity and the Hessians

The third major cause of American independence mentioned earlier was the deployment of Hessian mercenary soldiers to the American theater of war. Republican political theory opposed standing armies with vehemence because they were troughs of immorality that required extra taxes for their support and often resulted in military dictatorships. But if republicans hated standing armies, there was yet another holdover of absolutism for which they reserved loathsome horror: mercenary armies. The antithesis of citizen militias, mercenaries were piratical and barbarous, raping and pillaging for a paycheck. When the American colonists confirmed rumors of the impending arrival of Hessian mercenaries on their shores, no doubt lingered in their minds concerning Britain's intentions.

King George III never considered the reaction that his calling upon Hessian troops would elicit in the colonies; for him it was a plain matter of political necessity. Seen from the perspective of Britain, the recruitment of the Hessians provides a fuller insight into the tangled web of misunderstanding and miscommunication that jostled the reluctant Americans toward independence.

On August 23, 1775, the same day the king made his proclamation of American rebellion, John Wesley, the famous itinerant evangelist and founder of Methodism, wrote a letter to his patron, the Earl of Dartmouth. Wesley was pro-government, as would be seen shortly in his *A Calm Address to Our American Colonies* (1775), but having seen more of Britain than most politicians, he wrote Dartmouth with the express purpose of refuting those who claimed that the people of England sided strongly with the government. Wesley reported a nationwide opposition to the king and cautioned the ministry against believing exaggerated accounts of popular support. Most of the people he met in cities, towns, and villages were "dangerously dissatisfied" with the government and "do not so much aim at the ministry, as they usually did in the last century, but at the king himself." Wesley continued, "He is the object of their anger, contempt and malice," and nineteen in twenty persons "to whom I speak in defense of the King, seem never to have heard a word spoken for him before."[122] Two days later, Lord North conceded in a letter to the king, "The cause of Great Britain is not yet sufficiently popular." North thought "that the success of the War in America absolutely depends upon a considerable army being there early in the Spring," but he regretted that "there seems no way of having certainly an Army there of any magnitude."[123] After a series of Court-planted addresses failed to spirit up the people to enlist in the British service, George III and Lord North began to get desperate.[124] Their saber-rattling speeches and proclamations demanded a swift and decisive blow to the colonies, but they couldn't attract enough troops to carry out their plan.

Since they couldn't enlist enough British soldiers, they had to find soldiers somewhere, and the king's connections as a member of the Hanoverian dynasty provided a wealth of military resources. It was, therefore, an act of political necessity that led the king to request the help of his family members, the Landgrave of Hesse Cassel, Frederick II, and the Duke of Brunswick, Charles I.[125] The king guessed that the Duke of Brunswick would be disinclined to help, and he was right. The Landgrave of Hesse Cassel, ruler of a sizable German principality, was, however, glad to assist his nephew. On January 2, 1776, George III wrote a letter from St. James in which he officially accepted the Landgrave's offer of troops.[126] These negotiations took place under the colonial radar, but news of the preparations of Hessian troops and of their embarkation for America on May 15, 1776, sent the colonies into a panic that sealed the necessity of independence in the minds of many wavering Americans.[127]

It was a touch of irony, then, that the ties of hereditary monarchy that Paine had lambasted in *Common Sense* had in fact facilitated a decision that broke the will of proponents of reconciliation. The first two sections of *Common Sense* were concerned with the origins of government and a historical exposé of hereditary monarchy. These sections lack the zip of the last two sections or the Appendix, but they were absolutely crucial to the effectiveness of Paine's overall argument. Paine was digging up and destabilizing the foundation of the House of Hanover, and after he had removed the justifications for monarchy, stone by stone, the constitutional superstructure needed only the tap of corroborating events, and the entire building, at least in the American mind, came crashing down.

Signing the Petition of Independence

We will deal in Chapters Six through Eight with the particulars of the final decision for independence, but for the remainder of this chapter it will be helpful to skip ahead to July and August of 1776, the period just after the Americans declared independence. I noted in the Preface that a remarkable shift had taken place in American public opinion between July 1775 and July 1776. We can even see a shift in the representative documents from those two periods: the "Olive Branch" Petition referred to the king as his "Majesty" over twenty times, while the *Declaration of Independence*, admits of no titles whatsoever for the King of Great Britain and refers to him simply as "He" eighteen separate times. In this chapter we have begun to sketch the gradual dissolution of American affection for the king and for the function of monarchy in general. But before we can complete that picture, we must first ask a question that may seem initially out of place. Why did the Continental Congress sign the *Declaration of Independence*?

The Continental Congress had issued dozens of proclamations, and they were typically "signed" only by the President and the Secretary, in mid-1776, John Hancock and Charles Thomson. The Congress had debated the motion for independence in early July after its introduction by Richard Henry Lee the previous month. The motion for independence was voted in the affirmative on July 2—the day that John Adams thought should be remembered as "Independence Day"—but the *Declaration of Independence* was subjected to two *more* days of debate and revision. After the *Declaration* was approved, the Continental Congress ordered it to be printed, and the delegates issued instructions for the text to be read aloud in each colony and before each brigade. A round of elections during the month of July was changing the makeup of the Continental Congress. Some delegates had to return home to attend provincial congresses, to participate in elections, and to form new state governments. The cadre of delegates who remained or arrived in Philadelphia were consumed with treaties and a plan of confederation. For most, the act of signing the *Declaration* in early August was a sideline affair to be dispensed with before moving onto more important matters.

Why then do we remember the signing of the *Declaration*, on the surface an after-the-fact formality, rather than the vote that made independence a political reality? We refer to certain members of the founding generation as "signers" but not as "voters" or "debaters." One answer is straightforward: there was a mythic valiance about signing the *Declaration* that has made it stand out in our historical memory. The signers were casting their lot with the fledgling United States, and they realized the dire consequences of failure.

There is undoubted truth in this perspective. But there is another reason that signing the *Declaration* carries significance. John Adams always chafed that the ceremonial events of July and August 1776 eclipsed in significance what he thought was the "real" revolution that had occurred between the Massachusetts resistance of the early 1760s and the legislative maneuvering he spearheaded in late 1775 and early 1776. Late in life, in a comment tinged with self-aggrandizement, he inadvertently elucidated the very reason why the *Declaration of Independence* immediately began to occupy a paramount place in the national imagination. When he said, "The Revolution was in the Minds of the People," he was not referring to the summer of 1776, but he should have been.[128]

The Second Continental Congress, like its predecessor, was formed as a representative body whose power was strictly limited to recommendations and petitions. They had, as Paine said later, heaped "petition upon petition" in their pursuit of redress for colonial grievances.[129] The Congress did issue proclamations to the colonies, but compliance was solely at the discretion of an individual provincial assembly. Even the more artful ploys of the Continental Congress, like the Committee of Secret Correspondence, were elaborate mechanisms of placing requests for assistance. As a body, the Congress was restricted and muzzled by provincial instructions, and the delegates repeatedly begged in their June 1776 correspondence for explicit direction from their colonial assemblies on the question of independence.

This deferential body, always two steps removed from real power, operated within the dictates of a petitionary provincial culture, a culture where political agency was by and large confined to signing a petition addressed ultimately to the king. Scrawled names at the bottom of a petition signified the earnest consent of loyal subjects requesting changes and begging for redress in the language of abject humility.

The *Declaration of Independence* does not look, at first glance, like a conventional eighteenth century petition. Jefferson's composition refused to bow in deference to a king whom the Americans no longer regarded as their own. The *Declaration* was not addressed, as the "Olive Branch" Petition had been a year earlier, to "His Most Gracious Sovereign." In fact, the text bore no overt address at all in its introduction, but the extensive list of grievances followed the presentation of a petition. The *Declaration* was, in fact, a consummate example of John Locke's "appeal to heaven," a petition, a prayer, a supplication of last resort. These men had signed petitions before, but as they dipped the quill pen into the silver ink well, they understood that the *Declaration* they were signing was a very different sort of petition addressed to a very different Sovereign.

King of America

The pinnacle of Paine's fusion of religious and political imagery in *Common Sense* can be found in the dramatic paragraph where he identified the *real* king in America. Paine's casual introduction, "I'll tell you, friend, he reigns above," belied the sweeping panorama about to follow. The "King of America," Paine said, "doth not make havoc on mankind like the royal brute of Great Britain." Paine's appellation for George III was a scandalous oxymoron, since "brute" in his day connoted not "oaf" but "beast" or "animal." Like the biblical people of Israel to whom Paine had repeatedly referred, America needed no human to "play" God in an earthly role. Paine realized, though, that his American readers would sense an emotional and political vacancy without some sort of king. He suggested that the Americans could satisfy their psychological need for "earthly honors" by setting apart a solemn national holiday for "proclaiming the charter." He then described a ritual to be enacted on that occasion: the charter would be "placed on the divine law, the Word of God" and then a crown would be "placed thereon." He described this Bible-constitution-crown stack as a symbol "by which the world may know" that America intended to upend the logic of authority in absolutist states. Utilizing a rhetorical chiasmus whereby he could achieve maximum contrast between monarchies and republics, Paine said that elsewhere "the king is law," but in America, "the law is king." Paine then took his imagined ceremony one step further. "But lest any ill use" of the symbolic crown "should afterwards arise" by the hands of those who would scheme for its possession, Paine called for the crown "at the conclusion of the ceremony" to be demolished and "scattered among the people whose right it is." Paine's ceremony symbolized the redistribution of authority according to the residence of sovereignty in the people at large. During the Protestant Reformation, the textual laity had replaced the traditonary papacy as the primary bearer of divine religious sovereignty, and Paine was constructing an analogic call for the textual citizenry of America to replace the traditonary monarchy as the primary bearer of divine political sovereignty. The people, not kings, were the heirs and guardians of God's sovereignty on earth.[130]

Felling Monarchy

Beginning in July and extending through August 1776, in colony after colony, the *Declaration of Independence* was first read aloud to droves of excited Americans. Whenever these crowds heard the *Declaration*, they cheered their approval and then immediately turned to the task of enacting their newfound independence. Without fail, the first response of these crowds was the demolition of all public symbols of the British monarchy. In newly-minted state capitals up and down the

Atlantic coast, statue after statue of George III came crashing down and the Royal Arms were removed from courthouses and publicly burned. These were not the rash actions of angry mobs, nor were they indiscriminate acts of vandalism; these were symbolic enactments of the dissolution of royal authority in America.[131]

Common Sense had aggressively equated monarchy with idolatry: "And when a man seriously reflects on the idolatrous homage which is paid to the persons of Kings he need not wonder, that the Almighty, ever jealous of his honor, should disapprove of a form of government which so impiously invades the prerogative of heaven."[132] By unmasking the idolatry indelible to the monarchical system, Paine had done more than anyone else to loosen the grip of monarchy upon American minds.[133] The biblical record was sufficiently mixed on the subject of monarchy to empower ideologues on both sides of the issue with ample proof-texts. But the biblical precedent on the issue of idolatry was unequivocal.

The biblical narrative brims with instances of the Israelites being lulled into idolatry, gradually assimilating the gods of neighboring cultures. An idol was an ornamental fabrication ascribed with divinity and worshipped by the very men who had crafted it, and in biblical culture, an idol's falsity was marked by its unresponsiveness to supplication.[134] Time and again in the cycle of Old Testament history, a prophet would reveal to the people the error of their ways, and the Israelites would repudiate their attachment to idols and foreign gods. Breaking the cultural hold of idols often involved the physical task of tearing down shrines and statues that had been erected to honor the now-offensive deities.[135] Like a Hebrew prophet, Paine had already desecrated the shrines and symbols of monarchy, fouling the sacrosanct spaces of royal authority with offensive images and impolite language. *Common Sense* left the monuments of monarchy, now stripped of meaning and magic, for the people of America to topple and burn.

The Americans could have easily read the *Declaration*, cheered and celebrated their political autonomy, and then returned to their daily lives and their preparations for war. But this was not what happened. In Savannah, Georgia, as soon as the *Declaration* was received, it was read three times on the same day, first to the Provincial Council in its chambers, again "before a great concourse of people" in "the square before the Assembly House," and a third time at the Militia Battery. At the conclusion of the third reading, the council, the militia, and some other gentlemen "dined under the Cedar Trees, and cheerfully drank to the United Free and Independent States of America." As the sun began to set, several companies of the militia "with their drums muffled and fifes" began to march in "a very solemn funeral procession" followed by "a greater number of people than ever appeared on any occasion before in this Province." The crowd filed quietly to the Court House where they buried in effigy King George III. As soldiers dug the grave, one Georgia militia officer stood on a platform and spoke,

> For as much as George III, of Great Britain, hath most flagrantly violated his coronation oath and trampled upon the constitution of our country and the sacred rights of mankind, we therefore commit his political existence to the ground, corruption to corruption, tyranny to the grave, and oppression to eternal infamy, in sure and certain hope that he will never obtain a resurrection to rule again over these United States of America. But my friends and fellow-citizens, let us not be sorry as men without hope for tyrants that thus depart; rather let us remember America is free and independent; that she is, and will be, with the blessing of the Almighty, great among the nations of the earth. Let this encourage us in well-doing to fight for our rights and privileges, for our wives and children, for all that is near and dear unto us. May God give us his blessing, and let all the people say Amen![136]

By no means was this sort of dramatic display isolated to Georgia. Jeremy Belknap, in his groundbreaking *The History of New-Hampshire* (1784-1792), observed a remarkably similar performative rejection of monarchy in the behavior of New Englanders in the wake of independence:

> It is amusing to recollect, at this distance of time, that one effect of independence was an aversion to every thing which bore the name and marks of royalty. Sign boards on which were painted the king's arms, or the crown and scepter, or the portraits of any branches of the royal family, were pulled down or defaced. Pictures and escutcheons of the same kind in private houses were inverted or concealed. The names of streets, which had been called after a king or queen were altered; and the half-pence, which bore the name of George III, was either refused in payment, or degraded to farthings. These last have not yet recovered their value.[137]

The reaction was also not confined to major cities. In one inland New York town on July 18, 1776, the Declaration was "published at the Courthouse," to loud cheers, and "After which the coat of arms of his Majesty George the III was torn to pieces and burnt in the presence of the spectators."[138]

The king became the premise for every argument in favor of independence, and every official publication was strewn with grievances attributed to his person and his office. The Constitution of New Jersey began, "WHEREAS all the constitutional authority ever possessed by the Kings of *Great-Britain* over these Colonies…" and the Constitution of Virginia, likewise, "WHEREAS George the Third, King of Great-Britain and Ireland, and Elector of Hanover, heretofore, entrusted with the exercise of the kingly office in this government…"[139] The Americans were now submitting a long list of grievances *against* the king rather than *to* the king.

Less than a week after the *Declaration* was approved by the Continental Congress, it was read in New York "at the head of each brigade of the Continental army posted in and near this city, and every where received with the utmost demonstrations of joy." The King's Arms were pulled down and destroyed, "even those on Signs and Taverns." The Assistant Rector of Trinity Church, Rev. Charles Inglis, recalled that all ministers were ordered "to have the King's Arms taken down in the Churches, or else the Mob would do it."[140] That same evening, Colonel Peter Curtenius of the New York Militia ordered his men to topple the gilded lead equestrian statue of George III that had been erected by the order of the New York Assembly in Bowling Green only six years earlier. A large crowd cheered as the statue "was thrown from its pedestal and broken in pieces." Then, in one of the greatest moments of the entire American Revolution, the jubilant New Yorkers looked at the fractured body of George III upon his horse and had an epiphany. As it was reported in the newspapers, "We hear the lead wherewith this monument was made is to be run into bullets."[141]

Notes: Chapter 3

[1] "Eulogium sacred to the Memory of the late Major-General Warren, who fell June 17th, 1775 fighting against the ministerial army at Boston." PM, June 1775.
[2] CS 3.32, 2.23-2.24.
[3] CS 3.19.
[4] RM 2, CW 1:354.
[5] For a helpful discussion of Paine's involvement with English Methodism, see Keane, *Tom Paine*, 46-49.
[6] CS 2.3.
[7] [Middleton,] *True Merits of a Late Treatise*.
[8] Isaiah 40:15, 17.
[9] CS 2.4.
[10] CS 2.5.
[11] CS 2.6.
[12] CS 2.6-2.7.
[13] CS 2.8; Paine selectively cuts off his exposition before Gideon asks instead for all the gold earrings in the Israelites' plunder, which he promptly turns into an idolatrous ceremonial ephod.
[14] CS 2.9.
[15] Ibid.
[16] Ibid.
[17] Ibid.
[18] Ibid.
[19] This anti-Catholic bias obviously persisted in American politics for a long time—at least until Kennedy's presidency. After the American Revolution, the Federalists constantly suspected the Jeffersonian Democratic-Republicans of Francophile intrigue.
[20] CS 3.9, 2.9.
[21] CS 3.11.
[22] CS 2.5.
[23] CS 3.14.
[24] Paine quoted from Milton's *Paradise Lost* IV, 1.98, in CS 3.25.
[25] CS A.2.
[26] CS 3.48.
[27] CS 1.4.
[28] CS 3.50.
[29] CS A.15.
[30] CS 3.23.
[31] CS 4.22, 2.1.
[32] CS 3.48.
[33] Matthew 20: 22; Luke 23:34.
[34] CS 3.50; Ecclesiastes 4:12.
[35] CS 3.48; cf. Deuteronomy 33:2,17; Joshua 22:14; 1 Samuel 18:7-8, 21:11, 29:5; Psalms 3:6; Jude 14; Revelation 5:11.
[36] CS A.1; Isaiah 40: 3.
[37] CS 1.19.

[38] CS 1.15; cf. Matthew 12:24-37; Mark 3:22-27; Luke 11: 14-26. Paine was here the first to use this biblical metaphor in American political discourse, and *Common Sense* may have influenced the phrase's later invocation by Sam Houston, Daniel Webster, and, most famously, Abraham Lincoln.

[39] CS 3.28; Ecclesiastes 3: 1-8.

[40] The basic structures of synonymic repetition to which I refer may be easily identified, for example, in Psalms 136 (sustained lyric repetition) or in Proverbs 8 (proverbial couplets).

[41] CS 2.21.

[42] Anderson, *Imagined Communities*.

[43] This did not seem to bother Charles Carroll of Carrollton, Maryland, who was an advocate for independence and a Catholic. For more on the political marginalization of the Catholic minority, which wielded very little influence during the revolutionary period, except in small pockets of Pennsylvania and Maryland, see Metzger, *Catholics and the American Revolution*.

[44] See Warner, *Publics and Counterpublics*.

[45] An adaptation of the idea of "vulgar rights," a term coined by Breen, and "vulgar style" by Boulton.

[46] CS 4.22.

[47] CS 3.45.

[48] CS 4.21.

[49] CS 3.30.

[50] CS A.4.

[51] "The Will of Thomas Paine," CW 2:1500.

[52] CW 2:52-53.

[53] CS E.1.

[54] CS E.2.

[55] CS E.10.

[56] CS E.4.

[57] AR, CW 1:496-497.

[58] Barclay, *Barclay's Apology*.

[59] CS E.10.

[60] AC, No. 3, CW 1:83.

[61] The administration of August Henry FitzRoy, third Duke of Grafton, was replaced by that of Lord Frederick North, whose ministry extended through 1782.

[62] Cannon, *Letters of Junius*, xiii-xiv

[63] Appendix Two in Cannon, *Letters of Junius*, contains 84 letters between Junius and John Wilkes from 1771.

[64] In RM, Paine observed that this doctrine placed the king on the same legal footing as "idiots and persons insane." CW 1:339.

[65] Cannon, *Letters of Junius*, 160-161.

[66] Ibid., 166-167.

[67] Ibid., 173.

[68] Ibid., 172.

[69] Poole, *The Politics of Regicide in England*, 34.

[70] Poole, 34-35.

[71] Rickman, *Life of Thomas Paine*, 37-39.

[72] Williamson, *Wilkes: 'A Friend to Liberty.'*; Cash, *John Wilkes: The Scandalous Father of Civil Liberty*; Rudé, *Wilkes and Liberty*; Rudé, *The Crowd in History*; Boulton, *Language of Politics*.
[73] Quoted in Conway, *Life of Thomas Paine*, 1:37.
[74] Poole, 35-36.
[75] Ibid., 38.
[76] Ibid., 39.
[77] Ibid., 39.
[78] Bradley, *Popular Politics*, 43-46.
[79] Ibid.
[80] Ibid.
[81] CW 2:1128.
[82] Poole, 9-10.
[83] Ibid., 12.
[84] Ibid., 26-27.
[85] Ibid., 10-11.
[86] Ibid., 2-3.
[87] KGIII to LN, 26 July 1775. Fortescue, *Correspondence of King George the Third*, 3:235.
[88] In a contemporary American analogy, it was as if the United States Supreme Court were to stop hearing cases because they had grown weary of everyone's complaints. If this were to happen, their usefulness, intentions, and role as part of the government would be legitimately called into question.
[89] Bradley, *Popular Politics*, 12.
[90] Ibid., 25.
[91] Burke to Rockingham, 14 September 1775. Quoted in Bradley, *Popular Politics*, 17.
[92] Bradley. *Popular Politics*, 37-38
[93] Adams, *American Controversy*.
[94] Bradley, *Popular Politics*, 59, 93.
[95] British petitioners, it should be noted, generally were forced to choose one of two sides, *force* or *peace*, with both positions equally affirming total loyalty to the Crown.
[96] PEP, August 17, 1775.
[97] KGIII to LN, 18 August 1775. Fortescue, *Correspondence of King George the Third*, 3:247-248.
[98] Quoted in Commager and Morris, 281.
[99] Poole, 17.
[100] Bradley, *Popular Politics*, 210
[101] AC, No. 3, CW 1:88.
[102] KGIII to LN, 15 October 15 1775. Fortescue, 3:269
[103] KGIII to LN, 23 October 1775. Foretescue, 3:273
[104] KGIII to LN, 18 November 1775. Fortescue, 3:293-294.
[105] KGIII to LN, 11 December 1775, and 20 December 1775. Fortescue, 3:301-302.
[106] Hibbert, *George III*, 142.
[107] These are "pure" external causes. I will make the case later in this study for the causality of several other events, especially the Resolve of the Continental

Congress on May 10/15, 1776, the Virginia Resolves, and the Halifax Resolves. But each of these "events" was both a cause *and* an effect of earlier circumstances.

[108] CS A.11.

[109] NYG, January 8, 1776; PEP, January 9, 1776. The king's speech was given on October 26, 1775, and published in London on October 27, a fact that accounts for frequent misdating encountered in the historical record.

[110] CS A.1.

[111] Lords Proceedings. 26 October 1775. Simmons and Thomas, *Proceedings and Debates of the British Parliaments*, 6:69-70.

[112] CS A.2.

[113] CS A.2.

[114] CS A.1.

[115] CS A.1..

[116] SA to James Sullivan. 12 January 1776. Cushing, 257-258.

[117] SA to John Pitts. 21 January 1776. Cushing, 255-256.

[118] Dalrymple, *Address of the People of Great-Britain*.

[119] CS A.3.

[120] CS A.4.

[121] CS A.3.

[122] John Wesley to the Earl of Dartmouth, 23 August 1775. Quoted in Bradley, *Popular Politics*, 207.

[123] LN to KGIII, 25 August 1775. Fortescue, 3:249.

[124] LN to KGIII, 9 September 1775. Fortescue 3:255-256.

[125] KGIII to the Hereditary Prince of Brunswick, 8 October 1775; KGIII to LN, 18 November 1775. Fortescue, 3:263-264, 293-294.

[126] Stone, *Journal of Captain Pausch*, 5-6.

[127] Ibid., 19.

[128] JA to TJ, 24 August 1815. Cappon, *Adams-Jefferson Letters*, 455.

[129] AC, No. 3. CW 1:87.

[130] CS 3.47.

[131] The loyalist-leaning *Pennsylvania Ledger*, printed by James Humphreys, Jr. in Philadelphia, withdrew a woodcut of the Royal Arms from its masthead in June 1776; nonetheless, its publication was suspended for almost a year in November 1776.

[132] CS 2.6.

[133] CS A.3.

[134] See Jeremiah 10: 1-16 and 1 Kings 18: 25-29.

[135] See, for example, 2 Kings 23: 3-14.

[136] "Savannah [Georgia] Buries George III and Declares Independence," August 10, 1776. Quoted in Commager and Morris, 322-323.

[137] Belknap, *History of New-Hampshire*, 366.

[138] PEP, July 23, 1776.

[139] PG, July 17, 1776.

[140] Harris, *Charles Inglis*, 48.

[141] PG, July, 17, 1776. The conventional date for this event is July 9, but some accounts specify Wednesday, July 10. The lead from the statue was transported to Litchfield, Connecticut, to be made into bullets for the Americans. The

statue had been erected on August 16, 1770. The marble pedestal the statue had rested upon was in 1783 made into a tombstone for Major John Smith of the British Army, whose grave was leveled in 1804. Afterwards the slab was used as the front step of a mansion. NYHS.

Chapter Four

Mechanics of a Revolution

It is futile to expect a great advancement in the sciences from overlaying and implanting new things on the old; a new beginning has to be made from the lowest foundations, unless one is content to go round in circles for ever, with meager, almost negligible, progress.

Sir Francis Bacon
Novum Organum
1620

What Archimedes said of the mechanical powers, may be applied to reason and liberty: "*Had we,*" said he, "*a place to stand upon, we might raise the world.*" The Revolution of America presented in politics what was only theory in mechanics.

Thomas Paine
Rights of Man, Part the Second
1792

Part One
NATURAL PHILOSOPHY

Rational Mechanics

Amidst the tension and bustle of Philadelphia in early 1776, the ruling elite began to grow nervous about the swelling influence of the city's "mechanics," a group inclusive of everyone from staymakers (Paine's family trade) to cobblers, coopers, chandlers, blacksmiths, printers, carpenters, and anyone else who produced goods with his hands. "Mechanic" was synonymous with "artisan" or "craftsman," a "middling" class of workers who labored with their hands and gained skills through an extensive apprenticeship in their trades—in everything from clockmaking to plough repair. Mechanics as a group were trained but not educated, and most possessed only a basic competency in reading, writing, and mathematics as necessitated by their trade. The urban elite was concerned that this massive demographic was beginning to demand a more active role in colonial politics, even though they lacked the cultivation of a liberal arts education and the credentials of a landed estate.

Although these mechanics would play a crucial role in the course of American independence, there was *another* sense of "mechanics" in the eighteenth century that will be the focus of my analysis in this chapter. As we have already observed, Paine was attempting to replicate the conditions and effects of the Protestant Reformation in *Common Sense*, a translation from the religious to the political sphere. He was also attempting a further translation, one perhaps more important and pervasive, although more subtle. What Francis Bacon and Isaac Newton had done in the realm of natural philosophy—what we think of as science—Paine was attempting to accomplish in politics. Thus *Common Sense* was also a translation in principle and language from the scientific to the political sphere. Paine was seeking to observe, explain, and predict the political events of the British-American controversy with the accuracy and logic of "rational mechanics," the principles that had guided the scientific breakthroughs of the seventeenth and eighteenth centuries. To understand the role of science in early American culture and, in turn, the overwhelming import of scientific language and logic in *Common Sense*, we must first look at the giddy fascination displayed by a motley group of Philadelphia astronomers in 1769.

Useful Knowledge

Two separate Philadelphia scientific societies merged in 1769 to form "The American Philosophical Society, held at Philadelphia, for promoting useful Knowledge." Benjamin Franklin was elected the first president of the new American Philosophical Society and remained at its helm through 1790. In fact, the organization had only three presidents for the first 45 years of its existence: Franklin, David Rittenhouse, and Thomas Jefferson. The Philosophical Society's membership list was a who's-who of colonial and early republican elite. Proprietary politicians sat beside clergymen, prominent Quakers, college faculty, and leading lights from other American colonies. Honorary appointees from across the Atlantic provided a virtual connection to European scientific societies with whom these Americans participated in a "republic of letters."[1]

Meetings of the Philosophical Society were primarily symposia for papers on various topics in what we would term "applied science." The idea of "useful Knowledge" governed their "disquisitions" and emphasized "such subjects as tend to the improvement of their country, and the advancement of its interest and prosperity."[2] Knowledge was not useful when "confined to mere speculation" but rather when it was "reduced to practice" and "grounded upon experiments" that could be "applied to the common purposes of life."[3] Many presentations dealt with biology, chemistry, and pharmacology, such as Benjamin Rush's paper on the curative effects of the thorn apple and another paper from a physician in Antigua titled, "Remarkable Case of a Tetanus and Locked Jaw cured by amazing Quantities of Opium."[4] In its beginning, however, the dominant concern of the American Philosophical Society was astronomy and, specifically, the Transit of Venus on June 3, 1769.

At a meeting of the Society on February 7, 1769, fourteen members were selected as a committee for the observation of Venus's transit across the face of the sun.[5] With only four months until the event, the committee began preparations right away. The Society commissioned carpenters to build three observation decks: one in the State House yard in Philadelphia, one on the Rittenhouse farm in Norriton (now Norristown), and one on Cape Henlopen in Delaware.[6] As carpenters hammered away at the Philadelphia observatory, located in the open square south of the Pennsylvania State House (now Independence Hall), the observation team gathered regularly to make calculations, to adjust instruments, and to clear any possible obstructions to their view.

Transit of Venus and Scientific Culture

The Transit of Venus was an eighteenth century "space race." The transit generated worldwide scientific interest not because it was expected to reveal new facts about the planet Venus, but because it was the key for measuring the dimensions of the solar system. A careful observation of Venus's transit across the disc of the sun was the best method yet devised for measuring the solar parallax, an astronomical figure that would permit scientists to recheck the distance from the earth to the sun (the "absolute unit" in astronomy), which was used to calculate the size of the solar system. The planet Venus crosses the sun's face no more than twice per century because of the difference between the orbits of the earth and Venus.[7] Moreover, each transit is visible only from certain places on earth, and the transit of 1761 had not been visible from North America. The Transit of Venus was the most important astronomical problem of its day, and by conducting exemplary observations of the phenomenon in 1769, the Americans hoped to put themselves on "the map" of European scientific culture.[8]

Johannes Kepler had been the first to calculate the times of the Transit of Venus, but a mathematical error led him to the conclusion that the event would not be visible in 1639. An English minister, Jeremiah Horrocks, corrected Kepler's error, and along with his friend, William Crabtree, made the only observation of the transit in 1639. Although the clouds had parted just before Horrocks's observation, the accuracy of his results had been compromised because he was conducting church services when the planet first made contact with the sun.

Astronomers were ready for the next transit in 1761, which was a fiercely competitive affair, especially between Britain and France, who were then embroiled in the Seven Years' War. Cloudy weather in Europe hampered observations at all but a few stations in the northern and southern extremities of the continent, and well-funded expeditions to distant observation sites met with mixed success. Charles Mason and Jeremiah Dixon tried to abort their voyage to Sumatra after an attack by a French warship killed eleven of their crew. Their Royal Society patrons replied that abandoning their mission would "bring an indelible Scandal upon their Character, and probably end in their utter Ruin." After being forced to alter their course again, they ended up observing the transit from the Cape of Good Hope.

Around the world, astronomers awaited impatiently the next occurrence of the phenomenon in 1769 because it would allow them to check the correctness of the figures gathered from 1761 through repetition of the experiment.[9] Again, expeditions embarked for far flung locales specifically to view the transit in places like Norway, Hudson Bay, Baja California, and Tahiti, where then-Lieutenant James Cook and his crew timed the event as the main impetus for their first voyage of discovery.[10]

There were in 1769 two known methods of measuring the solar parallax. The first required only a single location but demanded perfect precision, instrumentation, and weather. Astronomers preferred a second method, proposed by the late Edmond Halley, who had referred to the Transit of Venus as "that sight which is by far the noblest astronomy affords." In this method, astronomers measured the difference of absolute time of the transit at a variety of locales and triangulated the results, along with precise longitudes and latitudes, to generate a figure acceptable to the world scientific community. The latter method did not demand advanced instrumentation, which relieved Thomas Pryor, a member of the Philadelphia observation team, because he used his own 18-inch reflecting telescope with a "magnifying power he does not certainly know, but supposes it to be at least an hundred times." Thus the Philadelphia team, armed with two 18-inch telescopes, one 12-inch telescope, and "a good time-piece," promised themselves "the pleasure of making accurate Observations, if the weather should prove favourable." And this last point was imperative. A stray cloud at the moment of contact could totally occlude the observation. The Philosophical Society team gambled, therefore, four months of effort on the weather conditions of just over eighteen minutes. They determined that the project was worth the risk, since the next transit would occur in 1874. For this band of amateur astronomers, the observation of the Transit of Venus was literally the chance of a lifetime.

Owen Biddle supervised the observation at Cape Henlopen. John Ewing and Hugh Williamson headed the Philadelphia team, and William Smith led the team observing the transit from Rittenhouse's farm in Norriton.[11] The day of June 3, 1769, proved clear at all three observatories, and the teams of amateur astronomers, equipped with telescopes and pocket watches, successfully observed the entry and exit of the tiny silhouette of Venus arcing across the sun's photosphere. Rittenhouse, an expert surveyor, had calculated the longitude and latitude of the observatories, and he had also predicted with fine detail the exact motion and duration of the event. Biddle, Ewing, and Smith composed reports of each respective observation, which were presented to the Philosophical Society, published in its *Transactions*, and circulated in Europe, where the results were compiled with others to produce a more accurate measurement of the distance between the earth and the sun.

The American Philosophical Society took pride in its "committee" of astronomers who had ably contributed to solving the greatest problem in the "most sublime" of sciences.[12] In the eighteenth century, one of the most important changes in the history of humankind's self-understanding was occurring. The vastness of the universe and the immensity of past time were just beginning to be grasped, and the paradigmatic impact of these discoveries changed the nature of human relations.[13] The Transit of Venus was an extraordinary alignment of the solar system, visible from only a few distinct spots on the planet. Under optimal conditions, amateur experimental scientists, aided by the instruments of chronometry and reflective optics, could observe and time this singular event. One epochal convergence in one fleeting moment, duly observed, held the key to unlocking the truths of the universe. This was a defining experience of Enlightenment culture, and by analogy, it explains Paine's construction of the decision for independence in *Common Sense*.

Paine later described America as "the only spot in the political world," where the "universal" principles of revolution could be at first adequately observed. In 1776 "an assemblage of circumstances conspired" to facilitate the discovery and advancement of political principles that would have been occluded anywhere else. Other pretended revolutions, he said, had "extended only to a change of persons and measures, but not of principles" and, therefore, were unable to escape the gravity of "the common transactions of the moment." The "independence of America" swelled in significance through the combined optical powers of perspective and observation. America "made a stand, not for herself only, but for the world," said Paine, because she "looked beyond the advantages herself could receive."[14] Paine did not begin to think in these terms at an advanced age. He never intended to become a political writer; he wanted to be a scientist.

PART TWO
A SCIENTIFIC TREATISE

Paine's First Audience

It has often been said that Paine geared his writings for the "lower sorts" in society. While this is true to a significant extent, it is important to remember that the artisans of the "middling class," the people with whom Paine had grown up and who shared his background and cultural vocabulary, were not necessarily the first audience he had in mind when he sat down to write *Common Sense*. He was, to be sure, writing a politics that made sense in an artisan's universe, a system that made intuitive sense to sharp but uneducated minds. It is safe to say that the *secondary* audience for *Common Sense* was the Philadelphia artisanal class, though Paine certainly kept near the front of his mind the inhabitants of the other American colonies—especially the afflicted Bostonians for whom he expressed direct sympathy.

But the primary audience for whom Paine wrote *Common Sense* was notably small. The only people (besides Paine and Robert Bell) whom we know read at least portions of *Common Sense* before it went on sale in Bell's book shop, were Benjamin Rush, David Rittenhouse, and Benjamin Franklin. Paine spent a great deal of time with Thomas Pryor during the fall of 1775, so it seems likely that he, too, was at least aware of Paine's composition. Though Samuel Adams and John Adams, along with Franklin, were often rumored to be the pamphlet's authors because of their radical reputations, Paine did not make the acquaintance of either Massachusetts delegate until after *Common Sense* reached the public.[15]

Franklin and Rittenhouse were not just famous American scientists, they were self-taught geniuses who had broken through the leather ceiling of their artisanal backgrounds and had risen to the highest ranks of eighteenth century natural philosophy without the privilege of an elite education. These were the men most esteemed by Philadelphia artisans, a printer turned physicist and a clockmaker turned astronomer, and Paine was eager to impress them. He wrote *Common Sense*, which required at some level their nod of approval, in a language that would have resonated with these men of science.

In the first sentence that Paine penned as the new editor of the *Pennsylvania Magazine* in January 1775, he described the "reigning character" of his adopted country as "the love of science." England's advances in agriculture and manufacturing, he continued, owed much "to hints first thrown out in some of their magazines" by "gentlemen whose abilities enabled them to make experiments." In order for science to flourish likewise in America, "the channels of communication" could not remain "so narrow and limited."[16]

Many of America's most prominent residents were, as we have observed, amateur writers and amateur politicians, but a remarkable number of them were also amateur scientists. It was the Enlightenment pastime of science or, as it was often called, natural or experimental philosophy, that consumed their aspirations and imaginations.

The Franklin Factor

Although Benjamin Franklin did not shepherd the process of composing and publishing *Common Sense*, his presence was felt the entire way. Paine addressed him with a reverential awe and treated him as an American father figure. Without "informing him what I was doing," Paine readied his draft for the press "as fast as I conveniently could, and sent him the first pamphlet that was printed off."[17] Without Franklin's patronage, Paine would never have written *Common Sense*, and one of Paine's major goals in writing *Common Sense* was to impress Franklin with his own "science of politics." When Paine published *Common Sense* anonymously, the pamphlet was most often rumored to be the work of Franklin, an untruth that served to bolster interest in *Common Sense* in America and, especially, in England.

At the beginning of October 1775, Franklin wrote a letter to his friend Richard Price, who was at that time composing what would become the bestselling British pamphlet of 1776, his pro-American *Observations on Civil Liberty*. Franklin wished "ardently" for peace, but confessed his frustration that "every ship from Britain brings some intelligence of new measures that tend more and more to exasperate." The British government, Franklin said, could not think of anything "far and reasonable" until they had "found by dear experience the reducing us by force impracticable." The Americans had "as yet resolved only on defensive measures" and would have mediated "nothing to injure" Britain if its troops were to be recalled. Franklin thought a little "cooling" time would have "excellent effects" on both sides, but knew that Britain would continue to "goad and provoke us" because they "despise us too much" and failed to understand "that there is no little enemy." Franklin continued,

> Our respect for them will proportionally diminish, and I see clearly we are on the high road to mutual hatred and destruction. A separation of course will be inevitable. 'Tis a million of pities so fair a plan as we have hitherto been engaged in for increasing strength and empire with public felicity should be destroyed by the mangling hands of a few ministers. It will not be destroyed, God will protect and prosper it. You will only exclude yourselves from any share in it. We hear that more ships and troops are coming out. We know you may do us a great deal of mischief but we are determined to bear it patiently as long as we can, but if you flatter yourselves with beating us into submission, you know

neither the people nor the country.. The Congress is still sitting and will wait the result of their last petition.[18]

Franklin's invective was not directed at Price but at the British ministry whom Franklin hoped would read the letter in the London press. The political views of Franklin were esteemed in America, but in Britain and in continental Europe, his opinions were often taken as singularly representative of American policy. Franklin had not ascended to this level of international respect by the conventional route of tutors, universities, grand tours, and appointments. He was an unschooled printer who had shown exceptional enterprise and ingenuity, turning a modest print shop into a media empire of sorts before he had turned forty. Franklin had "retired" from his printing business while still young to devote himself to science and diplomacy for the remainder of his long life. Franklin's story of obsessive self-improvement already held in the late eighteenth century a great deal of the mythic significance it would acquire after the publication of his *Autobiography*. Franklin's winsome personality, enviable wealth, and clever intellect made him an object of emulation for many Americans and Britons from working class backgrounds. Paine did not write *Common Sense* simply to *impress* Benjamin Franklin but, just as much, to *inhabit* the consummate Enlightenment identity of his patron.

Benjamin Franklin first made Paine's acquaintance through a mutual friend, George Lewis Scott, a famous mathematician, Fellow of the Royal Society, and a Commissioner of the Excise. Scott had been impressed with Paine's initiative and determination in the young officer's attempt to reform the Excise system. Benjamin Franklin wrote a letter of introduction for Paine, dated September 30, 1774, to his son-in-law, Richard Bache. Franklin said that Paine was "very well recommended to me, as an ingenious, worthy young man." Paine, he said, had "a view of settling" in Pennsylvania but required Bache's "best advice and countenance" because "he is quite a stranger there." Franklin requested that Bache find Paine employment as a clerk, an assistant tutor, or an assistant surveyor, "all of which I think him very capable." Franklin urged Bache, the husband of Franklin's only daughter Sarah, to help Paine "procure a subsistence" until he could "make acquaintance and obtain a knowledge of the country."[19]

Over the course of the decades Franklin spent in Europe, he had written several letters of introduction on behalf of young men who aspired to emigrate to America. The practice was so common, especially for someone of Franklin's social stature, that in 1777 the wit composed a humorous "Letter of Recommendation for all Occasions":

Sir,
The Bearer of this who is going to America, presses me to give him a Letter of Recommendation, tho' I know nothing of him, not even his Name. This may seem extraordinary, but I assure you it is not uncommon here. Sometimes indeed one unknown Person brings me another equally unknown, to recommend him, and sometimes they recommend one another! As to this gentleman, I must refer you to himself for his Character and Merits, with which he is certainly better acquainted than I can possibly be; I recommend him however to those Civilities which every Stranger, of whom one knows no Harm, has a Right to, and I request you will do him all the good Offices and show him all the Favour that on further Acquaintance you shall find him to deserve. I have the honor to be, &c.[20]

Franklin's real letter for Paine was both more generous and, as we have seen, more effective at opening doors in Philadelphia. In a show of thanks to his patron, Paine recounted his journey to America in a letter to Franklin dated March 4, 1775. Paine's trip aboard the *London Packet* proved precarious after a "Putrid Fever broke out," with five passengers dying and no more than five avoiding infection. The passage across the Atlantic took nine weeks. Paine became dreadfully ill with a fever, and he had "little hopes" that he would "live to see America." Dr. John Kearsley of Philadelphia attended the ship upon its arrival, and when he learned that Paine had been recommended by Franklin, he "sent two of his Men with a Chaise to bring me on shore," where he made special arrangements for the care of Paine, who "could not at that Time turn in my bed without help."[21] It took Paine six weeks to recover sufficient health to pay a visit to Richard Bache. Paine concluded the account of his journey with the eager observation of an amateur scientist, "I attribute the disease to the Impurity of Air between Decks, and think Ventilation would prevent it, but I am convinced it cannot remove the disease, after it has once taken place."

Paine could not resist taking the opportunity of his letter to ask Franklin a scientific question. He noted that, according to Joseph Priestley's *Experiments and Observations on Different Kinds of Air* (1774) and Franklin's "Letter thereon," new vegetation could recover the "former Purity" of air "rendered noxious by animal Substances decaying in it." He then asked, "Whether it will recover Air rendered Impure by Respiration only?" Paine proceeded to speculate whether air has "no vivifying Spirit" or whether it "acts only as a Cleanser," becoming foul "not by what it loses but by what it gains." He stopped himself, though, with a self-conscious admission: "I have not the Treatise by me, and may perhaps have made a useless remark."

Paine closed the letter with an account of the "many friends and much reputation" he had enjoyed because of Franklin's introduction. He had entertained several offers to tutor young men "on very advantageous Terms to myself" but had decided to assist Robert Aitken, "a Man of Reputation, and Property" with a new magazine. Subscriptions to the *Pennsylvania Magazine* had more than doubled since the second number, the first issue that Paine had been "Concerned in." Paine sent Franklin and Scott each a copy of the magazine, and requested that Franklin forward "any thing you may judge Serviceable to the Magazine." He also asked Franklin to purchase and bring him a copy of Oliver Goldsmith's eight volume *History of the Earth and Animated Nature* (1774) upon his return."[22] As we saw in Chapter Two, Paine began *Common Sense* as a "history of the present transactions." His composition was not a pure *political* history but, like Goldsmith's work, was a *natural* history that took as its object of study the forces and phenomena of imperial politics.

Paine and Science

Though the details of Paine's early life remain scant, we can be sure that the concatenation of events that led him to America and, likewise, to compose *Common Sense* had been governed by his interest in science. A preponderance of the men who had influenced Paine in the 1760s and 1770s were noted scientists, many of whom had been elected Fellows of the Royal Society, Britain's most distinguished scientific body. In England, Paine had attended the scientific lectures of Benjamin Martin and James Ferguson, FRS.[23] He became friends with John Bevis, MD, FRS, a physician and a celebrated astronomer. He met Benjamin Franklin, FRS, through the introduction of George Lewis Scott, FRS. In America, his early influences included Benjamin Rush, MD, Thomas Pryor, and David Rittenhouse, all members of the American Philosophical Society.[24] Most of these men had taken a major interest in the Transit of Venus, as did several other figures in the history of *Common Sense* and American independence, including Richard Price, FRS, Joseph Priestley, FRS, William Smith, Owen Biddle, and John Dickinson, to name a few.[25]

As a young man, Paine "had no disposition for what is called politics," but rather, he confessed, "The natural bent of my mind was to science." When in 1775 he first turned his thoughts toward the matter of government, he said, "I had to form a system for myself that accorded with the moral and philosophic principles in which I have been educated." What were those principles? As we have seen, he was deeply influenced by the moral frameworks of Quakerism and Methodism, but it was science, or "natural philosophy" that held the most intellectual salience for Paine. As soon as Paine could scrape together enough money, he purchased a pair of globes—the basic laboratory equipment of eighteenth century astronomy—and began attending the "philosophical lectures" of James Ferguson and Benjamin Martin in London.[26]

Paine was suckled on politics in the popular scientific community of London in the 1760s and early 1770s. He did not attend lectures on politics, *per se*, but the universal principles of Enlightenment science, he realized, applied as well to the "science of politics" as they did to every other branch of scientific inquiry. This is a point that cannot be overstressed: in *Common Sense*, Paine was attempting to delineate a political system that operated according to the principles of Baconian induction and was governed by the laws of Newtonian mechanics. During the seventeenth century, Francis Bacon and Isaac Newton had developed two distinct but complementary frameworks for studying the natural world that proved to be revolutionary in their implications. Bacon had prescribed a universal method for acquiring scientific knowledge, and Newton had discerned immutable laws that superintend the universe. In *Common Sense*, and in his later works, Paine's inventional logic, his political systems, and his prose style were greatly influenced by Baconian and Newtonian natural philosophy. Paine was attempting to translate the esoteric insights of these scientific giants into the practical problems of imperial politics.

Baconian Induction and Newtonian Mechanics

Francis Bacon and Isaac Newton, along with John Locke, combined to form the great triumvirate of thinkers held in highest regard by Voltaire and Thomas Jefferson. Bacon's *Novum Organum* (1620) was, according to Voltaire, the "most singular," the "most excellent," the "most useful," and "now the least read" of Bacon's works. Voltaire explained, "This is the scaffold by means of which the edifice of the new philosophy has been reared," explaining the general ignorance of Bacon's *magnum opus* as the discarding of the scaffolding "when the building was completed."[27] Voltaire made a similar comment about Newton. Only "a small number peruse" Newton's works, "because to do this the student must be deeply skilled in the mathematics, otherwise those works will be unintelligible to him." Voltaire famously observed of Newton's reputation among the English that he was "the Hercules of fabulous story, to whom the ignorant ascribed all the feats of ancient heroes."[28] When Jefferson, for whom "the tranquil pursuits of science" were his "supreme delight," became President of the United States, he commissioned portraits of Bacon, Newton, and Locke, and hung them prominently first in the State Department and then later at Monticello.[29] As these accounts demonstrate, Bacon and Newton were more worshipped than read. But the fact that their books were not perennial bestsellers is misleading. Their influence was everywhere, and the unending stream of discoveries, inventions, and publications by their disciples made an explosive impact on Western culture.

Bacon was a distinguished nobleman whose omnicompetence was dizzying. He had famously declared, "I have taken all knowledge to be my province," and he was serious about his territorial claim. In addition to serving as King's Counsel, Solicitor-General, Attorney-General, Lord Keeper of the Great Seal, and Lord Chancellor in the British government, he wrote on just about every subject imaginable in his time. His unfinished *New Atlantis* inspired the founding of the Royal Society of London for Improving Natural Knowledge. Though Bacon had been embroiled in numerous scandals and court controversies, Lord Bolingbroke once said that he was "so great a man that I do not recollect whether he had any faults or not."[30]

In Bacon's most popular work, *The Advancement of Learning* (1605), he assessed and classified the state of learning across Europe and laid out an agenda for intellectual progress. He famously recounted the tale of the philosopher who, "while he gazed upwards to the stars, fell into the water; for if he had looked down he might have seen the stars in the water, but looking aloft he could not see the water in the stars." He concluded that "mean and small things discover great, better than great can discover the small." As an empirical instance of this phenomenon, Bacon noted "how that secret of nature, of the turning of iron touched with the loadstone towards the north, was found out in needles of iron, not in bars of iron."[31]

Unlike Cicero and the later Academics, Bacon was not skeptical of sensory perception. He found the senses "very sufficient to certify and report the truth" if augmented "by help of instrument." He argued that the Ciceronians "ought to have charged the deceit upon the weakness of the intellectual powers, and upon the manner of collecting and concluding upon the reports of the senses." For Bacon, instrumentation was a key to accurate perception, since no one can make a completely "straight line or perfect circle by steadiness of hand," although it "may be easily done by help of a ruler or compass."[32]

In the *Novum Organum* (1620), Bacon unveiled an entirely new system of epistemology, the "New Instrument" he hoped would displace the deductive logic of Aristotle's *Organon* as the basis for philosophical inquiry. Bacon's method, he said, was designed to "establish degrees of certainty" and "to open and construct a new and certain road for the mind from the actual perceptions of the senses."[33] He excoriated the blindly deductive "art of logic" which "has had the effect of fixing [i.e., cementing] errors rather than revealing truth." The logicians were, in a "systematic and methodical act of insanity," applying their "bare hands" to problems that were impossible to solve without the "machinery" of an empirical methodology. Said Bacon,

> If men had tackled mechanical tasks with their bare hands and without the help and power of tools, as they have not hesitated to handle intel-

lectual tasks with little but the bare force of their intellects, there would surely be very few things indeed which they could move and overcome, no matter how strenuous and united their efforts.[34]

Anyone who endeavored to "improve the force of their minds with logic," which Bacon regarded as "a kind of athletic art," was like a group of "seriously demented" men who, unable to move a giant monument with their "bare hands," responded by trying again with "hands, arms, and muscles properly oiled and massaged according to the rules of the art."[35]

Bacon invited those who aspired "to conquer nature by action" and to acquire "sure, demonstrable knowledge" as "true sons of the sciences" to "pass the antechambers of nature which innumerable others have trod," and eventually open up access to the inner rooms. He referred to the method of the logicians as the "Anticipation of the Mind," while he named his method the "Interpretation of Nature."[36] Bacon's new system, what we now regard as the commonplace "Scientific Method" of empirical observation and experimental repetition was subversive of the entire educational structure of Europe. According to deductive logic, a person arrived at truth by beginning with a grand premise and reasoning *downward* toward particular conclusions. Bacon's system called for the careful observation of particular instances and reasoning *upward* from those to higher order "axioms."[37]

Isaac Newton utilized and built upon Bacon's system to construct his own definitive approach to natural philosophy. Like Bacon, Newton mastered a panoply of subjects and occupations. He served as a Member of Parliament, the Master of the Royal Mint, and the President of the Royal Society, a post he held for over two decades. He taught at Cambridge for over thirty years and wrote on chemistry, history, and theology, in addition to his famous works on mathematics, physics, and astronomy. Newton had deliberately constrained the original audience for his epochal *Philosophiae Naturalis Principia Mathematica* (1687) by writing with maximum scientific opacity, with the specific intention of preventing the meddling criticism of unqualified readers. Even though very few people could read or understand its combination of Latin prose and technical mathematical proofs, the *Principia* quickly became the most celebrated text of the age.[38] Newton explicated the roles of *mass* and *force* in the universe and proved with a level of unparalleled certainty the fundamental "laws" that govern the behavior of nature.[39] Though Newton's method in the *Principia* was more deductive than Bacon's by virtue of its reliance on mathematical propositions, theorems, and proofs, Newton's repudiation of hypotheses demonstrated an empiricist's commitment to achieving unbiased correspondence between his axioms and demonstrable natural phenomena.[40] Moreover, in Newton's *Optics* (1704), another work of lasting significance, his goal was "not to explain the Properties of Light by Hypotheses, but to propose and prove them by Reason and Experiments."[41] Toward the conclusion of Book III of the *Optics*, Newton reviewed his method:

> This Analysis consists in making Experiments and Observations, and in drawing general Conclusions from them by Induction, and admitting of no Objections against the Conclusions, but such as are taken from Experiments, or other certain Truths. For Hypotheses are not to be regarded in experimental Philosophy. And although the arguing from Experiments and Observations by Induction be no Demonstration of general Conclusions; yet it is the best way of arguing which the Nature of Things admits of, and may be looked upon as so much the stronger, by how much the Induction is more general. And if no Exception occur from Phenomena, the Conclusion may be pronounced generally.[42]

He continued, describing the epistemological framework of induction and its relationship to determining causality:

> By this way of Analysis we may proceed from Compounds to Ingredients, and from Motions to the Forces producing them; and in general, from Effects to their Causes, and from particular Causes to more general ones, till the Argument end in the most general.[43]

Newton anticipated that "by pursuing this Method" natural philosophy would "at length be perfected" in "all its Parts," and he reasoned that the same method would enlarge "the Bounds of Moral Philosophy"—an expansive term that encompassed what we would now partition as ethics, aesthetics, religion, political economy, sociology, psychology, and philosophy of the mind. Newton was implying that a method that had proven to carry unprecedented explanatory freight in the natural world should be equally applicable in human relations, which were simply a subclassification of the natural order. Other forms of truth, said Newton, would thus "appear to us by the Light of Nature."[44] In response to the inductive logics proposed by Bacon and Newton, John Locke, George Berkeley, and David Hume developed their influential systems of moral and political philosophy, as it were, "from the ground up" upon sensation, perception, and reflection.[45]

Part Three
LECTURES AND DEMONSTRATIONS

Secondary Education

Thomas Paine had not read either Bacon or Newton before he wrote *Common Sense*, but he didn't have to. Paine and his circle were swimming in their influence. Through the medium of James Ferguson's and Benjamin Martin's Newtonian philosophical lectures, Paine had entered into the world of British popular science, an intellectual subculture that promoted the basic principles of observation, experimentation, and inductive reason in a smorgasbord of visual demonstrations, tangible inventions, and plebian publications. Paine later exaggerated his inventional method in the composition of *Common Sense*: "I thought for myself." Even if he hadn't drawn his ideas from books or the opinions of others, as he claimed, his *thoughts* were nonetheless suffused with the vocabulary and logic of natural philosophy.

Before we take a closer look at the content of Paine's scientific influences, it will be helpful first to trace a broader pattern in his educational history. From the moment *Common Sense* was first published, Paine's readers have wondered how he did it. Even before his audience discovered his identity, eighteenth century Americans and Britons wondered who in America could possibly have written something with such verve. No American writer had ever approached this combination of vehement tenor, capital wit, and galloping cadence in any publication. If *Common Sense* was like anything early modern readers had seen before, it seemed closer to the biting style of Jonathon Swift or the narrative authenticity of Daniel Defoe, but it was unlike any contemporary piece of writing, even in England. When Americans and Britons learned that Thomas Paine, an untrained English castaway, was the author, most of them frankly didn't believe he could have written it.

Still today there is an air of mystery regarding how Paine learned to write and think the way he did without the benefit of any formal education beyond grammar school. Some historical detectives have sought to find cover-ups in Paine's humble beginnings, sensing that he must have read extensively in political theory and philosophy. Others have hypothesized that he received scholarly help from more learned patrons. In fact, the explanation for Paine's breadth of political knowledge is simple: while most of his contemporaries boasted of their abilities to read onerous primary texts, Paine focused on secondary sources of information. The "General Preface" to James Burgh's *Political Disquisitions*, one of only two works explicitly recommended by Paine to his readers in *Common Sense*, yields insight into this dynamic. Burgh gleaned the best quotations from works that would have been out of Paine's reach physically, financially, and temporally. Paine did not have to read Sir William Temple's *Preface to the History of England* (1695) to learn that "None can be said to know things well, who do not know them in their beginnings," because Burgh had relayed the information in a more convenient format.[46] Burgh's "General Preface" also demonstrates how vast stores of knowledge could be distilled for someone of Paine's background and means. Burgh described the sources for his work:

> That no important historical fact, nor valuable political remark, or as few as possible, might escape me, I went through a general course of such reading; particularly the following, *viz.* UNIVERSAL HISTORY, ANCIENT and MODERN, 68 Volumes, besides several of the *Greek* and *Latin* originals; *Rapin*'s, and two or three other *English* histories; MAGAZINES of the last 10 years; PARLIAMENTORY HISTORY, 24 Volumes; DEBATES of the Lords and Commons, 30 volumes; *Ancient* and *Modern* Republics, 27 volumes; the *Harleian* MISCELLANY, 8 volumes; *Somers*'s Tracts, 16 volumes; the political writings of *Sidney, Locke, Harrington, Gordon, Trenchard, Bolingbroke, St. Pierre, Hume, Montesquieu, Blackstone, Montague, Rymer*'s FOEDERA, STATUTES at LARGE, STATE PAPERS, &c.[47]

Paine's was a second-hand republicanism. He had learned his politics in the dissenting academies and popular scientific lectures of London and in the Headstrong Club of Lewes. Because he was an outsider to the circles of power and refinement, Paine had no incentive to stuff his writings with fawning self-deprecations and muscle-bound footnotes. He gathered his principles from reading widely in book shops and libraries, but he did not become constrained by his sources. He grew frustrated with the sesquipedalian style of conventional political discourse and attributed constipated decision making to convoluted modes of thinking and a blind adherence to the authority of precedence. Paine prided himself on his ability, within a basic framework, to reason unhindered.

We know that Paine had read widely by the end of 1775, and he paid special attention to works treating subjects of religion and natural philosophy. He had begun to get acquainted with more overtly political works such as Locke, Rousseau, Montesquieu, and the English republican writers. But there is no indication that he had read these works deeply or in their primary textual forms. He was a voracious reader of newspapers and magazines and picked up on the ubiquitous allusions to famous political thinkers well enough to grasp the basic concepts of their systems. In *Common Sense*, Paine quoted from Giacinto Dragonetti's *A Treatise on Virtues and Rewards* (1769), which had been published in its original Italian in London. Since Paine could not read Italian, he waited for translated excerpts to appear in the London press.⁴⁸

Translation is a key concept to understanding Paine's writing. Paine was not a gifted linguist; he never learned Latin and he never mastered French, even after living in France for years. But Paine's education had been conveyed by the principle of translation. Everything he learned in his early life, he learned from popular secondary sources that had been "translated" from inaccessible primary texts written by and for elites. Some of these primary texts, like Newton's *Principia*, had been written in a style that purposefully disqualified uneducated readers. The popular Newtonian movement of the eighteenth century took this text and translated its principles and logic into a format accessible to the masses. Because Paine had been educated according to this principle of translation, it was only natural that his political writing would take the erudite concepts of political theory and translate them into actionable decisions that made sense to the multitude.

If we take the case of Burgh's *Political Disquisitions*, we can see the process of translation at work. Burgh had read dozens of political treatises in preparation for his writing, and so Paine cherry-picked the best information of those volumes by reading a single trusted secondary source. Paine took this accrued information and translated it once again for an even wider reading audience. Paine may have been influenced by Burgh's denunciation of "laboured and cynical" style, and his aim for "perspicuity," but the *Disquisitions* was most influential as a source of content for Paine's pamphlet.⁴⁹ In *Common Sense*, Paine encouraged his readers to read the *Disquisitions* to "fully understand of what great consequence a large and equal representation is to a state." He was referring readers to Volume I, and specifically to Book I, "Of Government Briefly," and Book II, "Of Parliaments." Burgh there described a colony settled "in a new country" whose concern was "securing the happiness of the *whole*." If that same colony had made "the aggrandizement of the governor" its "supreme object," Burgh said, "all mankind would pronounce those colonists void of common sense." But this, he continued, was exactly the case in monarchies, where the "sense of the people" was so often betrayed.⁵⁰ Burgh's notions of sovereignty and equal rights likewise matched the arguments Paine used in *Common Sense*. All lawful authority, argued Burgh, "originates from the *people*." Likewise, "Every man has what may be called property, and unalienable property. Every man has a life, a personal liberty, a character, a right to his earnings," and "a right to a religious profession and worship according to his conscience."⁵¹

Though Paine was monolingual, he became an expert translator between the cultural registers of imperial Britain. This interpretive role was made easier by the synthetic character of early modern culture. Paine was socially located at the nexus of an integrated English culture of dissent that had bred in London in the 1760s and 1770s within the city's network of coffee houses, dissenting congregations, theaters, debating clubs, and dissenting academies.[52] The John Wilkes affair had initially attracted many Londoners to political agitation, and the escalating American controversy gave this radical element new reasons to oppose the British government. In this cultural context, the edges of politics, economics, religion, education, and science bled into each other. Into this inherited situation of discursive entanglement, the universalizing project of the Enlightenment ushered in Newtonian mechanics as a master trope, applicable to virtually any area of inquiry. Paine lived in a universe that acted and spoke in a Newtonian language. In the decade before he came to America, Paine imbibed the methodologies of eighteenth century science that would remain his lifelong aspiration, his compass, and ultimately, his religion.

Popular Newtonianism in England

Around the middle of the eighteenth century, a robust industry arose in London, touting and translating the principles of Newtonian physics in public lectures and textbooks aimed at the uneducated masses. It was in these popular scientific lectures that Paine, a corset maker by birth and a tax collector by profession, became engrossed in science, which, in turn, opened the door for his entry into politics. Applying the principles of Baconian induction to a coherent universe governed by the immutable laws of Newtonian mechanics, these street-level philosophers enacted in practical ways the theoretical agendas of high science, and thereby shattered the conventions of learning that had held sway since late antiquity.

James Ferguson and Benjamin Martin were two of the most successful of these Newtonian popularizers, and it was from them that Paine gained his first exposure to natural philosophy. Both Ferguson and Martin were self-educated polymaths who became itinerant lecturers in middle age.[53] Ferguson's formal education was limited to three months of grammar school in his native Scotland, and in spite of his disadvantaged circumstances, he had managed to teach himself mechanics, cartography, astronomy, anatomy, surgery, and medicine while supporting himself as freelance portrait artist. Once while traveling, Ferguson passed a man on the road who was holding a pocket watch. Ferguson had never seen one of these before and asked the man how it worked. The man opened up the watch and showed him the gears. Upon returning home, Ferguson became ill and was confined to bed for a few days. "In order to amuse myself in this low state," Ferguson managed to construct a clock of wood that "kept time pretty well." The bell, he recalled, "on which the hammer struck the hours, was the neck of a broken bottle." After working for a time as a physician in Scotland, he decided that astronomy was his true calling, and he began gazing at the stars and mapping constellations and eclipses. He managed to construct an orrery, a kind of mechanical planetarium, and was asked to read a lecture on it to a group of students. He moved to London, where he continued to refine the design of his orrery and other mechanical contraptions and soon thereafter began to publish short treatises on scientific subjects. His lectures consisted of reading these treatises aloud to students while demonstrating the principles using a wide variety of mechanical equipment.[54] Ferguson's modest demeanor and scientific renown by the late 1760s had earned him a royal pension and a Fellowship in the Royal Society.[55]

Benjamin Martin was a prolific author and inventor in addition to giving lectures on a staggering array of subjects, including optics, geometry, astronomy, and philology.[56] During the 1730s, Martin had run a boarding school and taught mathematics, and beginning around 1740, he became an itinerant lecturer in "Natural & Experimental Philosophy, from Town to Town in the Country." Martin eventually settled in London, where he continued to read lectures, publish books, and sell the apparatuses he invented. He set up shop as the "Optician, of Fleet Street," and from there he sold microscopes, telescopes, quadrants, sextants, reading glasses, and other optical equipment of his own design. Martin's incessant self-promotion attracted numerous critics and probably sealed his exclusion from the Royal Society.[57]

Paine paid a little over one pound total to attend a series of lectures by each of these men. Their lectures were usually presented in packed rooms of eager students whose interest in the subject matter was stoked by the theatrical spectacle of the lecturer's mechanical demonstrations. Curtains would be frequently drawn, and the rapt audience would witness the motions of stars, planets, and comets illuminated for effect and education. Sitting in the space-like darkness, Paine and his classmates witnessed the universe functioning, according to Newtonian mechanics, as an integrated system. He gawked at the descriptive power of natural philosophy, and as he contemplated what he would call in *Common Sense* "the universal order of things," he realized that the system of British imperial politics was manifestly *unnatural*.[58]

Machinery, Causation, and Motion

Paine would retain a lifelong belief in the statement from *Common Sense*, "He who takes nature for his guide is not easily beaten out of his argument."[59] He first came to this conclusion as he watched the scientific demonstrations of Ferguson and Martin and returned to his quarters to reflect and verify what he had learned against mathematics and experience. In the publications of Ferguson and Martin, we find a window into the "philosophical principles" from which Paine built his own political theory.

Ferguson realized that his science had political implications. The "vulgar and illiterate," he regretted, take "almost every thing, even the most important, upon the authority of others, without ever examining it themselves." This "implicit confidence" and "credulity" had been "much abused," especially "in political and religious matters" where it had "produced fatal effects."[60] He viewed his educational mission as enabling Britons to examine the natural world for themselves, and Paine's objective in *Common Sense* was to facilitate a popular examination of political alternatives using those same natural principles. After *examining* the defects of the British constitution, Paine asked his readers who favored reconciliation "To examine that connection and dependence, on the principles of nature and common sense, to see what we have to trust to, if separated, and what we are to expect, if dependant."[61]

Like the lecturers of London, Paine "demonstrated" the defects of the British Constitution according to mechanical principles.[62] Ferguson, who had constructed hundreds of different scientific instruments, always refined his designs by *simplifying* rather than *complicating* their operating mechanisms. As he put it in his *Select Mechanical Exercises* (1773), "The simpler that any machine is, the better it will be allowed to be, by every man of science."[63] Paine applied this ethic of simplicity to his examination in *Common Sense*. He listened carefully to "the simple voice of nature and of reason," and he drew his "idea of the form of government from a principle in nature, which no art can overturn, viz. that the more simple any thing is, the less liable it is to be disordered, and the easier repaired when disordered." He analyzed "the so much boasted constitution of England" with "this maxim in view."[64] Paine asked his readers "to examine the component parts of the English constitution," and he mocked the supposition that "a *union* of three powers reciprocally *checking* each other" was a strength of the system.[65] In the "exceedingly complex" British constitutional system, the suffering people had no idea "the head from which their suffering springs" and were "bewildered by a variety of causes and cures."[66] In any mechanical system, Paine argued, "the greater weight will always carry up the less" and "all the wheels of a machine are put in motion by one." He identified the Crown as "this overbearing part," the "power in the constitution" that "has the most weight" and, therefore, always "will govern." The notion that the Lords or the Commons could "clog, or, as the phrase is, check the rapidity of its motion" was both counterproductive and senseless, since "the first moving power will at last have its way, and what it wants in speed is supplied by time."[67] Even the "composition of monarchy," the driving force in the wheelwork of the constitution, was "exceedingly ridiculous" in its design. Paine argued, "The state of a king shuts him from the world, yet the business of a king requires him to know it thoroughly; wherefore the different parts, by unnaturally opposing and destroying each other, prove the whole character to be absurd and useless."[68] Paine was attempting to prove to his readers that the British Constitution was a flawed, broken, and dangerous machine that was unsalvageable and needed immediately to be discarded.

The relationship between Great Britain and America also defied the Newtonian law of gravity. Paine observed, "In no instance hath nature made the satellite larger than its primary planet," because the gravity of the object with greater mass will always dominate the lesser. Here he was regurgitating the language of his instructors, as Martin had said, "All the Primary PLANETS are here disposed about the Sun, and all the Secondaries, or SATELLITES, about their Primaries, in such Order as we see them in the Heavens."[69]

Paine looked at the vast landmass of America and found "something very absurd, in supposing a continent to be perpetually governed by an island." America, Paine noted, was "only a secondary object in the system of British politics" even though "England and America, with respect to each other, reverse the common order of nature." Based solely on a Newtonian logic applied to geographic placement, it was "evident" to Paine "that they belong to different systems. England to Europe: America to itself."[70] This principle also translated to the relationship between the King of England and the American people. The king, Paine saw, expected the entire political system to orbit around himself in bald defiance of rational mechanics, whereas the self-luminescent people were the orbital center in Paine's system.

The main body of *Common Sense* divides neatly into two halves. The first two sections are treatments of *causation*, and the last two sections deal with *motion*. Both principles were fundamental to the epistemology of popular natural philosophy. Ferguson had noted in his *A Dissertation upon the Phenomena of the Harvest Moon* (1747) that his pedagogical task was to make a deliberate connection between appearances and causes. Explaining his "design" for a treatise on the harvest moon, he said, "I have endeavoured to set it in so clear a Light, that any one who is but a little acquainted with the Use of a common Globe, may understand its Cause, and all the Varieties of its Appearances."[71] By simply looking at a model of the world as a whole, Ferguson promised to demonstrate the relationship between perception and causality.

Martin's *Course of Lectures in Natural and Experimental Philosophy, Geography and Astronomy* (1743) included his "Rules of Philosophizing," adapted from Newton's *Principia*. These "Rules" informed the core of Paine's theory of causation. Simplicity, again, was a dominant trope in *Common Sense*, echoing Martin's commentary, "For nature does nothing in vain, but is simple, and delights not in superfluous Causes of Things." Paine did not just degrade the British Constitution because of its complexity; he proposed alternatives on the basis of their simplicity. Since independence was a "single simple line, contained within ourselves; and reconciliation, a matter exceedingly perplexed and complicated, and in which, a treacherous capricious court is to interfere," the structural dissimilarity alone proved the advantage of independence "without a doubt."[72] Likewise, Paine's penchant for a unicameral legislature was not a direct repudiation of Montesquieu; it was a logical outworking of Paine's view that a legislature should be a simple and productive machine, not constrained by unnecessary internal "checking" and efficient in its output of laws.

Another of Martin's "Rules" invoked the Baconian scientific method. In experimental philosophy, Martin said, "Propositions collected from the Phenomena by Inductions" should be deemed "either exactly or very nearly true, till other Phenomena occur by which they may be render'd either more accurate, or liable to Exception."[73] When no substantive refutation of *Common Sense* appeared for over two months, Paine assumed a self-congratulatory tone in his publications that grated upon some of his audience. For Paine, however, the absence of opposition was a natural consequence of his inductive method. No "other Phenomena" had occurred in politics or in the press to dislocate his theory, and thus he claimed, "it is a negative proof, that either the doctrine cannot be refuted, or, that the party in favor of it are too numerous to be opposed."[74]

Other eighteenth century pamphlets, as we have seen, were deductive in their logic; *Common Sense* was inductive. Paine did not assume sophisticated erudition in his audience as his contemporaries had. Their aim was, most often, *to impress*, while Paine's objective was *to move*. Creating motion, Paine realized, was a problem of physics. Martin had defined mechanics as "the Doctrine of Motion, and all Kinds of Forces and Machines," and, at its core, Paine's mechanistic approach to politics was an explication of force and motion.

In the Newtonian system, all matter possesses certain immutable properties such as extension, solidity, attraction, repulsion, and divisibility, which Martin defined as "that Property by which the Particles of matter in all Bodies are capable of a Separation or Disunion from each other." More important for Paine's logical system were the properties of "Mobility" and "*Vis Inertiæ* (as Sir Isaac called it) or the Inactivity of Matter." Mobility was "that Property which all Bodies have, of being moveable or capable of changing their Situations or Places. This Property of matter is evident to all our Senses;" Martin added, "and to deny it would be an Absurdity too flagrant for any but a Cartesian Philosopher." Inertia, on the other hand, was the reciprocal property of matter "by which it endeavours to continue in its State either of Motion or Rest, or by which it resists the Actions and Impressions of all other Bodies which tend to generate or destroy Motion therein."[75] Here, in a nutshell, was Paine's task in *Common Sense*: to trigger the movement of thirteen sedentary colonies toward independence. These reciprocal properties, mobility and inertia, were governed in the Newtonian system by three general laws of motion:

> LAW I. Every Body will continue in its State of Rest, or moving uniformly in a Right Line, except so far as it is compell'd to change that-State by Forces impress'd.
> LAW II. The Change of Motion is always proportional to the moving Force impress'd, and is always made according to the Right Line in which that Force is impress'd.
> LAW III. Re-action is always equal and contrary to Action; or the Actions of two Bodies upon each other are always equal, and in contrary Directions.[76]

America was either in a "State of Rest," or, if it was moving at all, it was moving in the wrong direction.[77] No change would occur, Paine realized from his lessons in Newtonian mechanics, until a "moving Force" was applied. *Common Sense* was designed as that original force, and Paine benefited from the serendipitous synergy between his verbal force and the "forces" being applied by England. It was no surprise to Paine that the Pennsylvania proprietary interest would react in a manner "equal and contrary" to his action, but the combination of Paine's sustained force and the unwitting assistance of every utterance from London eventually overwhelmed the conservative opposition.

The American colonies not only lacked the property of mobility, they lacked solidity, which made them virtually impossible to move in a unified direction. Their "fatal and unmanly slumbers" exhibited softness in addition to stagnation.[78] At the beginning of 1776, America was, in Martin's terminology, a *fluid*, "A Body whose Parts move freely among themselves, and therefore yield to the least Force that is impressed upon them."[79] The colonies were in an amorphous state without law, government, or "any other mode of power than what is founded on, and granted by courtesy."[80] The stuttering Continental Congress and the dumbfounded populace had been disoriented by the course of events, and everyone, "left at random" in the "present unbraced system of things," pursued their own "fancy or opinion."[81] Paine proposed "that we may pursue determinately some fixed object," because he knew that pursuit would make the colonists themselves more "fixed," or more solid.[82]

Paine reached out to the broadest possible American audience to align the diffuse experiences, opinions, and interests that until then had broken along lines of religion, class, or geography. His compositional strategy fostered coherence among his diverse audience by targeting the least common denominators of colonial discourse. His advocacy of universality coaxed the Americans into uniformity. "Many circumstances have, and will arise, which are not local, but universal," he said, and Britain's "war against the natural rights of mankind" was "the concern of every man to whom nature hath given the power of feeling."[83]

Once Paine established this solidity, he could begin applying sufficient force to move the colonies to action. His Newtonian ethic of simplicity, however, dictated that Paine avoid the complex machinery of rhetorical contrivance or convoluted systems to apply his force. Paine had described the British constitution as an unnecessarily complex clockwork of pulleys and wheels. American political dynamics had to be different. The primary tools Paine used to apply his force were the wedge and the lever, two of the six simple machines in Newtonian mechanics.[84] The wedge was used "to separate the Parts of Wood, &c. which strongly cohere together."[85] The first two sections of *Common Sense* quietly performed this preparatory work of separating the affections of the Americans from the idea of the British Constitution, and especially from the Crown. The Americans had long despised parliament and leered at the king's ministers, but Paine focused his gaze on the king himself. By the end of the third section, Paine's wedge had even snapped the final tie to the constitution, the familial affection for "the people of England."[86]

Now that the American mind had been solidified and separated, Paine employed a second basic tool, the lever, to pry the colonies upward into action. Martin had defined a lever as "any inflexible Line, Rod, or Beam, moveable about or upon a fix'd Point (call'd the Prop or Fulcrum), upon one End of which is the Weight to be raised, at the other End is the Power applied to raise it."[87] Paine designed the final two sections of *Common Sense* and his Appendix to transform American popular opinion into a lever for independence. Separation and independence were discrete concepts in Paine's mind, even when compounded into a seamless movement. Separation was a *negative* movement away from Britain, while independence was a *positive* move toward "a continental form of government."[88] Paine quoted Giacinto Dragonetti's *A Treatise on Virtues and Rewards* (1769) to describe the fulcrum of the machine: "The science," said Dragonetti, "of the politician consists in fixing the true point of happiness and freedom."[89]

This "true point" was the "mode of government" most conducive to happiness, which Paine clearly identified as a republic. Paine's republican fulcrum was distinct from the classical republicanism that infatuated the colonial elite; he described a level of representation and participation that amounted to constitutional democracy. The power of the people, transferred through their representatives, was Paine's alternative "first moving power" that would "at last have its way."[90] The Continent's "great strength" lay not in raw numbers but "in unity," when the direction of its force was aimed toward the same object.[91]

The principle of the lever is instructive for Paine's mode of political mobilization. When a person attempts to lift an object using a lever, that person's strength is multiplied by his or her distance from the center. In Paine's system, "the people" included anyone *but* those at the center of politics. In fact, a person near the center of politics had very little power to affect change, but those, like Paine, who operated far from the privileged center possessed the most power to thrust America upwards. Paine realized that it was impossible to generate change from within the circles of power and privilege, since "The more men have to lose, the less willing are they to venture."[92] Paine utilized the logic of the lever—that distance is multiplicative of power—to gather power from the margins. By asking all colonists to identify with those "ruined by British barbarity" who had "nothing more to lose," he was pushing the Americans into a position of unified political leverage.[93]

The Radical Implications of Popular Science

Beyond the direct influence of lecturers like Ferguson and Martin upon Paine, the culture of popular natural philosophy in London had several radical implications that warrant explication in the context of *Common Sense*. Among others, two of the most important of those implications were the attitudes that popular science promoted toward gender and history.

In May 1774, Henry Laurens of South Carolina purchased for (and at the request of) his teenage daughter, Martha, who was then living in London, a "pair of the best eighteen inch" globes with "caps and a book of directions" along with "a case of neat instruments, and one dozen Middleton's best pencils, marked M.L." Laurens urged his daughter, "When you are measuring the surface of this world, remember you are to act a part on it," and then, remembering his South Carolinian social norms, he reminded her to "think of a plum pudding and other domestic duties."[94] Martha Laurens was not an isolated case of a young woman interested in scientific discovery; during the revolutionary period, the courses and demonstrations of Ferguson, Martin, and other popular lecturers were filled with both men *and* women. Because these sessions relied on stirring visual demonstrations rather than dry mathematical calculations, their content was accessible to a remarkably wide audience.

Ferguson and Martin had both published introductions to natural philosophy "for young gentlemen and ladies." Each book followed a similar format, composed as a series of informal conversations between a brother who had just returned from studying at the university and his curious sister. In Ferguson's *An Easy Introduction to Astronomy, for Young Gentlemen and Ladies* (1769), the sister, Eudosia, shared with her brother, Neander, that she would like to learn about "the sublime science of Astronomy" because "I have been told, that of all others, it is the best for enlarging our minds, and filling them with the most noble ideas of the GREAT CREATOR and his works." Eudosia was concerned that her brother would think her "too vain, in wanting to know what the bulk of mankind think our sex have no business with."[95] Her brother frowned upon this prejudice and commenced a series of conversations introducing her to the highlights of natural philosophy.

Martin's *The Young Gentleman's and Lady's Philosophy* (1772) mimicked the presentation of Ferguson's successful text. In Martin's dialogue, the brother Cleonicus, instructed his sister, Euphrosyne, in "Philosophy"—the "Knowledge of natural things in general," "the darling Science of every Man of Sense," and "a peculiar Grace in the Fair Sex."[96] Cleonicus informed his sister that "it is now growing into a Fashion for the Ladies to study Philosophy," and he expressed his delight "to see a Sister of mine so well inclined to promote a Thing so laudable and honourable to her Sex." Euphrosyne was worried that it looked too "masculine for a Woman to talk of Philosophy in Company," but her brother, Cleonicus, reassured her that he had known "several" women "remarkable for this new Cast of Thought" in "London, Oxford, and many other Places." Cleonicus compared one young woman he had known who was "now not more conspicuous for personal Charms and Beauty, than great and admirable for her singular good Sense and Judgment, in natural Science especially," to another young woman whose father had "bestowed no more Education on his Daughter than the Marking and making of Pastries." While the study of natural philosophy was "attended with some Difficulties," Cleonicus assured his sister that "those Parts of Philosophy which are perplexed with Schemes and Abstrusities, are generally such as may be either wholly neglected as useless to the generality of People; or else may be explained in a more easy and familiar manner by Experiments." Clenonicus concluded, "Fear not, Euphrosyne; the greatest and most delightful Part of this Science is within the Ladies' Comprehension."[97]

Both Ferguson and Martin were promoting a pedagogical system that eschewed the conventional prerequisites of a "liberal" education. Thus the two lecturers could teach all sorts of young men and women who, like themselves, did not have the advantages of a formal education. Martin applauded both "Gentlemen and Ladies" who "have the Happiness of a rational Curiosity, and are capable of the noblest Methods of improving it," in stark contrast to others who "trifle away their time in low, sensual, and unworthy Amusements."[98] When Benjamin Rush recalled late in life that Paine's initial "design" upon arriving in America "was to open a school for the instruction of young ladies in the several branches of knowledge," he was only partly right.[99] Paine had arrived planning "to establish an academy on the plan they are conducted in and about London, which I was well acquainted with"—schools which taught both young men and women. Rush fixated on the idea of teaching women because it was outside the norm of his educational experience.[100] Though Paine clearly wrote *Common Sense* in a style marked by "manliness," the fact that his ideas and prose followed the pattern of pedagogical accessibility he had learned in London meant, in point of fact, that his pamphlet invited women into the circle of readership. Paine realized that women were reading his work. In his first *American Crisis*, written at the end of 1776, Paine reflected on the case of Joan of Arc and implored, "Would that heaven might inspire some Jersey maid to spirit up her countrymen, and, save her fair fellow sufferers from ravage and ravishment!"[101]

Martin's dialogue included another point with equally radical implications. The sister, Euphrosyne, admitted that she had "not read much on the ancient Philosophy," but she supposed it "must needs come far short of the Modern." Her liberally educated brother, Cleonicus, affirmed her conjecture. Ancient natural philosophy fell "Very far short, indeed," of the modern, and "the Difference is not much greater between Dreaming and Reasoning." Though "Aristotle inquired in the Causes and Nature of Things," neither he nor his followers made any "great Discoveries, as being destitute of the proper Means, viz. Instruments and Experiments." Natural philosophy "was brought to no Perfection till within these 200 Years, or, I may more justly say, till within these last 50 or 60 Years." The "true Reason," he continued, "that many great and useful Inventions have been ascribed to several modern Names" was that the ancients lacked "a right Method of Philosophizing, and proper Means to conduct them in their Pursuits." Thus "my Lord Bacon's great Soul" was the first to "point out the Way to real Knowledge," Robert Boyle "indefatigably pursued it in numberless Experiments," and Isaac Newton and others "first improved the mechanical and mathematical Parts, and brought Astronomy to its greatest Perfection."[102]

The disrespect for antiquity Paine displayed in *Common Sense* was, in the eighteenth century, only commensurable with a scientific education. In no other field of inquiry had the principles of the ancients been so roundly discarded and disparaged. Bacon, Newton and their early modern peers had not only made Aristotle obsolete, the entire system of philosophical and pedagogical practice had been called into question. The ancients, to a starry-eyed follower of Newtonian science like Paine, were not merely dismissed for their ignorance of empiricism; they were culpable for two thousand years of epistemological sabotage. "Mankind have lived to very little purpose," said Paine in his *American Crisis, No. 5*, if "they must go two or three thousand years back for lessons and examples." If "the mist of antiquity be cleared away, and men and things be viewed as they really were," he argued, "it is more than probable that they would admire us, rather than we them."[103]

Especially for a tract that had begun as a "history," Paine showed in *Common Sense* a contemptuous disregard for historical precedence. The only history that passed muster in Paine's pamphlet was biblical history, and that showed, in Paine's construction, nothing but contempt for monarchy. Not only did he fail to summon the authorities of ancient political philosophy to his aid, he flatly ignored them. One of Paine's primary tasks in *Common Sense*, was to lift "off the dark covering of antiquity" which would lead his readers to the conclusion that "the antiquity of English monarchy will not bear looking into."[104] Paine found "traditionary history stuffed with fables" and filled with "superstitious" tales designed "to cram hereditary right down the throats of the vulgar."[105] Paine lamented that the Americans had "been long led away by ancient prejudices, and made large sacrifices to superstition.[106] The British constitution, in its reliance upon customary precedence and, in the person of the king, superstitious "pomp," embodied for Paine everything that was wrong with history and everything he hoped to correct in his new science of politics.

Not only did Paine shun ancient history, he declared all current history pointless as well. The "Volumes" that had been "written on the subject of the struggle between England and America" had proven patently "ineffectual." He pronounced, "the period of debate is closed," effectively branding everything written on the subject prior to *Common Sense* as unnecessary and irrelevant.[107] No antecedent political knowledge whatsoever was required to respond to *Common Sense*. Paine was arguing a point subverting the entirety of Western political thought: through careful observation and straightforward mathematical calculation, *anyone* could induce the proper course of political action. This political methodology required no specialized knowledge in the classics or prerequisite course of study in political theory. Making politics inductive opened it up to common people. Paine redirected the flow of legitimacy and sovereignty *upward* from the people to the rulers, following an inductive logic, rather than *downward* from the rulers to the people, following a deductive logic. Deductive systems of thought, when left to their own defenses, are particularly susceptible to argumentative attack, because the entire logical structure rests upon a few grand premises. Paine blasted those three or four pillars, and the whole system of thought began to teeter.

Paine attempted to neutralize the influence of "prejudice" in favor of the old system—precisely as Francis Bacon had done in his attack on Aristotle—because he knew that the tottering system of deductive politics was buttressed by an irrational popular bias.[108] Prejudice is a fundamentally deductive impulse, arriving at a conclusion in advance of examining the evidence. Paine sought, therefore, to "settle with the reader" that "he will divest himself of prejudice and prepossession, and suffer his reason and his feelings to determine for themselves."[109] The empirical philosopher *par excellence*, John Locke, had, in his *An Essay Concerning Human Understanding* (1690), recognized the philosophical challenge inherent in Paine's request. "'Tis not easy for the mind to put off those confused notions and prejudices it has imbibed from custom, inadvertency, and common conversation." Locke continued his observation that the mind "requires pains and assiduity to examine its ideas, till it resolves them into those clear and distinct simple ones." Until "a man doth this in the primary and original notions of things," Locke noted, "he builds upon floating and uncertain principles, and will often find himself at a loss."[110] Paine was drawing up the anchor of custom from American minds and steering them toward the solid ground of scientific certainty.

PART FOUR
EXPERIMENTAL PROSODY

Scientific Language

The "perspicuity" that Paine's contemporaries recognized in his writing was also in part a symptom of his attachment to scientific principles.[111] Benjamin Martin had written that the "Business of Experimental Philosophy" was the investigation of "the Reason and Causes of the various Appearances (or Phenomena) of Nature; and to make the Truth or Probability thereof obvious and evident to the Senses, by plain, undeniable, and adequate Experiments, representing the several Parts of the grand Machinery and Agency of Nature."[112] Martin's pedagogical objective, in turn, was "to render the BOOK of NATURE as legible as possible to every Capacity."[113] As popular lecturers like Martin demonstrated the truths of natural philosophy, they emphasized communicative clarity. The principles of the new science did not require rhetorical ornament to achieve validity; they needed only definitional precision and an accessible idiom to succeed in transporting concepts between minds.

A century earlier, Francis Bacon outlined his rules for collecting the observations of nature in his *Parasceve*, or *Preparation towards a Natural and Experimental History*, appended to the *Novum Organum*. The scientist, said Bacon, was to inspect nature first hand, doing away "with antiquities, and citations of authors." He urged a scientific language in which "ornaments of speech" and "suchlike emptiness" be "utterly dismissed." Bacon continued, "Also let all those things which are admitted be themselves set down briefly and concisely," and he added that "no man who is storing up materials for ship-building or the like, thinks of arranging them elegantly."[114] Bacon's call for an unadorned scientific language was heeded by his fellow natural philosophers. Thomas Sprat's account of the Royal Society included his observation that the scientists wished for a "native easiness" in their writing, the language of "Artisans" and "Merchants" rather than of "Wits, or Scholars."[115] John Locke had noted that "Vague and insignificant forms of speech" were "but the covers of ignorance" and a "hindrance of true knowledge."[116] Locke's philosophy of the mind and of language were both preparatory for Paine's method of politics and prose.[117] Ideas, for Locke, were not innate and instead originated only in experiential *sensation* and rational *reflection*, two mental processes that were central to Paine's argument in *Common Sense*.[118] Locke's philosophy of language was especially consonant with and even preparatory for Paine's perspicuity. Locke attributed most disagreements not to abstract ideas but to men who "confound them with words" which led to "endless dispute, wrangling, and jargon."[119] His prescriptive "ends of language" were three-fold: "to make known one man's thoughts or ideas to another," "to do it with as much ease and quickness as is possible," and "thereby to convey the knowledge of things." Language, Locke concluded, "is either abused, or deficient, when it fails of any of these three."[120] In *Common Sense*, Paine aimed for unequivocal, punchy language. He offered to his readers "nothing more than simple facts, plain arguments and common sense."[121] His first *American Crisis* paper, written at the end of 1776, echoed this sentiment: "I bring reason to your ears, and, in language as plain as A, B, C, hold up truth to your eyes."[122]

Rhetorical Poetry

Paine did write with a plainness uncommon in eighteenth century political discourse, but that did not mean that he eschewed all rhetorical devices. Because language is inextricably bound up with human subjectivity, any authorial claim of pure objectivity is a conscious or unconscious smokescreen. Thus we take Paine's "A, B, C" claim with a grain of salt and acknowledge that *Common Sense* was a profoundly rhetorical text, containing a rhetorical argument carried along by a small set of rhetorical techniques. Paine's scientific principles, his religious views, his political agenda, and his prose style were all cut from the same cloth, but the strength of his text did not rest solely in the congruity of his inventional sources. *Common Sense* was foremost a persuasive political text, not a work of aesthetic charm or philosophical rumination. It was a text that wore its agenda on its sleeve and measured success or failure not simply by copies sold but by minds changed and decisions made. Though Paine did not aspire to dispassionate data collection, he was in *Common Sense* applying the *structures* of scientific inquiry to early modern politics. One of those basic structures of Newtonian mechanics that deserves special mention is the concept of the "Balance of Nature." One of nature's defining characteristics in the Newtonian system, balance was evident in actions and reactions, in centripetal and centrifugal forces, in attraction and repulsion, and in motion and rest.[123] Balance was indicative of opposition, equivalence, and reciprocity, and it was best represented by the equal-sign in a Newtonian mathematical equation. Paine's prose and argument structure attempted to forge a natural balance that accorded with his scientific system of politics.[124]

But as we have seen, Paine's pamphlet was not simply or purely a scientific treatise. His prose and his arguments were influenced equally by his everyday life, his religious education, and his early "turn" for poetry. For most of Paine's 37 years of life before coming to America, he had been engulfed in the hackneyed colloquialisms of artisanal English, a fact he could not escape even in scientific lectures where he listened to James Ferguson's thick provincial Scottish accent. Like most early modern writers, Paine was heavily influenced by the imagery and syntax of the King James Bible and by the sermons he had heard and read. While he aspired to the sinewy clarity of scientific explanation, he had long been enamored with the wit and, sometimes, the sublimity he found in poetry. Though his parents discouraged his poetic bent, Paine had always loved to tinker with words, meter, and rhyme. Paine understood the ability of poetry to smooth the ingestion of language and, with it, the ideas it conveys. His rhetorical prose never lost that poetic sensibility. In 1775 Paine composed several poems for inclusion in the *Pennsylvania Magazine*, and his rhetorical style is hardly distinguishable from his poetic technique.

Operating at the intersection of Paine's religious, scientific, and poetic influences, the single most important element of Paine's prose style is its balanced phraseology. Everything he was able to accomplish with language was built upon the foundation of balance. Paine's writing did not possess the variations and metric exactitude of more polished wordsmiths, but the rough-hewn similitude of his cola allowed him to employ several derivative rhetorical schemes that require a balanced structure for their proper execution.

Balance and parallelism are syntactic constructions as old as language itself. They are the hallmarks of wisdom from ancient philosophy and prophecy. When a sentence is constructed in a balanced linguistic formation, it contains a built-in credential propensity. It *sounds* true. Only after a reflective pause can an adage or maxim be refuted, because the very structure of the saying works to shift the burden of proof to the reflective refutation of the hearer. *Common Sense* was so chock-full of these structures and adages that it became impractical for someone to refute them one by one. Paine's balanced rhetorical presentation, especially his summary zingers, vaguely smacked of "Truth" for his biblically-saturated audience, while they also mimicked the certainty of scientific axioms for his more philosophical readers. His style, like the secular proverbs of his mentor, Benjamin Franklin, followed a balanced and repetitive poetic structure characteristic of Proverbs and other Old Testament books.

Balance also allowed Paine to instantiate in language his ethic of commensurability. As we saw in Chapter Three, Paine advocated retributive justice according to a doctrine of ends and means. Commensurability was a theme Paine employed throughout the text as a rubric for political action. As he put it in the third section of *Common Sense*, "The object, contended for, ought always to bear some just proportion to the expence." Paine compared the cost of military resistance to Britain, if reconciliation was the colonies' only object, to "wasting an estate on a suit at law, to regulate the trespasses of a tenant, whose lease is just expiring." He continued,

> The removal of North, or the whole detestable junto,
>   is a matter unworthy the millions we have expended.
> A temporary stoppage of trade, was an inconvenience,
>   which would have sufficiently balanced
>   the repeal of all the acts complained of,
>   had such repeals been obtained;
> but if the whole continent must take up arms,
> if every man must be a soldier,
>   it is scarcely worth our while
>   to fight against a contemptible ministry only.
> Dearly, dearly, do we pay for the repeal of the acts,
>   if that is all we fight for;
> for in a just estimation,
>   it is as great a folly to pay a Bunker-hill price
>   for law, as for land.[125]

A balanced sentence structure is particularly amenable for rhetorical practice because it tends to partition a multitude of *possible* options into only two *actionable* decisions. If the writer's persuasive goal is to urge an audience toward a particular choice, then a balanced structure leaves readers or hearers with the impression that they must make a choice between only two options. After identifying only two sides of a question or two courses of action, the persuader must create a rhetorical separation between the more and less desirable options. In *Common Sense*, for example, Paine painted the advocates of reconciliation as walking anachronisms by utilizing an alliterative antithetical structure:

> the one proposing force,
>   the other friendship;
> but it has so far happened that the first has failed,
>   and the second has withdrawn her influence.[126]

Prior to the publication of *Common Sense*, the American colonists had two practical options: surrender-submission or resistance-reconciliation. Paine redescribed the reconciliation position as one that sought to restore "dependence" on Great Britain. This move allowed him to bifurcate new options in a balanced structure:

> To examine that connection and dependence,
>   on the principles of nature and common sense,
>   to see what we have to trust to, if separated,
>   and what we are to expect, if dependent.[127]

Employing a more complex balanced structure, Paine equated submission with dependence, showing that they produce the same outcome:

> any submission to,
> or dependence on,
> > Great Britain,
> > > tends directly to involve
> >
> > this continent
> > in European wars and quarrels,
> > > and sets us at variance with nations
> > > > who would otherwise seek our friendship,
> > > > > and against whom we have
> > > > > > neither anger
> > > > > > > nor complaint.[128]

Balanced linguistic structures allowed Paine to bifurcate political options through the use of secondary techniques such as antithesis, chiasmus, paradox, and parallelism. Paine inherited a debate in which the colonists were forced to choose between the actions of pacifist surrender and military resistance, and also between the objectives of submission (reconciliation at any cost) and redress of grievances (reconciliation with dignity and assurance). Through his balanced language, Paine brought the two previous options into closer alignment and then introduced a new option, attempting to demonstrate that the only two pragmatic options for political action were dependence or independence. Once he had recalibrated the debate, he continued to use antithetical verbal formations to funnel all evidence into one or the other of his new polarities. In the Appendix to *Common Sense*, Paine contrasted the king's October speech with the initial edition of his pamphlet:

> The bloody mindedness of the one,
> > shows the necessity of pursuing
>
> the doctrine of the other.[129]

To say that antithesis is a ubiquitous feature in *Common Sense* falls short of describing its significance. Balance and antithesis can both be found on every page of Paine's text, but to illustrate the principle and also the inherent rhythm of Paine's language, I will give one example from each section of the pamphlet:

> a long habit of not thinking a thing *wrong*,
> gives it a superficial appearance of being *right*,[130]

> Society in every state is a blessing,
> but government even in its best state is but a necessary evil;[131]

> Oppression is often the *consequence*,
> but seldom or never the *means* of riches[132]

that he will put *on*, or rather
that he will not put *off*, the true character of a man,¹³³

Common sense will tell us,
    that the power which hath endeavoured to subdue us,
    is of all others, the most improper to defend us.¹³⁴

A line of distinction should be drawn, between,
    English soldiers taken in battle,
    and inhabitants of America taken in arms.
        The first are prisoners,
        but the latter traitors.
            The one forfeits his liberty,
            the other his head.¹³⁵

We fight neither for revenge nor conquest;
neither from pride nor passion;
    we are not insulting the world with our fleets and armies,
    nor ravaging the globe for plunder.
        Beneath the shade of our own vines are we attacked;
            in our own houses,
            and on our own lands,
        is the violence committed against us.¹³⁶

What Paine was doing in his antithetical rhetoric, creating separation, was precisely what he was attempting to accomplish in his politics.

Solving for Time

July 8, 1776, proved to be a warm, clear day. John Nixon had been appointed by the Sheriff of Philadelphia and the Pennsylvania Committee of Safety to read the *Declaration of Independence* to the public in the State House yard in Philadelphia. This was the first of dozens of similar ceremonies in every part of America. Beginning at eleven in the morning, the various committees in Philadelphia began to converge, along with thousands of residents from the city and surrounding towns, upon the State House grounds. Just before noon, Nixon, who had been reviewing and remarking his copy of the *Declaration* to pronounce it with clarity to the multitude assembled before him, ascended a set of wooden steps. From his perspective, he could see the crowd's expanse filling the square like the stars would fill the Philadelphia sky that evening. He lifted the sheet of paper just below his chin, took a deep breath, and began. "When in the course of human events, it becomes necessary for one people…" For the first time, the gathered public heard their independence declared, and as Nixon continued, the hushed crowd listened with nervous expectation. No one in the State House yard that day knew how events would turn out, and no one could be sure that the Americans had made the right decision to declare independence at that particular moment in time. Some of the audience applauded politely, feigning support for a measure they thought premature. Others standing in the square that day, like Thomas Paine and John Adams, wondered in silence if the decision had come too late. Most of the auditors, however, were convinced that independence had arrived at just the right time. As John Nixon neared the end of the text, he raised his voice even more, "...in the name and by the authority of the good people of these colonies solemnly publish and declare, That these United Colonies are, and of right ought to be, *FREE AND INDEPENDENT STATES.*" When Nixon spoke the phrase introduced by *Common Sense*, the square erupted in cheers. Several members of the crowd that day looked up at the bright sunshine and then down at John Nixon standing atop the sturdy wooden platform that had been originally erected in 1769 as an observatory for the Transit of Venus.[137] They were reminded of a single extraordinary moment when the universe seemed to converge on that very spot, when space and time opened like a door that had been sealed for centuries. A group of amateur astronomers had stood on the very same platform seven years earlier and measured the breadth of the solar system. And the key to it all was time.

As we shall see in the next chapter, the most significant point of dispute in the debate over independence was *time*. Very few Americans had any problem with the idea of independence, but when *Common Sense* transformed the perpetual future of the *idea* into the immediate present of the *decision* for independence, many of the colonists balked. The decision for independence was, in Paine's mind, a very scientific question that could be solved using mathematics. He isolated *time* as the crucial variable in the independence equation. A large number of Americans anticipated independence in about a half century. Paine zeroed in on "this single position" and argued that if it was "closely attended to" it would "unanswerably prove" his theorem. "The argument turns thus," said Paine, "at the conclusion of the last war, we had experience, but wanted numbers; and forty or fifty years hence, we should have numbers, without experience." Since "the proper point of time, must be some particular point between the two extremes, in which a sufficiency of the former remains, and a proper increase of the latter is obtained," Paine concluded, "that point of time is the present time."[138]

Paine's lifelong passion, as we have seen, was science, but he was also an avid student of mathematics. While Paine served as an aide-de-camp to General Nathanael Greene in late 1776, the general noted that even in the midst of war, "Common Sense," as Paine was called by many Americans, was "perpetually wrangling about Mathematical Problems" with two of Greene's senior officers.[139] Paine had become infatuated with mathematics when he was studying for the entrance exam to qualify as an excise officer. Though he used only a limited set of mathematical skills in the excise, he demonstrated a sustained passion for complex mathematical problems that helped fuel his interest in natural philosophy. Direct mathematical arguments would not become a critical component of Paine's political writing until his later economic essays, but during his time as an exciseman we can witness the emergence of his ability to grasp the complex causality of systems. Paine made a reasoned argument in *The Case for the Officers of the Excise* (1772) that underpaid and exploited excise officers became more prone to corruption, which ultimately managed to clog Britain's revenue stream.

In late 1775 and early 1776, when Paine was writing *Common Sense* and his Appendix, he saw the mathematical logic of independence, but he also remembered his lecturers back in London who had translated Newtonian mechanics for an audience largely ignorant of mathematics. Men like James Ferguson and Benjamin Martin communicated and convinced, not by the means of mathematical proof, but by mechanical demonstration. In order to persuade his American audience to declare its independence immediately, Paine could not simply *describe* independence; he needed to help them *experience* independence. With this in mind, Paine strolled up Arch Street toward David Rittenhouse's shop.

Notes: Chapter 4

[1] A sampling of names from the early membership rosters: Joseph Galloway, Benjamin Chew, John Benezet, several members of the Biddle family, Thomas Bradford, Arthur Lee and Francis Lee from Virginia, and Comte de Buffon of France and Benjamin West of England.

[2] For a helpful account of the connection between Newtonian philosophy and the "practical" or "entrepreneurial" improvements of life, see Stewart, *Rise of Public Science*.

[3] Charles Thomson, "Preface," *Transactions of the American Philosophical Society, Volume 1*; cf. *Minutes of the American Society*, January 1, 1768. APS.

[4] *Transactions*, 1:318, 315.

[5] At the Society's meeting of February 7, 1769, two-thirds of the members present were appointed to the Transit of Venus Committee: Dr. John Ewing, Thomas Pryor, Joseph Shippen, Jr., Dr. Hugh Williamson, Provost William Smith, David Rittenhouse, John Lukens, John Dickinson, William Alexander, Owen Biddle, James Pearson, John Sellers, Charles Thomson, and William Poole. *Proceedings of the American Philosophical Society*, 1:31. APS.

[6] Biddle and John Bailey observed the transit from Lewestown (now Lewes), Delaware, at the mouth of the Delaware River.

[7] Because of the elliptical orbit of planetary bodies, transits of Venus occur in close pairs (e.g., 1761 and 1769) with more than a century transpiring between each subsequent set of transits.

[8] For a helpful overview of the transit's role in eighteenth century astronomy, see Teets, "Transits of Venus and the Astronomical Unit."

[9] Ford, *David Rittenhouse*, 35-36.

[10] For those interested in astronomical detail, the next Transit of Venus will occur on June 6, 2012, and the distance between the earth and the sun is approximately 93 million miles or 149.6 million kilometers.

[11] Ford, *David Rittenhouse*, 37. The APS holds Dr. John Ewing's copy of Benjamin Martin, *Venus in the Sun*.

[12] For other discussions of the Transit of Venus in the context of early American culture, see, Hindle, *Pursuit of Science*; and Wills, *Inventing America*.

[13] Gribbin, *The Scientists*, 193. In the twentieth century, the first photograph of the earth taken from the moon is often ascribed with this kind of significance for globalism.

[14] RM 2, CW 1:354-356.

[15] The Forester, "Letter II," CW 2:67; AC, No. 3, CW 1:88-89. John Adams was at home in Braintree, Massachusetts, when *Common Sense* was first published.

[16] CW 2:1109, 1111.

[17] TP to HL, 14 January 1779. CW 2:1160-1165.

[18] BF to Richard Price, 3 October 1775. Quoted in Peach, *Richard Price*, 306.

[19] BF to Richard Bache, 30 September 1774. Willcox, *Papers of Benjamin Franklin*, 21:325-326.

[20] BF, "A Letter of Recommendation for all Occasions," 2 April 1777. Quoted in Zall, *Franklin's Humor*, 120.

[21] In a touch of irony, Kearsley would become a prominent loyalist.

[22] TP to BF (Return addressed, "Opposite the London Coffee House Front Street. Philadelphia") 4 March 1775. Willcox, *Papers of Benjamin Franklin*, 21:515-518; Goldsmith, *History of the Earth and Animated Nature*.
[23] Martin campaigned with zeal to be admitted to the Royal Society but was denied, probably on account of his indecorous self-promotion. See Millburn, "Benjamin Martin and the Royal Society."
[24] DR would become a Fellow of the Royal Society in 1795.
[25] See, for example: Price, "A Letter from Richard Price, DD, FRS, to Benjamin Franklin, LLD, FRS, on the Effect of the Aberration of Light on the Time of a Transit of Venus over the Sun." *Philosophical Transactions* (1770), 536-540; James Ferguson, *A Plain Method of Determining the Parallax of Venus, by Her Transit over the Sun: and from thence, by Analogy, the Parallax and Distance of the Sun, and of All the Rest of the Planets* (1761); James Ferguson, "A Delineation of the Transit of Venus Expected in the Year 1769." *Philosophical Transactions* (1763), 30-40; Leeds, "Observation of the Transit of Venus, on June 3, 1769. In a Letter from John Leeds, Esquire, Surveyor General of the Province of Maryland, to John Bevis, MD, FRS." *Philosophical Transactions* (1769), 444-445; Bevis, "Observations of the Last Transit of Venus, and of the Eclipse of the Sun the Next Day; Made at the House of Joshua Kirby, Esquire, at Kew. By John Bevis, MD. FRS." *Philosophical Transactions*. (1769), 189-191; Wallis, "John Bevis," 211-225; Martin, *Venus in the Sun* (1761).
[26] AR, CW 1:496-497.
[27] Kramnick, *Enlightenment Reader*, 53.
[28] Ibid., 58-59.
[29] Cohen, *Science and the Founding Fathers*, 61, 57.
[30] Kramnick, *Enlightenment Reader*, 53. The most persistent of the charges against Bacon were bribery and sodomy.
[31] Bacon, *Advancement of Learning*, 76.
[32] Ibid., 130.
[33] Jardine and Silverthorne, *Francis Bacon: The New Organon*, 66.
[34] Ibid.
[35] Ibid., 66-67.
[36] Ibid., 68.
[37] This is a necessarily oversimplified, heuristic description of Bacon's aims and methodology. He realized that there must be a place for deduction in any rational system, and he saw his method as a corrective of a fallacious leap in the logic of the logicians from ordinary sensory experience to grand premises. He realized that observations would have to be deductively aggregated into "middle axioms," but his process accumulated and tested each step of certainty while the scholastic logicians practiced a divisive methodology that was wholly disembodied from experiential reality.
[38] Newton, *Mathematical Principles of Natural Philosophy*.
[39] Cohen, *Companion to Newton*.
[40] For the initial idea of partitioning the Newtonian system between the *Principia* and the *Optics*, I am indebted to Cohen, *Science and the Founding Fathers*.
[41] Newton, *Opticks* I, Part 1.
[42] *Opticks* III.
[43] Ibid.

[44] Ibid.
[45] Locke, *Essay Concerning Human Understanding*.
[46] Quoted in Burgh, *Political Disquisitions*, 1:xiii.
[47] Ibid., 1:vii.
[48] Dragonetti, *A Treatise on Virtues and Rewards*.
[49] Burgh, 1:xix.
[50] Ibid., 1:3, 35.
[51] Ibid., 1:3, 37.
[52] On the integrated culture of dissent in London during the period, see Lincoln, *Some Political & Social Ideas of English Dissent* and Levere, "Natural Philosophers in a Coffee House."
[53] Millburn, "Benjamin Martin and the Royal Society," 22.
[54] Lecturing was a lucrative business. James Ferguson charged a flat rate of 1 guinea (1 pound and 1 shilling) per person for a course of twelve lectures (or 1 shilling, 9 pence per lecture). In London, his classes met at least three days a week and enrolled a minimum of 25 students, guaranteeing him a minimum income of 26 pounds, 5 shillings in a month. He didn't change the price of the lectures when he traveled, but he raised the minimum enrollment. Within ten miles of London, he would read the lectures six days a week to no fewer than thirty people, guaranteeing him 31 pounds, 10 shillings in a two week period. Within a hundred miles of London, his minimum enrollment was 60 students over the same time span, guaranteeing him 63 pounds for two weeks of work. None of this included sales of equipment or publications that were required or recommended for many of the courses, and in Ferguson's case, he was also receiving 50 pounds per year from the Crown as a pension. When we take into consideration that the average *annual* salary around this time for a school teacher was about 25 pounds, it becomes obvious that the Newtonian lecture circuit was not a purely altruistic endeavor. For a complete list of the equipment Ferguson used for each of his twelve lectures, see the Appendix to Ferguson, *An Easy Introduction to Astronomy*.
[55] From the autobiographical "Short Account of the Life of the Author," in Ferguson, *Select Mechanical Exercises*.
[56] See, the Bibliography for an expansive list of Martin's publications.
[57] Millburn, "Benjamin Martin and the Royal Society." For criticisms of Martin's for-profit science, see Stewart, "Public Culture of Radical Philosophers."
[58] CS 3.25.
[59] CS A.10.
[60] Ferguson, *The Description and Use of a New Machine, Called the Mechanical Paradox*.
[61] CS 3.6.
[62] CS 1.8.
[63] Quoted in King and Millburn. *Geared to the Stars*, 178.
[64] CS 1.7-1.8.
[65] CS 1.10-1.11.
[66] CS 1.9.
[67] CS 1.16-1.17.
[68] CS 1.14.

[69] Martin, *Description and Use of both the Globes, the Armillary Sphere, and Orrery*, 181.
[70] CS 3.29, 3.35.
[71] Ferguson, *A Dissertation upon the Phænomena of the Harvest Moon. Also, the Description and Use of a New Four-wheel'd Orrery.*
[72] CS A.10.
[73] Martin, *A Course of Lectures in Natural and Experimental Philosophy, Geography and Astronomy*, 1-2.
[74] CS A.19.
[75] Martin *Course of Lectures*, 2-4
[76] Ibid., 12-13.
[77] CS 3.24.
[78] Ibid.
[79] Martin, *Plain and Familiar Introduction to the Newtonian Experimental Philosophy*, 109.
[80] CS A.11.
[81] CS A.11.
[82] CS 3.24, cf. CS A.11.
[83] CS F.4.
[84] Paine lists the two main arguments in his Appendix as separation and independence, which correspond respectively, following the argument in this section, to the wedge and lever. CS A.4.
[85] Martin, *Course of Lectures*, 26.
[86] CS 3.50.
[87] Martin, *Course of Lectures*, 24-25.
[88] CS 3.37.
[89] CS 3.46; Dragonetti, *Treatise on Virtues and Rewards*.
[90] CS 1.16.
[91] CS 4.3.
[92] CS 4.17.
[93] CS 3.38.
[94] HL to Martha Laurens, 18 May 1774. Ramsay, *Memoirs of the Life of Martha Laurens Ramsay*, 52-53.
[95] Ferguson, *An Easy Introduction to Astronomy.*
[96] Martin's works demonstrate the fluid vocabulary of eighteenth century natural philosophy. In his lexicon, "science" represented what we would think of as a system of "knowledge" or a "discipline," while "philosophy" was closer to what we now think of as "science." Here is how Martin put it: "The nature of Philosophy is Science itself; its Essence is Knowledge; and Wisdom, in all its various Branches, makes up its constituent Parts. These are all synonymous Terms, and (as is well known to the Literati) are implied in the Etymon of the Word…There are, indeed, other Professions whose Nature consists in Science, but in no respects comparable to that of Philosophy…Thus Poetry is the Science of versifying, Music of modulating Sounds: Grammar teaches the Use of Letters and Words, Rhetoric gives Rules for speaking floridly…" Martin, *Panegyrick on the Newtonian Philosophy*.
[97] Martin, *Young Gentleman and Lady's Philosophy*.
[98] Martin, *Panegyrick on the Newtonian Philosophy*.

[99] BR to James Cheetham, 17 June 1809. Quoted in Cheetham, *Life of Thomas Paine*, 34-40.
[100] TP to HL, 14 January 1779. CW 2:1161.
[101] AC, No. 1, CW 1:51.
[102] Martin, *Young Gentleman and Lady's Philosophy*.
[103] AC, No. 5. CW 1:123.
[104] CS 2.12, 2.15.
[105] CS 2.12.
[106] CS 3.9.
[107] CS 3.2.
[108] Bacon also worked to anticipate and counteract prejudice against his system. He asked that his critics not summarily dismiss his system "casually or while he is about something else" but after examining "the subject properly." Bacon urged the disbelieving to experiment with his method and to "get used to the subtlety of things which experience suggests." Only by trying his method out in little experiments could his readers correct "the bad mental habits which are so deeply ingrained." Jardine and Silverthorne, 68.
[109] CS 3.1.
[110] Locke, *Essay Concerning Human Understanding*, 174.
[111] According to Johnson's *Dictionary*, the definition of *Perspecuity (n.s.)*: "1. Transparency; translucency; diaphaneity. 2. Clearness to the mind; easiness to be understood; freedom from obscurity or ambiguity."
[112] Martin, *Course of Lectures*, 1.
[113] Martin, *Description and Use of an Orrery of a New Construction*.
[114] Quoted in Vickers, *English Science, Bacon to Newton*, 9.
[115] Ibid., 18.
[116] Locke, *Essay Concerning Human Understanding*, 11.
[117] For a treatment of Locke's aspiration toward a popular style, see Walmsley, *Locke's "Essay" and the Rhetoric of Science*.
[118] Sensation we have covered already at some length. For instances of the centrality of the mental process of reflection, see CS 2.6, 3.48, and A.17.
[119] Locke, *Essay Concerning Human Understanding*, 173.
[120] Ibid., 449.
[121] CS 3.1.
[122] CW 1:56.
[123] Ferguson, *Easy Introduction to Astronomy*.
[124] Even the concept of "nature," which Paine invoked 41 separate times in *Common Sense*, bridged the religious and scientific spheres of the eighteenth century.
[125] CS 3.32.
[126] CS 3.5.
[127] CS 3.6.
[128] CS 3.18.
[129] CS A.1.
[130] CS F.1.
[131] CS 1.2.
[132] CS 2.1.
[133] CS 3.1.

[134] CS 4.12.
[135] CS A.11.
[136] CS E.5.
[137] See entry for 8 July 1776, Marshall, *Diary*; Hart, "Colonel John Nixon."; Eckhardt, *Pennsylvania Clocks and Clockmakers*, 86.
[138] CS A.6.
[139] NG to Catharine Greene, 2 November 1776. Showman, *Papers of General Nathaniel Greene*, 1:329-330.

Chapter Five

Time and the Decision for Independence

See the sage RITTENHOUSE, with ardent eye,
Lift the long tube and pierce the starry sky;
Clear in his view the circling systems roll,
And broader splendours gild the central pole.
He marks what laws th' eccentric wand'rers bind,
Copies Creation in his forming mind,
And bids, beneath his hand, in semblance rise,
With mimic orbs, the labours of the skies.
There wond'ring crowds with raptur'd eye behold
The spangled Heav'ns their mystic maze unfold;
While each glad sage his splendid Hall shall grace,
With all the spheres that cleave th' ethereal space.

Joel Barlow
The Vision of Columbus
1787

This hour's the very crisis of your fate.
Your good or ill, your infamy or fame,
And all the colour of your life, depends
On this important now.

John Dryden
The Spanish Friar: Or, the Double Discovery
1681

Part One
THE CRAFTSMANSHIP OF TIME

An American Newton

In 1778, Thomas Jefferson penned what one historian has called "the authentic note of the Enlightenment" to David Rittenhouse, who at the time served as president of the Pennsylvania Council of Safety: "Writing to a Philosopher, I may hope to be pardoned for intruding some thoughts of my own, though they relate to him personally." Jefferson observed that, since 1776, Rittenhouse's attention had been consumed with "civil government" in Pennsylvania. The Virginian acknowledged "the authority our cause would acquire with the world from it being known yourself and Doctor Franklin were zealous friends to it," and Jefferson reiterated that he had been "duly impressed with a sense of the arduousness of government" and of "the obligation those are under who are able to conduct it." Nonetheless, Jefferson was convinced "there is an order of geniuses above that obligation, and therefore exempted from it." Though politics was a difficult and important business, Jefferson was saying, Rittenhouse was squandering his genius upon the mundane affairs of governance. "Nobody can conceive that nature ever intended to throw away a Newton upon the occupations of a crown." Jefferson continued, "I doubt not there are in your country many persons equal to the task of conducting government: but you should consider that the world has but one Rittenhouse, and that it never had one before."[1]

Jefferson did not reserve his praise of Rittenhouse for their private correspondence. One important section of Jefferson's *Notes on the State of Virginia* (1781-1782) refuted a scientific theory then circulating in Europe that the climate of America stunted the intellectual abilities of its inhabitants. Jefferson offered up three American "proofs of genius": in war, a Washington; in physics, a Franklin; and in astronomy, a Rittenhouse. In response to a speculative theory that the American continent was naturally hostile to genius, Jefferson paraded America's superstars as a conclusive empirical counterpoint. Washington, Franklin, and Rittenhouse were all "native" Americans: Washington of Virginia stock, Franklin from Massachusetts, and Rittenhouse from the German settlements of Pennsylvania.

Washington and Franklin, along with their admirer Jefferson, would become canonical "Founding Fathers," but Rittenhouse has been largely forgotten outside of the bustling square in Philadelphia that bears his name. Washington's legacy in America is, in a word, pervasive. Americans remember Franklin as a skilled diplomat, as an entrepreneurial wit, and as the rain-soaked, kite-flying discoverer of electricity. Rittenhouse, the other luminous mind of the age, was a clockmaker by profession and an astronomer by reputation. He was not just another "mechanic"; he was one of the world's greatest engineers, and his extraordinary mathematical and technical skills brought him tremendous respect and acclaim in America and Europe.

In his *Notes*, Jefferson withheld no superlatives when he spoke about Rittenhouse. America had "supposed Mr. Rittenhouse second to no astronomer living," said Jefferson, adding "that in genius he must be the first, because he is self-taught." In a compliment of infinite magnitude, Jefferson continued, "As an artist he has exhibited as great a proof of mechanical genius as the world has ever produced. He has not indeed made a world; but he has by imitation approached nearer its Maker than any man who has lived from the creation to this day."[2]

What had Rittenhouse done to merit such effusive praise? The answer is difficult for a twenty-first century mind to process: Rittenhouse had designed and produced a mechanical planetarium known as an orrery. Rittenhouse had not discovered, invented, or written anything new. He had simply improved the function of a clock-like machine. That was it. One historian of science, I. Bernard Cohen, looked at this situation and concluded, with ample justification, that "the fulsomeness" of Jefferson's praise for Rittenhouse "was an example of allowing his patriotism to overcome his normal critical faculties."[3] While I sympathize with Cohen's reaction, the problem with his conclusion is that Jefferson was not alone. Nearly everyone in eighteenth century America who viewed one of Rittenhouse's orreries, thought it was the most amazing thing he or she had ever seen, and, upon making Rittenhouse's acquaintance, those same persons were certain that he was the smartest person they had ever met. The fact that President George Washington appointed Rittenhouse in 1793 as the first Director of the United States Mint was as symbolic as it was functional: Isaac Newton had been Master of the Mint in England.

In this chapter, the mechanical and mathematical achievements of David Rittenhouse will be the *instrumental* vehicles by which I will analyze a facet of *Common Sense* that lies at the heart of this study. By comprehending the significance of Rittenhouse's achievements in their eighteenth century context, we will also grasp the paramount textual feature of *Common Sense*: Thomas Paine's treatment of *time*.

The perfect timing of the publication of *Common Sense* has become a commonplace of revolutionary history. The Reverend William Gordon, in *The History of the Rise, Progress, and Establishment of the Independence of the United States of America* (1788), described the pamphlet's impact:

> Nothing could have been better timed than this performance. In unison with the sentiments and feelings of the people, it has produced most

astonishing effects, and been received with vast applause, read by almost every American, and recommended as a work replete with truth, and against which none but the partial and prejudiced can form any objections. It has satisfied multitudes that it is their true interest to cut the Gordian knot by which the American colonies have been bound to Great Britain, and to open their commerce, as an independent people, to all the nations of the world. It has been greatly instrumental in producing a similarity of sentiment through the continent, upon the subject under the consideration of Congress." [4]

These effects were not solely the result of the *external* timing of *Common Sense*'s entry into the marketplace of discourse. Of equal importance was the *internal* construction of time in the reader's experience of Paine's text. Paine plainly advertised his rhetorical method in an aphorism at the end of the pamphlet's first paragraph: "Time makes more converts than reason."[5] Though he spoke of "reason" a goodly amount in *Common Sense*, Paine did not expect disembodied logic to convince his audience of the propriety of independence. Paine achieved their conversion through the textual manipulation of time. To facilitate our understanding of Paine's complex and multivalent treatment of time, it will help to engage intermittently with a few important scientific corollaries from Rittenhouse's early career.

A Rural Mechanic

Rittenhouse, the great grandson of a German immigrant who had established the first paper mill in America, had grown up on his family's farm outside of Germantown, Pennsylvania. A tinkerer from a very young age, Rittenhouse received his father's blessing to set up a roadside shop on his family's property in Norriton, where the seventeen year old began to make and sell clocks and surveying instruments.[6] Rittenhouse's sister married a young Anglican minister, Thomas Barton, who was responsible for introducing Rittenhouse to the "republic of letters," and, more directly, to Provost William Smith of the College of Philadelphia. Barton was leaving his position as tutor at the Academy of Philadelphia (chartered as a College in 1755) just as Smith was arriving as a professor. Barton sailed for London, where he received his ordination as a missionary for the Society of the Propagation of the Gospel and requested an assignment in rural Pennsylvania. Barton took a congregation in Lancaster and quickly reintegrated into the colonial Anglican world. Barton and Smith became friends over the next few years in their interactions as Anglican clergymen, and Smith honored his friend with an honorary master's degree from the College of Philadelphia in 1760.

Barton discerned the genius in his brother-in-law and urged his friend Smith to travel to Norriton to become acquainted with Rittenhouse and his mechanical skill. Smith was awed by the provincial autodidact from their first meeting. In addition to Smith's position as head of the College, he also lectured as a professor in astronomy and ethics, and he recognized Rittenhouse's mathematical sophistication and innovative craftsmanship. By 1763, Rittenhouse had acquired a strong reputation in rural Pennsylvania for his instrumentation and surveying. That year, he had demonstrated a cool demeanor and technical prowess in his survey of the boundary between Pennsylvania and Maryland, by which a contentious border dispute was quelled.[7]

Rittenhouse had managed to flourish with few resources and only limited encouragement, William Smith thought, and the provost wanted to increase his friend's exposure and stature in the colonies. Thus, in 1767, Smith awarded Rittenhouse an honorary master's degree from the college, a laurel that raised curiosity in urban Philadelphia about this "unknown" mechanic from Norriton. In 1768, Smith also sponsored Rittenhouse's nomination to the American Philosophical Society, and the two became collaborators on the Transit of Venus observation. Though Smith was the nominal leader of and spokesman for the Norriton observation team, everyone in the Society knew that the observatory's scientific success hinged on Rittenhouse's contribution. Rittenhouse built the observatory himself on his own land, and overcoming a dearth of astronomical instrumentation in the colonies, Rittenhouse made most of the equipment himself. Rittenhouse also calculated the precise longitude and latitude of the observatory and diagrammed Venus's path a full year in advance. Smith and John Lukens, the other lead members of the Norriton team, did not worry themselves with preparations, since they knew they had, said Smith, "entrusted them to a gentleman on the spot, who had joined to a complete skill in mechanics, so extensive an astronomical and mathematical knowledge, that the use, management, and even the construction of the necessary apparatus, were perfectly familiar to him."[8] Using optical and chronometric equipment of his own design and construction, Rittenhouse's observations of June 3, 1769, received accolades from European astronomers for their exquisite precision.[9]

After the transit, Rittenhouse's scientific skills began to receive further recognition, and with William Smith again leading the effort, Rittenhouse was persuaded in 1770 to move from Norriton to Philadelphia "to take a lead in a manufacture, optical and mathematical, which never had been attempted in America, and [which] drew thousands of pounds to England for instruments, often ill-furnished."[10] At the end of the year, Rittenhouse planned to settle at Seventh and Arch Streets, near the College of Philadelphia, but before he could move his shop from Norriton, he had to put the finishing touches on his first orrery.[11]

Admirers of Rittenhouse's scientific work and readers of Paine's pamphlet encountered two temporal experiences that shared much in common. Rittenhouse had been living in Philadelphia for about four years when Paine arrived from England. Both were rural mechanics who had been thrust into the cosmopolitan limelight because of their passion for scientific knowledge. As Paine sat in Rittenhouse's shop on Arch Street in Philadelphia during the fall of 1775, the two talked freely about politics and natural philosophy. Rittenhouse showed Paine his astronomical charts, his mathematical calculations, and his mechanical drawings. They met periodically to discuss experiments and saltpeter production, and they walked together to the College of Philadelphia and to the home of Thomas Pryor to inspect and discuss some of Rittenhouse's fabrications. On one occasion, Paine knocked on Rittenhouse's door holding a stack of loose foolscap sheets of linen paper. Paine requested his friend's candid opinion on a series of essays he had written that he hoped to publish in 1776 as a history of the conflict with Britain. Rittenhouse obliged him and read the pages of Paine's manuscript with characteristic attention to detail. Returning the essays to Paine a few days later, Rittenhouse commented that he found them very convincing. Rittenhouse wondered aloud if a bound book of history was the right outlet for their publication. He thought Paine's style and his arguments might be better served as a newspaper serial, a medium that would also reach a broader colonial audience with a shorter turnaround. Time, they agreed, was of the essence. Paine concurred with Rittenhouse's thoughts and promised to present the newspaper idea to their mutual friend and Paine's primary collaborator, Benjamin Rush. Rittenhouse politely excused himself, because he needed to return home to finish some astronomical and meteorological calculations for an almanac soon to be published in Philadelphia.

Causality and Temporality

Like so many famous political works before and after it, *Common Sense* failed to achieve the immediate rhetorical effect for which, it seemed, Paine was aiming. The pamphlet argued that America should declare independence immediately, but as it turned out, there was a seven month lag between the initial publication of the pamphlet and the publication of the *Declaration of Independence*—hardly a rousing or rapid success. Paine's inexperience with practical politics may have led him to underestimate the tedious foot-dragging of a twice-delegated political representation. Although Paine's objective was eventually met, his success, it would seem, was only partial because of the delay between the pamphlet's publication and independence's declaration. This lag forces us to face one of the chief difficulties in an analysis of textual history. Is it possible to prove textual effect or causality, or is correlation the pinnacle of analytical precision? It is impossible to isolate the variables of human decision in the same way we approach natural phenomena. Even if we could show that an eighteenth century American, hitherto in favor of reconciliation, read *Common Sense* from cover to cover, set it down, and marched off to agitate for political independence, we still could not know with certainty that the text *caused* this change in opinion or behavior. As David Hume pointed out in his famous illustration of billiard balls striking one another, there is "no interval betwixt the shock and the motion."[12]

It is one thing to claim agency for a text—that it is *doing* something—and another to claim textual causality—this it is *causing* something else to be done. Bernard Bailyn, in his elegant, short essay on *Common Sense*, pronounced this question of textual causality out-of-bounds. Though he gave no explicit rationale for his prohibition, it is clear that he was trying to preempt the speculative casuistry and ascriptions of textual magic so common in treatments of patriotic texts.[13] To establish textual causality in complex societies is difficult, he seemed to be saying, and the track record of failure led him to the conclusion that the venture should not be attempted.[14]

There were in late colonial America an abundance of factors urging the colonies to break with England. Necessities of war became impossible to obtain because they had always come to the colonies through British merchants who were now largely forbidden from colonial ports. There was a lack of domestic production of the materials of war such as saltpeter and gunpowder. The materials of communication, like the linen rags required to make paper, were desperately scarce, and too few mills existed in the colonies to produce paper in sufficient quantities. There was the British siege of Boston, the proclamation of martial law in Virginia by Lord Dunmore, and the burning of Falmouth and Norfolk. There were repeated proclamations and speeches by King George III, his ministry, both houses of parliament, and even some English associations, painting the American colonists as rebellious vagrants in need of swordpoint discipline. These came on top of a cool British silence in response to all petitions from the Continental Congress. The employment of mercenary Hessian troops to fight against the Americans was a catastrophic violation of the principles of civility. This complex causality, what Paine labeled optimistically in *Common Sense* the "general concurrence, the glorious union of all things," was the circumstantial convergence of literally dozens of factors that contributed to a mounting sense of colonial American angst. But angst is an insufficient cause of political revolution. In traditional republican theory, citizens were called to be virtuous and vigilant, to hail the freedom of the press and to rue standing armies. But there was little guidance for the disciples of English republicanism beyond dutifully transcribing their private consternation into public objections.

The reluctant decision of the Continental Congress to form a committee to draft a declaration was initiated as each provincial assembly changed its instructions to its delegates on the question of independence. For months, the provincial assemblies had expressly forbidden their delegates to support any plan that would lead to independence. As local public opinion in each colony swung from reconciliation to independence, this opinion infected elected assemblymen. In cases where the assemblies remained staunchly opposed to independence, such as Pennsylvania, voters elected new pro-independence representatives. Delegates to the Continental Congress were bound to follow the instructions of their respective assemblies, and the assemblies, sooner or later, were bound to follow the instructions of their constituents. By late May of 1776, the majority opinion in each colony was becoming unanimous. Because of the nebulous political structure of interregnum America, street-level public opinion was the only legitimate source of authority. The necessary, but not solely sufficient *cause* of American independence can thus be located at the ground level of public opinion, as a community of readers interacted with texts to achieve shared understandings of collective decisions.

The causal significance of texts is not located solely in quantitative markers such as sales volume. Though we may infer that any text that goes through several impressions and sells an unusually large number of copies has struck a chord with its intended audience, all those copies may have shifted hands and landed unread on bookshelves and garbage heaps. Thus we also need an evaluative indication of the qualitative components of the text. Some texts are forgotten with the turn of a page, while others prove life-changing, and we cannot grasp the qualitative differential between the two without careful attention to internal textual mechanisms and to external public reactions. By engaging both interpretive and archival evidence, this book is attempting to explicate the causal role of *Common Sense* in the British Colonies' decision to become American States.

One of the most remarkable aspects of American public discourse in 1776 was the absolute vacuum of any public call for independence that was not in some way a response to *Common Sense*. John Adams claimed that he had paved the way for independence in the Continental Congress starting in the fall of 1775, but a majority of delegates would stonewall the idea for months to come. And the debates of the Second Continental Congress can hardly be considered "public" with any candor. The only printed call for American independence prior to *Common Sense* was actually written and published in England and received limited circulation in the colonies.[15] During the spring of 1776, every event and publication crossing the Atlantic from England—whether supporting or opposing the American cause—was received as a corroboration of *Common Sense*. So although the soil of

American public opinion was tilled and fertile, no one else was planting the seeds of independence.

What would have happened if Thomas Paine had never written *Common Sense*? Perhaps someone else would have written a plea for independence in the absence of *Common Sense*, but would it have been an effective piece of persuasion? Would it have stoked the fires of public debate? Would it have translated across the disparate colonial cultures? The best pamphlet writers of the revolution besides Paine were ineligible: John Dickinson, because he opposed independence to the point of refusing to vote for or sign the *Declaration*, and John Otis, because he had gone mad. Without wandering too far into speculative territory, it appears unlikely that any other American could have written anything approaching the white-hot clarity of *Common Sense*. The conditions for a chemical reaction may be perfect, but without the right catalyst, nothing happens.

Only by entertaining this null hypothesis or counterfactual scenarios can we clarify the role of *Common Sense* in the turn from reconciliation to independence during the spring of 1776. Paine himself believed that America would have still declared independence without his pamphlet, but likely months later and under different auspices. Independence, he argued, was inevitable, but lingering would prove disastrous. As a historical fact, the Americans almost lost the war during the winter of 1776-77 because, as Paine had predicted, they were underprepared and undersupplied. If a declaration of independence had been postponed beyond July 1776, the colonies' indeterminate situation would have exacerbated matters further. Therefore, a more relevant and, perhaps, more fair historical question for us to ask is: To what extent did *Common Sense* speed up the process leading to a declaration of independence? Among a parade of causal factors, *Common Sense* was certainly in the first rank. The text was a *necessary* but not wholly *sufficient* cause of the *Declaration of Independence* of July 1776. In publishing his pamphlet, Paine initiated a vigorous debate that inclined the majority opinion of the colonies toward independence. He was not creating rhetorical effect *ex nihilo*; he was simply accelerating political discourse to force a decision at his estimation of the right time.

To understand how *Common Sense* accelerated the debate over independence, we need to investigate the experience of time that Paine created for his readers. Paine employed four distinct kinds of time in *Common Sense* that, with some overlap, correspond to four of David Rittenhouse's most important mathematical and mechanical productions. These four modes of textual temporality and their respective scientific artifact-events are: clock time (*chronos*): the Potts-Pryor Astronomical Clock; seasonal time (*kairos*): *Father Abraham's Almanac*; epic time (*epos*): the Norriton observation of the Transit of Venus; and crisis time (*krisis*): the famous Rittenhouse Orrery. I will now treat each of these modes of temporality in turn.

PART TWO
CHRONOS

Clock Time and the Potts-Pryor Astronomical Clock

By 1774, Rittenhouse had been building clocks for over two decades. On the face of one of his earliest productions, he had inscribed, "Time is fleeting," an intimate principle for a man who, like Paine, had lost his first wife in childbirth.[16] The mechanical clock was a mature invention by the late eighteenth century, and pocket watches were even becoming a common sight on the streets of Philadelphia. But a Rittenhouse clock was not just a clock.

In the spring of 1774, Thomas Pryor paid 640 Pennsylvania dollars for what is still considered Rittenhouse's horological masterpiece, a nine foot, Chippendale case clock. Pryor had purchased the clock after the wealthy, loyalist forge owner for whom it had been made, Joseph Potts, refused it. Potts, a man notorious for his frugality and simple tastes, balked at Rittenhouse's final price and requested a half-clock instead.[17] During the British occupation of Philadelphia, Pryor would refuse British General Sir William Howe's offer of 120 guineas for the clock as well as a second offer of 800 Pennsylvania dollars from a Spanish minister.[18]

This clock, one of the most complex chronometric devices ever made in America, measured time with unparalleled precision along multiple dimensions. The main dial plate recorded time with four filigreed hands indicating the seconds, minutes, hours, and months. A lunarium in the center dial showed the corresponding phases of the moon, and an aperture in the dial showed the numerical date. The uppermost dial was a small orrery that displaying the positions of Mercury, Venus, Earth, Mars, Jupiter, and Saturn (the six then-known planets), while the four corner dials exhibited the positions of the sun and the moon in the Zodiac, the lunar orbit around the earth, the equation of time (the difference between solar and actual time), and a ten-song tune selector. The clock could even be adjusted so that its fifteen bells would play four songs at the same time. Most clocks during this era required daily or weekly winding, but Rittenhouse's astronomical clock was capable of running for an entire month.[19] While other clock and watch-makers in Philadelphia carried on the "business in all its branches as usual," Rittenhouse transcended the bounds of his trade and marked time by the stars.[20]

A typical clock marked the forward march of time in seconds, minutes, and hours. This clock time (*chronos*), represented by hands on a watch and dates on a calendar, imposed a modern sense of order upon human events. It cannot be forgotten that precise timekeeping was a relatively new development, even in the latter half of the eighteenth century. Just a century and a half before, Galileo Galilei was still timing his scientific experiments by taking his pulse or by singing songs with a familiar beat. The dates of a conventional British calendar were only officially converted from the "old" Julian to the "new" Gregorian style—the latter format we still use—in 1752. Paine used clock time to his advantage with subtlety in *Common Sense*. America's knowledge was "hourly improving" and its manufactories were "every day producing" the articles of war, although the timber necessary for ship-building was "every day diminishing."[21] Likewise, "Every day wears out the little remains of kindred between us and them," America and Britain, and "the relationship expires," implied Paine, like the waning ticks of a manual-crank clock.[22] The chronological slowness of transatlantic imperial governance would "in a few years be looked upon as folly and childishness." In an interlocking escalation of figures that pointed toward infinite absurdity, Paine mocked the idea of "always running" a "tale or a petition" across "three or four thousand miles" of ocean and "waiting four or five months for an answer, which, when obtained, requires five or six more to explain it in."[23]

The distinctive feature about clock time was its straightforward, mundane factuality—the sense that every minute, hour, or day was the same as every other. Every tick of a clock came on at a uniform pace, and every hourly chime was barely distinguishable from the one preceding. The real significance of clock time in *Common Sense* was not in its employment of standard chronology but in the embedded textual structures that Paine used to disrupt it.

Though the Potts-Pryor Astronomical Clock was as accurate as it was complex, the experience of a person encountering the clock for the very first time was actually temporal disorientation. This was not a normal clock, and all of its spinning dials and overlapping chimes seemed initially like a cacophony of information and noise. But in Rittenhouse's pursuit of an integrated temporal experience, he had first to defy viewers' limited expectations of what a clock could do.

Dismantling and Reconstructing Time

In order for Paine to create a special sense of textual time in *Common Sense*, he had to untrammel his readers from any regular sense of time to which they clung. In other words, to accomplish a temporal *reorientation*, he needed simultaneously to effect a temporal *disorientation*. The kaleidoscopic past-present-future continuum in *Common Sense* confused, collapsed, and reconfigured political time according to Paine's own devices. He construed the quasi-factual norms of entrenched British culture as fundamentally temporal and thus mobile rather than indelible. Paine portrayed his pamphlet as "not *yet* sufficiently fashionable" and predicted that his proposals would "at first seem strange and difficult," but, like the habitual customs he was opposing, his arguments "in a little time" would become "familiar and agreeable."[24] In the interim, Paine was busy creating a temporal vertigo for his readers. *Common Sense* self-consciously initiated the public debate on independence but declared, "The period of debate is closed."[25] Halfway through the pamphlet, Paine wrote a second general introduction at the beginning of the third section, where he again covered "preliminaries to settle with the reader."[26] After this second foreword, he never again referred to any material from the preceding two sections. They were now in the past, and he was focused on the present and future. It was as if Paine imagined himself so effective at washing away justifications for monarchy that both he and his readers were starting from scratch.

Although *Common Sense* followed a loose past-to-future progression in its overarching structure, Paine blended the grammatical tenses and moods of his arguments with a stupefying effect. As we saw in Chapter One, Paine managed to describe a hypothetical past perfect "state of nature" with a combination of present indicative and future subjunctive language. Likewise, throughout *Common Sense*, the future existed in a state of maximum contingency as a present imperative fork in the road. At the same time, the subjunctive, conditional mood freighted Paine's descriptions of the future with possibility while siphoning any sense of security. Paine was doing two things here: first, he was strengthening the logical relationship between past, present, and future. By shifting grammatical gears so often, he was blurring the imaginary lines demarcating *what was*, *what is*, and *what will be*. He needed his audience to *feel* the impact their present decisions would have on the future. Secondly, he was demonstrating the pliability of the temporal justifications for British government. The relationship between America and Britain, he argued, was built solely upon the shifting sands of custom, habit, and prejudice, which were nothing more than past illegitimacies loitering in the present. By rearranging the tattered furniture of the past, Paine was demonstrating for his flummoxed readers that governmental structures were not, in fact, bolted to the floor and could be discarded and replaced. Though the past had governed the Americans' melancholy indicative present, Paine was showing how the future could begin to govern their sanguine subjunctive present. Paine thus yanked the carpet of temporal normalcy out from under the languid deliberations over America's future.

In the first paragraph of both the foreword and the third section of the pamphlet, Paine encouraged his readers to divest themselves of a distorted past-fixation characterized by *prejudice*, where the past trumps and blockades the present.[27] Instead he urged the Americans to assume a sound past-orientation characterized by *reflection*, where the memory of past experience informs present action. Paine stressed the presentness of his audience's decision and the necessity of reflection: "Should we neglect the present favorable and inviting period, and independence be hereafter effected by any other means, we must charge the consequence to ourselves, or to those rather whose narrow and prejudiced souls are habitually opposing the measure, without either inquiring or reflecting."[28] Delay and "backwardness" encouraged Britain to "hope for conquest" and tended "only to prolong the war." Looking ahead to the future, independence was the only guarantee of perpetual union, "the only bond that can tie and keep us together."[29]

Common Sense distorted the norms of temporality like a funhouse mirror, and Paine shifted the relations of past-present-future like a street artist playing a shell game. In one sentence, Paine connected the past, present, and future in a bleak diatribe against reconciliation. The present, he said, was the same as the past, because of the illusory effect of reconciliation: "the advantages of reconciliation, which, like an agreeable dream, has passed away and left us as we were." In the very same sentence, he cast the present as identical to the future: "the many material injuries which these colonies sustain, and always will sustain, by being connected with and dependant on Great Britain." Therefore, the past and the future would be identical as long as the connection remained intact.[30] But no sooner had he made this connection than he began to dissociate the past, present, and future. The present was not like the past after all: "We are not the little people now, which we were sixty years ago; at that time we might have trusted our property in the streets, or fields rather, and slept securely without locks or bolts to our doors and windows."[31] Looking forward, Paine decided that the present was stagnated in the future, "we should be no forwarder a hundred years hence," but concluded the present was, in fact, superior to a degenerative future in which America's resources were "every day diminishing."[32] He painted the continuance of the "unsettled and unpromising" reconciliation path as precipitating a future state of anarchy that would initiate the exodus of all but the most base of inhabitants and lead to constant "civil tumult."[33] The future may be very different from the past, he said, since "The next war may not turn out like the last." In that case, "advocates for reconciliation now," in the present, "will be wishing for a separation then," in the future. Paine had sufficiently diced the connections between past, present, and future that he had destabilized his readers' sense of temporal normalcy. Within the text of *Common Sense*, it was easy for a reader to get lost and ask, *What time is it?* Paine's response to his disoriented readers was simple enough: "'TIS TIME TO PART."[34]

History and Expediency

Paine's two main targets for temporal demolition in *Common Sense* were the political functions of history and expediency. He identified a particular conception of history as essential to the existence of the British Constitution, while the short-sighted expediency he witnessed in British imperial affairs revealed the corrupting influence of self-serving interest. Paine lambasted customary history as a perversion of the past and political expediency as a fetishism of the future.

In his treatment of expediency, Paine appeared to be speaking out of both sides of his mouth—as he did on several other issues. Paine railed against political expediency in others and then sold independence on the basis of its expediency as "the easiest and most practicable plan." Though measures "only of a temporary kind" and a "temporary expedient" were anathema to Paine, he was certainly not calling for slow deliberation. In one passage, he even warned that the king might *slow down* British aggression as a means of political expediency. He warned that the king, by repealing the offensive acts "at this time" could accomplish by "Craft and Subtlety" in the "Long Run" what he could not "do by Force and Violence in the Short One."[35] This apparent inconsistency was reflective of Paine's differentiation between behavior and thought: he advocated fast action but slow thought. In other words, Paine was *for* expedient action, but he *opposed* expedient motives.[36]

Paine could not expand the boundaries of the public within a customary historical framework. The discursive justifications of traditional British political culture were, like the Latinized language of politics, patently inaccessible to the common folk. The collusion of formal speech and archived precedent ensured the preservation of a partitioned British society, since "the many" were thereby systematically excluded from engaging in the logic of "the few." The people's rights were buried in the labyrinthine annals of common law government and the "ancient" British Constitution.

When one makes an argument using history or custom as a mode of proof, as was the case with British common law and constitutional history, the fastest way to compromise the credibility of that custom is to displace its origins. Truth, in such structures, hinges on historical precedence. In *Common Sense*, Paine was evacuating the authority of a traditionary past by crippling the legitimacy of its origins and the logic required to uphold the current system. Even if Paine's audience did not assent to his every argument, their very observation of Paine's dissection made them complicit in the demystification or, in Weberian terms, the "disenchantment" of their sacrosanct nationalist mythology.[37]

Paine lambasted the institution of monarchy by first delegitimizing the origins of monarchy during Biblical times and then by bringing a harsh realism to the mythic days of William the Conqueror. Paine's wicked characterizations of George III were derivative to his argument; he poisoned the well of monarchy by employing the antedating authority of scripture and English history. If God detested monarchy and if William the Conqueror, the first King of England, was a "French bastard landing with an armed banditti," then to his audience of pious Protestants, haters of Catholic France, hereditary monarchy was exposed in its naked pretension.

Some of Paine's statements indicated that he had entirely disregarded history as a legitimate form of proof. For instance, the Americans' situation was "without a precedent," said Paine, and since "the case never existed before," historical arguments were useless.[38] In fact, though, Paine *was* writing history, but he was writing it on his own terms as a popular Protestant Christian History: "Monarchy is ranked in scripture as one of the sins of the Jews, for which a curse in reserve is denounced against them. The history of that transaction is worth attending to."[39] Though secular history was obscured by "the dark covering of antiquity," and "traditional history" was "stuffed with fables," religious history was a valid form of precedence.[40] Historical time was marked following the "Mosaic account of the creation," and the distant past was only known via the Bible.[41] The "early ages of the world" were revealed by "the scripture chronology," and "antiquity" was the "quiet and rural lives of the first patriarchs" in the Old Testament.[42] His strategic objective here was to pit "profane" nationalist mythology versus "sacred" religious mythology in a manner that forced most of his audience to choose one or the other. He was not ignoring precedence, but he was discombobulating historical conventions and substituting religious history for political.

Even when history was admitted into his arguments, it was merely a temporal auxiliary to his emphasis on natural proof. For example, Paine repudiated the idea that America should remain a subordinate cluster of colonies on the basis of violations against reason, nature, and history, respectively: "It is repugnant to reason, to the universal order of things, to all examples from former ages, to suppose, that this continent can longer remain subject to any external power."[43]

Paine replaced the pristine prehistory of England and the chronological justifications for the British Constitution with an alternative configuration of authority composed of ancient religious history (past), practical expediency (present), and the interest of posterity (future). Clock time in *Common Sense* was purposefully abnormal. Though a typical eighteenth century clock marked the time as the succession of seconds, minutes, and hours, Rittenhouse's complex astronomical clock depicted time as the interlocking rhythms of the universe. When Paine wrote the Appendix to *Common Sense*, he started, "Since the publication of the first edition of this pamphlet," and then he stopped himself.

He was describing his pamphlet in the language of precedence that was typical of British political discourse. He then redirected the same sentence, continuing, "or rather, on the same day on which it came out, the king's speech made its appearance in this city."[44] Sequential order was much less important for him than momentary conjunction. Paine was demolishing historical custom, the foundation of the British constitutional system, in order to reorient his readers to an altogether different conception of time. In Paine's system, the temporal justification of *precedence* was replaced with *concurrence*.

Part Three
KAIROS

Seasonal Time and Father Abraham's Almanac

Unlike Benjamin Franklin, David Rittenhouse never published or authored any almanacs. But by the 1770s—Franklin having long since retired from his *Poor Richard's* amusements—Rittenhouse's name graced the title page of several leading American almanacs. By far the bestselling publications in the colonies, almanacs were localized miscellanies printed and sold in every town of even modest size. The most essential feature of an early modern almanac was the astrometeorological calculations figured for each particular latitude and longitude. This laborious technical task was often outsourced to a resident expert, or the publisher would acquire figures syndicated from a city of comparable latitude. John Dunlap's *Father Abraham's Almanac*, James Humphreys's *Universal Almanac*, Francis Bailey's *Lancaster Almanac*, and several other almanacs outside of Pennsylvania all advertised during the 1770s their association with Rittenhouse as a differentiating feature of their contents. As Rittenhouse's friend, John Dunlap, boasted on the title page of his *Father Abraham's Almanac*, "Our customers are requested to observe, that the ingenious David Rittenhouse, A.M. of this city, has favoured us with the astronomical calculations of our Almanac for this year, and therefore they may be most firmly relied on."[45] Rittenhouse may have been known to the colonial elite as a renowned scientist, but most Americans knew him as their weatherman.[46]

Almanacs are the most perplexing of early modern texts for historians and literary critics. Although they were, besides the Bible, the most ubiquitous textual forms circulating in the Anglo-American world, they are virtually ignored by scholars. They invite dismissal because they were so intrinsically ephemeral, and their pastiche agrarian contents are so *foreign* to our post-industrial sensibilities. But there were *reasons* why American colonists who purchased no other printed material bought an almanac every year, and, to avoid a form of revisionist arrogance, we should at least pay these publications some attention.

Almanacs had been central to American life since the early colonial period. Cotton Mather, the prolific New England Puritan minister, recorded in his own almanac in 1683 that "such an anniversary composure comes into almost as many hands, as the best of books," by which he meant the Bible. Almost a century later, almanacs were still the second most important book in every house. As historian Marion Barber Stowell put it, "The Bible took care of the hereafter, but the almanac took care of the *here*."[47]

The almanac was a repository of *useful knowledge*, containing something for every person in the family to consult freely and regularly.

Its contents functioned as a practical guidebook for vocations of every stripe, including sailors, merchants, fishermen, farmers, lawyers, teachers, clergymen, physicians, and mothers. Commonplaces of colonial American almanacs included conversion tables for currencies; tables calculating payments at six and seven percent interest; lists of provincial courts and assemblies; postal delivery schedules; lists of holidays; and travel distances along major roads. They also included a potpourri of "receipts" [recipes] and curatives for all kinds of ailments, including frost-bite, corns, constipation, toothaches, canker sores, various kinds of coughs, "consumption," colic, nose-bleeds, vomiting, and gangrene. Cures for the "staggers in horses" were mixed with recipes for making currant wine, farmyard maintenance, and the European method of dying woolen cloth blue. Poems, maxims, and short moralistic essays shared pages with gardening tips and baking techniques.

The breadth of the contents of a colonial American almanac was invariably displayed on its title page. One New Jersey almanac typical of most others contained, "The motions of the Sun and Moon; the true places and aspects of the planets; the rising and setting of the sun; the rising, setting and southing of the moon." The title page continued its detailed list of the almanac's further contents: "The lunations, conjunctions, eclipses, rising, setting and southing of the planets; length of days; judgment of the weather; festivals, and other remarkable days; high water at Burlington; Quakers' general meetings; fairs; courts; roads, &c. Together with very useful tables, chronological observations, and a variety of instructive and entertaining Matter both in Prose and Verse."[48]

Much of the material toward the end of this list was just "filler." Early Americans didn't *need* to purchase entertainment on an annual basis, though they certainly enjoyed reading the jokes and stories wedged into the white space on many of the pages. But the bulk of an almanac's text—and the means of Rittenhouse's involvement with the almanac publishing industry—they *did* consider to be worth the investment of a few pence each year. Americans purchased almanacs because they contained astronomical, meteorological, and chronological information. And this is the most problematic aspect of almanacs for historians of the period: the most popular texts in the revolutionary period were handbooks of astrology.

Though Rittenhouse practiced *astronomy*, the scientific observation of celestial objects and events, his results were used in almanacs to create a system of *astrology*, the less-than-scientific interpretation of the effects of celestial events upon human affairs. The origins of astronomy are bound up with astrology in much the same way that the modern discipline of chemistry arose out of the medieval practice of alchemy. Johannes Kepler's astronomical discoveries were propelled by his astrological beliefs, and even Isaac Newton first became interested in astronomical subjects because he wanted to test "judicial astrology," the art of forecasting future events by means of planetary and stellar motion with respect to the earth.

Every colonial almanac began with a list of upcoming eclipses (the most significant astrological events) followed immediately by an anatomical illustration connecting the Signs of the Zodiac with individual parts of the body to be used by practitioners of folk medicine. The astrological calendar that made up the bulk of an almanac's text included in a columnar table: days of the month (sometimes in "old" and "new" style); days of the week; fasts, festivals, and other remarkable days; time of the moon's "southing" (used to find high-tide and evening times); time of the moon's rising and setting; time of high-water at a particular landmark bridge or port; planets, aspects, and variations of the weather; phases and signs of the Moon; rising and setting of the Sun; increase or decrease of day-length; and accounts of "the probable Influences of some of the planetary Aspects." The five major astrological "Aspects," the relative angle between two heavenly bodies, were: conjunction (0°- 10° apart), sextile (60°), square (90°), and trine (120°), and opposition (180°). Many colonists believed that these celestial relations bore direct influence on human affairs, and they kept astrological and meteorological information with religious regularity. Writing in their journals, diaries, or almanacs (many of which included "Diary" in their titles), they recorded their observations of the weather and the stars with abbreviations and astrological glyphs.

The practice of astrology was primarily a medieval cultural holdover and would decrease in prominence as the principles of rational science, especially in the areas of agriculture and medicine, diffused through the broader populace. Almanac readers did not think of themselves as occultists; in fact, most were fervent Christians, but they required a rubric for important decisions unaddressed by the Bible. Thus meteorological astrology attempted to forecast medium and long-range weather in order to know the time to plant crops, to find the best navigational routes on the seas, and to predict harsh winter seasons that would require advance preparation. If meteorological projections promised to prevent failed crops, shipwrecks, or frostbite, then, in the absence of any alternative, following the almanacs' dictates was worth a try. Likewise, medical astrology associated various parts of the body, the course of diseases, and the efficacy of remedies with the influence of the heavens. In an era with very high infant mortality rates, frequent epidemic diseases (e.g., small pox and yellow fever), and medical doctors who routinely prescribed blood-letting with leeches, it is no surprise that common people looked to the stars and to their almanacs for guidance. These people saw their destinies as humans as part of the interwoven fabric of creation.[49] Like tiny gears in the wheelwork of the universe, their lives were connected to the same mechanisms that spun the night sky above their heads.⁵⁰

Almanacs demonstrated a fascination with space, but spatial relationships attained significance vis-à-vis temporal relationships. John Dunlap led his *Father Abraham's Almanac* for the year 1775 with the following stanza:

> With the earnest and exploring eye
> I point my tube to scan the sky:
> Sun, Moon, and Stars, I nicely view,
> And bring down all that's rare and new.⁵¹

But collecting curiosities with a telescope was not an end in itself. As the same almanac put it two years later:

> Think, O my soul, how much depends
> On the short period of a day;
> Shall Time, which Heav'n in mercy tends,
> Be negligently thrown away?⁵²

Time was at the heart of the colonial almanac; indeed the astrological data were read like an owner's manual to the clockworks of the universe. From tables of sunrises and sunsets to nifty poems about "The Equation of Time" and reminders about designated feasts and court days, almanacs were inexpensive paper clocks. Indeed, colonial Americans shoved almanacs into their pockets more readily than they did mechanized watches. Minutes and seconds were less important in colonial life than seasons, and it was in conveying seasonal time that almanacs excelled.

Open Season

A tremendously important temporal descriptor in *Common Sense* was seasonal time (*kairos*), the passage not of fixed seconds, hours, or years, but of variable moments, seasons, and ages. Seacoast American cities like Philadelphia, New York, and Boston were, in the late eighteenth century, exceptional pockets of cosmopolitanism amidst vast tracts of countryside. The urban luxuries of scientific societies, subscription libraries, bookshops, and colleges were unavailable to most American colonists. The colonies were, and would remain for decades, largely agrarian societies, and almanacs were indispensable to plantation farmers and plot gardeners alike. Paine, who grew up in rural Thetford, England, capitalized on this latent sense of seasonal time throughout *Common Sense*, and this component of its argument helped Paine to connect with audiences along wagon-grooved dirt roads as well as with his immediate neighbors along the cobblestone streets of Philadelphia.

Seasons are, by their nature, fleeting windows of distinct activity. In agrarian culture, there was always some work to be done: sowing, weeding, harvesting, clearing, plowing. Many colonial farmers, especially tobacco growers, worked their farms 365 days per year.[53] Twice in *Common Sense*, Paine used a "seed time" metaphor to discuss the pressing matter of continental union, and his audience would have recognized that a seed time lasts only a few short weeks. As Paine put it, "Youth is the seed time of good habits, as well in nations as in individuals. It might be difficult, if not impossible, to form the Continent into one government half a century hence."[54] On the other end of the planting-harvesting cycle, the inaction of the Americans threatened to let the fruit of independence rot on the vine. Paine said, "And there is no instance, in which we have shewn less judgment, than in endeavouring to describe, what we call, the ripeness or fitness of the Continent for independence."[55]

Paine's most famous deployment of seasonal time in his career came at the end of the *Rights of Man, Part the Second* (1792) in "a figure easily understood." Disputing that his political principles were "a new fangled doctrine," he described an idyllic "turn into the country" where he found the trees to have a "leafless, wintry appearance" because of "the vegetable sleep," but he anticipated the revolution of the seasons. Although the exact arrival of "the political summer" was impossible to predict, he contented himself with the easy perception "that the spring is begun."[56] In the dedication of that work to his friend, the Marquis de Lafayette, Paine said,

> The only point upon which I could ever discover that we differed was not as to principles of government, but as to time. For my own part, I think it equally as injurious to good principles to permit them to linger, as to push them on too fast. That which you suppose accomplishable in fourteen or fifteen years, I may believe practicable in a much shorter period.

Paine added, "Mankind, as it appears to me, are always ripe enough to understand their true interest, provided it be presented clearly to their understanding."[57]

In late 1775, Paine saw the ripeness of America for independence, and in *Common Sense* he was urging the people to begin gathering the harvest. Like a farmer inspecting his fields, Paine pointed to the evidence of the impending peak ripeness:

> As I have *always* considered the independency of this continent,
>   as an *event* which *sooner or later* must arrive,
> so from the *late rapid progress* of the continent *to maturity*,
>   the *event* cannot be *far off*.[58]

The seasonal window of independence had been flung wide open by the outbreak of war at Lexington and Concord. The Americans needed to act "while we have it in our power" rather than leaving events "to time and chance."[59] The Continental Army and provincial militias "at this time" had "just arrived at that pitch of strength, in which no single colony is able to support itself, and the whole, when united, can accomplish the matter, and either more or less than this might be fatal in its effects."[60] Likewise, the conditions were perfect to build an American navy which would "in time excel the whole world." Paine described a perfect storm for building a fleet, since "we never can be more capable to begin on maritime matters than now, while our timber is standing, our fisheries blocked up, and our sailors and shipwrights out of employ."[61]

Everything had changed for America, argued Paine, on April 19, 1775. The "independency of America should have been considered," he said, "as dating its era from, and published by, *the first musket that was fired against her*."[62] Paine was describing what Ralph Waldo Emerson would memorialize as the "shot heard 'round the world." This shot referred "the matter from argument to arms" and thereby struck "a new era for politics." Before that moment, the "advocates on either side of the question" agreed that they were pursuing "a union with Great-Britain," and "the only difference between the parties was the method of effecting it; the one proposing force, the other friendship." But now, said Paine, "All plans, proposals, &c. prior to the nineteenth of April, *i.e.* to the commencement of hostilities, are like the almanacs of the last year; which, though proper then, are superseded and useless now."[63] *Common Sense* was, in many ways, a functional almanac, a seasonal guidebook, for this new period.

Paine later remarked that "the disposition of the people" after Lexington and Concord, did not seem favorable "at this crisis, to heap petition upon petition." The "Olive Branch" Petition, Paine remarked, "was submissive even to a dangerous fault, because the prayer of it appealed solely to what is called the prerogative of the crown, while the matter in dispute was confessedly constitutional." The Americans miscalculated their efforts because their concept of seasonal time was askew, and they were using a backdated almanac. Paine saw evidence in "every circumstance" following April 1775 "that it was the determination of the British court to have nothing to do with America but to conquer her fully and absolutely."[64]

Facing such aggressive opposition, observed Paine in *Common Sense*, the Americans must be equally proactive in their planning and preparation. For farmers, winter was a time of vigorous activity without which the produce of the coming seasons would be hampered by hardened soil and broken tools. Paine had this agricultural metaphor in mind as he wrote a crucial passage describing the situation of America:

> The present winter is worth an age if rightly employed, but if lost or neglected, the whole continent will partake of the misfortune; and there is no punishment which that man will not deserve, be he who, or what, or where he will, that may be the means of sacrificing a season so precious and useful.[65]

Here was the culmination of seasonal time in *Common Sense*. This "precious and useful" season possessed a multiplicative effect "if rightly employed" but, "if lost or neglected," might prove to be America's undoing. Paine did not forget his temporal forecast, and he returned to this passage later in 1776 in his *American Crisis, No. 1*. Quoting the paragraph from *Common Sense* in a footnote, Paine confided, "We did not make a proper use of last winter, neither could we, while we were in a dependent state. However, the fault, if it were one, was all our own; we have none to blame but ourselves."[66] As he said in *Common Sense*, the Americans' "military ability, *at this time*" was at its peak, while experienced officers from the French and Indian War were still in a condition to provide tactical leadership. Those who hoped for America to hatch "forty or fifty years hence, instead of *now*," were foolishly inattentive to "this single position" that, by itself, "unanswerably" proved "that the present time is preferable to all others."[67]

Popular History

Because almanacs functioned as calendars and miscellanies, it is not surprising that they did traffic in history, albeit in a unique way that emphasized seasons and ages as much as days and dates. Paine's approach to time is further elucidated by comparing his references to "ancient history" in *Common Sense* to the curious historical snapshot included in a typical British almanac for the year 1776. In "A Compendious Chronology of Memorable Things since the Creation to this present Year," the London almanac, *The English Apollo*, listed only *sixteen* "memorable things" that had happened between "The Creation of the World" and the "Passion and Resurrection of Jesus Christ," or about *four* per thousand calendar years in the popular estimation.[68] Of those events listed for a period spanning four millennia, only two, the fall of Troy and the death of Alexander the Great, were extra-biblical events. Besides accounts from the biblical narrative like "Noah's Flood began" and "The Israelites' Departure out of Egypt," ancient history was veiled from the sight of common British subjects. Paine thus assumed this preponderant biblical influence on his audience's worldview as he spoke in *Common Sense* of beginning "the world over again" as in "the days of Noah," and as he referred to George III as "the hardened, sullen tempered Pharaoh of England."[69] In the London almanac, only *ten* more "memorable things" occurred in the next one thousand years between the death of Christ and the conquest of England by William, Duke of Normandy, who was to Paine nothing more than a "French bastard landing with an armed banditti" and "a very paltry rascally original."[70] Two events listed in the almanac for the first millennium AD revealed popular contempt for Catholicism and Islam: "The wicked Phocas [a Byzantine emperor] makes Pope Boniface Head of the Church," and "Mahomet [Muhammad] broaches his Imposture at Mecca." In Paine's pamphlet, monarchy was "the Popery of government," and its fabulous ancient history was nothing more than a "superstitious tale, conveniently timed, Mahomet like, to cram hereditary right down the throats of the vulgar."[71] In the almanac's popular historical timeline, other "memorable" events tended to trickle in until about 1600 AD, when page after page of "memorable things," including the births of every member of the British royal families, began to occur.[72]

Paine's approach to popular history revealed the intellectual background of his audience. He was most *explicit*, and often parenthetically explanatory, when he wrote about technical or current political events, assuming a minuscule knowledge of the names of British ministers, political tracts, and contemporary history. On the other hand, his *implicit* references to the Bible and to Aesop's *Fables* demonstrate the epistemic enthymeme—the suppressed premises and assumed knowledge—that allowed him to communicate at the level of his popular audience. Though Paine never referred overtly to Aesop's *Fables* in *Common Sense*, he assumed a familiarity with their subject matter and symbolism. Whether his readers owned a collection of the *Fables* or had just read them excerpted—as they often were—in almanacs, Paine expected his audience to "get" his allusions, as we can see in his two references to the *Fables* in the second section of *Common Sense*. Nature had disapproved of monarchy, Paine said, as evidenced by her "so frequently" turning it "into ridicule by giving mankind an *ass for a lion*."[73] In folklore, the ass was always a stupid beast of burden and the lion, a cunning, fearsome king. Paine was referencing "The Ass in the Lion's Skin," the story of an ass who roamed about the forest disguised as a lion to frighten all of the foolish animals. He tried to frighten a wise fox, who shrugged, "I might possibly have been frightened myself, if I had not heard your bray."[74] Two paragraphs later, Paine folded in another fable, "The Ass Carrying the Image," where an ass, carrying a famous wooden idol to a temple, thought the crowds were bowing their heads with respect to himself.[75] Paine declared it "needless to spend much time in exposing the folly of hereditary right, if there are any so weak as to believe it, let them promiscuously worship the ass and lion, and welcome. I shall neither copy their humility, nor disturb their devotion."[76] By conjuring up the images of the ass and the lion, Paine was also invoking the famous morals of several other ass-and-lion fables by

Aesop, such as "Might makes right," "In quarreling about the shadow we often lose the substance," "Conquer, but conquer to your cost," and "Happy is the man who learns from the misfortunes of others."[77] These timeless narratives were for many of Paine's readers a surrogate form of practical moral instruction that replaced classical or even contemporary history as a profane auxiliary to biblical instruction.

In the eighteenth century Anglo-American popular imagination, history was understood as seasonal lived experience. Because all of early modern life, especially for the rural American majority, was framed by the cycles of nature, there was a draw toward mimicking those cycles in politics. Paine advocated annual elections in *Common Sense* for this very reason, to allow politicians to revolve at the same rate as the earth progressed around the sun. The rhythmic cycles of life created a sense of opening or completion in different cultures. Paine knew this dynamic well, and he used it to predict events with curious accuracy. For example, Paine wrote to General Washington in 1782 that he thought the war would conclude soon because of "the peculiar effect which certain periods of time have, more or less, upon all men." He described the British people as accustomed "to think of seven years in a manner different to other portions of time." They acquired this belief "partly by habit, by reason, by religion, and by superstition." The war was then in its seventh year, which would have carried symbolic meaning for Britons:

> They serve seven years apprenticeship—they elect their Parliament for seven years—they punish by seven years transportation, or the duplicate or triplicate of that term—they let their leases in the same manner, and they read that Jacob served seven years for one wife, and after that seven years for another; and this particular period of time, by a variety of concurrences, has obtained an influence in their minds.

Unless, Paine quipped, Parliament could pass an act "'to bind TIME in all cases whatsoever,' or declare him a Rebel" then the British would soon grow exasperated with the fruitless war.[78]

The annual almanacs of America had this same effect on colonial minds. A year was a new beginning, and Paine wanted to publish *Common Sense* early in January to start "the new year with a new system." But 1776 wasn't just any year, as American almanacs for the year (printed at the end of 1775) attest on their title pages. There were three demarcations of time at the head of almost every American almanac that year, and these three were amalgamated in the text of *Common Sense*. First, the almanac described "the year of our Lord 1776," the religious calendar that dated time from the birth of Christ. By implicating the language of popular religious history in *Common Sense*, Paine associated American independence with this sacred marker of time.

Second, every almanac also marked "The Sixteenth Year of the Reign of King George III," the official political marker of regal time in the British dominions.[79] This denotation of temporality would be noticeably absent from the title pages of almanacs the following year. Third, each almanac applied to a "Bissextile or Leap-Year," an intercalary corrective to the discrepancy between imprecise calendrical time and actual astronomical time. In the vulgar imagination, a leap year did not signify anything predetermined, but it was an extraordinary temporal event that caused their ears to perk for something new. Paine's seasonal depiction of time held forth the opportunity for the common people to insert their corrective presence into American politics and together to take the riskiest leap of their lives.

Part Four
EPOS

Epic Time and the Norriton Observation of the Transit of Venus

As William Smith related the situation in his account of the observation of the Transit of Venus, "The great discouragement which the different Committees" of the American Philosophical Society endured at first "was the want of proper apparatus, especially good telescopes."[80] The Pennsylvania Assembly agreed to fund some of the necessary equipment, most of which was directed (for political reasons) toward the Philadelphia observatory in the State House Yard. Owen Biddle used the Library Company of Philadelphia's reflecting telescope for the Cape Henlopen observation. William Smith received word that colonial proprietor Thomas Penn was sending him from London a Gregorian reflecting telescope with a micrometer to be given to the College of Philadelphia when the observation was finished. John Lukens used a refracting telescope that Rittenhouse had assembled using "glasses" sent with Smith's telescope from England. Rittenhouse himself observed the transit using a refracting telescope with a magnifying power of about 144 times. Lukens, the surveyor-general of Pennsylvania, had obtained from the surveyor-general of New Jersey an astronomical quadrant, a device used to measure the altitude of celestial objects above the horizon. The Norriton team also utilized, according to Smith's account, "An excellent clock; a transit telescope, nicely moving in the plane of the meridian; and a very accurate equal altitude instrument, supported, in the observatory, on a stone pedestal." Each of these last three items, as well as Rittenhouse's refracting telescope and the observatory itself, were "Mr. Rittenhouse's private property, and made by himself."[81]

Rittenhouse had begun building his observatory in November 1768 but, "through various disappointments from workmen and weather," did not complete it until mid-April 1769. It was a primitive but sturdy wooden structure with an earthen floor, large windows, and openable shutters on its roof. Rittenhouse had hoped to receive an equal altitude instrument from Philadelphia, but, he reported, "Finding I could not depend on having it, I fell to work and made one, of as simple a construction as I could contrive." His poor health kept him from conducting evening observations, so he was "obliged to content myself" with taking equal altitudes of "the Sun only." On May 20, Rittenhouse installed thin perpendicular wires on the lens of his equal altitude instrument rather than the conventional scalp-plucked "crosshairs." That day he began a series of exacting daily observations with the equal altitude instrument and his "meridian or transit telescope," which he continued uninterrupted for at least a month and a half. Rittenhouse half. Rittenhouse also paid special attention to an astronomical clock that he had made for the occasion; between March and May 1769, Rittenhouse "altered" his clock several times, took it down once for cleaning, and returned it to the observatory to be "regulated anew."[82]

When Smith and Lukens arrived at Norriton on June 1, 1769, two days before the transit, they found "every preparation so forward, that we had little to do but to examine and adjust our respective telescopes to distinct vision. Mr. Rittenhouse had completed his observatory, fitted up the different instruments, and made a great number of observations, for fixing the latitude and longitude of the observatory, and ascertaining the going of his time-piece."[83] The team coordinated a methodical scheme for their observation. With the purpose that "each of us might the better exercise our own judgment, without being influenced, or thrown into any agitation or surprise by the others," they agreed to "transact every thing by signals" and in silence. John Sellers and Archibald McClean leaned out one window of the observatory to take signals from Lukens. Two members of Rittenhouse's family who "had been trained by him to services of this kind" stood in another window "to count the time, and take his signals." Smith was inside the observatory and "within the hearing of the beats of the clock," so he was "to count and set down my own time."[84]

At two o'clock, everyone moved to their stations, but "a great concourse of many of the principal inhabitants of the county" made them apprehensive that "that our scheme of silence and order might be interrupted by the impatience and curiosity natural on such occasions." Smith informed "the gentlemen, who had honoured us with their company, that the accuracy and success of our observations would depend on our not being disturbed with the least noise, till the contacts were over." During the twelve minutes between Smith's announcement and the first contact, "there could not have been a more solemn pause of expectation and silence, if each individual had stood ready to receive the sentence that was to give him life or death." Smith further described the scene,

> So regular and quiet was the whole, that, far from hearing a word spoken, I did not did not even hear the feet of the four counters, who had passed behind me from the windows to the clock; and I was surprised, when I rose up and turned to the clock, to find them all there before me, counting up their seconds to an even number; as I imagined, from the deep silence, that my associates had yet seen nothing of Venus.[85]

As Smith sat in the cool shade of the observatory scanning the edge of the sun, the only sound he heard, besides the beating of his heart, was the ticking of a clock.

Rittenhouse's telescope was set up farthest from the observatory, and laying on the ground for maximum stability, he peered through the long tube of his refracting telescope. At the moment of first contact, he gave a hand signal to his assistant, Thomas Barton, who in turn waved a handkerchief "to the counters at the window, who, walking softly to the clock, counting as they went along, noted down their times separately, agreeing to the same second."[86] Rittenhouse had signaled at the time "to the best of my judgment" when "the least impression made by Venus on the Sun's limb could be seen through my telescope," but his estimate of the time was earlier than that of his colleagues.[87]

Even though the air was "beautifully serene and quiet" and the Sun's edges "perfectly defined" and "free from any tremulous motion," the observation was not so clear-cut as they had hoped. As Smith put it, "The idea I had formed of the contact was—that Venus would instantaneously make a well-defined black and small dent or impression on the Sun." In fact, the actual "appearance was so different" that he "was held in suspense for five or six seconds"—an eternity in the calculation of the astronomical unit—"to examine whether it might not be some small skirt of a watery flying cloud." In fact, what Smith, Rittenhouse, Lukens, and every other observer of the transit saw was what is now called the "black drop effect." Smith described "the disturbance on the Sun's limb" as "so undulatory, pointed, ill-defined, waterish, and occupying a larger portion of the limb than I expected."[88] The "internal contact," or the exit of Venus from the sun's disc was no better, as Smith said, "The thread of light, coming round from both sides of the Sun's limb, did not close instantaneously, but with an uncertainty of several seconds, the points of the threads darting into each other, and parting again, in a quivering manner, several times before they finally adhered." Smith claimed to wait "for this adherence with all the attention in my power" but still differed "a few seconds" from Lukens, "who took the same method of judging."[89] The Norriton team, it turned out, was among the first to attribute this bleeding "undulatory motion" to the presence of an atmosphere on Venus, "varying the refraction of the rays" of the sun.[90]

Lenses and Mirrors

Eighteenth century telescopes were either made with refracting lenses or reflecting mirrors. Smith used a high-end reflecting telescope that was kept inside Rittenhouse's observatory to view the transit through the open shutters in the roof, while Rittenhouse and Lukens viewed the transit in the open air several feet from the observatory with more pedestrian models of refracting telescopes. A reflecting telescope works by bouncing light between an objective mirror and an angled reflecting mirror and through an eyepiece. A refracting telescope, on the other hand, bends light through a convex objective lens and a concave eyepiece lens, functioning like a high-powered magnifying glass. Because mirrors are cheaper and easier to fabricate than lenses—and therefore can be fused into larger telescopes—reflecting telescopes have generally been preferred by astronomers. Both kinds of telescopes were useful for the transit observers, and the functions of those devices, especially *reflection*, *perspective*, and *magnification*, were instrumental for Paine's argument in *Common Sense*.

Paine saw the reticence of the insecure colonists to even entertain the question of independence, and he diagnosed that their coyness stemmed from the pressure they felt to discern the precise time for independence. Paine insisted that their hand-wringing was wasted, and he handed them his pamphlet as a new ocular instrument. The text of *Common Sense* became the instrument that focused their diffuse sensory impressions into a clarified picture. As Francis Bacon had mocked the logicians a century and a half earlier, Paine handed the Americans his text as a scientific tool that merged optical precision and temporal sophistication. In his rhetorical language, he sought to heighten and focus their dulled senses to view the political system from the proper perspective.

To *reflect*, as Paine used it in *Common Sense*, was to take pause and to give something serious thought.[91] Paine in fact equated the capacity for reflection with basic human rationality, which meant to him that anyone who could think clearly could make a wise political decision.[92] Conversely, in Paine's estimation, foolish decisions were most often made by those who were unreflective.[93] Normally, we think of reflection as a purposeful examination of the past via memory, and this was certainly an element of Paine's scheme. Thus Paine's loathed trio of prejudice, custom, and habit were at their root mnemonic maladaptations blockading unhindered reflection. For Paine, though, the concept of reflection also allowed looking forward. "We ought to reflect, that there are three different ways, by which an independency may hereafter be effected; and that *one* of those *three*, will one day or other, be the fate of America."[94]

The most important precondition for accurate reflection as Paine conceived it was achieving the proper mental perspective. Reflection was the mental equivalent of visual observation, and the two were intertwined in Paine's system. The internal process of reflection, like the external process of observation, was corruptible. Paine's criticism of political expediency was based upon its perspectival perversion, because it was a myopic future orientation that could not see past its own interested motives. For Paine, genuine perspective was a view of the present in light of the distant future.

Paine had to bring faraway things nearer to his readers. He accomplished this *spatially* through affective sentiment, as we saw in Chapter Two. He cultivated an imaginative immediacy and a transporting empathy with the suffering Bostonians and startled many who "live distant from the scene of sorrow" by bringing the barbarity "to *their* doors" and making "*them* feel the precariousness with which all American property is possessed."[95] He also had to close vast *temporal* distances. He had to introduce his readers to their great, great, great grandchildren.

Paine, imagining himself as a parent, communicated the "painful" futility of "looking forward" to a "merely temporary" form of government. "As parents, we can have no joy, knowing that *this government* is not sufficiently lasting to ensure any thing which we may bequeath to posterity." Since the current generation was "running the next generation into debt," he said, "we ought to do the work of it, otherwise we use them meanly and pitifully." The colonists' children would be paying for this war, he was saying, so it would be doubly tragic to stick them with the bill *and* the unfinished task. Like a navigator surveying with his sextant the course for the ship of state, Paine advocated, "In order to discover the line of our duty rightly, we should take our children in our hand, and fix our station a few years farther into life; that eminence will present a prospect, which a few present fears and prejudices conceal from our sight."[96] The "eminence" Paine described was not *upward* spatially but *forward* temporally, and the optical instruments he urged the colonists to take in hand, through which they would see beyond the occluding horizon, were their children.

The colonists' delay, "being formed only on the plan of present convenience," was "bringing ruin upon posterity," "leaving the sword to our children, and shrinking back at a time, when, a little more, a little farther, would have rendered this continent the glory of the earth."[97] The future was an exponential expression of the present. Those who opposed "independence now" were "opening a door to eternal tyranny."[98] The Americans' immediate progeny and their distant posterity would suffer because of the present generation's inaction. Paine was tapping his audience's protective impulse and threatening the security of their honor. If the American's pursued a "fatal and unmanly" course of temporary measures, designed only to "*last my time*," then "the names of ancestors will be remembered by future generations with detestation."[99]

Paine was magnifying contemporary events to make them larger than life. He did not content himself with constructing the momentary urgency of seasonal time, but he pushed the theater of action further, creating for his reading audience a sense of Providential, prophetic-fulfillment, or, to use a term from literary theory, epic time (*epos*).[100] Paine expanded the scope of the conflict to epic proportions, playing on the colonists' self-conception as a special people chosen by God. This expansion infused the situation and, importantly, the audience, with a divinely-sanctioned power to decide the course of the future. Paine's readers were not ragamuffin soldiers bumbling into a war in which they were grossly overmatched; they were quasi-divine heroes, and upon their actions hung the fate of world civilization.

Paine used the most expansive language he could find: "We have it in our power to begin the world over again." Comparing the Americans' situation to the ancient history with which they were familiar, he said, "A situation, similar to the present, hath not happened since the days of Noah until now." Eighteenth century theologians spoke of antediluvian and postdiluvian civilizations—before and after "The Flood"—and Paine was depicting American independence in equally epochal terms. "The birthday of a new world is at hand," Paine said, "and a race of men, perhaps as numerous as all Europe contains, are to receive their portion of freedom from the event of a few months."[101] This statement was a *double-entendre*, since Paine *did* harbor the belief that the downfall of monarchy in America would infect European nations, but he was also looking to "a race of men" living in the future. Paine was awed by this "Reflection," and he urged his readers to evaluate affairs from this expansive "point of view." Looking across the generations from the Paine's promontory, "How trifling, how ridiculous, do the little, paltry cavilings of a few weak or interested men appear," especially when compared to "the business of a world."[102]

In epic time, there is no hyperbole. Little decisions in the epic present, the "least fracture now," carried overwhelming consequences in the future. As Paine put it in his first *American Crisis* at the end of 1776, "There are cases which cannot be overdone by language, and this is one."[103] The correspondence between description and experience was not violated by Paine's soaring rhetoric because the colonists felt such crushing pressure in their circumstances. The Americans knew they were not living in ordinary times, and Paine was articulating the extraordinary nature of what they perceived as an inchoate impression.

Because Paine was employing epic time, he justified the most sweeping passages in *Common Sense* as reflective of a special reality. In one significant example, Paine created an escalating taxonomy that ran parallel through geography, time, and nature. He also framed the present as the crossroads of eternity, linking the "end of time" to the "proceedings now." Toward the close of this passage, Paine even forged a hybrid epic-seasonal time that translated epic grandiosity into common experience. The scalar progressions and metrical balance of the passage become more evident when we view the text in poetic form:

> The sun never shined on a cause of greater worth.
> 'Tis not the affair of
> > a city,
> > > a county,
> > > > a province,
> > > > > or a kingdom,
> > > > > > but of a continent—
> > > > > > > of at least one eighth part of the habitable globe.
> 'Tis not the concern of
> > a day,
> > > a year,
> > > > or an age;
> > > > > posterity are virtually involved in the contest,
> > > > > > and will be more or less affected,
> > > > > > > even to the end of time,
> > by the proceedings now.
> > Now is the seed time
> > > > of continental union, faith and honor.
> > The least fracture now
> > > will be like a name engraved
> > > > with the point of a pin
> > > > > on the tender rind of a young oak;
> > > > > > the wound will enlarge with the tree,
> > > > > > > and posterity read it in full grown characters.[104]

If we look closely at Paine's poetic construction, we can identify an interactive mirror-like structure in the sounds and syntax of his prose that created an aural palindromic effect for those who heard *Common Sense* read aloud:

> > time, by the proceedings now.
> > > > > Now is the seed time

This mirrored transition fused together Paine's epic time argument and his seasonal time argument. Unless the colonies planted *now* in the seed time, their descendants would never harvest perpetual freedom. Time would amplify—for better or worse—the consequences of America's youth. Carve a full grown tree, and the inscription will retain its original size and character, but every "wound" on the "tender rind of a young oak" would be multiplied for future generations.

Benjamin Rush certainly felt empowered by a sense of epic time. Rush wrote to his wife, Julia, at the end of May 1776 that he and a handful of colleagues were working "for the salvation of this province," and confided, "It would be treason in any one of us to desert the cause at the present juncture." Rush looked forward to a time in the future of America "when freedom shall prevail without licentiousness, government without tyranny, and religion without superstition, bigotry, or enthusiasm." He exclaimed, "Oh, happy days! To have contributed even a mite to hasten or complete them is to rise above all the Caesars and Alexanders of the world."[105]

Paine likewise embraced the realization that his writing was prophetic. Observing that *Common Sense* was published in Philadelphia on the same day as the king's October speech, Paine noted in the first paragraph of his Appendix, "Had the spirit of prophecy directed the birth of this production, it could not have brought it forth, at a more seasonable juncture, or a more necessary time."[106] This perspective widened the eyes of many colonists. A writer in the *Boston Gazette* at the end of April wrote, "Had the spirit of prophecy directed the birth of a publication, it could not have fallen upon a more fortunate period than the time in which 'Common Sense' made its appearance. The minds of men are now swallowed up in attention to an object the most momentous and important that ever yet employed the deliberations of a people."[107]

The Americans may have chattered with nervousness prior to reading *Common Sense*, but the degree to which they embraced Paine's epic temporal argument influenced the stiffness of their resolve. "Providence," Paine would say in 1777, "chose this to be the time, and who dare dispute it?"[108] Because Providence had selected an American David to defeat the British Goliath, the colonists had only to step forward with confident assurance. They may have been outsized and outarmored, but by carrying the divinely-sanctioned sling of representation, Paine later noted, their "human faculties act with boldness" and acquired "a gigantic manliness."[109] In *Common Sense*, the providential justification embedded in Paine's use of epic time carried an epistemic authority, making the "*present time*" the "*true time*" for establishing independence.[110]

The Experience of Textual Time

As mentioned earlier, Paine signaled his approach to the role of time in a pithy sentence at the end of the pamphlet's first paragraph: "Time makes more converts than reason." Reason and "common sense" may have contributed to the about-face in public opinion during the period, but as Paine claimed from the outset, it was *time*—not just the external time of history, but also the time internal to the reader's experience of the text—that carried his argument. In Paine's construction, time was not merely a passive marker of the progression of events; it was a persuasive agent: it *convinced*, and it *redressed*.[111] Time governed the act of writing, "the Time needful for getting such a Performance ready for the Public being considerably past," and in the augur of reading, it activated the latent agency of language, "every line convinces, even in the moment of reading."[112] Paine's concept of temporal agency was an extension of his usage of providential epic time in *Common Sense*. In the text, time was not only the *scene* of the epic movement toward independence; it was also an *actor* in the drama.

To read—and not merely to skim—a text is to enter into its world, whether for a few moments or for a few hours. As a reader inhabits that alternate world constituted within the text, the spatial and temporal relationships of extra-textual "real life" become suspended, and the reader succumbs to an experience framed by the author. The parameters of reality are bent by the nature of particular language formations, and the hiatus of extra-textual experience is filled by the reader's participation in the text. When critics speak of a text "prefiguring" its audience, this dynamic is more than a selective circumscribing of eligible readers; also implied is the creation of a reading identity that reciprocates the pseudonymous inertia of all authorship. The identity of the author is other than the identity of the person who writes, and the identity of the reader is distinct from the identity of the person who reads.[113] Because rhetoric is largely concerned with the production of belief, a component of the action within a rhetorical text is to move the reading identity and the actual identity of an audience closer together. I may be a coward, but when I read the speech of a valiant general, *within the text* I believe myself to be brave. For rhetoric to be effective, my reading identity must escape the bounds of the text and penetrate my sense of identity outside the text. I must remember my reading identity, and the mnemonic stickiness of a text allows it to reverberate beyond the cessation of the act of reading.

Human experience is bounded by the dimensions of space and time. Likewise, any reading experience is governed by these same dimensions. When an author uses, for example, an architectural metaphor or refers the reader to a portion of the text "above" or "below", then he or she is signaling a reading experience in which *spatiality* is in the foreground. Space and time occur in every text as an amalgam, but one dimension often gains prominence while the other falls into relief. *Common Sense* strutted *temporality* as its primary experiential dimension. As it attempted to elicit the action of political judgment in the face of apathy and confusion, the pamphlet constructed a textual reality within which time was creased, skewed, and even folded back upon itself to serve the political interests of its author.

Paine did not, of course, invent the concept of temporal agency. One political antecedent to the republican usage he sometimes employed was the Machiavellian concept of fortune (or, *fortuna*). Paine recognized "the precariousness of human affairs," and he advocated action "while we have it in our power," rather than trusting "such an interesting event to time and chance."[114] Fortune, a concept English commonwealthmen culled from the writings of Florentine republicanism, construed time as an agent of political entropy. In this Machiavellian framework, time was an enemy, an irreparable crack in the foundation of a politician's fragile claim to power. According to this school of classical republican thought, the cyclical nature of time tended toward disorder, and, therefore, time was vilified as the centrifugal force against which politicians tugged to enact their agendas.[115] A politician's only hope for counteracting the fickle force of fortune was to overwhelm it with virtue. While the Machiavellian *virtù* had sometimes implied sheer luck, the meaning of virtue that carried into eighteenth century Anglo-American politics was the enactment of a benevolent public character. Paine's political thought was, obviously, much more influenced by the English concept than the Italian. He demonstrated no familiarity with Machiavelli specifically, but his citation of Dragonetti and his narrative of the populist tyrant Tomasso Aniello evince an interest in and a basic understanding of the history of Italian republicanism. Regardless of the ideological genealogy of the term, the malignant effects of fortune were, in Paine's view, a symptom of passivity. Virtuous political activity could stave off these effects, especially if applied at the right moment and location. Paine was preoccupied in *Common Sense* with helping his audience to discern this right moment, and his "timely and well-intended hints" were tracking the trajectories of both fortune and virtue.[116]

Paine believed that there was a fleeting moment of agency that, if missed or refused, would cede to passivity, and he believed that time was *now*. He placed this dynamic in the context of national history:

> The present time, likewise, is that peculiar time which never happens to a nation but once, viz. the time of forming itself into a government. Most nations have let slip the opportunity, and by that means have been compelled to receive laws from their conquerors, instead of making laws for themselves.[117]

Though Paine was the first to characterize the spring of 1776 in such terms, he was joined by a chorus of voices within a few months. The written correspondence of pro-independence delegates in the Continental Congress, for instance, during the spring of 1776, demonstrated an affinity for the following poignant lines from William Shakespeare's *Julius Caesar* (1623):

> There is a tide
> in the affairs of men,
> Which, taken at the flood, leads on to fortune;
> Omitted, all the voyage of their life
> Is bound in shallows and in miseries.[118]

After quoting these lines, Richard Henry Lee urged Patrick Henry in April to join him in "leading our countrymen to embrace the present flowing tide."[119] Jonathon Dickinson Sergeant wrote from Princeton in April to John Adams, "There is a Tide in Human things & I fear if we miss the present Occasion we may have it turn upon us."[120] Adams, who had observed upon his return to Philadelphia in February a striking change in "the Tide of Political Sentiment," wrote that spring to William Heath, then a Brigadier General in the Continental Army stationed in New York, "It is now perhaps the most critical Moment that America ever saw. There is a Tide in the affairs of Men—and Consequences of infinite Moment depend upon the Colonies assuming Government at this Time."[121]

Many essays published in the colonial press during those heady days carried a similar temporal tone. "A Friend to Posterity and Mankind," for example, wrote in the *Pennsylvania Packet* during February 1776 of the seriousness of the debate over reconciliation and independence, "Do not trifle on this occasion, all your other legacies must derive their true value from the part you now take in this contest." This pro-independence writer warned against mischievous schemes of accommodation, "Swallow the bait and you are undone forever."[122]

In the fall of 1775, when no one in America dared mutter a word about independence, Paine had the audacity to write in *Common Sense* that "all men allow the measure." He had declared independence to be a self-evident proposition and, thus, a consensual premise before anyone had really discussed it as a practical course of action. Many colonists had, of course, talked about independence behind closed doors as an *idea*, but even the idea did not garner unanimous assent. Paine did not need, he thought, to investigate the opinions of "all men" on the subject, because his "natural" logic had led him to what he considered to be an irrefutable conclusion. What Paine saw was a general tendency among the colonists to affirm the eventual independence of America as a philosophical idea, but a reluctance to approach the topic as a viable political decision.

He understood that the evasive prudence of colonial politicians masked an underlying fear of an uncertain future. The "Moderate" proponents of reconciliation during the spring of 1776 repeated again and again that the colonies needed to *wait* for commissioners to arrive from Britain before they made a rash decision for independence. If the colonies would *wait* a little longer, the Moderates said in a thousand different ways, then they would be able to ascertain Britain's intentions. In truth, they were displaying a common human tendency to forestall a difficult decision until every easier option has been exhausted. The Moderates required more data, more information, more communication, and, ultimately, *more time* to allay their fears. Paine realized that there would *always* be more intelligence to gather, and that certainty in politics was an idealistic mirage and a volitional excuse. Moreover, the British government, he argued, was stringing the colonies along, because they knew that a disunited America would be easily conquered. The people and politicians of colonial America were frozen by fear, and their collective window of opportunity was already beginning to close.

Paine identified the fears that stifled American political action, and he attempted to address any legitimate concerns. But his chief method of addressing fear was in his construction of time. Paine endeavored, on behalf of the anxious Americans, "to find out the *very time*" when an independence should be declared. He continued, "But we need not go far, the inquiry ceases at once, for the *time hath found us*."[123] Paine was crafting for his readers an agential understanding of time that metonymically represented the working of Providence. By imbuing time with a sense of providential agency, Paine was channeling that agency to his readers. This is a crucial dynamic in *Common Sense*: the text was empowering readers, especially those on the margins of politics, with an agency they had never possessed. The American colonists had been, as it were, hand-picked to stand at the crossroads of world history. This rhetorical move had profound practical consequences. If the colonists—even those of a low station—believed Paine, as surely many did, they must have swelled with courage at this tremendously empowering chiasmus: they thought they were finding the right time to act, but instead "the time hath found us." Paine's readers were not bound by the conventions of normal human experience; they were fundamentally special, selected by *Time* for an uncommon task. The Americans could not fail, and they need not fear, because their own inadequacies and uncertainties had been eclipsed by the alignment of events and time.

PART FIVE
KRISIS

Crisis Time and the Rittenhouse Orrery

David Rittenhouse, as mentioned earlier in this chapter, did not invent the orrery. The original design of a modern orrery was executed around 1704 by George Graham, who turned to instrument maker John Rowley of London to construct a working prototype. Rowley showed the device to his patron, Charles Boyle, fourth Earl of Orrery in Ireland, who commissioned a copy. When Richard Steele trumpeted in his periodical *The Englishman* that Rowley, "that worthy and ingenious Artificer," had called "his Machine the Orrery, in Gratitude to the Nobleman of that Title; for whose Use and by whose Generosity and Encouragement he began and accomplished the Undertaking," the name stuck. Steele described this "Orrery" as "a Machine which illustrates, I may say demonstrates, a System of Astronomy, as far as it relates to the Motions of the Sun, Moon, and Earth, to the meanest Capacity." Steele tried to describe this machine for his audience: "It is like receiving a new Sense, to admit into one's Imagination all that this Invention presents to it with so much Quickness and Ease. It administers the Pleasure of Science to any one." Although this original model was crude and inaccurate, Steele thought it so stunning that any "Family of Distinction" ought "to have an *Orrery* as necessary as they would have a Clock."[124]

Orreries became the trademark instruments of the Newtonian popularizers in London, like James Ferguson and Benjamin Martin, both of whom designed, built, and sold multiple orreries. The orrery allowed these popular lecturers to demonstrate rather than merely to explain the concepts of astronomy. The orrery enabled the dissemination of Newtonian natural philosophy by making a heliocentric, gravity-bound solar system seem intuitive. Though planetary reproductions like globes and orreries illustrate principles we now find commonplace, in the eighteenth century they were fantastic and new. Watching the earth turn on its axis, and watching the planets orbit the sun was, in every sense of the word, a *revolutionary* experience.

In America, Harvard College received an English-made orrery in 1732 to use in its natural philosophy courses, and Thomas Clap, President of Yale College, built the first American-made orrery out of wood in 1743.[125] Orreries remained a novelty in America for most of the eighteenth century. Fabricated by London instrument-makers like Benjamin Martin and imported to American colleges accompanied by English textbooks, orreries were imported classroom demonstration equipment, heuristic tabletop curiosities that illustrated only general astronomical concepts. The young David Rittenhouse, however, saw potential for the orrery beyond this role as an astronomical visual aid; he imagined the orrery as the most advanced clock ever made.

At the beginning of 1767, Rittenhouse began planning to construct an orrery of his own design. Dissatisfied in particular with the design of Martin's orrery, Rittenhouse hoped to make "my Orrery really useful, by making it capable of informing us, truly, of the astronomical phenomena for any particular point of time; which, I do not find that any Orrery yet made, can do."[126] The orreries that were becoming ubiquitous in London were constructed as pedagogical devices, so their imprecision was easily overlooked by novice audiences. Rittenhouse saw the opportunity for the orrery to become a research tool, in which case it would require the utmost precision. By March 1767, Rittenhouse's design was starting to come together. He would put the machine in motion by turning a single crank, and the orrery's indexes would display the hour of the day, the day of the month, and the year, while, at the same time, demonstrating "that situation of the heavenly bodies which is then represented." By simply turning the crank in one direction or another, Rittenhouse's orrery would represent the locations of astronomical objects "for a period of 5000 years, either forward or backward." Over ten millennia, Rittenhouse's design promised unwavering accuracy. "It must be understood," he wrote, "that all these motions are to correspond exactly, with the celestial motions; and not to differ several degrees from the truth, in a few revolutions, as is common in Orreries."[127]

Rittenhouse made good progress on the orrery in 1767 and 1768, and in the spring of 1768, William Smith communicated a description of the orrery to the American Philosophical Society, which in turn had a description published in the *Pennsylvania Gazette*.[128] Rittenhouse's progress on the machine halted in 1769 as he became preoccupied with observations of the Transit of Venus in June and of the Transit of Mercury in November, along with overseeing a survey that clarified the boundary between New Jersey and New York.

Though 1769 was a hiatus in Rittenhouse's progress on the orrery, as he reflected on his experience with the Transit of Venus, he became motivated to finish the machine in 1770. Astronomy, "the most sublime of human Sciences" had "at length arrived to a great degree of perfection." Yet it was still "not complete," and many "yet unthought-of discoveries" required better "accuracy of our Astronomical Instruments" or a long series of "good Observations." In 1771 Rittenhouse described his orrery's function as an instrument of accurate observation:

> It is well known that there are certain times particularly advantageous for making such Observations as may serve to ascertain such parts of Astronomy as still remain doubtful. The new Orrery lately erected in this City, is designedly adapted to save the laborious task of calculating

those times, for by an Easy Motion of the hand, it will in the space of a few Minutes, point out the times of all remarkable phenomena of the Heavenly Bodies for years to come.[129]

The "new Orrery lately erected" in Philadelphia was actually Rittenhouse's *second* orrery. William Smith had assumed that Rittenhouse would offer his orrery first to the College of Philadelphia, but while Smith was on a voyage to London, John Witherspoon of the College of New Jersey had offered Rittenhouse 300 pounds for his machine. Smith returned to Philadelphia a month later, and as he relayed it to Thomas Barton, "I never met with greater mortification, than to find Mr. Rittenhouse had, in my absence, made a sort of agreement to let his Orrery go to the Jersey College." Smith and his Philadelphia associates "regretted" that Rittenhouse's "noble invention" would remain in the secluded "village" of Princeton. Smith told Barton, in an effort to save face, "As I love Mr. Rittenhouse, and would not give a man of such delicate feelings a moment's uneasiness, I agreed to waive the honour of having the first Orrery, and to take the second."[130] Rittenhouse, writing about the same time to Barton, was less concerned, "I am to begin another immediately, and finish it expeditiously, for the College of Philadelphia. This I am not sorry for; since the making of a second will be but an amusement, compared with the first: And who knows, but that the rest of the colonies may catch the contagion."[131]

Space and Time Machine

To understand the significance of Rittenhouse's orreries in eighteenth-century American culture, it may be helpful first to relate an eye-witness account of the machine from a nonscientific perspective. Oliver Wolcott of Connecticut paused from his busy schedule in the Continental Congress during the spring of 1776 to write a lengthy letter to his wife, Laura, describing the city of Philadelphia. He related his observations of the city's geography, architecture, and culture. Though he had seen "Many Things here which discover great Ingenuity and Design," said Wolcott, "Nothing Struck my Mind in any Degree like the Amazing Orrery of Mr. Rittenhouse" on display at the College of Philadelphia. The Connecticut delegate was "but little acquainted with astronomy or Mechanism," and, therefore, "could only View it with the strange Wonder of a Barbarian for such I could only consider myself when compared to such a Matchless Genius." Wolcott described the orrery for his wife, "The whole Solar System is here represented, the comparative Distances and Magnitude of every Planet and their Satellites, and all their true Motions made by turning a small crank in the manner a Man turns a Grind stone, each turn Makes a day." The "outer Circle" on the face of the orrery, marked with the Signs of the

Zodiac, made a complete revolution "once in Twenty five Thousand years," and this mechanism "moves so inconceivably Slow as to require Nine Million one hundred Twenty five Thousand Turns" of the crank "to bring this Circle once round." Rittenhouses's orrery, said Wolcott, "has a Vast Number of Wheels and an Infinity of Indentations and Teeth and is capable of representing the Exact Position of every Moon and Planet at any Period for eighteen hundred years forward." The complexity of the invention made Wolcott's head spin. "How Such a Complicated tho't could ever enter into, or be retained by a human Soul, and if retained how Such an Amazing Design could ever be executed, infinitely exceeds all my Comprehension." Wolcott thought the work "calculated to Make an ordinary Genius humble, while it leads [us] to adore that fountain of Wisdom that has darted such a bright Ray of himself upon any human Soul." Wolcott saw Rittenhouse and "Viewed him with great Curiosity" looking for some "Mark of Genius Stamped upon him" but found him "extremely Modest and rather what We call Shamefaced." Regardless, said Wolcott, Rittenhouse "has erected a Monument which will be admired while learning lasts, or Man is capable of adoring the Creator."[132]

Upon seeing Rittenhouse's first orrery during a tour of the College of New Jersey, John Adams called it "a most beautiful Machine," and noted, "It exhibits almost every Motion in the astronomical World."[133] Thomas Paine, who in London "had made myself master of the use of the globes and of the orrery, and conceived an idea of the infinity of space, and the eternal divisibility of matter," explained the concept of an orrery thus:

> It is a machinery of clock-work, representing the universe in miniature, and in which the revolution of the earth round itself and round the sun, the revolution of the moon round the earth, the revolution of the planets round the sun, their relative distances from the sun, as the center of the whole system, their relative distances from each other and their different magnitudes, are represented as they really exist in what we call the heavens.[134]

The idea that a "machinery of clock-work" could *represent* "the universe in miniature" was significant of its own accord, but this Enlightenment aspiration was characteristic of any orrery. The key phrase in Paine's description was "represented as they really exist," and it was in this respect that Rittenhouse's orreries excelled every other design.

Rittenhouse's orreries were built upright, like a triple-wide tall-case clock, which allowed the machine "to be adapted to and kept in motion by a strong pendulum clock." Since the regular swing of a pendulum is the result of its length and the force of gravity, Rittenhouse's orrery was powered by the very forces that it described. The brass and ivory balls on the face of the orrery, representing the planets, moved "in elliptical orbits, having the central ball," representing the sun, "in one focus." The orbital motions of the planets were "sometimes swifter, and sometimes slower, as nearly according to the true law of an equable description of areas as is possible without too great a complication of wheel-work."[135] The "advantage" which this design had over "common Orreries," said Rittenhouse, was owed "to the exact proportion which has been preserved in the Motions and disposition of its parts, & which it is very difficult to preserve. For the velocities and distances of the planets are so disproportioned and incommensurable to each other, than it is not easy to represent any two of them with tolerable accuracy by wheel-work." Rittenhouse saw the accuracy of his orreries as an aid for those who wanted to use them to teach "young beginners in Astronomy." Because it conveyed "a true idea of the relative distances of several parts of the Solar System" as well as "the various inclinations of the planes of the planets' Orbits, which cannot be well explained by lines drawn on paper, and which are falsely represented by common Orreries," he hoped his design would "facilitate the Study of Astronomy" by "removing some of the greatest difficulties."[136]

Though Rittenhouse advertised the educational purposes of the orrery, his personal interest lay in the research aspects of the device. Besides a circle representing the Zodiac, Rittenhouse's design discarded simplistic circles and used only the more accurate ellipse. Rittenhouse wrote,

> I did not design a machine which should give the ignorant in astronomy a just view of the Solar System: but would rather astonish the skilful and curious examiner, by a most accurate correspondence between the situations and motions of our little representatives of the heavenly bodies, and the situations and motions of those bodies, themselves.[137]

When William Smith ordered a second orrery from Rittenhouse, he raised the money by having groups of about ten persons pay five pounds each to hear Rittenhouse lecture using the first orrery (not yet delivered to Princeton). Rittenhouse described the over-twenty such lectures he gave as a "drudgery" that was partly soothed by "the satisfaction" his students "universally express."[138] Rittenhouse was a researcher, an experimenter, and an engineer, not a lecturer or teacher—although he would be often thrust into the role of professor because of his scientific excellence. What Rittenhouse found interesting about the orrery— besides the immense mathematical and engineering challenge it presented—was its function as an instrument of observation. No other device in the world at the time depicted the relationship between space and time with such accuracy. And Rittenhouse's design was not limited in its description to the present. Though Rittenhouse's orreries functioned normally by the motion of a "strong pendulum clock," the winch that initiated its motion could likewise be turned "at liberty" and "adjusted to any time, past or future."[139]

Textual Orrery

As we saw in Chapter Four, Thomas Paine's worldview had been deeply influenced by the scientific cultures of London and then Philadelphia. The principles of Enlightenment natural philosophy were for him a universal template that applied equally well to political bodies as to celestial bodies. Paine thus conceived of *Common Sense* as a largely scientific text that sought to recalibrate its readers' perspective on the *system* of Anglo-American politics in much the same way that Nicolaus Copernicus had challenged the ancient Ptolemaic theory. Following the Copernican Revolution, Francis Bacon, Isaac Newton, and scores of other philosopher-scientists assembled a coherent system that described and predicted the behaviors of the universe with unprecedented accuracy. Once Newton had discovered the law of universal attraction, or gravity, the motions of the universal system became explainable. Rittenhouse's orreries attempted to recreate the experience of universal gravity by depicting the ellipses and eclipses of the solar system. Planetary orbits are elliptical and vary in their speeds because of the effective pull of gravity, and ecliptic phenomena occur as those orbital paths intersect from a given vantage point. The fact that Rittenhouse mimicked these natural occurrences in wheelwork was an illustrious achievement in the eighteenth century. Rittenhouse's machine "did the math" for its users, who could predict astronomical occurrences with the simple turn of a crank. Rittenhouse's orrery design unlocked the shackles of time, allowing astronomers to experience virtual astronomical events in the distant past or future. Thus the design breakthrough of Rittenhouse's orrery was not merely in its precise replication of space, but in its manufacturing of the interconnected effects of time.

What Rittenhouse had accomplished in mechanical form, Paine knew he must enact in textual form for *Common Sense* to generate political effect. In 1777, in his *American Crisis, No. 2*, Paine addressed Lord Howe, who had "published a proclamation," while Paine had "published a *Crisis*." Paine described the two texts in the language of mathematical astronomy,

> As they stand, they are the antipodes of each other; both cannot rise at once, and one of them must descend; and so quick is the revolution of things, that your lordship's performance, I see, has already fallen many degrees from its first place, and is now just visible on the edge of the political horizon.[140]

At the close of the War of Independence, Paine looked back on America's uniquely aligned situation "on the theatre of the universe" in 1776, a position that amounted after independence to "a new creation entrusted to our hands." In his *American Crisis, No. 13*, the last of the series, Paine saw the union, first of the colonies, and then of the states, as "the great hinge on which the whole machine" of the Revolution turned. Returning to a major theme of *Common Sense*, Paine wrote of America, "The world is in her hands." He continued, "The struggle is over, which must one day have happened, and, perhaps, never could have happened at a better time." This last phrase triggered Paine's memory, and he inserted a footnote that demonstrates the coherence of his political thought during the American Revolution. "While I was writing this note," said Paine, "I cast my eye on the pamphlet, *Common Sense*, from which I shall make an extract, as it exactly applies to the case."[141] He then proceeded to quote at length from the beginning of the fourth part of his 1776 pamphlet, a passage already touched upon in this chapter but meriting a full quotation, because it contained the crux of *Common Sense*'s argument:

> I have never met with a man, either in England or America, who hath not confessed his opinion, that a separation between the countries, would take place one time or other: And there is no instance, in which we have shewn less judgment, than in endeavouring to describe, what we call, the ripeness or fitness of the Continent for independence. As all men allow the measure, and vary only in their opinion of the time, let us, in order to remove mistakes, take a general survey of things and endeavour, if possible, to find out the *very* time. But we need not go far, the inquiry ceases at once, for, *the time hath found us*. The general concurrence, the glorious union of all things prove the fact.[142]

Here was Paine's textual orrery, his instrument for accurate observation of events in the political system. As Paine's most recent biographer, John Keane, has noted, "No account of the extraordinary impact of *Common Sense* should... neglect its original attempt to transform its readers' sense of time."[143] Of the four major modes of temporality discussed in this chapter, crisis time (*krisis*) was the most important contributor to *Common Sense*'s unprecedented success. In many respects, Paine's deployment of crisis time in the pamphlet subsumed the other three modes of temporality, as Rittenhouse's orrery was the pinnacle of all his other innovations.

Again like Rittenhouse, Paine did not *invent* the concept of crisis, but he perfected its use in political discourse.[144] Paine's concept of a "concurrence" or a "union of all things" was related on a popular level to the early modern astrological-medical idea of a "crisis," the notion that all natural events, from planetary alignment to physical health, were infused with meaning by their connection. Thus, an infirm, like

Paine upon his arrival in America, reached a "crisis" at the precise point in his or her illness when the course of recovery or death was determined, often by phenomena external to the immediate medical situation. This was, once again, the popular language of the almanac at work in Paine's argument, but it took seasonal time a step further and infused it with a sense of judgment.

Paine had certainly read *The Crisis*, a London serial from 1774-75 that was widely republished in the colonies and was likely the titular inspiration for his own series of papers, *The American Crisis*. In the introductory number to *The [London] Crisis*, the anonymous author addressed his "Friends and Fellow Subjects" in both England and America at "this great, this important crisis," a "crisis big with the fate of the most glorious empire known in the records of time." The author created a stark binary for his transatlantic audience, "by your firmness and resolution you may preserve to yourselves, your immediate offspring, and latest posterity, all the glorious blessings of freedom given by Heaven to undeserving mortals," but "by your supineness and pusillanimity, you will entail on yourselves, your children, and millions yet unborn, misery and slavery."[145] Samuel Johnson's *Dictionary* (1776), a useful conservative counterpoint, included two definitions for *Crisis, n.s.* The first was "The point in which the disease kills, or changes to the better; the decisive moment when sentence is passed." The second definition, arising out of the first, was "The point of time at which any affair comes to the height."[146] Johnson's own royalist propaganda piece on the American controversy, *Taxation no Tyranny* (1774), was itself an archetypal anticrisis text, attempting to defuse the heightening situation by substituting methodical denotations for emotive connotations and, thereby, hosing down inflammatory discourse.

Rittenhouse's orrery was designed as an integrated mechanism for demonstrating the concurrence of celestial bodies with such ease that someone untrained in mathematics could, by the turn of a single crank, estimate the motions of the universal system with astonishing precision even into the distant past or future. *Common Sense* aspired to the same utility. By connecting multiple modes of temporality within the same textual mechanism, Paine was trying to create a model political system, accessible even to those with no historical or political knowledge, in the interlocking wheelworks of the reading experience. He was demonstrating, by turning the crank of temporality backward into the past and forward into the future, that the most perfect concurrence of political events favoring independence was the present moment.

Declaring Crisis

Through his complex construction of time within his audience's experience of reading or listening to the pamphlet, Paine had created a sense of crisis in the minds of colonial Americans. To take such a precarious step as declaring independence, it took Paine's roundhouse argument and unreserved manipulation of time to shake the Americans from their polite deference and misplaced reverence. The temporal language of Paine's *Common Sense* initiated the separation from Britain in 1776, a decisive separation that occurred first in the minds of his American readers.

A crisis may be rooted in external realities, but it is not itself a tangible event. It only exists as an internal interpretive experience, whether it is a crossroads of private or public import. A person separated from an experience by apathy or distance of any kind is impervious to crisis. The ambulance speeding toward a hospital with the victim of an automobile accident is responding to an *emergency*, but as a disconnected bystander, my life will return to normal very shortly, and I did not experience the event as a *crisis*. If that same ambulance contains a friend or family member clinging to life, then the emergency is infused with deeper meaning and becomes for me a crisis. The archetypal crisis of our time, 9/11, was only a crisis insofar as we experienced it as a meaningful event. To an Eskimo in northern Greenland, news of the event would have held only marginal significance. Two tall buildings collapsed and many people died: a solemn and sad event, yes, but not a crisis. For an American, and especially for a resident of New York or Washington, DC, the event was of infinitely greater significance. It was an attack on the United States, a surreal experience of heroism and tragedy, an irreplaceable loss of loved ones, and dozens of other interpretive meanings that were heightened by the degree of experiential proximity to the event. Returning to the eighteenth century, *Common Sense* instantiated, in textual form, a defining crisis for the American colonists in early 1776. A crisis was, for Paine's readers as it has become in a demystified sense today, an urgent moment of decision, steeped in meaning, pregnant with consequences for the future, and involving the foreclosure of the *status quo*.

Every syllable of *Common Sense* was geared toward crafting *an urgent moment of decision* between reconciliation and independence. Creating such a moment is a fundamental skill of democratic governance. Writing in the context of the late Athenian democracy, Aristotle had identified *krisis*, or political judgment, as the end goal of rhetorical practice.[147] When a public or deliberative body is called upon to make a decision, myriad factors work to forestall and complicate the process. The difficulty of achieving consensus or majority, the crystallization of infinite variables and alternative courses into a small set (most often two) of actionable options, finding a balance between curt and interminable debate, and several other complexities of public discourse stifle the decision-making process. The proliferation of endless possibilities fuels an endemic collective apathy and indecisiveness. One of rhetoric's most basic functions, then, is to initiate situational or periodic remissions of societal paralysis that sustain themselves long enough to facilitate collective decisions on particular questions. The most common method for achieving collective political judgment within the art of rhetoric has been the creation of a sense of urgency in the minds of audiences. If no decision is required immediately, then few tools of persuasion are sufficient to overcome the complex obstacles constipating collective decisiveness.

Common Sense thus focused on winnowing a host of possible options into a hardened binary of mutually exclusive, actionable, immediate courses of action: reconciliation or independence. Paine collapsed former categorical enemies—loyalist Tories and moderate Whigs—into the same pro-reconciliation ideological camp, and he resurveyed the boundaries of Whig politics to include only pro-independence Whigs. The choice as Paine demarcated it in *Common Sense* was between Whig-independence and Tory-reconciliation, and he demanded nothing short of immediate and wholehearted assent. Those who favored *independence later* instead of *independence now* were branded as saboteurs who failed to recognize the special opportunity of the immediate present. *The time for independence is now*, Paine was saying, in every way he could contrive to present his case. These three words, *Time* (used 74 times), *Independence* (used 37 times), and *Now* (used 41 times) dominated his argument.[148] The Americans must decide *immediately* whether they would choose reconciliation or independence. "And if something is not done in time," Paine warned, "it will be too late to do anything, and we shall fall into a state in which neither *Reconciliation* nor *Independence* will be practicable."[149] He was replacing an infinity of cloned *seconds* with a single unique *moment*. If one time is no different from the next, then in "our present state we may quarrel on forever," a suspicion Paine held as the objective of some Anglophile moderates.[150] He argued that America alone possessed the power of victory or defeat within temporal constraints: "It is not in the power of Britain or of Europe to conquer America, if she does not conquer herself by *delay* and *timidity*.[151] Drowsiness and passivity—sins of omission—amounted to culpability during the crisis period. Paine pointed to men with "passive tempers" whose "fatal and unmanly slumbers" and "idle and visionary" plans of reconciliation were no more than "a fallacious dream" manifesting the "heart of a coward and the spirit of a sycophant."[152] Because independence would happen at "one time or other," and because "the longer it is delayed, the harder it will be to accomplish," the "independence of this country on Britain or any other" was "now the main and only object worthy of contention, and which, like all other truths discovered by necessity, will appear clearer and stronger every day."[153] England's hubris and America's paralysis were to Paine the height of futility: "England is, at this time, proudly coveting what would do her no good, were she to accomplish it; and the Continent hesitating on a matter, which will be her final ruin if neglected."[154] The "present favorable and inviting period" was, in fact, so unique, said Paine, that "We ought not now to be debating whether we shall be independent or not, but, anxious to accomplish it on a firm, secure, and honorable basis, and uneasy rather that it is not yet begun upon. Every day convinces us of its necessity."[155]

As we have seen in our discussion of epic time, the decision for independence was both *steeped in meaning* and *pregnant with consequences for the future*. The Americans were fighting a war of vital necessity and lasting significance, and the objective of their sacrifice should "bear some just proportion to the expence."[156] If "the whole continent must take up arms, if every man must be a soldier," only to precipitate a change in the "contemptible ministry" or "the repeal of the acts," then the Americans were pitiable fools. Only "the independency of this continent" was adequate compensation for the colonists' payment in blood.[157] World civilization threatened to crumble, argued Paine, if America did not embrace "freedom," a "fugitive" that had "been hunted round the globe." Paine called America to oppose tyranny and tyrants, oppression and oppressors, and to "prepare in time an asylum for mankind."[158] Likewise religious freedom, required as the culmination of the Protestant Reformation, would be choked out without America's nurturing protection.[159]

Future generations would, likewise, either bless or curse the American colonists depending upon their choice for independence or reconciliation. Paine asked each reader "to generously enlarge his views beyond the present day," for by doing so the Americans would stop "using posterity with the utmost cruelty" by "leaving them the great work to do, and a debt upon their backs, from which, they derive no advantage." [160] When the matter was referred "from argument to arms," the terms of engagement changed. Paine saw the conflict dragging on in perpetuity unless the Americans made a decisive stand. He said, "Wherefore, since nothing but blows will do, for God's sake, let us come to a final separation, and not leave the next generation to be cutting throats, under the violated unmeaning names of parent and child."[161] The "present union" of the American colonies was an "intimacy" that had been "contracted in infancy" and a "friendship" that had been "formed in misfortune." These "characters" were "of all others, the most lasting and unalterable." The colonies were "young" and had been "distressed," but their "concord hath withstood our troubles, and fixes a memorable era for posterity to glory in."[162] Other nations had "let slip the opportunity" of first forming "the articles or charter of government" and then delegating the execution of that government, but instead had settled for governments foisted upon them by conquerors. The Americans, Paine said, should "lay hold of the present opportunity—*To begin government at the right end.*"[163] By keeping future consequences always before his readers, Paine was replacing the historical justification for government with a progenerative rationale.

A final element of Paine's crisis argument was *the foreclosure of the status quo*. The strongest arguments in favor of reconciliation involved the ostensibly straightforward request to return the colonies to the flourishing state of past affairs they remembered with fondness and yearning. After the close of the French and Indian War in 1763, an indebted British government began to seek recompense through a series of taxes and duties on goods consumed in America. If those taxes and the related encroachment of the parliament would be rescinded, argued the pro-reconciliation moderates, then the colonies would gladly drop their weapons and return to life as normal. Paine identified this position as problematic on temporal grounds, because the moderates' definition of normal was obsolete, and, fundamentally, anachronistic. "Put us, say some, on the footing we were in sixty-three: To which I answer, the request is not *now* in the power of Britain to comply with," asserted Paine.

> To be on the footing of sixty-three, it is not sufficient, that the laws only be put on the same state, but, that our circumstances, likewise, be put on the same state; Our burnt and destroyed towns repaired or built up, our private losses made good, our public debts (contracted for defence) discharged; otherwise, we shall be millions worse than we were at that enviable period. Such a request, had it been complied with a year ago, would have won the heart and soul of the Continent—but now it is too late, "The Rubicon is passed."[164]

When the Roman general, Julius Caesar, crossed the Rubicon with his army, he had passed a line of symbolic and political significance demonstrating his intention of establishing himself as absolute emperor over Rome. King George III, by authorizing the British Army to fire upon his own loyal subjects, signaled in Paine's mind a Caesarian thirst for total conquest and subjugation. Paine thus described the outbreak of war at Lexington and Concord as a similar symbolic "point of no return," irrecoverable because of the forward march of time. "Ye that tell us of harmony and reconciliation, can ye restore to us the time that is past? Can ye give to prostitution its former innocence? Neither can ye reconcile Britain and America."[165] Legal restoration may have been feasible, but circumstantial restoration would require turning back the clock on the conflict. Rewinding time was a practical impossibility, but

Paine did turn the crank of his textual orrery forward and backward to demonstrate that an independent future held more promise than a dependent past. By burning the bridge back to 1763, Paine was, in fact, giving his audience only one directional option: forward into nationhood.

Part Six
THE TIME IS NOW

No Time Like the Present

How did *Common Sense* influence the trajectory of independence? Paine himself admitted that the Americans would have declared independence eventually; in fact, he declared a consensus on the issue: he had "never met with a man" in either England or America who would not admit that "a separation between the countries would take place one time or other."[166] Beginning in 1774, Americans and Britons used the words "separation" or "independence" with regularity, but they discussed the subject only as an idea or a general tendency. The British government suspected the Americans of harboring thoughts of independency, and the Americans repeated time and again that their intent was self-protection, not self-government. The greater the American military resistance, the more vehemently the British accused the colonists of aiming at independence. The Americans were so frustrated at this misinterpretation of events that they hushed any mention of the subject in public discourse to prove unequivocally that they wanted to reconcile.

Insofar as Americans mentioned the word "independence" in late 1775 or early 1776, they concerned themselves with the *rightness* or *wrongness* of declaring independence. General Nathaniel Greene and John Adams both made a case for independence in the fall of 1775, the former in a private letter and the latter in the cloistered deliberations of the Continental Congress. Paine catapulted this nascent debate, taking the rightness of independence for granted. The general progression of Paine's argument reveals the essential point of *Common Sense*. The first and second parts of *Common Sense* are a treatise on separation; the third, on the propriety of independence; the fourth part and the Appendix are chiefly arguments about the correct time to declare independence. The earlier sections are instrumental to the latter, and Paine reiterated this primacy by devoting his entire Appendix, published one month after the pamphlet's initial appearance, to the same subject—the timing of independence—as its original conclusion. The flow of his arguments and the construction of his language make it clear: time is at the heart of *Common Sense* from the first page to the last. Paine did not compose *Common Sense* as an answer to the question of *whether* America should declare independence, but rather to answer *when* America should declare independence.

When was the right time? In one passage, Paine said he believed that the colonies should have declared independence in the early fall of 1775, around the time he began writing the pamphlet. In another passage, he said that America should have become independent the day the news arrived of the Battle at Lexington and Concord, around the time he claims to have become convinced of the necessity of independence.[167] Paine was projecting onto the general population of America his own experience of achieving *sentimental* independence from Britain. Both of the points in time that Paine proposed as ideal for a declaration of independence shared the same practical discrepancy: they had already expired. The ideal time, he seemed to be arguing, had already come and gone. Since the ideal time was foregone and irretrievable, most of Paine's argument toward the end of *Common Sense* was devoted to finding the best *possible* time. Paine was trafficking not in the lofty ideals of philosophy, but rather in the mundane contingency of political rhetoric.

And his answer to the question of the right time was an age-old rhetorical response: *now*. Paine could have declared a month or set a calendrical deadline, but he refused to allow his arguments to be bridled by the external calendar and clock time that frames the historical experience of modern sociality. Paine referred to events and persons from that external world, but he was busy crafting an alternate habitation for his readers, one internal to the text of *Common Sense*. In this alternate intratextual world, each reader's experience of the text was as fresh and vibrant as Paine's own epiphanies concerning independence. Whether *Common Sense* was read in January or April, in New Hampshire or South Carolina, the moment of reading was always *now*. As a reader or an auditor of a rhetorical text, one experiences the words and arguments as perpetual presence. The moment one reads or listens is *now*, and *now* is precisely the moment when Paine advocated action.

Independence now: these two words sum up the entirety of Paine's groundbreaking argument in *Common Sense*. All his clever turns of phrase, all his hortatory flourishes, were subordinate to or derivative of this end. Paine's goal was not simply to declare independence and to establish a republican and constitutional form of government. His goal was to declare independence and establish a new government *now*. The problem and the benefit with "now" as a temporal textual construct is its eternal presence. The text is impervious to the passage of calendrical time. It operates on a plane internal to the reader's experience. "Now" is the moment of reading, but it doesn't necessarily connote "this very second" but instead implies a looser "without delay or hesitation."

At the time *Common Sense* was first published, even the most powerful of Paine's readers did not possess sufficient agency to declare independence or to establish a new government. Until late June 1776, most delegates to the Continental Congress were bound by orders from their respective provincial assemblies *not* to declare independence. Thus, the only body that *could* declare independence was convinced it *could not* declare independence. The individual provincial assemblies possessed more discretionary power, but they tended to be controlled by propertied or proprietary members who were resistant to change and affectionate toward Great Britain. Most provincial assemblymen interpreted their very presence as elected members of the legislature as a *de facto* popular mandate against independent tendencies. Because they had run on a platform of filial affection and a desire for restoration with the parent state, their election expressed the will of the people until the expiration of their terms of office. Political stagnation was justified because, in the colonial calculus, opinions and time stood still between elections.

By crafting a mission in the "now," Paine was locating the crucial decision for independence within each reader's experience. Therefore, Paine's readers, though powerless at the moment to declare independence in a collective sense, were being asked to declare independence on an individual basis, within their own minds. Before America could declare independence, Paine realized, Americans had to declare themselves Independents.

Temporal Virtue

Many political theorists and historians of the American Revolution purport to deal with time; often, these discussions of time are abstracted commentaries on history and custom. Among the most notable of these scholars, John Pocock described in *Politics, Language, and Time* (1989) the early modern fear that time (*i.e.*, fortune) would inevitably sap civic virtue. Pocock wrote, "We recognize also that the aim of politics is to escape from time; that time is the dimension of imperfection and that change must necessarily be degenerative."[168] Pocock's interest in conservative historical figures, from Machiavelli to Hobbes and Burke, certainly colored his analysis of time, and his sweeping characterization of time as the betrayal of a Platonic political ideal reveals a broader conservative antipathy to the progression of time. Political conservatism, often caricatured by its opponents as a struggle to maintain the *status quo* (the precarious present), has devoted its primary energies toward the recovery of a particular lost golden age of politics (the forgotten past). Paine, like countless progressive, liberal, or radical politicos, rejected this postulated propensity and embraced time (especially, the anticipated future) *as an agent of political change*. Politics must have, Paine said, "a unity of means and time, and defect in either overthrows the whole."[169]

One of the basic differences between political conservatives and liberals in the modern era is evident in their respective attitudes toward time. Since only rulers are ever satisfied with the politics of their own period, the political discourse of an unsatisfactory present is perpetually preoccupied with the search for an ideal referent, a standard and a target. Conservatives categorically locate their political golden age in the past, while liberals believe that political perfection lies somewhere in the future. This is not to say that liberals eschew the past or that conservatives abdicate the future. Both perspectival categories point to historical precedent and make plans for the future, but conservatives fixate upon what we have lost, and liberals upon what we have not yet found. We see the divisive effect of political time in the radical divergence of former allies like John Adams and Thomas Jefferson, or Edmund Burke and Thomas Paine. These men disagreed on a number of issues, but at the core of their contentions lay incommensurable attitudes concerning the temporal direction of "the good ol' days."

Fortune and time were, for traditionalist Whigs, entropic political forces that could only be staved off by the force of public virtue and tradition. The progression of time was an enemy, and ensconced traditions slowed down its degrading influence. Pocock argued that the "repudiation of tradition," even of particular traditions, was viewed in republican culture as a slippery slope to the complete abolition of all references to the past.[170] In Pocock's interpretive framework, any erasure of the past was interpreted as a concession to the anarchic contingency of the future. Paine, of course, proves an aberration to Pocock's typology of republican engagement with historical time. In *Common Sense*, Paine railed against custom as a perversion of history and a false justification for monarchy, hereditary succession, the British constitution, and imperial commercial ties. Paine devoted the first half of the pamphlet to exploding, via recourse to an idiosyncratic popular history, the English conception of customary justification. In the very first sentence of the foreword, Paine contended that "a long habit of not thinking a thing *wrong*, gives it a superficial appearance of being *right*, and raises at first a formidable outcry in defence of custom." He preempted the bristling reaction of many of his readers by addressing their customary prejudices head-on, and he commenced his pamphlet with dual appeals to religious and natural histories, narratives that superseded political custom in the popular mind of colonial America.

Paine's sense of political time first obliterated the relevance of custom, and then it created an innovative framework in which time was cast as the accomplice of virtue. A central tenet of eighteenth century civic republicanism, as sketched by Pocock and others, was its emphasis on virtue, specifically on the public virtue of economically independent citizens. As Richard Henry Lee recounted in a 1775 letter to his friend, the celebrated Whig historian Catherine Macaulay, "Lexington, Concord, and Bunker Hill opened the tragic scene; and clearly proved to the whole world that N. America had no reliance but on its own virtue in Arms." He continued, "The inhumanity with which this war (unprovoked as it has been on this side) is prosecuted, is really shocking."[171] By maintaining "virtue in Arms" as well as virtue in their public deliberations, the Americans expected to be preferred by Providence in the struggle with Britain. Yet the lingering problem for every closet republican in America, especially those harboring theologies inclusive of Calvinist natural depravity, was the manifest *lack* of virtue among the people at large. The ideal of virtue proliferated in political theory, but virtue's too-frequent empirical absence made republicans cringe.

Classical English republicans influenced by Machiavelli's *Discorsi* (1531) discussed this dilemma in terms of fortune, a Renaissance concept (*fortuna*) that attempted to describe the volatility of political culture.[172] One way to overcome the combined ill effects of fortune, the corrupting impulse of power, and the evident lack of virtue was by setting up a system of reciprocal checks to quarantine and cancel out the degradation and abuse of power. This was the method preferred by the originators of the constitutions of Britain and, later, of the United States. Gordon Wood, in *The Creation of the American Republic*, described the *United States Constitution* as a systemic innovation of the republican model that substituted structural for popular virtue. The Federalists were trying to create, said Wood, "a republic which did not require a virtuous people for its sustenance."[173]

The other method for solving the virtue conundrum entailed a completely different approach. Paine was neither a misanthrope nor a social utopian, and he understood the corruptibility of humanity as well as anyone; in fact, during the Revolutionary War, he endured vicious attacks because he had been the first to detect the malfeasance of the American emissary to Europe, Silas Deane. "Virtue," asserted Paine twice in *Common Sense*, "is not hereditary, neither is it perpetual."[174] Paine's republicanism described not only a *people*, but also a *time*, solving the dilemma of a people not virtuous enough to sustain a republic. There are no indelibly virtuous people, he was saying; there are only people who live up to virtuous moments. Many of Paine's respondents (especially John Adams) expressed anxiety and skepticism over the unbuffered republicanism of *Common Sense*. But republicanism to Paine was less about guarding the deleterious impulses of humanity and more about creating the temporal conditions for true representation. Paine's republican time reinforced a self-conception of American virtue, if only for the revolutionary moment.

There are times when men who are otherwise mired in the expediencies and exigencies of their circumstances become actuated by a sense of duty and calling that allows them to perform acts of selfless heroism totally out of their character. No one is intrinsically virtuous, Paine argued. In the final decade of the eighteenth century, Paine's chief criticism of his one-time friend, George Washington—a criticism that, along with the *Age of Reason*, sealed Paine's infamy in America—was the austere prudence that the general and president cultivated as an indelible character trait. Washington's detached indifference, thought Paine, dressed up as virtuous disinterestedness and gave people the artful impression that Washington's virtue was constant. Paine's analysis of human nature, and his personal experience with Washington, led him to believe that virtue ebbed and flowed with the tide of affairs. A person's virtue could not be manifest in the mundane activities of eating breakfast or performing daily chores—that was simply morality and discipline. Virtue was a public quality that only surfaced during "the times that try men's souls."

Paine's most revealing description of temporality and crisis came later in 1776 in his *American Crisis, No. 1*.[175] The first lines of that essay are among the most famous and oft-repeated lines in American history. The remainder of the pamphlet and, indeed, the rest of that thirteen-part series was an extended exploration into the rhetorical construction of political crisis. The first clause, consisting of eight monosyllabic words, is now so familiar that we hardly give it a second thought, but the words in their original context encapsulated Paine's conception of crisis:

> THESE are the times
> that try men's souls:

The most curious word in this clause was "try." Paine meant it in the juridical sense, that "men's souls" were being put on trial by "the times." The iconic structure of this proposition, it should be noted, was an inefficient grammatical construct. "These times try men's souls," or "This time tries men's souls" would have been more succinct, but such alternatives would have lost Paine's essential meaning and metrical balance.[176] The reading present ("THESE") was identified ("are") as a temporal plurality ("the times"). Crisis does not happen in chronological "time" but in critical "times." The plural, active, and agential "times" were calling the "souls," the characters of men, before a tribunal to be tested in the crucible of crisis. The fickle and the fashionable would fail, as Paine continued in his metrical phrasing:

> The summer soldier and
> the sunshine patriot will,
>   in this crisis,
>   shrink from
>   the service
> of his country;[177]

While those who endured the present calamities with fortitude would deserve lasting acclaim:

> but he that stands it NOW,
> deserves the love and thanks
>   of man and woman.

> Tyranny, like hell,
> > is not easily conquered;
> > > yet
> > we have this consolation
> > > > with us,
> > > that
> > the harder the conflict,
> > the more glorious the triumph.

As in his *American Crisis* pamphlets, Paine was crafting in *Common Sense* a textual environment of temporality that fostered virtuous action. He understood that in both declaring independence and in spiriting up the public during the war, the morale of the conflicted and afflicted reading public was lifted according to the gravity of the moment. In *Common Sense*, Paine had disoriented and discarded traditional modes of marking time, and he had created within the reading experience a fleeting and agential window of opportunity with exponential consequentiality for better or worse. Extraordinary times called extraordinary people to do extraordinary things. It was the "necessity of the times" that had "dragged and driven" Paine's authorial talents "into action" in the first place, and those same times would make the Americans capable of declaring independence and supporting a republic government.[178] Frequent revolutions of elected representatives in their "proper rotation" would ensure natural equity and would maintain through regular concurrences with the people a sustainable virtue.[179]

Following Lexington and Concord, Paine recognized, "It was time for every man to stir," but the colonies' policies and deliberations remained, month after month, slothful and confused.[180] *Common Sense* startled and roused the American colonists from their political somnolence, and the text shoved its groggy audience toward a political reality of which it had only dreamed. Paine had replicated multidimensional political temporality in the textual mechanism of *Common Sense*, just as Rittenhouse had accomplished the mechanical description of astronomical temporality in his scientific works. *Common Sense* translated political time into the dialects of its colonial audience, and it thereby quickened the pace of American political discourse.[181] The contentious debate over independence that followed was halting in its progress, as pro-independence colonists mashed the temporal accelerator and their pro-reconciliation opponents stood on the political brakes. In the end, it was the "people out of doors" who would push the decision in favor of independence. Maryland, for example, was one of the last colonies to sanction independence. At the end of June 1776, a "committee of freemen" from Charles County, Maryland, sent strict instructions to their delegates to the Provincial Convention, the *ad hoc* intermediary body that would, in turn, issue new instructions regarding independence to the Maryland delegates in the Continental Congress. The men of Charles County wrote, "We are of the opinion that *the time has fully arrived* for the colonies to adopt the last measure for our common good and safety, and that *the sooner* they declare themselves separate from and independent of the Crown and parliament of Great Britain, *the sooner* they will be able to make effectual opposition."[182] As is evidenced by these instructions, independence was a decision framed ultimately by temporality. The upward and forward pressure from popular committees such as this one eventually dislodged the elite blockade of independence. In *Common Sense*, Paine empowered readers through an experiential recalibration of time, and he transformed even common people, whom Edmund Burke had called "the swinish multitude," into virtuous politicians. Thus Paine hastened the arrival of independence one reader and one crisis at a time.

Notes: Chapter 5

[1] Commager, "Science, Learning, and the Claims of Nationalism," 80. 80; TJ to DR, July 19, 1778, Boyd. *The Papers of Thomas Jefferson*, 2:202-203.

[2] TJ, *Notes on the State of Virginia*, from Peterson, *Thomas Jefferson: Writings*, 190-191.

[3] Cohen, *Science and the Founding Fathers*. 85-86.

[4] Gordon, *The History of the Rise, Progress, and Establishment of the Independence of the United States of America*, 2: 275.

[5] CS F.1.

[6] Rice, *The Rittenhouse Orrery*, 21-23.

[7] Ibid., 22-23. Owing largely to his success in this tense situation, in 1769 he was called in to survey the boundary between New York and New Jersey.

[8] Quoted in Rufus, "David Rittenhouse," 511.

[9] Both the astronomical clock and transit telescope fabricated by Rittenhouse and used in the transit observation are held in the collection of the APS. Rittenhouse had been grinding lenses and making telescopes and other surveying equipment since the mid-1750s, but some historians suggest that this transit telescope was the first astronomical telescope made in the United States. See Mitchell, "Astronomy during the Early Years of the American Philosophical Society." The Zenith Telescope made sometime before 1786 by David Rittenhouse and Andrew Ellicot, using an objective lens donated by Thomas Pryor, now held by the Smithsonian Institution's National Museum of American History, is often regarded as the most precise scientific instrument built in America during the eighteenth century. See, Ellicott, "Astronomical and Thermometrical Observations," 204-205; and Ellicott, "Observations for Determining the Latitude and Longitude," 447-450.

[10] See, Hindle, *David Rittenhouse*; Rice, 22-23; and Jeff Locke, "Construction Details of Rittenhouse Compasses," 28-34.

[11] Rice, 22-23.

[12] Hume, "Abstract of a Book Lately Published," in Kramnick, *Enlightenment Reader*, 197.

[13] The early hagiographies of "Parson" Mason Locke Weems were among the first in a long tradition of nationalist writing that, to this day, portrays the "Founding Fathers" as towering demigods whose "original intent" was timelessly infallible.

[14] Bailyn, "Common Sense."

[15] Cartwright, *American Independence*.

[16] Ford, 76.

[17] Potts announced his intention to Israel Pemberton that he would sail for England or Ireland at the end of March 1776. This was common practice among wealthy Tories in the spring of 1776. Joseph Potts to Israel Pemberton, 16 February 1776. Pemberton Papers, 28:170, HSP.

[18] Eckhardt, George H. *Pennsylvania Clocks and Clockmakers*. New York: Devin-Adair, 1955, p. 141.

[19] See Bailey, *Two Hundred Years of American Clocks*, 33. The clock is now owned by Drexel University in Philadelphia, where it is displayed in a gallery in the Main Building.

[20] Advertisement for John Wood, Clock and Watch-Maker, PJ, May 1, 1776.

[21] CS 4.15, 4.3.
[22] CS 3.49.
[23] CS 3.28.
[24] CS F.1, 4.28.
[25] CS 3.2.
[26] CS 3.1.
[27] CS F.1, CS 3.1. For a thorough treatment of the concept of "prejudice" in *Common Sense*, Hoffman, "Paine and Prejudice."
[28] CS A.17.
[29] CS A.18.
[30] CS 3.6-3.7.
[31] CS 4.11.
[32] CS 4.3.
[33] CS 3.36-3.38.
[34] CS 3.19. This colloquialism was the eighteenth-century equivalent to our, "It's time to go."
[35] CS 3.35.
[36] "Every thing done as an expedient grows worse every day, for in proportion as the mind grows up to the full standard of right it disdains the expedient. America has nearly been ruined by expedients in the first stages of the Revolution, and perhaps would have been so, had not *Common Sense* broken the charm and the *declaration of Independence* sent it into banishment." TP to John Breckenridge [Jefferson's spokesman in the U.S. Senate, about the Louisiana Purchase], 2 August 1803. Paine Papers, CL.
[37] *From Max Weber: Essays in Sociology.*
[38] CS A.11.
[39] CS 2.7.
[40] CS 2.12; 3.19.
[41] CS 2.6.
[42] CS 2.3.
[43] CS 3.25.
[44] CS A.1.
[45] *Father Abraham's Almanack, for the Year of our Lord 1778* [1777].
[46] Rittenhouse continued to perform calculations for almanacs through the late 1770s. See, Ford, 64; *Father Abraham's Almanack, For the Year of our Lord 1778; Being the Second after Leap-Year. Containing, The Motions of the Sun and Moon; the True Places and Aspects of the Planets; the Rising and Setting of the Sun; and the Rising, Setting and Southing of the Moon. Also, The Lunations, Conjunctions, Eclipses, Judgment of the Weather, Rising and Setting of the Planets, Length of Days and Nights, &c. &c. Fitted to the Latitude of Forty Degrees, and a meridian of near five Hours West from London.* By Abraham Weatherwise, Gent. ***Our customers are requested to observe, that the ingenious David Rittenhouse, A.M. of this city, has favoured us with the astronomical calculations of our Almanack for this year, and therefore they may be most firmly relied on. Lancaster: John Dunlap [1777].
[47] Stowell, *Early American Almanacs*, ix-x.

[48] *The Burlington Almanack for the Year of our Lord 1776. Being Bissextile or Leap-Year. And the 16th Year of His Majesty's Reign, after the 25th of October 1775.* By Timothy Trumean, Philom. Burlington [NJ]: Isaac Collins, [1775].

[49] British almanacs of the 1770s tended to indulge more than American almanacs in "judicial astrology," the practice of forecasting political events by the stars. One London almanac found the appearance of two "Mock Suns" on April 27, 1775, "being a few Days after the embarking of the Generals to North America," to be a significant omen for the coming year. In the author's "astrological Judgment," these "unusual Signs" were "the Precursors of Divisions, Clandestine Plots, Treacheries, Breaches of Leagues and Covenants, and sudden Commotions against Authority." Because the sun, "the true Representer of Kings, Princes, &c." was involved, the author was convinced that in 1776 "the Honour and Grandeur of Kings, Princes, Magistrates, &c. will much advance and increase" regardless of "all Machinations and envious Designs framed against them." The author predicted that "Such rebellious Spirits, whether in North America or elsewhere, as will not love, obey, and submit to Authority, will be constrained to fear it, and also to feel its Coercion." Saunders, Richard. *The English Apollo: or, Useful Companion: Assisting all Persons In the right Understanding the Science of Time, Past, Present, and to Come. Particularly Applied to this Present Year 1776; Being the Bissextile, or Leap-Year.* London: George Hawkins, 1776.

[50] Stahlman, "Astrology in Colonial America," 551-563.

[51] *Father Abraham's Almanack, for the Year of our Lord 1775; Being the Third after Leap-Year. (The fifteenth Year of the Reign of King George III.) ....that the ingenious David Rittenhouse...has favored us with the astronomical calculations for this year....* Philadelphia, John Dunlap, [1774].

[52] *Father Abraham's Almanack, for the year of our Lord 1777 ... Fitted to the latitude of forty degrees, and a meridian of near five hours west from London.* By Abraham Weatherwise, gent. ... Philadelphia: John Dunlap, [1776].

[53] Breen, *Tobacco Culture.*

[54] CS 4.18; see also, CS 3.4.

[55] CS 4.1.

[56] RM2, CW I, 453-454.

[57] RM 2, CW I, 347.

[58] CS 3.32 (emphasis added).

[59] CS 3.48.

[60] CS 4.3.

[61] CS 4.10.

[62] CS A.15.

[63] CS 3.5.

[64] AC, No. 3, CW I, 87.

[65] CS 3.24.

[66] AC, No. 1. CW I, 50.

[67] CS A.6.

[68] Saunders, Richard. *The English Apollo: or, Useful Companion: Assisting all Persons In the right Understanding the Science of Time, Past, Present, and to Come. Particularly Applied to this Present Year 1776; Being the Bissextile, or Leap-Year.* London: George Hawkins, 1776.

[69] CS A.16, 3.32.
[70] CS 2.13.
[71] CS 2.9, 2.12.
[72] Saunders, *The English Apollo.*
[73] CS 2.10.
[74] Aesop, *Fables*, 245.
[75] Aesop, 118.
[76] CS 2.13.
[77] "The Wild Ass and the Lion," "The Ass and His Shadow," "The Ass and His Driver," "The Lion, the Fox, and the Ass." Aesop, 101, 126, 310, 161.
[78] TP to His Excellency General Washington, 7 September 1782. CW II, 1212.
[79] See, for example, *Poor Will's Almanack, for the year of our Lord, 1776; Being bissextile, or Leap-year, and 16th year of the King's Reign, till October 26.* Philadelphia: Joseph Crukshank, [1775]; *The Lancaster Almanack, for the Year of Our Lord, 1776; Being Bissextile; or Leap-Year. The sixteenth year of the reign of K. George, III. ...by Anthony Sharp, Philom.* Lancaster: Francis Bailey, [1775]; *The Philadelphia Newest Almanack, for the Year of our Lord 1776, Being Leap Year. ...By Timothy Telescope, Esq.* Philadelphia: R. Aitken, [1775]; *The Universal Almanack, for the Year of our Lord 1776; Being Bissextile or Leap-Year. (The Sixteenth Year of the Reign of King George III...... The ingenious D. Rittenhouse, A.M. has again favour'd us with the calculations. Fitted to the latitude of forty degrees north, and near five hours west from London.* Philadelphia: James Humphreys, Jr., [1775]; *Poor Richard improved: Being an Almanack and Ephemeris of the Motions of the Sun and Moon; the True Places and Aspects of the Planets; the Rising and Setting of the Sun, and the Rising, Setting, and Southing of the Moon, for the Year of our Lord 1776. Being Bissextile or Leap-Year. ... Fitted to the latitude of forty degrees, and a meridian of near five hours west from London; but may, without sensible error, serve all the northern colonies. By Richard Saunders, philom.* Philadelphia: Hall and Sellers, [1775]; *Father Abraham's Pocket Almanack for the Year 1776.* Philadelphia: John Dunlap, [1775].
[80] *Philosophical Transactions* (1769), 291.
[81] Smith, William. "Account of the Transit of Venus Over the Sun's Disk, as Observed at Norriton in the County of Philadelphia, and Province of Pennsylvania, June 3, 1769." *Philosophical Transactions* (1769), 293. A transit telescope was a refracting device mounted to a horizontal axis and designed to follow the meridian plane, while an equal altitude instrument was similar to a transit telescope but had the added feature of a graduated vertical circle or arc that made it easier to measure the altitude of celestial bodies at various times of the day.
[82] Ibid., 298
[83] Ibid., 294.
[84] Ibid., 308-309.
[85] Ibid., 309-310.
[86] Ibid., 310.
[87] Ibid., 310.
[88] Ibid., 314.
[89] Ibid., 315.
[90] Ibid., 316-317.

[91] CS 2.6, 3.48.
[92] CS 1.6, A.11.
[93] CS A.6, A.17.
[94] CS A.16.
[95] CS 3.22.
[96] CS 3.20.
[97] CS 3.23, 3.30.
[98] CS 3.48.
[99] CS 3.3.
[100] Bakhtin, *Dialogic Imagination*, 14.
[101] CS A.16.
[102] CS A.16.
[103] AC, No. 1, CW I, p. 56.
[104] CS 3.4.
[105] BR to Mrs. [Julia Stockton] Rush, 29 May 1776. Butterfield, *Letters of Benjamin Rush*, 1:99-100.
[106] CS A.1.
[107] *Boston Gazette*, April 29, 1776. Quoted in Tyler, *The Literary History of the American Revolution*, 1: 473-474.
[108] AC, No. 3, CW I, 86-87.
[109] RM, CW I, 338.
[110] CS 4.18.
[111] CS A.17, CS 3.32.
[112] CS F.5, CS A.2.
[113] For a wonderful treatment of this phenomenon, see Borges, "Borges and I," 246-247.
[114] CS 3.48.
[115] Pocock, *The Machiavellian Moment*.
[116] CS A.16.
[117] CS 4.19.
[118] This quotation, spoken by Brutus, comes from Act IV, Scene III. In modern rhetorical theory, Chaim Perelman's concept of the "locus of the irreparable" is a useful analogue to the concepts I am discussing here. See Pereleman and Olbrechts-Tyteca, *The New Rhetoric*, and Cox, "The Die is Cast."
[119] RHL to [Patrick Henry], 20 April 1776. Ballagh, *Letters of Richard Henry Lee*, 1: 176-180.
[120] Jonathan Dickinson Sergeant to JA, 11-12 April 1776. LDC, 3:508.
[121] JA to James Warren, 14 February 1776. LDC, 3:253-254; JA to William Heath, 15 April 1776. LDC, 3:525.
[122] DPP, February 12, 1776.
[123] CS 4.2.
[124] Steele, *The Englishman*, October 29, 1713, quoted in Rice, 6-8.
[125] Rice, 11-12.
[126] DR to Thomas Barton, 28 January 1767, quoted in Rice, 28-29.
[127] DR to Thomas Barton, 27 March 1767, quoted in Rice, 30.
[128] Smith's report was delivered to the APS on March 22, 1768, and the description published in the PG on April 28, 1768. See Rice, 33-34.

[129] From DR's "Little Paper" on the Orrery, February 1771. Quoted in Rice, 84-85.
[130] WS to Thomas Barton, 13 May 1770, quoted in Rice, 33-34.
[131] DR to Thomas Barton, 12 May 1770, quoted in Rice, 34.
[132] Oliver Wolcott to Laura Wolcott, 8 March 1776. LDC, 3:360.
[133] 27 August 1774, *John Adams Diary* 21:28, Adams Family Papers, MHS.
[134] AR, CW I, 498.
[135] DR, "Description of a New Orrery," March 1767, quoted in Rice, 82-84.
[136] From DR, "Little Paper" on the Orrery, February 1771, quoted in Rice, 84-85.
[137] DR to Thomas Barton, 28 January 1767, quoted in Babb, "The Relation of David Rittenhouse and His Orrery to the University," UPL.
[138] DR to Thomas Barton, 15 March 1771, quoted in Babb.
[139] DR, "Description of a New Orrery," March 1767, quoted in Rice, 82-84.
[140] AC, No. 2, CW I, 59.
[141] AC, No. 13, CW I, 231, 233-234.
[142] CS 4.1-4.2.
[143] Keane, 113. For another approach to this same question, see Vincent, *The Transatlantic Republican*, especially Chapter 1, "The Strategy of Time in *Common Sense*."
[144] The concept of *krisis* in rhetorical theory dates back at least to the Greek sophists. See, for example, Poulakos, *Sophistical Rhetoric in Classical Greece*.
[145] *The [London] Crisis*, No. I. "To the People of England and America." *The Crisis, Numbers I-XI*. New York, 1775. APS.
[146] Johnson, *Dictionary of the English Language*.
[147] Aristotle, *On Rhetoric*; Black, *Rhetorical Criticism*; Beiner, *Political Judgment*.; and Kahn, *Rhetoric, Prudence, and Skepticism in the Renaissance*.
[148] I have included in my tallies related morphologies such as "independence" and "independent," "time" and "times."
[149] CS A.12.
[150] CS 4.26.
[151] CS 3.24.
[152] CS 3.23-3.27.
[153] CS A.5.
[154] CS A.5.
[155] CS A.17.
[156] Paine uses *necessary* or *necessity* 28 times in CS.
[157] CS 3.32.
[158] CS 3.51.
[159] CS 3.19.
[160] CS 3.1, 4.5.
[161] CS 3.26.
[162] CS 4.18.
[163] CS 4.19.
[164] CS A.14.
[165] CS 3.50.
[166] CS 4.1.
[167] CS 3.24, 3.32, A.15

[168] Pocock, *Politics, Language, & Time*, 88.
[169] AC, No. 7, CW I, 143.
[170] Pocock, *Politics, Language, & Time*, 260-261.
[171] RHL to Mrs. [Catherine] Macaulay, 29 November 1775. Ballagh, *Letters of Richard Henry Lee*, 1:160-164. Macaulay had written *The Address to the People of England, Scotland, and Ireland, on the Present Important Crisis of Affairs* in 1775.
[172] See Biener, *Political Judgment*, and Kahn, *Prudence*.
[173] Wood, *Creation*, 475.
[174] CS A.16.
[175] AC, No. 1, Philadelphia: Steiner and Cist, 1776.
[176] Notice the balanced, four-syllable clauses and the repetition of key sounds such as "th" and the long "i."
[177] Observe Paine's emphasis on the hissing "s" of the serpent and the hushing "sh" by which he hoped to silence the loyal opposition.
[178] AC, No. 7, CW I, 143-144.
[179] CS 3.43.
[180] AC, No. 7, CW I, 143-144.
[181] A relevant modern analogy to this accelerating function of *Common Sense* may be found in the description of the American electoral cycle in the first sentences of Bill Clinton's First Inaugural Address (1993): "Today we celebrate the mystery of American renewal. This ceremony is held in the depth of winter. But, by the words we speak and the faces we show the world, we force the spring."
[182] Emphasis added. Scharf, *History of Maryland*, 228-229.

Chapter Six

Declaration of Independents

I find it impossible in the small compass I am limited to, to trace out the progress which independence has made on the minds of the different classes of men, and the several reasons by which they were moved. With some, it was a passionate abhorrence against the king of England and his ministry, as a set of savages and brutes; and these men, governed by the agony of a wounded mind, were for trusting every thing to hope and heaven, and bidding defiance at once. With others, it was a growing conviction that the scheme of the British court was to create, ferment and drive on a quarrel, for the sake of confiscated plunder: and men of this class ripened into independence in proportion as the evidence increased. While a third class conceived it was the true interest of America, internally and externally, to be her own master, and gave their support to independence, step by step, as they saw her abilities to maintain it enlarge. With many, it was a compound of all these reasons; while those who were too callous to be reached by either, remained, and still remain Tories.

Thomas Paine
The American Crisis, No. 3
1777

The exertions which we had made, and the blood which we had shed, were deemed too great a price for reconciliation to a power which still claimed the right "to bind us in all cases whatsoever," and which held out to us unconditional submission, as the only terms on which we were to expect even a pardon. Subjection to a prince who had thrown us out of his protection; who had ruined our commerce, destroyed our cities and spilled our blood; and who would not govern us at all, without the interposition of a legislative body, in whose election we had no voice, was an idea too absurd to be any longer entertained. These sentiments, being set in their just light by various publications and addresses, had such force as to produce a total change of the public opinion. Independence became the general voice of the same people, who but a few months before had petitioned for reconciliation.

Jeremy Belknap
The History of New-Hampshire
1784-1792

PART ONE
DODGING BULLETS

Divided by the Sword

There was a hypocritical chasm between the policy and rhetoric of the American colonies in late 1775 and early 1776. The dissonance between the colonies' *independent* actions and *dependent* addresses was patently obvious to most outside observers. Leading members of the British government interpolated cunning subterfuge into the perplexing gap between rebellious deeds and loyal words and thereby convinced themselves of the colonists' diabolical scheme to attempt independence. On the western side of the Atlantic, an overwhelming majority of Americans harbored no such intentions, and, moreover, they were oblivious to the inconsistency of their position.

While the colonies were *acting* remarkably independent, they still did not *feel* independent. The imperial conflagrations of the 1760s and early 1770s edged the American colonies into a gradual manifold independence from Britain in the spheres of economics, law, religion, and military defense. The functional dissolution of royal government in several of the colonies by late 1775 amounted to political independence, but the colonies refused to admit the fact. Events were fast reaching a precipice, but most Americans saw independence as a blind leap over the political ledge. Indeed, most of the colonies were functioning as independent states at the end of 1775, but they could not bring themselves to declare their independence.

Common Sense exhorted the Americans to declare independence in the one area where they remained most dependent upon Britain: in their *sentiments*—their thoughts, opinions, and feelings. Paine made them *feel* independent by crafting a rhetorical experience that highlighted the otherness of Britain and the sameness of the American colonies, and he helped them to *believe* that independence was both achievable and advantageous. As colonist after colonist read Paine's pamphlet, for the first time they envisioned a united and independent America, and for the first time they thought, "We can do this. We *are* doing this." The Reverend Ashbel Green of New Jersey observed that *Common Sense* was advertised that spring "at every place of public resort," and that the pamphlet "struck a string which required but a touch to make it vibrate." In a concise summary, Green said, "The country was ripe for independence, and only needed somebody to tell the people so, with decision, boldness, and plausibility."[1]

Before America could declare independence, Americans had to declare *themselves* independents. The colonists had to disavow dependence upon Britain in every sphere of their lives. Prior to cutting the collective cord, Americans had first to become personally convinced that political independence was a necessary step. Reaching this conclusion was a process that occurred one person at a time, sometimes in a flash, but more often in stages over the course of several months. Independence was not a procedure; it was a realization.

As late as the spring of 1776, American independence was not a foregone conclusion, and opinions on the subject varied widely with location and occupation. The people who remained the staunchest advocates for political dependence on Great Britain were merchants, lawyers, and ministers whose livelihoods and identities were bound up in some way with the transatlantic connection. On the other hand, officers and soldiers in the Continental Army were the first to realize that independence was an absolute necessity, because the lived experience of these men emphatically disproved a return to colonial dependence and subordination.

The number one categorical determinant of a general favorability toward independence in early 1776 was the proximity of armed conflict to a particular colony or person. Armed combat soiled all of the highfalutin political theories about allegiance and protection, and it mocked bow-and-curtsy court diplomacy. Even in the eighteenth century, war was hell, and under-equipped Continental soldiers lived in that hell of frostbitten digits, rancid rations, empty powder pouches, and best friends lying face-down in crimson mud. The officers and soldiers of the Continental Army and the colonial militias witnessed firsthand the catastrophic ramifications of delaying independence, while the risk involved in declaring independence was no greater than what they already faced.

The same propensity operated among civilian colonists as well: the closer the proximity to war, the more receptive a person or community was to independence. Virginia, the colony that would take the lead in the push for independence, had endured a standoff with its royal governor, and the town of Norfolk had been burnt to the ground on the first day of 1776. In North and South Carolina, residents would become dramatically more open to independence after local battles and with each successive rumor of the arrival of British troops. Likewise, every new threat of British naval action against Philadelphia snapped a link in the heavy chain that restrained the Pennsylvania independence movement.

The hot-headed retaliation of New England against parliamentary taxation had attracted Britain's initial military retribution, and the inhabitants of Massachusetts felt the necessity of independence more acutely than residents of colonies who had yet to taste battle. Massachusetts had been under attack for almost a year when *Common Sense* began to circulate through the colony. Continental soldiers and besieged Bostonians endured cannonades and musket fire, the loss of friends and extended separation from their families, blistering winter wind and flagging provisions. If *Common Sense*, as one commentator noted, "was meant for plain men, in desperate danger, and desperately in earnest, then it was clearly meant for soldiers and Bostonians, people who *felt* the war happening around them, and who knew that independence was the only acceptable alternative that would make it stop."[2] But Paine wasn't writing just for soldiers and Bostonians; he was writing for residents in every other colony who had yet to beat their ploughshares into swords. Paine's rhetorical task was to replicate the conditions of battle in the minds of his readers—to create a crisis—because those conditions tended to precipitate a consensus in favor of independence. *Common Sense* thus closed the experiential distance in the American colonies between the horrors of war and the dalliance of peace.

In this chapter I will begin my exploration of the turn in colonial opinion toward independence in the wake of *Common Sense*. Specifically I will illustrate how American colonists read *Common Sense* during the first half of 1776. As colonial readers engaged with Paine's text and shared it with others, individuals and communities were steered toward the realization of independence. The responses of readers to *Common Sense* constitute a remarkable window into the colonial mind in the morning of the American Revolution. The friction between *Common Sense* and entrenched colonial opinion sparked small flickers of change in each community, and the public debate the pamphlet ignited, fanned into flame by the perceived obstinacy of Britain, caught in every colony until it became what Paine later called "the blaze of 1776."[3]

Massachusetts and Common Sense

The obstreperous residents of the Massachusetts Bay Colony had grown accustomed to wearing the epithet of "rebels," so while other colonies cringed at the king's accusations in the fall of 1775, the Massachusetts colonists just rolled their eyes. But despite their comfort with the character of "rebels," they were more hesitant to become "revolutionaries." On January 13, 1776, Samuel Adams—among the most notorious of American rebels—wrote from Philadelphia to James Warren in Boston, "I have sent to Mrs. Adams a Pamphlet which made its first Appearance a few days ago. It has fretted some folks here more than a little. I recommend it to your Perusal and wish you would borrow it of her." Adams cautioned that Warren may "find the Spirit of it totally repugnant with your Ideas of Government," but he asked his friend to "Read it without Prejudice, and give me your impartial Sentiments of it when you may be at Leisure."[4]

Adams's hesitation proved unnecessary. Warren read the pamphlet with glee. In a letter thanking another Massachusetts delegate, Elbridge Gerry, for the gift of an extra copy of *Common Sense*, Warren wrote, "It is really a most Excellent thing. I admire every part of it." Warren lauded the book's title and contents as "more strongly connected by nature and Reason" than anything he had ever read. *Common Sense* had "done a most Eminent Service" to the American cause, said Warren, "It has Convinced, Converted and Confirmed in every place, and has prepared us for the Grand decisive measure my Soul has longed for."[5]

James Warren and his wife, playwright and historian Mercy Otis Warren, were enthusiastic acolytes of *Common Sense*'s principles and sent the pamphlet to their friends. James Bowdoin, one of those recipients, wrote at the end of February 1776 to Mercy Otis Warren that he was "much obliged for the loan of it." Bowdoin expressed his confidence in the pamphlet's ability to proselytize many, noting, "The more it is contemplated, the stronger is the conviction of the truth of it, at least this is the case with respect to myself and my dear Rib, we having been much confirmed in it since reading the Pamphlet."[6] Bowdoin expressed a wish that the pamphlet be "republished in all the Newspapers" in which case "it would have an extensively good effect." Bowdoin found the author's "doctrine" had a benevolent tendency "to confirm the real Christian, recover the doubting, and convert the ignorant and unbelieving to the true faith."[7] A month later Bowdoin again wrote to Mercy Otis Warren, referring any objector to a declaration of independence "to that excellent Pamphlet entitled *Common Sense*" which would "probably silence all his objections, and disciple him to the author's doctrine" of the absolute necessity of independence.[8]

In mid-April, Samuel Adams wrote to James Warren of "the Necessity of proclaiming Independency." Adams stressed the timing of the measure: "The Salvation of this Country depends upon its being done speedily. I am anxious to have it done. Every Day's Delay tries my Patience. I can give you not the least Color of a Reason why it is not done." The colonists had constructed a commonplace binary of "Liberty or Slavery," but Adams indicated a crucial shift in the structure of the decision when he declared, "The only Alternative is Independence or Slavery." Adams said that he no longer corresponded with "our moderate prudent Whigs" whose "Moderation has brought us to this Pass" and who would choose to "continue the Conflict a Century." The principles of "such moderate Men" in Philadelphia, he said "are daily going out of Fashion." In a Mosaic metaphor reminiscent of *Common Sense*, Adams added, "The Child Independence is now struggling for Birth. I trust that in a short time it will be brought forth and in Spite of Pharaoh all America shall hail the dignified Stranger."[9]

Common Sense reverberated throughout Massachusetts society in 1776. On March 21, the Reverend Samuel Cooper of Boston wrote to Benjamin Franklin asking, "How is *Common Sense* relish'd among you? It is eagerly read and greatly admir'd here."[10] Major Joseph Hawley of Massachusetts wrote to his friend in the Continental Congress, Elbridge Gerry, "I beg leave to let you know that I have read *Common Sense* and that every sentiment has sunk into my well prepared heart."[11] Deacon Palmer observed, "I believe no pages were ever more rapturously read, nor more generally approved. People speak of it in rapturous praise." Joseph Ward called it a "glorious performance," and Abigail Adams's cousin, William Tudor surmised that the "doctrine it holds up is calculated for the climate of New England, and though some timid *piddling* souls shrink at the idea," a hundred times more "wish for a declaration of independence from the Crown."[12] Two things are especially notable about Tudor's comment: first, that he read *Common Sense* as a local text, and second, that the majority of New Englanders urged independence not just from Britain, but "from the Crown."

Another New Englander reflected Paine's temporal argument in a newspaper essay: "This is *the time* for declaring independence," the writer said, adding, "we never have had such a favorable moment before, and 'tis not likely we shall have such another if we neglect this."[13] The *Boston Gazette* from April 29 included a letter that lifted the language of *Common Sense* to assert, "Had the spirit of prophecy directed the birth of a publication, it could not have fallen upon a more fortunate period than the time in which *Common Sense* made its appearance. The minds of men are now swallowed up in attention to an object the most momentous and important that ever yet employed the deliberations of a people."[14]

On May 27, the residents of Malden, Massachusetts, sent pointed instructions to their representative in the Massachusetts Provincial Congress. While Great Britain "continued to act the part of a parent state," they said, "we felt ourselves happy in our connection with her, nor wished it to be dissolved." But now, they said, "our sentiments are altered." In words clipped from *Common Sense*, the people of Malden rebuked a king who could "unfeelingly hear of the slaughter of [his] subjects, and composedly sleep with their blood upon his soul!" It was now their "ardent wish" for America to "become a free and independent state." They were also "confirmed in the opinion that the present age would be deficient in their duty to God, their posterity and themselves, if they do not establish an American republic." A republic was "the only form of government we wish to see established," because they could "never be willingly subject to any other King than he who, being possessed of infinite wisdom, goodness and rectitude, is alone fit to possess unlimited power."[15]

In the correspondence of these Massachusetts colonists, then, we find a heuristic snapshot of the manner in which *Common Sense* wound its way through America in early 1776.[16] The Warrens had received multiple copies from friends in Philadelphia and had, in turn, forwarded those and other copies they could obtain to their friends, neighbors, and family. Letters were written, copied, and excerpted, and essays were published in newspapers. American colonists did not argue for independence "because *Common Sense* said so," but rather they infused their conversations, speeches, and writings with the pamphlet's vocabulary, imagery, and structure.

We are not surprised by the receptivity of Massachusetts firebrands to *Common Sense*; our textbook histories of the American Revolution have prepared us to anticipate patriotism in Boston and its surrounds. The purpose of this chapter, and the reason I have begun in Massachusetts, is not to take us on a predictable tour of nationalistic platitudes, but to come face-to-face with the contemporaneous response of the colonists to *Common Sense* unembellished and uncensored by hindsight. If the arguments of *Common Sense* were old hat in Massachusetts, then what merited the cautious introduction of the pamphlet by Samuel Adams, the colony's leading radical, in a private letter to a close friend?[17] If *Common Sense* had merely expressed, like a greeting card, what the people of Massachusetts had been thinking all along, then why did they testify to its conversional power? Paine's pamphlet did not possess monolithic causality, but we should not undersell its impact on colonial minds. We need to understand the reasons why American colonists embraced or rejected independence in early 1776, because these are the reasons they chose to summon the United States of America into existence. The reactions to *Common Sense*—in marginalia, in diaries, in handwritten letters, in newspapers, and in pamphlets—are the central archive of the decision-making process that birthed the American nation. Before we open the door to the blizzard of opinions surrounding *Common Sense* beginning in January 1776, we need first to know how colonists encountered Paine's text.

PART TWO
COLONIAL READING

American Literacy

The first question we musk ask is not "*How* did Americans read *Common Sense?*", but "*Who* could read *Common Sense?*" The latter is a question of access and literacy, because Americans could not read a text they were unable to obtain, and a wagonload of pamphlets would be wasted upon an illiterate target audience. I will begin by clarifying our notions of colonial American literacy.

As I have repeated earlier in this study, to be "literate" in the eighteenth century was to read and write in Latin, the official language of the transnational republic of letters (*res publica litterarum*). As Enlightenment popular science began to displace the Renaissance cult of the ancients as the epicenter of philosophical discourse, facility with the classics became less functional and more ornamental. By the end of the eighteenth century, reading and writing Latin had become primarily a performance that partitioned elites from commoners. Thomas Paine dismissed this conception of literacy as frivolous self-indulgence, and his prose style aimed at perspicuity for monolingual speakers of vernacular English like himself.

The question of vernacular English literacy in early America is a contentious point among scholars. One reason for the dispute is the fuzzy definition of modern "literacy": does it require the ability to read, to write, to sign one's own name, or some combination of the three? Reading was considered easier to teach than writing, and we can be sure that a large number of colonial adults—both men and women—were able to comprehend uncomplicated English texts, even if many of those same adults lacked the ability to compose a basic letter. Certainly, literacy rates varied from colony to colony, depending upon the particulars of a culture such as laws, schools, occupations, and religious denominations that would either encourage or discourage activities associated with reading and writing.[18] The sizable German population in colonial Pennsylvania promoted their native tongue to the detriment of English fluency and literacy, but the February 23 edition of *Gesunde Bernunft*, the German-language translation of *Common Sense* printed by Melchior Steiner and Carl Cist in Philadelphia, did ensure a measure of textual access for the "Pennsylvania Dutch" community.

A 1774 census of the twelve colonies who participated in the First Continental Congress (from which Georgia abstained) generously estimated a population of just over three million people.[19] That estimate was probably more accurate by early 1776. Though the population had been doubling every twenty years for most of the eighteenth century, the start of the war saw a temporary dip in population as numerous loyalists fled to England. Roughly sixty percent of Americans were of English descent, twenty percent were Africans (mostly slaves and a few freemen), and ten percent were of German stock, concentrated in Pennsylvania and the southern backcountry.[20] It is safe to estimate that about one-sixth of the adult population in the American colonies, or approximately 500,000 people, had achieved basic reading literacy by the mid-1770s.[21] By contrast, no more than one in every thousand Americans had ever attended college, and accordingly a college degree conferred automatic status.[22] Only this most elite sliver of early American society—a total population of less than 3,000—possessed a comprehensive literacy, including the cumulative skills of reading English, writing English, and reading and writing Latin. Traditional American pamphlet culture targeted this thousandth part of the colonial population, and considered a sold out single edition a smashing success.

We cannot know exactly how many copies of *Common Sense* were published in America during 1776. Paine claimed a preliminary total of 120,000, and one contemporary account in the London press estimated at least 46,000. Because scant records survive from colonial print shops and because the pamphlet's publication was so decentralized, verifiable statistics elude us. We do know that the earliest editions of Robert Bell and William and Thomas Bradford totaled not less than 12,000 copies available for purchase in Philadelphia by mid-February. A normal pamphlet run in the late eighteenth century was 500, and a proven seller would easily be double that quantity. Even if we assumed a conservative average of 1,000 copies for each of the 25 known editions of *Common Sense* printed in America during 1776, then no fewer than 25,000 copies of the pamphlet—exclusive of newspaper and broadside extracts—made their way into the hands of American colonists. In the eighteenth century, one could assume at least twenty readers per pamphlet, as they were left in taverns and coffee houses, on workbenches and kitchen tables, and as they were passed between friends and family.[23] These conservative estimates would still have amounted to a readership of 500,000, or roughly the estimated literate population of America.

A Community of Readers

Since no compositional manuscript of *Common Sense* survives, the proliferation of editions and publishers make locating *the* text of the pamphlet impossible. This is a serendipitous difficulty because it would be disingenuous to simply refer to *a* text of *Common Sense* as *the* text of *Common Sense*. Yes, there was a mostly-unchanged core of the work, but it is important to remember that the experiences of readers—solitary and corporate, Massachusetts and South Carolina, male and female, artisan and elite, early-1776 and mid-1776, closely read and quickly scanned—were as diverse and fluid as the composition of the text held in their hands. I have paid attention to markings and book plates on as many surviving copies of the pamphlet as I could leaf through, in order to stitch together a picture of how an unprecedented number of readers encountered this kaleidoscopic text.

When contemporary author Scott Liell refers to *Common Sense* as "46 pages," he is implying that the pamphlet's brevity belied its influence.[24] This can be a bit misleading, though, because *Common Sense* was quite large compared to other pamphlets of the day and, more obviously, because its page count varied from printer to printer. John Carter of Providence printed the pamphlet with ample margins, while other printers squeezed the margins close to the edge. Several printers included supplemental materials in their editions, while Solomon Southwick of Newport, Rhode Island, printed an edition that lopped off the first two sections and concentrated only on what he thought were the most salient parts. And even the inescapable language of "editions," begun by Robert Bell and perpetuated in contemporary scholarship by Paine überscholar Richard Gimbel, clouds the fact that many copies of *Common Sense* were a hodge-podge of paper qualities, typefaces, or, in several cases, of print runs. The apprentice charged with the task of stitching the pamphlet together simply took the next sheet off the top of the stack with little concern for precision matching. And those customers of Robert Bell and others who purchased early copies of *Common Sense* often hand stitched the later "Large Additions" together with the original. In this way, many of Paine's readers found themselves constructing the *material* as well as the *semantic* text.

Just as the language of a text often contains hints of its audience, so too the physical pages of a text often retain an audience's engagement with the printed word. As part of the research for this book, I have read and analyzed 136 extant copies of *Common Sense*, housed in archives and research libraries around the United States. Reading *Common Sense* in a glistening twenty-first century paperback reprint is a very different experience from reading it in an eighteenth century edition on linen rag paper loosely stitched with hemp twine. Turning the pages of an eighteenth century pamphlet is a very tactile experience; in many instances the page surfaces feel Braille-like from the deep impressions of the wooden press. The pages themselves often tell a story. Scattered spark burns recall the colonists reading beside a crackling fire on a frigid February evening in 1776. Smoke stains speak of glowing candles and puffing pipes, and hurried chicken-scratch calculations on back covers remind us of paper's short supply and the mundane tug of meeting financial obligations. The practiced signatures and silly poems of young boys and girls are the traces of literary education at the dawn of the republic.

Sometimes adult readers would annotate their copies of *Common Sense*, yielding greater insight into the immediate reactions of Paine's audience. One Massachusetts man wrote copious notes throughout his copy of Bell's second edition. For example, next to the passage in *Common Sense* where Paine was refuting Britain's status as "the parent country," the reader jotted, "Parent. Mamma! Mother in Law." The first word represented the reader's observation—a bare transcription of the key word in the paragraph—while the second and third comments signaled his own facetious interpretation of Paine's argument.[25] Another reader wrote beneath the last paragraph of the Appendix, a passage that called for the extinction of "the names of Whig and Tory" and also proposed the new title, the "Free and Independent States of America":

> This Pamphlet is in part fulfilled,
> That Whig and Tory is no more
> America is free, Come let us yield
> To him we should adore.[26]

But discussions of colonial literacy and the circulation of *Common Sense* often ignore a fundamental element of eighteenth century American culture: oral reading. The most vivid surviving account of oral reading practices in early America comes from the autobiography of Olaudah Equiano, a manumitted slave who would later play a significant role in the British abolition movement. Equiano described his first encounter with printed books while a slave in colonial Virginia. Not long off the slave ship from Africa, Equiano spied his master "employed in reading." The awestruck young African "had a great curiosity to talk to the books," because he assumed that his master was conversing aloud with the text. Equiano recalled, "For that purpose I have often taken up a book, and have talked to it, and then put my ears to it, when alone, in hopes it would answer me; and I have been very much concerned when I found it remained silent."[27] Equiano's fresh perspective and his ethnographic lens help focus our attention on an aspect of early American culture that is easy to overlook. In the twenty-first century, silent reading is the norm, but in the eighteenth century and for most of antecedent literary history, written texts were usually vocalized in the course of reading.[28]

Many colonists read *Common Sense* as we would today, alone and silent. But these people tended to be elites who also read more erudite works of history and philosophy. The common reader, the artisan or small farmer, would have shared the experience of reading with friends and associates. Though *Common Sense* was not written for liminal audiences like women, free and enslaved blacks, indentured servants, or children, the oral performance of the text likely allowed individuals on the fringes of public life to glean pieces of its arguments as the sound drifted freely into adjacent kitchens and workrooms.

A *de facto* oral culture existed in all but the highest levels of the educated colonial elite, and even when the written language was employed, it was no more than a pen and ink representation of the suprareality of the spoken word, subordinated as sheet music is to a symphony. When a text is read or recited aloud, the listening audience yields control to the author or orator for structuring the presentation. The auditors cannot flip back or forward a few pages to refresh or preview an argument. Their intake of the text is governed, as even the inflection and emphasis of the presentation and the structure of arguments are more strictly controlled by others.

Paine's emphasis on temporality fit well into an oral culture where the acts of both writing and reading were governed primarily by spoken time rather than by printed space. Paine thought it "needless to spend much *time* in exposing the folly of hereditary right," rather choosing a reference to wasted space, ink, or paper. When he did include a spatial figure, such as "every line convinces," it was often modified by a temporal construct like "even in the *moment* of reading."[29] Paine also wrote for an aural rather than a visual audience, because he was himself an auditory learner. In *Common Sense* he said, "I have frequently amused myself both in public and private companies, with silently remarking, the specious errors of those who speak without reflecting," and he continued his comment with a telling clause: "And among the many which I have heard…" This generalized source citation—reiterated in different forms throughout the pamphlet—demonstrated Paine's reliance upon aural data collection. In one instance, he had "heard some men say," while in another, he had "heard it asserted by some"—phrases that revealed the source of his education: the classroom of conversation.[30]

The prose style of *Common Sense* was reflected in its printed typography, and both were well-suited for oral presentation, increasing the potential audience of the text beyond the bounds of traditional pamphlet culture.[31] The frequent italicization in *Common Sense* was not superfluous but, instead, demonstrated the pervasive orality of the piece. Italics functioned for Paine like linguistic stress marks that prescribed the meter and meaning of his prose. By following the italics, readers would vocalize the text with the emphasis that Paine had intended—and spoken aloud himself—as he wrote. Italics and the rarer block capitals enabled Paine to make overt correspondences between words and ideas, most often to reinforce antithetical structures. Even Paine's idiosyncratic punctuation made sense in an oral culture. *Common Sense* was littered with what appear to be extraneous commas. But when we remember that Paine had no interest in following the dictates of grammarians, we understand that he took a purely functional approach to the usage of commas: they were breathing marks.

One commonality across all eighteenth century versions of *Common Sense* that is absent in later reproductions is a marginal word, called a catchword, in the lower right-hand corner of every other page. At first glance this convention of eighteenth century pamphlet culture seems just another quirk of early modernity, like the now-obsolete "f" representing a long- or medial-"s." But the subtlety of the catchword belies its importance as a key to understanding how *Common Sense* and other pamphlets were read by contemporaneous audiences. The word at the bottom of the page is a duplication of the lead word on the next page, and it served a dual purpose. For the printer it facilitated quick checking of the collation of a text. For the reader, the catchword's purpose was to smooth the transition between turns of the page, an unnecessary feature for silent reading but extremely helpful for public reading. *Common Sense* was not intended for solitary study but for public performance, and as colonists read the pamphlet to other colonists, scattered personal opinions began to align into a distinguishable community opinion.

Readers of *Common Sense*, then, were not depositing knowledge via the optic nerve into their brains; they were reciting and enacting a performance of *Common Sense* before an audience of their friends and family. The most salacious passages elicited giggles and gasps, while Paine's ringing perorations merited applause and even an occasional "Amen!" Readers would enunciate a section and then stop to discuss it, going back over their favorite parts or disputing with one another on a point of disagreement. *Common Sense* was often the evening's entertainment, read by one man to a group of three or four others swilling beer or coffee after dinner. The orality of the performance allowed the arguments of *Common Sense* to waft beyond the perimeter of gentlemanly culture as wives, children, servants, and slaves overheard all or part of the performance regardless of their visual literacy. Family Bible reading was an entrenched practice in colonial American culture, and the oral performance of *Common Sense*, with its strong biblical cadences and images, was a political instantiation of that deeply religious practice.

Literary historian Jay Fliegelman has pointed out the significance of Jefferson's calculated breathing marks in the original manuscript version of the *Declaration of Independence*.[32] Jefferson's attention to the orality of the performance was both indicative of the rhetorical culture of the time and also of the Virginian's recognition that most Americans would first learn of their independence by hearing the *Declaration* read aloud. *Common Sense* was not composed, like the *Declaration*, to be read before a large concourse of people. Instead, it was read in homes, in shops, in coffee houses and taverns, and even on one occasion in a Connecticut church as the Sunday sermon.[33] These were intimate gatherings of family, friends, and coworkers, not impersonal mass audiences filled with would-be auditors cupping their ears and shushing other bystanders. *Common Sense* was read in community, and this made the decision whether and how to act on its principles strategically personal. Husbands and wives, fathers and children, and cadres of close friends determined, in dialogue with the text, where they stood on the issue of independence. When a decision was made, it was often made in the presence of those whose support would be vital to follow-through on the decision, whether that meant gathering linen rags, enlisting in the Continental Army, traveling to a provincial convention, or supplying the local militia.

PART THREE
MARKETPLACE OF DISCOURSE

Economies of Print

Beyond Robert Bell's newspaper ads for *Common Sense*, the first surviving mentions of the pamphlet came on Saturday, January 13, 1776, a market day in Philadelphia. The scandalous pamphlet on sale at Bell's shop was the topic *du jour* as residents from the city and county converged on the sprawling commercial shantytown north of Market Street. Philadelphia druggist Christopher Marshall, later a local leader in the independence movement, mixed with the crowds at the market that brisk morning. The gregarious apothecary stopped to talk with artisans as well as Congressional delegates, and men of both vocations shared with him their spirited opinions about the king's speech and the first new pamphlet printed in Philadelphia in recent months. These conversations piqued Marshall's interest, and he decided to run one more errand before heading home. He made a nonchalant note in his diary for that day, "Went to Bell's; bought a pamphlet called *Common Sense*."[34]

It was fitting that Paine's pamphlet entered the marketplace of discourse via the marketplace of goods, because *Common Sense* was in large measure a study in political economy. The pamphlet laid out a series of economic arguments in favor of political independence, as well as political arguments in support of economic independence.[35] Paine explicitly called on the colonies to diversify their economic supply chain, and his arguments wrought a diversification of the political supply chain. No one entity could meet every colonial need, he said, but the Americans could thrive in an interdependent horizontal relationship with each other rather than through a dependent hierarchical relationship with Britain. *Common Sense* painted a picture of plenty and possibility, and it reassured the colonists that any gaps in domestic supply could be filled by commercial ties with a decentralized European market. America could be self-sustaining, Paine assured the colonists, but only if their collective conception of "self" shifted its referent from isolated colonies to a confederated union of American states. Especially in the area of naval shipbuilding, that "nice point in national policy in which commerce and protection are united," the abundant natural resources of America ensured that "We need go abroad for nothing."[36] *Common Sense* clearly anticipated the commercial ascendancy of America, but Paine stressed that America's success hinged upon broadening its market from an English monopsony to a multilateral European exchange. "Our plan is commerce," said Paine, "and that, well attended to, will secure us the peace and friendship of all Europe, because it is the interest of all Europe to have America a *free port*," and he assured agrarian America that its produce "will always have a market while eating is the custom of Europe."[37]

Paine's thinking on the diversification of supply and the broadening of markets carried over into the circulation of *Common Sense* in the colonies. Circulation of *anything*—crops, goods, texts, soldiers—was a challenge in colonial America. Under normal circumstances, the surest, fastest means of travel between the colonies was by boat between seaports, but beginning in 1775, the threat of attack from British naval vessels forced many Americans who would otherwise have sailed to their destinations to travel on horseback along primitive trails or by stagecoach down teeth-chattering roads. When the North Carolina delegates to the Continental Congress traveled home from Philadelphia in early 1776, they described the eighteen-day journey as "fatiguing beyond all description."[38]

Since nine out of ten colonial Americans were what we would consider remote rural dwellers, overland travel was a basic requirement for survival. Under optimal conditions, a trip "to town" to attend church or court-days, to purchase supplies and dry goods, or to sell livestock or produce at market was an arduous affair. A cracked wagon wheel, a gimpy horse, or a hard rain could easily turn a day's journey into a week's detainment. But slow travel was usual for the majority of colonists who made their living off of the land. In the thirteen colonies, there were only twenty towns with populations over 3,000, and only five could realistically be called cities: Philadelphia, New York, Boston, Charleston (South Carolina), and Newport (Rhode Island). These modest cities had a combined population of just over 100,000, with Philadelphia alone accounting for nearly half that number, and yet even this largest city in the colonies accounted for only one-tenth of the population of Pennsylvania.[39] Though the cities were few and small by our standards, they dominated regional politics, commerce, culture, and communication.[40] Since people and goods moved with great difficulty through early America, these primary seaport cities accrued their disproportionate influence not because of their vast populations or wealth, but by virtue of their function as the major connecting hubs of colonial life.

While America was fully integrated into imperial Britain, imported goods arrived from London and fanned out regionally from seaport cities to secondary towns and then to tertiary villages and farms, while exported goods were funneled in the opposite direction. The gradual economic estrangement between the London metropole and the colonial periphery forced the Americans to look to their neighbors as intercolonial trading partners. The stoppage of transatlantic trade cut off the flow of goods between London and the seaport cities, but the regional distribution infrastructures remained intact, and a handful of American cities still set the agenda for news, commerce, and politics.

Philip Freneau depicted the rural circulation of texts and information in late eighteenth century America in his poem, "The Country Printer" (1791).[41] The county seat or shire town was the place of meeting for the vast majority of Americans who made their living as rural farmers. A coach might pass through the town "Three times a week, by nimble geldings drawn," but it "scarcely deigns to stop" unless the driver needed to pull into the blacksmith's shop for repairs. When a coach did stop, the country printer leapt at his "harvest-time of news," and he would wander over to the shop and strike up a conversation with any passenger willing to talk to him, "Hoping, from thence, some paragraph to find,"

> Some odd adventure, something new and rare,
> To set the town a-gape, and make it stare.

But if travelers had no interesting morsels for him, he would watch longingly for "the weary post-boy traveling through" town on horseback. The rider carried with him "letters, safe in leathern prison pent," as well as newspapers "wet from press, full many a packet sent." The printer's shop was a "poor lonely shed" where "wretched proofs by candle-light are read," and

> Inverted letters, left the page to grace,
> Colons derang'd, and commas out of place.

The printer's "ink-bespangled press" gave "to the world its children with a groan." His publications may only "live a month—a day—some less;" while the almanac was the printer's "longest-living brat."[42] Freneau's caricature of the printer's desperation for news reflected a basic fact of eighteenth century American life: in a society populated primarily by scattered small farmers, information was scarce and communication was slow.

This isolation was true at the micro-level of communities, but it also described the macro-level relationships between colonies. Perhaps the largest hurdle that threatened to prevent *Common Sense* from swaying American public opinion, was the fact that in January 1776 American public opinion did not exist. Literary historian Moses Coit Tyler's diagnosis of the colonial period that "we find in this country, not one American people, but many American peoples" was still a reality for most colonists at the beginning of 1776.[43] The historically atomistic colonies had never before relied upon each other, because their needs had been wholly supplied by Britain.

The British monopoly had made "colonial isolation," as Tyler observed, "the prevailing fact in American life." Beginning with the Stamp Act, however, the crimped imperial lifeline forced the colonies to begin tapering off their absolute dependence upon Britain, a decade-long process that disrupted the transatlantic supply of goods, ideas, discourse, and identity. But undeveloped intracolonial infrastructure and stifled European relations hampered the colonies' ability to locate a singular substitute that could fill the cavernous British absence. Thus the fitful struggle of colonial resistance prior to 1776 seemed only to reinforce the depth of the colonies' addiction to Britain and the absence of an inclusive *American* identity.

The *circulation* of *Common Sense* capitalized upon the disconnected situation of the American colonies, even as the *text* of *Common Sense* worked to transform isolated colonies into united states. A single colonial print shop, using medieval labor practices and Renaissance technologies, could not set, wet, ink, pull, sort, and stitch enough pamphlets to supply the entire continent. Even if every printer in Philadelphia had been employed in the work, an insufficient supply of paper would have idled the presses. Also, transporting tens of thousands of pamphlets from a central distribution point to the end of every dirt road in America would have been a logistical impossibility. *Common Sense* could not succeed by imposing a macroeconomic model where it did not exist, but instead the text infiltrated the existing microeconomic networks of supply and demand that defined colonial American life.

Networked Printers

With the enthusiasm of Freneau's fictional country printer, in the first few months of 1776, printers and booksellers in other colonies caught wind of the *Common Sense* phenomenon and scurried to grab profits of their own. The ever-struggling colonial printers longed for the elusive sure-seller, and the buzz surrounding *Common Sense* almost guaranteed an audience. By January 20, William Green, a friend of Robert Bell, was selling copies of *Common Sense* in New York.[44] Paine and the Bradfords placed an advertisement for their forthcoming edition in the *New York Journal* on February 1, and a week later William Green was advertising his "2nd Edition" and John Anderson, a new edition "Printed on a good paper."[45]

When Paine began to issue his new edition of *Common Sense* on February 14, using William and Thomas Bradford as his nominal publishers, the lid blew off the pamphlet's circulation.[46] Paine and the Bradfords managed to slash the price of the pamphlet in half, even as they added more content, by shrinking the typeface, farming out the printing to other shops, and selling the finished pamphlets at very low margins. There was no talk of mittens and blankets after the Bradford edition because, at the new one shilling price, the author and publishers were simply covering their costs.

Paine later claimed to have "granted" the copyright to *Common Sense* to the other colonies; in fact, he took a *laissez faire* approach to the republishing of his work. Copyright laws at the time lie somewhere between vague and nonexistent, and an author had even less statutory authority than a printer to prosecute pirated editions. Paine realized, though, in the wake of his controversy with Bell, that his number one priority should be a wide distribution, and the combination of a low price and a decentralized publishing network accomplished that objective.

On February 17 the *Providence Gazette* announced a run of *Common Sense* to be sold in the Rhode Island capital for one shilling each, adding "This Pamphlet is in such very great Demand, that in the Course of a few Weeks three Editions of it have been printed in Philadelphia, and two in New-York, besides a German edition."[47] Though it had been promised earlier, the German edition, *Gesunde Bernunft*, did not, in fact, come out in Philadelphia until February 23, when Steiner and Cist advertised it for sale in their shop as well as in four others.[48]

In cases where a local edition had not yet been printed, booksellers scrambled to gather as many copies as they could from elsewhere. The printers of the *Norwich Packet* offered "A few Copies of a Pamphlet, Entitled, *Common Sense*" to readers in late February, and in early March, the *Boston Gazette* announced "A few of the celebrated Pamphlets" for sale in Cambridge and Watertown "if applied for soon."[49]

When a printer failed to obtain a sufficient number of pamphlets to resell, he tried to spike the circulation of his newspaper by publishing excerpts. The *Norwich Packet*, with a circulation in Connecticut, Massachusetts, New Hampshire, and Rhode Island, reprinted extracts of *Common Sense*, including the Appendix and the Epistle to the Quakers, on the front page of nine consecutive issues, beginning in February and ending in late April.[50] The *Connecticut Courant*, published in Hartford, was more efficient in its reprinting of *Common Sense*. The publisher devoted most of three issues in late February and early March to reprinting the pamphlet. Each issue carried the full text of the second, third, and fourth sections of *Common Sense*.[51] Alexander Purdie and John Pinkney both printed an extract of the pamphlet's third section in their Virginia papers in early February.[52] In most cases this third section was considered the "meat" of the pamphlet and elicited the strongest reactions on both sides of the question. In March the *New-England Chronicle* reprinted Paine's Appendix and the Epistle to the Quakers as a service to its readers who had purchased or read an earlier edition of the pamphlet. As the editor put it, "The Public in General Having Read, and (excepting a Few Timid Whigs or Disguised Tories) Loudly Applauded that truly excellent pamphlet," his readers would "doubtless be pleased with the perusal" of the new sections by "the same ingenious author."[53]

By the beginning of March, another pamphlet edition with the Appendix was selling in New York for "Eighteen Coppers Only," or as retailers would announce to their customers, "*Common Sense* for Eighteen Pence." A new Connecticut edition was advertised in New London, with the note: "Such has been the Demand for this Pamphlet, that eight Editions of it have been printed in different Colonies, in the Course of a few Weeks only."[54] Massachusetts readers, who had endured a full year of battle in their colony, gobbled up editions of *Common Sense*. By the end of March, Ezekiel Russell had printed two editions in Salem, and by mid-April new editions were being sold "by the bundled dozen" in Andover and Newburyport.[55] "The Book so much admired" continued to sell, along with other "Pieces on the Times," in New England through June and July.[56]

Most editions of *Common Sense* printed outside of Philadelphia sold for less than Bell's original two shilling price, and many maintained the Bradfords' one shilling price in spite of the rampant scarcity and, therefore, the steep price of paper. The low price of *Common Sense* was critical to its wide circulation, a point that Robert Bell, an aficionado of fine books, never seemed to grasp. As aggressively as the Bradford edition had driven down the price, Bell drove his prices up. When he published *Plain Truth* at the end of March, Bell and his New York distributor, William Green, charged three shillings for the pamphlet, and the duo attached the same price to their "Third Edition, in large Print" of *Common Sense*.[57] Bell and Green clung to these decidedly unpopular prices because they were publishing *Common Sense* (and its textual competitors) as a small *book*, while the Bradfords and others published *Common Sense* as a large *pamphlet*. The distinction may seem piquant, but the mentality of book publishing prioritized quality over quantity and sanctioned inefficient printing techniques. Robert Bell saw himself as a craftsman of books and a purveyor of refinement, while William and Thomas Bradford embraced their role as a node on the network of colonial information distribution. Bell had tried to control *Common Sense*, while the Bradfords were satisfied to convey it.[58] *Common Sense* met an existing demand and then created an additional demand for its ideas by its accessibility and availability. As a result, it was not uncommon in early 1776 for the Bradfords to receive requests, like one from Annapolis, Maryland, "to send down by the Post three or four dozen Pamphlets of *Common Sense* with the Additions."[59]

Continental Congress: Gathering and Scattering

For about a month after it was first published, *Common Sense* remained primarily a Philadelphia phenomenon. Of course, to be a

Philadelphia phenomenon in 1776 meant that it attracted the attention of America's most populous city as well as the delegates Philadelphia was hosting from every other American colony. The spirited controversy between Paine and Robert Bell focused the attention of a *Philadelphian* audience on the text, but the correspondence of the Continental Congress helped *Common Sense* to develop an *American* audience. The delegates of the Continental Congress were a crucial mechanism for facilitating the distribution of *Common Sense*. They wrote letters talking about the pamphlet, and they sent copies to their friends and family.

The Continental Congress existed primarily as a hub for intercolonial communication. As a body, it issued formal proclamations, resolutions, and recommendations, and it provided a central point for coordinating the actions of the Continental Army with the separate colonial militias. These formal communications were supplemented by the informal conveyance of information between the expatriate delegates and their correspondents back home. The turnstile representation of each colony in the Continental Congress boosted *Common Sense*'s circulation. Delegates came and went from Philadelphia on a constant basis, either because of new elections, sickness, fatigue, militia duty, or their concurrent responsibilities in their respective colonial governments. It was not uncommon for a delegate in the Continental Congress to be also a simultaneous member of every possible committee of inspection, committee of safety, colonial assembly, colonial court, provincial congress, and militia battalion, in addition to supervising their farms, businesses, and families. These were busy, influential men whose social networks, family connections, and, in some cases, material fortunes multiplied their political clout by orders of magnitude over most American colonists. When Paine advertised his "New Edition" at the end of January, noting that "Several hundreds are already bespoke, one thousand for Virginia," he made it sound natural.[60] But this was estimated and not actual demand, and someone had to subsidize the production of those pamphlets. One thousand pamphlets, even at the printer's cost, would have exceeded the annual salary of an average Philadelphia craftsman. Thus the support and encouragement of the Continental Congress was a crucial factor in the pamphlet's wide circulation.

On January 13, New Hampshire delegate Josiah Bartlett wrote home after reading a report in a Philadelphia newspaper that depicted, he thought, the town of Portsmouth as "very much afraid of the idea conveyed by the frightful word *Independence!*" Bartlett informed his correspondent of "a pamphlet on that subject" printed in Philadelphia that week and "greedily bought up and read by all ranks of people." Bartlett sent a copy of *Common Sense* home with his letter, "which you will please to lend round to the people." Bartlett hoped that upon "consideration there may not appear any thing so terrible in that thought as they might at first apprehend."[61]

That same day, Samuel Adams sent a copy of *Common Sense* to his wife, Elizabeth, and asked his friend, James Warren, to have a look at it. Adams noted that "It has fretted some folks here more than a little. I recommend it to your Perusal and wish you would borrow it of her. Don't be displeased with me if you find the Spirit of it totally repugnant with your Ideas of Government. Read it without Prejudice and give me your impartial Sentiments of it when you may be at Leisure."[62] It is revealing that even Samuel Adams in a letter to his good friend did not express unabashed admiration for *Common Sense*. These were dangerous waters, and prudent delegates preferred to dip their toes into the controversy rather than diving in headfirst. That same weekend, Henry Wisner of New York sent a copy of the pamphlet to his friends and some members of the New York Committee of Safety, asking their "opinion of the general spirit of it." He said he would have commented more thoroughly on the pamphlet, "but the bearer is waiting."[63]

The following Wednesday, January 17, John Hancock enclosed to Thomas Cushing "a pamphlet which makes much Talk here," which he was sending for the "Amusement" of Cushing and his friends. Hancock, the President of the Continental Congress, made it his business to learn the author's identity, which he revealed well before it became common knowledge. The pamphlet, Hancock disclosed, is "said to be wrote by an English Gentleman Resident here by the name of Paine, and I believe him the Author."[64]

The mood inside the Continental Congress shifted more slowly than it did "out of doors," but it was clearly shifting. According to the diary of Richard Smith, a delegate from New Jersey, on the same day that *Common Sense* was first published in Philadelphia, James Wilson had "moved and was strongly supported that the Congress may expressly declare to their Constituents and the World their present Intentions respecting an Independency, observing that the King's Speech directly charged US with that Design." Wilson expected near unanimous support for his measure, but there was greater uncertainty than in the past. New party lines were just beginning to form within the Continental Congress on the issue in the wake of the king's threats. During the January 9 debate over Wilson's measure, "Several Members said that if a Foreign Force shall be sent here, they are willing to declare the Colonies in a State of Independent Sovereignty."[65] The measure was tabled for two weeks, and in the meantime the tenor of discourse in Philadelphia continued to escalate. The second week of January brought word of the burning of Norfolk, Virginia, and in the third week of January, the Congress's session was interrupted with "the unfortunate news" of the defeat at Quebec and the death of General

Richard Montgomery, regarded universally as a "gallant Soldier and amiable Man."[66]

Oliver Wolcott, a new delegate from Connecticut, sent his wife on January 24 "the Journals of Congress together with a Pamphlet lately published in this City entitled *Common Sense*. It has had a great Sale and has been Variously Animadverted upon. Said to be Wrote by one Mr. Paine."[67] On that same day, as Paine's inductive argument continued its rapid dissemination through the colonies and events seemed to corroborate his arguments, James Wilson resumed his proposal "to address the People of America our Constituents deducing the Controversy *ab initio*." Wilson, John Dickinson, and others again took up the conciliatory torch in long speeches about "the Mode and Propriety of stating our Dependence on the King," although "much was said about Independency" by a growing contingent of delegates.[68] A committee appointed that day to prepare a draft in accordance with Wilson's motion consisted of five conspicuously conservative members: Robert Alexander, James Duane, William Hooper, Dickinson, and Wilson. Most congressional committees at that time were balanced to represent competing perspectives, and the uniformity of this committee indicated that a solid majority of delegates did not anticipate endorsing its work. When the committee submitted its report on February 13, the measure elicited little comment and was quietly tabled. As Richard Smith recorded it, Wilson's report "was very long, badly written and full against Independency." Smith continued parenthetically, "Wilson, perceiving the Majority did not relish his Address and Doctrine, never thought fit to stir it again."[69]

In the interval between Wilson's initial motion of January 9 and his embarrassing rejection on February 13, the independence movement had continued to build steam. On February 3, Oliver Wolcott had written to Samuel Lyman of Litchfield, Connecticut, "*Common Sense* Operates pretty well, but all Men have not common Sense."[70] The following day, Virginia delegate Thomas Nelson wrote to Thomas Jefferson, who had yet to come to Philadelphia, "I send you a present of 2 shillings worth of Common Sense. I had liked to have omitted to send you a present from the Quakers also," referring to the *Ancient Testimony* that Paine was at that moment preparing to refute.[71]

On the evening of February 13, after the pronounced defeat of Wilson's measure, Joseph Hewes of North Carolina sent a single copy of *Common Sense* to his friend, Samuel Johnston. "The only pamphlet that has been published here for a long time I now send you, it is a Curiosity, we have not put up any to go by the Wagon, not knowing how you might relish independency. The Author is not known. Some say Doctor Franklin had a hand in it, he denies it."[72] The next day, John Penn, also of North Carolina, sent "a pamphlet called *Common Sense* published here about a month ago" to Thomas Person in the North

Carolina Provincial Congress, a gentlemen who would become a chief architect of the pro-independence Halifax Resolves in April.[73] Around this same time, John Adams, who had not yet arrived in Philadelphia, sent Abigail "from New York a Pamphlet entitled *Common Sense.*"[74] Though most of the delegates refrained from explicitly endorsing the pamphlet, there was growing doubt about the likelihood of reconciliation, and they sent copies abroad to test the political waters.

On February 19, Josiah Bartlett detailed the pamphlet's rapid circulation, and he noted that "by the best information" *Common Sense* "has had a Great Effect on the minds of many here & to the southward."[75] That same day, Benjamin Franklin wrote to General Charles Lee that Paine was "the reputed, and I think the Real, Author of *Common Sense*, a pamphlet that has made a great Impression here."[76] Also on February 19, Samuel Ward of Rhode Island wrote to his brother, Henry,

> I see no Advertisement in the Providence Paper for reprinting *Common Sense*; that Pamphlet ought surely to be distributed throughout all the Colonies if it was even at the public Expense. It has done immense Service; I am told by good Judges that two thirds of this City & Colony are now full in his Sentiments; in the Jerseys & Maryland &c. they gain ground daily.[77]

Joseph Hewes wrote again to Samuel Johnston on February 20. Only a week earlier Hewes had explained his hesitancy to send multiple copies of *Common Sense* to North Carolina, but this time he said,

> I mentioned to you in my Last per express that we had not sent any copies of the Pamphlet entitled *Common Sense* but finding Brother [John] Penn had a fondness for them have agreed some should be sent, the Council can Judge of the propriety of distributing them. Let me know your opinion on that head.

Hewes had arranged to put "live horses to the Wagon" and hoped the cargo, including seven barrels of gunpowder, three boxes of drums, and "three Boxes of Pamphlets" would "all be delivered safe to you."[78] In the first week of March, Samuel Ward—who would die of small pox before the end of the month—sent the Appendix to *Common Sense* to his brother, saying "I think it has been in the middle Colonies of immense Service and doubt not but it will [be] so with you." He asked his brother, Henry, to have John Carter of Providence "print the Appendix separately to complete the work."[79]

On March 16, Oliver Wolcott wrote that *Common Sense* "has had a Surprising run, which is an evidence it falls in with the general Sentiments of the People." He continued, "Court Measures may necessitate the Colonies to realize these Sentiments in general."[80] On March

19, Francis Lightfoot Lee of Virginia prefaced a letter to Landon Carter with the supposition that "you have received a Copy of *Common Sense* which I sent you some time ago; if not, I now send a parcel to Col. [John] Tayloe of whom you may have one." Lee then proceeded to deploy the arguments of *Common Sense* in his letter:

> Our late King & his Parliament having declared us Rebels & Enemies [and] confiscated our property, as far as they were likely to lay hands on it; have effectually decided the question for us, whether or not we shou'd be independent. All we have now to do, is to endeavour to reconcile ourselves to the state it has pleased Providence to put us into; and indeed upon taking a near & full look at the thing, it does not frighten so much, as when view'd at a distance. I can't think we shall be injured by having a free trade to all the world, instead of its being confined to one place, whose riches might always be used to our ruin. Nor does it appear to me that we shall suffer any disadvantage, by having our Legislatures uncontrolled by a power so far removed for us, that our circumstances can't be known; whose interest is often directly contrary to ours; and over which we have no manner of control...The danger of Anarchy & confusion, I think altogether chimerical, the good behaviour of the Americans with no Government at all proves them very capable of good Government.... There is such an inveteracy in the [King] & his advisers, that we need not expect any other alternative, than slavery or separation. Is it not prudent therefore, to fit our minds to the state that is inevitable?[81]

On April 2, William Whipple wrote to New Hampshire to inquire "how the politics of Portsmouth stand," specifically asking about independence: "Can they yet reconcile themselves to that illustrious stranger that was so much feared?" Whipple added, "*Common Sense* has made all the Southern Colonies his friend, and I hope the Northern Colonies will soon open their arms to receive him. It's my opinion under the rose that the salvation of America depends on him."[82] The following week, Whipple rejoiced that "The army have converted all the Yankees" in New York to independence, and, borrowing a slur from *Common Sense*, he said, "I expect the statue of the Royal Brute now standing in Bowling Green will soon be demolished."[83]

By the end of April, Samuel Adams noted, "The Ideas of Independence Spread far and wide among the Colonies." He pointed to a number of favorable developments in several colonies, and then turned his attention to "this populous and wealthy Colony" where "political Parties run high." Adams told his correspondent, the Rev. Samuel Cooper of Boston, "The Newspapers are full of the Matter, but I think I may assure you that *Common Sense* prevails among the people."[84]

By early June, Elbridge Gerry had become a friend of "Mr. Paine Author of *Common Sense*," and the two shared the opinion that George III's answer to the March 22 petition of London in Common

Council Assembled had "given the *Coup de Grace* to all Expectations of Reconciliation in the middle Colonies." Gerry regretted that the middle colonies' "Knowledge was so shallow as not to have discovered the Designs of the Ministry which were equally apparent to every discerning Person in the Beginning of the present Year."[85]

One week after the *Declaration* had been read in Philadelphia, Benjamin Rush wrote to Patrick Henry, congratulating him upon his appointment as the Governor of Virginia but more so "upon the declaration of the freedom & independence of the American colonies." Rush said, "I tremble to think of the mischiefs that would have spread thro' this country had we continued our dependence upon Great Britain twenty years longer." Paine's early collaborator was about to take his seat in the Continental Congress, and Rush's opinions still rung with the themes of *Common Sense*. "The contest two years ago found us contaminated with British customs, manners & ideas of government. We begin to be purified from them. In particular we dare to speak freely & justly of royal & hereditary power," and he added a plug for democracy, "In a few years we shall vie I hope for wisdom with the Citizens of Athens." Rush commented upon the virtuous response of the Pennsylvania Militia to the "late Alarm from New York," and he observed greater bravery and virtue in the regular soldiers than in the officers. "Were our officers equal to our men, I believe we might drive a whole Army of Howes & Burgoynes into the Ocean in a few days." Of these citizen-soldiers, Rush noted, "War, liberty & independence is the common language of them all."[86]

Samuel Adams wrote on July 27, that "I have tho't that if this decisive Measure had been taken six months earlier, it would have given Vigor to our Northern Army & a different Issue to our military exertions in Canada. But probably I was mistaken." He continued,

> The Colonies were not then all ripe for so momentous a Change. It was necessary that they should be united, & it required time & patience to remove old prejudices, to instruct the unenlightened, convince the doubting, and fortify the timid. Perhaps if our Friends had considered how much was to be previously done, they would not have been, as you tell me some of them were, 'impatient under our Delay.'

The elder Adams then turned his attention to the formation of governments:

> New Gov'ts are now erecting in the several American States under the Authority of the people. Monarchy seems to be generally exploded, and it is not a little surprising to me, that the Aristocratic Spirit which appeared to have taken deep Root in some of them, now gives place to that of Democracy.[87]

Common Sense had been the loudest advocate in 1776 of everything that Samuel Adams described: it had ripened, united, exploded, unrooted, and popularized. Through the pamphlet's crisis language and the bifurcation of colonial discourse, Paine had replicated within his text the experience of war, even for those who had yet to witness it firsthand.

John Witherspoon addressed the Continental Congress at the end of July on the subject of the confederation of states. Witherspoon asked,

> Does not all history cry out, that a common danger is the great and only effectual means of settling difficulties, and composing differences. Have we not experienced its efficacy in producing such a degree of union through these colonies, as nobody would have prophesied, and hardly any would have expected?[88]

The "common danger" of war did not fully unite the American colonies for more than a year after Lexington and Concord, because the threat was unevenly distributed between colonies. It took the arguments of *Common Sense* and the reverberating debate of the spring of 1776 to fashion an unprecedented "degree of union" in America on the topic of political independence.

John Adams wrote at the beginning of August 1776, describing "the Exultation at a Declaration of Independence." He asked, "Is not the Change We have seen astonishing? Would any Man, two Years ago have believed it possible, to accomplish such an Alteration in the Prejudices, Passions, Sentiments, and Principles of these thirteen little States as to make every one of them completely republican, and to make them own it? Idolatry to Monarchs, and servility to Aristocratical Pride, was never so totally eradicated from so many Minds in so short a Time."[89] Adams would never have admitted it, but the assault of *Common Sense* upon "the Prejudices, Passions, Sentiments, and Principles" of the American colonies, and specifically their "Idolatry to Monarchs" and "servility to Aristocratical Pride" owed its eradication "from so many Minds in so short a Time" in large part to Paine's text.

PART FOUR
FRONT LINES

A General's Perspective

The interpretive burden of this study demands that I recount not just *what* colonial American readers said about *Common Sense*, but also *why* they said it. The best entrée into that subject is a man who did not, as far as we know, mention *Common Sense* during the early part of 1776. Brigadier General Nathanael Greene of Rhode Island, encamped with the Continental Army in late 1775 and early 1776 outside of Boston, probably read *Common Sense*, but no commentary survives detailing his reaction to the pamphlet. What is relevant about General Greene in this chapter is how he arrived at the conclusion of independence, a political stance for which the general was among the clearest and earliest American advocates. When we understand why Nathanael Greene began to call for a declaration of independence in late 1775, we will better see the parallel rhetorical logic at work in *Common Sense*.

As early as October 23, 1775, Greene wrote from his camp at Prospect Hill, Massachusetts, to his wife's uncle, Samuel Ward, Sr., a delegate in the Continental Congress, that the soldiers in the Continental Army were beginning "heartily to wish a Declaration of Independence."[90] Greene wished the Continental Congress could "behold the distresses and wretched condition of the poor Inhabitants driven from the Seaport Towns" because it would "kindle a blaze of Indignation" against the British. Greene said he would "make it Treason against the state to make any further Remittances to Great Britain." He encouraged the opening of colonial ports "to all that has a mind to come and Trade with us." More significantly, Greene stressed the need for a "separation" rather than an "accommodation" because of the dire need for France's aid. The French, he said, would refuse to "intermeddle" in American affairs as long as there was hope of an accommodation, because, he said, "Should France undertake to furnish us with Powder and other Articles we are in need of, and the breach between Great Britain and the Colonies be healed, She will incur the displeasure of Britain without reaping any solid Advantage from her plan of Policy."[91]

Upon hearing of the burning of Falmouth by the British, Greene said, "Fight or be Slaves is the American Motto."[92] In the fall of 1775, there was "a black Cloud" hanging over "this once happy Land, but now Miserable and Afflicted People."[93] Greene grew frustrated in November at this "most alarming Crisis of American Affairs," that the "present disposition of the Troops" from New England was to quit the service in "lukewarm indifference." Greene thought the "present backwardness the Troops discover in engaging in the service again will in all probability protract the War for Years, by encouraging the Ministry to hold out in hopes of our getting sick of the dispute and divided amongst ourselves." Greene called the New England troops' behavior an "infamous desertion" that would make the residents of the northern colonies "the vilest Paltroons in the Universe," a "laughing Stock," and a "subject of derision for all Europe." Greene explained, "After they had insulted the King and Ministry in bidding defiance to their Unconstitutional Laws, after they had engaged the whole Continent in support of their Opposition," with "every thing prospering beyond their most sanguine expectations" they were choosing "to basely desert the cause and at a time too when every thing round us promises success."[94]

At the end of 1775, the army struggled with the absence of a common cause. New Hampshire's recruiting efforts had been successful, but there was still a "great defection" among their troops. Massachusetts was beginning finally "to exert itself," but troops from Connecticut were "going home in Shoals" and Rhode Island's regiment had "hurt our Recruiting amazingly" because "they are fond of serving in the Army at Home" and refused to leave their families to fight on behalf of another colony. Of his own colony, Rhode Island, Greene surmised, "No Public Spirit prevails." The town of Newport, he had learned, was hedging its bets and would "Observe a strict Neutrality this Winter, and join the strongest party in the Spring."[95]

Greene observed that most recruits had arrived from "the Country" and lacked "the Sentiment of honor, the true Characteristic of a Soldier," and were still driven by "Interest." Greene described the backcountry men as "Naturally brave and spirited as the Peasantry of any Country," but they were yet a "Raw Militia." General Washington, he said, had believed the people of New England "a superior Race of Mortals," but their evident vices had caused them to "Sink in his Esteem." Washington had been too busy to acquaint himself with "the Genius of this People," Greene said, which was, because of "the long intercourse of Trade," at its best, a commercial savvy and, at its worst, "exceeding" avarice.[96]

By late December, Greene was calling for Congress "to put a finishing stroke to this dispute" by acting with one accord and giving "every measure an Air of decision." Greene prayed that "we may not lose the critical moment." Since "Human Affairs are ever like the Tide constantly upon the Ebb and flow," a few resolute actions would "draw in the weak and wavering" and to "give such a turn to the minds of People" that they would remain focused despite minor setbacks.[97]

At the beginning of January, after reading a copy of the king's October speech to parliament, Greene declared, "The War begins to grow very Serious. The Tyrant's last Speech closes all hopes of an Accommodation." He continued, "There is no Alternative but Freedom or

Slavery," adding, "the latter is too horrible to think on, the former too desirable to lose." As a general, he saw the "Great Preparations" being made for battle by both sides and grimly predicted, "The Plains of America will be stained with Human Blood the next Campaign. The Moments are swiftly Rolling on" before the opening of "this Tragic Scene." After reading the speech, Greene placed the blame for present and coming miseries squarely on the king. "The King," he said, "is as Obstinate as the Devil and as Cruel as a Turk. His boundless Ambition has plunged two happy Countries into an endless train of Misery."[98] The "last Graceless Speech," he said in a bilious tone, "to that Stupid, Ignorant, wicked, Pensioned, Perjured Parliament" emphatically shut "the Door of hope for a Reconciliation." He then referred to independence as the next obvious step, "One thing more and then, 'Who raw' for America."[99]

A letter from Greene to Samuel Ward on January 4, 1776, was remarkable for the way the general anticipated the arguments of *Common Sense*. Greene told Ward, a congressional delegate from Rhode Island, that the king's speech confirmed that George III was "determined at all Hazards to carry his plan of Despotism into Execution." In a remarkable statement, Greene said, "Indeed it is no more than common sense must have foreseen long since had we not been blinded by a too fond attachment to the Parent State. We have consulted our wishes rather than our Reason in the indulgence of an Idea of accommodation."

The general then opened his "Mind a little more freely" on the subject of international alliance. Greene described the benefits of a treaty with France and Spain and urged Congress to "embrace them as Brothers." Because of the urgent need of foreign aid, Greene recommended "from the Sincerity of my Heart, ready at all times to bleed in my Country's Cause," that the Continental Congress make "a Declaration of Independence." Such a statement would "call upon the World and the Great God who Governs it to Witness the Necessity, propriety and Rectitude" of their cause. Reminding Ward that he stood as a "Representative not of America only but of the Whole World," Greene scoffed at the misguided frugality of the Continental Congress. Because the king's speech "hath convinced us that to be free or not depends upon ourselves," he asked, "How can we then startle at the idea of Expense when our whole Property, our dearest Connections, our Liberty, nay Life itself is at stake?" He urged the Congress to "Act like Men, Inspired with a Resolution that nothing but the Frowns of Heaven shall Conquer us." He lambasted the timidity and loquacity of the Congress: "It is no time for Deliberation, the hour is swiftly rolling on when the Plains of America will be deluged with Human Blood; Resolves, Declarations and all the Parade of Heroism in Words will never obtain a Victory." An army "properly furnished" and "fighting in the best of Causes" would "bid defiance to the United force of Men and Devils."[100]

Speaking as both a general and a former politician, Greene observed that "The populace borrow almost all their opinions." All a politician could do, he said, was to "watch the temper of the times, and the disposition of the people, and take our measures from them." He realized that he could not "drive mankind into measures," even if those measures were "necessary to promote their own interest and happiness."[101]

By the early summer of 1776, as Greene awaited the arrival of British and Hessian troops in New York, he had grown frustrated by the "narrow and Economical" policy of Congress in levying more troops. "They do not seem," he said on June 7, "to have any Systematical plan. The Delegates of some Governments Clog the necessary measures suggested by others; and thus the Chariot goes heavily on." He gaped at "That dam'd Idea of Reconciliation" that was "continually damping and dividing the Assembly" and wished "the Devil would fetch it" and its advocates out of Congress.[102] Greene did not know that the very same day Richard Henry Lee was introducing in Congress a resolution for American independence.

Although Greene's surviving papers do not give any indication of the general's response to *Common Sense*, the sentiments expressed in his letters were strikingly consonant with the pamphlet's arguments. We can be sure that the similitude between Greene's letters and Paine's pamphlets was strong enough to merit an introduction of the two men later in the year. After Greene was promoted to Major General in August 1776, Paine became his aide-de-camp. While under Greene's command and, as the legend goes, using the head of a drum as a writing desk, Paine composed the *American Crisis, No. 1* in December 1776.

Something Worth Fighting For

Nathanael Greene's silence about *Common Sense* manifests an important facet of public discourse in the period of independence: the general did not need to read *Common Sense* in order to become convinced of the necessity of independence. Greene had been convinced by experiencing firsthand the realities of war.

Every soldier in the Continental Army and in the colonial militias shared a perspective on the conflict that had been shaped by the scene at the frontlines of battle. James McHenry, a young Irishman who had studied medicine under Benjamin Rush in Philadelphia, was serving in early 1776 an assistant surgeon in the Continental Army. At the beginning of the year, McHenry, writing from camp in Cambridge to his younger brother, said, "A declaration of Independency may not be far off." The army surgeon continued,

> We can hardly suppose a reconciliation between England and America. Both are too far engaged to recede. Our terms of accommodation would be too humiliating to the false dignity of Britain, and theirs too ignominious for the sons of freedom. Strength must decide the present dispute. I have few fears of the scales turning against us. We have within ourselves materials for carrying on a war of any duration: We have many more natural resources than the ministry will confess. And may, if wanted, have foreign assistance. Under such circumstances, it would be foolishness in the extreme to accept of less than *absolute independency*. For in short we are only to be subjugated by pusillanimity and disunion.[103]

America had been engaged in open combat with Britain since April 19, 1775, but, as Paine later put it, she was "without either an object or a system; fighting, she scarcely knew for what, and which, if she could have obtained, would have done her no good."[104] The Americans were "startled at the novelty of independence," he said, "without once considering that our getting into arms at first was a more extraordinary novelty." Paine added that the hesitant colonists had not reflected on the fact "that it required the same force to obtain an accommodation by arms as an independence."[105]

In late 1775, Paine lacked any real military experience and had not yet ventured beyond the bounds of Philadelphia, yet he grasped better than anyone in America the importance of public opinion for the war effort (as his *American Crisis* papers would later demonstrate). He knew that a delayed independence would vanquish the Americans' fleeting tactical advantages, further depress troop morale and enlistment numbers, and lead to sure defeat. It was for these reasons that General George Washington and his field generals were some of the most enthusiastic early fans of *Common Sense*.

The last day of 1775 and the first day of 1776 marked significant events for the Continental Army. On December 31, 1775, encouraging news arrived in Cambridge, Massachusetts, at General George Washington's headquarters that the Virginians had soundly defeated Lord Dunmore's makeshift loyalist army. Yet even as the troops in Boston cheered for Virginia, a reciprocally discouraging battle was taking place in Canada. Also on December 31, the Americans failed in their effort to take Quebec City and General Richard Montgomery, arguably Washington's most respected general and a man "fired with a noble ardor" had been killed by a musket ball as he stormed the city wall. Montgomery's troops, ably led by Colonel Benedict Arnold had, up until that point, met with remarkable success in their Canadian expedition, and hopes had been high that "the reduction of the city of Quebec would have been the finishing stroke." Montgomery may have pressed matters too quickly in order to capitalize on the momentum and experience of his forces, many of whom would be free to return home the next day. January 1, 1776, "presented a great change in the American army" as new regiments of soldiers arrived at the same time "the old regiments were going home by hundreds and by thousands." In Boston, this change took place without event "in the very teeth of an enemy."[106]

Military news in 1775 and 1776 was susceptible to dramatic swings and frequent mixed reports. It seemed that every victory was followed by a loss, every advance by a retreat. Even the success in Virginia proved mixed as the coastal town of Norfolk burned to the ground. And such was the case throughout the Revolutionary War, though it must be remembered that no such war existed at the start of January 1776. The soldiers were fighting as rebellious subjects in what they construed a civil war. The object of this civil war was typically described under the murky heading of "a redress of grievances," but the manner and extent of this redress, it was assumed by most, was the business of politicians, not soldiers.

The Continental Army was an awkward mishmash of smarmy stableboys posing as enlisted soldiers, silver spoon collegians performing the role of gallant officers, and ragtag colonial militiamen who refused to pretend allegiance to anyone from a colony other than their own. Militiamen "trained" for battle by purchasing and reading a military manual. Troop levels fluctuated wildly with the ebb and flow of recruitment bonuses, desertions, casualties, disease, harvest obligations, and uncertain reinforcements. A handful of senior officers, most of whom were veterans of the French and Indian War, attempted with varying degrees of success to bring order to this chaos.

The experience of the Continental Army was critical to the movement for independence. In the smoky swirl of musket fire and cannonades, the soldiers realized that they were embroiled in a war. This seems patently obvious in hindsight, but at the time it was a startling revelation. They were not engaged in a romanticized "defense of their liberties"; they were dodging lead bullets that had been aimed at their heads. The most powerful army on earth was attempting to obliterate them and every gory casualty put a restoration of the colonies "on the footing of 1763" further out of reach. What was worse, the British regulars charging their garrisons served the same king with whom the Americans had exchanged allegiance for protection. American civilians and politicians had to read the king's speeches to learn that they were excluded from his protection, but the Continental soldiers had *felt* that exclusion on a daily basis since Lexington and Concord.

The reluctance of the colonies to admit the nature of the military conflict had palpable consequences for the Continental Army. The American troops faced a rigorously disciplined and abundantly supplied force of British regulars, but their own provisions were grossly inadequate. The Continentals lacked proper clothing, sufficient munitions, decent nutrition, and even basic compensation. Only foreign alliance promised reinforcement and resupply, but the reluctance of colonial politicians to separate from Britain effectively blockaded all hopes of aid from other European powers. The colonists were trying to win a war without ammunition, and, as we have seen, the American obsession with gunpowder and saltpeter in 1776 transcended the battlefield and became symbolic of a pervasive political deficiency.

In a state of imperial dependence, winning the war carried with it no positive incentive, because there was no shared objective in the fighting that was commensurate with the blood already spilled. The reconciliation movement was an elaborate effort to pretend that the last twelve years had never happened, sealed with a promise that Britain would never do *that* again. The fantasy that the colonies could erase their collective memories in exchange for an apology was only fungible off of the battlefield, where losses were solely financial and could therefore be recouped. Fallen soldiers and broken families were beyond the scope of reparations. It is no surprise, then, that the Army was at the forefront of the independence movement.

Pockets of military resistance had existed in the colonies in 1775, but in the spring of 1776 all of America became militarized. Robert Aitken, Paine's former employer and a man who always kept politics at arm's length, sold piles of military manuals during the spring of 1776 to colonists who sensed the pressing urgency to train themselves for battle.[107] Headlining an April 29 ad for "goods to be sold" by John Sparhawk at his Philadelphia bookstore was "ENTICK's naval history," the source of Paine's longest intertextual quotation in *Common Sense*.[108]

Captain John Paul Jones recounted to Benjamin Franklin in 1779 the risk he had taken in joining the embryonic Continental Navy in an expedition against Lord Dunmore at the end of 1775. "I had not then heard the doctrine of Independence even in a whisper." Jones then added an insightful explanation: "as the Pamphlet called *Common Sense* did not Appear till a considerable time afterwards," he noted, "I could have no views of protection from a new Government."[109] According to revolutionary America's most famous naval officer, *Common Sense* gave the colonists a common military objective: they were fighting for a new government.

Paine, of course, did not write *Common Sense* to circulate only among the Continental Army. For *Common Sense* to succeed as a persuasive text, it had to approximate for its civilian readership the path by which soldiers in the colonial militias and the Continental Army had arrived at independence. Paine attempted to replicate the sentimental experience of battle in the minds of his readers by employing a full rhetorical battery of crisis temporality, vivid description, and antithetical structures, along with a series of commercial and diplomatic arguments favoring independence.

As we shall see in coming chapters, *Common Sense* did not convert every colonist to its doctrine, but a sizable number of Americans pointed to their reading of the pamphlet as a major step along the path to independence. At the beginning of May 1776, a combined meeting of the Pennsylvania Militia company and "a number of other inhabitants" of Faun, in York County, Pennsylvania, issued the following resolution:

> *Resolved unanimously,*
> That the independent principles of *Common Sense* are what we wish to see established, as soon as the wisdom of the Hon. Continental Congress shall think proper, as we look upon it to be the only alternative left us to secure our liberties, and screen us from the disgraceful epithet of rebels in the eyes of all the world."[110]

Americans who had taken up arms supported independence by a landslide. On June 10, "the grand question of INDEPENDENCY" was "proposed" to the first, second, fourth, and fifth battalions of the Pennsylvania militia from Philadelphia and the surrounding suburbs. In a gathering of about two thousand officers and enlisted soldiers, the response to this informal referendum was: "Against it, in the first battalion, four officers and twenty-three privates—second, two privates—fourth and fifth, unanimous for independence."[111]

When news of America's independence reached the Continental Army in New York on July 6, a "choir" of the officers "went to a Public House to testify our Joy at the happy news" by drinking wine all afternoon.[112] At roll call on the evening of July 9, the Declaration of Independence was "published," or read aloud, at the head of every brigade, and the soldiers responded with three loud cheers and "the utmost demonstrations of joy."[113]

The *Declaration of Independence* was proclaimed in every town in America accompanied by a full military procession. The soldiers of the Continental Army and from every local militia company were, in that moment, transformed from "rebels" into "patriots." They were no longer disloyal subjects fighting on the wrong side of a civil war; they were now virtuous citizens fighting to perpetuate their right to self-governance. In Easton, Pennsylvania, "a great number of spectators" assembled at the court house on July 8 to hear the *Declaration* "read aloud." The procession of the *Declaration* was led by a local militia battalion with "drums beating" and "fifes playing." The entire congregation "gave their hearty assent" to the *Declaration* "with three loud huzzas, and cried out MAY GOD LONG PRESERVE and UNITE the FREE and INDEPENDENT STATES of AMERICA," a national neologism, like the later "United States of America," crafted by Thomas Paine.[114]

The End of Britishness

Some Americans glanced at *Common Sense* and rejected independence out of hand, while others flung their arms open to embrace Paine's proposals wholesale. Most colonists, however, fell between those two extremes. They occupied an undecided middle ground and adopted a wait-and-see attitude, mulling over each new conspiratorial factoid with circumspect caution. Those Americans who were closest to armed conflict realized that the archetypal Whig vigilance of the moderate majority was, in fact, a self-justifying guise for timidity. For soldiers and civilians who awoke every morning in plain view of the British military, *Common Sense* was a welcome validation of their lived experience and a manifesto clarifying the inchoate reasons why they refused to surrender or defect.

Most colonists who lived beyond firing range chose to partition military necessity from political discourse. By late 1775 an emphatic majority of Americans had attained a certain level of mental comfort with *fighting to be reconciled*—oblivious to their oxymoronic policy and unaware how easily it could be construed as hypocrisy. The colonists spoke as though they were inhabiting a political mansion with a few controllable leaks, but Paine, pointing to the thundercloud gathering over their heads, demonstrated that the American political system was a roofless lean-to slated for demolition by a royal landlord.

As we saw in Chapter Five, Paine created a textual crisis in *Common Sense* in order to press millions of American colonists into concerted action. A crisis is an experience born of textual interpretation and designed to replicate the bifurcating conditions of war. The Americans had held their position since April 1775, but they could not crouch in their ammunition-bare bunkers forever. The British were preparing to call their bluff. Just as in battle, argued Paine, the colonies now had to choose to advance or to retreat.

In order to survive the coming battle, Paine emphasized, the colonies needed to advance together. Achieving continent-wide independence would require some degree of colonial unanimity, and so Paine's crisis rhetoric needed to level the cultural topographies that divided America into thirteen separate "countries." At the start of 1776, the Americans shared a *Continental* Congress and a *Continental* Army and little else beyond their common connection with Britain. Because the political charters, religious denominations and economic situations of each colony were not even commensurable, much less aligned, Paine had to subsume all inferior concerns and quibbles with his overawing text, and thus he had to point the barrel of every American musket at the same object: the British Constitution.

Henry Middleton of South Carolina, one of Paine's American critics in 1776, revealed that the "great Aim" of *Common Sense* was "to overthrow the [British] Constitution."[115] At the beginning of 1776, most Americans considered the British Constitution as inviolable and sacrosanct, not unlike the way in which subsequent generations of Americans have viewed the *United States Constitution* of 1787. American disaffection toward British policy had been accumulating since 1763, but by early 1776 there remained still a visceral prepossession in the colonies in favor of the British ideal. The Americans had become practiced in partitioning the malevolent *acts* of parliamentary policy from the benevolent *constitution* of British government. The official standoffishness of George III toward the colonies prior to 1775 led most Americans to assume that, since the king was not *against* them, he must be *for* them. All along the American colonists earnestly believed that the beloved "Father of his People" was contending behind the scenes for their rights against a power-hungry parliament. When *His Majesty's* Army opened fire upon the residents of Lexington and Concord, and when the king began to issue a series of proclamations and addresses expressing contempt for the American cause, the startled colonists began to grasp that they had, in fact, no advocate at all within the British government. The House of Commons, the House of Lords, and the Crown had each shut its ears to the Americans' grievances, but the colonists managed to miss the obvious connection among these three entities: they represented all three parts of the British Crown-in-Parliament system. Most Americans already regarded British colonial policy as unjust, but they believed it was an unfortunate aberration from the venerable British Constitution.

Common Sense did not present any new evidence against Great Britain, but Paine arranged the pamphlet's arguments in such a way that it gave the Americans a new interpretive framework with which to view transatlantic affairs. Paine's degradation of the practical British government was only truly radical insofar as it served his goal of vaporizing the Americans' cherished ideal of the British Constitution. And this was the fundamental task of *Common Sense*: to obliterate that constitutional ideal from the American political calculus. As Moses Coit Tyler fittingly observed, "Thomas Paine did not take up his pen in the service of amenities."[116] *Common Sense* did not argue for a new parliament, a new ministry, or a new king. It argued for a new constitution of government and a brand new political identity. Historian Edward Countryman said it well: "Paine attacked not one policy or another but the whole structure of Britishness, subordination, and monarchy within which colonial Americans lived. The problem was not to explain what had gone wrong in a good system; it was to explain why the system itself was the problem."[117]

Becoming politically independent of Britain was the culmination of a decades-long process that involved severing ties with the mother country in every sphere of colonial life.[118] *Common Sense* initiated this last phase of independence because it targeted the sentimental attachment of the American colonists to the British ideal. Other pamphlets, said Paine, had tried to be diplomatic and had failed; *Common Sense* was intended as a textual replication of war. The pamphlet's style and arguments were markedly more violent than other eighteenth century political tracts, because Paine was engaging in a verbal battle. He barreled over ornamental delicacies, stripped the royal draperies, and sacked the first American dream: to become fully British. Paine had to pry loose the sentimental attachment to Great Britain—one reader, one will at a time—or the colonies would never choose independence. The struggle between reconciliation and independence took place in minds even more than it did on battlefields, and *Common Sense* attacked the pillars of Britishness as a strategic maneuver. Paine knew that until the colonists ceased imagining themselves as Britons, they could never fully become Americans.

Notes: Chapter 6

[1] Green, *Life of Ashbel Green*, 47.
[2] Tyler, *Literary History of the American Revolution*, 1:469.
[3] AC, No. 9. CW 1:176.
[4] SA to James Warren, 10/13 January 1776. *Warren-Adams Letters*, 1:204.
[5] James Warren to Elbridge Gerry, 7 March 1776. Gardiner, *A Study in Dissent*, 8-9.
[6] "Rib" is a reference to his wife, a common Puritan adaptation of Genesis 2: 21-23.
[7] James Bowdoin to Mercy Warren, 28 February 1776. *Warren-Adams Letters*, 1:208-209.
[8] Ibid., 23 March 1776. *Warren-Adams Letters*, 1:215.
[9] SA to James Warren, 16 April 1776. *Warren-Adams Letters*, 1:224-225; cf. CS A.16, CS 3.32, Exodus 1:15-22.
[10] Samuel Cooper to BF, 21 March 1776. Willcox, *Papers of Benjamin Franklin*, 22:387a.
[11] Quoted in Commager and Morris, 283.
[12] Quoted in Smith, *A New Age Now Begins*, 682-683.
[13] Ibid., 684.
[14] Quoted in Tyler, *Literary History*, 1: 473-474.
[15] Quoted in Commager and Morris, 297-298, and in Maier, *American Scripture*, 79.
[16] I am not taking the social standing of the Adams or Warren family as typical or normative, but rather as an example of the network of relationships that governed the spread of *Common Sense*. The remainder of this chapter will demonstrate how the pamphlet circulated among individuals of lesser notoriety—whose extant private correspondence may not be as complete as those of leading colonial families.
[17] While letters, especially those sent to and from delegates in the Continental Congress, were an insecure form of communication in 1776, Samuel Adams wrote several other letters during this period wherein he displayed far more candidness.
[18] Monaghan. "Literacy Instruction and Gender in Colonial New England." See also Lockridge, *Literacy in Colonial New England* and Davidson, *Revolution and the Word*.
[19] From a map of the colonies by Thomas Jefferys, London, 1775, Map Division, NYPL.
[20] The remaining ten percent were a mixture of other Europeans and some integrated Native Americans. Stout, *The Perfect Crisis*, 1-2, 11.
[21] Ibid., 147.
[22] Ibid., 12.
[23] In *The Spectator, No. 10*, Joseph Addison wrote, "My Publisher tells me, that there are already Three thousand of them distributed every Day: So that if I allow Twenty Readers to every Paper, which I look upon as a modest Computation, I may reckon about Threescore thousand Disciples in London and Westminster." Steele and Addison, 210.
[24] Liell, *46 Pages*. Though Liell has been the most numerically specific, he is by no means alone in the enterprise of emphasizing the pamphlet's brevity. It has

long been a commonplace of American historiography to frame discussions of *Common Sense*'s influence in terms of its page count.

[25] *Common Sense*. Philadelphia: Robert Bell, 1776. MHS E187.

[26] CS A.19. NUL.

[27] Sollors, *Life of Olaudah Equiano*, 48.

[28] Augustine's narrative of Ambrose in the *Confessions* is a famous example of the opposite phenomenon: Augustine, a trained rhetorician, had never seen anyone read in silence before Ambrose.

[29] Emphasis added. CS 2.13, A.2.

[30] CS A.6, 3.38, 3.7.

[31] Almost a century later, Abraham Lincoln's public speaking was, reciprocal to Paine, well-suited to written presentation at the moment when advances in publishing and telecommunication technologies were ushering in another shift away from orality.

[32] Fliegelman, *Declaring Independence*.

[33] Corner, *Autobiography of Benjamin Rush*, 114-115.

[34] 13 January 1776. Marshall, *Diary*.

[35] The anonymous 1776 pamphlet, *Civil Prudence*, was dedicated to *Common Sense*. The author noted that his pamphlet had been originally written soon after the repeal of the Stamp Act but thought that his proposals for trade might now be useful in light of the prospect of colonial independence.

[36] CS 4.9.

[37] See CS 3.7, 3.16-3.18, 4.9, 4.14, A.5.

[38] Morgan and Schmidt, *North Carolinians in the Continental Congress*, 22.

[39] Contemporaneous estimates of the population of Pennsylvania clustered around 400,000. See for example, "For the PENNSYLVANIA PACKET. QUERIES addressed to the writer who signs himself CATO," DPP, March 18, 1776.

[40] Stout, 5.

[41] Though Freneau's poem was written in 1791, it described cultural practices that remained largely unchanged for several decades. Besides the disruptions of the Revolutionary War, the circulation of texts and goods in the America interior did not change substantially until after the turn of the nineteenth century.

[42] Pattee, *Poems of Philip Freneau*, 3:60-65.

[43] Tyler, *History of American Literature*, 522, 538.

[44] *Constitutional Gazette*, January 20, 1776, and NYG, January 22, 1776.

[45] NYJ, February 1, 1776; NYJ, February 8, 1776.

[46] Especially in Virginia, the broad circulation of *Common Sense* was facilitated by an influx of Bradford editions. See, for example, James Madison's copy of the Bradford edition now held in the Chapin Library at Williams College.

[47] *Providence Gazette*, February 17, 1776.

[48] PS, February 23, 1776.

[49] *Norwich Packet*, February 19, 1776; *Boston Gazette*, March 4, 1776.

[50] Some editions call the "Epistle" an "Address." *Norwich Packet*, February 19/26, 1776 through April 15/22, 1776.

[51] *Connecticut Courant*, February 19, 1776 through March 4, 1776.

[52] Purdie's *Virginia Gazette*, February 2, 1776, and Pinkney's *Virginia Gazette*, February 3, 1776.

[53] *New-England Chronicle*, March 21 and 28, 1776.
[54] "Eighteen Coppers" equaled one and a half shillings. NYJ, February 29, 1776; *Connecticut Gazette*, March 1, 1776.
[55] *New-England Chronicle*, March 28, 1776; *Essex Journal*, April 19, 1776.
[56] *Freeman's Journal* (New Hampshire), June 29, 1776; *American Gazette* (Massachusetts), July 16, 1776.
[57] PEP, March 19, 1776, and March 28, 1776; NYG, April 22, 1776.
[58] To a large extent, Paine drove the high-volume, low-margin economics of *Common Sense*'s publication. Philiadelphia's printing community, on its own volition, had no desire to do more work for less money. Robert Aitken, Paine's former employer, like Bell suffered the consequences of inefficient, "fine" printing. The Continental Congress contracted with Aitken to publish its proceedings beginning in February 1776, but two months later, the Congress ordered him to stop printing and reset both completed volumes in a smaller typeface. Aitken sold the spoiled reams of paper to the Army as cartridge paper. See Spawn, "R. Aitken: Colonial Printer of Philadelphia." Another piece of evidence that Paine deflated the monetary value of his pamphlets to increase their circulation is the scant , nine-pence price of *Four Letters on Interesting Subjects*, the first original-edition pamphlet Paine wrote following *Common Sense*. on See PEP, July 16, 1776. Following Aldridge, *Thomas Paine's American Ideology*, I attribute *Four Letters on Interesting Subjects*, at least in part, to Paine's pen. I have found no hard external evidence of Paine's authorship of the short pamphlet, but the text bears Paine's unmistakable stylistic imprint. Why did Paine never "claim" the pamphlet as his own? He may have considered it an incidental or provincial piece, or he may have co-authored it with another Philadelphian. We know that *Four Letters* was first published in July 1776 by Styner and Cist, the German-American printers who (along with Benjamin Towne) had printed the first run of the Bradford edition of *Common Sense*, and who would also print the first copies of Paine's *American Crisis* (later "No. 1") in December 1776.
[59] William [Whiterush?] of Annapolis to Bradfords, 19 February 1776. Bradford Family Papers, HSP.
[60] PEP, January 25, 1776.
[61] Josiah Bartlett to John Langdon, 13 January 1776. Mevers, *Papers of Josiah Bartlett*, 36-37.
[62] SA to James Warren, 13 January 1776. *Warren-Adams Letters*, 1:204.
[63] Henry Wisner to John McKesson, [13 or 14 January 1776.]. LDC, 3:90-91.
[64] John Hancock to Thomas Cushing, 17 January 1776. LDC, 3:105-106.
[65] 9 January 1776. "Diary of Richard Smith in the Continental Congress, 1775-1776. Part I," (Hereafter RS 1), 307.
[66] 17 January 1776. "Diary of Richard Smith in the Continental Congress, 1775-1776. Part II," (Hereafter RS 2), 493.
[67] Oliver Wolcott to Laura Wolcott. 24 January 1776. LDC, 3:146.
[68] January 24, 1776. RS 2:495.
[69] Wednesday, 24 January 1776, RS 2:495, and Tuesday, 13 February 1776, RS 2:501-502.
[70] Oliver Wolcott to Samuel Lyman, 3 February 1776. LDC, 3:191.
[71] Thomas Nelson to TJ, 4 February 1776. LDC, 3:194.

[72] Joseph Hewes to Samuel Johnston, 13 February 1776. LDC 3:247.
[73] John Penn to Thomas Person, 14 February 1776. LDC 3:256.
[74] JA to AA, 18 February 1776. LDC, 3:271.
[75] Josiah Bartlett to John Langdon, 19 February 1776. Mevers, 48-50.
[76] BF to Charles Lee. 19 February 1776. Willcox, 22.356a.
[77] Samuel Ward to Henry Ward, 19 February 1776. LDC, 3:285.
[78] Joseph Hewes to Samuel Johnston, 20 February 1776. LDC, 3:289-290.
[79] Samuel Ward to Henry Ward, 4 March 1776. LDC, 3:329-330. See, Stillman, *Death, the Last Enemy, Destroyed by Christ*.
[80] Oliver Wolcott to Samuel Lyman, 16 March 1776. LDC, 3:389-390.
[81] Francis Lightfoot Lee to Landon Carter, 19 March 1776. LDC, 3:407-408.
[82] William Whipple to John Langdon, 2 April 1776. LDC, 3:479.
[83] William Whipple to John Langdon, 11 April 1776. LDC, 3:510.
[84] SA to Samuel Cooper, 30 April 1776. LDC, 3:600.
[85] Elbridge Gerry to James Warren, 6 June 1776, LDC, 4:151-153.
[86] BR to Patrick Henry, 16 July 1776. LDC, 4:473-474.
[87] SA to Benjamin Kent, 27 July 1776. LDC, 4:552.
[88] John Witherspoon, "Speech in Congress," [30 July 1776]. LDC, 4:585-586.
[89] JA to Richard Cranch, 2 August 1776, LDC, 4:604.
[90] The October 23 letter itself refers to a previous letter to Samuel Ward as the source of Greene's original statement, thus placing the general's observation even earlier. This early date is corroborated by the journal of Jeremy Belknap—at the time a chaplain in the army—who noted on October 19 and 22, 1776, that a "plan of independence was becoming a favorite point with the army, and that it was offensive to pray for the King" (*Proceedings of the MHS*, 4: 78-84). In Greene's correspondence, he used the word "People" to refer to the soldiers of the Continental Army; the general had very little civilian contact at the time.
[91] NG to Samuel Ward, Sr., 23 October 1775. Showman, *Papers of General Nathaniel Greene*. 1:138-142.
[92] NG to Deputy Governor Nicholas Cooke of Rhode Island, 24 October 1775. Showman, 1:142-143.
[93] NG to Catherine Greene, 26 October 1775. Showman, 1:144-145.
[94] NG to Governor Nicholas Cooke of Rhode Island, 29 November 1775. Showman, 1:154-156.
[95] NG to Samuel Ward, Sr., 10 December 1775. Showman, 1:160-161.
[96] NG to Samuel Ward, Sr., 18 December 1775. Showman, 1:163-166.
[97] Ibid.
[98] NG to Christopher Greene, [ca. 20 December 1775]. Showman, 1:168-169. The actual date of this letter is on or after January 4, 1776, because that is the earliest date Greene would have possessed a copy of the king's speech.
[99] NG to Catharine Ward Greene, 13 January 1776. Showman, 1:181-184.
[100] NG to Samuel Ward, Sr., 4 January 1776. Showman, 1:176-180.
[101] NG to Jacob Greene, 22 January 1776. Showman, 1:185-186.
[102] NG to Christopher Greene. 7 June 1776. Showman, 1:230-234.
[103] Steiner, *Life and Correspondence of James McHenry*, 6-7. McHenry would later serve as Secretary of War under both Washington and Adams, in addition to several other political posts.

[104] "Letter to Messrs. Deane, Jay, and Gérard [On the Silas Deane Affair]," DPP, September 14, 1779. CW 2:182.
[105] AC, No. 3. CW 1:88.
[106] 1 January 1776 and 17 January 1776, Abbatt, *Memoirs of Major-General William Heath*, 27-29.
[107] Aitken, "Wastebook." See also Spawn and Spawn, "R. Aitken: Colonial Printer of Philadelphia."
[108] DPP, April 29, 1776.
[109] John Paul Jones to BF, 6 March 1779. Willcox, 29:63a.
[110] PEP, May 4, 1776.
[111] PEP, June 11, 1776.
[112] Bangs, *Journal of Lieutenant Isaac Bangs*, 56.
[113] Abbatt, 41; PG, July 17, 1776.
[114] PEP, July 11, 1776; cf. CS A.19. On the "Union of the States" and on Paine's emphasis upon the sovereignty of America as "United States," see AC, No. 13, CW 1:233-234.
[115] [Middleton,] *True Merits of a Late Treatise*.
[116] Tyler, *Literary History*, 1:469.
[117] Countryman, *American Revolution.*, 111.
[118] Tyler, *History of American Literature*, 522; For example, the long taxation controversy initiated the extrication of most Americans from economic dependence on Britain. The emphasis on religious liberty, the heritage of dissenting Protestantism, the resistance to an American episcopate, and the outcry over the Quebec Act of 1774 were a multi-stage severing of religious ties with London. The training of military and militia during the French and Indian War lessened the dependence of the colonies on British military leadership, and the outbreak of war sealed the military independence of America.

Chapter Seven

Common Sense and Independence

Extreme distress, which unites the virtue of a free people, embitters the factions of a declining monarchy.

> Edward Gibbon
> *The History of the Decline and Fall of the Roman Empire*
> 1776-1788

There is no instance in the world, where a people so extended, and wedded to former habits of thinking, and under such a variety of circumstances, were so instantly and effectually pervaded, by a turn in politics, as in the case of independence; and who supported their opinion, undiminished, through such a succession of good and ill fortune, till they crowned it with success.

> Thomas Paine
> *American Crisis, No. 13*
> April 19, 1783

PART ONE
TEXT AND MOVEMENT

Reception and Progress

The chicken-or-egg relationship between *Common Sense* and independence has long frustrated historians of the American Revolution. Did *Common Sense* simply reflect a growing colonial consensus in favor of independence, or did the text in some measure generate the independence movement? The documentary record from 1776 unequivocally affirms the latter position, but the untidy progress of independence through the colonies challenges our simplistic assumptions about textual causality. As we shall see in this and coming chapters, individuals did not read *Common Sense* and then call a meeting to become independent; they read *Common Sense* and approached the problems of imperial domination and political legitimacy in entirely new ways. To put it another way, *Common Sense* did not cause independence, but it reorganized colonial society to facilitate the groundswell that *did* cause independence.

There were only two scenarios in the first months of 1776 that created avowed independents: experiencing war and reading *Common Sense*. That spring, one could not be pro-independence and anti-*Common Sense*. Indeed, it is telling how few advocates of independence in 1776 expressed, even privately, a hint of dislike for *Common Sense*.[1] There were a substantial number of colonists who ignored, did not like, or in some cases openly disdained Paine's pamphlet, but most of these individuals comprised the opposition to independence, at least until after the *Declaration of Independence* made it a political fact.

Some 1776 commentators claimed to have arrived at the conclusion of independence when they read the king's August proclamation or October speech. Reverend Ezra Stiles of Connecticut did not read *Common Sense* until the end of February but echoed Paine's sentiments when he wrote in mid-January that the king's speech "convinces me that nothing but Blood is before us in America."[2] Stiles confessed in his diary that "My secret *Hope* that the Veil would be removed from the Eyes of the Parent State, is *now at an End, since the Kings Speech*, & the Disputes thereon in Parl't are come over."[3] When he heard the news that Norfolk, Virginia, had been burned, he reflected, "Thus we see what Effect the national Hostilities have in alienating Americans from the Parent State, & reconciling them to Measures they little tho't of."[4]

What Stiles, and others like him, experienced when they read the king's addresses was a vague feeling that *this* was "the last straw." In the moment of reading the king's speech, some Americans did give up their hope for a reconciliation, but *independence* implied much more than an exasperated desire for political separation. As the movement played out in 1776, American independence meant forsaking the *desire* for a reconciliation, and it also entailed creating foreign trade and military alliances, forming republican governments upon the basis of popular sovereignty, entering into a lasting union with other American states, and announcing the entrance of a new nation onto the world stage. These were not logical conclusions to be drawn from the king's speech, but they *were* the central topics of *Common Sense* and the continent-wide debate the pamphlet instigated that spring.

When we track the circulation and reception of *Common Sense* alongside the political events of 1776, a discernible trend emerges. There was a strong correlation between the reception of *Common Sense* and the progress of independence in individuals and communities. This is not to say that vocal support for *Common Sense* within a particular colony equated to official support for American independence. In several colonies, the most powerful individuals were also those who most loathed *Common Sense* and independence, and existing political bodies proved formidable obstacles to independence. But even as moderate and loyal politicians strove to halt the progress of independence, *Common Sense* was excavating and dismantling the very foundations of their authority.

Common Sense and independence, the text and the movement, were cut from the same cloth. In this chapter I will continue to survey the colonial response to *Common Sense*, beginning with a scan through several colonies. Then, I will focus my analysis on just two colonies: Virginia and New York. Virginia was at the head of the independence movement, and New York was its most reluctant tail. We will witness the responses to *Common Sense* in each colony and then transition to a comparison of the course of the independence movement in both cultural contexts.

An Uncommon Sensation

Every colony, every town, every family, every person was different. American colonists made their decisions about independence based upon a localized calculus reflective of their different backgrounds, cultures, urgencies, and prognostications of success. Yet the fact remains that *most* Americans opposed independence at the beginning of 1776, and *most* Americans supported independence by the end of that spring. On the first day of 1776, "An English American" had written from Philadelphia to Lord Dartmouth, then the British Secretary of State for America, "I know the Americans well; their strongest and ruling passion was their affection to their Mother Country; the honor, the glory of Great-Britain they esteemed as their greatest happiness; a large portion of the same affection remains."[5] Another writer, a conservative Virginian, summed up the prevailing attitude in the colonies prior to the spring of 1776, saying, "It may with certainty be affirmed, that among the ends which the colonies, from South Carolina to New York inclusively, had in view, when they began the present contest, independence held no place; and that the New England governments, if they had it in view at all, considered it as a remote and contingent object."[6] Yet by late March, newspapers across the country carried word that "A favourite toast, in the best companies, is, 'May the INDEPENDENT principles of *COMMON SENSE* be confirmed throughout the United Colonies.'"[7]

The colonists warmed to independence as they discussed and debated the subject between January and May. And whether those conversations took place in homes, taverns, or letters, or if they occurred in the northern, middle, or southern colonies, *Common Sense* was the discursive touchstone of American independence. A letter from Maryland on February 6 requested, "If you know the author of *COMMON SENSE*, tell him he has done wonders and worked miracles, made TORIES WHIGS, and washed Blackamores white. He has made a great number of converts here. His style is plain and nervous; his facts are true; his reasoning just and conclusive."[8] The author of the letter knew only three in his county who disapproved of the piece, all of whom opposed it only because they heard Daniel Dulany, a notorious loyalist, say it might be easily answered. The author requested two dozen copies of the second edition and added, "Since the King's speech, and the addresses of both Houses of Parliament, I look upon the separation as taken place. Some time past the idea would have struck me with horror; I now see no alternative...Can any virtuous and brave American hesitate one moment in the choice?"[9]

One correspondent from Charleston, South Carolina, wrote in mid-February to his friend in Philadelphia, asking "Who is the author of COMMON SENSE? I can scarce refrain from adoring him. He deserves a statue of gold."[10] On February 26, a New Jerseyan wrote a public letter of appreciation "To the Author of *Common Sense*" showering praise on "your famous pamphlet, entitled *Common Sense*, by which I am convinced of the necessity of Independency, to which I was before averse."[11]

One gentleman from Connecticut relayed his eyewitness account of a conversation that took place on March 7 in Norwalk. While on business, the gentleman had observed a conversation between a clergyman and a trader that "sets the characters of the friends and enemies to *Common Sense* in a striking contrast." The clergyman struck up the conversation "in a pleasant facetious manner, by asking the trader if he had read *Common Sense*." The trader had only negative comments about the pamphlet, in response to which the clergyman "enlarg'd somewhat in vindication of *Common Sense*, and the American cause in general." The clergyman said he did not know the author but found the pamphlet "wise and judicious," "practicable," and "possessed of a good share of sense and learning." The clergyman then remarked that "he hoped the colonies would soon universally come into" the plan laid out in *Common Sense*. To this "the sullen trader replied in a very frowning and angry tone, that his horse had more sense than the said piece, or its author, whom he treated with the utmost scorn, indignation, and contempt; intimating that he was a mean, mischief-making fellow, that dare not set his name to his book." The clergyman retorted that neither the trader "nor his horse together with him, were capable of such a performance." This comment provoked the trader into "a most violent rage, and passion" and "with parliamentary or ministerial vengeance in his eyes," the trader "seem'd determined to decide the controversy with his fist, which had more weight in it than any argument he could produce." When he realized he was about to strike a clergyman, who stood his ground with "gravity, sedateness, and composure," the trader "felt his heart and courage fail," and he "retreated back like a bullying pusillanimous Tory." After the trader cast several more aspersions "on the Author of *Common Sense*, on the Clergyman, and on our Colleges, and public seminaries of learning," the clergyman saw "it was no purpose to reason with a madman" and with that "the debate abruptly ended, and the disgusting scene was closed."[12]

Another Connecticut writer addressed the author of *Common Sense*, "In declaring your own, you have declared the sentiments of Millions." The writer described Paine's "production" as "a land-flood that sweeps all before it." Referring to the conversion of the Apostle Paul in the Book of Acts, he said, "We were blind, but on reading these enlightening works the scales have fallen from our eyes," and he added that "even deep-rooted prejudices take to themselves wings and flee away." He continued, "The doctrine of Independence hath been in times past, greatly disgustful; we abhorred the principle—it is now become our delightful theme, and commands our purest affections." This Connecticut Yankee claimed to express the opinion of "MILLIONS" who "revere the author, and highly prize and admire his works." *Common Sense* had a "peculiar virtue" that it could "convert Tories" and, like Noah's Ark, provided a cover "for different species of animals." Americans of different creeds and cultures, he added, "like the radii of a circle, may meet in this common centre, and become one in the great cause of liberty." Should the Continental Congress "think as we do," he observed, "the business would be done—the free and independent states of America fixed on an immoveable foundation."[13]

By late May, one Connecticut town had "in a full meeting" voted to adopt "the principle of independence contained in *Common Sense*," and they also voted that delegates to the Continental Congress "ought to be elected by the freemen of the colony, and not by their representatives."[14] In the spring of 1776, America was not just turning toward independence; it was turning toward democracy.

Part Two
NEW YORK OR VIRGINIA

New York and Common Sense

No American colony was more deeply divided in 1776 than New York. The wealthy merchants and lawyers who made up the colony's ruling class shrugged off the opinions of anyone of lesser means. As a lot, New York politicians predictably loathed *Common Sense*, while the general populace embraced it. Like Landon Carter in Virginia, some New York aristocrats saw it as their moral duty to refute Paine's pamphlet.

The difficulty of refuting *Common Sense* in a pamphlet was exemplified in the failed attempt of one group of New York politicians. When *Common Sense* first arrived in Albany, several leading members of the New York Provincial Congress, "alarmed at the boldness and novelty of its arguments," met "for the purpose of writing an answer." They gathered in the evening, and one of them "read the pamphlet thro'" to the others. The group agreed that it was both "necessary and expedient to answer it immediately, but casting about for the necessary arguments they concluded to adjourn and meet again." They continued to meet for several successive evenings, "but so rapid was the change of opinion in the colonies at large in favour of independence, that they ultimately agreed not to oppose it."[15]

Outside the circles of power, New York was electric with enthusiasm for *Common Sense*. A writer in the *New-York Journal* of February 22 had "just finished the second reading of that incomparable pamphlet," and he effused, "You can scarce put your finger to a single page, but you are pleased, though, it may be, startled, with the sparks of an original genius." The writer continued, "It answers to the name" it was given, and he welcomed the fact that the pamphlet skipped over all but the most important subjects, being "only highly charged with that matter, which as the electrical fire, is universally diffused."[16] Another New Yorker wrote on February 25 of the combined effect of Paine's text and the corroborating news from Britain:

> Your COMMON SENSE operates most powerfully upon the minds of the people, but its effects are trifling compared with the effects of the folly, insanity and villainy of the King and his Ministers. Their last acts have given the *finishing stroke* to dependence. The man who now talks of reconciliation and reunion, ought to be pelted with stones, by the children, when he walks the streets, as a town fool.

This writer demanded that "some treaty should immediately be entered into with France" so that America would be negotiating from a position of prosperity instead of waiting until "the proposal of an alliance would have the air of a solicitation for protection."[17]

The common people of New York ran well ahead of their aristocratic leaders. One writer, calling for "activity, vigilance, and resolution" in a letter to the *New York Journal*, berated the provincial congress as a bunch of do-nothing cowards. At the beginning of the new year, Hugh Hughes of New York wrote to Samuel Adams, "The people are constrained, disappointed and discouraged here by the timidity or treachery of their leaders" in the New York Provincial Congress. Hughes recounted how two separate members of the New York legislature had approached John Holt to discourage him from reprinting *Common Sense*, "the people's minds not being prepared for such a chance &c." Rumors were floated in New York that *Common Sense* had been written by a crafty Tory. Hughes concluded, "Let them say and do what they please, the people are determined to read and think for themselves. It is certain, that there never was any thing published here within these thirty years, or since I have been in this place, that has been more universally approved and admired."[18]

An essay in the [New York] *Constitutional Gazette* on February 24, described the experience of reading *Common Sense*:

> This animated piece dispels, with irresistible energy, the prejudice of the mind against the doctrine of independence, and pours in upon it such an inundation of light and truth, as will produce an instantaneous and marvelous change in the temper, in the views and feelings of an American. The ineffable delight with which it is perused, and its doctrines imbibed, is a demonstration that the seeds of independence, though imported with the troops of Britain, will grow surprisingly with proper cultivation in the fields of America.[19]

Another essay contributed in March to Samuel Loudon's *New York Packet* required, in Loudon's estimation, a disclaimer about its "strong and indecent expressions" that the printer thought did not help the American cause. The passionate writer broadcast his approval of Paine's pamphlet:

> The late excellent pamphlet, entitled, *Common Sense*, justly estimated to be of more worth than its weight in gold, has made a very rapid progress into the country, and meets with universal approbation and applause. The sentiments it contains are eagerly imbibed, by every one possessed of any tolerable share of that rare commodity. It has become the topic of the day, and engrosses conversation in all companies, and not a single objection has as yet, to my knowledge, been raised against the proposed plan of American separation and independency.

The writer described how the once "stupid and sleeping" Americans had been awakened to "the exercise of this *Common Sense*," the most valuable and "safest conductor thro' the perils and dangers of life." He continued, "Indeed, the striking arguments offered by the worthy author of *Common Sense*, against the doctrine of reconciliation, and in favour of immediate separation, are fully convincing, as far as my acquaintance reaches, and doubt not they will be so to all unprejudiced minds." He advocated assembling "the true sons of America" whose domestic "interest and connections" unclouded their judgment. If this crowd of Americans had "*Common Sense* publicly read and explained to them," then "at least nineteen in twenty, if not ninety-nine in a hundred would hold up both hands in favour of an immediate separation from Great Britain."[20] Another New Yorker neatly summarized the popular reaction to the pamphlet in a letter written on April 12, "A pamphlet entitled *Common Sense* has converted thousands to Independence, that could not endure the idea before."[21]

Virginia and Common Sense

Public rumblings of a separation began in the Virginia press as early as December 13, 1775. A writer in Purdie's *Virginia Gazette* on January 5, for example, had recommended the colonies "lay aside that childish fondness for *Britain*, and that foolish, tame dependence on her."[22] But the debate over independence did not really launch in Virginia until early March when the first shipment of over a thousand copies of the "New Edition" of *Common Sense* began circulating in the colony. Virginia, the most populous American colony in 1776, was flooded with cheap Philadelphia editions of the pamphlet. In fact, wagonloads full of *Common Sense* had so quickly saturated the Virginia market that none of the Williamsburg printers bothered to republish it.

Near the end of January, John Page, the vice-president of the Virginia Assembly then meeting in Williamsburg, received a Robert Bell edition of the pamphlet in the mail. Page observed that the cover had already been "quite worn off" and realized that he had received the pamphlet in error. Richard Henry Lee, for whom the copy had been intended, had not yet arrived in Williamsburg, but Page was certain that Lee "would wish to propagate the Doctrine it contained." Page made it a point to read *Common Sense* aloud to John Pinkney, who made "some Extracts of it" for publication in his *Virginia Gazette*, and Alexander Purdie followed suit, printing "valuable Parts" in his newspaper.[23] Around that time, an Englishman staying in Alexandria recorded with disgust that among Virginians "Nothing but Independence will go down. The Devil is in the people."[24]

It is true that agrarian Virginians, deeply indebted to British merchants and in desperate need of an outlet for their crops, were among the fastest colonists to jump on the independence bandwagon.

When, at the end of 1775, the exiled royal governor, Lord Dunmore, tried to turn slaves against their masters, and when British troops attacked Norfolk, the Virginians realized that they were at war. Prior to the arrival of *Common Sense* in the colony, though, Virginians struggled to channel their animosity into a productive vision or a plan of action. *Common Sense* gave vent to their emotions and focused their attention upon the necessity of independence. One Virginian, writing on February 20, called *Common Sense* "admirable," and concurred, "I perfectly agree with the author that the time has found us. It would seem as if heaven had favoured us by bringing on the struggle before it was too late." The writer reiterated Paine's concern that if a separation had developed "more gradually and calmly" then Britain would have realized the colonies' "importance as well as our weakness." Finding the colonists "apt subjects for the pestilence of corruption," any effort toward independence would be easily thwarted by a few well-placed bribes.[25]

By early March, Virginians had fully discarded their 1775 innuendos and began to speak frankly and openly about independence. "Phil-Americus," for instance, wrote on March 8 in a Virginia paper, "We have a hard alternative, either to be slaves, or to fight for independence." Fielding Lewis had written two days earlier to General Washington, "The opinion for independency seems to be gaining ground, indeed most of those who have read the Pamphlet *Common Sense* say it's unanswerable."[26] Another Virginian claimed on March 23 that *Common Sense* had made "a number of disciples here," and he added, "Indeed, I know of none who disapprove, save a few dastard souls" who are "chiefly displeased" that they are incapable of "the furnishing of an answer." This writer noted, "Men in general begin to consider Independency with satisfaction." Though independence was "a noble idea," most minds required some preparation "e'er they can cordially, and with ease, embrace so dignified a stranger."[27]

Still another Virginian corresponding with a resident of Philadelphia read *Common Sense* "with much pleasure," adding that the "author's arguments may be caviled at, but many of them, in my opinion, will never be fairly answered." This Virginian reported the testimony of his countrymen that *Common Sense* "has made many converts here. Indeed every man of sense and candor, with whom I have had an opportunity of conversing, acknowledges the necessity of setting up for ourselves, having already tried in vain every reasonable mode of accommodation." The published letter called Paine's arguments against the probability of civil wars and against leaving vacant the seat of government "new and striking." The Virginian said that *Common Sense* had not made "any material alteration" in his personal sentiments, because his "political creed" had been "firmly fixed" since he first saw the king's proclamation of August. Though he had been long prejudiced in favor of "what we have been used to call our Mother tution and form of government, "they have passed away as a tale that is told, and are now obliterated by the stronger motives of self-preservation."[28]

In early April, John Lee of Essex County wrote, "Independence is now the Topic here, and I think I am not mistaken when I say, it will (if not already) be very soon a Favorite Child."[29] A letter from Petersburg, Virginia, written on April 12, described Virginia's inhabitants as "warm for Independence." A long conversation with a South Carolinian had convinced the writer that the residents of South Carolina "have no expectation of ever being reconciled with Britain again but only as a foreign state." Several letters he had received from North Carolina confirmed that their provincial convention was "quite spirited and unanimous" in favor of independence and for the repeal of their former instructions. Among North Carolinians was heard "nothing praised but *Common Sense* and Independence," while the people manifested a determination "to die hard." The letter's author assured his correspondent that "the vehemence of the Southern Colonies will require all the coolness of the Northern ones to moderate their zeal." He was not at all surprised by this reaction, saying "that whenever they were urged," he had suspected the southern colonies "would go great lengths."[30]

By April, said one Virginian, "The independence of the colonies daily becomes more and more a topic of very anxious disquisition."[31] On April 20, William Aylett wrote from King William, Virginia, that "the People of this County almost unanimously cry aloud for independence," and on the very same day John Adams relayed from Philadelphia the report of North Carolina delegate John Penn that "*Common Sense* and Independence" was "the Cry, throughout Virginia."[32] Four days later, a majority of the "freeholders" of James City County in Virginia, "being desirous of expressing their sentiments on the important subject of independency," assembled at a local tavern and published their instructions in Purdie's *Virginia Gazette*. They had reasoned "from justice, policy and necessity" that "a radical separation from Great-Britain" was the best choice for America. In one part of their instructions, they argued that independence was the only just response to American casualties. Paraphrasing *Common Sense*, they said, "For the blood of those who have fallen in our cause cries aloud, 'It is time to part.'"[33]

Not every Virginian embraced *Common Sense*. Colonel Landon Carter hated the pamphlet before he had read more than a couple of pages of it. He suspected, because of its attribution to "an Englishman," that among "its secret intentions" was "to fix an ill impression that the Americans are resolved not to be reconciled." He had read the extracts printed in Purdie's *Virginia Gazette*, and found the matter "encouraged under the most absurd arguments in the world." He had already written "an answer to the Extracts," but, since the Bradford edition promised "many additions," he thought it best to "wait to see what they are." His "present impression," on February 14, was that the pamphlet was "quite scandalous and disgraces the American cause much."³⁴ Ten days later, Carter visited two friends who introduced *Common Sense* "as a most incomparable performance." Carter responded that "it was as rascally and nonsensical as possible, for it was only a sophisticated attempt to throw all men out of principles." The author exhibited "as much the random of a despot as anything could be" because "he declared every man a damned scoundrel that didn't think as he did," and he reduced "mankind to a mere brutish nature, that of an implacable and unforgiving temper," which he had the audacity to call the "image of God at first implanted in us."³⁵ Carter described Richard Henry Lee as "a prodigious admirer, if not partly a writer in the pamphlet *Common Sense*." Lee and Carter corresponded throughout the spring, and the two had disputed about the benefit of an alliance with France, while Carter had urged "that the Pure British Constitution was not to be so reprobated as *Common Sense* had done it."³⁶ Carter "could not help expressing my detestation at so brutish an author" who seemed to him "a very fit person to head an aristocratic power which must generate from this independency reduced into ever so formal a republican show." Carter planned to write a letter that would "strive to disappoint these artists" and send it by his son to Williamsburg.³⁷ By mid-April, Carter was convinced that *Common Sense* had been "written by a member of the Congress" because every publication in opposition to its principles was met with the "comical" threats of someone, "perhaps a member of the same club," who spread "the terrors of disuniting the colonies and offending the majesty of the people." Unlike his tremulous cohort, the "creature" who had written *Common Sense*, Carter remarked, had "no uneasiness of this sort," even while he was advancing "new and dangerous doctrines."³⁸

New York and the Spirit of '87

The political situation in New York was a study in contrast. At the end of February 1776, British General Henry Clinton and Captain Hyde Parker of the British Navy together decided against firing upon the town of New York because of their confidence, Parker explained to Vice Admiral Molyneux Shuldham, "that the Majority of the Citizens, particularly those of *Property* are faithful to the King."³⁹ Parker described his perplexing situation, "Convinced as I am of the Attachment to His Majesty of many Men of great Property in this Town, at the same time knowing that it is Garrisoned by Rebels" who "even had the Audacity to place Sentinels immediately before Me." The British naval officer had declined to cannonade them and "involve the

City in ruins" because of his determination "to make the Act of committing Hostilities theirs and not Mine." He worried, though, that "this lenity on my side" could be "Misconstrued as a want of Zeal in carrying on the King's Service."[40]

The city of New York had grown rapidly in population and affluence in the decades preceding the American Revolution. In spite of hiccups in trade caused by the imperial taxation dispute, New York had blossomed into the rising star of transatlantic commerce as a result of the city's protected ports and central location. While the city and especially the merchants of New York basked in their prosperity, the rest of the colony hobbled slowly along. Tench Tilghman, a lieutenant in the Pennsylvania Militia and later Washington's aide-de-camp, recorded in his journal only disdain for the colony of New York, where the young officer was stationed during the fall of 1775. New York was "far behind any other of the Colonies in public spirit," noted the soldier, adding, "her Roads are narrow, her Bridges loose logs dangerous to pass, and everything bears the Mark of the true situation of the Bulk of the People, A State of Tenancy."[41]

New York was a colony of haves and have-nots, and political preferences broke cleanly along the lines of economic class. Like most other colonies, New York's official political system was dominated by elites, but the colony's dense concentration of powerful merchants was especially effective at excluding opposition. Thus, in spite of clamorous popular support for independence in the colony, by May 31, the New York Provincial Convention had not yet said "a word" on "the subject of a declaration of Independence."[42] In begrudging compliance with the recommendation of the Continental Congress, they had begun setting up a new form of government. To do so, the Convention realized that it had to call the people of the colony "either to give them proper powers for the purpose, or to add to their number and give the increased body powers, or to choose a new Convention and give the powers to them."[43] The provincial convention moved gingerly into such a step. Though an appeal to "the people" was required to maintain the convention's legitimacy, most New York elites found "the people" to be inconveniently and insufferably *popular*.

Gouvernor Morris, the New York aristocrat and lifelong loather of populist sentiment who would become a primary draftsman of the *United States Constitution*, wrote in 1774, "Reunion between the two countries is essential to both—I say essential. It is for the interest of all men to seek reunion with the parent State."[44] He worried that the "spirit of the English constitution" was dissolving in America, and he grumbled that the colonies were saying, "farewell aristocracy." He added with a foreboding tone, "I see, and I see it with fear and trembling, that if the disputes with Britain continue, we shall be under the worst of all possible dominions—the dominion of a riotous mob!"[45]

By May 1776, Morris began to sound a more populist tone in a speech to the New York Provincial Congress. He acknowledged that "Some, nay many, persons in America dislike the word Independence," but claimed that the hazardous path of independence was preferable to the infallible ruin of a sustained connection with Great Britain. He questioned the colonies' hesitation and trust in the expected commissioners. "Trust crocodiles, trust the hungry wolf in your flock or a rattlesnake near your bosom, you may yet be something wise. But trust the King, his Ministers, his Commissioners, it is madness in the extreme." America needn't worry about the invasion of other European powers, assured Morris, because they knew that "an American war is tedious, expensive, uncertain, and ruinous." Unless New York consented to an immediate declaration of independence, "this miserable country" would "be plunged in an endless war," that would result in all of America bidding "farewell liberty, farewell virtue, farewell happiness!"[46]

Morris was able to divorce his preference for aristocratic governmental control from his affection for Great Britain. John Jay did not make the leap with as much ease. When pressed to acknowledge British wrongdoing, Jay, like other moderates in 1776, placed the blame on Lord North's ministry and never on King George III. Jay showed extreme caution in all of his letters from Philadelphia and remained tight-lipped about his opinions. He realized that anything he wrote as a congressional delegate could surface unexpectedly in a newspaper or in a parliamentary debate. Jay wrote in roundabout terms to his brother, James, a physician in England, on January 4, "I can say in general that Everything with us is in a good Way, and, tho' We desire Reconciliation, are well prepared for contrary Measures."[47] This was an empty and oblique threat, intended by Jay to induce the belief that Americans weren't negotiating from a point of desperation. Jay had no interest in independence, either in January or July.

By the spring of 1776, Jay had been away from his New York home and in constant attendance at the Continental Congress for what was approaching a full year, and therefore, he was eminently qualified to speak about its deliberations. In April 1776, Jay said of the Continental Congress that "no pains have been spared to traduce that respectable assembly and misrepresent their designs and actions." The chief of the "aspersions cast upon them" was "an ungenerous and groundless charge of their aiming at Independence, or a total separation from G. Britain." Jay concluded that "to charge the Congress with aiming at a separation of these Colonies from Great Britain, is to charge them falsely and without a single spark of evidence to support the accusation." He insinuated that the public had been "duped by men who are paid for deceiving them."[48]

Jay finally returned home in May 1776 to attend to his personal business and then to attend the New York Provincial Congress.

On June 11, four days after Richard Henry Lee moved in the Continental Congress that the United Colonies "are, and of right ought to be, free and independent states," John Jay moved in the New York Provincial Congress, "that the good people of this Colony have not, in the opinion of this Congress, authorized this Congress, or the Delegates of this Colony, in the Continental Congress, to declare this Colony to be and continue independent of the Crown of Great Britain."[49]

Jay, like many New York elites, had been alarmed by what he saw as popular excesses in the city during 1775. On November 23, 1775, a group of men from Connecticut, recruited by Captain Isaac Sears of the New York Sons of Liberty, attacked the "dangerous and pernicious" print shop of loyalist James Rivington, confiscating his press and his types. This was the second mob attack on Rivington, publisher of the *New-York Gazeteer*, within the year, and the climate of radicalism in the city made many men of property uneasy.

The young Alexander Hamilton, who would soon become a captain in the New York Artillery and in 1777 Washington's aide-de-camp, wrote to John Jay shortly after the attack on Rivington's press. Hamilton worried of the "great danger of fatal extremes" during "times of such commotion as the present" when "the passions of men are worked up to an uncommon pitch." The passionate multitude, he said, lacking "a sufficient stock of reason and knowledge to guide them," were easily led from an "opposition to tyranny and oppression" to "a contempt and disregard of all authority." When the minds of the "unthinking populace" become "loosened from their attachment to ancient establishments and courses," Hamilton noted, "they seem to grow giddy and are apt more or less to run into anarchy." Hamilton attributed "a principal part of the disaffection now prevalent" in New York to the "antipathies and prejudices" that had "long subsisted between this province and New England."[50]

The functional dichotomy for Hamilton, Jay, and other conservative New Yorkers was not reconciliation or independence, but reconciliation or rebellion.[51] Thomas Jefferson was so convinced of Hamilton's hostility to the core principles of the American Revolution that he attributed *Plain Truth* to Hamilton's pen.[52] Paine likewise would later mince no words concerning Jay's antagonism to independence, "If America had no better friends than himself to bring about independence, I fully believe she would never have succeeded in it" and would have become "a ruined, conquered and tributary country."[53]

Virginia and Independence

As demonstrated in New York, overwhelming popular support for *Common Sense* did not automatically translate into official support for colonial independence. A resident of Williamsburg in March described Virginia's "great misfortune" that "the most obdurate and hardened sinners, in political matters, are men in high trust." These political leaders "were shocked with the bare mention of opposition to Parliament; and these men now reject with abhorrence the idea of Independence." In a phrase descriptive of landed elites across America, including many members of the Continental Congress, the writer said, "They have been constantly dragged into every virtuous measure." The Virginian aristocrats, he continued, "remain sunk in that political turpitude" that makes them always prone "to skulk off" and pursue their "rascally purpose": to have America's chains "riveted faster than before."[54]

The most influential of these anti-independence Virginians were Carter Braxton, Landon Carter, Richard Bland, and Robert Carter Nicholas, the provincial treasurer. Braxton and Carter both composed tracts in 1776 opposing *Common Sense* and preserving the colonial aristocracy.[55] Bland had called Paine "a blockhead and ignoramus" for his "grossly mistaken" views on theocracy.[56] John Page wrote on April 12 that "almost every Man except the Treasurer," referring to Nicholas, "is willing to declare for independency."[57]

Even some who were not explicitly opposed to independence continued to hesitate. In April, General Charles Lee, one of the period's most colorful and controversial characters, wrote of Edmund Pendleton, then President of the Virginia Committee of Safety, that, though he was "certainly a Man of sense," when pressed on the subject of independence, "He talked or rather stammer'd nonsense that would have disgraced the lips of an old Midwife drunk with Bohea Tea and gin."[58] In this the Virginia gentry mirrored the elite position across America. Virginian Thomas Nelson, Jr., had written in mid-February that the words "Independence, Confederation & foreign alliance" were as fearful to a majority of congressional delegates as "an apparition to a weak and enervated Woman."[59]

The performative culture of Virginia's landed gentry inculcated a deep reverence for duty, disinterestedness, virtue, and the "public good" in its members—something that had not shaped the New York merchant class or elites in several other colonies to the same degree. For a decisive majority of Virginia planters, the abiding values of their cultural education overrode raw economic interest and even the fear of an uncertain future.[60] Jefferson and Washington would become the two most famous actors in the events of 1776, but two other Virginians, George Mason and Richard Henry Lee, placed Virginia at the forefront of the movement toward independence. Mason, who had been detained from attending the beginning of the Virginia Assembly's session by "a smart fit of the Gout," arrived in Williamsburg in time to pen one of the most important texts of the American Revolution. The Virginia *Declaration of Rights*, drafted by Mason, would influence Jefferson's *Declaration*, several of the other American bills of rights, and the French *Declaration of the Rights of Man and the Citizen*.[61] During the spring of 1776, Richard Henry Lee joined with John Adams of Massachusetts as the two most indefatigable proponents of independence in the Continental Congress. In June, Lee stood up before the Continental Congress and moved that the American colonies become "free and independent states." The actions and opinions of George Mason and Richard Henry Lee in 1776 reveal the mentality that drove Virginia to the head of the drive toward independence.

The Virginia Resolves and the Spirit of '76

On May 15, 1776, an epic day for the American Revolution, the 112-member Virginia Convention, meeting in Williamsburg with Edmund Pendleton presiding, reached a unanimous decision. They described the "state of extreme danger" facing the American colonies, and concluded that "we have no alternative left but an abject submission to the will of those over-bearing tyrants, or a total separation from the Crown and government of Great-Britain, united and exerting the strength of all America for defense, and forming alliances with foreign powers for commerce and aid in war." They appealed "to the SEARCHER OF HEARTS for the sincerity of former declarations expressing our desire to preserve the connection with that nation," and they stressed that they had been "driven from that inclination" by the "wicked councils" of Britain and "the eternal laws of self-preservation." With that prelude, the Virginia Convention instructed its delegates in the Continental Congress "to propose to that respectable body TO DECLARE THE UNITED COLONIES FREE AND INDEPENDENT STATES, absolved from all allegiance to, or dependence upon, the Crown or Parliament of Great-Britain." They also instructed their delegates to "give the assent of this colony to such declaration and to whatever measures may be thought proper and necessary by the Congress for forming foreign alliances and A CONFEDERATION OF THE COLONIES."[62] The Virginia Convention also resolved unanimously that day to appoint a committee to prepare "A DECLARATION OF RIGHTS and such a plan of government as will be most likely to maintain peace and order in this colony, and secure substantial and equal liberty to the people."[63]

The measures that would become known as the Virginia Resolves were "universally regarded as the only door which will lead to safety and prosperity." A group of wealthy Virginians took up a collection for "treating the soldiery" the next day, and a large crowd gathered to hear the "resolution being read aloud to the army," who "partook of the refreshment prepared for them by the affection of their countrymen." The Virginians lingered well into the evening enjoying multiple toasts, discharges of the artillery and small arms, and "illuminations." A report of the event described every one present as "pleased that the domination of Great-Britain was now at an end, so wickedly and tyrannically exercised for these twelve or thirteen years past, notwithstanding our repeated prayers and remonstrances for redress." The day following the celebration, May 17, the Virginia militia announced that they were "now well provided with arms and ammunition" and were "ready, at a call, to march to the relief of any part of the country which is invaded, or to assist their brethren in the neighbouring provinces."[64]

George Mason and Richard Henry Lee were the two Virginian gentlemen upon whom the burden fell to bring the Virginia Resolves into execution. Mason wrote to Lee from Williamsburg on May 18 that he was dissatisfied with the "tedious, rather timid, & in many Instances exceptionable" preamble to the new resolution, but he hoped "it may answer the purpose." Mason took satisfaction in the unanimity with which the Assembly had carried "the first grand Point," the opponents to the measure "being so few, that they did not think fit to divide or contradict the general Voice."

Mason told Lee that the task yet before them, preparing a plan for the government of Virginia, was "the most important of all Subjects," and he despaired that the committee appointed to draft a proposal was "according to Custom, overcharged with useless Members" who would inevitably submit "a Plan form'd of heterogeneous, jarring & unintelligible Ingredients." Mason believed that the only way to countermand this disaster was to recruit "a few Men of Integrity & Abilities, whose Country's Interest lies next to their Hearts" to steer the process, "defending it ably thro' every stage of opposition." Mason pressed for Lee's attendance in Williamsburg, telling Lee that he presumed it would be "some time' before the Continental Congress, with which Lee was sitting, "can be fully possess'd of the Sentiments & Instructions of the different Provinces, which I hope will afford you time to return."[65] Lee obliged his friend's request to return to Williamsburg, but only after taking care of his lingering business in Philadelphia.

In a letter two years later, Mason vehemently denied the rumor, propagated by the British ministry during the war, that a faction or "junto of ambitious men" had designed the independence movement "against the sense of the people of America." He described how the people had, in fact, "outrun their leaders; so that no capital measure hath been adopted, until they called loudly for it." Then, in language profoundly reminiscent of *Common Sense*, Mason said, "To talk of replacing us in the situation of 1763, as we first asked, is to the last degree absurd, and impossible." He continued,

> Can they raise our cities out of their ashes? Can they replace, in ease and affluence; the thousands of families whom they have ruined? Can they restore the husband to the widow, the child to the parent, or the

father to the orphan? In a word, can they reanimate the dead?—Our country has been made a scene of desolation and blood—enormities and cruelties have been committed here, which not only disgrace the British name, but dishonor the human kind, we can never again trust a people who have thus used us; human nature revolts at the idea!—The die is cast—the Rubicon is passed—and a reconciliation with Great Britain, upon the terms of returning to her government, is impossible.[66]

Mason claimed, "No man was more warmly attached to the Hanover family and the whig interest of England, than I was, and few men had stronger prejudices in favor of that form of government under which I was born and bred, or a greater aversion to changing it." His opinion had been that "no good man would wish to try so dangerous an experiment" unless it was driven by "an absolute necessity." He had opposed "all violent measures" with his utmost power "as long as we had any well founded hopes of reconciliation." When, however, "reconciliation became a lost hope, when unconditional submission, or effectual resistance were the only alternatives left us," Mason began to make decisions in view of the latter option. From the moment "when the last dutiful and humble petition from congress received no answer" besides "declaring us rebels, and out of the king's protection, Mason's mind was made up. He "looked forward to a revolution and independence, as the only means of salvation." To fight a powerful nation while "still professing ourselves her subjects" and "without the reins of government in the hands of America" was "too childish and futile an idea to enter into the head of any man of sense"—an opinion, he said was shared by "more than nine tenths of the best men in America."[67]

Mason spent the latter half of May 1776 composing the Virginia *Declaration of Rights*. The second of sixteen enumerated rights in Mason's *Declaration* reflected a new approach to political sovereignty: "That all power is vested in, and consequently derived from the people; that magistrates are their trustees and servants, and at all times amenable to them." The people, wrote Mason, had not bequeathed their sovereignty to an unaccountable perpetual ruling class; as "trustees and servants," politicians would be judged by their seasonal cultivation of the people's rights. Most importantly, the origin and exercise of the people's rights were derived from *nature*, and not granted on the basis of a charter or contract between rulers and ruled. The Virginia Convention adopted the *Declaration of Rights* unanimously on June 12, 1776, just five days after Richard Henry Lee stunned the Continental Congress with a resolution for revolution.

Richard Henry Lee and the Gauntlet of Independence

Much of Thomas Paine's political perceptiveness stemmed from his knowledge of both sides of the imperial conflict. Richard

Henry Lee of Virginia enjoyed a similar benefit from the steady stream of information he received from his two brothers, Arthur and William, who lived in London. John Adams described Richard Henry Lee as "a masterly Man," and noted in his diary that the Lee brothers—Richard Henry, Francis Lightfoot, William, and Arthur—were all "sensible, and deep thinkers."[68] During the fall of 1775, both Arthur and William Lee sent Richard Henry Lee intelligence that shaped the congressional delegate's expectations of British policy.

On September 4, Arthur Lee, a physician and member of the American Philosophical Society, expressed his regret that "Philosophy and physics" were "silent" in America, and "nothing discussed of but war." The British ministry, said Arthur Lee, were busy attempting to arm "every hand, Protestant & Catholic, English, Irish, Scotch, Hanoverian, Hessian, Indian & Canadian against the devoted Colonies." Nonetheless, the ministry's recruiting efforts met "with very little success" because of the "general repugnance" of "this unnatural war." Though "the ministry have sought & forc'd this quarrel," they were "endeavoring to transfer their own guilt to others" by their threatened prosecution of all who correspond with the Americans "in arms." The principle by which "their pension'd writer Dr. Johnson" defended the "Boston port Bill" in *Taxation no Tyranny* (1775)—"that where they are satisfied of guilt, there is no occasion for evidence or trial"—was the same principle according to which "they would punish all those who oppose their tyranny."

Arthur Lee warned his brother and others in the Continental Congress, "The quantity of Artillery, Arms & Ammunition shipp'd against New England is greater than ever went from this Country before." An army of 24,000 soldiers and fifty warships "intended to carry destruction thro' those Provinces next spring." The coast of America would be ravaged and all commerce stopped, he predicted, and small armies would attempt to invade Virginia and South Carolina. Arthur Lee urged the colonies "to prepare against the storm that is intended to pour down destruction upon them." He also added a somber note about the fate of the "Olive Branch" Petition. After "a great many days delay & debate," the ministry had "condescended to receive the petition from the general Congress, but they have refused to give an Answer." The petition, he averred, was "sufficiently answered by the Proclamation, which was forced some days after they had a copy of the Petition." By the proclamation, he said, America would understand "that she has nothing but her own virtue & firmness in which she can trust."[69]

Richard Henry Lee's other brother then living in London, William, had been active in London politics during the early 1770s and was well positioned to convey confidential information. In a letter sent to Richard Henry from London on September 22, 1775, William accurately predicted the imminent "horrors of war" in Virginia. "What the

Ministry intend against you and the rest of America," said William Lee, "cannot be exactly ascertained before the meeting of the Parliament" in October. He was, however, sure that "The ensuing Session of Parliament, will decide whether [Virginia will] have actual War or not." William conveyed information "that the war is to be carried into Virginia, as well as in the northern Provinces, next spring." William Lee advised his elder brother, "This winter will be employ'd in providing every means that can shield you from the destruction to which your merciless enemies have destined you." He stressed that speed and decisiveness were essential: "No precautions can be too great against the dangers that threaten you, especially as no one can tell what foreign foes, taking the advantage of the present state of things, may invade you." William estimated a force of 30,000 men would be "intended against America, next year," and he said, "I am afraid a total disconnection between the two Countries will be the consequence of these hostile measures." He regretted, "It seems that Liberty is never to be procured, or maintained, but by the Sword," adding, "Be vigilant in providing for your safety against the probable attempts of next Spring; and let not the Philistines come upon you unprepar'd."[70]

Richard Henry Lee's actions in the Continental Congress in early 1776 demonstrated his commitment to heeding his brothers' advice. In early April, Richard Henry Lee wrote from Philadelphia to Patrick Henry that "whilst people here are disputing and hesitating about independancy, the Court by one bold Act of Parliament, and by a conduct the most extensively hostile, have already put the two Countries asunder."[71] The king's speech and the responses to it in both houses of Parliament, along with "their infamous retrospective robbery Act" proved to Lee "the design of the British Court to subdue at every event, and to enslave America after having destroyed its best Members," while the Prohibitory Act had "to every legal intent and purpose dissolved our government, uncommissioned every magistrate, and placed us in the high road to Anarchy." As Lee saw it, "We cannot be Rebels excluded from the King's protection and Magistrates acting under his authority at the same time."

Lee's letter to Patrick Henry illustrates the convoluted flow of sovereignty in America on the eve of independence. Lee instructed Patrick Henry to lead the charge in "taking up government immediately, for the preservation of Society" in Virginia, and he promised that Virginia's initiative would be followed by North Carolina, Maryland, Pennsylvania, and New York. Setting up governments free of the king's authority would "effectually remove the baneful influence of Proprietary interests from the councils of America." After this step had been taken, Lee continued, "give peremptory instructions to your Delegates," of whom Lee was one, "to take every effectual step to secure America from the despotic aims of the British Court." Lee was chiefly concerned that Britain would attempt to partition America with France and Spain, and he argued that a "timely alliance with proper and willing powers in Europe" was the Americans' only chance to foil Britain's ambitions. As long as they considered themselves British subjects, though, "no State in Europe will either Treat or Trade with us" until "we take rank as an independent people." The American colonies found themselves in a "present undefined unmeaning condition," and their clearest interest and "very existence as freemen" required that "we take decisive steps now, whilst we may, for the security of America."[72]

No direct record survives of Lee's response to *Common Sense*, but other contemporaneous sources attested to his hearty approval of the pamphlet. According to Landon Carter, Lee's correspondence had revealed that he was a "prodigious admirer" of *Common Sense*.[73] Lee also rejoiced in April when he heard that the "people of New-York have collected and burnt publicly every copy they could find" of the *Deceiver Unmasked*, written in opposition to *Common Sense*. He added that "Cato," the signature used by Provost William Smith in a series of newspaper essays opposing *Common Sense*, "still continues to write nonsense and the other Tories to forge lies about the Commissioners."[74]

From April through mid-June, Lee immersed himself in the Philadelphia movement for independence, and though he wanted to attend the Virginia Convention, he thought it "impossible to leave this place" at the height of affairs. His letters during this period were "so hurried that I scarcely know what I write." General Charles Lee had written to ask him why Congress hesitated in declaring independence, and Richard Henry Lee responded, "I'll tell you my friend, because we are heavily clogged with instructions from these shamefully interested Proprietary people." He said this situation would continue until Virginia "Sets the example of taking up Government, and sending peremptory Orders to their delegates to pursue the most effectual measures for the Security of America." Lee presaged the domino effect this would have in the middle colonies, since "the people in these Proprietary Colonies will then force the same measure, after which Adieu to Proprietary influence and timid senseless politics."[75]

By late May, Lee was growing more optimistic by the day. His time continued to be occupied with "excessive writing and constant attention to business," but his spirits were high "in the great cause of America." He saw the "mischievous instructions from some Colonies" that had long fettered the Continental Congress now falling away one by one, and he testified that the resolution of the Congress urging the colonies to set up governments had "wrought a great change hereabouts."[76] Lee maligned Maryland's representative bodies as "a Conclave of Popes," who continued in May to call for a reunion with Great Britain "on constitutional principles." He claimed that he did not understand what they meant, "nor do I believe the best among them have any sensible ideas annexed to these terms." He dismissed them, though, "being satisfied they will never figure in history among the Solon's, Lycurgus's, or Alfred's."[77] Lee rejoiced at the "sensible and spirited resolve of my Countrymen on the 15th," referring to Virginia's call for independence, and he expressed confidence that the resolve "will have a wonderful good effect on the misguided Councils of these Proprietary Colonies."[78]

As Paine had done months earlier, in June Richard Henry Lee began to shift his description of the situation away from a vocabulary of decision to one of response. He said, "It is not choice then, but necessity that calls for Independence, as the only means by which foreign Alliance can be obtained and a proper confederation by which internal peace and union may be secured."[79] On June 7, Lee stood in the Continental Congress and introduced, on behalf of the Virginia delegation, the following motion:

> *Resolved,*
> That these United Colonies are, and of right ought to be, free and independent States, that they are absolved from all allegiance to the British Crown, and that all political connection between them and the State of Great Britain is, and ought to be, totally dissolved.
> That it is expedient forthwith to take the most effectual measures for forming foreign Alliances.
> That a plan of confederation be prepared and transmitted to the respective Colonies for their consideration and approbation.[80]

After a spirited debate, a majority in the congress agreed to appoint committees to flesh out each clause of the resolve over the next three weeks. Lee left Philadelphia on June 13, confident in the direction of events there, and headed to Williamsburg to participate in the Virginia Convention. At the end of June, he wrote to General Charles Lee, "I have not the least doubt but that Independence will, in a few days, be publicly announced by the General Congress." All of the impediments had been removed except for Maryland's "restraining instructions," but there "the people were up, and instructions sending from all parts to their Convention, which met 10 days ago, expressly directing to rescind their instructions and pursue a different line of political conduct."[81] A week later he reported, "The Convention of Maryland has rescinded the mischievous instructions with which they had bound their Delegates, empowered three of them to join the other Colonies in a vote of Independence, Foreign Alliance, Confederation, &c. By this time I expect the two former are settled in Congress."[82] Lee's apprehensions about Maryland further subsided as their new convention had excluded from Congress "all those that have been famous for *Moderation* as it is strangely called."[83]

On July 29, Lee shared his frustration with Samuel Adams that although "we are forever parted," the New Jersey government considered "their present state as a transient thing!" Using a phrase from Paine's "Dialogue between the Ghost of General Montgomery and a Delegate" from February 1776, Lee asked, "Shall we never cease to be teased with the Bugbear Reconciliation, or must we hang on forever on the 'haggard' breast of G. Britain?"[84]

Though Richard Henry Lee came from one of the most prominent families in Virginia, he held remarkably democratic political views. Lee sent Patrick Henry a copy of John Adams's "sensible" *Thoughts on Government* chiefly because "it proves the business of framing government not to be so difficult a thing as most people imagine."[85] Lee thought a refutation of Adams's pamphlet, written anonymously by Carter Braxton, a "Contemptible little Tract" marked by "confusion of ideas, aristocratic pride, contradictory reasoning, with evident ill design." It was so poorly executed, Lee said, that it was "out of danger of doing harm."[86] After returning to Williamsburg in June, Lee described the new state government as "very much of the democratic kind."[87]

PART THREE
AMERICAN CONTROVERSY

From Text to Discourse

Unlike Richard Henry Lee, most American colonists did not have access to confidential information sent from their politically savvy expatriate brothers or from official communiqués directed to the Continental Congress. All humans, regardless of social standing, make decisions based upon readily available information, but elites often have privileged access to sources of information. In late colonial America, only a gentleman "with connections" could acquire the kind of rich, private information that helped shape Lee's perspective on the controversy. While the upper echelons of American society supplemented their stores of political data with private communications, most Americans based their political decisions solely on information they received from public texts.

Common Sense was an important agent of change in 1776, but its influence was not limited to a discrete exchange between author and reader. The agency of Paine's pamphlet lay not only in its personal textual impact, but also in its public discursive effect. In other words, the pamphlet did not just persuade; it stirred controversy and recruited others to persuade on its behalf. To craft a new collective identity for the American populace, Paine's pamphlet needed more than calm nods of approval. Paine had shattered the ideal of British America, but he still had to mobilize a fragmentary colonial population to choose independence together. Paine needed the crisis of his text to spill over into the arena of public discourse. There is embedded in the etymology of *discourse* the idea of opposition; discourse is a back-and-forth exchange between competing viewpoints.[88] In the beginning of 1776, there was no public discourse in America on the issue of independence. There was a public consensus against it. To succeed in uniting America in favor of independence, *Common Sense* first needed to divide America on the subject of reconciliation.[89] For independence to emerge victorious from "the crucible of public debate," *Common Sense* needed to attract both acolytes and adversaries.[90]

Finally, a Pamphlet Challenge

Paine had boasted at the end of his February Appendix to *Common Sense*, "And as no offer hath yet been made to refute the doctrine contained in the former editions of this pamphlet, it is a negative proof, that either the doctrine cannot be refuted, or, that the party in favour of it are too numerous to be opposed."[91] This audacious statement needled proponents of reconciliation up and down the coast of America, and yet no formal pamphlet reply surfaced until March 13, almost a full month after Paine's swaggering challenge. When the first pamphlet published in opposition to *Common Sense*, James Chalmers's *Plain Truth*, finally arrived, it had a ready-made audience.[92] Dr. Thomas Young rushed out to Robert Bell's to purchase *Plain Truth* on March 13, the same day it was published, and the doctor stayed up late that night reading it aloud to Christopher Marshall. The two concluded that *Plain Truth* was "very far from coming up to the title."[93]

Chalmers, a wealthy Maryland landowner who would later become a lieutenant colonel in a Maryland battalion of loyalist fighters, dedicated his pamphlet to John Dickinson to pay tribute to the legacy of moderation displayed by the "Pennsylvania Farmer." The dedication may also have signaled Chalmers' intent to persuade the "swing voters" from the moderate middle toward a hardened advocacy of reconciliation.

Chalmers' authorial persona, "Candidus," glowed "with the purest flame of Patriotism" in his indignation at the "Insidious Tenets" of *Common Sense*. In a passage rife with overt anti-Semitism, Chalmers dismissed the authority of the Old Testament to undercut Paine's anti-monarchical arguments. Chalmers recognized Paine's "indecent attack" on the British constitution and defended it as "the pride and envy of mankind" in spite of "all its imperfections." He used copious quotations from Rousseau, Hume, and, in particular, Montesquieu to defend his principles on government with a special emphasis on the inadequacies of "a democratical state."

"The many unmerited insults offered to our gracious Sovereign," he declared, "by the unprincipled Wilkes, and others down to this late Author" would "forever disgrace humanity" by their "execrable flagitious jargon." He lamented "that the King did not receive the last excellent petition from the Congress," but he placed partial blame on the impropriety of "the Gentlemen of the Congress" in addressing themselves "at that juncture, to the people of Ireland." In one of his best points, Chalmers questioned whether the Continental Congress could "be so deluded, to expect aid from those princes" whose subjects would be inspired by America "with a relish for liberty" that "might eventually shake their arbitrary thrones."

Chalmers called "the specious science of politics" the "most delusive" of all, and he implied that *Common Sense*'s phrase, "the time hath found us," was a flight of imagination. The author of *Common Sense* was, he said, a "Political Quack" who attempted "to cajole the people into the most abject slavery, under the delusive name of independence." Like most subsequent opponents of independence, he painted the bleakest picture possible of the future. "Volumes," he said, were "insufficient to describe the horror, misery, and desolation, awaiting the people at large in the siren form of American independence." The argument of *Plain Truth* was best summarized in the pamphlet's final sentence, printed for emphasis in all capitals, "INDEPENDENCE AND SLAVERY ARE SYNOYMOUS TERMS."

A New Jerseyan writing under the signature of "Rusticus" published in May a formal reply to Chalmers's arguments, *Remarks on a Late Pamphlet entitled Plain Truth* (1776). Rusticus had read *Common Sense* "and must confess that I could not withhold my assent to the arguments of the victorious author, notwithstanding I was at first much alarmed at the novelty of his ideas." Rusticus read *Plain Truth* expectantly, because he said, "I would always choose to keep my mind open to conviction, especially in a matter of so great importance as the present contest," and he continued, "I was glad of an opportunity of seeing those arguments to which I had for the present yielded, scrutinized and brought to the test of a counter examination."[94]

Rusticus was, however, severely disappointed by *Plain Truth*. He chafed that Candidus would "impose upon" John Dickinson—to whom Chalmers had dedicated his pamphlet—and "upon us, no less than 65 pages and an half of his '*crude remarks*' at this important era of the American constitution!" After criticizing Candidus's misplaced dedication, Rusticus proceeded to "the author's introduction, of which, the best that can be said, is that it is short."[95]

Rusticus suspected that the author was "labouring in behalf of your oppressors, either in gratitude of favours received or in expectation of future emolument." He exclaimed,

> Can it be possible that any man should presume to place the words PLAIN TRUTH in capital letters at the head of a page filled with ungenerous sneers, wicked falsehoods and gross misrepresentations? I would recommend it to the printers in their future editions of this work, and also to those whose business it may be to translate it into foreign languages, to erase the words *Plain Truth*, and in their room insert the words *Energetic Description*.[96]

In a newspaper commentary, "Aristides" noted that *Plain Truth* sold "at a very high price" but for a curious reason: because, according to advertisements, "only a small number of copies were printed of this *first* edition." Aristides pointed out the oddity of calling a brand new publication the "first" edition, comparing it to calling "my wife, who is still alive and well," "my first wife." Printing few copies made *Plain Truth* "unreasonably dear" and amounted to "an unlucky stumble at the threshold" by Candidus and "an unexpected lapsus of the illustrious and exalted R. B. provedore (as he calls himself) to the sentimentalists," both of whom were acting, as well as writing, "in direct opposition to *Common Sense*."

In spite of the limited edition of *Plain Truth*, Aristides had received two copies from friends, but found "the reading of three pages gave me the opinion of it which all who read it afterwards concurred in, and which all who had not read it easily acquiesced in," that its execution was "so contemptible that it could not procure a reading on a subject as to which the curiosity of the Public was at the greatest height." *Common Sense*, he said, "sometimes failed in grammar, but never in perspicuity," but *Plain Truth* "was so ridiculously ornamented with vapid, senseless phrases, and feeble epithets, that his meaning could hardly have been comprehended." Though *Common Sense* "in some places wanted polish," *Plain Truth* was "covered from head to foot with a detestable and stinking varnish." The conclusion to which *Plain Truth* led its readers, said Aristides, was "that we ought immediately to send an embassy with ropes about their necks, to make a full and humble surrender of ourselves and all our property to the disposal of the Parent State." Aristides framed the looming question with great succinctness: "Shall we make resistance with the greatest force as Rebel Subjects of a government which we acknowledge, or as Independent States against an usurped power which we detest and abhor?"

By April, *Plain Truth* had missed its chance. It was "a performance," chided Paine "which hath withered away like a sickly unnoticed weed, and which, even its advocates are displeased at, and the author ashamed to own."[97] But the pamphlet's author, James Chalmers, was not entirely to blame for his text's embarrassing failure. While Chalmers had been writing and making arrangements to publish *Plain Truth*, American public discourse had accelerated beyond the limits of his chosen medium. Colonial newspapers, not pamphlets, were the main stage of the independence controversy.

The Circulation of Colonial Newspapers

Common Sense shared more in common with newspapers than it did with other American pamphlets. The similarity between *Common Sense* and colonial newspapers was not limited to style and idiom; newspapers were also the closest corollary to the mechanisms of *Common Sense*'s print circulation. For the ideas in *Common Sense* to receive maximum exposure, the text of *Common Sense* needed to reach a maximum audience—a perspective on publishing that Paine had held since his editorship of the *Pennsylvania Magazine*. The dainty circulations of other American pamphlets were no model to follow, but the networks by which newspapers traveled through the colonies showed more promise.

William and Thomas Bradford's subscription lists for the *Pennsylvania Journal* are a great entrée into the dynamics of newspaper circulation in the colonies. In February 1776, the month that the Bradfords' "New Edition" of *Common Sense* began selling, the *Pennsylvania Journal* had 244 "downtown Subscribers," some of whom took multiple copies. A handful of women joined a host of militia captains, reverends, merchants, and printers on the list.[98] Beyond the borders of Philadelphia, the *Pennsylvania Journal* circulated through a vast informal network of relationships. The papers saturated the towns and cities of America: Exeter, Gloucester, Springfield, Albany, Burlington, Bordentown, Fredericktown, Alexandria, and Williamsburg, to name a few. According to the Bradfords' records, the *Pennsylvania Journal* was delivered to 155 distinct towns or locales, usually by an individual who would leave a stack of papers at someone's shop or home to be picked up by individual subscribers. James Bailey picked up papers at the Fountain Tavern on Chestnut Street in Philadelphia and delivered them to about 100 subscribers around Nottingham, Newark, and "Various" locations. Most towns in America and every county in Pennsylvania received at least one copy sent to the local post office or tavern. Copies also went to Antigua, Barbados, St. Kitts, Jamaica, Grenada, and Dominica in the Caribbean and across the Atlantic to Bristol and London. During the 1760s, there was even a copy of the *Pennsylvania Journal* (published at the London Coffee House) sent to a subscriber at the Pennsylvania Coffee House in London.[99]

There were six newspapers printed in Philadelphia in 1776, five in English and one in German. Most colonial newspapers were, like the *Pennsylvania Journal*, weeklies with tiny circulations by our standards, around 1,500 per issue. At its peak in October 1774, loyalist James Rivington's *New York Gazetteer* boasted the largest subscription in the colonies, about 3,600, but just over a year later, the New York Sons of Liberty destroyed his press, burned his house, and confiscated his types to be made into bullets.[100] The *Boston Chronicle* was published twice weekly and Benjamin Towne's *Pennsylvania Evening Post* was the only paper with three editions per week.

A year's subscription to a typical colonial newspaper cost ten shillings in 1776, a price maintained by the Bradfords' *Pennsylvania Journal* until the end of October 1776, when inflation and the imminent invasion of Philadelphia motivated them to raise the rate to fifteen shillings.[101] William and Thomas Bradford were businessmen who set their prices according to market conditions. They did not sell the *Pennsylvania Journal* at a bargain rate, and they weren't trying to increase the newspaper's popularity by economizing its circulation. Lowering the price of *Common Sense* was Paine's idea, not his publishers'.

Newspapers were not yet "popular" to the extent that they would become in the nineteenth century, when advancing press technologies and cheaper newsprint lowered their price, increased their throughput, and widened their reach. But they were decidedly more popular than pamphlets, not only because of their price, but because of their circulation.¹⁰² An established postal route was all that was required for Philadelphia newspapers to arrive with regularity as far away as Virginia.¹⁰³ Anyone who could afford to subscribe to multiple newspapers did so, a practice that facilitated fact-checking and weighing of different editorial perspectives. Local printers subscribed to every paper possible in search of "the freshest advices, foreign and domestic." Letters, quotations, intelligence, and stories from one colony thus resurfaced sporadically in other colonies over the span of several months. Many colonists came to coffee houses and taverns to catch up on local gossip and to thumb through the newspapers. The sturdy rag paper held up to dozens of readers per copy, and each patron would glean the most interesting or relevant information to report back home around the dinner table or the fireplace.

Philadelphia Flashpoint

Compared to today's graphical four-color editions, colonial newspapers were visually drab and stylistically dry. The typical four-page weekly paper functioned primarily as an imperial data service, republishing a cut-and-paste medley of stories from the London press. There were no beat reporters on staff, conducting interviews and hunting for the local scoop. News often came in the form of letter extracts and parliamentary snippets, peppered with any other information a printer could cajole out of passers-through. On occasion a reader would submit an essay commenting on current events, but local color was rare, and most newspapers, colony-to-colony, looked practically identical.

The only exception to this vanilla tone was to be found in the copious advertisements on every page. Advertising was so central to the solvency of colonial newspapers that most included "Weekly Advertiser" or "General Advertiser" in their full masthead titles. The ads, more than anything else, gave a newspaper its personality and provided a window into the daily lives of its readership. A newspaper like Hall and Sellers's *Pennsylvania Gazette* revealed its conservative elite readership by the disproportionate number of ads for horses and estates. Most papers carried sensationalist ads for "cure-all" tinctures, ointments, and drops. Maredant's Anti-Scorbutic Drops promised cures from "inveterate scurvy, leprosy, pimpled faces of ever so long standing," "old obstinate sores or ulcers," and, "by purifying the blood," promised to "prevent malignant humors of every kind from being thrown upon the lungs."¹⁰⁴ Likewise, "Dr. Ryan's Incomparable Worm-Destroying Sugar Plumbs" were "Necessary to be kept in all Families."¹⁰⁵ Booksellers and general merchants promoted their potpourri inventories in exhaustive detail. Notices of bounties for runaway slaves, indentured servants, and "apprentice lads" were commonplace prior to the war, after which they tended to be replaced with identical ads for runaway soldiers, sometimes for entire detachments gone absent without leave.

The most humorous ads were often the most personal, such as an exasperated husband notifying the public that he would not be responsible for the outstanding debts of his charge-happy estranged wife: "Whereas the wife of Daniel Stevens has left him, and plundered him of every thing she could conveniently carry away, and has declared that she will ruin him—I do hereby forewarn all persons from trusting her on my account, as I will pay no debts of her contracting after this date."[106] Such rare tabloid flashes were engulfed, however, by the drone of imperial news that embodied the tedium of a transatlantic voyage with every duplicated British paragraph. In the spring of 1776, however, the Philadelphia newspapers were transformed from a mere "wire service" to the hub of the independence controversy.

One of the most curious aspects of the furor over *Common Sense* during the spring of 1776 is that it played out primarily in newspapers instead of pamphlets. There were a handful of pamphlet responses, yes, but as a lot they proved grossly inadequate to the task of comprehensive refutation. Colonial newspapers were the primary arena where advocates for and against independence exchanged verbal blows.

Why newspapers? The first reason was that the publishing scrape between Robert Bell and Thomas Paine had taken place in paid advertisements for *Common Sense*. The independence controversy began in the most profitable part of a newspaper, a fact that would not have escaped the scrimping colonial printer. Benjamin Towne of the *Pennsylvania Evening Post* had no incentive to stop the harangues of Bell and Paine, because he made money from the debate even if no one read it. A newspaper publisher did not have to edit a prepaid advertisement's contents with the same appeasing caution as pure "news," so ads were generically more open to descriptive flourishes.

A second reason for the discursive location of the independence controversy in newspapers related to the embedded temporality of Paine's text. *Common Sense* had sped up the debate to a level that pamphlet culture could not abide. Most pamphlets were methodical compositions designed for cool deliberation, and, therefore, they took time to write, time to print, and time to read. Because Paine had yanked the rug of slow deliberation out from under the moderates' feet, the debate over independence outpaced a pamphlet's fastest turnaround and thus precluded a measured response.[107] Early on in the text's composition, Paine had abandoned his plan of writing a history and had instead framed *Common Sense* as a newspaper serial, only later adapting its contents to a pamphlet format. Paine's text took the form of a pamphlet but retained a style more typical of a contributed newspaper essay.

A third reason for debating independence in newspapers was access. Pamphlets required an advance fee that was out of reach for most would-be American authors. To place an essay in a newspaper was often free, and, even in those cases where publishers expected under-the-table placement fees, the charge was considerably less than the alternative of a pamphlet run. Newspapers also offered the less ambitious politico the chance to chime in on an important point without the necessity of composing an elaborate treatise.

As one Pennsylvanian, signing his letter "Aristides," opined in the May 13 issue of John Dunlap's *Pennsylvania Packet*, "*Common Sense* has been read by many, yet the newspapers are read by many more." Aristides provided a lucid account of "the manner of conducting what is now called the Independent controversy in the newspapers." As Aristides pointed out, "nobody was obliged to read" *Common Sense* except those "willing to pay for it, and that pretty dearly too," referring to Bell's expensive editions. That it was "read very generally" owed not to "the beauty and elegance of the composition" but to "the truth and importance of the matter contained in it." The subject of *Common Sense*'s argument "was proposed to the world under every disadvantage but that of its own manifest importance and apparent truth or probability." In the spring of 1776, those who chose to broadcast their thoughts on *Common Sense*—both positive and negative—preferred to utilize the established network of colonial newspaper publication.[108]

Propaganda and Critique

While the "question of Independency" had been "lately started, in a pamphlet entitled *Common Sense*," as one commentator observed, it was brought to a head as colonists debated the pamphlet and its implications in newspapers.[109] As we saw in Chapter Two, Robert Bell and Thomas Paine exchanged verbal blows in an advertising duel conducted primarily in Benjamin Towne's *Pennsylvania Evening Post*. The first published commentary on *Common Sense*, besides the author-publisher fracas, was an oblique censure by some Pennsylvania and New Jersey Quakers printed in the *Pennsylvania Ledger* on January 27. Though the Quakers did not mention *Common Sense* directly, their conclusion left no doubt regarding the impetus for their public statement. The Quakers urged,

> May we therefore firmly unite in the abhorrence of all such writings and measures, as evidence a desire and design to break off the happy connection we have heretofore enjoyed with the kingdom of Great-Britain, and our just and necessary subordination to the king, and those who are lawfully placed in authority under him.[110]

It would be a gross inaccuracy to imply that *Common Sense* and the independence movement blew through the American colonies unhindered. Paine's ideas were subjected to furious debate that spring, but it took more than two weeks after the pamphlet went on sale for private whispers to become public discourse. The inhabitants of Philadelphia seemed to wait for someone to make a move.

A "Salus Populi" broke the awkward silence with an essay in support of *Common Sense* in the *Pennsylvania Gazette* of January 24, 1776. Addressing the "People of North America," he saw the "present unsettled state of government in the several provinces" as "one of the fairest opportunities ever offered to any people of correcting constitutional errors." Because the colonies were "without any settled form of Government" they were also "at present in a state of absolute independence" and "fully convinced of the imperfection of those forms we have heretofore enjoyed." This writer said that the colonies had been "obliged, for our own safety and preservation" to "dissolve our present forms of government and to create new ones." He took this as evidence that "the forms we have hitherto lived under are by no means equal to the task of preserving our liberties," and he recommended to his readers, "That form of government alone can give us security which puts all the servants of the public under the power of the people."[111]

We do not know the identity of "Salus Populi," but we can be certain that he was a close associate of Paine's. Three weeks *before* Paine would use similar arguments and language in his Appendix to *Common Sense*, Salus Populi pointed out the futility of the Continental Congress's prayer "to have the colonies put into the situation they were in before the year 1763, *i.e.* liable to an attack whenever a British ministry and parliament choose to begin it." Using a graphic image redeployed by Paine in the Appendix to *Common Sense*, Salus Populi said no future security could be guaranteed, "even granting that our burnt towns, and depopulated and destroyed cities, our slain friends and distressed countrymen would be restored to the very state they were in before the present struggle began."[112] The author also previewed Paine's arguments about the structural corruption of the British Constitution, snidely praying, "May God therefore preserve us from the dependence and connection of 1763, until he has purged British ministers and British parliaments of all corruption and iniquity, and made British Kings detest ambition and injustice as much as any monarch ever loved them."[113]

The second public approbation of *Common Sense* came in Towne's paper on February 3. A "Candidus" (not to be confused with the later author of *Plain Truth*) wrote, "Mr. Towne, When the little pamphlet entitled *Common Sense* first made its appearance in favor of that so often abjured idea of independence upon Great-Britain, I was informed that no less than three gentlemen of respectable abilities were engaged to answer it." The Quaker piece opposing *Common Sense* had, in Candidus's opinion, "offered nothing to the purpose," and he contributed some thoughts of his own from early formal political theory. While he was inclined to uphold the position of *Common Sense*, Candidus requested that "any arguments in favor of returning to a state of dependence on Great-Britain" would be "timely offered, that they may be soberly considered, before the cunning proposals of the cabinet set all the timid, lazy and irresolute members of the community into a clamor for *peace at any rate.*"[114]

The Philadelphia newspaper debate began to escalate in the middle of February. A "Demophilus," writing in the *Pennsylvania Packet* on February 12, picked up the crisis language of *Common Sense*: "I am bold to assert, that such a favourable combination of circumstances as they are blessed with at this important conjuncture, never did take place among any people with whom history has made us acquainted." Demophilus said, "How quickly the most important revolution of the fundamentals of our policy can pervade a continent, may be guessed at by the progress of the idea of Colonial Independency in three weeks or a month at farthest!" He argued that "thousands and tens of thousands of common farmers and tradesmen" were "better reasoners than some of our trammeled *juris consultors*" who showed a "reluctance to part with the abominable chain" that would "in a very little time drag the colonies into the most abject slavery." The connection with Britain, "tho' modified by all the wisdom and caution of the greatest men now living" would prove fatal to the colonies. Demophilus added, "Many profess themselves zealous for the liberties of America, yet declare an abhorrence of the idea of independency on Great Britain. If this be not a solecism, as absurd and irreconcilable as ever was obtruded on mankind, I know not the meaning of the term!"[115]

"Salus Populi" published a second letter "To the FREEMEN of the PROVINCE of PENNSYLVANIA" in the February 14 issue of the Bradfords' *Pennsylvania Journal*. The timing of this piece is another sure sign of close collaboration between the writer, Paine, and the Bradfords, who began selling the "New Edition" of *Common Sense* the very same day. Salus Populi felt compelled to dispute the "excellence of the English constitution" that had been "spoken of with such warmth, eagerness and seeming devotion" by advocates for reconciliation. The British Constitution did not provide "any effectual method of securing the rights of the people from the encroachments of the Crown, *i.e.*, from tyranny," but even if Britain's constitution were "ever so good, it is little to us." The "constitution of the Colonies" did not even have "vigour sufficient to support itself against the slightest attack." He continued, "Mercantile combinations have done more in a few months for the preservation of the liberties of America than all your constitutional powers would have effected in ten thousand years." He argued that Tories and the British Ministry wanted the colonies to see "every thing pass thro' what they affect to call a constitutional channel" because they understood that the colonies, in fact, had no constitutional protection.

The call for a restoration of the situation in 1763, Salus Populi said, was the song "with which they hope to lull us to rest on the lap of an abandoned government, which knows no right but the pleasure of an obstinate and blood-thirsty Prince and his courtly sycophants." The past "happiness" of America did not arise from "a state of dependency on Great-Britain," but instead, "It sprung from the fertility of the soil, and the sobriety, industry and equality of the inhabitants alone," adding, "Our dependence on Great-Britain never did, nor ever could add the ten thousandth part of a grain to that happiness which flowed so abundantly to us" from those sources. Salus Populi put it succinctly, "We enjoyed happiness *in* a state of dependence, but not *from* that state."

Even the protection that American trade ships received from Britain was not worth the cost of British wars and customs restrictions. Pointing out the two million pounds American vessels paid in customs to the port of London, the writer asked, "How many Londons America may contain a century hence if she now becomes independant, God only knows." Salus Populi picked up on the themes of shipbuilding and maritime commerce from *Common Sense*, and he stressed that after the war had concluded, "Our trade will protect itself." America's free trade with multiple European countries would ensure that her fleets would sail undisturbed for fear that "a hornet's nest" would swarm on any nation that tried to interrupt American commerce. Because America had "no haughty neighbouring tyrant to disturb our internal repose," the "consequence of independency to America, if she makes right use of the present occasion, will be a perfect state of political liberty, a good sound wholesome constitution, a free and enlarged trade, and peace to the end of time, unless our sins should bring down the Divine vengeance upon us." According to Salus Populi, "every prospect of the future" and "every providential occurrence for more than twenty years past" seemed to invite "us to embrace independency." He concluded his letter with his assessment of what "the voice of God" was saying to America:

> If you will remain free and happy, if you wish not to entail a civil war or slavery on your offspring, if you spill not your blood at present in vain, and despise not what I have been doing for you these twenty years past, tho' you knew it not; fix a constitution which will give perfect Liberty to all my people now in, or that hereafter shall fly to America for shelter from tyranny and oppression, and declare for independency immediately, and put your trust in me alone for success.[116]

Regardless of the precise identity of "Salus Populi," Paine and his pro-independence cohort were attempting to steer public opinion by turning the wheel of Philadelphia's newspapers.

On February 17, the author of an unsigned article titled "Questions and Answers" asked, "What will be the probable benefits of independence?" He then described at length the benefits as they would become manifest in the areas of commerce, manufacturing, science, and property. Supposing the war would last for six years and cost America three million a year, he concluded the essay, "We cannot pay too Great a Price for Liberty, and Posterity will think Independence a Cheap Purchase at Eighteen Millions."[117]

Not everyone agreed with these enthusiastic pronouncements. The most incisive early commentary on *Common Sense* came in an essay by "Rationalis" published in the moderate-leaning *Pennsylvania Gazette* at the end of February. Quoting Voltaire to begin the paper—"The Republican Spirit is indeed at Bottom as ambitious as the Monarchical"—Rationalis described Philadelphia as lately "amused with a new political Pamphlet" that, "though it has taken a popular name, and implies that the contents are obvious and adapted to the understandings of the bulk of the people," is "equally inconsistent with learned and common Sense." Unlike many subsequent writers, Rationalis did not and cared not to know the author's "name or character" because "the book, and not the writer of it, is to be the subject of my animadverions."[118]

Rationalis praised Pennsylvania's freedom of the press because it allowed "the sentiments and opinions of the meanest, equally with those of the greatest" to be aired. The "rich and high-born are not the monopolizers of wisdom and virtue," he reminded his audience, declaring that "the middling class in every country" tends to be "less dissipated and debauched than those who are usually called their betters" and, therefore, can "apply themselves with more industry to the culture of their understandings, and in reality become better acquainted with the true interests of the society in which they live." Nonetheless, Rationalis cautioned, he had "too often seen instances of persons in every class of life, whose publications" had attempted "by the cadence of words, and force of style, a total perversion of the understanding."

With the attuned eye of a critic, Rationalis parsed the intent of *Common Sense*. The pamphlet was "plainly calculated to induce a belief of three things," which were:

> 1st. That the English form of government has no wisdom in it, and that it is by no means so constructed as to produce the happiness of the people, which is the end of all good government.
> 2d. That monarchy is a form of government inconsistent with the will of God.
> 3d. That now is the time to break off all connection with Great-Britain, and to declare an independence of the Colonies.

Rationalis employed arguments from scripture and history, the sacred and the profane, to counter the assertions in *Common Sense* that were derisive of the British Constitution and monarchy. Toward the end of the essay, Rationalis expressly disagreed with Paine's opinion "that this is the time to declare an Independence of the Colonies," and he added, "This ought to be the dernier resort of America." The colonists should "not yet lose sight of the primary object of the dispute," which was "a safe, honourable and lasting reconciliation with Great Britain." He warned his readers not to give up hope of an "advantageous accommodation" until "we are under a necessity of doing it." Demonstrating his psychological distance from the battles that had already been fought, Rationalis promised, "But if justice is still denied us, and we are to contend for liberty by arms, we will meet them in the field, and try our manhood against them, even to spilling the blood of every brave man we have." Then he made an important caveat: "Should the ministry have recourse to foreign aid, we may possibly follow their example; and, if it be essential to our safety to declare an Independence, I would willingly embrace the necessity."[119] Rationalis's contingency clause would take on increased relevance when word reached America of the enlistment of Hessian soldiers in the British cause.

In the following week's issue of the *Pennsylvania Gazette*, a member of the growing Independent bloc refrained from a "formal answer" to Rationalis but desired to inform the public of what he called "the plan of the moderate man." The writer had been "in a company where the important doctrine of Independency was pretty thoroughly agitated, a few evenings ago" where he said, it was clarified for him that the moderate party pushed for "bearing arms and repelling the force that might be sent against America, till Great-Britain would grow weary of the enterprise, and be willing to make up with us on equitable terms." The primary argument of the moderates, he said, hinged first on the connection to Britain "by blood, interest, language, laws, constitutions, religion, commerce, &c.," second, on America's "need of the national protection, if attacked by any foreign power," and third, on "the lullaby of our having been a very happy and flourishing people during our dependence upon the parent state."[120]

"A Common Man" writing in the *Pennsylvania Packet* on April 1 and 8, provided an impartial perspective on the controversy. This writer, probably a wealthy businessman, did not care "whether I live under an Emperor, a pope, a Bashaw, a King of England, or a Republic, provided I can be convinced, by irrefutable arguments, that such or such a state contained the greatest quantity of happiness for the people at large, and for individuals in particular." Since he, like "99 out of every 100 in the world," did not expect to ride "upon the top of the machine" but only "to contribute my proportion of labour to wheel it along," he desired a governmental machine designed "to move with as little labour as possible" and not prone "to get out of order in the variety of rough and smooth roads through which we must inevitably pass." He reminded "all the Writers on the Independent Controversy" of the gravity of their subject matter: "Be pleased to remember, Gentlemen, you are pleading at the bar of the public, upon a cause of greater importance than ever came before any tribunal on earth, no less, than whether it is expedient or inexpedient to make a total separation in government between the New and the Old World." He requested that both sides of the argument state their case "by full and positive demonstration," avoiding general assertions in favor of a list of benefits "particularized in a number of plain, clear instances." If they would "Stick to the matter, and neglect the man," then he promised to "read your controversy with great attention" as would "thousands beside me." If then, "upon an impartial hearing, it should appear to be for the real interest of America" to tie a "Gordian Knot and establish Independence," he declared, "with utmost sincerity and solemnity, that I will give it my hearty concurrence."[121]

Echoes of Common Sense

The newspaper debate sometimes revealed the influence of *Common Sense* in subtle ways. An essay addressed in mid-April to the inhabitants of New Jersey picked up the either-or crisis language of *Common Sense*, saying, "I think we are now visibly reduced to the alternative of Independency or Submission; And I am sure we had better never have engaged in this controversy than not to have the courage to go through with it. To submit after having once resisted! to be treated as a conquered country! 'tis horrible!"[122]

"A Pennsylvania Countryman" in May excused his intervention in the debate and described the purpose of accumulating opinions on the subject of independence, "tho' most should advance nothing new, yet the *general sense* is the more known."[123] His "plain account" revealed how "I, and many I converse with in the country, view these melancholy affairs." His argument was most remarkable for its *lack* of originality; he was simply trying to convey the topics of a normal conversation in his circle of interaction.

The Pennsylvania Countryman said, "If the Colonies have thriven under connection with Britain, this was as some industrious tenants do under oppressive landlords; they would have been much better without it, and there is no hope of tolerable living under them hereafter." The writer ended each of his paragraphs with punchy summaries like, "The Colonies must be *independent* or they are *undone*" and "nothing but *independence* can save us from them." He laid out all the alternatives in dichotomous terms, saying Britain "will not treat but conquer, and so lay a necessity on the Colonies *now* to shake off the yoke or be conquered slaves; to become independent on the British Parliament, or submit to merciless, enraged tyranny." The author foreclosed the "hope of accommodation" advised by cautious men who had not sufficiently weighed the state of affairs. He added, "But whatever apparent reason there was for this some time ago, it is vanished now; what might have been prudent a while since, might be destructive now, and should be no longer insisted on." The Pennsylvania Countryman argued that open commerce was the key to a self-sustaining America, and he said "the repeal of some acts" was not worth "this bloody contest." Finally, he advised, "If declaring for independence *now* might gain advantages to the cause that would render success surer, perhaps shorten the struggle, and save blood, then delay is hurtful and dangerous."[124]

Here was a man whose opinions had been shaped by *Common Sense* on a level deeper than perfunctory quotation. He was following the logic, employing the same topics, and even echoing the diction and syntax of *Common Sense*. He framed the decision—four months after the first publication of *Common Sense*—with Paine's sense of urgency and tracked with Paine's argument the entire way.

Realizing Independence

Independence was both a decision and an experience. By late June, Ezra Stiles of Connecticut wrote in his diary, "All the Country is in Motion," and he recorded the account of a young man from North Carolina who had "journeyed thro' & seen the whole spirit from Wilmington thither." According to the North Carolinian, "Independency" was "high everywhere, especially in Virginia."[125] Because newspaper accounts were often contradictory or biased, Stiles wrote "Doubtful" next to his diary entries on the earliest reports of independence. When, however, someone brought to Connecticut an authenticated copy of the *Declaration of Independence*, Stiles was spellbound. "This I read at Noon, & for the first time realized Independency." After a rapturous prayer for the new "*Independent Republic*," Stiles expressed the gravity of the moment, "And have I lived to see such an important & astonishing Revolution?"[126]

Notes: Chapter 7

[1] John Adams, as we shall see in Chapter 11, was a cautious fan of *Common Sense* in 1776. Only later in life did Adams conflate his opinion of the pamphlet with his antipathy for Thomas Paine.
[2] 19 January 1776 and 24 Feburary 1776. Stiles, *Literary Diary*, 1:657, 662.
[3] 23 January 1776. Stiles, 1:658.
[4] 29 January 1776. Stiles, 1:659.
[5] PEP, February 10, 1776.
[6] Purdie's *Virginia Gazette*. April 12, 1776.
[7] *New-England Chronicle*, March 28, 1776. This piece was reprinted in several other colonial newspapers.
[8] "Blackamores" was a racial slur originating as a description of the inhabitants of Northern Africa, "Black Moors," but applied generally to dark-skinned people, especially to slaves.
[9] PEP, February 13, 1776.
[10] Extract of a letter dated February 14, 1776, and published in the PEP, March 26, 1776, and also in the PJ, March 27, 1776.
[11] "Essex." "To the Author of *Common Sense* [26 February 1776]," NYJ, March 7, 1776. "Essex" published a series of "hints" on the subject of independence in the New York papers throughout the spring. See also NYJ, March 19, 1776.
[12] "Extract of a Letter from a Gentleman at Norwalk, to His Friend at Danbury," NYJ, April, 11, 1776.
[13] *Connecticut Gazette*, March 22, 1776.
[14] *Massachusetts Spy*, May 31, 1776.
[15] Rickman, 61.
[16] NYJ, February 22, 1776.
[17] PEP, March 2, 1776.
[18] Hughes to SA, 19 December 1775, January 8, 1776, and February 4, 1776; "The Monitor," No. 7. NYJ, December 21, 1775. Quoted from Mason, *Road to Independence*, 112-113.
[19] Quoted in Scott, *Trumpet of a Prophecy*, 120.
[20] "Z. F.," *The New York Packet and the American Advertiser*. (Printed by Samuel Loudon, in Water-Street, between the Coffee-House and the Old Slip.) March 7, 1776. NYHS.
[21] From Almon's *Remembrancer* for 1776. Quoted in Tyler, *Literary History*, 1:473.
[22] Scribner and Tarter, *Revolutionary Virginia*, 5:20.
[23] Ibid., 6:284. Extracts from the third section of CS appeared in Alexander Purdie's *Virginia Gazette* on February 2, 1776, and in John Pinkney's *Virginia Gazette* on February 3, 1776.
[24] 26 January 1776. *Journal of Nicholas Cresswell*, 136.
[25] PJ, March 27, 1776.
[26] Scribner and Tarter, 6:284-285.
[27] DPP, April 8, 1776.
[28] PEP, April 9, 1776.
[29] Scribner and Tarter, 6:284-285.
[30] DPP, April 22, 1776.
[31] Purdie's *Virginia Gazette*. April 12, 1776.

[32] Scribner and Tarter, 6:284-285.
[33] Purdie's *Virginia Gazette*, April 26, 1776. Reprinted in PEP, May 11, 1776. It should be noted that Purdie's reprinted extract of *Common Sense* from February replaced Paine's colloquial contraction "'tis time to part" with "It is time to part." Cf. CS 3.19.
[34] 14 February 1776, "Diary of Colonel Landon Carter." 149-152, 258-264.
[35] 24 February 1776, "Diary of Colonel Landon Carter."
[36] RHL to Landon Carter, 2 June 1776, LDC, 4:118n. Carter's comments were written on the cover of Lee's letter.
[37] 29 March 1776, "Diary of Colonel Landon Carter."
[38] 13 April 1776, "Diary of Colonel Landon Carter."
[39] General Henry Clinton had spent much of his childhood living in New York, where his father, George, was royal governor.
[40] Captain H. Parker to Vice Admiral Molyneux Shuldham, 25 February 1776. Neeser, *The Despatches of Molyneux Shuldham*, 110.
[41] Tilghman, *Memoir of Lieut. Col. Tench Tilghman*, 82.
[42] The following broadside indicates the kind of artisanal support for independence that was building in New York during the spring of 1776: *The Mechanicks in Union, and their associates, are earnestly requested to attend the general committee of mechanicks in union, at Mechanick Hall, on Monday evening next, to consult with them on Business of Importance. By order of the committee. Nathaniel Tylee, Chairman. New-York, April 12, 1776. God and the Righteous agree that all the Good should be Free. Keep your watch light burning.* Mechanicks. New York: 1776.
[43] "Extract of a letter from New-York, dated May 31, 1776." DPP, June 3, 1776.
[44] In a 1779 speech, Morris described Paine as a "mere adventurer from England, without fortune, without family or connexions, ignorant even of grammer [sic]." Morris's speech was part of a Congressional debate over Paine's authorship of a piece in the January 2, 1779, *Pennsylvania Packet*, entitled "Common Sense to the Public." Sparks, *Life of Gouverneur Morris*, 1:200-204. Morris' venomous dislike for Paine and his political principles was enduring. While ambassador to France in the 1790s, Morris refused to demand Paine's release from a French prison. James Monroe, upon taking over Morris' role, promptly worked for Paine's freedom.
[45] Morris, *Diary and Letters of Gouverneur Morris*, 1:3-4.
[46] Fragments of a speech he made to the New York Provincial Congress in May 1776. Morris, *Diary and Letters of Gouverneur Morris*, 1:5-6.
[47] John Jay to James Jay, 4 January 1776. LDC, 3:29.
[48] Fragment on "Congress and Independence." [April 1776?]. Johnston, *Correspondence and Public Papers of John Jay*, 1:52-56.
[49] Morris, *John Jay*, 1: 263-264.
[50] Alexander Hamilton to John Jay, 26 November 1775. Syrett, *Papers of Alexander Hamilton*, 1:176-178.
[51] Alexander, *A Revolutionary Conservative*.
[52] See Morgan, *Meaning of Independence*, 59. See also, Lipscomb and Bergh, *Writings of Thomas Jefferson*, 1:324.
[53] "Letter to Messrs. Deane, Jay, and Gérard. [On the Silas Deane Affair.]" *Pennsylvania Packet*, September 14, 1779. CW 2:182.

[54] DPP, April 8, 1776.
[55] Landon Carter's diary indicates that he was writing a refutation of *Common Sense* that spring, but it is unclear whether he ever had it published, either as a pamphlet or in a newspaper essay. Carter Braxton wrote a pamphlet against John Adams's *Thoughts on Government* later that spring. See the section on RHL later in this chapter.
[56] Scribner and Tarter, 6:285-286.
[57] Ibid., 286.
[58] Ibid., 285.
[59] Ibid., 284-285.
[60] See Breen, *Tobacco Culture*, and Isaac, *Transformation of Virginia*.
[61] The Virginia Convention made some minor syntactical changes to Mason's draft, but most of the text is of Mason's composition. To illustrate the changes, here is a comparison of Mason's version (from a report in the PEP, June 6, 1776) of the first point (in *italics*), followed by the final version adopted by the convention: GM: 1) "*That all men are born equally free and independent, and have certain inherent natural rights, of which they cannot, by any compact, deprive or divest their posterity; among which are the enjoyment of life and liberty, with the means of acquiring and possessing property, and pursuing and obtaining happiness and safety.*" VC: 1) "That all men are by nature equally free and independent, and have certain inherent rights, of which, when they enter into a state of society, they cannot, by any compact, deprive or divest their posterity; namely, the enjoyment of life and liberty, with the means of acquiring and possessing property, and pursuing and obtaining happiness and safety."
[62] PEP, May 28, 1776; PJ, May 29, 1776.
[63] PEP, May 28, 1776; PJ, May 29, 1776.
[64] PJ, May 29, 1776.
[65] GM to RHL, 18 May 1776. Rutland, *Papers of George Mason*, 1: 271-272.
[66] GM to George Mason V [his son], 2 October 1778. Niles, *Principles and Acts of the Revolution*, 125-126. Cf. CS 1.14, 2.21, 3.19, 3.50, and especially A.14.
[67] Niles, 126.
[68] 3 September 1774. JA, *Diary*, MHS. Elder brothers Phillip Ludwell Lee and Thomas Ludwell Lee, along with elder sister Hannah Ludwell Lee Corbin, were not involved in Continental politics. Sister Alice Lee Shippen participated in the events of the Revolution alongside her husband, Dr. William Shippen, Jr.
[69] AL to ? and intended for John Dickinson and RHL, 4 September 1775. Arthur Lee Papers, HL.
[70] WL to RHL, 22 September, 1775. Ford, *Letters of William Lee*, 1:173-175.
[71] RHL to Landon Carter, 1 April 1776. Ballagh, *Letters of Richard Henry Lee*. 1:172-174.
[72] RHL to [Patrick Henry], 20 April 1776. Ballagh, 1:176-180.
[73] See RHL to Landon Carter, 2 June 1776. Ballagh, 1:197-200.
[74] RHL mistakenly thought the New Yorkers had burnt *Plain Truth*, the only loyalist pamphlet with which he was familiar. He had never seen a copy of the *Deceiver Unmasked* because the New Yorkers had burnt the whole edition. RHL to Charles Lee, 1 April 1776. LDC, 4:471-472. Francis Lightfoot Lee pointed out the same event in a letter the next week, noting that even in "the

temperate City of N. York" the burning of "a Pamphlet written against *Common Sense*" was enacted "by a vast majority of its inhabitants." Francis Lightfoot Lee to Landon Carter, 9 April 1776. LDC, 4:501.

[75] RHL to [General Charles Lee], 22 April 1776. Ballagh, 1:181-183.

[76] RHL to General [Charles] Lee. 21 May 1776. Ballagh, 1:192-193.

[77] RHL to General [Charles] Lee. 27 May 1776. Ballagh, 1:193-195.

[78] RHL to Thomas Lud[well] Lee, 28 May 1776. Ballagh, 1:196-197.

[79] RHL to Landon Carter, 2 June 1776, Ballagh, 1:197-200.

[80] "Resolution of Independence. Moved by R. H. Lee for the Virginia Delegation." Boyd, *Papers of Thomas Jefferson*, 1:298-299.

[81] RHL to General [Charles] Lee, 29 June 1776. Ballagh, 1:203-205.

[82] RHL to [General Charles Lee], 6 July 1776. Ballagh, 1:205-206.

[83] RHL to the Governor of Virginia [Patrick Henry], 20 August 1776. Ballagh, 1:213-214.

[84] Cf. DPP, February 19, 1776. RHL to [SA], 29 July 1776. Ballagh, 1:211-212.

[85] RHL to [Patrick Henry]. 20 April 1776. Ballagh, 1:176-180.

[86] RHL to [Edmund Pendleton?]. 12 May 1776. Ballagh, 1:190-192. Braxton, *An Address to the Convention of the Colony and Ancient Dominion of Virginia*. Braxton's pamphlet was also printed in Dixon and Hunter's *Virginia Gazette* on June 8 and 15, 1776. See Adams, *American Independence*, 151. According to the Diary of Richard Smith, Braxton first took his seat in the Continental Congress on February 23, 1776. RS 2:505-506. See also, Dill, *Carter Braxton.*.

[87] RHL to General [Charles] Lee, 29 June 1776. Ballagh, 1:203-205.

[88] "Discourse" comes from the Latin word meaning "to run to and fro." In contemporary usage, we use "discourse" to refer to all types of conversations and symbolic exchanges. But two related words with eighteenth-century curreny, "intercourse" (to run between) and "concourse" (to run together), demonstrate an important etymological distinction that is neglected in our one-size-fits-all use of "discourse."

[89] For the spirit of this statement, I owe a debt to Kenneth Burke's formulation: "identification is compensatory to division." See Burke, *Grammar of Motives*.

[90] I borrow this phrase from Zarefsky, *Lincoln, Douglas, and Slavery: In the Crucible of Public Debate*.

[91] CS A.19.

[92] I use the word "publish" in the sense of "to make available to the public," a criterion thwarted by opponents to *The Deceiver Unmasked*. See Adams, "The Authorship and Printing of *Plain Truth* by Candidus."

[93] 13 March 1776. Marshall, *Diary*.

[94] Rusticus. *Remarks on a Late Pamphlet Entitled Plain Truth*.

[95] Ibid.

[96] Ibid.

[97] The Forester, "Letter II. To Cato." PJ, April 10, 1776.

[98] Thomas Paine, Benjamin Rush, Robert Bell, Robert Aitken, Thomas Mifflin, Robert Morris, George Clymer, Joseph Shippen, Thomas Mifflin, and Joseph Dean were among the Philadelphia subscribers.

[99] Subscription Books for the *Pennsylvania Journal*, 1766-1782. Bradford Family Papers, HSP.

[100] Stout, 6; Pierce, "A Revolutionary Masquerade."
[101] Subscription to the PG in *Receipt Book of John Paschall 1747-1776*, Paschall Papers, HSP. Paschall paid for three years, but his payment was seven months late. The PJ raised its rate on October 30, 1776.
[102] The price per issue of a typical colonial newspaper was a little over two pence, compared to the price of a typical pamphlet of between one and two shillings. A small stack of pamphlets would cost the same as an entire year's worth of newspapers.
[103] See RHL to Landon Carter, 2 June 1776. Ballagh, 1:197-200.
[104] PJ, March 12, 1777.
[105] PL, March 23, 1776.
[106] PJ, January 28, 1777.
[107] The best contemporary metaphor I can think of is an academic journal article response to a blog.
[108] "Aristides," DPP, May 13, 1776.
[109] DPP, April 1, 1776.
[110] "The Ancient Testimony and Principles of the People Called Quakers, Renewed, with Respect to the King and Government" was signed by John Pemberton on behalf of a group of Quakers that had met in Philadelphia on January 20. It was later published in pamphlet form. PL, January 27, 1776.
[111] PG, January 24, 1776.
[112] CS A.14.
[113] PG, January 24, 1776; cf. CS A.14. Based upon internal stylistic evidence, I don't think Paine composed the letters of "Salus Populi," but it is possible that one of his collaborators, even Benjamin Rush, did. Salus Populi published his second letter of support for *Common Sense* in the Bradfords' newspaper on the very same day as the Bradfords' edition of *Common Sense* went on sale, a fact that indicates that the writer was closely coordinating his efforts with Paine and the Bradfords.
[114] "Candidus," PEP, February 3, 1776.
[115] DPP, February 12, 1776.
[116] Salus Populi, "To the FREEMEN of the PROVINCE of PENNSYLVANIA." PJ, February 14, 1776.
[117] PEP, February 17, 1776.
[118] PG, February 28, 1776.
[119] PG, February 28, 1776.
[120] PG, March 6, 1776. This essay was signed "Candidus," and it is possible that the writer was the same as the contributor to PEP on February 3. "Candidus" was, however, a common classicized pseudonym during the period.
[121] DPP, April 1 and 8, 1776. Writers in the Revolutionary era often used the metaphor of the Gordian Knot as loosely indicative of a bond that cannot be untied, rather than appropriating the ancient myth (in the conventional sense) to describe an intractable problem that must be severed rather than untied.
[122] "Cimon." "To the Inhabitants of New-Jersey." *Postcript* to the DPP, April 15, 1776.
[123] DPP, May 13, 1776.
[124] "A Pennsylvania Countryman," DPP, May 13, 1776.
[125] 21 June 1776 and 8 July 1776. Stiles, *Literary Diary*, 2:17, 21.

[126] 8 July 1776 and 13 July 1776. Stiles, *Literary Diary*, 2:21-22.

Chapter Eight

Transatlantic Resistance

You are shocked by Accounts from the Southward of a Disposition in a great Majority, to counteract Independence. Read the Proceedings of Georgia, South and North Carolina, and Virginia, and then judge. The Middle Colonies have never tasted the bitter Cup—they have never Smarted—and are therefore a little cooler—but you will see that the Colonies are united indissolubly. Maryland has passed a few eccentric Resolves, but these are only Flashes which will soon expire. The Proprietary Governments are not only encumbered with a large Body of Quakers, but are embarrassed by a proprietary Interest—both together clog their operations a little: but these clogs are falling off, as you will Soon see.

John Adams to Benjamin Hichborn
May 1776

I observed that in writing *Common Sense* however easy it may appear now it is over, the necessity of knowing both countries was so material, that no person who had reflected only on one could have sufficiently succeeded in a proposition for their political separation: and though that pamphlet has much to say respecting England, it has never been attacked in that country on the score of error or mistake, which scarcely would have happened had the writer known only one side of the water.

Thomas Paine to a Committee of the Continental Congress
1783

PART ONE
LOYALIST WHIGS AND PATRIOTIC TORIES

The Gamble of Loyalism

In this chapter I shall begin folding into my analysis of the independence movement more detail on the resistance to *Common Sense* and independence. Gaining a clearer picture of the political movement that led to American independence requires a thickened description of "loyalists" as well as "patriots." To understand the American Revolution at over two centuries' distance, one of the first things we must do is forget the end of the story. To grasp the motives and to make sense of the behaviors of political actors in the period, we must remember the uncertainty of outcomes and the contingency of political affairs. We have a tendency to confuse our hindsight and the revolutionaries' foresight. No one alive at the end of the eighteenth century could have foretold how America would grow in size and significance, but many had vague intimations that they were launching an experiment of massive consequence. To inhabit the "mind" of the time period as a student of early American history is to participate in wild swings of military momentum, constant anxiety for the safety of friends and family, frustration at the ineptitude of leaders and fickle public resolve—all punctuated with glimmers of expectant confidence.

Surviving in a world of manifold uncertainty required measured risk-taking, and loyalism was, in this climate, a very sensible posture based upon cool calculation. Imagine yourself, for example, a wealthy colonial merchant in New York. Your material abundance is tied up in the transatlantic trade in consumable goods between your small city (the third largest in provincial America) and the billowing metropolis of London. Maybe you are a lifelong Anglican, and you possess, from childhood forward, dozens of fond memories associated with the Church of England: baptisms, weddings, friendships, moving sermons, etc. You were raised by your parents to adore the king and to respect his decisions as innately just, even if those decisions become burdensome on occasion. Because you are, in your mind, an Englishman who *happens* to live in America, you endure hardship for the greater good of your parent and protector, Britain. In fact, to be a "patriot" means remaining loyal to Britain at all costs.

Now imagine that a bunch of "middling class" activists—in your eyes, a flock of nobodies—begin canvassing for support to cut off all imports and exports to your largest market, and they begin disparaging a country of which you are a happy subject. When they begin to talk about declaring a political separation between the countries, you get squeamish. You have much, and, therefore, have much to lose. The world's most devastating army and navy are now on your shores on a mission to quiet this hotheaded bombast. The likelihood that a ragtag army and a potluck colonial militia led by a stoic Virginia planter will effectively repulse legions of professional, well-supplied troops is minuscule. *When*—not *if*, in your mind—the plans of the colonial rabble-rousers are squashed, then they will all be hung. Trade will be restored, and you will be rewarded for your steadfast commitment to the Mother Country with a bounty of vacant property and favorable trade contracts. This scenario is so certain, in fact, that all you need to do is keep your head down and wait out the storm. In practical political affairs, you advocate against rash measures and prefer instead to wait for terms of an accommodation from England. The operative word here is "wait," because any slowdown in the course of political change would sap momentum from the reckless radical movement and bide time for a decisive British victory and a restoration of your imperial market and sumptuous lifestyle.

The most famous traitor of the American Revolution, whose name has become synonymous in American lore with "turncoat," Benedict Arnold was in 1780, like our imagined New York merchant, simply playing his odds. In 1776 Arnold was a heroic officer in the Continental Army, displaying his valor and capacity for field command in the Quebec campaign and beyond. Over time, however, seasoned with disaffection toward his aloof commanding general—an experience so very common among Washington's colleagues—and calculating a swing in the war strongly favoring the British, Arnold decided that his prospects were brighter on the other side of the firing line. He no doubt betrayed the American cause, but like many Americans, he realized that the consequences of treason against both sides were not equal. If America won, and Arnold had joined the British, he could simply retire to a life of ease in London. If the British won, however, he could expect to hang from the gallows in New York.

There was no predictable "profile" of loyalists in America. Loyalists tended to be more affluent than "Continentals," but there was no one-to-one correspondence between wealth and loyalism. Some loyalists were people of modest means who objected to the American rebellion as an immoral usurpation of God-granted political authority. Loyalists did not look or dress differently from other Americans. Moreover, *most Americans* were loyal to the Crown at the beginning of 1776, so any difference was a matter of degree. Before the institution of "test oaths," the only way a loyalist could be positively identified as such was by the careful observation of his or her actions and speech, but most loyalists were smart enough to act and speak in their communities with great caution. As the independence movement grew during the spring of 1776, pronounced caution in a person's behavior became grounds for suspicion of "disaffection."

If a loyalist was unwilling for whatever reason to uproot his family and return to England, then he was forced to keep his head down to avoid the wrath of the populace. James Moody, a militant loyalist throughout the war who eventually settled in Nova Scotia, exemplified the bitterness that set in as a result of silent affection for Britain. Though Moody was a middle class farmer living in New Jersey in 1776, when he spoke of his "most ardent love for his country and the warmest attachment to his countrymen," he was referring to England. Moody "resolved to do anything, and to be anything, not inconsistent with integrity—to fight, to bleed, to die—rather than live to see the venerable Constitution of his country totally lost, and his countrymen enslaved."[1] Many Independents made statements like this during 1776, but they were talking about *America*, not Britain. Moody held that the conflict had not originated "with the *people* of America, properly so called." A "great majority of the peasantry in America," said Moody, "felt no real grievances." Moody was unclear in his definition of "peasantry," because he did blame a sizable number of common people for complicity with the independence movement. He pointed to the "multitudes"—specifically those "with little property and perhaps still less principle"—who had been "easily wrought upon and easily persuaded to enlist under banners of pretended patriots and forward demagogues."[2] When, in 1774 "the whole continent" was thrown "into a ferment" by "these popular leaders," the rest of the country responded "with *Associations, Committees*, and *Liberty-poles*, and all the preliminary apparatus necessary to a *Revolt*." In the months following the outbreak of war, said Moody, "The "general cry was *Join or die!*" Moody "relished neither of these alternatives, and, therefore, remained on his farm a silent, but not unconcerned, spectator of the black cloud that had been gathering, and was now ready to burst on his devoted head."[3]

Maryland's Resistance

Along with Pennsylvania and New York, Maryland was one of the last holdouts on the issue of independence. Like Pennsylvania, it was a proprietary colony and had been shielded, at least in theory, from the capricious rule of a royal governor. One of the chief reasons that Pennsylvania and Maryland delayed the authorization of independence longer than other colonies was that, unlike most other colonies, they still had functioning governments. The governments in most of the royal colonies had dissolved by 1775, and the stoppage of trade undercut the legitimacy of government in the commercial colonies. The colonies run by proprietary families had no reason to alter a form of government that still worked. Thus the assemblies of Pennsylvania and Maryland were the last to perceive the crisis of their political legitimacy.

Loyalism was a perfectly acceptable course of policy in Maryland—the ideological home of James Chalmers's *Plain Truth*—until the middle of 1776. William Eddis, a staunch loyalist living in Annapolis during the early stages of the American Revolution, had expressed in a February 1775 letter to the *Maryland Gazette*, his "deepest concern" for the "present unhappy contention between the mother country and her colonies." Eddis objected to the principle of "parliamentary taxation over this extensive part of the empire," but he expected "a perfect reconciliation" between Britain and America. He calmly identified finding "the most eligible method to obtain redress" as "the grand subject of controversy."[4] While Eddis's optimism waned following the outbreak of war, the Maryland gentleman's perspective on the causes and objects of the imperial dispute remained unmoved.

By the beginning of January 1776, Eddis's personal correspondence, like that of most loyalists at the time, painted a bleak picture of America. Harbors and rivers were deserted, and the "cheerful sound of industry" had been replaced with "warlike preparations" by a people whose faces were "clouded with apprehension." Though "a continued succession of aggravated reports" tended to "agitate the mind and foment the general discontent," Eddis rested in the remaining possibility "that a reconciliation may be constitutionally effected," and he reiterated the duty of "the servants of government not to relinquish their respective situations."[5]

Eddis had hoped that the tension in the seaport town would subside, but it only worsened. In March 1776, he described the inhabitants of Annapolis as "exceedingly alarmed." When Eddis's neighbors learned of a British ship passing up the bay not far from the city, he said, "The consternation occasioned by this information exceeds description." In spite of a "tempestuous, extremely dark" night in which "the rain descended in torrents," the streets of Annapolis "were quickly crowded with carriages laden with furniture and property of various kinds."[6]

As the spring wore on, Eddis was becoming more cynical. When news of the British evacuation of Boston reached Maryland, Eddis expressed his skepticism of the "industriously circulated" opinion that the event was "a preliminary towards a reconciliation." He was beginning to find fault only with the American side of the conflict. He had "faint hopes of a speedy reconciliation," because he was certain that "greater requisitions" would be made "than, I fear, can consistently be complied with." Political evils, like moral indiscretions, "imperceptibly" descended a slippery slope, and the "original limited boundary" of the dispute had been "cast far behind," with "new claims and new pursuits" being "sanctified by the fallacious plea of justice and necessity."[7]

Still, Eddis applauded Maryland's "spirit of moderation," and he observed that "every endeavor" of his province's government was "directed to restore a constitutional connection with the parent state." But by the end of March he worried that "in several populous and powerful provinces, doctrines are industriously promulgated and eagerly received which will effectually bar every avenue to a pacific accommodation." Not even "the most sanguine adherents to the interests of Great Britain" could "indulge the faintest idea that any single colony" would be able "to stem the torrent should it unhappily tend to the establishment of an independent government." Eddis predicted that "the day cannot be far distant when it will be necessary for those to abandon this country who cannot consistently coincide with the popular measures."[8]

By May 20, Eddis expressed his displeasure with the May 15 recommendation of the Continental Congress urging the establishment of new governments in each colony. He wondered if "any of the provinces, by their delegates in Congress, have dissented from a measure which must inevitably be productive of the most serious consequences." Eddis was even more flummoxed by the Virginia declaration of the same date, which he believed was "extraordinary and premature" because of the daily expectation of commissioners "to adjust and regulate the terms of reconciliation." He contented himself with the possibility that the commissioners' "powers may be ample," and thought it unwise to "preclude a possibility of entering upon a negotiation" before their arrival. Eddis hoped that men of influence in each province would "prevent the final declaration of independence until, in their opinion, it becomes an unavoidable expedient and immediately necessary for the interest, the happiness, and the freedom of America."[9]

The experience of William Eddis was characteristic of the Maryland elite during the early months of 1776. On January 18, 1776, the Maryland Provincial Convention issued its formal response to the king's October 26 speech to parliament. The delegates were aghast that their "necessary preparations for defense" had been misconstrued as an indicator of the colonies' "purpose of establishing an Independent Empire." The elite-controlled Maryland convention then published a declaration intended "to remove from the mind of the King an opinion which we feel to be highly injurious to the people of this province." The convention declared,

> That the people of this province, strongly attached to the English constitution, and truly sensible of the blessings they have derived from it, warmly impressed with sentiments of affection for, and loyalty to, the house of Hanover, connected with the British nation by the ties of blood and interest, and being thoroughly convinced, that to be free subjects of the King of Great Britain, with all its consequences, is to be the freest members of any civil society of the known world, never did, nor do entertain any views or desires of Independency.

Because the Marylanders considered "their union with the mother country" as "their highest felicity," they viewed any "fatal necessity of separating from her" as a "misfortune" second only to death.[10]

Charles Carroll, a wealthy planter from Maryland, provided a window into the material realities of political involvement. Carroll's first reaction to reading the king's October speech was economic: in late January, he said, "I make no doubt Tobacco will bear a great price as all hopes of peace have vanished." In June of the same year, his agricultural livelihood remained at the front of his mind. While he was in attendance at the Maryland Provincial Convention, he wrote a letter assuring his father that the convention session would be short due to "the impatience of the members to get home time enough for harvest."[11]

On paper, Charles Carroll was a prototypical Maryland loyalist: rich and Catholic. But Carroll consistently defied expectations. In January 1776, he stressed the Americans' inclination "to listen to just and honourable Terms of Accommodation, but such the ministry & Parliam't seem not disposed to offer, and thus this unnatural & destructive Civil war may be continued till the whole British Empire is ruined."[12] Carroll served as a Maryland delegate to the Continental Congress, and like Samuel Chase, leaned toward independence and against official Maryland policy. The Continental Congress, in particular, valued Carroll for his equal devotion to the Roman Catholic religion and the Continental cause, and he was appointed as a member of the Franklin-led congressional delegation that traveled to Catholic Quebec in February 1776.

On March 18, Charles Carroll, who had by then returned to Philadelphia, wrote to his father in Annapolis, "The Difficulties and objections to reconciliation & dependence are every day increasing—the restraining bill, or rather the bill for confiscating American property, breathes such a spirit of depredation & revenge, that I am satisfied, peace with Great Britain is at a great distance, & Dependence out of the question."[13] Even two months later, Carroll's colleagues back in Maryland did not agree. On May 15, the same day that the Continental Congress called upon the colonies to set up new governments and also the day that Virginia effectively declared its independence, the Maryland Convention took a defiant step backwards. The convention published the following resolution:

> *Resolved unanimously*,
> That as this Convention is firmly persuaded that a re-union with Great-Britain, on constitutional principles, would most effectually secure the rights and liberties, and increase the strength, and promote the happiness of the whole empire, objects which this province hath ever in view, the said Deputies are bound and directed to govern themselves by

the instructions given to them by this Convention in its session of December last, in the same manner as if the said instructions were particularly repeated.[14]

Carroll's personal opinion on the subject of independence was irrelevant. As a delegate, he was bound by the instructions of his provincial government. But the rigid stance of the Maryland Convention backfired; it served as proof that the opinions of an increasingly pro-independence populace were being entirely disregarded by their elected representatives. By early June, Carroll was confident that in Maryland, "The desire of Independence is gaining ground rapidly."[15] By the end of June, the independence movement in Maryland culminated in a new set of instructions authorizing the province's delegates to vote for independence.

Charles Carroll was committed to the Continental cause, but the hectic scene in early 1776 had exhausted him—along with the rest of the Maryland delegation in Congress. In late June, Carroll expressed his hope that he wouldn't be elected to the Maryland Council of Safety, "I really begin to be sick of this busy scene & wish for retirement," acknowledging that his political service was motivated by duty, not pleasure.[16] Unexpectedly, and much to his chagrin, Carroll was again appointed a delegate to the Continental Congress in early July. He had less than a week to arrive in Philadelphia, because "Mr. Johnson can't go [because] his wife is nigh her time—Mrs. Chase is too ill to permit [Mr.] Chase to go—Mr. Tilghman is prevented by something or other, so I am reduced to the necessity of being there very soon as we have now no Representation."[17]

By mid-July Carroll had returned to Philadelphia, where the next month he would sign the *Declaration of Independence*. The Maryland delegate had grown weary of the push-and-pull of representing a loyalist colony in the midst of a revolutionary movement. But he was vindicated in his position when he read Lord Howe's declaration of pardon for those who "lay down their arms & return to duty." Carroll said, "I believe every man's eyes must now be open: the blindest & most infatuated must see, & I think, detest the perfidy & Tyranny of the British Constitution, Parl't & Nation." He added, "It is remarkable that even these harsh terms of submission & pardon have not been offered to the N. England Gov'ts—they, I suppose, must expect no mercy."[18]

In the public discourse of 1776, the opposition to independence in Maryland and other colonies was not called "loyalism," and support for independence was not called "patriotism." Those are terms that gained currency later in the American Revolution. In the parlance of 1776, William Eddis was a "Tory" and Charles Carroll was a "Whig." We are tempted, as twenty-first century Americans accustomed to a two-party political system, to assume that these terms corresponded to the dominant parties of the era. But "Whig" and "Tory" were not only the two most common words in the debate over American independence; they were also the era's most confusing and contested descriptive categories.

Redefining Whig and Tory

The partisan labels of "Whig" and "Tory" did not translate directly from England to America. In England, the basic differentiation between Whig and Tory rested on the interpretation of the hierarchy within the British Constitution. Whigs emphasized the legislative supremacy of parliament, while Tories preferred to centralize power in the king. As a rule, Whigs leaned toward republicanism, while Tories were royalists. In British politics, Whig partisans had established a reputation as supporters and protectors of the people's rights, but the John Wilkes affair and the American controversy had splintered the Whigs into several camps. Even "Radical" Whigs varied widely on these important questions, with some supporting the Wilkesite movement and others holding to the position that parliament should remain a thick filter on popular politics. Because the American controversy was bound up with the issue of parliamentary supremacy—a central tenet of Whiggism—then a majority of Whigs joined with the Tories in condemning the American rebellion.

Though "Whig" and "Tory" were familiar and convenient partisan labels for the American colonists, the ideological fault lines between parties had not been demarcated and reinforced with the specificity of English political culture. Before 1765, the American ideas of Whig and Tory were mostly decorative and resembled a group of contemporary sports fans rooting for one team over another. Lacking as they did a deep ideological foundation, when partisan labels achieved political relevance in the colonies during the taxation controversies, they became subject to American redefinition.

In the political discourse of late colonial America, Whig and Tory were treated as fixed, occupiable stances and immutable identities, but most colonists clustered somewhere near the center of a fluid continuum between these two imaginary poles: a Tory "right" and a Whig "left." In fact, the political norms in the colonies had traditionally occupied a range on the right of the continuum, since the Americans who appealed to the king over the parliament were, by the British definition, more Tory than Whig. When royal governments began disintegrating in the colonies in 1774 and 1775, most Americans were forced to become nominal Whigs to demonstrate their support for the last vestige of legitimate British authority, the colonial assemblies. Thus on one level, the debate over independence occurred as an exchange between competing groups of Whigs—conventionally termed "Radical" and

"Moderate"—rather than Whigs versus Tories.[19] But this standard account overlooks a nuance in late colonial political culture. American "Radical Whigs" were not tethered to the British "Radical Whig" tradition, and the American "Moderate Whigs" were actually closer to their British "Radical" counterparts. By 1775, so few Americans accepted the contentious authority of the British Parliament that colonial Whig sentiment had lost all reference to the functional core of British Whiggism. The American Whigs—whether "Radical" or Moderate"—thus shifted their predilection for legislative supremacy from the British Parliament to the individual provincial assemblies and, to a lesser extent, to the Continental Congress.

During the debate over independence in the wake of *Common Sense*, American public discourse crystallized political affiliations and, for the first time, considered individual judgments on a single question—independence or reconciliation?—as a sufficient litmus test for determining partisan affiliation. The political bifurcation during the spring of 1776 was largely a result of the crisis language of *Common Sense*. Paine had removed the shuffling middle ground from the debate through his structural antitheses and temporal acceleration. Like a bulldog prosecutor, Paine forced the colonists to answer yes-or-no questions and preempted any narrative justifications. While this technique was not strictly fair or even completely accurate, it achieved Paine's rhetorical objective: to generate a *decision*, not a discussion. As Paine put it in 1777, "A person, to use a trite phrase, must be a Whig or a Tory in a lump." If a man "says he is against the united independence of the continent, he is to all intents and purposes against her in all the rest; because *this last* comprehends the whole." There was no "neutral ground, of his own creating" that a man "may skulk upon for shelter, for the quarrel in no stage of it hath afforded any such ground; and either we or Britain are absolutely right or absolutely wrong through the whole."[20] How could Paine tell apart Tories and Whigs? He said, "As *disaffection* to independence is the badge of a Tory, so *affection* to it is the mark of a Whig." Some Whigs "nobly contribute everything," while others "have nothing to render but their wishes," but they "tend all to the same center." He stressed, "All we want to shut out is disaffection." And he reinforced his point, "All we want to know in America is simply this, who is for independence, and who is not?"[21]

This kind of talk was a profound departure from colonial politics of the preceding decades. For example, textbook American history tends to remember Benjamin Franklin as a Whig, John Dickinson as a Moderate, and Joseph Galloway as a Tory. Franklin and Galloway had been allies in the Tory opposition to Pennsylvania's Proprietary party and had lobbied hard for a royal government in the colony.[22] Dickinson held more traditional Whig values and as a member of the landed gentry, sparred with both Franklin and Galloway over their drive to cash-in proprietary government. Dickinson said that Franklin and Galloway wanted all the privileges of a proprietary charter to "be consumed in the blaze of royal authority."[23] In the 1760s, no one could have predicted that Franklin, Dickinson, and Galloway would have taken the courses that they did, because no one could have predicted the question of independence upon which they would split.

Galloway had served as Speaker of the Pennsylvania Assembly in an uninterrupted term from 1766 to 1774. When the First Continental Congress convened in Philadelphia in 1774, Galloway was among its delegates, and offered the Congress full use of the Assembly Room in the Pennsylvania State House. The New York delegates agreed, but a majority of the delegates assembled at the City Tavern decided that they would rather meet in Carpenters' Hall, ostensibly "to please the mechanics" of the city. The real reason the delegates had declined Galloway's offer was to stay off his home court. As events in America escalated in 1774 and 1775, Galloway's political influence was beginning to wane. In over a decade at the helm of the Pennsylvania Assembly, Galloway had demonstrated that he preferred enforced law and order, even if he had to accept parliamentary taxation, over liberty with lawlessness. The tyranny of the mob was far more fearful to him than the tyranny of parliament.[24] All government subsists in the tension between liberty and order, and Galloway, like most devoted loyalists, placed more value in security than he did in freedom and rights. But the loyal statesman's positions did not fit in the zeitgeist of parliament-bashing, and his star began to fade.

In 1779, when Galloway was questioned in the British Parliament by Lord George Germain, the former Pennsylvania politician claimed that less than "one-fifth of the people had independence in view" when the Americans first took up arms. Later in the examination, he lowered his estimate: "I think I may safely say, not one-tenth part had independence in view." Galloway described "the progress of the spirit of independence" as "very gradual." As early as 1754, he claimed, some men in Boston, New York, Philadelphia, and Williamsburg "held independence in prospect" and used "the gentlemen of the law in every part of America" as a "stalking-horse" during the Stamp Act controversy of the 1760s. These conspirators pressed "their designs" though they knew "that the great bulk of the people of North America was averse to independence." The resolves of Congress "down almost to the very period of their declaration of independence" used "the same language, the same pretence of obtaining a redress of grievances." Even the *Declaration*, said Galloway, argued that the Americans' "distress for want of a great many foreign necessaries," not "a view to a total separation of the two countries," forced the issue of independence. Galloway told his parliamentary inquisitors that the Continental Congress and "the very small part of the people" whom they had convinced "to take up arms" had misrepresented the views of the majority of Americans by disarming "all persons whom they thought disaffected to their measures, or wished to be united to this country, contrary to their scheme of Independence."[25]

A Rational Choice

Most Americans in 1776 weighed the costs and benefits on each side of the question of independence before determining their political affiliations.[26] In 1777, Benjamin Rush distilled five reasons why individuals had become Tories the year before: 1) "from an attachment to power and office," 2) "from an attachment to the British commerce which the war had interrupted or annihilated," 3) "from an attachment to kingly government," 4) from an attachment to the hierarchy of the Church of England, which it was supposed would be abolished in America by her separation from Great Britain," and 5) "from a dread of the power of the country being transferred into the hands of the Presbyterians." Rush noted that the fourth reason "acted chiefly upon the Episcopal clergy, more especially in the Eastern states," while the fifth reason "acted upon many of the Quakers in Pennsylvania and New Jersey" and upon Anglicans in those states where the Church of England had been "in possession of power, or of a religious establishment."[27]

Rush's parsimonious list—part scientific taxonomy and part medical diagnosis—displayed uncommon clarity amidst great political turbidity. Especially after the publication of *Common Sense*, most loyal colonists kept their political cards close to their chests. In a February 12 letter to the *Pennsylvania Packet*, "A Friend to Posterity and Mankind" urged the Americans to rise above party line politics. "Whig and Tory should be out of the question," said the writer, adding, "Private pique, party faction and animosity ought to subside. He who thinks should think for posterity, and he who acts should act for his children." This writer shared Paine's sense of perspective and scope, but he cautioned against reckless partisan epithets. He believed that some of the individuals "who are denominated Tories by the more zealous Whigs" were, in fact, merely chagrined because their measures "did not go down with the people" and were "uniform, open, and not very dangerous." But this even-handed essayist harbored suspicions of shifty-eyed moderates, "who, under the cloak of friendship for the cause, harbour the bitterest rancour and malice in their hearts." These men, said the writer,

> talk favourable in general, though their discourses mostly terminate with a doubt, suspicion, or "but," which gives those with whom they converse, reason to dread some hidden design, or approaching evil, which most men have not properly attended to. They artfully recall your attention to a certain period, when all was peace and quietness,

and by pathetically lamenting the unhappy alteration, endeavour to impress your minds with an opinion that all our troubles arose from ourselves. They carefully avoid mentioning the iniquitous measures of the British government that produced them, and by keeping those out of sight, they gradually lead the unwary into the belief that the men who have been most active on the present occasion in opposing the tyrannical proceedings of Great Britain and who have hazarded their all in defense of their country, have been actuated by sinister motives in all they have done.

The "Friend to Posterity and Mankind" lamented such men "who would sell the whole continent and all the blood on it for private advantage and with whom a few thousand guineas with a title would be esteemed an equivalent for the lives, liberty and property of the freemen of a colony." He urged his audience in crisis language, "Do not trifle on this occasion: all your other legacies must derive their true value from the part you now take in this contest." He added a foreboding reference to rumors of reconciliation, "Swallow the bait, and you are undone forever."

This writer then turned to the king and to Lord North, both of whom demonstrated by their "language" that they were insensible "of the justice of their proceedings and the wrongs they have done us." The king had lamented "so pathetically" the exorbitant cost of the war, while he had "not a single tear to shed, not a groan, nor as much as a sigh for all the blood he has already spilt and yet means to spill" against his American "rebels." The writer exclaimed, "Oh! George! The day thou utteredst that sentiment in the face of the sun, thou gavest up all title to humanity."

The "Friend to Posterity and Mankind" concluded his letter with an entreaty to "all PARENTS in the THIRTEEN UNITED COLONIES," that "you never desert your present opposition until you obtain such a plan of constitutional vigour as shall put it at all times in your power to secure yourselves and your descendants from tyrannical encroachments." He noted, "This you never had nor ever can have on the plan of your former dependence." He wished success to those who acted "from a principle of humanity and benevolence to mankind" while he prayed that "the schemes of hypocrites be blasted."[28]

The essayist was trying to partition America on the basis of underlying motives, a technique that would prove practically impossible. Were the colonists cunning hypocrites or simply confused? In early 1776, only the dogmatic extremes of colonial political culture—the *most* loyal Tories and the *most* independent Whigs—benefited from absolute clarity in their perspective on the conflict. The lion's share of American colonists were reluctant to make a decision, and yet they felt increasing pressure to choose a definitive course of action. This uncertain middle made up a huge percentage of the American population, and many who had initially cheered for *Common Sense* settled into a sober assessment of the odds of success. Later in this chapter, as well as in the following chapter, we will take a close look at the arrival of clarity among the American public. But first we must turn our attention to the other side of the Atlantic Ocean. The Americans were confused during the early months of 1776, but so were the British, and the two sides of the imperial controversy managed to confuse one another into a political separation.

Part Two
BRITISH *COMMON SENSE*

A Useful Distraction

Common Sense did not spark British public discourse in the same way it had in America. In fact, the pamphlet did not even meet with significant opposition in the British press for a surprising reason: it was not the most important pamphlet on the American controversy published in Britain in 1776. That honor fell to Richard Price's pamphlet, *Observations on the Nature of Civil Liberty, the Principles of Government, and the Justice and Policy of the War with America* (1776), which first appeared in London on February 12, 1776, and became an instant bestseller. Price had originally planned to print only 500 copies of his pamphlet, but when his printer learned that Price, a famous dissenting preacher and Fellow of the Royal Society, was willing to sign it, together they decided to double the first run to 1,000 copies.[29] Price's friend Joseph Priestley grabbed one of the last remaining copies to forward to Benjamin Franklin, noting, "An edition of a thousand has been nearly sold in two days." Priestley sent it immediately to Franklin in hopes that the ideas in Price's pamphlet would "unite us."[30]

Price's *Observations on Civil Liberty* went through five editions within a month and had a sale of over sixty thousand in six months. The pamphlet went through a total of 20 British editions in 1776, and it was translated into German, French, and Dutch, and reprinted in Philadelphia, New York, Boston, and Charleston.[31] In contrast to the case of *Common Sense*, the popularity of *Observations on Civil Liberty* hinged upon its author's identity. One response to Price's pamphlet, the anonymous *Experience Preferable to Theory* (1776), mentioned that John Cartwright's *American Independence* (1774) had expressed the "same sentiments, style, or mode of expression" as Price but "had less notice taken of it" because of its anonymity. Price's reputation "as a man of ingenuity and learning, increases that éclat to the book, which the spirit of party would have raised, had the author been unknown."[32]

Richard Price had been educated at various dissenting academies and was ordained to the nonconformist Presbyterian ministry, a vocation to which he was devoted above all else. Price preached to dissenting Presbyterian congregations in London at Poor Jewry Lane and north of the city at Newington Green, where his neighbor, James Burgh, was a schoolmaster.[33] Price leaned toward Arian theology, a movement within dissenting sects away from orthodoxy and toward "rational Christianity."[34] Price's personal system of theology, ethics, and politics was driven largely by his commitment to the "freedom of choice and the autonomy of the individual."[35]

Amidst the demands of the ministry, Price found time to write extensively on mathematical probability and other subjects, and he was elected to the Royal Society for his contribution to the solution of a problem in the doctrine of chances. Price went on to write several actuarial pamphlets and a two-volume book on reversionary payments, compositions for which he is regarded by some as the forefather of modern life insurance and retirement pensions.[36]

By 1776, Richard Price and Benjamin Franklin had been friends for two decades. Franklin had sponsored Price's nomination as a Fellow of the Royal Society in 1765, and the pair often engaged in private and public correspondence on scientific subjects. Along with Joseph Priestley and James Burgh, the two were members of what Franklin called in 1775 his "Club of Honest Whigs," a group made up mostly of dissenting ministers and tutors from the dissenting academies who met for dinner and philosophical conversation fortnightly.[37] One London dissenting minister boasted in January 1775 that he had dined with Price, Franklin, and Priestley, "no bad company you will say," and he added, "We began and ended with the Americans."[38]

The close relationship between Price and Franklin made some Londoners suspect that Price was a British proxy for Franklin's schemes. Thomas Hutchinson, the late governor of Massachusetts, said that Price's pamphlet "makes great noise" and "is calculated to do mischief." In his diary, Hutchinson labeled Price "a tool of F[ranklin]'s."[39] There was a grain of truth in Hutchinson's comment. The ubiquitous Franklin orchestrated many of the events of 1776 via his vast transatlantic social network and his mastery of the power of suggestion. Franklin rarely told his associates *what to do* in a direct, prescriptive manner. But he and Price had talked round and round the American controversy, and there is a strong likelihood that Franklin mentioned, at some point before returning to America in 1775, that it would be an immense help to both sides of the issue if Price would set some of his private political thoughts down in writing. Franklin cultivated his cryptic influence in such a way that his friends took an oblique suggestion as a positive injunction. Toward the end of the Revolutionary War, after the North ministry fell from power, Franklin sent a letter of congratulations to Price, in which he noted the "evident effects of your writings, with those of our deceased friend Mr. Burgh, and others of our valuable club."[40]

Price received "a great deal of abuse" in England because of *Observations on Civil Liberty*, but he consoled himself with the warm encouragement of his friends in America and elsewhere. *Observations on Civil Liberty* was the first in a series of pamphlets on the American conflict for which Price was offered honorary American citizenship by the Continental Congress in 1778. By Price's own account, he had been driven to write on the American controversy for reasons framed by his Enlightenment humanism, not from a general prepossession to root for the underdog or from a specific affection for America. Price recognized that the "interest of mankind depends so much" on the political establishment of America as "an asylum for the virtuous and the oppressed in other countries," or in other words, as a safe harbor for dissent.[41]

Price's *Observations on Civil Liberty* did not contain any earth-shattering arguments or incendiary language. Like its author, the pamphlet was modest in its tone and deliberate in its arguments. Much of the attention garnered by the pamphlet in England related to its economic arguments. In particular, Price's stress on the ruinous financial implications of the war alarmed many in Britain's financial circles. Because of Price's intellectual status and the domestic row over the competing agendas of military and trade policy, *Observations on Civil Liberty* generated 30 pamphlet responses in London in 1776.[42] As events played out in the spring of 1776, and in the broader context of the American Revolution, the pamphlet's most important function was to divert attention from *Common Sense*. Because the British press was so consumed with debating Price's pamphlet, and because Britons were accustomed to over-starched and dismissible American writing, *Common Sense* was instantly relegated to secondary status. By the time the wider British public began reading *Common Sense*, the Americans were already preparing to declare independence.

In *Observations on Civil Liberty*, Price expressed his hope that a peaceful solution to the conflict could be reached. Price's friend, Joseph Priestley, was less sanguine about the course of events. In a letter to Franklin accompanying the gift of a copy of *Observations on Civil Liberty*, Priestley lamented the conduct of the ministry—especially of the minister for American affairs, Lord George Germain. The ministry, said Priestley, "breathes rancour and desperation," and mutual catastrophe could only be halted by "absolute impotence" on both sides of the conflict. Priestley had concluded, then, that Britons should "look upon a final separation from you as a certain and speedy event."[43]

Price's comparative optimism was not just a glass-half-full attitudinal difference between him and Priestley. Price had written his pamphlet under the assumption that the colonies desired to be reconciled with Britain, because he had no reason to think otherwise. Besides the conciliatory petitions of the Continental Congress and the anti-independence instructions of the Pennsylvania legislature, Price had been the direct recipient of multiple letters from America in late 1775 and early 1776 that expressed without hesitancy a colonial consensus in favor of reconciliation.

One letter Price received from New York, dated August 3, 1775, tried to correct the misconception in England that the Americans desired independence. The writer referred to "a lie current last week that the congress had finally agreed upon independence to take place the 10th of March next, should not our grievances be redressed before that time." The New Yorker was so concerned by this rumor that he wrote to one of the delegates in New York who replied, "upon his honour, that he believed there was not one man in the Congress who would dare to make a motion tending to independence or, that if any one did, two could not be found to support the motion."[44] The same correspondent wrote again to Price on January 3, 1776, that the ministry could "annihilate all our disputes by restoring us to the situation we were in at the conclusion of the last war. If this is done we shall immediately return to our allegiance." Price's friend warned of "an awful scene" that would come that spring unless something was done soon. He said, "Let me repeat a caution to you; believe not the insinuations of our enemies, who would make you all believe that independence is what America aims at. It is an insidious falsehood."[45]

Price had received another letter from New York written November 2, 1775, that couldn't have been clearer about the intentions of America. Price's friend said, "We love and honour our King. He has no subjects in all his dominions more attached to his person, family and government, notwithstanding the epithet of rebels bestowed upon us." He continued, "No charge is more unjust than the charge that we desire an independence on Great Britain. Ninety-nine in a hundred of the inhabitants of this country deprecate this as the heaviest of evils." But the American colonists saw independence as an unfortunate inevitability if the "administration will persist in their present measures," because submission "to the present claims of the British parliament, while unrepresented in it" was unconscionable. Americans of all denominations were "much employed in prayer to God" for a successful resolution of the military struggle, and considered "their cause as the cause of God and, as such, they humbly commit to him, confident of success in the end, whatever blood or treasure it may cost them."[46]

Price later observed that between the writing of those letters and the *Declaration of Independence,* "the sentiments of America, with respect to independence have been much altered." He attributed the change to the combined effect of the rejection of the "Olive Branch" Petition, the Prohibitory Bill, and the employment of foreign troops. The last of these, said Price, "produced a greater effect in America than is commonly imagined. And it is remarkable that even the writers in America who answered the pamphlet entitled *Common Sense* acknowledge that should the British ministry have recourse to foreign aid it might become proper to follow their example and to embrace the necessity of resolving upon independence."[47] Price also observed that "the answer to the last petition of the City of London, presented in March 1776, had no small share in producing the same effect." Price had been assured by an American correspondent that the colonies "were not perfectly unanimous till they saw this answer." By all of these measures "those colonists who had all along most dreaded and abhorred independence were at last reconciled to it." Though an accommodation remained a possibility well into the spring of 1776, "our rulers preferred coercion and conquest," and therefore America and Britain were "now plunged" into "desolating calamities."[48]

A Gross Misunderstanding

In 1783 at the close of the war, Paine commented upon the inadequate understanding of America displayed in "all the English papers, publications and politics" during the contest. The British comprehension of American affairs vacillated between a "state of profound ignorance" in some cases and "only a loose uninformed notion in others." Because their information was corrupted, the British government, observed Paine, had attempted to conquer America "on the ground of delusion." For the most part, the only Americans in Great Britain at the time were, like Joseph Galloway, "on the wrong side," and the British people thus received very distorted eyewitness accounts of American politics. Parliament experienced gridlock on the issue, and, said Paine, "We frequently saw that even those who were against the war were, in many instances, as wrong as those who were for it."[49]

There had been contention in the British Parliament since the inception of the American controversy, but the hard-liners won most of the political battles in the mid-1770s. The North administration and the king were aggressive in building a strong majority in favor of forcing the Americans to submit, and they used every available means—from propaganda to threats to bribery—to achieve their policy agenda.[50] George III had no kind words for parliamentary supporters of the American rebels, calling Charles James Fox "as contemptible as he is odious," Lord Chatham a "trumpet of sedition," and Edmund Burke, simply, "a pest."[51] Like any other weak minority, all that this Whig opposition could do in 1775 and 1776 was voice their criticisms and attempt to decelerate measures they considered reprehensible. Besides a handful of members in each house, parliament was in the pocket of King George III and Lord North.

The House of Lords, in particular, walked in lockstep with the king on the American question. After the king's October 26, 1775 speech, the Lords "adjourned during Pleasure to unrobe" and, returning to their seats, immediately tabled a petition from the Lord Mayor, Aldermen, and Commons, of the City of London, in Common Council assembled that prayed, "Their Lordships would be pleased to adopt such measures for the Healing of the present unhappy Disputes between the Mother Country and the Colonies, as may be speedy, permanent, and honourable."[52]

After brushing aside this conciliatory petition from the most powerful extraparliamentary political body in the British Empire, the Lords quickly agreed on an affirmative "humble Address" in response to the king's speech. The Commons composed a similar address to "return His Majesty the Thanks of this House for His most gracious Speech from the Throne." The Commons said, "That since the Rebellion is now become more general, and manifests the Purpose of establishing and maintaining an independent Empire, we cannot but applaud His Majesty's Resolution to vindicate the Rights, the Interests, and the Honour of His Kingdom, by a speedy and most decisive Exertion" of military strength.[53] In trying to squash an independence movement that did not yet exist, parliament was creating a self-fulfilling prophecy about the course of American affairs.

But the Commons did not merely duplicate the consensus of the landed aristocracy. While the Lords rubberstamped their address to the king, the Commons vigorously debated its reply, and it did not adjourn until one o'clock in the morning after debating their "humble Address" for an additional two days. The opposition in the House of Commons tried to include an amendment to the address, stressing that

> this Misfortune has, in a great Measure, arisen from the Want of full and proper Information being laid before parliament of the true State and Condition of the Colonies, by reason of which, Measures have been carried into Execution injudicious and inefficacious, from whence no Salutary End was reasonably to be expected, tending to tarnish the Lustre of the *British* Arms, to bring Discredit on the Wisdom of His Majesty's Councils, and to nourish, without Hope of End, a most unhappy Civil War.[54]

The opposition motion was defeated after a long debate, but the amendment made a cogent point. During the peak of the conflict with the American colonies, the British Parliament *did* receive information that, if it was not *bad*, was at least slanted and lagging. Besides Benjamin Franklin's clever responses to a parliamentary interview, the information channels of the British government depended upon partial sources. Pennsylvania proprietary governor Richard Penn, for example, had presented the "Olive Branch" Petition to the Earl of Dartmouth on September 1, 1775, but Penn wasn't called before the House of Lords until November 10, 1775, two months after his arrival and half a month after the parliamentary session had opened. Penn's examiners asked him if the American people "wish to support the measures of Congress at present," and Penn answered, "It is firmly my Opinion that they do, but wish at the same Time for a Reconciliation with this Country."[55] By the time Penn's interview circulated back in the colonies, his statement sounded like a wishful anachronism.

Most Britons recognized that the Prohibitory Bill of December 1775 amounted to a declaration of war against America. In the parliamentary struggle between coercion and conciliation in 1775 and 1776, force always trumped negotiation. The sweeping nature of the Prohibitory Bill bugled the British government's determined course of policy: military subjugation at all costs. As one contributor to the *London Evening Post* put it that December, "The dies are thrown, and the game is lost. The addressers have won."[56] The Prohibitory Bill was a legal requisite for the British government to wage war against the Americans; it revoked their British subjecthood. The Americans had displayed—or, so thought the British government—faltering allegiance to the Crown, and, therefore, had absolved the king of his reciprocal obligation to protect them. In point of fact, the Americans reasoned in exactly the opposite manner: they had been unwavering in their allegiance to the Crown until he had revoked his affection and protection. The Prohibitory Bill was thus the pretext for the Continental Congress's call in May for each colony to set up new governments, a major step toward *de jure* independence.

The British Parliament recessed for most of January and in February again took up the matter of suppressing the American rebels. One of the most important events in the final push for American independence occurred on March 14, 1776, in the House of Lords. The Duke of Grafton introduced the following motion to the house:

> That an humble Address be presented to His majesty, beseeching His Majesty, that in order to prevent the further Effusion of Blood, and to manifest how desirous the King of *Great Britain* and His Parliament are to restore Peace to all parts of the Dominions of His Majesty's Crown, and how earnestly they wish to redress any real Grievance of His Majesty's Subjects, His Majesty would be graciously pleased to issue His Royal Proclamation; declaring, that in case the colonies, within a reasonable Time before or after the Arrival of the Troops destined for *America*, shall present a Petition to the Commander in Chief in *America*, or to the Commissioner or Commissioners to be appointed by His Majesty under the Authority of [the Prohibitory Act]... and setting forth in such Petition, which is to be transmitted to His Majesty; what they consider to be their just Rights and real Grievances, that in such Case His Majesty will consent to a Suspension of Arms; and that His Majesty has Authority from His Parliament to assure them, that such their Petition shall be received considered, and answered.[57]

The relief felt by pro-reconciliation Americans who read Grafton's resolution in May was, however, quickly displaced with dread as they continued to read the parliamentary record. The Earl of Dartmouth was the most vociferous opponent to Grafton's motion. Dartmouth replied to accusations of inconsistency in his hardening view of the colonies: "if unconditional submission be a resolution on our part, not to cease hostilities till America submits so far as to acknowledge the supreme authority of this country, I am still consistent." Dartmouth continued,

> I ever was, and ever shall be of opinion, that this country cannot, with propriety, concede, nor can we, consistent with the honour, dignity or most essential interests of this country, consent to lay own our arms, or suspend the operations now carrying on, till the Colonies own our legislative sovereignty; and by acts of duty and obedience, show such a disposition, as will entitle them to the favour and protection of the parent state.

Dartmouth had assumed "that the disorders in that country were local, and had chiefly pervaded the hearts of an inconsiderable number of men, who were only formidable, because they possessed the power of factious delusion and imposition." He said further, "I all along expected, that the *body* of the people, when they came to view the consequences closely, and consider them attentively, would soon perceive the danger in which they were precipitating themselves, and of course return to their duty."

Dartmouth pronounced, "The surest way to prevent a calamity, which I as earnestly deprecate as any lord in this House, will be to send the armaments, now destined for that country, with all possible expedition." He was certain that the colonists' "fears may exact a conduct, which I am persuaded their duty or obedience would never have inspired. They will be convinced that we have the ability, as well as the inclination, to compel them to acknowledge the true subordinate and constitutional relation they bear to the mother-country." Dartmouth was set on a plan that would "awe the Colonies into submission."[58] After "long Debate" Grafton's pacific motion was "Resolved in the Negative," and it became unequivocally clear that parliament meant to "reconcile" the Americans by force.[59]

The April arrival of *Common Sense* in London did not help those in parliament who hoped to avert a prolonged armed conflict; in fact, Paine's pamphlet furnished the North administration with a necessary piece of evidence. For several members of the British government, *Common Sense* was the long-coveted unequivocal "proof" of a general plot for American independence. In an April 24 speech before the Committee of Ways and Means in the House of Commons, Paymaster of the Forces Richard Rigby "was extremely violent against America and contended that Great Britain ought never to make any specific promise or agree to any previous conditions till the people of America threw down their arms; and if they should obstinately persist, Britain ought to persevere till America was subdued." Rigby excused his malevolence because "America aimed at independence," as he said, "It was plain, from the pamphlet called *Common Sense*, written by a member of the congress."⁶⁰

Both houses of parliament, the ministry, and the king stood firm in their commitment to smashing the American rebellion. In a speech at the close of the parliamentary session on May 23, 1776, George III said he would "still entertain a Hope that My rebellious Subjects may be awakened to a Sense of their Errors," but, he warned, "if a due Submission should not be obtained from such Motives and such Dispositions on their Part, I trust that I shall be able, under the Blessing of Providence, to effectuate it by a full Exertion of the great Force with which you have entrusted Me."⁶¹

David Hartley, a Member of Parliament, wrote from London to his friend Benjamin Franklin in June 1776. Hartley still hoped for "the restoration of peace," but he feared the "stoppage of communication between the two countries" had produced the "very worst of consequences." The British ministry, he said, had taken the opportunity to send "their own irritating information to America" while at the same time "withholding the knowledge of all the good dispositions which there are in this Country towards their fellow Subjects in America." Hartley saw the "fatal Effect" of a litany of "angry Addresses" that had been sent "with all the parade of Authority to America" while "the petitions in favour of peace have not been Suffered to appear in the gazettes." Hartley paraphrased the passage from *Common Sense* where Paine noted that the people of England were presenting addresses against America, resulting in the "last cord" of connection being broken. Hartley objected that "the general sense of the people of England" was "full as favorable to America" as it had been when Franklin was in London a year and a half earlier. The ministry, Hartley said, had been unsuccessful in its attempts "to raise any national Spirit of resentment against America," adding, "The generality of the people are cold upon the Subject." Though there were "many Zealous and principled friends to America" in Britain, "Nine Men in ten content themselves with an indolent wish for peace." In fact, the only "bitter enemies" to America were the ministry and those who profited from the war. Hartley acknowledged that "it is easy to Reason like Philosophers" for "those who neither see nor feel the horrors of War." He made "all allowances for the Sufferings of America," but he still thought "reconciliation and peace the best bargain to both sides." He knew nothing of the commissioners' instructions of powers, and he trusted that "Time would secure and confirm all the rights of America."⁶²

As Edmund Burke listened to the speeches in parliament that spring, he realized that he was witnessing the unraveling of the British Empire. The entire conflict had arisen, he observed, "from a total misconception of the object" of each opposing side. "The whole of those maxims upon which we have made and continued this war must be abandoned. Nothing indeed," he said, "can place us in our former situation. That hope must be laid aside."[63] Burke warned of the unintended consequences of parliamentary and royal grandstanding. He said, "Declaiming on rebellion never added a bayonet or a charge of powder to your military force, but I am afraid that it has been the means of taking up many muskets against you."[64]

In early 1777, Burke pointed out that, "For a long time, even amidst the desolations of war and the insults of hostile laws daily accumulated on one another, the American leaders seem to have had the greatest difficulty in bringing up their people to a declaration of total independence." But the "outrageous language" and "disingenuous compilation and strange medley of railing and flattery" had "accomplished what the abettors of independence had attempted in vain." Burke noted that when the "court gazette" began to be "adduced as proof of the united sentiments of the people of Great Britain" against the colonies, "there was a great change throughout all America." Burke continued, pointing to *Common Sense* as a linchpin in this change,

> The tide of popular affections, which had still set towards the parent country, began immediately to turn, and to flow with great rapidity in a contrary course. Far from concealing these wild declarations of enmity, the author of the celebrated pamphlet, which prepared the minds of the people for independence, insists largely on the multitude and the spirit of these addresses; and he draws an argument from them which (if the fact was as he supposes) must be irresistible.[65]

Burke understood that Paine's argument hinged upon the disaffection of the people of England. Paine had asserted, "The last cord now is broken, the people of England are presenting addresses against us," and the implication was clear to his readers: if the political connection to the king was invalid, and if the sentimental connection to the people and culture of England had been cut on the eastern side of the Atlantic, then only an unreciprocated sentimental attachment to England perpetuated the Americans as British subjects.[66] Paine encouraged the Americans to take the hint: the colonists were being denied the constitutional rights of Englishmen, because no one in England considered them to *be* Englishmen. First, parliament had been the Americans' enemy, and then the ministry. When *Common Sense* pointed the finger at the king and then at the English people, every element in the British Constitution had become complicit in the oppression of America.

At the end of May 1776, Edmund Burke left the parliamentary session wearing a bewildered daze and slumped shoulders. He wrote, "Our Session is over; and I hardly can believe, by the tranquility of everything about me, that we are a people who have just lost an Empire. But it is so."[67]

Almon's Hiatuses

Ralph Izard of South Carolina was living in London in mid-1776.[68] By early May he had read *Common Sense* and described it as "by much the cleverest and most ingenious performance I ever saw." Izard noted that John Almon "had a copy of it, but it was taken from him," probably confiscated by royal officials.[69] Almon managed to obtain another copy, and he quietly began to set the type for a London edition of *Common Sense*.

Of the original copies of *Common Sense* extant today, a disproportionate number are London editions published by John Almon. No one in Britain was surprised that Almon, a Wilkesite radical printer who had already printed numerous pro-American tracts, decided to publish the London edition of *Common Sense*. Almon, known equally as a bookseller, publisher, and pamphleteer, began operating *The Gazetteer* in 1761, the same year he first made the acquaintance of John Wilkes, and two years later set up a bookshop in Piccadilly. In 1770 Almon was fined for selling a paper containing a reprint of the infamous *Letter of Junius* addressed to the king.[70]

Almon, a lifelong member of the political opposition, was taken aback by the force of *Common Sense*. He took the considerable risk of printing *Common Sense* in London, but he was careful to cover himself by expunging the pamphlet of its most offensive passages, primarily those that included slanderous attacks on the king. Almon left the controversial passages as lacunae in the printed text, because he was less interested in saving space than in saving time. The decision to insert hiatuses was a typesetting convenience that circumvented the need to perform extensive reformatting from the American source edition and thus enabled a speedy production turnaround.

The lacunae in the London editions make for one of the most fascinating episodes in the history of political writing. Because Almon—and other publishers in Edinburgh, Stirling, and Belfast who copied his edition—left the offensive passages as space-filling hiatuses rather than condensing them with ellipses, British readers were tempted to treat *Common Sense* as a fill-in-the-blank puzzle. In a time when all books, even pamphlets, were still relatively expensive, it was rare for readers to annotate their books beyond an inscription on the title page. In this instance, however, copies of *Common Sense* looked more like a copy book or an annotated almanac than a political treatise. Often with the aid of a circulating copy of an unexpurgated French or American edition of *Common Sense*, reader after reader filled in the salacious passages in manuscript. Instead of remaining arms-length spectators of *Common Sense*'s seditious libel, hundreds—and quite possibly thousands—of Britons participated in Paine's royal evisceration with their own hands. Whether they were motivated by curiosity or contempt, these readers signed, as it were, the most vicious rhetorical attack against the dual institutions of the British Crown and Constitution ever yet written.

Almon and his fellow London printers were careful to expurgate *Common Sense*'s harshest criticisms before placing extracts from the pamphlet in their newspapers, because they realized that Paine's attacks on monarchy exceeded the norms of British political criticism and smacked of outright indecency.[71] William Woodfall, who published long excerpts of *Common Sense* in his *Morning Chronicle*, explained the hiatuses in the text to his readers. If he were to publish the whole work, said Woodfall, he would justly be accused "of printing more foul mouth'd abuse against our gracious Sovereign than ever yet issued from the press of this country."[72]

As soon as Almon got the chance, he published an expanded edition of *Common Sense* along with *Plain Truth*. Including both pamphlets under the same cover increased the credibility of Almon's argument that he was simply relaying current colonial opinion. But Almon did not just publish *Plain Truth* as an alibi. Like most other "radical" Whigs of his day, Almon didn't know what to do with *Common Sense*. He found it patently offensive and alarming. At the time it arrived in London, even the most ardent British supporters of American liberties hoped for a reconciliation between daughter colonies and the mother country. The John Wilkes affair had convinced many of the British of the endemic corruption of parliament, and the bumbling ministry was widely regarded as a cadre of sycophants, but, as in America, openly criticizing not just the *person* of George III but the *institution* of the Crown was taboo.

Almon's nervousness showed in the editor's introduction to his dual edition of *Common Sense* and *Plain Truth*, published later in 1776:

> The public have been amused by many extracts from the Pamphlet entitled *Common Sense*, which have been held up as Proof positive that the Americans desire to become independent; we are happy in this opportunity of publishing *Plain Truth*; which we take to be as good a Proof that the Americans *do not* desire to become independent. After all, the public can only judge from the reasonings of two private gentlemen in North America, whether the Americans are, or are not prepared for a state of independence; and whether it is probable they may betake themselves to such a state.[73]

Paine's authorial anonymity helped the pamphlet's popularity in London as it had under different circumstances in Philadelphia.[74] Benjamin Franklin's identification with the American cause was so strong that most British writers and editors ascribed authorship of *Common Sense* to him. The *Morning Post* reported in June 1776 that an outraged George III had commissioned Samuel Johnson to answer "Dr. Franklin's *Common Sense*."[75] Franklin's friends, however, noted that the "abusive style and illiberality of sentiment" in the pamphlet was "inconsistent with the good sense and spirit of the writings of the great philosopher."[76]

Because of the confident tone of *Common Sense*, Britons looked upon this cogent treatise as a philosophical justification of the Americans' rebellion written by one of its top leaders. The *Morning Post* inferred, "Hancock, Adams, and Franklin are the men...and common sense abounds among them."[77] The *General Evening Post* of April 6 had assumed that *Common Sense* was written "by one of the leading MEMBERS of the CONTINENTAL CONGRESS."[78] Thomas Hutchinson, deposed as Governor of Massachusetts in 1774, was living in London in 1776. On April 8, he picked up the *Public Advertiser* and read "some extracts from an American pamphlet said to be wrote by John Adams," Hutchinson's avowed enemy. In his diary for that day, Hutchinson noted that the extracts amount to an "open declaration against all plans of reconciliation," but moreover, he recorded, "the book contains the most shocking abuses of the King—*Royal Brute, &c.* This a loyal subject would not reprint."[79]

Especially considering the furor over *Common Sense* in the American colonies, reaction to Paine's pamphlet in Britain was comparatively mute. Only four pamphlets published in Britain during 1776 can justly be called "responses" to *Common Sense*, none of which were English in origin. Two of the pamphlets, James Chalmers's *Plain Truth*, and Henry Middleton's *The True Merit of a Late Treatise* were written and published originally in America. The other two pamphlets *Free Thoughts on the American Contest* and *A Sequel to Common Sense* were published in Edinburgh and Dublin, farther away from ministerial controls on the press.[80]

The breadth of the arguments in *Common Sense* made it difficult to refute *in toto*, especially from across the Atlantic. Franklin's friend William Doyle, by his own admission "not very much a Republican," undertook but never completed a refutation of *Common Sense*, which he viewed as "quite inconsistent with any Government this Day upon the Earth."[81] Since no one in London could manage a comprehensive response, most British newspapers were eager to publish any letter, fact, or figure that would refute even a single argument in *Common Sense*. For example, the *St. James Chronicle* reprinted an article from the *Jamaica Gazette* wherein a retired admiral disputed *Common Sense*'s calculations of the British naval force.[82]

Though *Common Sense* was overshadowed in the British context by *Observations on Civil Liberty*, Paine's pamphlet still had a sizable circulation in Britain and in Europe. There were at least thirteen printings of *Common Sense* in London in 1776, four of which were combined editions including *Plain Truth*. Other editions of *Common Sense* were published that year in Newcastle upon Tyne, Edinburgh, and Stirling, while a French edition originated in Rotterdam.[83] The attention of the British reading public was focused on America during 1776, and *Common Sense* was the main textual import that year. The British press was not ignoring America; in fact, between 1773 and 1778, the American controversy was the primary topic of 60 percent of the pamphlets published in Britain.[84]

In Britain, *Common Sense* was a bestseller but not a defining text as it was in America. Almon never divulged any statistics about *Common Sense*'s circulation in England, but by late August, the *Morning Post* expressed the opinion that every segment of British society had been affected by the work. But in America the over 46,000 copies of *Common Sense* printed and circulated among the colonists had been "attended with greater effect than any other public performance of the kind that ever appeared in any country, and gave the decisive spirit for independency."[85] The limitations of transatlantic pamphlet culture ensured that *Common Sense* did not become a phenomenon in Britain until *after* the Americans had declared independence, but by then, of course, the time for response had expired. Americans read *Common Sense* to figure out what to do, while Britons read *Common Sense* to figure out what just happened.

Paine was a rhetorical practitioner, and his persuasion was specific to a particular time and a particular audience. *Common Sense* was an American, not a British, pamphlet. Paine immigrated to Philadelphia with a native knowledge of British political culture, but he wrote *Common Sense* as an American, not as an Englishman. Likewise, he imagined an American audience for *Common Sense*—the only audience who could *decide* to declare independence—and he did not pander to British delicacies.

Paine always considered his American *Common Sense* and his later British *Rights of Man* to be cut from the same cloth. Of the *Rights of Man*, he said, "The principles of that work were the same as those in *Common Sense*," adding, "As to myself, I acted in both cases alike."[86] He *acted* alike in both cases, and he *wrote* alike as well. Though *Common Sense* did not garner voluminous British critical commentary because of the distraction of Price's pamphlet and the issues of audience and timing, we can understand something of the British reception of Paine's idiosyncratic prose style by responses to the *Rights of Man* in the 1790s. Though *Common Sense* and the *Rights of Man* were separated by an ocean and fifteen years, Paine's style remained remarkably consistent.

After reading the *Rights of Man*, Charles James Fox, one of Britain's more radical Whigs, appreciated Paine's writing, saying, "it seems as clear and simple as the first rule in arithmetic." Working class Britons as a rule adored the *Rights of Man* because it was the first political tract written in their vernacular, but most members of the British establishment, even if they sympathized with Paine's political positions, loathed the way he wrote. The *Monthly Review* described Paine's politics as "just and right on the whole," but his style was "desultory, uncouth, and inelegant." Likewise, "His wit is coarse, and sometimes disgraced by wretched puns; and his language, though energetic, is awkward, ungrammatical, and often debased by vulgar phraseology." Horace Walpole, son of Sir Robert Walpole, described Paine's style as "so coarse, that you would think he means to degrade the language as much as the government."[87] Sir Brooke Boothby thought Paine had "the natural eloquence of a night-cellar," and the baronet found *Rights of Man* to be "written in a kind of specious jargon, well enough calculated to impose upon the vulgar." Boothby gibed that Paine wrote "in defiance of grammar, as if syntax were an aristocratic invention."[88] When Paine was tried *in absentia* for seditious libel, His Majesty's Attorney-General urged the jury "to take into your consideration the phrase and the manner as well as the matter."[89]

Thomas Paine wrote in a style that was unlike anything his American or British audiences had ever seen. Because his prose was so foreign, Americans assumed it was British in origin, and Britons assumed it was American in origin. In point of fact, it was neither. It was a vernacular style that arose from Paine's artisan background, was cultivated by the cadences of dissenting religion, was hewn by the discipline of scientific inquiry, and was sparked by the American opportunity to form a democratic polity. Literary critic James Boulton perceived "a philosophical claim inherent in the language used" by Paine. The author's "choice of idiom, tone, and rhythm" suggest "that the issues he is treating can and ought to be discussed in the language of common speech; that these issues have a direct bearing on man's ordinary existence."[90] "Paine's manner," said Boulton," was radical in both literary and political terms," since the nature of Paine's theory required that he "eschew the literary methods associated with an aristocratic culture linked, in its turn, with the politics of the establishment."[91] Boulton's analysis focused on the *Rights of Man*, but the same principles were driving Paine's philosophy, politics, and prose in 1775 and 1776.

While Paine's prose was not a direct British import, his perspective on the conflict was. Letters from England at the end of 1775—not received in America until the next year—mirrored the arguments in *Common Sense*. For example, one anonymous letter from London, dated December 10, 1775, accused the British ministers of a determination "to force you to the formation of a new and independent government. That, I presume, *will be the work of this winter.*"[92] This anonymous English correspondent was so convinced that America would require a "new constitution" that he entreated his American friend to forbid "hereditary titles of honour" as an "absurdity." He said, "That a vicious or immeritorious son should enjoy that distinction and those privileges, which were given to the virtue and merit of his father, is at once preposterous and pernicious."[93] Paine took advantage of his dual perspective to exploit the opportunity that only a few could see.

Common Sense may not have been the riptide in Britain that it had been in America, but the *Declaration* had a visible effect on British culture. In September 1776, the Virginian William Lee observed from London that "The *Declaration of Independence* on the part of America, has totally changed the nature of the contest between that country and Great Britain." In Britain, the war was now exclusively "a scheme of conquest which few imagine can succeed." The *Declaration* had "altered the face" of politics in London. He said, "The Tories, and particularly the Scotch, hang their heads and keep a profound silence on the subject," while "the Whigs do not say much, but rather seem to think the step a wise one on the part of America, and what was an inevitable consequence of the measures taken by the British Ministry."[94]

It is clear from the historical record that people in Great Britain thought about American independence far more than the American colonists did prior to 1776. Paine brought this assumption with him from England, and this foreordained conclusion was one of his most significant "imports." Even Benjamin Franklin, a man who had achieved fortune and fame as a participant in royal culture, brought with him back from England the dawning assumption of colonial independence.

The actions of the British government in 1775 and 1776 were based upon the mistaken assumption that the colonies were aiming for total independence. The Americans had, it is true, wanted to be independent *of parliament* ever since they became convinced that their pleas for direct colonial representation had been rejected *by parliament.* But before 1776 the colonists had never imagined themselves as independent *of the king.* The Americans associated the malevolence of the ministry with *parliament*, not the *king.* The colonists had, for over a decade, parsed the British Constitution to fit their predicament, and they did not realize that the king was complicit in their treatment until he began to describe them in the third-person as "my rebellious subjects." When viewed from St. James's, the escalating American resistance looked like a stiff-necked rejection of the totality of British constitutional authority. The colonists' pathetic petitions and determined resistance didn't line up, and the former came across as the most absurd farce playing in the theaters of Drury Lane. It was clear that the Americans were faking loyalty to take advantage of an irresolute British response. Thus a decisive majority in the British government thought that a well-applied surge of force could squash the nascent independence movement in

America—a movement that, in fact, did not exist until the provocations of war created it.

Part Three
FOG OF LOYALTY

Reconciliation or Independence

With the help of the malevolent communications of the British government, by the spring of 1776 Paine had effectively forced the colonists to equate "Whig" with independence and "Tory" with reconciliation. The base definitions of independence and reconciliation thus defined revolutionary partisan categories. Especially among the common people of America, nuanced interpretations of political theory did not make a person a "Whig" or a "Tory." Only a single question could define an individual's affiliation: "Reconciliation or independence?"

This was, of course, an oversimplified and sometimes unfair question, especially because "reconciliation" harbored multiple meanings. The British Tory lexicographer, Samuel Johnson, serendipitously conveyed the dictional conundrum of pro-reconciliation Americans in his tripartite definition of *reconciliation (n.s.)*: "Renewal of friendship; Agreement of things seemingly opposite, solution of seeming contrarieties; or Atonement, expiation." The first two options sounded safe enough, but the third implied an admission of guilt—even *American* guilt—a definitional loophole exploited by hard-line loyalists. When a 1776 writer spoke on behalf of a "reconciliation," the black box term encompassed everything from amicable equality to prostrate submission.[95] As the independence debate wore on, the three distinct definitions became conflated, and any reference to reconciliation became a tacit admission of Tory principles. By the spring of 1776, "Tory" was no longer a partisan self-identification in America; it was an epithet ascribed by opponents.

I will close this chapter with a sketch of the murky political culture in New Jersey, one of the middle colonies that stalled the question of independence as long as possible. The confused reaction to *Common Sense* and independence in New Jersey will serve as a fitting segue into our fuller exploration of colonial moderation in the next chapter.

The Other Franklin and an Unwelcome Innuendo

Royal governors in late colonial America served two masters, the King of England and the people of America, and those masters were increasingly at loggerheads. In most colonies during the 1760s, as long as royal governors acted like reluctant arbiters of imperial policy rather than parliamentary bedfellows, the Americans viewed them as inoffensive necessities.[96] The outbreak of war in 1775, however, forced the royal governors to pick sides, and invariably they chose to support the British government against the American "rebels." By the end of

1775, most royal governors had either fled to England or were attempting to subvert the rebels and govern their colonies from a British ship anchored off the coast.

Governor William Franklin of New Jersey retained a semblance of power longer than most of his peers. Franklin, an ardent Tory and the son of Benjamin Franklin, wrote to Lord George Germain at the end of March to update him on the American situation. Governor Franklin thought the New Jersey Provincial Congress "appeared inclined to adopt an independency should it be recommended by the Continental Congress," but he was satisfied that such an event was remote given "the present members of the New Jersey Assembly." His surety was tempered however by the fact "that the minds of a great number of the people have been much changed in that respect since the publication of a most inflammatory pamphlet in which that horrid measure is strongly and artfully recommended." Franklin said the "one good effect" of *Common Sense* was its "opening the eyes of many people of sense and property who before would not believe that there were any persons of consequence, either in or out of the Congress, who harboured such intentions." These "alarmed" elite, he said, were finally beginning "to venture to express their fears and apprehensions." Franklin sent Germain a copy of *Common Sense* and *Plain Truth*, apologizing for the error laden printing of the latter. Franklin closed his letter in a somber mood and with a quote from *Common Sense*, contrasting "the merciful and benevolent intentions of the supreme legislature" with America's "artful and designing men," who "already, as your lordship will see, represent 'reconciliation and ruin as nearly related.'"[97]

Around the same time, William Franklin composed another letter to the New Jersey Assembly to exhort them "to avoid, above all things, the traps of Independency and Republicanism now set for you, however temptingly they may be baited." New Jersey, he said, would never be happier than in its "ancient constitutional dependency on Great-Britain." He reminded them of his earlier warnings against "many pretended patriots" who, behind "the mask of zeal for reconciliation," had been "insidiously promoting a system of measures" calculated to widen the breach between the two countries "so far as to let in an Independent Republican Tyranny—the worst and most debasing of all possible tyrannies." Franklin knew that his address did not contain "language to the times," but he asserted that "A real patriot can seldom or ever speak popular language."[98]

In April 1776 came the first real test of the collective attitude of the residents of New Jersey toward independence. That month an anonymous newspaper advertisement invited each county in New Jersey to send delegates to New Brunswick for a meeting "on matters which greatly concerned the province." The New Jersey counties sent delegates as a matter of course, assuming the meeting pertained to establishing a market for "Home Manufactures." Elias Boudinot, who would later serve as President of the United States in Congress Assembled at the close of the war, traveled to the meeting as a representative from his county. When the delegates arrived in New Brunswick, Reverend Doctor John Witherspoon met them, acknowledged his authorship of the announcement, and informed them "that the Design of the Meeting was, to consider the peculiar Situation of the Province, and the Propriety of declaring a Separation from Great Britain, and forming an independent Constitution for ourselves." The delegates, recalled Boudinot, were stunned. The meeting adjourned until the afternoon to allow each member time to think seriously about the subject. Boudinot already knew what he thought. He had first entered public life as a representative in the New Jersey Provincial Congress in 1775 and had opposed, along with "all Men of Note & Understanding," a call for raising a regiment of troops. Boudinot had sneered at the "few weak and violent men" who had dared to introduce "a Measure wholly against our Duty of Allegiance to Great Britain" and "contrary to every Sentiment or Desire of our Constituents."[99]

When Witherspoon's meeting reconvened that April afternoon, the Presbyterian minister and President of the College of New Jersey "rose and in a very able, and elegant Speech of one Hour & half endeavored to convince the Audience & the Committee of opposing the extravagant demands of Great Britain, while we were professing a perfect Allegiance to her Authority and supporting her Courts of Justice." Boudinot was "astonished" at the effect of Witherspoon's speech on the assembly, recalling, "There appeared a general Approbation of the measure, and I strongly suspected an universal Acquiescence of both Committees & Audience in approving the doctor's scheme." Boudinot claimed to have never found himself "in a more mortifying Situation" because the proceedings smacked of a "preconcerted Scheme" by the Presbyterian interest, with which Boudinot and his traveling companion, William P. Smith, were affiliated.

Boudinot decided to speak against the measure and rose "at my Wit's End, to extricate myself from so disagreeable a Situation, especially as the Measure was totally against my Judgment." His speech of over an hour intended to demonstrate "the Fallacy of the Doctor's Arguments" and consisted primarily of a principled deference to the Continental Congress, who were "the only proper Judges of the Measures to be pursued" because to them "we had resigned the Consideration of our public Affairs" and that only they could "represent all the Colonies now thus united." Boudinot stressed the privileged knowledge of the Congress "with regard to Finances, Union & the Prospects we had of a happy Reconciliation with the Mother Country" and "of our relative Circumstances with regard to the other nations of Europe." He concluded that the New Jersey committee gathered there had "no right to involve them in Distress & Trouble by plunging ourselves into a Measure of so delicate a Nature until they should advise us in what Manner to Proceed."[100]

Boudinot recalled that Witherspoon "was a good deal out of Humour, & contended warmly against a Vote," but the vote proceeded, and Witherspoon's proposition was defeated 32 to 4. "Thus ended," said Boudinot, "this first Attempt to try the Pulse of the People of New Jersey on the Subject of Independence." He added a quick justification, however, that "when advised by the Continental Congress, no Part of the Union was more hearty, than the State of New Jersey."[101]

Witherspoon had read a copy of Paine's "well known pamphlet" in the Bradford edition, but he was no fiery radical. The minister included a lengthy footnote in the printed version of his fast day sermon preached at Princeton on May 17, 1776.[102] Witherspoon had no quibbles with *Common Sense*'s politics, but he took exception to its theology. The Calvinist Witherspoon recoiled at the section in *Common Sense* where hereditary succession was compared to original sin.[103] He worried that the author had represented "the doctrine of original sin as an object of contempt or abhorrence." Witherspoon mistakenly assumed that Paine was attacking the *doctrine* of original sin, when in fact Paine was simply comparing the generational transference of monarchy to the perpetuation of original sin. If the educated Witherspoon could misinterpret *Common Sense* because of his denominational biases, it is not surprising that Witherspoon's meeting unraveled as a result of the misunderstandings and political biases of his conferees.

The independence movement progressed in New Jersey, as it did in other colonies, in fits and starts. The question of independence versus reconciliation was often clouded, as we can see in Witherspoon's meeting, in a fog of uncertainty over sovereign legitimacy in a post-royal context. Boudinot was certain that the Continental Congress would instruct the colonies whether they should declare independence, even as the Continental Congress awaited instructions from the colonies. There was a great deal of confusion in America that spring over who had the requisite authority, information, and desire to declare or to forbid independence.

Notes: Chapter 8

[1] Moody, *Lieutenant James Moody's Narrative*, 3.
[2] Ibid., 5-6.
[3] Ibid.
[4] Borden and Borden, *American Tory*, 21; cf. *Maryland Gazette*, February 14, 1775.
[5] 1 January 1776. Land, *William Eddis' Letters from America*, 131.
[6] 14 March 1776. Land, 137.
[7] 29 March 1776. Land, 142-143.
[8] Ibid.
[9] 20 May 1776. Land, 145-146.
[10] "Extract from the Proceedings of the Convention of the Province of Maryland, held at the city of Annapolis, on Thursday the 7th of December, 1775," [Article dated "Annapolis, January 18, 1776."] DPP, March 4, 1776.
[11] CCC to Wallace, Davidson, and Johnson. 25 January 1776, and CCC to CCA, 28 June 1776. Hoffman, *Papers of Charles Carroll of Carrollton*, 2:859-860, 923-925.
[12] CCC to Wallace, Davidson, and Johnson. 25 January 1776, Hoffman, 2:859-860.
[13] CCC to CCA, 18 March 1776. Hoffman, 2:878-882.
[14] "Proceedings of Maryland Convention, May 15, 1776." PG, May 29, 1776.
[15] CCC to CCA, 11 June 1776. Hoffman, 2:919-920.
[16] CCC to CCA, 28 June 1776. Hoffman, 2:923-925.
[17] CCC to CCA, 5 July 1776. Hoffman, 2:926-927.
[18] CCC to CCA, 20 July 1776. Hoffman, 2:928-929.
[19] Lucas, *Portents of Rebellion*, 157, 262.
[20] AC, No. 3, CW 1:76.
[21] AC, No. 3, CW 1:90-91.
[22] Ferling, *The Loyalist Mind*; Newcomb, *Franklin and Galloway*.
[23] See Jacobson, "John Dickinson's Fight Against Royal Government, 1764."
[24] Baldwin, "Joseph Galloway, The Loyalist Politician."
[25] "Joseph Galloway, Esq, called in and examined by Lord George Germaine (Published June 16, 1779). Baldwin, *Joseph Galloway: Selected Tracts*.
[26] In the heading, I use "rational" in the technical sense of "a pattern that is logically discernible," as opposed to the colloquial connotation of "emotionless."
[27] "Classes of Tories" from Benjamin Rush's 1777 Notebook. Quoted in Borden and Borden, 67. A similar list appears in Corner, *Autobiography of Benjamin Rush*, 117-119.
[28] "A Friend to Posterity and Mankind," "To all Parents in the Thirteen United Colonies," DPP, February 12, 1776.
[29] Adams, *American Controversy*, 1:433.
[30] Joseph Priestley to BF, 13 February 1776. Willcox, 22:347-350.
[31] Adams, *American Controversy*, 1:433-440; Peach, 9; Price, *Observations on the Nature of Civil Liberty*.
[32] *Experience Preferable to Theory* (1776).
[33] Crane, "The Club of Honest Whigs," 217.
[34] Ibid.
[35] Ibid., 232.

[36] Peach, 13-14.
[37] Thomas, *Richard Price and America*, 6-7; Crane, 210.
[38] Crane, 222.
[39] Ibid., 232.
[40] Ibid., 233.
[41] Richard Price to Arthur Lee, January 1779. Quoted in Peach, 313-314.
[42] Adams, *American Controversy*, 2:923.
[43] Joseph Priestley to BF. 13 February 1776. Willcox, 22:347-350.
[44] New York, 3 August 1775. Quoted in Price, *The General Introduction and Supplement to the Two Tracts on Civil Liberty, the War with America, and the Finances of the Kingdom*. [1778], Peach, 169.
[45] New York, 3 January 1776. Quoted in Price, *General Introduction*. Peach, 169.
[46] New York, 2 November 1775. Quoted in Price, *General Introduction*. Peach, 169-170.
[47] Price was here referring to the essay by "Rationalis" from PG, February 28, 1776.
[48] Peach, 168-172.
[49] TP to a Committee of the Continental Congress, [October 1783]. CW 2:1231.
[50] See the exchanges between LN and KGIII from 1775-1776 in Fortescue, *Correspondence of King George the Third*, Volume 3.
[51] Hibbert, *George III*, 142.
[52] Simmons and Thomas, *Proceedings and Debates*, 6:70.
[53] Ibid., 71.
[54] Ibid., 72, 122-142.
[55] Ibid., 220.
[56] *London Evening Post*, December 19-21, 1775. Quoted in PL, March 23, 1776, and also in Bradley, *Popular Politics*, 204.
[57] Simmons and Thomas, 6:465.
[58] Ibid., 470.
[59] Ibid., 465.
[60] 24 April 1776. Ibid., 504.
[61] Ibid., 596-597.
[62] [David Hartley] to BF, 8 June 1776. Willcox, 22:451-452.
[63] Burke, "A Letter to John Farr and John Harris, Esqrs, (Sheriffs of the City of Bristol)," 3 April 1777. Quoted in Peach, 268.
[64] Ibid., 269.
[65] Burke, *Speeches and Letters on American Affairs*, 206-207.
[66] CS 3.50.
[67] Burke to Champion, 30 May 1776. *Burke Correspondence*, 3:269; Bradley, *Popular Politics*, 204.
[68] Also in 1776, Izard worked as an American diplomat in France and Tuscany. He was later a member of the Continental Congress and the United States Senate.
[69] London, 4 May 1776. Deas, *Correspondence of Mr. Ralph Izard*, 1:213.
[70] In 1786, while publisher of *The General Advertiser*, Almon was tried for libel and fled to France. Plomer, et al., *A Dictionary of Printers and Booksellers*, 4-5.

[71] Almon printed long extracts of *Common Sense* in his *Evening Post* on May 28 and 30, 1776, passages that were hawked and reprinted in the *Morning Post* on June 13, 1776. Lutnick, *American Revolution and the British Press*, 45.
[72] *Morning Chronicle*, June 5, 1776. Quoted in Lutnick, 46.
[73] *Common Sense* and *Plain Truth*. London: J. Almon, 1776.
[74] See for example, Tucker, *A Series of Answers to Certain Popular Objections* [written no earlier than December 22, 1776].
[75] *Morning Post*, June 12-13, 1776. Quoted in Lutnick, 45.
[76] *Morning Chronicle*, June 5, 1776. Quoted in Lutnick, 45.
[77] *Morning Post*, June 12, 1776. Quoted in Lutnick, 45.
[78] *General Evening Post*, April 6, 1776. Quoted in Lutnick, 46.
[79] 8 April 1776. Hutchinson, *Diary and Letters of Thomas Hutchinson*, 2:32.
[80] Adams, *American Controversy*, 1:448.
[81] William Doyle to BF, 10 July 1784. Willcox, 42:u30.
[82] *St. James Chronicle*, August 27, 1776. Quoted in Lutnick, 47.
[83] It is difficult to trace precise printing locations, because the threat or practice of censorship encouraged murky publishing information. One of the "London" editions, for instance, was probably printed in Dublin but purposefully mislabeled. There is also a strong likelihood that the "Rotterdam" edition cloaked the actual origin in Paris or another French city.
[84] Adams, *American Controversy*, 1:xiv.
[85] *Morning Post*, August 19, 1776. Quoted in Lutnick, 46-47.
[86] TP to the Citizens of the United States, 15 November 1802. CW 2:910.
[87] Boulton, *Language of Politics*, 137-138.
[88] From Boothby's *Observations on the Appeal from the new to the Old Whigs, and on Mr. Paine's Rights of Man*. Quoted in Boulton, 138, 147.
[89] Quoted in Boulton, 250.
[90] Boulton, 139.
[91] Ibid., 258.
[92] Cf. CS 3.24.
[93] "Extract of a letter from London, December 10, 1775." PJ, April 3, 1776.
[94] WL To C. W. F. Dumas, 10 September, 1776. *Letters of William Lee*, 182-184.
[95] Johnson, *Dictionary*. On a related note, Johnson's dictionary includes "independance" as an alternative spelling of "independence." In American discourse from 1776, including in Paine's writing, the two were used with equal frequency. In this study I have normalized the spelling to align with our conventional spelling, but I must confess a certain interpretive pull toward the performative morpheme indepen-*dance*.
[96] Stout, *The Perfect Crisis*, 8.
[97] Cf. CS 3.35. Governor William Franklin to Lord George Germain (No. 2), 28 March, 1776. Davies, *Documents of the American Revolution*, 12:99-100.
[98] Governor William Franklin to the New Jersey Legislature, 1776. Ricord and Nelson, *Documents Relating to the Colonial History of the State of New Jersey*, 10:726-728.
[99] Boudinot, *Life, Public Services, Addresses, and Letters of Elias Boudinot*, 13.
[100] Ibid., 14-17
[101] Ibid., 18.

[102] Witherspoon, *The Dominion of Providence over the Passions of Men.*
[103] CS 2.14.

Chapter Nine

A Conflict of Interest

THEIR Petitions thus answered—even with the Sword of the Murderer at their Breasts, the Americans thought only of new Petitions. It is well known, there was not then even an Idea that the Independence of America would be the work of this Generation: For People *yet* had a Confidence in the Integrity of the British Monarch. At length subsequent Edicts being also passed, to restrain the Americans from enjoying the Bounty of Providence on their own Coast; and to cut off their Trade with each other and with foreign States—*the Royal Sword yet REEKING with American Blood*, and the King still deaf to the Prayers of the People for "Peace, Liberty and Safety." It was even so late as the latter End of the last Year, before that Confidence visibly declined; and it was generally seen, that the Quarrel was likely to force America into an immediate State of Independence. But, such an Event was not expected, because it was thought, the Monarch, from Motives of Policy, if not from Inclination, would heal our Wounds, and thereby prevent the Separation; and it was not wished for, because Men were unwilling to break off old Connections, and change the usual Form of Government.

William Henry Drayton
A Charge, on the Rise of the American Empire
October 1776

The Novelty of the Thing deters some, the Doubt of Success others, the vain Hope of Reconciliation many. But our Enemies take continually every proper Measure to remove these Obstacles, and their Endeavours are attended with Success, since every Day furnishes us with new Causes of increasing Enmity, and new Reasons for wishing an eternal Separation; so that there is a rapid Increase of the formerly small Party who were for an independent Government.

Benjamin Franklin to Josiah Quincy, Sr.
April 1776

Part One
DIVIDED LOYALTIES

Irreconcilable Differences

We investigated in the last chapter the multiplicity of confusions that exacerbated the rift that would result in political separation. We saw that the revolutionary-era labels, "Whig" and "Tory," do not translate directly to our respective broad-brush tags, "liberal" and "conservative." We also encountered the confusion created in the public debate by these terms. Whiggism and Toryism were, in the American colonial context, both matters of degree. Men like Alexander Hamilton and John Jay, for example, considered themselves Whigs in late 1775, at least when compared to the "insolent and clamorous" Tories of New York.[1]

In this chapter I want to explicate the grey area between the imagined ideals of Whig and Tory. To understand why American colonists supported, rejected, or acquiesced to independence, we cannot ignore the formidable bloc of "Moderate" opinion. Political moderates in 1776 were caught in a tug-of-war between their incommensurable loyalties toward Britain and toward the American colonies. Political reconciliation was the only solution that would prevent these colonists from the most feared forced choice of their lives.

In much the same way that proximity to armed conflict predisposed Americans to embrace independence, there was an opposite force pulling colonial opinion toward reconciliation with Great Britain. On the surface, it seems like a tautology: the deeper an individual's or a community's dependence upon Britain, the slower they warmed to independence. Overt loyalism and subtle hesitation were alike rooted in dependence. In the realms of economics, law, religion, and sentiment, the harshest reactions against independence came from those who had the most to lose by severing the connection with Britain. Imperial merchants stood to lose their preferred trade contracts with London. British-trained lawyers risked losing their upper-hand knowledge of the British Constitution. Anglican clergymen were threatened with losing their congregations. And sentimental Anglophiles faced losing a major piece of their identities. Most colonists who opposed independence did so as an act of self-preservation.

As Paine observed in 1777, only after "every prospect of accommodation" seemed "to fail fast," did men begin "to think seriously on the matter" of independence. With "their reason being thus stripped of the false hope which had long encompassed it," the subject "became approachable by fair debate: yet still the bulk of the people hesitated; they startled at the novelty of independence." They also doubted "the ability of the continent to support" the measure, "without reflecting that it required the same force to obtain an accommodation by arms as an independence."[2]

We will look in this chapter at exemplars of each of four areas of tenacious dependence: sentimental, mercantile, legal, and clerical. Of the individuals we will describe in this chapter, only one, Reverend Charles Inglis, used political moderation as a front for resolute loyalism. Everyone else we will here encounter was sincerely grappling with the decision between independence and reconciliation.

PART TWO
SENTIMENTAL DEPENDENCE

Out of Edenton

The North Carolina delegates were typical of the Second Continental Congress; they had been sent to Philadelphia to prevent a revolution, not to start one. In June 1775, delegates William Hooper, Joseph Hewes, Richard Caswell, and John Penn urged the people of North Carolina, "Look to the reigning monarch of Britain as your rightful and lawful Sovereign; dare every danger & difficulty in support of his person, Crown & dignity."[3]

In early 1776, Hooper and Penn both expressed grave apprehensions about independence, but by March Hooper was condemning George III as a haughty monarch, Hewes saw "no prospect of a reconciliation," and Penn actively urged foreign alliances.[4] What had caused this change of position? Certainly, each of these men had read *Common Sense* in the interim, but they also found their colony had experienced another persuasive event: the North Carolinians' baptism into the war.

On February 27, 1776, the Battle of Moore's Creek Bridge between a loyalist Scots militia battalion and the assembled North Carolina Continentals changed the complexion of affairs for the North Carolina delegates. Exiled Royal Governor Josiah Martin had bribed a formidable number of Scottish Highlanders to muster behind the rallying cry of "King George and Broad Swords," but the outnumbered Continentals routed the loyalist force in an early morning battle. The decisive Continental victory spirited up the American cause in North Carolina and beyond. Convinced that they could succeed in battle, North Carolinians now began to consider the merits of independence in earnest.

Samuel Johnston, President of the North Carolina Provincial Congress meeting in Halifax, wrote to his friend and former legal apprentice, James Iredell, on April 5, 1776. The two North Carolina lawyers lived and practiced in Edenton, North Carolina, also the adopted home of Joseph Hewes, a delegate to the Continental Congress with whom they both corresponded regularly. Johnston had received a letter from Hewes written March 20, but Hewes had "no news except what you have in the newspapers." According to Johnston, Hewes "seems to despair of a reconciliation" since no commissioners were appointed before the parliamentary recess at the beginning of the year. Johnston seemed unfazed by the news, reporting that "All our people here are up for independence."[5]

By April 12, the Provincial Congress had approved the Halifax Resolves, empowering North Carolina's delegates "to concur with the delegates of the other Colonies in declaring Independency, and forming foreign alliances." Penn, who was in attendance at the Provincial Congress, wrote John Adams that in North Carolina "all regard and fondness for the King or the nation of Great Britain" had evaporated and "Independence," he added, "is the word most used."[6] This sentiment would carry over into the North Carolina constitution, ratified later that year. The new constitution included after its opening address the first principle of American politics in 1776: "That all Political Power is vested in and derived from the People only."[7]

Most elite colonial politicians did not immediately grasp what was happening around them. By the end of April, James Iredell wrote to Joseph Hewes that the colonies were now driven "to the brink of precipice. Scarcely any hope of reconciliation can now be entertained." Iredell was an Anglophile who then saw "things in the most melancholy aspect." He faced the competition of internal values that roiled inside most colonists at one point or another. "My first attachment is to the liberty and welfare of America; my next to the happiness of Great Britain. If these can yet be found compatible most happy should I be in seeing the blessed union; if they cannot, notwithstanding the extreme bitterness of the struggle, it would be our duty to support the former against the latter."[8]

Hewes, who had remained in Philadelphia, received a copy of the Halifax Resolves late in April, but delayed presenting it to the Continental Congress until May 27, when the Virginia delegates laid their colony's strong resolutions before the body.[9] On June 9, Iredell wrote to Hewes that "Our situation is so unhappy that a declaration of absolute independence may become necessary, before a distant body can be collected, and therefore I think the members of the Congress ought to have full powers to declare it, when the melancholy exigency shall arrive."[10] Each of these North Carolinian gentlemen supported independence when it was finally declared, but like so many other colonists who *believed* in the ultimate beneficence of Britain, they first exhausted every other possibility. Men like Hewes and Iredell joined in the toasts and celebrations following the public readings of the *Declaration*, but they returned to their private quarters, sat on their beds, and let out a deep sigh.

Henry Laurens and the Inner Conflict of Separation

It is easy for us to forget that the American colonists made individual and collective decisions in the face of mortal risk. At the end of February, Henry Laurens of South Carolina wrote to his teenage daughter Martha in London "with an aching heart and overflowing eyes." Everywhere he looked, Laurens beheld "increasing preparations for civil war" and he considered every estate in South Carolina "as being on the very precipice of bankruptcy." Having already lost his wife and a young son, Laurens worried what would happen to his sister and daughters if he and his brother both died in the oncoming war. "Not only tears, but irresistible groans accompany this afflicting inquiry," wrote a sobbing Laurens. He described the "melancholy" scene in Charleston "of many good houses in this town, which are now made barracks for the country militia, who strip the paper hangings, chop wood upon parlor floors, and do a thousand such improper acts; but alas, they are still good enough for burning," which either the king's troops or the militia were prepared to do to prevent the other side from using the town as a garrison.[11] By the middle of March, Laurens wrote to Martha, "The sound of war increases, and the danger seems to be drawing nearer and nearer." He expected "a visit very soon" from the British forces. He concluded the short letter with a foreboding tone, "Under these circumstances, every man here holds his life by the most precarious tenure; and our friends abroad should prepare themselves for learning that we are numbered among the dead."[12]

The eloquent reaction of Henry Laurens to the independence controversy demonstrates that not all colonists fell into the terminological polarities of the day. Laurens was a reluctant independent, one of many who eventually acquiesced in the *Declaration* but only after their desperate hopes of reconciliation were disintegrated. These moderates were not disguised Tories feigning moderation as a procrastination device favoring British rule. They were Americans with equally divided loyalties—and often equally divided families—between America and Britain. These British-Americans found themselves embroiled in a civil war, and they dreaded with all their hearts being forced to choose a side.

Henry Laurens was a southern planter who in the years ahead would become close friends with Thomas Paine and also President of the Continental Congress, but the South Carolinian had no kind words for *Common Sense* in 1776. Laurens's correspondence with his family and friends on both sides of the Atlantic catalogues one man's agonized decision to support independence. At the beginning of January, Laurens wrote to his brother, James, that he "had no share nor part in bringing forward the distress" of the colonies but was "willing to bear my full proportion & more without murmuring & will always be thankful for the good Days which I have enjoyed."[13] Laurens knew that worse lay ahead, "I Shudder at the thought of what may happen," but he held out hope for divine intervention: "I pray [for] God at this critical time to interpose, to Soften the Hearts of the King & his Counselors." He underscored, "the Americans are not desirous of independence—they wish to remain in obedience to the King & to acknowledge & Submit in every reasonable degree to the Authority of parliament," but the colonists, on the other hand, "Seem determined to

Maintain Such Rights as they have ever held & enjoyed at the hazard of Life & Fortune."[14]

In early February on behalf of the South Carolina Council of Safety, Laurens forwarded a copy of *Common Sense* to a sister committee in Georgia at the request of Colonel Christopher Gadsden. Laurens hadn't read the pamphlet at the time but noted for the Georgians that Gadsden "begs your acceptance of it."[15] Gadsden had returned to South Carolina with the pamphlet, Laurens told his brother in late February, and "he is wrapped up in the thought of separation & independence, & will hear nothing in opposition." Laurens had by then read *Common Sense* and did not share Gadsden's enthusiasm. When Laurens pointed out that part of *Common Sense*'s argument had been "stolen" from a sixteenth century royal address, Gadsden shrugged and said, "I don't dislike it on that account."[16] At the time, Laurens was uncertain "how the Doctrines contained in it are relished in the Northern Colonies," but he was certain that the people of South Carolina would "subscribe to them" only if forced to by the "repeated & continued persecution by Great Britain." Laurens acknowledged that *Common Sense*'s "reasoning, tho' not all original; is strong & captivating & will make many converts to Republican principles." Still, Laurens had "already borne my testimony against" the doctrine contained in *Common Sense* in the provincial assembly and "more against those indecent expressions with which the pages abound."[17]

Laurens, who had at the time two children and a brother in England, continued throughout February to "hope, though seemingly against hope, that a happy reconciliation may yet be effected," but he confessed that his "Love of both Countries Britain & America" affected his judgment.[18] By the end of February, though, Laurens began to accept the inevitable, "I am confirmed in my opinion & weep for Great Britain—I love & reverence her Still—but alas I perceive that I am to be Separated from her." He lamented that his Children would not be called "British" and commented on the suddenness of the turn toward independence. Even still, he clung by a thread to the prospect of reconciliation, "I think there is Still a possibility to bring forward a reconciliation," but he admitted that it "would have been easy twelve aye Six months ago," but would "now be uphill." He realized that America might yet be conquered by military force but stressed that "Men's minds cannot be conquered." Laurens' inner conflict was heightening. In one sentence he told a correspondent that the principles of *Common Sense* "are not relished with us yet" and in another, "The Cry is, 'Let us resist against violence. We cannot be worse off than we are—one Year more will enable us to be Independent.'" His anxiety welled up within him, "Ah! that word cuts me deep, I assure you I feign not, when I Say, the bare expression has caused tears to trickle down my Cheeks—We wish not for Independence, but Britain will force a Separation & Independence will Soon follow."[19]

In August, a month after the *Declaration* was approved in Congress, Laurens was still stunned by the events that had transpired. "The sound of Separation was six Months ago harsh & ungrateful to us & even at this very moment every Man of common understanding must See that acceding to the *Declaration*," he said, "will be embracing much certain difficulty & distress with great hazard of Life."[20] "The great point is now settled," he wrote to his son, John, coloring his description of the *Declaration*'s proclamation in Charleston with his own emotions. The *Declaration* was read "with great Solemnity," he said, adding with exasperation, "amidst loud acclamations of Thousands who always huzza when a Proclamation is Read." Laurens's inner conflict had not abated. "The scene was Serious, Important & Awful.—even at this Moment I feel a Tear of affection for the good old Country & for the People in it whom in general I dearly Love." He expressed sympathy for "your King," whom Laurens felt had "been greatly deceived & abused." He still lamented "the downfall of an old friend, of a Parent from whose nurturing Breasts I have drawn my support & strength" and candidly admitted, "If my own Interests in my own Rights alone had been concerned, I would most freely have given the whole to the demands & disposal of her Ministers in preference to a Separation." He had been forced, though, to protect "the Rights of Posterity" and had chosen against his interest, because "I happened to stand as one of their Representatives & dared not betray my Trust." Alas, Laurens said, "I am now by the Will of God brought into a new World & God only knows what sort of a World it will be."[21] He urged his daughter, Martha, to pray for peace between "the Country in which you reside & that to which you more particularly belong." He asked her too to mourn "your Father's unhappy Lot to be engaged in War, Civil War—God's Severest Scourge upon Mankind." Still conflicted to his core, Laurens held out for the first time a new hope, "It is not impossible but that the Separation lately announced may produce great benefit to both."[22]

For many colonists like Henry Laurens and the aforementioned North Carolina politicians, dependence was largely an emotional attachment to Great Britain. These men may have benefited in other areas of their lives from the imperial connection, but their hearts were rent by the decision to turn away from the mother country. Paine had emphasized sentiment so incessantly in *Common Sense* for this very reason: until the Americans surrendered their emotional bond to Britain, they were destined to surrender themselves into iron bonds. Paine's pamphlet stimulated this sentimental disentanglement for many colonists, but others clutched their dependence until the summer of 1776.

Part Three
MERCANTILE INTEREST

Interest and Disinterest

As a rule, the propertied elite of the colonies despised the convulsions that disrupted their livelihoods. One anonymous American wrote in August 1775 to a friend in London, "You would hardly conceive, without seeing it, to what a height the political fury of this country is arrived." This gentleman wished to be "home among freeborn Englishmen, not among this tyrannical and arbitrary rabble of America." He felt indignation "every day, when I hear my King and country vilified and abused by a parcel of wretches, who owe their very existence to it." He was "amazed at the stupor and supineness of your Admiralty," and asked, "Are the friends of Great Britain and their property to be left exposed at this rate, to the dictates of an inhuman rabble?" He expected, if he did not soon "join in the seditious and traitorous acts in vogue, to be hauled away and confined in a prison with the confiscation of all I have in the world." The loyalist closed his letter, "Words cannot paint the distress of a sober people who have property, and wish for peace and quietness."[23]

In the early modern republican ideal, both the electors and the elected had to be men of property because that property was seen as insulation against the corrupting influence of "interest." The rationale was that an independently wealthy person would be less susceptible to bribery and more capable of even-handed judgment. John Adams expressed the conventional republican wisdom in a March 1776 letter to Massachusetts assemblyman James Sullivan. Adams asked, "Is it not equally true, that Men in general in every Society, who are wholly destitute of Property, are also too little acquainted with public affairs to form a Right Judgment, and too dependent upon other Men to have a Will of their own?" Adams argued that, like women and children, "very few Men who have no Property have any Judgment of their own." The unpropertied masses "talk and vote as they are directed by Some Man of Property," said Adams, "who has attached their Minds to his Interest." Adams thus discouraged altering the "Qualifications of Voters" in Massachusetts, because it would open a Pandora's Box of "Controversy and altercation." He said,

> There will be no End of it. New Claims will arise. Women will demand a Vote. Lads from 12 to 21 will think their Rights not enough attended to, and every Man, who has not a Farthing, will demand an equal Voice with any other in all Acts of State. It tends to confound and destroy all Distinctions, and prostrate all Ranks, to one common Level.[24]

Adams was not being particularly mean-spirited according to the standard of his day; he was simply reflecting the political norms he had inherited and studied as a New England lawyer.

"Interest"—applied both in national and in individual contexts—was a very important word in early modern politics, and one that figured prominently into the debate over independence. As the term was used in international affairs, a state's interest reflected what was most beneficial to the present and future of the political community. Thus arguments for and against a particular policy were often couched in the commonplace language of interest. The idea of national interest received top billing in several pamphlets published on the subject of independence, as indicated by the titles of Dean Josiah Tucker's *The True Interest of Britain, set forth in regard to the colonies* (1776), Major John Cartwright's *American Independence; The Interest and Glory of Great Britain* (1774), and both versions of Charles Inglis' pamphlet, *The Deceiver Unmasked; or, Loyalty and Interest United* (1776) and *The True Interest of America Impartially Stated* (1776).

On a personal level, an "interested" person was prone to corruption and under-the-table deals with a view toward personal benefit. A "disinterested" person, on the other hand, retained his independent judgment unsullied by motives of personal profit or advancement. Disinterestedness was a core component of public virtue and genteel character, and this single principle explains much of George Washington's later standing above the pantheon of founders. Washington was lauded as the American embodiment of Cincinnatus, a Roman general who quit his sword and returned to his farm when he could have become dictator. George Washington's disinterested reluctance to assume power—a repeated recurrence throughout his career—was the very vehicle by which he attained it. In stark contrast to the disinterested Washington, most loyalists were viewed as highly interested individuals.

Thomas Paine's public refusal to profit from his writings was a display of this ideal of disinterestedness. Because Paine arrived in America as an "unconnected" Englishman, he was vulnerable to allegations of mercenary behavior: that he was just a Grub Street "hack" or a pen-for-hire. By eschewing profit with such theatrical flair in early 1776, Paine was signaling his commitment to an ethic of disinterestedness.[25] Paine's subordination of his own economic interest showed, in his words, "that there may be genius without prostitution."[26] But republican disinterestedness required ample resources, which is why Paine spent much of his life teetering on the brink of bankruptcy. In truth, Paine wanted *not* to care about money, but his ethical dogma constrained him to forfeit his single most profitable source of income, his pen. His life consisted of a predictable cycle that began with each of his famous pieces of prose. He rode high on the public adulation for a time, but then struggled to repress his desire for financial gain as the applause quieted. After brooding for a time, he would explode in a letter to one of his associates about how he had been taken for granted and forgotten. Paine spent much of his life bitter and, in his opinion, unappreciated, because he had expected to be compensated liberally by the beneficiaries of his textual "donations." As Paine's experience illustrated, disinterestedness was an ideal, while possessing an interest was an unavoidable facet of real life. Most of the time, Paine was able to ignore his economic ambitions while pursuing his other goals. Even in these seasons of productivity, though, Paine *did* have an interest, but it was neither personal nor local. Paine's interest was *humanity*. He thought in universals, and he reasoned with Enlightenment values. He wrote about basic subjects like "rights," "equality," and "nature," and he legislated on behalf of a constituency made up of "mankind," "the world," and "posterity."

In 1776 the classical republican political equation was flipped on its head. Wealth was supposed to foster *disinterest*, but in the midst of revolution, property became an albatross of *interest* around the colonists' necks. Thus the very people *most qualified* to superintend a classical republican government became the *least qualified* to man the helm of a revolution. Men of independent means became themselves the means of keeping the colonies dependent.

Class Consciousness

The early stages of the revolutionary struggle had been a struggle between competing American oligarchies. Colonial governments were controlled by the "leading" families in each respective colony, and the primary difference between the "Whig" oligarchy and the "Tory" oligarchy was in their preferred arena of political action. As we saw in the last chapter, the power of the Whig oligarchy was centralized in the colonial assemblies, while the Tory oligarchy attempted to maintain its power by controlling the governorship and executive council. The boundaries between the Whig and Tory oligarchies were fluid and their cultures were often indistinguishable.[27]

A daily reality of colonial oligarchic culture was tension between "haves" and "have-nots," regardless of partisan affiliation. Some historians have attempted to brush aside class distinctions in early modern America, but such an interpretive move requires a selective reading of textual evidence. American class structures were not articulated in the eighteenth century as they would become in the century following, but there was a deep consciousness in late colonial America regarding the parameters of wealth. Class need not be nuanced to be universally perceived. John Adams, no egalitarian himself, described tidewater politics in April 1776 as a study in class conflict: "The Gentry are very rich, and the common People very poor. This Inequality of Property, gives an Aristocratical Turn to all their Proceedings, and occasions a strong Aversion in their Patricians, to *Common Sense*. But the Spirit of these Barons, is coming down, and it must submit."[28]

Colonial class consciousness was not just a fact in Virginia and the Carolinas. In most colonies, lower economic classes pressed for independence in the spring of 1776, while upper economic classes snarled the movement's progress. As "middling class" Philadelphia artisans wrested political power from the Pennsylvania landed aristocracy, it was only natural for class resentment to bubble to the surface of public discourse. A satirical advertisement in the April 8 issue of the *Pennsylvania Packet* demonstrated with biting wit the growing antipathy for the proprietary party among the Philadelphia working class.[29] The ad for a book entitled *The Way to Reconcile All Parties to Independency* posed as a conventional subscription proposal and included detailed contents of its twelve chapters. The first chapter, for instance, promised to show "that this world and the government thereof was originally vested in the rich, and that the poor have no right to intermeddle in its affairs." The satirist proposed that a monarchy and landed nobility should be erected of the wealthiest men in each colony, followed with an "act of oblivion" whereby the Americans would forget how it happened. The final paragraph of this act, said the contributor, "invests the Kings, Princes, and Nobles with the power of knowing the thoughts of all below the rank of Nobility as soon as they see their faces, effectually to secure a full submission to the act."

In a mock printer's note at the bottom of the ad, the satirist detailed a plan for delineating ranks of American society by dress. All inhabitants of America "not worth a thousand per annum in landed estate" would be required to wear specific uniforms fit to their low station in life. Most "wives and daughters" would wear humiliating outfits of sandals, jackets, petticoats, and cotton caps, while all "men and their sons not worth the forementioned sum" would wear wooden shoes, a Scotch night coat, and "a tin label on each of their breasts with this inscription, ARE NOT WE YOUR ASSES."

At the end of the ridiculous advertisement, the author promised that his book would be dedicated "to all those who are ambitious and possess more power than is for the good of the common people," and also to those who "got possession of power" by means other than the people's "free voice." The book would be dedicated to these men, said the jeering author, because "it is hoped they will patronize and encourage the work."[30]

In over half of the American colonies, the heated contest over independence of April, May, and June of 1776 became as much a conflict between the common people and aristocrats for political control as it was a conflict between the colonies and Great Britain for the right to establish a separate government."[31]

Loyal Merchants

Historian Thomas Doerflinger conveyed the role of colonial merchants in the revolutionary movement in pointed terms: "If it had been left to the city's merchants, the Revolutionary movement would have been more circumspect and cautious, more judicious and temperate, less eager to make the final break with Britain. In short, it would not have been a revolutionary movement at all."[32] If there was a discrete economic subset of Americans that tended to eschew independence *en masse*, it was the colonial merchants. We have already seen how the influence of the merchant interest in New York shaped that colony's loyalist policies, and Pennsylvania was not much different.

Thomas Clifford, Jr., a wealthy Philadelphia merchant whose political views were shaped by his economic interests, demonstrated the turn in Pennsylvania politics in the course of two months in the spring. On March 7, 1776, he wrote a lengthy account of "the Situation of Public Affairs" to an associate in England, including his apprehensions about "the Disposition of many who are inclined to widen the breach between the two Country's" and the common concern that "the Commissioners that are coming over... will not avail much towards settling matters." Clifford noted that he expected "all intercourse between the two Countries" to come to a halt at the order of the Congress and requested for that reason to have his English accounts settled as much as possible. Nonetheless, Clifford expressed without reservation his "hope that in Due time, the Eyes of the People will be opened, to see their true Interest, and that England and America may again be united upon a firm and solid Basis."[33] Clifford wrote another letter to his associate on May 16, 1776, that demonstrated the escalated tension among Pennsylvania loyalists and moderates. Clifford's protracted reflection on politics in the last letter was replaced with a curt "the times are such as will not permit us saying much on Public Affairs."[34] For Clifford and other colonial merchants, independence was primarily an economic consideration, not a political one. According to Clifford, "the present Contest is very unnatural and will assuredly prove unprofitable."[35]

Only one colony, New York, abstained completely from the vote on independence in the Continental Congress, because its delegates had not received explicit instructions from the New York Provincial Congress. Besides this single colony, two individuals also chose to abstain from the vote. Robert Morris, one of those abstainers, was among the wealthiest of Philadelphia merchants and a political ubiquity in revolutionary Pennsylvania. Morris had received instructions that authorized and even encouraged a vote for independence, but on July 2, the merchant king chose to absent himself from the voting as a silent protest. Morris became famous after 1776 as the leading domestic financier of the Revolutionary War, and his commitment to the American cause has not been called into question by subsequent generations.[36] What is more curious than Morris's refusal to vote for independence is Morris's place in history as the first Pennsylvanian to sign the *Declaration of Independence*, something he did in bold, unwavering manuscript. Why did Morris oppose the *Declaration* to the point of refusing to vote for it, and then consent to sign the document the next month?

The first reason was, as we have seen, Morris's occupation as a transatlantic merchant. He was *willing* to declare independence, but he recognized that his commercial fiefdom would be placed in grave jeopardy by such a move. Thus he had a financial disinterest in moving too quickly with a step that might be a slippery slope to bankruptcy. Like any investor, Morris wanted to hedge his risk by evaluating the best data on the prospects of success. This economic impulse, then, leads us to the second reason for Morris's reluctance to embrace independence. He had received information from a trusted American source residing in Bristol, England, in late February 1776 that would influence his opinions and his actions throughout the spring. According to Morris's expatriate correspondent, "the Whigs are under the Marquis of Rockingham and will desert Us if We aim at Independency." The British Whigs would stand by the Americans, according to Morris's best information, if the colonists maintained a position for reconciliation. Morris's informant also assured him "that Commissioners are certainly coming out to treat."[37] Morris held fast to these spurious morsels of information through mid-July, and he opposed any action on the part of America that would subvert either the support of British Whigs or the favorability of British peace terms.

The third reason that Morris opposed independence in early July lay in his interpretation—as we see once again—of the proper *timing* of the measure. Morris justified his opposition to independence in a letter to Joseph Reed on July 20, 1776, in which he detailed this rationale. Morris wrote,

> I have uniformly voted against and opposed the *Declaration of Independence*, because in my poor opinion it was an improper time, and will neither promote the interest nor redound to the honor of America, for it has caused division when we wanted union, and will be ascribed to very different principles than those which ought to give rise to such an important measure.

Morris acknowledged that "the councils of America have taken a different course from my judgment and wishes." He did not wish to be "a bad subject" of America just because "its councils are not conformable to his ideas," so he submitted to "follow, if he cannot lead."[38]

PART FOUR
CONSTITUTIONAL OPPOSITION

An Excess of Moderation

Robert Morris did not stand alone in his principled opposition to independence as a member of the Pennsylvania delegation to the Continental Congress. He was joined in his abstention from the vote for independence by an even greater force in Pennsylvania politics: John Dickinson. Dickinson was a lawyer and Morris was a merchant, but they both enjoyed a vast family fortune and immense political clout.[39] Together their presence was felt everywhere in late colonial politics: both held concurrent offices at every level of American political life and were active in military affairs. Their combined opposition to a declaration of independence was a virtual blockade by two of America's wealthiest and politically influential men.

At the beginning of 1776, there was no more famous "patriot" in America than John Dickinson. In both England and the colonies, Dickinson's pen name, "A Pennsylvania Farmer," was equated with the constitutional logic of American resistance. In the third number of *Letters from a Farmer in Pennsylvania to the Inhabitants of the British Colonies* (1767), Dickinson had highlighted the extreme difference between "the resistance of a people against their prince" during the English Revolution and "the case of the colonies against their mother country." Dickinson claimed that the "illustrious house of Brunswick" seemed "to flourish for the happiness of mankind" after replacing the Stuart line of kings, but the Pennsylvanian applauded the seventeenth century English revolutionaries for "retaining their ancient form of government." The American colonies, Dickinson argued, were in a completely different situation. He asked, "But if once we are separated from our mother country, what new form of government shall we adopt, or where shall we find another Britain, to supply our loss?" Dickinson did not hide his desperate attachment to the mother country, "Torn from the body, to which we are united by religion, liberty, laws, affections, relation, language and commerce, we must bleed at every vein."

Dickinson laid out arguments in his letters from the 1760s that would be resurrected in 1776. He staunchly defended the principle that "the prosperity of these provinces is founded in their dependence on Great-Britain," and he reiterated America's "duty and interest" to promote the welfare of Britain. Dickinson described George III as "an excellent prince, in whose good dispositions towards us we may confide," and the British nation as "generous, sensible and humane." British anger, he assured his American audience, would not be "implacable," and he urged the Americans to "behave like dutiful children, who have received unmerited blows from a beloved parent." He added, "Let us complain to our parent; but let our complaints speak at the same time the language of affliction and veneration." The quintessential moderate urged his audience, "We cannot act with too much caution in our disputes," and he closed the letter with the assurance, "*Nil desperandum*. Nothing is to be despaired of."[40]

Dickinson believed deeply in the British Constitution.[41] He had been trained as a lawyer at the Middle Temple in London, and his skill as a political theorist rested on his education in British legal culture. Dickinson's was an ironic patriotism: the very beliefs that earned him such fame as a defender of American rights in the 1760s ensured that in 1776 he would be smeared as an opponent of American rights. He was celebrated as a Whig one decade and derided as a Tory the next, but his political values remained unchanged.

Because of Dickinson's fame as a political writer, he was selected as the primary draftsman for several crucial late colonial texts. Dickinson had composed in July 1774 a set of instructions for Pennsylvania's delegates in the First Continental Congress. Dickinson wrote on behalf of a conference of committees then meeting in Philadelphia to discuss issues such as nonimportation and the constitutionality of shutting up the port of Boston. He had been led "into the train of sentiments" evident in his instructions by the "mere accidents of meeting with particular books and conversing with particular men." Of the sixteen resolutions, written by Dickinson and agreed upon by the meeting, the first three were approved unanimously:

> I. That we acknowledge ourselves, and the inhabitants of this province, liege subjects of his majesty king George the third, to whom they and we owe and will bear true and faithful allegiance.
> II. That as the idea of an unconstitutional independence on the parent state is utterly abhorrent to our principles, we view the unhappy differences between Great Britain and the Colonies with the deepest distress and anxiety of mind, as fruitless to her, grievous to us, and destructive of the best interests of both.
> III. That it is therefore our ardent desire, that our ancient harmony with the mother country should be restored, and a perpetual love and union subsist between us, on the principles of the constitution, and an interchange of good offices, without the least infraction of our mutual rights.

Dickinson's 1774 instructions to Pennsylvania's delegates in the First Continental Congress included extensive footnotes that often consumed two-thirds of the printed page. Dickinson wrote on behalf of the people of Pennsylvania, "Our judgments and affections attach us, with inviolable loyalty, to his majesty's person, family and government." The instructions advocated "at this alarming period" the necessity of exerting "our utmost ability, in promoting and establishing harmony between Great Britain and these colonies, ON A CONSTITUTIONAL FOUNDATION." Dickinson hoped that "our mother country may regard us as her children" well into the future, when "her colonies like dutiful children may serve and guard their aged parent forever revering the arms that held them in their infancy and the breasts that supported their lives while they were little ones."[42]

Dickinson had also written the "Olive Branch" Petition on behalf of the Continental Congress in July 1775, and four months later, he composed the response of the Pennsylvania Assembly to King George III's August proclamation of rebellion. The latter text, written in November 1775, included the infamous instructions of the Pennsylvania Assembly that practically forbade the colony's delegates from even *entertaining* thoughts about independence. As events in Pennsylvania turned during the spring of 1776, Dickinson's influence in and out of the Continental Congress waned. The gentleman lawyer stated time and again during 1775 and 1776, "The first wish of my soul is for the Liberty of America. The next is for constitutional reconciliation with Great Britain. If we cannot obtain the first without the second, let us seek a new establishment."[43] He was open—or so he said—to independence, but he wanted to be *absolutely certain* that his two highest values were incommensurable before taking a step.[44]

When in June 1776 the Pennsylvania Assembly gave in to public pressure to rescind their instructions from the prior November, Dickinson again sat at his writing desk to draw up new instructions. Yet even amidst crushing calls from the Pennsylvania populace for independence, Dickinson managed to compose the cagiest instructions imaginable under the circumstances. His new instructions lifted the restriction on acceding to measures productive of independence, but they included no positive injunction to vote *for* independence. Here it must be remembered that Dickinson was essentially drafting instructions for himself in his dual capacity as assemblyman and delegate. An overwhelming majority of Pennsylvanians had, by late June, grown so frustrated with this begrudging behavior that they circumvented the assembly's reluctance by calling a popular convention to issue new instructions of their own. After Dickinson and Morris recused themselves from the vote on independence, Dickinson—also a colonel in the First Philadelphia Battalion of Associators—made preparations to march off with his troops to New Jersey instead of remaining in Philadelphia to vote for and sign the *Declaration of Independence*.

John Dickinson's behavior confused most eighteenth century Americans. They could not reconcile his magnanimous patriotism with his molasses moderation, and they subjected him to vicious verbal attacks throughout the next several years. In 1783 at the end of the Revolutionary War, Dickinson finally defended himself against these attacks on his patriotism in a series of essays in *The Freeman's Journal*, a Philadelphia newspaper printed by Francis Bailey. Dickinson's public explanation of his 1776 behavior was a remarkable chronicle of events and confessional of motivations by a man at the center of late colonial political culture. Dickinson admitted that he had opposed independence for the very reason that *Common Sense* had urged it. Dickinson clarified, "I opposed the making the declaration of independence *at the time when it was made*. The right and authority of Congress to make it, the justice of making it, I acknowledged. The policy of *then* making it I disputed." All of his actions in 1776, he said, had been "actuated by a tender affection for my country," and he hoped that "my country will excuse the honest error."

Dickinson recalled his decisions and motives with exact detail even eight years later. When the Continental Congress began considering independence, Dickinson had tried to act as "a *trustee for Pennsylvania* immediately, and in some measure for the rest of America." He realized that "The business related to the happiness of millions then in existence, and of millions who were unborn, and he "felt the duty and endeavoured faithfully to discharge it." In the 1760s, Dickinson reminded his readers, he had been "among the very first men on this continent, who by the open and decided steps we took, staked our lives and fortunes on our country's cause." At that point in the conflict, "no reserve, no caution was used by me," and, he said, "I frankly pledged my *all* for her freedom." Dickinson did not mind adventure when he "was risking only *my own*," but when "a point of the last importance to you and my other fellow citizens, and to your and their posterity" became the point of dispute, "*then*, and not till then, I became guilty of reserve and caution." It was Dickinson's hope "that not one drop of blood should be unnecessarily drawn from American veins, nor one scene of misery needlessly introduced within American borders."

The reason Dickinson opposed the Declaration "*at the time when it was made*" had been "acknowledged in the debate, that the first campaign would be decisive as to the final event of the controversy." He had insisted that a "declaration would not strengthen us by one man or by the least supply" in that first campaign, and might, on the contrary, "inflame the calamities of the contest." As he reasoned in 1776, Dickinson thought, "We ought not, without some prelusory trials of our strength, to commit our country upon an alternative, where, to recede *would be* infamy, and to persist *might be* destruction."

He could find no historical precedent "of a people, without a battle fought or an ally gained, abrogating forever their connection with a great, rich, warlike, commercial empire" and "bringing the matter finally to a prosperous conclusion." He thought a declaration "was informing our enemies what was the ultimate object of our arms" before the Americans "were better prepared for resistance." He feared that the measure would "unite the different parties" in England "against us, without our gaining anything in counterbalance." Likewise, a declaration might create "disunion" among the colonies and even "rather injure than avail us" in the eyes of foreign powers. He wanted to act out of "prudence" rather than "passion."

If it was "the interest of any European kingdom or state to aid us, we should be aided without such a declaration," but "by our actions in the field." Dickinson knew that "The erection of an Independent Empire on this continent was a phenomenon in the world—Its effects would be immense, and might vibrate round the globe," but in his opinion, the Americans had not then sufficiently asked how their new empire "might affect, or be supposed to affect old establishments." He thought the *Declaration* "disrespectful" to France or "some competent power." To "break" with the power of Great Britain "before we had compacted with another, was to make experiments on the lives and liberties of my countrymen, which I would sooner die than agree to make." In the best case, "it was to throw us into the hands of some other power, and to lie at mercy; for we should have passed the river, that was never to be repassed." He wanted to wait until the colonies had received assurance and approval from another power before proceeding.

Dickinson acknowledged, "True it is, that we have happily succeeded, without observing these precautions," but he asked his enemies to point to "an example from history" of the "justice, wisdom, benevolence, magnanimity, and good faith" displayed in the permissive conduct of the King of France. Dickinson also thought that "the formation of our governments and an agreement upon the terms of our confederation ought to precede the assumption of our station among sovereigns." Such a "sovereignty" as the American states claimed "had never appeared" before in history. Dickinson viewed the "forming of our governments" as "a new and difficult work" that "ought to be rendered" perfectly acceptable to the people, followed by a confederation, and then independence. Dickinson wanted to fix "the boundaries of the states," to mutually guarantee "their respective rights" and to appropriate "the unallocated lands" to the "benefit of all the states" before a declaration. Dickinson summarized, "Upon the whole, when things should be thus deliberately rendered firm at home, and favourable abroad, then let America advance with majestic steps and assure her station among the sovereigns of the world."

Dickinson recalled, "I spoke my sentiments freely," and "yet, when a determination was made upon the question against my opinion, I received the determination as the sacred voice of my country." Within a week after the *Declaration*, he said, "I was the *only* member of Congress that marched with my regiment to Elizabeth Town against our enemies, then invading the state of New York." Dickinson took this as "a strong proof of my devotion to the *independence* of America, when once it became the *resolution* of America." All of his arguments "concerning *the time* of making the declaration, were in my judgment and conscience done away, and were of no more use, *after it was made*, than the rubbish caused in erecting a palace." He continued, "Reasons that were proper in a *debate*, were useless after a *decision*; and the nature of *these* evinces that they opposed only *the time of the declaration*, and not *independence itself*."[45]

Because of his political mobility, Dickinson was probably the single most important opponent of independence from the end of 1775 through the early summer of 1776. Just as *Common Sense* had tried to accelerate the inevitable, Dickinson's inexhaustible moderation attempted at every turn to apply the brakes to the independence movement. He was not a loyalist, but he was doggedly loyal. Like many of his aristocratic peers, Dickinson wanted every step in 1776 to follow his path of prescribed perfection, but *real politick* would not abide his theoretical deductions. The Pennsylvania lawyer was a man of consummate wealth, connections, erudition, and deliberation—the antitype of Thomas Paine in 1776. As Paine's sun rose in America that spring, Dickinson's began slowly to set.

PART FIVE
CONFLICTED CLERGY

Ministers of the Administration

A final set of colonists, the Church of England clergy in America, found themselves in perhaps the most contorted position of all. In July 1775 Pennsylvania's proprietary governor, Richard Penn, carried with him to London two petitions, the first from the Continental Congress, the "Olive Branch" addressed to the King of England, and the second from the Philadelphia Anglican clergy to the Bishop of London. The address to the bishop, signed by six clergymen, including Reverend Doctor William Smith, Provost of the College of Philadelphia, expressed a "deep affliction of mind" on a subject "in which the very Existence of our Church in America seems to depend." Through the clergymen's "*private* Influence and Advice" they had worked for a reconciliation, but their "*public* Advice" had been muted because they had decided to "keep our Pulpits wholly clear of every Thing bordering on this Contest; & to pursue that Line of Reason and Moderation, becoming our Characters." The ministers had hoped to avoid "whatever might irritate the Tempers of the People, on the one Hand; or create a Suspicion that we are opposed to the Interest of the Country in which we live, on the other."[46] Their policy of public abstention was, however, not working. The clergymen told their bishop, "But the Time is now come, my Lord, when even our Silence is misconstructed; and when we are called upon to take a more public Part." Their "Congregations of all ranks have *associated* themselves" and were "*determined never to submit to the Parliamentary Claim of taxing them at Pleasure*." The "Blood already spilt, in maintaining that Claim," they added, "is unhappily alienating the Affections of *many* from the Parent Country, and cementing them closer in the most fixed Purpose of a Resistance dreadful even in Contemplation."

In this situation "our People call upon us," said the ministers, "and think they have a Right to our Advice in the most public Manner, from the Pulpit." And here was their dilemma: "Should we refuse, our Principles wou'd be misrepresented, and even our Religious Usefulness among our people destroyed. And our Complying may, perhaps be interpreted to our Disadvantage, in the Parent-Country."[47]

The Continental Congress had recommended that each colony observe a "Day of general Humiliation, Fasting & Prayer" to seek God's guidance in the heightening state of affairs. The Philadelphia ministers felt that they had no choice but to comply with the proclaimed fast day, although they knew their behavior during the solemn services would be scrutinized by their congregants, including the congressional delegates in attendance. The Philadelphia clergy decided to participate in the fast day services but "did scrupulously conduct ourselves consistently with out Duty, as loyal Subjects and Ministers of the Church of England." The clergymen were torn, they said, between being "hearty and steady Friends of the Constitution both in Church and State" and "faithful Ministers of the Gospel of Love and Peace." The nervous clergymen were teetering in the middle of a tightrope strung between the rites of the Church of England and the rights of the people of America.

In October 1775, while Paine was busy composing *Common Sense*, Provost William Smith led another group of Anglican clergymen to compose a similar letter to the Bishop of London. Ministers from several colonies had gathered in Philadelphia for the annual conference of "The Corporation for the Relief of the Widows & Children of Clergymen in the Communion of the church of England in America," and the meeting afforded an ideal opportunity for the group to produce a general address from the "Church of England clergy in America." For the most part, this joint statement simply reiterated the arguments introduced at the end of the summer by the Philadelphia clergy. The twelve ministers present joined with their Philadelphia brethren "in the Prayer contained in their Letter to your Lordship" that men in both countries "may be directed to pursue such truly salutary Measures as may produce a speedy and permanent Reconciliation between the Mother-Country and her Colonies." They requested "your Lordship's paternal prayers, Advice and Protection" amidst a state of difficulties under which they labored "at this important Crisis" wherein even "the Preservation of our Church in America" was in question. Among those who signed the letter "Your Lordship's dutiful Sons & Servants" was the assistant rector of Trinity Church in New York, Reverend Charles Inglis.[48]

Textual Sabotage

James Chalmers's *Plain Truth* had squandered its opportunity to stymie the independence movement, but another pamphlet refutation, the *Deceiver Unmasked*, never even got the chance.[49] On March 18, 1776, the following ad appeared in the *New-York Gazette*:

> On Wednesday next will be Published and Sold by SAMUEL LOUDON, *The Deceiver unmasked, or Loyalty and Interest united; In answer to a Pamphlet, entitled, COMMON SENSE*. Wherein is proved that the Scheme of INDEPENDENCE is ruinous and delusive, and that in our Union with Great-Britain on liberal principles consists our greatest glory and happiness.[50]

The very next evening, March 19, an angry band of the New York Sons of Liberty stormed into Loudon's print shop, confiscated 1,500 copies of *The Deceiver Unmasked*, and proceeded to the Commons where they torched the pamphlets before cheering crowds.[51] Popular opinion in the colonies—even in ostensibly loyal New York—was by mid-March squarely on the side of *Common Sense* and independence. The New Yorkers had only to read the advertisement and title page of *The Deceiver Unmasked*, signed "By a Loyal American," to ascertain that it was an audacious assault on the principles laid out in *Common Sense*. Because these Sons of Liberty concurred with *Common Sense*'s pronouncement that "the period of debate is closed," they perceived such flaunted loyalism as a mischievous affront to the public.[52] They gave no thought to their infringement on the liberty of the press; instead, they determined to prevent the loyalist tract from what they considered to be an insidious agenda: to fracture the nascent consensus in favor of independence.[53]

Thus the most intellectually formidable pamphlet opposing *Common Sense* faltered at the starting block. The pamphlet's author, the Reverend Charles Inglis of New York, remained determined to air his arguments.[54] According to Inglis, "The Author, with much Trouble & no less Hazard, conveyed a Copy to Philadelphia, after expunging some Passages that gave greatest offense, softening others, inserting a few adapted to the Spirit of the Times, & altering the Title Page" had it printed by James Humphreys as *The True Interest of America Impartially Stated, In Certain Strictures on a Pamphlet Entitled Common Sense* (1776).[55]

But even after making these modifications, including the conspicuous absence of the word "loyal" on the new title page, Inglis's reply never managed to attract much discursive attention. In the swift moving currents of public opinion, events were passing Inglis by. Though his preface had been completed on February 16, relatively early in the debate over independence, *The True Interest* did not become available to the reading public until the end of May. If the publication of *Common Sense* was perfectly timed, Inglis's pamphlet was its temporal inverse. By the time it was reissued in Philadelphia, the debate over independence had been decided nearly everywhere but in Congress.[56] It is not surprising then that Humphreys and Hugh Gaine in New York continued to offload their unwanted stock of the pamphlet in newspaper ads throughout the following fall and winter.[57]

The initial act of sabotage by the Sons of Liberty did precipitate the three and a half month delay in the publication of Inglis's pamphlet, but there were other reasons why *The True Interest* proved ineffective in combating *Common Sense*. First, Inglis's penchant for thoroughness glutted *The True Interest* with long blocks of quotations from its competitor, making any thorough refutation impracticable. A second reason for Inglis's ineffectiveness is understandable coming from a loyalist Anglican minister: he expended most of his energy refuting the first two sections of *Common Sense* that deal with theology and history. These sections were crucial in setting up Paine's argument, but they also happened to be the most theoretical passages that waned in importance during the spring with each new report of practical political enmity. Third, Inglis's haughty tone and overly-technical arguments bled through every page, and the author thereby failed to ingratiate himself to his audience, and bored them with a tedious presentation. Related to this miscalculation, a fourth reason for Inglis's failure was that he embarked on his mission to expose Paine's logical fallacies without realizing that *Common Sense*'s sloppy, street-level reasoning was one of its strong suits in the eyes of its popular audience. Lastly, *The True Interest* also failed in its persuasive goal because Inglis incorrectly assumed that Paine was educated in the political classics. Paine would never have engaged Inglis in a debate on classical political theory, because, in part, his modest educational background forbade it.

Common Sense, said Inglis in *The True Interest*, was "one of the most artful, insidious and pernicious pamphlets" the minister had "ever met with." It was "addressed to the passions of the populace, at a time when their passions are much inflamed." During "such junctures," said Inglis, "Positive assertions will pass for demonstration with many, rage for sincerity, and the most glaring absurdities and falsehoods will be swallowed." *Common Sense* had proposed "that we should renounce our allegiance to our Sovereign, break off all connection with Great-Britain and set up an independent empire of the republican kind." The author of *Common Sense* was "Sensible that such a proposal must, even at this time, be shocking to the ears of Americans," and, therefore, "he insinuates that the *novelty* of his sentiments is the only *obstacle* to their success." Inglis claimed that the title of Paine's pamphlet was best described "by a figure in rhetoric, which is called a *Catachresis*, that is, in plain English, an abuse of words." Inglis found "no Common Sense in this pamphlet, but much uncommon frenzy."

Inglis held that "a Reconciliation with Great-Britain, on solid, constitutional principles, excluding all parliamentary taxation" was the only arrangement under which "the happiness and prosperity of this continent, are only to be sought or found," while the plan of *Common Sense* was, in one of Inglis's favorite phrases, "big with ruin." Paine had exhibited himself as "an avowed, violent Republican, utterly averse and unfriendly to the English constitution," and the "few faint glimmerings" of genius in the pamphlet were "but a poor compensation for its malevolent, pernicious design, and serve only to raise our indignation and abhorrence."[58]

Inglis said, "I look upon this pamphlet to be the most injurious, in every respect, to America, of any that has appeared since these troubles began." It was written, observed Inglis, in direct opposition to the utterances of the "Continental Congress, the several Provincial

Congresses and Assemblies." Each of those bodies had "unanimously and in the strongest terms, disclaimed every idea of Independency." They had "repeatedly declared their abhorrence of such a step; they have as often declared their firm attachment to our Sovereign and Parent State." Against these unequivocal statements, "here steps forth a writer, who avers with as much assurance as if he had the whole continent on his back, and ready to support his asseverations—That Independency is our duty and interest." Inglis felt compelled to compose a pamphlet reply "to vindicate my injured countrymen from this disgrace, which they deserve not" as well as "to oppose the destructive project of Independency…a project which is as new as it is destructive." Inglis said, "I am fully, firmly, and conscientiously persuaded, that our author's scheme of Independency and Republicanism, is big with ruin—with inevitable ruin to America." Moreover, Inglis accused Paine of closed-mindedness, "The author of *Common Sense* is a violent stickler for Democracy or Republicanism only—every other species of government is reprobated by him as tyrannical." This "Incendiary's pamphlet" recommended "a new, untried, romantic scheme, at which we would at first have shuddered—which is big with inevitable ruin, and is the last stage of political frenzy." Inglis tried to infuse the situation with his "cool reason and judgment" that "America is far from being yet in a desperate situation."

Inglis's was a learned and technical piece, in which he was primarily concerned with tracing the intellectual antecedents of *Common Sense*. He argued that *Common Sense*'s ideas about monarchy were related to *The Grounds and Reasons of Monarchy considered and exemplified in the Scotch Line* by John Hall ("a pensioner under Oliver Cromwell"), a treatise often bound together with Harrington's works. He says that "the principal outlines" of *Common Sense*'s sketch of government "seem to be taken from Mr. Harrington's *Rota*, which was too romantic even for the times of Cromwell."

No Man Can Serve Two Masters

By 1776, Inglis had worked for a decade as the assistant rector at Trinity Church, one of the most prestigious clerical positions in America.[59] Inglis had received an honorary doctorate from Oxford and, before the outbreak of the war, had even served for a short time as the acting president of King's College (later Columbia) in New York. Standing alongside William Smith, Inglis had been a chief proponent for the establishment of an American episcopate in the 1760s, a position he may have envisioned occupying himself one day. After defecting to the British side during the Revolutionary War, Inglis would settle for an appointment as the Bishop of Nova Scotia in 1787.[60]

Inglis's pamphlet was part of a larger strategy of loyalist propaganda. In 1774, Inglis and a handful of other New York ministers resolved together "to watch and refute all publications disrespectful to Government and the Parent State tending to a breach." Inglis had written a series of letters in the *New York Gazette*, beginning in the summer of 1774, over the signature of "A New York Farmer."[61] He and the other clergymen tried to utilize "constitutional" means and focused their attention on "legally organized bodies." Looking back on the events of 1776, the ministers were sure that their "positive remedies" could have secured eventually "every demand of the Whigs except independence."[62]

As independence became the touchstone issue of 1776, Inglis's strategy became more and more tenuous. Like the rest of the loyalist clergy in America, "amidst this Scene of Tumult and Disorder" Inglis tried to preach sermons that were confined "to the Doctrines of the Gospel, without touching on politics," and he tried to use his "Influence to allay our heats and cherish a Spirit of Loyalty" among the people. Though his conduct, he thought, was "harmless," he acknowledged that it "gave great offence to our flaming Patriots who laid it down as a maxim, 'That those who were not for them, were against them'."[63]

It was almost impossible for loyal clergymen to preach on the occasion of the May 17, 1776 fast. While many ministers were compelled to choose between incurring danger or departing from their duty, Inglis said, "I endeavoured to avoid both, making Peace and Repentance my Subject, and explicitly disclaimed having any Thing to do with Politics." But even this tack was unsuccessful. He said, "I have frequently heard myself called a Tory, and Traitor to my Country, as I passed the Streets, and Epithets joined to each, which decency forbids me to set down." Inglis and his fellow ministers endured "Violent threats" that they would regret praying for the king in public.[64]

One instance in particular conveys the mounting tension between Inglis's views and New York popular opinion. According to Inglis, one Sunday while he was "officiating and proceeded some length in the Service, a Company of about one hundred armed Rebels marched into the Church, with Drums beating and fifes playing, their Guns loaded and Bayonets fixed as if going to Battle." The solemn congregants were "thrown into utmost Terror, and several Women fainted, expecting a Massacre was intended." Inglis "took no Notice of this and went on with the Service," and only responded by exerting his voice, "which was in some Measure drowned by the Noise and Tumult." Inglis said, "The Rebels stood thus in the aisle for near fifteen Minutes, till, being asked into Pews by the Sexton, they Complied." Even when this happened, the people in the congregation "expected that, when the Collects for the King and the Royal Family were read, I should be fired at, as Menaces to that Purpose had been frequently flung out." As Inglis recorded it, the matter "passed over without any Accident."[65] When George III received word of Inglis's "fearless devotion," the king sent the minister a "magnificent" Bible and Prayer Book with the royal monogram on the cover, as a token of appreciation.[66]

After the equestrian statue of the king in Bowling Green was toppled, remembered Inglis, "All the King's Arms, even those on Signs and Taverns, were destroyed. The Committee sent me a message, which I esteemed a Favor and Indulgence, to have the King's Arms taken down in the Churches, or else the Mob would do it, and might deface and injure the Churches. I immediately complied."[67] Inglis had borne "the Imputation of being notoriously disaffected," but he also was "known and pointed at as the Author of several Pieces against the Proceedings of the Congress." He later paraphrased his pamphlet of 1776 when he remembered *Common Sense* as "one of the most virulent, artful, and pernicious Pamphlets I ever met with, and perhaps the Wit of Man could not devise one better calculated to do Mischief. It seduced thousands." Inglis knew that he answered it at the risk, "not only of my Liberty, but also of my Life." He paid for *The Deceiver Unmasked* to be printed in New York, but his pamphlet "was no sooner advertised, than the whole Impression was seized by the Sons of Liberty, and burnt." Not lacking in fortitude, Inglis "then sent a Copy to Philadelphia, where it was printed, and soon went through the second Edition" in its new form as *The True Interest of America Impartially Stated*. This pamphlet "swelled the Catalogue of my Political Transgressions" and placed him "in the utmost Danger."[68]

The "embarrassments of the clergy" were only made worse by the *Declaration of Independence*. As Inglis put it,

> To officiate publicly, and not pray for the King and the royal family according to the liturgy, was against their duty and oath, as well as dictates of their conscience; and yet to use the prayers for the king and royal family would have drawn inevitable destruction on them. The only course which they could pursue to avoid both evils, was to suspend the public exercise of their function, and shut up their churches."[69]

Inglis was a notorious loyalist, and he was not alone in his profession. But most Anglican ministers could not muster Inglis's stony resolve. A well-known Philadelphia Anglican, Reverend Jacob Duché, exhibited a chameleon nature that was despised even by ardent Tories. In 1776, Duché was Rector of both St. Peter's and Christ Church in Philadelphia, Chaplain to the Continental Congress, and Professor of Oratory at the College of Philadelphia. When the British took possession of Philadelphia in 1777, Duché became nervous and changed his political affiliation from "Whig" to "Tory." Alexander Graydon, a Tory himself, observed that Duché switched allegiances when he was convinced "his country was in a fair way of being subdued." Graydon found Duché "weak and vain, yet probably not a bad man: his habits, at least, were pious; and with the exception of this political tergiversation, his conduct exemplary."[70] William Bradford, very much a Whig, preferred the preaching of Duché to that of William Smith. Bradford described Duché's homiletic style on the Fast Day on May 17, 1776: "His Delivery was excellent but the matter not extraordinary. He is an amiable man & every feature of his face expressive of benevolence. This joined to an harmonious voice cannot fail of pleasing in the pulpit."[71] But Duché's eloquence could not steady his jumpy political compass, and while he wandered between sides of the conflict, American independence had become the colonists' true north.

Part Six
TREATING WITH BARBARIANS

Waiting for Commissioners, or: The Hessians are Coming

The argument of moderate politicians hinged upon the viability of an expected envoy of British commissioners. If the call of *Common Sense* and the Independent bloc was "Now!" then the response of the Moderate bloc was "Wait!" The colonists anticipated that a group of commissioners would arrive *any day* to offer peace terms to the colonies. The commissioners became the focal point of the moderate call to delay independence. The moderates feared that a preemptive independence would close the door to negotiations, and they remained hopeful of "favourable terms."

On March 26, a letter in the *Pennsylvania Evening Post*, signed "T***L," provided a stinging commentary on *Common Sense* and one of the strongest rationales offered for waiting on British commissioners. The writer mocked *Common Sense* as opposed to "common policy" and "so mad for the important NOW." He picked up on the urgency in Paine's writing, "there is no time to be lost—this winter is worth an age—let not a moment more escape you," and, cautioned against an imprudent rush into measures. "Surely," he told the advocates of independence, "you don't conceive there is something magic in the word Independence, and that the moment Great-Britain hears the sound, her heart will sink into the bottom of the ocean, and all her forces be blown up into the air." The Americans had nothing to fear from "protractions," because they were "not quite so ready to defend" as Britain was "to attack." The writer spurned "the baseness of the thought" that Britain's commissioners came only to bribe the colonial leaders, and he advocated a balanced approach to their arrival, "Let us hear her proposals, and treat them as they deserve." In an important caveat at the end of the essay, the author agreed to hold up his hand "most earnestly for Independence" whenever it "becomes necessary," specifically, "when a reunion with Great-Britain cannot take place with advantage to America."[72]

This essayist embodied the strand of opinion that frustrated many political insiders who had become convinced that independence was the colonies' only viable option. On March 3, Joseph Reed expressed wonderment at the "strange reluctance in the minds of many to cut the knot." This curiosity was especially the case in Pennsylvania "and to the southward," where "no man of understanding expects any good from the commissioners, yet they are for waiting to hear their proposals before they declare off."[73]

As each successive month passed without the commissioners' arrival, more and more Americans grew skeptical of the commissioners' mission. A short article in the *Pennsylvania Packet* on April 22 included the parliamentary clause that empowered the commissioners to grant pardons "by proclamation in His Majesty's name" for the express purpose of encouraging "all well affected persons in any of the said Colonies to exert themselves in suppressing the rebellion therein, and to afford a speedy protection to those who are disposed to return to their duty." At the end of the piece, the contributor noted, "Now, Sir, if any man, idiots and lunatics excepted, can imagine any *good* is to be expected from Commissioners, I am myself deprived of reason."[74]

The moderates themselves knew that their clock was ticking. By the end of April, Maryland delegate Thomas Stone worried, "If the Commissioners do not arrive shortly and conduct themselves with great candor and uprightness" in view of a reconciliation, then "a separation will most undoubtedly take place." Stone wanted "to conduct affairs so that a just & honorable reconciliation should take place, or that we should be pretty unanimous in a resolution to fight it out for Independence."[75] An indication of the withering influence of the reconciliation camp in the Continental Congress can be seen in the place of commissioners in their recorded debates. After May 6, the Continental Congress gave no attention to commissioners until two months after independence. When the commissioners did finally arrive, hamstrung with unsatisfactory powers and in a political climate exulting in its newfound independence, the negotiations were fruitless.[76]

By June 1776 the evidence began to pile up against the commissioners, and still more Americans gave up hope for a peaceful reconciliation. A "Republicus," writing in the *Pennsylvania Evening Post* at the end of June, confessed, "EVERY moment that I reflect on our affairs, the more am I convinced of the necessity of a formal Declaration of Independence." He added, "Reconciliation is thought of now by none but knaves, fools and madmen." Even if Britain conquered America, said Republicus, "I would, for my own part, choose rather to be conquered as an independent state than as an acknowledged rebel." America "may be benefited by independence, but we cannot be hurt by it," he said, adding, "and every man that is against it is a traitor."[77]

But it was not the inadequacy of the commissioners that sealed the American decision for independence. If there was any single event that dashed the colonists' hopes of reconciliation, it was the news that Hessian troops had embarked for the western shore of the Atlantic. Different persons in different places had placed different degrees of hope in the arrival of a conciliatory commission from Britain, but word of the imminent arrival of foreign mercenary soldiers, recruited expressly to subdue the Americans, evaporated any presentiment in favor of British benevolence. The idea of foreign mercenaries was anathema to eighteenth century civilization; it represented piracy and barbarity to the highest degree and was perceived as the equivalent of unleashing hordes of rabid wild animals on the American colonists.

A May 6 report in the Philadelphia press of British and Hessian troops setting sail for America elicited the humorous editorial interjection, "*Oh GEORGE*! Are these thy commissioners of peace and reconciliation?"[78] The week after the Continental Congress's May 15 resolution, disbelieving colonists could read for themselves in their newspapers a translation of treaties between King George III and the Duke of Brunswick, the Landgrave of Hesse-Cassell, and the Count of Hanau.[79]

The arrival of German mercenaries was terrible, but the duplicitous juxtaposition of mercenaries and commissioners raised the Americans' ire like nothing else. A "Committee of Freemen of Charles County" in Maryland was one of many local committees that sent new instructions in May and June to its delegates in their respective provincial conventions. The Charles County Committee made a special point of the relationship between commissioners and mercenaries. Their instructions expressed anger that "instead of commissioners to negotiate a peace, as we have been led to believe were coming out," the British government was sending "a formidable fleet of British ships, with a numerous army of foreign soldiers."[80]

The May 1776 news of coming mercenary forces convinced most colonists that Paine's military predictions in *Common Sense* had been spot on. But the transcolonial unanimity crystallized by a looming invasion had been preceded and prepared by the peak of the newspaper controversy over independence in March and April. *Common Sense* and the independence movement met their most formidable public challenger in the person of a clergyman and educator, Provost William Smith of the College of Philadelphia.

Notes: Chapter 9

[1] Alexander Hamilton to John Jay, 26 November 1775. Syrett, *Papers of Alexander Hamilton*, 1:176-178.
[2] AC, No. 3, CW 1:88.
[3] Morgan, and Schmidt, *North Carolinians in the Continental Congress*, 17.
[4] Ibid., 19.
[5] Samuel Johnston to James Iredell, 5 April 1776. Saunders, *Colonial Records of North Carolina*, 10:1032.
[6] Morgan and Schmidt, 22-24.
[7] Ibid., 116.
[8] James Iredell to Joseph Hewes. 29 April 1776. Saunders, 10:1036-1037.
[9] Morgan and Schmidt, 24.
[10] James Iredell to Joseph Hewes. 9 June 1776. Saunders, 10:1038-1040.
[11] HL to Martha Laurens, 29 February 1776. Chesnutt, *Papers of Henry Laurens*, 11:53-55.
[12] HL to Martha Laurens, 14 March 1776. Chesnutt, 11:56.
[13] HL to James Laurens, 6 January 1776. Chesnutt, 11:4-7.
[14] HL to Robert Deans, 8 January 1776. Chesnutt, 11:10-12.
[15] HL to Georgia Council of Safety [Addressed to A. Bullock & George Galphin], 13 February 1776. Chesnutt, 11:99-100.
[16] The pamphlet Laurens referred to was *An Apology or Defence of William the First, Prince of Orange, in answer to the proclamation against, and proscription of him by the King of Spain. Or An Apology for the Revolt of the Low Countries* (1580). London, 1707.
[17] HL to John Laurens, 22 February 1776. Chesnutt, 11:114-121.
[18] Ibid.
[19] HL to William Manning, 27 February 1776. Chesnutt, 11:122-128.
[20] HL to Babut & Co., 5 August 1776. Chesnutt, 11:216-220.
[21] HL to John Laurens, 14 August 1776. Chesnutt, 11: 222-246.
[22] HL to Martha Laurens, 17 August 1776. Chesnutt, 11:252-256.
[23] A letter from Philadelphia, August 1, 1775, in the *London Chronicle*; reprinted in Willard, *Letters on the American Revolution*, 179-183. Also quoted in Borden and Borden, 36.
[24] JA to James Sullivan. 26 May 1776. LDC 4:73-75. To be fair to Adams, he did in this letter advocate dividing land into smaller parcels so that it would be affordable to a larger percentage of the populace.
[25] Paine's note: "I did not, at my first setting out in public life, nearly seventeen years ago, turn my thoughts to subjects of government from motives of interest; and my conduct from that moment to this, proves the fact. I saw an opportunity in which I thought I could do some good, and I followed exactly what my heart dictated." RM 2, CW 1:406.
[26] From AC, No. 13, CW 1:235.
[27] Benton, *Whig-Loyalism*, 14-17.
[28] JA to AA, 14 April 1776. Butterfield, et al. *Book of Abigail and John*, 122.
[29] The assortment of trades in Philadelphia during 1776 can be glimpsed in an order of procession from the next decade. The common types of late colonial and early republican craftsmen included: cordwainers, coach painters, cabinet and chair-makers, brick-makers, painters, watch-makers, fringe and ribband

weavers, bricklayers, tailors, instrument-makers, turners, and Windsor chair-makers, carvers and gilders, coopers, plane makers, whip manufacturers, black smiths, bell-hangers, coach-makers, potters, hatters, wheel-wrights, tin-plate workers, skinners, breeches-makers and glovers, tallow-chandlers, butchers, printers, stationers and book-binders, saddlers, stone-cutters, bakers, gun-smiths, copper-smiths, gold-smiths, silver-smiths and jewelers, distillers, tobacconists, brass-founders, stocking manufacturers, tanners, druggists, upholsterers, sugar-refiners, brewers, barbers, ship-chandlers, engravers, plasterers. See, *Order of procession, in honor of the establishment of the Constitution of the United States. To parade precisely at eight o'clock in the morning, of Friday, the 4th of July, 1788*. Philadelphia: Hall and Sellers, [1788]. HSP/LCP.

[30] Supplement to the DPP, April 8, 1776. The prevailing republican interpretive framework in early American historiography has fostered the idea that social and economic classes were unimportant in the era of the American Revolution, a thesis called into question by the events of 1776. Bernard Bailyn: "the American Revolution was above all else an ideological, constitutional, political struggle and not primarily a controversy between social groups undertaken to force changes in the organization of the society or the economy." (*Ideological Origins*, x); and Gordon Wood: "And ultimately such a stand was what made their Revolution seem so unusual, for they revolted not against the English constitution but on behalf of it." Wood, again: "'Happy above all Countries is our Country,' he exulted, 'where *that equality* is found, without destroying the necessary subordination.' For most Americans, as for [Thomas] Shippen, this was the deeply felt meaning of the Revolution: they had created a new world, a republican world." (*Creation of the American Republic*, 10, 47-48).

[31] Friedenwald, *The Declaration of Independence*, 80.

[32] Doerflinger, "Philadelphia Merchants and the Logic of Moderation," 198.

[33] [Thomas] Clifford to Thomas Frank, 7 March 1776. Clifford Correspondence, Pemberton Papers, HSP.

[34] [Thomas] Clifford to Thomas Frank, 16 May 1776. Clifford Correspondence, Pemberton Papers, HSP.

[35] Doerflinger, 223.

[36] See Ver Steeg, *Robert Morris*, and Young, *Forgotten Patriot, Robert Morris*.

[37] 27 February 1776. RS 2:506.

[38] Oberholtzer, *Robert Morris*, 20-21.

[39] On Dickinson: Jacobson, *John Dickinson and the Revolution in Pennsylvania*; Wolfe, *John Dickinson, Forgotten Patriot*; Flower, *John Dickinson, Conservative Revolutionary*. On Morris: Ver Steeg, *Robert Morris, Revolutionary Financier*; Young, *Forgotten Patriot: Robert Morris*; Gould, *Life of Robert Morris*.

[40] Letter III. *Letters from a Farmer in Pennsylvania to the Inhabitants of the British Colonies*. Philadelphia: William and Thomas Bradford, 1767.

[41] See, Dickinson, *An Essay on the Constitutional Power of Great-Britain over the Colonies in America*.

[42] Extract from the Minutes of the Committee. "Resolutions, &c. At a provincial meeting of deputies chosen by the several counties in Pennsylvania.," July 15-18, 1774.

[43] Dickinson Papers at HSP and LCP. Quoted in Flower, 143.

⁴⁴ See Powell, "Speech of John Dickinson Opposing the Declaration of Independence, 1 July, 1776.
⁴⁵ Dickinson, "To my Opponents in the late Elections of Councillor for the County of Philadelphia, and of President of the Supreme Executive Council of Pennsylvania." *The Freeman's Journal: or, the North-American Intelligencer.* Philadelphia: Francis Bailey, January 1, 1783.
⁴⁶ It is worth noting that the ministers did not equate the "Tempers of the People" with the "Interest of the Country in which we live."
⁴⁷ The Bishop didn't like the phrase "Religious Usefulness" as indicated in his reply and noted in Smith's memorandum book. "Letter of the Philadelphia Clergy to the Bishop of London," 30 June 1775. William Smith Papers. UPA.
⁴⁸ "Letter to the Bishop of London from a meeting of Church of England clergy in America," 5 October 1775. William Smith Papers. UPA.
⁴⁹ [Charles Inglis], *The Deceiver Unmasked; or, Loyalty and Interest United: In Answer to a Pamphlet Entitled Common Sense. By a Loyal American.* New York: Samuel Loudon, 1776; NYHS, APS. See also, [Inglis, Charles]. *The True Interest of America Impartially Stated, In Certain Strictures on a Pamphlet Entitled Common Sense. By An American.* Philadelphia: James Humphreys, Jr., 1776.
⁵⁰ NYG, March 18, 1776.
⁵¹ A very few copies of this edition survive, salvaged either from the unburned edges of the pile or by virtue of being tucked away in Loudon's shop. The NYHS has a full copy and the APS a partial copy.
⁵² CS 3.2.
⁵³ Wall, "The Burning of the Pamphlet 'The Deceiver Unmasked' in 1776."
⁵⁴ Inglis, *The True Interest of America Impartially Stated.* The Preface is dated February 16, 1776.
⁵⁵ Lydekker, *Life and Letters of Charles Inglis*, 152.
⁵⁶ NYG, March 18, 1776; PL, June 1, 1776.
⁵⁷ PL, September 14, 1776. Gaine continued to advertise the pamphlet in New York newspapers through December 1776.
⁵⁸ *True Interest.* From the Preface.
⁵⁹ Cuthbertson, *The First Bishop: A Biography of Charles Inglis*; Harris, *Charles Inglis, Missionary, Loyalist, Bishop*; *The Claim and answer with the subsequent proceedings, in the case of the Right Reverend Charles Inglis, against the United States.*
⁶⁰ Harris, 34-35.
⁶¹ Ibid., 40.
⁶² Ibid.
⁶³ From a report written by Inglis in October 1776, Quoted in Harris, 42.
⁶⁴ Harris, 45.
⁶⁵ Ibid., 45-46.
⁶⁶ Ibid., 47.
⁶⁷ Ibid., 48.
⁶⁸ Ibid., 48-49.
⁶⁹ Ibid., 43.
⁷⁰ Borden and Borden, 4.
⁷¹ Bradford, "A Memorandum Book and Register for the Months of May and June, 1776." Bradford Papers. HSP.

[72] "T***L." PEP, March 26, 1776.
[73] 3 March 1776. *Reed's Reed*, 1:163; quoted in Friendenwald, *Declaration of Independence*, 63-64.
[74] DPP, April 22, 1776.
[75] *Journal and Correspondence of the Maryland Council of Safety*, 383. Quoted in Friedenwald, *Declaration of Independence*, 65.
[76] See JCC, May 6, 1776. Friedenwald, *Declaration of Independence*, 66.
[77] PEP, June 29, 1776.
[78] Postcript to the DPP, May 6, 1776.
[79] Supplement to the PJ, May 22, 1776.
[80] Scharf, *History of Maryland*, 228-229.

Chapter Ten

A War of Words

But if there appears among you any new book, the ideas of which shock your own—supposing you have any—or of which the author may be of a party contrary to yours—or what is worse, of which the author may not be of any party at all—then you cry out "Fire!" and all is noise, scandal, and uproar in your small corner of the earth. There is an abominable man who has declared in print that if we had no hands we would not be able to make shoes nor stockings. The devout cry out, furred doctors assemble, alarms multiply from college to college, from house to house, whole communities are disturbed. And why? For five or six pages, about which no one will give a fig at the end of three months. Does a book displease you? Refute it. Does it bore you? Don't read it.

Voltaire
Philosophical Dictionary
1750

NOW, TORIES—now, is the time—the COMMISSIONERS are coming, and ye shall all be well paid.—At it again, my boys—that's right, my lads—letter the first—letter the second—letter the second—letter the third—well done, CATO—at it again, CATO—now, CATO, huzza!

"Old Trusty"
"For the *Pennsylvania Evening Post*"
March 1776

Part One
DUELLING PENS

A Defining Debate

In this chapter I will describe the complex spike in American public discourse during March and April 1776. William Smith and Thomas Paine positioned themselves in the middle of the independence controversy and dozens of other writers piled onto the public scrum. I will focus here on two phases of the debate between Smith and Paine: the first, an indirect conflict over the death of General Richard Montgomery, and the second, the head-to-head newspaper exchange of "Cato" and "The Forester." Smith was the only direct respondent to *Common Sense* whom Paine viewed as posing any serious challenge to the snowballing independence movement. In fact, Paine's friends recalled him from New York in March 1776 specifically because they had begun to worry that Smith's serial essays were sapping momentum from the independence camp. By taking a close look at the causes, content, and discursive reverberations of this high-profile publication controversy, I will continue to flesh out the complex dynamics of the American decision for independence. Before plunging again into the 1776 fray, though, I need first to provide some contextual background for Smith's entry into the debate.

A Man of Conflict

During the summer of 1775, William Smith sent a flurry of letters to London and to his fellow clergymen in America. He suspected that opponents of the Anglican Church were planning "to ruin it and draw off our People, at this Crisis" by propagating rumors that the clergy were "Tools of [the] Administration to inculcate Slavish Principles." He thus encouraged his friend, Reverend Thomas Barton of Lancaster, "The Time is now come when we must speak."[1]

Barton's reply to Smith demonstrated, according to Smith's manuscript annotations, that the two "seem not essentially to differ in Principles." Those principles, as Barton conveyed them, were:

> There is a maxim, which I have somewhere met with, that the "Profundity of Politics is so great that men of plain Sense cannot fathom it." This has taught me not to venture my little Bark into the stormy Ocean—I therefore *paddle* my Canoe, as much as possible, in quiet Waters, along the Shore; and so, by that means, I hope to *steer* without Danger into the Port of Peace.

Barton added, "As the American Ideas of Whig and Tory have never been properly defined, I have not yet assumed the Name of either."[2]

Smith included a private letter to the Bishop of London in the packet to be delivered by Richard Penn in the fall of 1775, and in that letter Smith testified that he had attempted "to promote Conciliatory measures" as early as the summer of 1774. Smith described his reticence to "appear cold to the Interests of America, or the Parent Country, which," he thought, "are certainly the same." He reiterated to the bishop his theory that "some in this Country" wished to color the Anglican clergy as *Tools of Power*, slavish in their own Tenets, and privately Enemies to the *Principles of the Revolution*." If this design succeeded, he warned, "it would give a deadly wound to the Church in this Country. Indeed, I question whether we should have the appearance of a Congregation in it."[3]

The case of William Smith illustrates the deep conflict of loyalties that worked just beneath the surface of late colonial politics, especially for those who, like Smith and other clergymen, served two masters. Though Smith had lived in America for over two decades by 1776, he was a thoroughgoing Briton. Smith had been educated for the ministry at the University of Aberdeen in Scotland, and he received honorary doctorates from Oxford, Aberdeen, and Trinity College in Dublin. He received money, prestige, religious authority, and his sense of identity from his ties to Great Britain, but he lived among American colonists, taught their sons, and preached to their congregations. He was neither fully British nor fully American.

Benjamin Franklin, a royalist for much of his early life, had been William Smith's Pennsylvania patron. Franklin had been inspired by Smith's educational treatise, *A General Idea of the College of Mirania* (1753), to transform the Academy of Philadelphia into the College of Philadelphia, and so Franklin recruited Smith to lead the new institution.[4] While other American colleges emphasized the training of ministers, Smith and the college's early trustees saw themselves as managers of an elite English preparatory school, one that would train loyal colonial young men in the classical languages and natural sciences in preparation for their return to England to study "useful" subjects like law or medicine.[5]

By Franklin's design and in opposition to the norms of eighteenth century higher education, the college had been led originally by a nonsectarian Board of Trustees. Smith had traveled to England in 1762-1763 on a very successful fundraising campaign, but the Church of England placed one condition on its substantial financial backing: Smith had to "freeze" the composition of the Board of Trustees of the College of Philadelphia to "preserve its diversity." In actuality, this gave the Anglicans a four-to-one majority on the board and an unrivalled sway over college policies.[6] This Anglican majority persisted until 1779 when the Pennsylvania legislature revoked and then replaced the college's charter, making it a public institution subject to the oversight of *ex officio* legislators and renaming it "The University of the State of Pennsylvania." The first action of the new overseers in 1779 was to fire Smith.

During the Revolutionary War, Smith was reprimanded, ostracized, and always closely watched by the Americans, but he never officially defected to the British side. In late 1776, Smith was taken into custody for his refusal to sign a letter of association, and again in 1777, the Executive Council of Pennsylvania made him promise not to do anything "injurious to the United Free States of North America, by Speaking, Writing, or otherwise."[7]

In 1782, shortly after the Battle of Yorktown, the ever-opportunistic Smith founded a college in Maryland and named it after the triumphant General George Washington. By 1788, the populist "Spirit of 1776" had begun to wane, and Smith returned to Philadelphia with his sights set on returning to his former post. He and a few other "Federalists" capitalized upon the spirit of the Pennsylvania "counter-revolution" and applied to the state legislature to replace the university charter of 1779 with a new, more conservative charter. Smith then returned to his position as provost, but he was again fired in 1791. After Smith's second ouster, the university's charter was returned closer to its substance of 1779, although it remained a private institution.[8]

Part Two
SPEAKING FOR MONTGOMERY

Remembering the General

As we saw in Chapter 6, news of the loss of General Richard Montgomery momentarily knocked the wind out of American morale. Montgomery was held by the colonists in the highest esteem for his personal character and his military leadership. Like General Joseph Warren who had died earlier that year at Bunker Hill, Montgomery became an instant martyr for the American cause.

Once the colonists overcame their initial shock and disappointment over Montgomery's death and the loss at Quebec, the deceased general took on a new role as a symbol for opposition to monarchy. As a poem, "On the Death of General Montgomery," in the February 17 *Pennsylvania Ledger* eulogized,

> WHEN haughty monarchs quit this chequer'd scene,
> When cruel tyrants fall a prey to death,
> Their actions may employ the venal pen,
> Their praise may sound upon the venal breath.
>
> But when the Hero and the Patriot fall,
> (Heroes and Patriots must submit to fate)
> Then may the mournful verse their virtues tell
> And elegy their fame may celebrate.[9]

The colonists did not confine their tributes to Montgomery's symbolic utility, but instead they took their memorials a step further: they ventriloquized the general's voice in direct support of their political positions. William Smith and Thomas Paine joined others in indulging this tactless impulse, each in a text presented to the public on February 19, 1776.

William Smith's Oration

The Continental Congress had originally planned to invite Reverend Jacob Duché to compose and deliver "an Oration in Praise of the General," but Duché was unavailable, so on January 25, the congress asked Provost William Smith instead.[10] The resolution requested that Smith deliver a funeral oration "in honor of General Montgomery, and of those Officers and Soldiers who magnanimously fought and fell with him in maintaining the principles of American Liberty."[11] Smith collected all of Montgomery's correspondence with the congress and composed his address with characteristic exactitude.

The provost intended to make a political splash with his speech, and accordingly he sent a special note to the Continental Congress a week before the memorial service. Smith requested that the congress invite "the General Assembly, Corporation, Associators, &c. to hear the Oration" the following Monday.[12] The congress complied with Smith's request, and the service became the hottest ticket in Philadelphia. In addition to reserved seating for every politician and military man in Philadelphia, a four hundred person gallery was designated "for Ladies and Strangers, whose public Spirit may induce them to honor the Solemnity" by purchasing a ticket.[13]

After taking care of "some little Business" during the morning of February 19, the Continental Congress, "attended by the Pennsylvania Assembly and other invited bodies with a vast Crowd of Spectators, proceeded in State to the Dutch Calvinist Church where Dr. Smith pronounced an Oration for Gen. Montgomery." The Pennsylvania Light Infantry and Rifle Rangers flanked the Continental Congress in their procession up Fourth Street to the church.[14] Delegate Richard Smith of New Jersey observed that, once everyone had packed inside the church, "the Band of vocal and Instrumental Music was good but played too low for the Place."[15]

William Smith claimed in his oration that Montgomery had acted in "the spirit of reconciliation," a character trait that gave Smith "particular satisfaction." Smith went so far as to say that only the general's commitment to reconciliation "induced me to appear in this place on this occasion." Smith made his own political stance unequivocal, and he spoke on behalf of his distinguished audience, quoting from the "Olive Branch" Petition as proof of their concurrence. Smith was "happy" to know that "the delegated voice of the continent, as well as of this particular province supports me in praying for a restoration 'of the former harmony between Great Britain and these Colonies upon so firm a basis as to perpetuate its blessings, uninterrupted by any future dissensions, to succeeding generations in both countries.'"[16]

After the service, many of those present murmured their dissatisfaction with Smith's performance, and especially with the imputation that he was speaking on behalf of General Montgomery, the Pennsylvania Assembly, and the Continental Congress. Samuel Adams wrote to his wife that "Certain political Principles were thought to be interwoven with every part of the Oration which were displeasing to the Auditory. It was remark'd that he could not even keep their Attention."[17] This was a common indictment of Smith's oratory. The reverend doctor often preached at the Anglican Church on Arch Street, causing William Bradford "no small Dissatisfaction," and often lulling the congregation to sleep with his "droning" sermons. As Bradford recorded it in his diary, "There is something in that man's voice which, like the manner of bees, invites to sleep."[18]

As a matter of courtesy, some Pennsylvanians of a more loyal stripe thanked Smith for his address and asked him if they would be able to purchase a printed copy. Smith took their genteel signal and began polishing his draft copy for pamphlet publication.[19] Smith showed his manuscript to Benjamin Franklin and William Livingston of New Jersey and requested their criticisms. The two congressional delegates suggested a number of minor stylistic changes and urged him to delete the most controversial paragraph in the oration. Smith accepted their minor suggestions but refused to strike the paragraph.[20]

Franklin and Livingston did not edit Smith's oration in a vacuum, and the changes they suggested had been first outlined in a debate within the Continental Congress. On the Wednesday following the memorial service, William Livingston had moved that the Continental Congress express its thanks to Doctor Smith in a public manner—a common courtesy in eighteenth century politics—but "this was objected to for several Reasons" by a majority of delegates; "the chief [reason] was that the Dr. declared the Sentiments of the Congress to continue in a Dependency on Great Britain which Doctrine this Congress cannot now approve." Livingston was backed by James Duane, James Wilson, and Thomas Willing, and opposed by John Adams, George Wythe, Edward Rutledge, Oliver Wolcott, and Roger Sherman. Before the body reached a vote, Livingston withdrew his motion.[21]

John Adams described Smith as "one of the many irregular and extravagant Characters of the Age. I never heard one single person speak well of any Thing about him but his Abilities, which are generally allowed to be good."[22] Recalling the motion to thank Smith for the oration, John Adams wrote that the "insolent Performance" was "opposed with great Spirit and Vivacity from every part of the Room" in congress. The motion was withdrawn "lest it should be rejected, as it certainly would have been with Indignation."[23]

In the pamphlet version of *An Oration in Memory of General Montgomery*, Smith attached an explanatory footnote to the speech's most controversial paragraph wherein he declared the Pennsylvania Assembly and the Continental Congress to be resolute in their opposition to independence. As Smith put it, his original statement had "been either misrepresented or misunderstood by some." He had not made "the least declaration concerning the present sentiments of either of these bodies," and he stressed that his references to the Congress's petition and the Assembly's instructions both pointed "to a past period." Smith assured his readers that he had not precluded "the taking into the terms of an accommodation, so far as may be thought reasonable, the redress of whatever grievances or losses we may have sustained since that period." Smith claimed that his oration contained only points that were "fully consonant to every declaration of Congress which has yet appeared." He dared not "impute to them, or even suspect, the least change of sentiment, before they themselves have declared it."[24]

Thomas Paine's Dialogue

The same day that Smith delivered his oration, Paine published in the *Pennsylvania Packet* an anonymous "Dialogue between the Ghost of General Montgomery and a Delegate, in a Wood near Philadelphia."[25] In the imaginary encounter, General Montgomery's ghost wandered up to an unnamed delegate to the Continental Congress and struck up a conversation. Montgomery said, "I am sent here upon an important errand, to warn you against listening to terms of accommodations from the Court of Britain."

The delegate was still anticipating "just and honourable" terms from Britain, but Montgomery asked, "How can you expect these, after the King has proclaimed you rebels from the throne, and after both houses of parliament have resolved to support him in carrying on a war against you?" Montgomery saw "no offers from Great-Britain but of PARDON," adding, "The very word is an insult upon our cause," since it was offered by "a ROYAL CRIMINAL" to "virtuous freemen" who had flown "to arms in defense of the rights of humanity." Montgomery would "rather have it said that I died by [the king's] vengeance, than that I lived by his mercy."

When the delegate objected, "But you think nothing of the destructive consequences of war," Montgomery replied, "I think of nothing but of the destructive consequences of slavery. The calamities of war are transitory and confined in their effects. But the calamities of slavery are extensive and lasting in their operation."

The delegate recognized that Montgomery was "for the independence of the colonies on Great-Britain," but Montgomery clarified, "I am for permanent liberty, peace, and security to the American colonies." This could not be maintained by simply restoring the colonies to a mythic 1763, said Montgomery, adding the query, "Can no hand wield the scepter of government in America except that which has been stained with the blood of your countrymen?" Montgomery's ghost attributed all distinctions between king and ministers to "political superstition." The colonists "shun the streams, and yet you are willing to sit down at the very fountain of corruption and venality." To the objection of the delegate that their colonial charters would protect them, Montgomery rebuffed, "Charters are no restraints against the lust of power." From the moment of their conversation forward, said the fictional Montgomery, "the only aim of administration" would be "the seduction of the representatives of the people of America."

Paine reiterated in the "Dialogue" the core arguments of *Common Sense*: on the endemic corruption of monarchy, on the necessity of independence *at this time*, on the role of America as an asylum for religious liberty, and on the benefits of establishing a commercial empire. He expressed, through the persona of Montgomery's ghost, the opinion that "there are now, I believe, but few prejudices to be found in this country in favour of the old connection with Great-Britain. I except those men only who are under the influence of their passions and offices."[26]

The ghost of Montgomery continued, correcting the delegate's misconception that the Americans had "many friends" in both houses of parliament: "You mean the ministry have many enemies in Parliament who connect the cause of America with their clamours at the door of administration." The general claimed that any of the conciliatory measures proposed by the "friends" of America in parliament would "have ruined you more effectually than Lord North's motion."

As a political theorist, Paine was not heavily invested in the strict ideological framework of republicanism; it was simply the only available alternative to monarchy. The imaginary delegate shivered at the prospect of becoming "a commonwealth" if independent. Montgomery replied, "I maintain that it is your interest to be independent of Great Britain, but I do not recommend any new form of government to you." The Americans naturally possessed sufficient "wisdom to contrive a perfect and free form of government," since they had displayed "virtue enough to defend themselves against the most powerful nation in the world." The colonies were so virtuous, said Montgomery, that "did not some of them still hang upon the haggard breasts of Great-Britain, I should think the time now come in which they had virtue enough to be happy under any form of government."

His only specific recommendation concerning government was reminiscent of a Rittenhouse clockwork mechanism: "All the wheels of a government should move within itself—I would only beg leave to observe to you, that monarchy and aristocracy have in all ages been the vehicles of slavery." He reminded the colonists that "in a commonwealth only" could they "expect to find every man a patriot or hero." All of the illustrious names of Greek and Roman history, he postulated, "would never have astonished the world with their names had they lived under royal governments."

The general's ghost had grown tired of reasoning with the delegate and ordered him, "Go, then, and awaken the Congress to a sense of their importance; you have no time to lose." From Montgomery's celestial vantage point, he could see that "The decree is finally gone forth, Britain and America are now distinct empires. Your country teems with patriots—heroes—and legislators, who are impatient to burst forth into light and importance." God had not excited, said Montgomery, "the attention of all Europe—of the whole world—nay of angels themselves to the present controversy for nothing. The inhabitants of Heaven long to see the ark finished in which all the liberty and true religion of the world are to be deposited." Montgomery closed his peroration with the statement that he "would rather die in *attempting* to obtain permanent freedom for a handful of people, than survive a conquest which would serve only to extend the empire of despotism." He was certain that "America is the theatre where human nature will soon receive its greatest military, civil, and literary honours."

PART THREE
COMMISSIONERS AND COMMITTEES

Loyal Moderation

In July 1774, William Smith sat down to write a letter to the Bishop of London "under deep anxiety of mind."[27] Smith had hoped to hide "in the Silent vale of Life, unnoticed and unknown," but the "Connections and Influence which twenty years' Employment in public Life" had garnered him had finally driven him to engage with the imperial controversy. The provost viewed his role in the dispute in straightforward terms: to "Seek & Propagate *Peace*, by all lawful means." "British America" had, "from one End to the other" been alarmed by the treatment of Boston, said Smith, and the "Dangerous Precedents" set by Parliament had "led the Colonies generally to adopt the Cause of Boston as their own." The "Cool and dispassionate men" of the colonies did not agree with "the Conduct of the People of Boston in all things," especially "those impudent Publications & rash actions, which seem even to tend towards *Independency*," but neither did they think the harsh retribution of Britain was justified.

Smith was concerned that the people of Philadelphia, in "the first Heats of Resentment" could "be worked up into desperate Conduct." Philadelphia, noted Smith, was "the first City on this Continent, & a Place to which others look up for that wisdom & moderation of Councils, which have hitherto generally Distinguished its Conduct." Unless "Men of Prudence and Discretion" stood forth, "the Multitude might here fall into such rash & violent Measures, as might disgrace our Country & be the Cause of much future Trouble." Smith and some members of his church had been solicited by "Sundry of the best Characters in this Government" to support only "moderate and reasonable measures" by advising the popular committees, "who think they have a right in urgent Cases, to meet and *resolve* upon their own public Concerns."

Smith called "a very large and respectable meeting" on the issue, offering "to act in their Behalf," but the a majority of the audience was composed of "various Tempers" whose "Zeal might be greater than their Knowledge." Smith found it difficult in that setting to say anything "worthy of a grave man to Say, & yet not give offence." He chose to "say little," and what he did say "might have come from the Pulpit" except for a sentence where he condemned the ministry. Smith backpedaled before the prospect of the bishop reading that statement in the newspapers. He stammered, "But I had no Particular minister in view that now is, or ever was, and thought it the best way to gain attention by Showing that at whatever the administration might be, if we wished to make any Impression upon them it must be by the weight of Cool and dispassionate measures; and I think it did Good." Smith summarized for the bishop his political principles, "that allegiance and Subordination we owe to the Crown & Empire of Great Britain," and he committed to "declare off" if American policy ever went "beyond that Line." The aim of Philadelphia in the "very fruitless" dispute, he said, was that matters "Should be brought to an Explanation."

Smith argued that it dishonored Britons and defiled the "Protestant Religion" to attempt to rule "so great a Body of men, descended from their own Loins" by "arbitrary or Slavish Principles." He told the bishop, "I have long had even an Enthusiastic Persuasion that this great Continent—is designed by Providence to be the last Seat of Liberty and Knowledge, & I believe no human Purpose, or human Power, shall be able finally to defeat this gracious Intention of Heaven towards this Country." The first Continental Congress then assembling in Philadelphia, he said, met "to devise ways & means of Reconciliation with Great Britain, and an Explanation & Settlement of disputed Points."[28]

Cassandra's First and Cato's Second

The Philadelphia newspaper controversy over independence during the spring of 1776 was a strange entanglement. The height of the debate stretched from early March through late May and frustrated colonial readers with its itinerancy and duplication. The exchange involved multiple authors, erratic insertions in various newspapers, convoluted serial numbering, deliberate addressing of different audiences, and blatant mud-slinging. The principal debaters were James Cannon, writing as "Cassandra," William Smith, writing as "Cato," and Thomas Paine, writing as "The Forester."[29] The disorienting public argument began with the first essay of Cassandra—a piece that would be followed almost three weeks later by his "first" numbered letter to Cato. Cato's *second* letter came out in the *Pennsylvania Packet* on March 11, and his *first* in the same paper a full week later. In the interim, the *Pennsylvania Gazette* published Cato's first two letters in the same issue. Smith frequently published two Cato's letters at a time, and almost every Philadelphia newspaper carried each of his eight full letters. Paine was late to enter the debate: his first Forester's letter did not appear until April 1, in the same issue of the *Pennsylvania Packet* as Smith's fifth number in the Cato series.

The immediate catalyst for Smith's series of letters by "Cato," was the first essay by "Cassandra." James Cannon, writing as "Cassandra," was a friend of Paine's and a tutor in mathematics at the College of Philadelphia. We should not overlook the fact that the stakes of the spicy exchange between Cassandra and Cato were raised by the simple fact that Smith was Cannon's *boss*.

Cannon published his first Cassandra essay, "On Sending Commissioners to treat with the Congress," in the *Pennsylvania Evening Post* on March 2, 1776. Cassandra argued that "Great-Britain has steadily and invariably pursued one course of conduct towards these colonies for the last twelve years, and yet politicians have constantly charged her with fickleness and want of a regular plan." He argued that Britain's "inconsistent consistency" demonstrated "the firmest steadfastness" in a complex imperial scheme to subjugate the colonies. The British government was constantly switching the tones of its addresses, Cassandra postulated, to confuse and disunite the colonies. He said, "The King and his cabal go to work with all the secrecy and vigour they are masters of, and Lord North assumes his new character, which is that of the deceiver of America, and amuser of the nation." The proposals may vary from month to month and year to year, but they were all calculated "for the same purposes." The highest levels of the British government were executing a standard cavalry maneuver and flanking the colonies in a divide-and-conquer strategy. As Cassandra put it,

> The two parties now divide, each going to his own proper business. The King and his secret Cabinet, to arraying the greatest military force they can muster, and dispatching them to butcher us with the utmost expedition; Lord North, and the Parliament, to amuse the nation, and distract and divide the colonies by every hypocritical art in their power.

Cassandra chastised Pennsylvania moderates, "All ye timid, irresolute, terrified and double-faced Whigs, who have, by one means or other, crept into authority, open your mouths wide, and bawl stoutly against every vigorous measure until the Commissioners arrive." The commissioners would "bring pockets well lined with English guineas; patents for places, pensions, and titles in abundance will attend them." Cassandra assured the moderates, "Your palms will be first greased. You are the only men who can complete the Parliamentary plans for raising an American revenue!" He continued to rail against the veiled agenda he ascribed to political moderates, "*COMMON SENSE* says this winter is worth an age; rejoice that it is now past, do all in your power to pass the spring in inactivity, and matters may yet go to your minds." Cassandra was convinced that "*divide & impere*" was the "instruction of every Commissioner," and he predicted that the main task of the negotiators was to "divide and distract as much as possible, until the forces are all arrived," at which point the British delegation would inform the colonists of fresh orders to break off the treaty. In the final paragraph of this first Cassandra essay, Cannon called for a course of action that made temperate colonists bristle. Cannon urged the Continental Congress to preempt the schemes of the British government by ordering the

Continental Army immediately to seize the commissioners upon their arrival.[30]

It is likely that some miscommunication or an editorial decision by John Dunlap of the *Pennsylvania Packet* hampered the initial order of publication for Smith's letters. Whatever the precise cause, the first letter by Cato to appear in the Philadelphia press was "Letter II," a response to Cassandra. Like a modern newspaper columnist, Cato took up his subjects "as they rise out of the times." This allowed him to "leave to my next letter the further defense of our Assembly"—referring to "Letter I" and "Letter III," neither of which had yet surfaced—and provided a sufficient transition away from his original agenda for his serial letters toward a critique of the first essay by Cassandra, which Smith regarded as "highly disgraceful to America and pernicious to society in general."

Cato accused Cassandra of being drunk on "the *cup of independence*" and "too ready to sacrifice the happiness of a great continent to his favourite plan." In a phrase that would be repeated incessantly in the debate, Cato was "bold to declare" that "the true interest of America lies in *reconciliation* with Great-Britain, upon *constitutional principles*."

Cato turned his attention to "the many publications in favour of *independency*, with which our presses have lately groaned." Rather than admitting that they had been unanswered, he subtly turned the silence into a defense of why they had "passed hitherto unnoticed." In times like the present "when public affairs become so interesting," Cato said, "every man becomes a debtor to the community for his opinions, either in speaking or writing." When "an *appeal* was pretended to be made to the COMMON SENSE of this country," he speculated, "perhaps it was thought best" by opponents to the doctrine "to leave the people for a while to the free exercise of that good understanding which they are known to possess." Cato was "confident that nine-tenths of the people of Pennsylvania yet abhor the doctrine." He accused *Common Sense* and its adherents of acting "like true quacks" by "constantly pestering us with their additional doses, till the stomachs of their patients begin wholly to revolt." He, on the other hand, encouraged his audience to "act the part of skillful physicians, and wisely adapt the remedy to the evil."

Cato investigated why "some among us" had been "constantly enlarging their views, and stretching them beyond their first bounds, till at length they have wholly changed their ground" from "the origin of the present controversy." Some men, he said "may have harboured the idea of independence from the beginning of this controversy," but no one was sure whether "this scheme" was supported by any "men of consequence." Cato called *Common Sense* "the first open proposition for independence" that had been "published to the world." The sentiments of the Congress and the Colonies were, he said, "directly repugnant" to the idea of independence, and those who worshipped that "idol" wished, in fact, "to subvert all order among us, and rise on the ruins of their country!"[31]

The Constitutions of the People

Smith had written "Letter I" in response to popular agitation in Philadelphia about the inadequacy of the Pennsylvania Assembly as a legitimate representative body in interregnum America. By choosing the *nom de plume* of Cato, Smith was strategic in his selection of a Roman republican martyr who had been memorialized in Joseph Addison's *Cato, A Tragedy* (1712) and in John Trenchard and Thomas Gordon's celebrated collection of English republican tracts, *Cato's Letters* (1720-1723). This first letter, Smith's second to be published, pitted the Committee of Inspection and Observation of the City and Liberties of Philadelphia versus the Pennsylvania Assembly. Because Smith had been involved as a tempering influence upon Philadelphia committees in 1774, it was natural that his attention would be grabbed by the issue again in 1776. Smith had not begun writing that spring to register his direct dissent to independence, but rather to take issue with the function of "extra-legal" committees in Pennsylvania politics. The provost recognized that Pennsylvania could stave off the independence movement only by squelching the popular enthusiasm embodied in the local committees.

Cato worried that the Pennsylvanians had "too quietly yielded to a *few* who have been claiming one *power* after another" and "prostituting the cry of public necessity to cloak an ambition which needs as much to be checked in the *lowest* as the *highest*."
This group had "now the astonishing boldness to aim at a total destruction of our chartered constitution, and seizing into their own hands our whole domestic police, with legislative as well as executive authority."

Cato identified "this most ruinous design" and warned that the schemers had "grievously wounded" the "MAJESTY OF THE PEOPLE OF PENNSYLVANIA" in "the persons of their legal Representatives" through "repeated attempts to intimidate them in the discharge of the great trust committed to them by the voice of their country." Cato said that "individuals of our Committees" had, "by the bait of power thrown out to them," been "led out of their line, to interfere in matters foreign to their appointment." The people of Pennsylvania had "given their sanction" to existing policies "by reelecting the same men, since the contest with England had advanced into open war."

Cato waxed about the "great privilege which we enjoy, of giving our free unbiased voice annually in the choice of an Assembly, who, from that moment, by charter, become a constitutional body, vested with the authority of the people, and can meet when they please, and sit as long as they judge necessary." He asked, "Would any wise people, enjoying such a constitution, ever think of destroying it with their own hands; or does any other colony, whose Assemblies can exercise their authority, ever think of committing the conduct of affairs to Conventions?"

Cato was making an argument about the locus of "the people" in revolutionary Pennsylvania, and he focused on elevating the Pennsylvania Assembly and undercutting the Philadelphia Committee of Inspection. Even if the Assembly were "really chargeable with any culpable neglect of duty," the "present Committee, who are so loud in their clamours against them," could not legally "step into their seats." The "Committee of *Inspection*" was not chosen for the purpose they were assuming, and "few people gave themselves any concern" about their election, since the hundred members "should be thankfully indulged with the office" if they were willing to "take the trouble." Now the committee was aspiring, said Cato, "at the powers vested in an Assembly, fairly and constitutionally elected" by a larger number of votes than had been cast in the by-election for committeemen. Cato warned that "whatever may be pretended about the necessity of a Convention," such a body would vest all the powers of government "in the hands of a few men, who consider themselves as leaders in the city of Philadelphia," effectually excluding the voice of "the province in general."[32]

Sometimes the private correspondence of colonists added another dimension to the public exchange. For example, the day after the first two letters of "Cato" surfaced in the *Pennsylvania Gazette*, William Smith wrote a letter to London addressed to Juliana Penn, the widow of former proprietary governor Thomas Penn. Smith apologized for his epistolary negligence, "The times are such that I have long declined all Correspondence in England." He promised to renew his correspondence "when I see what Situation Affairs are like to be in, upon the Arrival of the Commissioners expected from England." Smith prayed that the commissioners would offer "proper Terms" and that "Reconciliation may yet take Place," but he acknowledged the likelihood of unfavorable terms, in which case "The Mouths of the most zealous Friends of Peace will then be shut."[33]

James Cannon steamed as he read Smith's first two letters, and he spent most of two weeks writing a reply. Cassandra blasted Cato from the first sentence of his second letter, published in the *Pennsylvania Packet* on March 25. In the first of many *ad hominem* attacks and low-blows, Cassandra made it clear that he knew the real identity of Cato. Cassandra wondered if Cato "had forgotten the fatal 7th of Nov. 1774" when "all your ambitious projects" had been "blasted" by a public vote in favor of secret ballot voting and separating the populist Philadelphia City committee from the aristocratic Philadelphia County committee. Smith had preferred to select committee men "by holding up of hands" because voters could be intimidated or bribed "to serve the purposes of your party." Now that the people of Philadelphia had been protected from the "undue influence" and "electioneering attempts" of Pennsylvania aristocrats, Cato's "masterly pen is called forth into the field of political controversy." A sardonic Cassandra congratulated Cato that only "a few dashes" of his pen had overset our Committee of Inspection, demolished the whole tribe of patriotic scribblers in Newspapers, and hid *Common Sense* in the dirt, taken a catalogue of all the whigs and tories in the province, converted 36 Commissioners, about to be sent over to insult us with terms no one can accept, into Ambassadors of peace, and poor Cassandra into an enthusiast, madman, barbarian and drunken independent.

Cassandra lamented the "wretched" lot of any Whig who fell "into the hands of this fiery defender of ministerial stratagems." Cato, rather than defending "the MAJESTY OF THE PEOPLE OF PENNSYLVANIA" was, in fact, provoking it "by the bold flourishes of a pen which pays no respect to truth." Cassandra criticized Cato's argument that Pennsylvania had no reason to alter its constitution. Cassandra said,

> This assertion might pass for truth on the coast of Labrador, or in the deserts of Siberia; but the People of *Pennsylvania* must have drunk deep of the waters of oblivion, and laid aside all pretensions to recollection, before they can consider such assertions in any other light than insults on their understanding.

According to Cassandra, Cato could not point to a "single measure" of colonial resistance "that can be pursued in the line of our charter constitution." Cassandra listed every genuinely patriotic act of the Pennsylvania Assembly and argued that they were all strictly *illegal*. The assembly could not legislate without the approval of "the King's Representative," the Pennsylvania Governor, who would never "give his sanction to our opposition," and, therefore, confining political legitimacy to the assembly effectively restricted all political resistance in the colony. Cassandra concluded, "The interest of the Governor, and not of the people, is plainly Cato's."

Cassandra reiterated his argument against receiving the British Commissioners. He could find no historical precedent or legal principle that led him to welcome "Ambassadors of Peace attended with Acts of Parliament to confiscate, and Royal Proclamations to divide, the property of those they are to treat with, and backed by immense armies of Ministerial Cut-throats, to enforce their demands." He challenged Cato to "supply the public with a few instances" of this situation from the storehouse of his "great reading." Cassandra was "greatly concerned for our virtue, lest we should be cajoled, deceived, and corrupted. Cato is not so. Corruption may be more familiar to Cato, which will fully account for our difference in sentiment."

Cassandra promised to "spare the Printer much of my intended lucubrations" if Cato would simply change his pen name to one "correspondent with your designs," such as "Iago" or "Sempronius."[34] Cassandra claimed to know "no guide but reason and the love of mankind," and, turning one of his opponent's attacks back against him, testified that the "cup out of which Cassandra had drunk was never employed to offer libations at the altar of Royal despotism or Proprietary influence." Cassandra, unlike his nemesis, "neither wishes nor expects to be Prime Minister to any future *would-be* King of Pennsylvania."

Cassandra challenged Cato to "lay aside groundless declamation" and "speak a language which facts will support." He continued, "The people of Pennsylvania, I trust, will ever have the good sense to prefer COMMON SENSE to the appeals of any government tool." Cato was among a group of "men who sell their consciences for the prospect of future advantages." He urged Cato to "Give your name to the public, and I will stand corrected if I have missed my object." Cassandra snidely closed his letter by expressing his support for "the sentiments of the celebrated Dr. Smith," who had said in his May 1775 address to the graduates of the college, "'The glory of every country is its LIBERTY, its INDEPENDENCY, and its Improvements in Commerce, Arts and Religion.'" Cassandra concluded that "the sentiments of this Gentleman are as much esteemed among those of your party as the sentiments of Cato."[35]

Cato versus Conventions and Common Sense

Cato's third letter demonstrated that he was beginning to move on from his original subject matter. To his audience, "The People of Pennsylvania," he said, "When I sat down to address you, a resolve or vote of our *Committee of Inspection* for calling a CONVENTION had alarmed many good friends of the province, on account of our Charter-constitution." When the committee began to agitate for a formal convention, Smith rightly concluded that they were attempting to declare the existing colonial charter invalid. Smith responded by examining "the right of the Committee to convene such a body, the necessity of their being convened, the powers which they might assume, and the confusion such a measure must produce." The Committee of Inspection and the Pennsylvania Assembly had reached a compromise in late March that appeared to address the committee's concerns about equal representation while preserving the assembly's political stature in the province. The two bodies agreed to hold a by-election on May 1 to increase the number of representatives in the Pennsylvania Assembly—specifically enlarging the delegations from Philadelphia and the back counties in order to rebalance what had become a cartel of the affluent collar counties.

Because the Philadelphia committee had agreed to postpone its call for a Convention, Cato would "likewise for the present forebear sending to the press everything which I had prepared in vindication of our injured Representatives, except so far as relates to INDEPENDENCY." Cato would handle independency "at some length" because he found "the chief resentment leveled against" the Assembly was "on account of their instructions to their Delegates." These instructions were "in the eyes of some men," an "insurmountable barrier in the way of their destructive purposes." Without proof, said Cato, of "the clear sense of an uncorrupted majority of the good people of this province," the Assembly "can neither consent to any change of our constitution, or to make the least transfer of our allegiance." The "full proof" of this sentiment "ought to be more pure than what can flow through the foul pages of interested writers or strangers intermeddling in our affairs, and avowedly pressing their republican schemes upon us, at the risk of all we hold valuable."

Cato took to task "A Lover of Order" who had written in the *Pennsylvania Evening Post* of March 9, that the First Continental Congress "was nothing but the ECHO OF *Committees* and *Conventions*. In the present important question concerning INDEPENDENCE, the Congress SHOULD *only*, as in the former case, ECHO back the sentiments of the people." The assumption of "A Lover of Order," as Cato pointed out, was that "the sentiments of the people" were best expressed by "Committees and Conventions." Cato replied, "And thus we may be ECHOED and RE-ECHOED out of our liberties, our property, our happiness, and plunged deeper and deeper into all the growing horrors of war and bloodshed, without ever being consulted." Cato heartily disagreed that committees were accurate expressions of the people's voice: "For I insist upon it, that no Committees were ever entrusted with any authority to speak the sense of the People of Pennsylvania on this question." He reiterated that low voter turnouts for committee elections weakened the legitimacy of their office, and he found an extreme example to prove his point, "I know some counties where the whole Committee was named by six or seven voices only."

The debate over the representative legitimacy of the Philadelphia Committee of Inspection and the Pennsylvania Assembly—a focal point in my upcoming argument in Chapter Eleven—was a landmark in the groundswell toward independence. But Cato began halfway through his third letter to shift his attention away from the particulars of local politics and toward more continent-wide concerns—specifically a frontal assault on *Common Sense* and independence.

In this third letter, Cato recommended the "just published" *Plain Truth* to his readers' "perusal, as containing many judicious remarks upon the mischievous tenets and palpable absurdities held forth in the pamphlet so falsely called *Common Sense*." Cato restated again in his third letter the "*political creed*" that governed his actions (for any who missed it in his second): "That the true interest of America lies in *reconciliation* with Great-Britain, upon Constitutional Principles, and that I wish it upon none else." He objected to the "pernicious, though specious plans which are every day published in our news-papers and pamphlets."

Cato admitted that Britain's "late conduct towards us" resembled "a cruel Step-dame, and not of a fostering Parent," but, he said, that conduct did not give him the right, as an American, to "quarrel with the benefits I may reap from a connection with her." Without mentioning any specifics or context, Cato threw in a controversial assertion into the midst of his argument. In a statement that Paine would shred in the next month, Cato said that "a few weeks ago" some "gleams of reconciliation began first to break in upon us."

Once again, the question of timing was central to Cato's argument. To declare independence "as our own act, before it appears clearly to the world to have been forced upon us by the cruel hand of the Parent-state," was tantamount to admitting that the Americans were "a faithless people in the sight of all mankind." He also implied that a preemptive decision for independence was being driven by the lower economic classes. In a swipe at Paine and other immigrants, Cato pointed to the likelihood of failure for independence and noted, to "see America reduced to such a situation may be the choice of adventurers who have nothing to lose."

Cato ended his third letter with a direct attack on *Common Sense*. According to Cato, *Common Sense* had asserted "that a confederacy of the Colonies into one great *republic* is preferable to *Kingly government*, which is the appointment of the *Devil*, or at least reprobated by GOD." *Common Sense* had "boldly asserted" but not "fully proved" that "the [English] nation itself is but one mass of corruption, having at its head a *Royal Brute*, a hardened *Pharaoh*, delighting in blood." In a statement of terrific significance for our understanding of the revolutionary era, Cato declared that the doctrines of *Common Sense* "contradict everything which we have hitherto been taught to believe respecting government."

Smith was far from finished with his project. In a teaser at the end of the third letter, Cato hoped that his "dear countrymen" would keep "one ear open to hear what answer may be given in my future letters."[36] He planned to keep writing for as long as possible, because he knew that his political agenda would only be benefited by stalled deliberations. And he had a lot to talk about, including the actual identity of his antagonists. As we saw in the case of Robert Bell and his "By an Englishman" innuendo, eighteenth century readers and publicists were consumed with discerning the underlying identities, connections, and interests of pseudonymous writers. In the Philadelphia newspaper debate of March through May, Cassandra had initiated the authorial exposé by alluding to Smith's authorship of the pieces by Cato. Smith returned the favor in his fourth Cato's letter.

This fourth letter began with a pun on Hamlet's soliloquy: "To write, or not to write; that is the question." Cato's purpose in including the soliloquy was to identify "the authors" of "what is called *Common Sense*." An excerpt from the soliloquy:

> With a *dry quill?* Who would endure this Pain,
> This foul discharge of wrath from Adam's sons
> Marshall'd in dread array, both old and Young,
> Their pop-guns here, and there their heavy Cannon,
> Our labor'd pages deem'd not worth a Rush

In case the references were lost on some of his readers, Smith included a footnote after "Pain": "Some writers, in imitation of our ancestors, yet spell this word Payne." Smith was exposing Thomas Paine, Samuel Adams, John Adams, Christopher Marshall, Thomas Young, James Cannon, and Benjamin Rush as the men whom he believed had collaborated on *Common Sense*. The soliloquy, said Cato, "was really put into my hands by a friend." The "*authors*, or if I must say *author*" had been allowed "full time" by "the sale of his pamphlet, to reap the fruits of his labours, and gratify that avidity with which many are apt to devour doctrines that are out of the common way—bold, marvelous and flattering." The lack of a response to *Common Sense*, said Cato, "was intended as a compliment to the public—to give them time to gaze with their own eyes, and reason with their own faculties, upon this extraordinary appearance," but "the author's vanity has construed wholly in his own favour." If *Common Sense* lived up to its name, said Cato, it would be "invulnerable" and "every attack upon it will but add to the author's triumph," but "if it should be proved, in any instances, to be *Non-Sense*, millions will be interested in the discovery; and to them I appeal."

Cato conceived the question of independence "of the greatest importance that ever came before us," and he stressed that the question was "not yet decided" and "ought therefore to be fully discussed." Cato held that the question of independence "cannot but employ the most serious thoughts of men whose *all* is at stake in the resolution of them." Americans deserved to have their questions "answered to the general satisfaction, before we are launched out into a tempestuous ocean, of which we know not the other shore."

Cato positioned himself as an arbiter of information whose main task was to balance the scales of the debate. Cato pointed out that "one side of a great question has been held up to us. He continued,

> We are told that it can never be our interest to have any future connection with Great-Britain, and are pressed immediately to declare our total separation, for now is the time—*and the time has found us*. Could it be expected that all America would instantly take a leap in the dark, or that any who had not a predilection for the doctrine, or were capable of reasoning upon it, would swallow it in the gross, without wishing to hear the arguments on the other side?

Cato's defenders invariably fell back upon this argument as ample justification for plodding deliberation and exhaustive argumentation. But while Cato demanded that his side of the question be heard in its entirety, he had no patience for the questions posed to him by others. Referring to two sets of "Queries" directed toward him in the *Pennsylvania Evening Post*, Cato claimed that he could not possibly answer the endless "silly *queries* and daily scribble" of his opponents.

In his fourth letter, Cato specifically attacked the position held by *Common Sense* that a declaration of independence was a necessary step toward "procuring foreign assistance, especially that of France." Cato raised a weighty question for the Francophobic Protestant majority in America, "Under whose wing is Pennsylvania to fall—that of the most *Catholic* or most *Christian* King?" In fact, said Cato, "The matter of foreign assistance is a mere decoy." What the Independents really desired was "to shut the door against all future reconciliation" by the "precipitate step" of "an immediate *declaration* of independence."

Cato took exception to almost every assumption in *Common Sense*. He objected to being told that his entire worldview was "mere prejudice," and he bristled at the implication

> that we must divest ourselves of every opinion in which we have been educated, in order to digest his pure doctrine; and throw down what our fathers and we have been building up for ages, to make room for his *visionary fabric*—I say to be told this, is only insult instead of argument; and can be tolerated by none but those who are so far inflamed or interested, that separation from Great-Britain at any risk is their choice, rather than reconciliation, upon whatever terms.

Cato could not "understand what is meant by a *declaration of independence*, unless it is to be drawn up in the form of a solemn *abjuration* of Great-Britain, as a nation with which we can never more be connected; and this seems the doctrine of the author of *Common Sense*."

Cato believed that *Common Sense* had "made but few converts to this part of his scheme; for who knows to what vicissitudes of fortune we may yet be subjected?" In fact, said Cato, "We have already declared ourselves *independent*, as to all useful purposes, by *resisting* our oppressors, upon our own foundation." He closed his letter in a foreboding tone about the implications of leaving the shelter of the British monarchial system: "What may be the consequences of another form we cannot pronounce with certainty; but this we know, that it is a road we have not traveled, and may be worse than it is described."[37]

Cassandra's Final Parry and Thrust

Cassandra argued in his third essay from early April that the subject of independence "demands a clear, plain, full, rational and manly discussion, and it ought to have it." He had put all of his labor into the question, because "*Liberty* or *Slavery* is *now* the question." The task of the writers on both sides of the question, said Cassandra, was to "fairly discover to the inhabitants of these Colonies on which side Liberty has erected her banner," and then to allow the colonist to "choose liberty tho' accompanied with war, or Slavery attended by peace." Such loaded constructions were, in Cannon's "Cassandra" essays, interspersed among perceptive observations. For example, Cassandra pointed out, "The present contest is a contest of constitutions, and the war a war of legislatures." The war had initially been "between the British Parliament and the colonies' Assemblies," but it had become "a war between the people of Great-Britain and the people of America."

In the "contest of constitutions," the parliament had "evidently won the field," but the Americans had "in no one instance been able to call forth the strength of our legislatures to oppose, nay, we have constantly had them against us ready to join the foe." Cassandra prodded, "how happens this, Cato?" and answered for himself, "It is because our legislatures are dependent on our very enemy and theirs is independent of us." The colonies' "constitutional connection with Britain," argued Cassandra, "gives her so prodigious an advantage over us, that if we had strictly adhered to our chartered constitutions, we would have been enslaved before this time. And it will ever be so, as long as we are dependent." Cassandra hoped "in a short time to prove every assertion of *Common Sense*," and he wished that "every position of Cato was equally consistent with Common Sense."[38]

Cannon published his final Cassandra essay at the end of April. Since Paine had entered the debate, Cannon's contributions were pushed to the edge of the controversy, and he knew it was time for him to make an exit. He used his final Cassandra essay to review his earlier points and to renew his call for a concrete plan for reconciliation from Cato. Cassandra had "engaged in the present political controversy with a design to be of service to my country." He had opposed a "reunion" with Britain on the grounds that "the *present* state of the British constitution" did not give the Americans "*security* for the future enjoyment of our *rights* and *liberties*." He was arguing for a contextual constitution for the colonies; it was a matter "of small consequence to America" if "God has granted a King to the people of Britain or not" or whether the British Constitution "answers excellently to the inhabitants of that island." Dependence upon "that excellent form of government" was "big with *slavery* and *ruin* to America," he said, and thus every other theoretical consideration was irrelevant.

Cassandra insinuated that Cato was holding his "countrymen in suspence until the day of salvation is past," and he demanded that Cato "prove that Great-Britain can offer *any plan* of *constitutional dependence* which will not leave the future enjoyment of our liberties to *hope, hazard, and uncertainty*, as the Forester has finely expressed it."
He also enjoined Cato to further prove that even "if she *can* there is a probability she *will*." He added further, "If the one is impossible, or the other *altogether* improbable, [you] yourself must acknowledge it is *time to part*."

Cassandra confessed that his objections were "radical, reaching to the root of the evil." The British Constitution in America was sick and infected, and "To skin over the wound would be madness." Liberty "will never flourish" in a political system where officers of the government were nominated by someone disconnected from the people. Cato needed "either to point out a complete remedy" for the defects in the colonies' constitutional relationship with Britain and "prove it more easily attainable than a complete delivery by a Declaration of Independence," or he needed "to give no further opposition to the measure."[39]

The opening exchange between Cassandra and Cato helped to set the stage for the main intertextual event of the independence controversy: the gloveless verbal brawl between Cato and The Forester, William Smith and Thomas Paine. But the themes of the early debate between Cassandra and Cato carried significance in their own right. As we shall see in the next chapter, the contention between the Philadelphia Committee and the Pennsylvania Assembly proved to be far more than a semantic spat. At stake was the very definition of the American people.

Part Four
THE BATTLEGROUND OF PRINT

Cato on Alliances and Government

The engagement of William Smith and Thomas Paine pitted two of the most formidable arguers in the colonies against one another in a gladiatorial showdown. This is no exaggeration: a large number of colonial readers waited upon the outcome of the debate between Cato and the Forester before deciding finally to support reconciliation or independence. Like two armies watching their champions battle to the death as a representation of full battle, the American colonists waited to see which giant, Cato or The Forester, would be the first to fall.

Cato tipped his political hand in a brief letter to "Tiberius" in the *Pennsylvania Ledger* on March 23. "The question," said Cato, "is whether the liberty and happiness of America can be best secured by a constitutional reconciliation with Great Britain or by a total separation from it?" He continued in the third person, "Cato is willing to be judged by his countrymen, when the whole of his arguments shall be submitted to them. Whatever may be insinuated before that time he will scarce think worthy of regard." William Smith intended to write about undisclosed topics for an undisclosed amount of time—and for undisclosed purposes. Writing as Cato, he thought his meaning was easily "picked out," and he claimed to despise "a *war* about *words*."[40]

One week after the intercalary letter to "Tiberius," the fifth of Cato's letters "To the People of Pennsylvania" began with a full exposition of a point he had initially brought up in his fourth letter. Cato again cautioned his readers against "the dangerous proposition held up to us by the author of *Common Sense*, for having recourse to foreign assistance, and mixing the virtuous cause of these Colonies with the ambitious views of France and Spain." History attested, said Cato, to the ease by which any people had recourse to such "an expedient of this kind" that they ended up "having their *allies* at last for their MASTERS." Cato had by this fifth letter focused his entire attention on "answering" *Common Sense*. That pamphlet, argued Cato, had not made a sufficient distinction between commercial and military protection and, therefore, opened the door to "the unholy violence of mercenary soldiery."

Cato did not know at the time that he was setting a trap for himself by attempting to scare his readers into moderation with the threat of rapacious mercenaries. He wrote in direct opposition to evidence that would soon surface in America, "The administration of Great-Britain itself, daring as they seem to be, have not yet dared to recur to the desperate measure of calling in foreign aid," and he added accurately that whichever "side, Great-Britain or America, shall first call in foreign assistance, will but force the other into the same desperate measure." Cato assumed that his ominous message applied only to rash American actions, and he therefore slathered on bathetic imagery about the ravishment of wives and daughters. All sorts of evil consequences would be the Americans' fault if they pursued foreign alliances and declared independence. Cato said, "But, I repeat it once more—by the former measure of calling in foreigners to decide our quarrels, we shall bleed, not in a few parts only, but at every pore; and the present generation will not probably see the end of the contest."

Conscious that his writing might be perceived as over-the-top, Cato paused, "Let it not be said that I am here drawing a horrible picture to frighten this country into an absolute submission to Great-Britain." He persevered in his belief that the Americans could not be forced "on our present plan of resistance," into either "submission or reconciliation, but upon such terms as the united wisdom of the colonies shall deem safe and honourable."

Cato was "well persuaded" that the idea in *Common Sense* of foreign alliances was "not yet adopted by many persons of much consideration in this country, much less by any Public Bodies." In general, Cato considered *Common Sense* as something "thrown out to collect the sentiments of America upon it." He considered the pamphlet—even at the end of March—to be advocating "a dangerous as well as unreasonable question at this time," and he wished that "it had not been brought before the public." But, since independence was now a public question, "it ought now to be fairly discussed."

Cato pretended to be open to independence, *eventually*. He balked at the presentation of *Common Sense* as he explained,

> When we shall be generally convinced, by better arguments than declamation, and the abuse of things venerable and ancient, that future connection with Great-Britain, is neither possible nor safe; then we shall be fully *united* and prepared, at every risk, to pursue whatever measures the sense of the community, fairly collected, shall think necessary to adopt. But even then, before we launch forth, many domestic concerns are to be adjusted.

William Smith, like the earnest moderate John Dickinson, placed very strict conditions upon his acceptance of independence. Smith likewise wanted every event to be fully settled and in the proper order before even considering independence. Unlike Dickinson, however, Smith's commitment to exhaustive detail barely concealed his true intentions. Cato started to list out question after question about confederation, constitutions, territorial disputes, treaties, and representation, but he displayed no interest in answering them. The uncertainty created by asking them was sufficient to accomplish his purposes. And he promised more: "I might propose more questions of this kind; and when the necessity comes, they will rise thick enough upon us." Cato was sure that "the author of *Common Sense*, who labours to prove that the *necessity is already come*," would soon be scuttled by the general public. With this, Cato claimed that he had "dispatched" the "main argument for Independence" in *Common Sense*, the question of the propriety of foreign alliances.

In the second half of his fifth letter, Cato moved on from the issue of alliances to the issue of government. Cato revolted at the idea that the early sections of *Common Sense* had "leveled the English constitution in the dust, together with all our American constitutions, which are formed on similar models" and had "thereby *led us past the Rubicon*." The first sections of the origins of government and monarchy, said Cato, "appear to be the strangest medley of inconsistencies and contradictions, which were perhaps ever offered to the *Common Sense* of any people." Cato then zeroed in upon the general arguments about society and government in Paine's pamphlet. Cato could agree that government was unnecessary "if all men were perfectly virtuous and followed the pure dictates of right reason," in which case he would have complimented the author on "clothing an old truth in a spruce metaphor." But Cato disputed *Common Sense*'s assertion that "monarchies were any more founded on the ruins of paradise than Republics." The Reverend Doctor Smith then launched into an extensive biblical commentary to show that monarchy did not appear in the scriptures until much later. *Common Sense*, joked Cato, paid "but a poor compliment to Satan's cunning," since the devil "was a long while in hammering" out monarchy, even though one would assume that, "being a King himself from the beginning," Satan should have "hit upon it sooner" as his most prosperous invention for promoting idolatry.

Cato pointed out that *Common Sense* refuted its "own first doctrine" and demonstrated that "instead of *Palaces for Kings*, State Houses for WHOLE COLONIES were built on the ruins of Paradise; nay more, that these ruins, in the case of the Jews, were near three thousand years tossed up and down into various forms, before they were converted into *Royal Edifices*!"

Cato, enraptured by his own wit, stumbled at the finish line of his fifth letter. After poking holes in the exegetical technique of Common Sense, he closed with a paragraph on the only "modern" king that he had found in scripture to be "particularly rejected by Heaven," the "Monsieur, the King of France." Through a loosely strung association of linguistic resemblances among Hebrew, English, and French, Cato recast the biblical prophecy against Mount Seir as a censure of the French king. Smith was trying to illustrate in a facetious manner the lack of interpretive rigor in *Common Sense*, but his poor comedic execution made Cato come across as a court jester.[41]

In his sixth letter, published on April 8, Cato continued down the path of scriptural refutation to show that monarchy was "officially" sanctioned by God in Israel. Cato called the author of *Common Sense* "a perverter of scripture and of the fundamental principles of mixed government." Cato was, by early April, the target of vociferous criticism, and he began in his sixth letter to expend more effort in his own personal defense. His critics had asked him to arrive at his point, and he called for their patience. He was pursuing his "siege" of the "citadel" of the independence movement in his "own way," namely by trying to "sap or overturn your foundations" after which "the aerial part of your fabric would tumble to the ground." Cato here made his political objective explicit: "a safe return to a connection with our ancient friends and kindred, accompanied with all the advantages we have formerly experienced, and perhaps more." He trusted that his plan was "yet practicable," but even if it "should prove otherwise, we can lose nothing by the exercise of deliberation and wisdom in the meanwhile."[42]

The Forester Enters the Fray

Paine launched into his first Forester's Letter, published on April 1 in the *Pennsylvania Packet*, with a blunt aphorism that presaged the famous opening of the *American Crisis, No. 1*. "To be *nobly wrong* is more manly than to be *meanly right*," he said, continuing, "Only let the error be disinterested—let it wear, *not the mask*, but the *mark* of principle and 'tis pardonable." The Forester loathed the first four letters that had "appeared under the specious name of Cato," and he clarified the authenticity of his emotions in a biblical paraphrase, "And if the sincerity of disdain can add a cubit to the stature of my sentiments, it shall not be wanting."

He saw no commonality between the pretentious writer and the Roman martyr, but The Forester contented himself "with contemplating the similarity of their exits." While each of Cato's four letters promised another, the writer kept "wide of the question" and preferred to "loiter in the suburbs of the dispute." Cato would not show "the numerous blessings of reconciliation" or prove them "*practicable*," because "The moment he explains his terms of reconciliation the typographical Cato dies." Cato's "general and unexplained expressions" were intended to "allure the Public" but would have the same success attempting "to catch lions in a mousetrap." The Forester stressed, "It is now a mere bug-bear to talk of *reconciliation* on *constitutional principles* unless the terms of the first be produced and the sense of the other be defined; and unless he does this he does nothing."

The Forester observed that Cato's letters were addressed "'To the People of Pennsylvania' only: In almost any other writer this might have passed unnoticed, but we know it hath mischief in its meaning."

The "great business of the day is Continental," and Cato, asserted The Forester, was endeavoring to "withdraw this province from the glorious union by which all are supported."

Cato's first letter, he wrote, was "insipid in its style, language, and substance" and "crowded with personal and private innuendoes." Cato was fond of "impressing us with the importance of our *'chartered constitution,'*" said The Forester, but, "Alas! We are not now, Sir, to be led away by the jingle of a phrase." If the colonies had "framed our conduct by the contents of the present charters, we had, ere now, been in a state of helpless misery." Alluding to a North Carolina loyalist general killed in the Battle of Moore's Creek Bridge, The Forester asserted that the Pennsylvania charter was "transparent with holes; pierced with as many deadly wounds as the body of McCleod." In a vicious exposé of Cato's authorial identity, The Forester said, "Disturb not its remains, Cato, nor dishonour it with another funeral oration." Paine was trying to force Smith to commit to a particular partisan stance: "Who submitted, Cato? we Whigs, or we Tories? Until you clear up this, Sir, you must content yourself with being ranked among the rankest of the writing Tories."

The Forester said the Prohibitory Bill clearly proved that the expected commissioners would not be "*Ambassadors of Peace*, but the distributors of pardons, mischief and insult" on a mission of "down right bribery and corruption." Because the present war was carried out "under the authority of the whole legislative power united," even if the King of England came to America in person, "he could not ratify the terms or conditions of a reconciliation," because the barriers to negotiation were "not proclamations but acts of parliament," and the king could not "stipulate for the repeal of any *acts* of parliament."

Though Cato had professed that the Americans were contending "against an arbitrary Ministry for the rights of Englishmen," The Forester countered, "No, Cato, we are *now*, contending against an arbitrary King to get clear of his tyranny. While the dispute rested in words only, it might be called 'contending with the Ministry,' but since it is broken out into open war, it is high time to have done with such silly and water-gruel definitions." It was in Cato's "interest to dress up the sceptred savage in the mildest colors" because "Cato's patent for a large tract of land is yet unsigned." The Forester closed his first letter by noting that he had seen "thy soliloquy and despise it. Remember, thou hast thrown me the glove, Cato, and either thee or I must tire."[43]

Identity, Causality, and Sentiment

Paine prefaced his second Forester's letter, published on April 10 in both the *Pennsylvania Journal* and the *Pennsylvania Gazette*, with a statement on the question of "How far personality is concerned in any political debate." The Forester clarified that he was concerned with "measures, and not men," but "the political characters, political dependencies, and political Connections of men, being of a public nature" necessitated some acquaintance with a person's *public* character. "We have already too much secrecy in some things, and too little in others;—were men more known, and measures more concealed, we should have fewer hypocrites and more security."

The Forester clarified "the chief design of these letters" was "to detect and expose the falsehoods and fallacious reasonings of Cato," of whom The Forester said that "a grosser violation of truth and reason scarcely ever came from the pen of a writer." Referring to Cato's commentary on *Common Sense*, The Forester said that Cato's "imposed" interpretations had "never existed in the mind of the author, nor can they be drawn from the words themselves." Rather than supporting his assertions with definitive facts, The Forester observed that Cato had flown from his argument with "plump declarations" of a consensus against *Common Sense*.

Cato had described the pro-independence publicists as political quacks who manipulated the colonists with unnecessary "additional doses" of their medicinal propaganda. The Forester turned Cato's accusation of quackery back against his opponent. The Forester testified that the author of *Common Sense* hadn't "published a syllable on the subject from that time, till after the appearance of Cato's fourth letter." This statement, of course, wasn't precisely true, but Paine was prone to rationalizing technicalities when it served his larger argument. He certainly hadn't published *much* in that time period, and whatever he did publish may have been indirect or collaborative. Nonetheless, Cato had no room to talk, since he was busy publishing "two letters in a week" and even stooped to place "them both in one paper. Cato here, Cato there, look where you will." Cato's publication strategy was akin to his prose style, said the Forester: "Cato's manner of writing has as much order in it as the motion of a squirrel."

The Forester again turned Cato's argument against him. Cato had claimed that independence was "directly repugnant to every declaration of that respectable body," the Continental Congress. The Forester pointed to "an extract from the Resolves of the Congress, printed in the front of the Oration delivered by Dr. Smith, in honor of that brave man General Montgomery." Smith had been appointed to compose and deliver the speech, said the Forester with a deliberate double entendre, "in the *execution* of which, the orator exclaimed loudly against the doctrine of independence," and when the customary motion of thanks was made in the Congress, "the motion was rejected from every part of the house and thrown out without a division."

The Forester would not let pass Cato's standard argument that America had flourished because of its connection with Great Britain.

"All writers on Cato's side have used the same argument, and conceived themselves invincible," said The Forester. He continued, "nevertheless, a single expression, properly placed, dissolves the charm, for the cheat lies in putting the *consequence* for the *cause*." If the Americans had "not *flourished*, the *connection* had never *existed*, or never been *regarded*," argued the Forester, "and this is fully proved by the neglect shewn to the first settlers, who had every difficulty to struggle with, unnoticed and unassisted by the British Court."

This causal argument marked Paine's return to several themes from *Common Sense*. All of Cato's best arguments, he said, "now amount to nothing. They are out of date. Times and things are altered." The Forester continued, "The true character of the King was but little known among the body of the people a year ago;—willing to believe him good, they fondly called him so, but have since found, that Cato's Royal Sovereign, is a Royal Savage."

The Forester excoriated Cato for his lack of feeling. "But the cold and creeping soul of Cato is a stranger to the manly powers of sympathetic sorrow. He *moves* not, nor *can* he move in so pure an element." Cato had grown so "Accustomed to lick the hand that has made him visible, and to breathe the gross atmosphere of servile and sordid dependence," that "his soul would *now* starve on virtue, and suffocate in the clear region of disinterested friendship." The Forester said,
Paine said, "We feel the same kind of undescribed anger at her conduct, as we would at the sight of an animal devouring its young: and this particular species of anger is not generated in the transitory temper of the man, but in the chaste and undefiled womb of nature."

In a final blow against the lack of sentiment in Cato's letters, The Forester crushed his adversary's comparison of the imperial controversy to a lovers' quarrel as "one of the most unnatural and distorted similes that can be drawn." The Forester asked,

> What comparison is there between the soft murmurs of an heart mourning in secret, and the loud horrors of war—between the silent tears of pensive sorrow, and rivers of wasted blood—between the *sweet* strife of affection, and the *bitter* strife of death—between the curable calamities of pettish lovers, and the sad sight of a thousand slain! "Get thee behind me," Cato, for thou hast not the feelings of a man.

And this was ultimately Paine's most scorching critique of Cato, that "many of his expressions" discovered "all that calm command over the passions and feelings which always distinguishes the man who hath expelled them from his heart."[44] Cato, argued The Forester in his third letter, had "not virtue enough to be angry."

At the Point of the Pen

The third Forester's letter, published initially in the *Pennsylvania Packet* on April 22, swept through Cato's fourth through seventh pieces, which Paine dismissed with "little trouble and less formality" because "they contain but little matter." The Forester pointed to Cato's "punning soliloquy" in his fourth letter and he scoffed, "Cato's title to soliloquies is indisputable; because no man cares for his company." The Forester followed that derisive sentence with a curious footnote that revealed Paine's democratic assumptions about his newspaper-reading audience. "As this piece may possibly fall into the hands of some who are not acquainted with the word 'soliloquy,'" said Paine, "for their information the sense of it is given, viz. 'talking to one's self.'"

The Forester continued his harried critique of Cato's prolix corpus, noting that Cato's fourth and fifth letters were "constructed on a false meaning uncivilly imposed on a passage quoted from *Common Sense*." Smith had construed Paine's call for "foreign assistance" as an invitation for a pan-European invasion. The Forester reiterated that America had a "natural right" to "erect a government of our own, *independent of all the world*." He clarified, "The assistance which We hope for from France is not armies, (we want them not) but arms and ammunition," and he reminded his readers that France had already supplied Pennsylvania with "near two hundred tons" of saltpeter and gunpowder and a large supply of muskets. Paine stressed, "At *this time* it is not only illiberal, but impolitic, and perhaps dangerous, to be pouring forth such torrents of abuse, as [Cato's] fourth and fifth letters contain, against the only power that in articles of defense hath supplied our hasty wants."

The Forester was "fully persuaded that Cato does not believe one half of what himself has written," but that "he nevertheless takes amazing pains to *frighten* his readers into a belief of the whole." Cato had, in fact, expended "near two letters in beating down an idol which himself *only* had set up." *Common Sense* said "not a syllable" about "calling in foreign assistance, or even forming military alliances." In fact, *Common Sense* "constantly holds up" the position that America should "have nothing to do with the political affairs of Europe." Cato had built his "air-built battery against independence" on a "bubble" that *Common Sense* advocated foreign troops. The Forester looked at this "poor foundation" and noted that "even the point of a pin, or a pen, if you please, can demolish with a touch, and bury the formidable Cato beneath the ruins of a vapor."

Government, said The Forester, was "a matter of convenience, not of right." He reiterated the scriptural argument against monarchy and identified that "A republican form of government is pointed out by nature" while "kingly governments by an inequality of power." In a patently antithetical structure, Paine contrasted the role of votes and violence in the two forms:

> In republican governments, the leaders of the people, if improper, are removable by vote; kings, only by arms: an unsuccessful vote in the first case leaves the voter safe; but an unsuccessful attempt in the latter, is death. Strange, that that which is our *right* in the *one*, should be our *ruin* in the *other*.

Because "the balance hangs uneven" in monarchial governments, they were "the most subject" to disorders, while a republican government displayed *"true grandeur,"* since "it is far nobler to be a ruler by the choice of the people, than a king by the chance of birth."

The Forester called George III both a fool and a tyrant, and reminded his readers that when "the history of Creation and the history of kings [is] compared," they would find "that God hath made a world, and kings have robbed him of it." Then The Forester took his argument a step further: "But that which sufficiently establishes the republican mode of government, in preference to a kingly one, even when all other arguments are left out, is this simple truth, that all men are republicans by nature, and royalists only by fashion." The proof of this assertion, claimed The Forester, was "that passionate adoration which all men show to that great and almost only remaining bulwark of natural rights, *trial by juries*, which is founded on a pure republican basis." He added, "Here the power of kings is shut out. No royal negative can enter this court. The jury, which is here supreme, is a *Republic*, a body of *Judges chosen from among the people*."

As The Forester reviewed "the ground which I have gone over in Cato's letters," he made the following "material charges" against Cato:

> 1. He hath accused the Committee with crimes generally; stated none, nor proved, or attempted to prove any.
> 2. He hath falsely complained to the public of the restraint of the press.
> 3. He hath wickedly asserted that "gleams of reconciliation hath lately broken in upon us," thereby grossly deceiving the people.
> 4. He hath insinuated, as if he wished the public to believe, that we had received "the utmost assurance of having all our grievances redressed, and an ample security against any future violation of our just rights."
> 5. He hath spread false alarms of calling in foreign troops.
> 6. He hath turned the Scripture into a jest. Ez[ekiel] 35.[45]

The Forester included a note after the first of his summary points that would prove fundamental to the final push toward independence. He wrote, "Cato and I differ materially in our opinion of committees: I consider them as the only constitutional bodies at present in this province." He reasoned that "they were duly elected by the people, and cheerfully do the service for which they were elected." The Pennsylvania Assembly, though "likewise elected by the people," occupied their time with "business for which they were not elected." The authority of the assembly, said The Forester, "is truly unconstitutional, being self-created." To make certain that he was expressing a political and not a personal argument, he emphasized, "My charge is as a body, and not as individuals."

Paine appended to his third Forester's Letter a "well-meant, affectionate address *To the People*." He began with another trademark sentence: "*It is not a time to trifle.*" Though some men, like Cato, had held out to them "the false light of reconciliation," he said, "There is no such thing. 'Tis gone. 'Tis past. The grave hath parted us—and death, in the persons of the slain, hath cut the thread of life between Britain and America."

The Forester continued his address, "Conquest, and not reconciliation, is the plan of Britain." Paine employed one of his most common argumentative techniques, readmitting a previously-refuted premise to cripple further any counter-argument. "But admitting even the last hope of the Tories to happen, which is, that our enemies after a long succession of losses, wearied and disabled, should despairingly throw down their arms and propose a reunion; in that case, what is to be done? Are defeated and disappointed tyrants to be considered like mistaken and converted friends? Or would it be right, to receive those for governors, who, had they been conquerors, would have hung us up for traitors? Certainly not."

America and Britain did not need to reunite as friends, argued The Forester, but to make peace as enemies. Only then could America hope for "eternal peace." Then, he said, "America, remote from all the wrangling world, may live at ease. Bounded by the ocean, and backed by the wilderness, who hath she to fear, but her GOD?"

The Forester warned, "Be not deceived. It is not a little that is at stake. Reconciliation will not now go down, even if it were offered. 'Tis a dangerous question; for the eyes of all men begin to open." The decision between reconciliation and independence "concerns every man, and every man ought to lay it to heart. He that *is* here, and he that was *born* here are alike concerned." The Forester dismissed those like a "Common Man," a contemporaneous newspaper essayist, who "split the business into a thousand parts, and perplex it with endless and fruitless investigations." Though a "Common Man" may "mean well," the "unparalleled contention of nations" could not be "settled like a schoolboy's task of pounds, shillings, pence, and fractions."

The Forester asked if America could "be happy under a government of her own," and his answer was "short and simple, viz. As happy as she please; she hath a blank sheet to write upon. Put it not off too long." And at the end of this sentence, Paine included one of the most famous footnotes in American history: "Forget not the hapless African."

Paine proclaimed it "the duty of the public, at this time, to scrutinize closely into the conduct of their committee members, members of Assembly, and delegates in Congress; to know what they do, and their motives for so doing." Unless this was done, said Paine, "we shall never know who to confide in; but shall constantly mistake friends for enemies, and enemies for friends, till in the confusion of persons, we sacrifice the cause."

Cato's Grand Finale

Paine's prose style, in the eyes of his friends, fostered retributive empathy, while the very same writings, in the eyes of his enemies, festered uncontrolled anger. Cato, of course, fell into the latter interpretive camp. He said, "The author of *Common Sense* stands singular in his rage for condemning the English constitution in the lump, and the administration of it from the beginning."[46]

Cato's final essay, "Letter VIII," first surfaced in the *Pennsylvania Gazette* on April 24. In this last letter, Cato unloaded his full arsenal against *Common Sense* and independence. Cato acknowledged that "men, in general, may be said to *feel* better than they can *see*," and he condemned his opponents for unethically stoking the fires of sentiment. His opponents had exaggerated, concealed facts, and stated "but one side of a question." Every writer who attempted, he said, "to warp the judgment by partial representation, to give railing for reason, invectives for arguments, and to urge a people into hasty resolutions, by addressing the inflamed passions, rather than the sober reason" was insulting his distressed country and abetting "its enemies to hasten its ruin." If the author of *Common Sense* had considered this, said Cato, then "his performance would have been of a different nature." Instead, *Common Sense* had irreverently manipulated "the judgment or feelings of a great and enlightened people."

Cato made explicit a commonplace argument in America during the spring of 1776. Political moderates argued that an expedited independence could be proposed only by a British mole who was trying to lure the colonies into a position whereby they could be easily and—according to the laws of nations—legitimately crushed. Cato wrote,

> If the British administration has a tool here, labouring to forward their ruinous purposes by divisions and distractions, THOU ART THE MAN—even thou the author of *Common Sense*, who hast started thine *ignis fatuus* to draw the unwary into untried regions, full of tremendous precipices and quagmires treacherous to the foot; whither the wise and considerate think it not safe to follow.

Cato mocked the urgency of *Common Sense* and The Forester: "Thou sayest that now is the exact time for adopting thy plan, and holdest up ruin as the sure consequence of the least delay!—Thou said'st the same, and did'st threaten the same, near three months ago, if we hesitated a moment to follow thy advice." He continued, "Possibly any time may be thy NOW, especially if thou should'st have nothing to lose, and peradventure may'st hope to gain something by the change." When "the Almighty shall be pleased to say NOW," argued Cato, "thy interpretations will be unnecessary. He will send conviction along with it, in circumstances so clear and unambiguous, that they *who run may read them*."[47]

Cato then turned to his opponents. Although "near a dozen answers have been given in one shape or another to my two or three first letters," in his opinion "nothing has been yet offered worthy of a particular reply." When The Forester entered the debate, however, it became clear that he was "the chief champion against me." Cato acknowledged The Forester's verbal skill and creative editing: "He makes me write what he pleases, that he may answer as he pleases."

Cato was unsurprised by The Forester's wily partial quotations, as he said, "But what can I expect from one who uses the immortal *Milton* much in the same way?" Cato proceeded to point out one of the most damning missteps in *Common Sense*—something that many of Paine's readers had probably overlooked unless they had ready access to a copy of *Paradise Lost*. In a passage from the third section of *Common Sense*, Paine had made an "unlucky" quotation that Cato compared to a coal snatched from the altar by a foolish eagle who "thereby set her nest on fire, which consumed herself and her brood." Paine had quoted from Milton "to establish his favorite doctrine, that reconciliation with Great-Britain is now impossible, and urging us on to blood, whatever terms may be offered," but he had extracted the quotation from its context as "fit to be copied in the conduct of a Christian people." Cato gave the citation for the passage and alerted his readers, "You will find that it was *the speech of the Devil*, mediating the destruction of mankind." Cato then turned to The Forester, "'Get thee behind me,' thou abandoned writer; and take back another of thy compliments!"

Cato moved on to remark upon The Forester's "furious antipathy to mixed governments, in which thou hast surpassed all the writers I have met with." Cato compared his opponent to the "popular leaders" of the English Revolution, who used the label of republicanism only "to procure the favour of the people; and whenever by such means they had mounted to the proper height, each of them, in his turn, began to kick the people, from him, as a ladder then useless." Cato discussed mixed government and republicanism in an extended commentary on Cromwell, Sidney, and Gordon, and he promised to discuss Montesquieu in his next letter—which never appeared.

Cato concluded his eighth letter with a cagey statement of his openness to independence. He said,

> When it shall clearly appear, that we can be no longer *free* nor secure in our *rights* and *property*, in connection with Britain, or that we can be more secure in any other connection (and the time which will enable us to judge of this cannot be very remote) the author of these letters shall not then lisp a word against whatever measures the sense of the majority of this country, fairly taken, shall adopt for the common good; and will be ready to give his best assistance for carrying them into execution.

But Cato insisted that he would "ever bear his testimony against being surprised into public decisions, by misrepresentations, ungrounded suggestions, and delusive arguments." When "the happiness of a great continent is involved," he finished, politics must never proceed from "prejudice or predetermination of a question," as advocates of immediate independence had done.[48]

Although Cato had hinted at a fuller explication of Montesquieu's position on mixed government in a future letter, he realized that his series was nearing its end. He refrained from including a teaser concluding paragraph as he had in most of his other letters. The next week would bring the Pennsylvania by-election, and Smith would either be vindicated or condemned by the results. When the moderates won three of four positions in the Pennsylvania Assembly, Smith congratulated himself and considered his series a success. With the exclusion of most pro-independence candidates from the assembly, Smith retired Cato's pen and basked in his victory. But Paine and his fellow independents were far from admitting defeat.

Post Mortem on the Election

Paine had started the independence controversy of 1776, so it was fitting that he would have the last word in the newspaper debate that spring. Paine's fourth and final Forester's letter was an exposition of the political dynamics of the May 1 election, an event that I will treat in more detail in the next chapter.[49] The Forester began his final letter with an important discourse on time, nature, and reason:

> Whoever will take the trouble of attending to the progress and changeability of times and things, and the conduct of mankind thereon, will find that *extraordinary circumstances* do sometimes arise before us, of a species, either so purely natural or so perfectly original, that none but the man of nature can understand them. When precedents fail to spirit us, we must return to the first principles of things for information; and

think, as if we were the *first men* that *thought*. And this is the true reason that, in the present state of affairs, the wise are becoming foolish and the foolish wise."

The Forester blamed the Pennsylvania Quakers for the setback suffered by the Independents in the May 1 election. The Quakers, though "wise in other matters," had shown "unanswerable ignorance" in the present contest. They had begun walking down the wrong path, and The Forester was calling them "back to the first plain path of nature, friends, and begin anew." The Quakers had already traveled "to the summit of inconsistency, and that with such accelerated rapidity as to acquire autumnal ripeness by the first of May." The Quakers, he said, had been insensible of the changing political seasons, and "Now your *resting time* comes on."

Paine looked at the election of May 1 with horror. He asked, "Who can look, unaffected, on a body of *thoughtful* men, undoing in *one rash hour* the labor of seventy years: Or what can be said in their excuse, more, than that they have arrived at their second childhood, the infancy of three-score and ten," which he explained in a footnote about the Quakers' resistance in 1704 "against the encroaching power of the Proprietor." Referring to these early Quakers, The Forester asked, "Would these men have elected the proprietary persons which you have done?"

The Forester said that his "chief design" in the fourth letter was "to set forth the inconsistency, partiality, and injustice of the *dependent faction,* and like an honest man, who courts no favor, to show to them the dangerous ground they stand upon; in order to do which, I must refer to the *business, event,* and *probable consequences* of the late election." The "business of that day" was to "elect four burgesses to assist those already elected, in conducting the military proceedings of this province, against the power of *that Crown* by whose authority they pretend to sit." The first act of those elected would be "to take an oath of allegiance to serve the same King against whom this province, with themselves at the head thereof, are at war." Likewise, "a necessary qualification required of many voters was, that they likewise should swear allegiance to the same King against whose power the same House of Assembly" had obliged them either to "take up arms" or to pay a fine. Paine exclaimed, "Did ever national hypocrisy arise to such a pitch as this!"

In fact, "under the pretense of moderation" the colonies were "running into the most damnable sins. Good God! Have we no remembrance of duty left to the King of Heaven! No conscientious awe to restrain this sacrifice of sacred things?" He asked, "Is this our chartered privilege? this our boasted Constitution, that we can sin and feel it not?" Said The Forester, "It is now the duty of every man, from the pulpit and from the press, in his family and in the street, to cry out against it."

The Forester noted that a "motion was sometime ago made to elect a convention to take into consideration the state of the *province*," and he called it a "judicious proposal," because the "alarming" condition of Pennsylvania made it "worse off than other provinces." Though an inquiry into the condition of the province was "highly necessary," Paine asserted, "The House of Assembly in its present form is disqualified for such business, because it is a branch from that power against whom we are contending." The assemblymen were "in intercourse with the King's representative, and the members which compose the House have, as members thereof, taken an oath to discover to the King of England the very business which, in that inquiry, would unavoidably come before them." The minds of the assemblymen were "warped and prejudiced by the provincial instructions they have arbitrarily and without right issued forth."

The Forester instructed his readers, "In times like these, we must trace to the root and origin of things; it being the only way to become right, when we are got systematically wrong." Although "the motion for a convention alarmed the Crown and proprietary dependents," to "every man of reflection, it had a cordial and restorative quality." The Forester advised a plan of action, "First, we are got wrong; secondly, how shall we get right?" He answered, "Not by a house of assembly; because *they* cannot sit as *judges, in a case,* where their *own existence* under their *present form and authority is to be judged of.*"

The by-election of May 1 had been hammered out as a compromise between a group calling for a provincial convention and a group of "objectors" to the measure in the Pennsylvania Assembly. The "objectors," argued The Forester, had managed to evade the convention issue "by promoting a bill for augmenting the number of representatives" in the Assembly, but they did not perceive "that such an augmentation would *increase* the *necessity* of a convention." The issue, it turned out, was not the equality or the distribution of representation, but the *source* of representative authority. Any power, said The Forester, "which derives its authority from our enemies" became only "more unsafe and dangerous" when "augmented." The Forester emphasized, "Far be it from the writer of this to censure the individuals which compose that House; his aim being only against the chartered authority under which it acts." In both Pennsylvania and England, he clarified, "there is *no constitution*, but only *a temporary form of government*."

As The Forester recounted the events of the spring, he construed the postponement of the motion for a convention as an attempt "to show the inconsistency of the House in its present state." Four "conscientious, independent gentlemen" had been proposed as candidates for the augmented assembly with the agreement that, if they were elected, they would refuse to take "the oaths necessary to admit a person as a member of that assembly." When that would happen, "the House would have had neither one kind of authority or another, while the old part remained sworn to divulge to the king what the new part thought it their duty to declare against him." That, said The Forester, was the plan of the Independents "on the morning of the election."

He admitted that his party "had to sustain the loss of those good citizens who are now before the walls of Quebec and other parts of the continent," while "the Tories, by never stirring out, remain at home to take the advantage of elections." The Forester added, "this evil prevails more or less from the Congress down to the committees." At the election a "numerous body of Germans of property, zealots in the cause of freedom," were "excluded for non-allegiance," while "the Tory nonconformists, that is, those who are advertised as enemies to their country, were admitted to vote on the other side." Additionally, the "testimonizing Quakers" who had been "duped by the meanest of all passions, religious spleen," tried to infect the Roman Catholics with "the same disease."

The combined, nominally "Moderate" parties "were headed by the proprietary dependents to support the British and proprietary power against the public." The proprietary alliance had "pompously given out that nine-tenths of the people were on their side," but, he continued,

> notwithstanding the disadvantages we laid under of having many of our votes rejected, others disqualified for non-allegiance, with the great loss sustained by absentees, the maneuver of shutting up the doors between seven and eight o'clock, and circulating the report of adjourning, and finishing the next morning, by which several were deceived—it so happened, I say, that on casting up the tickets, the first in numbers on the dependent side, and the first on the independent side, viz., Clymer and Allen, were a tie: 923 each.

This conclusion required some creative tabulation on The Forester's part, as he mentioned in a footnote that Samuel Howell, the highest overall vote-getter, "though in their ticket, was never considered by us a proprietary dependent."

The Forester contrasted the unity of the two parties in the election as one of expedience and another of principle. Those "who are against us" had "neither associated nor assisted" but were "a collection of different bodies blended by accident, having no natural relation to each other." They "agreed rather out of *spite* than right; and that, as they met by chance, they will dissolve away again for want of a cement." On the independent side, "our object was single, our cause was one." The Independents had "stood the experiment of the elections, for the sake of knowing the men who were against us."

The Forester asked of the moderate coalition, "When the enemy enters the country, can they defend themselves? Or *will* they defend themselves?" He continued, "And if not, are they so foolish as to think that, in times like these, when it is our duty to search the corrupted wound to the bottom, that we, with ten times their strength and number (if the question were put to the people at large) will submit to be governed by cowards and Tories?"

The Forester concluded his fourth letter with the observation that the "English fleet and army have of late gone upon a different plan of operation to what they first set out with; for instead of going against those colonies where independence prevails *most*, they go against those only where they suppose it prevails *least*." He said, "They have quitted Massachusetts Bay and gone to North Carolina, supposing they had many friends there." For this same reason, they were expected soon at New York, "because they imagine the inhabitants are *not* generally independents." In that colony, "the large share of virtue" in its inhabitants had been overshadowed by "the odium" of its aristocratic assembly.

The Forester reasoned from this last point that the election of James Allen, "the King's attorney, for a burgess of this city is a fair invitation" for the British to arrive in Philadelphia. The Forester asked provocatively, "in that case, will those who have invited them turn out to repulse them?" Since "there will not be found more than sixty armed men" among all of their partisans, the inadequate physical force of the Pennsylvania loyalists might be compensated for, proposed The Forester, by levying "the expense attending the expedition" against the British troops "*on the estates of those who have invited them.*"[50]

An Unfair Advantage

To this point I have confined the discussion of the Philadelphia newspaper controversy to its three principal contributors: Cassandra, Cato, and The Forester. There were, however, dozens of other writers who weighed in on the issues then in play. In this section, I will provide some highlights from those contributions, while acknowledging that the proliferation of contributing essays prevents an exhaustive catalogue of the controversy. Since most of these secondary disputants responded to issues from the letters of the three primary writers, I will focus mainly upon the metacritical commentary of these ancillary writers.

A May 6 note on the front page of the *Norwich Packet*, summarized the Philadelphia newspaper controversy well: "For some Weeks past the Pennsylvania Papers have abounded with Disputes concerning the present State of America, some have held up Independency as the best Mode, others advise Reconciliation with Great-Britain." The editor apologized "that it has not been in our Power to insert the whole of those Productions," but he promised to "insert such Pieces, from Time to Time, on BOTH SIDES of the QUESTION as, we apprehend, will be satisfactory to the FRIENDS of FREEDOM and an IMPARTIAL PRESS."[51]

The next week, "Aristides" provided readers of the *Pennsylvania Packet* with a cogent, bird's-eye view of the metastasized controversy. After commenting upon the inadequacy of *Plain Truth* as a pamphlet response to *Common Sense*, Aristides noted the shifting scene of the controversy. A "new set of antagonists appeared against *Common Sense*," he said, appearing not in "first editions of pamphlets" but in newspapers. Aristides then discussed the "propriety" of this turn in the controversy. With so much talk of the "liberty of the press," Aristides hoped to say "a few words for the liberty of readers." An exchange between pamphlets, he said, is a fair and impartial trial, but when a pamphlet "has so shamefully failed" as *Plain Truth* had, to repackage its arguments in "various detached pieces in the news-papers" was inequitable.

Aristides said he paid for the *Packet* and two other newspapers and had grown tired of these authors "cramming [their] sense or nonsense" down his throat, sometimes "four or five times over." Because the newspapers reprinted pieces from each other, Aristides had paid "three times for the most part of Cato's letters, and if they were to be published in a pamphlet I would not give a rush for them all together." Aristides suspected that printers were being paid to insert these essays and were being bribed "to deceive your readers." Aristides opposed this practice because "those who pay best will have the preference." The pay-to-play newspaper publishing system was creating "a new standard of literary merit" that forced "nonsense upon us which could not make its appearance in any other mode of publication." Aristides mocked Cato's "ridiculous pun upon Mount Seir" and his "wretched parody upon Hamlet's soliloquy" as "egregious trifling." He added, "To answer a whole book by a series of letters in the news papers is like attacking a man behind his back, and speaking to his prejudice before persons who never saw or heard of him, nor are ever likely so to do."

Aristides asked that pieces "might stand or fall by their own merit and the judgment of the Public" instead of artificially propping up limp arguments. In his view, the "tedious, trifling, indecent altercation" over independence was "occasioned by handling this subject in the newspapers." Aristides implied that Cato was stalling the colonies' decision by forcing readers to wait till he "has done speaking." More importantly, Cato's arguments evade the essential points of discussion, which Aristides demanded should "be the hinge of the controversy." Those questions, said Aristides, were: "Is there a probable prospect of reconciliation on constitutional principles? What are these constitutional principles? Will anybody shew that Great-Britain can be sufficiently sure of our dependence and yet we sure of our liberties?" Aristides closed his letter with a request of the *Pennsylvania Packet*'s printer, John Dunlap, "If you please, you may insert" this letter, but Aristides reminded his readers that "neither money nor promise of good deeds" would pave his letter's way, "so that its fate is wholly uncertain."[52]

Aristides was not the first to identify the ease of newspaper publication as an obstacle to ethical public discourse. In the March 25 issue of the *Pennsylvania Packet*, an anonymous writer composed an imaginary "Conversation between Cato and *Plain Truth*." The writer of the "Conversation" had Cato say, "Our cause will never appear to advantage in a pamphlet. If you begin a series of letters in a news-paper you are at full liberty to say as much or as little as you please, to suspend your operations for a time and strike in again when occasion serves." The imaginary Cato continued,

> When you write a pamphlet you are expected to say the best, if not all that can be said on the subject, and if it contains a few weighty arguments the author is despised and the subject suffers. There you are obliged to come to a period, but you may write a twelve month in a news-paper and yet make the public believe that your main argument has not yet appeared.[53]

The Object of Attack

Many of the contributors to the newspaper controversy expressed their frustration with the style of the debate. Moderate writers tried to defend Cato against *ad hominem* attacks and demanded that his opponents let him finish his argument. A writer signing himself "Aesop, Junior" in the *Pennsylvania Gazette* of April 3 retold Aesop's fable about "The FORESTER and the LION" to show that "the Forester of Aesop's day, as well as he of ours, was a person who could not argue the matter in dispute fairly with his opponent, but relied on the work an ingenuity of others of his own side to prove the matter in controversy." Addressing The Forester directly, the writer said, "Cato and thyself are disputing whether these Colonies will be happier in a state of independence, or in a state of reconciliation with Great-Britain, on constitutional principles." The writer continued, "and when Cato had produced his arguments in favour of the side he took, and they seemed to bear hard on thee, thou, like thy name-sake in the fable, for want of argument, shewest the book called *Common Sense*, and takest it for granted that thy point is already proved, whereupon Cato tells thee, let him write, and he will shew thee that that book is not to be depended on." But The Forester would not grant "this reasonable request, and when Cato "sets about writing thou endeavourest to interrupt him." The writer concluded, "I would therefore recommend to thee to wait till Cato has finished his work, and then the judges will determine the matter between you, upon a full examination on both sides."[54]

A contributor to the *Pennsylvania Evening Post* on April 18 wrote a long article in defense of Cato against the Forester. The writer thought The Forester was trying to divert Cato's attention "from the subject of which he treats" or, "if that should fail, to intimidate him and others from a candid examination of the pieces which have, without any opposition whatever, been handed to the public in favor of independence." The Forester may have taken "for granted that the point is settled in favour of independence, and that Cato and *his faction* are not of sufficient consequence 'NOW to turn the scale,'" but, the writer continued, "the *Good Sense* of the inhabitants of this province, *nay of this continent*, is not to be led captive by the assumed title and pompous style of *Common Sense*, or its inferior advocates." The writer quoted a pamphlet written by William Blackstone during the John Wilkes controversy, and insinuated that the Independents were trying to deceive the "*Good Sense*" of the people "by the arts of false reasoning or false patriotism."[55] Americans demanded, said the writer, to "read and hear everything that can be written and said on both sides, and after a full deliberation" would "form an opinion of which they will have no occasion to repent." The writer discussed the doctrine of independence and then said,

> In order to propagate this doctrine, a pamphlet has been written, and honored with the title of *Common Sense*, containing perhaps the most artful misrepresentations of facts that has appeared since the commencement of our disputes.—This pamphlet is printed and scattered throughout the Continent, it is suffered to remain uncontradicted in the hands of the people for many weeks, aided by a troop of auxiliaries, in order to be tried by that test the *Good Sense* of the reader.

Common Sense had been given "every chance of gaining proselytes and admirers," and now those rabid Independents prohibited "a single writer, a Cato" to "combat the doctrines it contains," to "shew the arguments which may be sued on the other side," and to "furnish the *Good Sense* of the readers with materials to work on." Cato was "attacked on every side; he is questioned as by an inquisition; his person is attempted to be pointed out to the resentment of the people; he is contradicted when he relates facts as notorious as the sun." These were serious charges, implied the writer, but "to crown all," Cato had been "branded with the odious, the obnoxious name of *Tory* and threatened in more than one publication with being 'dragged a culprit before the bar of the public.'"

The writer then bucked the shift in partisan lines that was happening during the spring of 1776:

> These writers affect to think that a *Whig* and an *Independent* are convertible terms, but I trust they are mistaken, for there are thousands in this country who would spill the last drop of their blood in this contest rather than the arbitrary designs of the Parliament should take effect, but would throw down their arms in an instant, if they were satisfied that an offer of Parliament of an accommodation, placing us in our former envied situation, and ensuring a future enjoyment of our liberties, would be rejected.

If Cato "is really a *Tory*, and deserves the character given him by the Forester and his coadjutors, his cloven foot will soon discover him." On the other hand, "if he is really a *sound constitutional Whig*, and aims only at stating the arguments against Independence, in a fair point of view for your consideration," then "your own *Good Sense* demands that he should be fairly heard, and will prevent every possibility of his deceiving you."[56]

On the pro-independence side of the question, The Forester did not benefit from the direct defense of his partisans. As a rule, they assumed that he did not require their assistance in defending himself, and many had earlier chimed in their public approbation of *Common Sense*. Most of the attention, therefore, of auxiliary writers on the independence side of the question was targeted at Cato. One of Cato's numerous detractors, "Eudoxus," referred to him as "the redoubted stickler for the supremacy of the British Parliament over the North-American Colonies." Eudoxus had grown impatient with Cato's inconstancy. He had expected a work written "under the signature so much honoured by the works of the patriotic Gordon and Trenchard" to have set forth "in terms so clear and striking" all of the "great advantages of maintaining *a constitutional dependence on the land that gave birth to our forefathers*." Instead, "the seventh letter has already appeared" and "not a syllable of the argument in favour of this same constitutional dependence is yet offered to our view." Moreover, "Cato is now in the *porch* of another *subject*, and for perhaps ten or twelve letters more, we shall be favoured with general encomiums and panegyrics upon the English constitution." Even if the Americans allowed, "without dispute or hesitation, that the *present* English constitution, was, for that island, the best that human wisdom could invent," Eudoxus asked, "what will that prove respecting a country in circumstances so different from England?"

Cato and other moderates were trying to spook the American populace, said Eudoxus, by referring to independence and republican government as an "untried experiment." According to Eudoxus, nowhere on earth had a government "yet been tried, that has for any long time answered the end of securing the people's liberty." He assigned this historical black eye to the fact that "the people have never been sufficiently careful of their delegated power." They have "often bestowed, often sold, and often surrendered" their sovereignty" to "very unworthy persons, who having once obtained it, used it as their own property, and deemed it an inheritance [transferable] to their children." The only "effectual remedy for this intolerable evil" was "the new experiment Cato and his party so earnestly combat." He added, "This is the faction, sedition, agrarian law, leveling scheme, anarchy, democratical power, they so bitterly hate and oppose."[57]

Another commentator included a pretended loyalist oath in his essay in the *Pennsylvania Evening Post*. The writer spoke of "the savage treatment we have met with from the king of Britain" and "the impossibility of the colonies being ever happy under his government again," and he gaped that "we still find some people wishing to be *dependent* once more upon the crown of Britain." Since he held "too good an opinion of the human understanding to suppose that there is a man in America who believes that ever we shall be happy again in our old connection with that crown," he concluded that all "advocates for dependence" had other reasons for their political stance. He included eleven itemized quotations that would prod all such loyalists "to speak for themselves." The reasons he listed for advocating reconciliation:

1. I shall lose my office.
2. I shall lose the honor of being related to men in office.
3. I shall lose the rent of my houses for a year or two.
4. We shall have no more rum, sugar, tea, nor coffee, in this country, except at a most exorbitant price.
5. We shall have no more gauze, nor fine muffins imported among us.
6. The New-England men will turn Goths and Vandals, and overrun all the southern colonies.
7. The church will have no King for a head.
8. The Presbyterians will have a share of power in this country.
9. I shall lose my chance of a large tract of land in a new purchase.
10. I shall want the support of the first officers of government, to protect me in my insolence, injustice, and villainy.
11. The common people will have too much power in their hands.

After the eleventh point, the writer included a note that "The common people are composed of tradesmen and farmers, and include nine tenths of the people of America." The loyalists, asserted the writer, refused to "submit to the chance" of these eleven "probable evils." Instead, he continued, they would rather "have our towns burnt, our country desolated, and our fathers, brothers, and children be butchered by English, Scotch and Irishmen; by Hanoverians, Hessians, Brunswickers, Walbeckers, Canadians, Indians and Negroes." And after all of this, "such of us as survive these calamities" will be forced to submit to whatever "terms of slavery" as King George III and the British Parliament may choose to "impose upon us." The writer signed this statement, "HUTCHINSON, COOPER, CATO, &c. &c.," lumping together notorious loyalists as coauthors of colonial destruction.[58]

For most of the newspaper controversy over independence, no clear victor emerged. Both sides had ample representation from a variety of writers, and depending upon the particular week of the debate and the sampling of newspapers one chose to read, it would have been easy to reach divergent conclusions about which side had prevailed. Both sides of the debate were bruised and bloodied, but neither had fallen to the mat. The irony of the newspaper debate over independence was that neither side was debating its ostensible opponent. Writers on both sides of the question acknowledged that they had little interest in debating each other directly, because Cato defeating Cassandra or vice versa amounted to only a minor personal victory or defeat. Every essay in the newspaper controversy was either attacking or supporting *Common Sense*, the inescapable epicenter of the entire conflict.

The most captivating essay written by a proponent of reconciliation appeared in the *Pennsylvania Ledger* on April 27. Rather than the typical oblique references to *Common Sense*, the "Moderator" weaved together his reading of the newspaper controversy with his experience of Paine's pamphlet. The Moderator confessed to reading "with great attention the various productions of the several writers, who have favoured the public with their sentiments, on the important subject of Independence." But the Moderator did not dwell upon these minor pieces and instead went into great detail about his shifting reaction to *Common Sense*. When he first read Paine's pamphlet, the Moderator found himself "stagger'd with the high wrought declamations against Monarchy in general, and of Britain in particular." He started to view, he recalled,

> the 'Royal Brute' with an indignant frown, and began to new-mould my monarchical sentiments, into those of a common-wealth, whose virtue should reign triumphant, and vice be expelled from the land, where Liberty like the mighty branches of the spreading oak, should extend her protecting arms, and shelter me from the scorching heats and beating storms of Slavery.

The Moderator had discussed *Common Sense* with "every man I met (with whom I had the least acquaintance)," because he wanted to find out if "the theme which was uppermost in my mind" was shared by his friends. Many of his acquaintances had "been convinced by the appearance of the late wonderful phenomenon" and had, like the Moderator himself, drunk deep from the stream of independence. Others of his circle, men "of more cautious tempers," had "perused the performance with calm attention, and pronounced it an artful, well wrought deception, calculated to alarm the passions, rather than convince the reason." These opinions gave the Moderator pause, and so he read the pamphlet "a second time with more deliberation and uninfluenced by those impressions which are generally made by novelty." He confessed that he was "one of those who have a wonderful aptitude to be smitten with any thing that is grand," and "such had been my situation of mind, when I surrendered the reins of my imagination to the guidance of the ingenious author of *Common Sense*." Together, they "soar'd aloft into the wilds of fancy, the dull beaten tracks of monarchy we left far behind us, and found a republic amidst the stars." Said the Moderator, though the sun might appear "to admiring mortals below, the grand monarch of the heavenly bodies," he and the author of *Common Sense* "found other suns and other worlds innumerable, who might only be considered as *Presidents*, not *Monarchs*, of the vast system." Rapt in their textual adventure, the Moderator and the author of *Common Sense* looked out across space and "everywhere shone a republic, the various constellations which enspangle the sky, united upon the principles of perfect equality; and gravitating towards each other, with wonderful adjustment, mutually attracted and mutually repelled."

The Moderator admitted to his "gentle reader" that thus had his imagination been "led captive, with fiery velocity, through a pleasing, unknown, and mighty expanse, till at length, fatigued with the rapidity of my course, I alighted in my easy chair, and took a recollective view of my journey." When he reviewed his wonderful trip, he "could not call to mind a single stage on which I had given rest to the sole of my foot." No part of his "airy progress" between stars and planets was sufficiently "fraught with happiness" to sustain "a being that had so much of mortality about him."

Switching his metaphors, the Moderator then found himself like Noah's dove, waiting "till the waters were assuaged" and hoping "for a pleasing prospect of the former verdure which had spread the plains and crowned the mountain." Thus, said the Moderator, he "stood on the second reading of *Common Sense*," fully determined "to remain in the ark, that is, to continue our present opposition to Great-Britain till a firm basis of liberty can be established," and he said, "then to review those pleasing happy haunts, which I frequently had visited in the innocent days of my youth, where joys unmolested smiled around me, and plenteous fields broke in upon my wondering sight."

The Moderator beheld "a tedious and expensive war" as the result of "a total separation." He saw "the blood of thousands bedewing the ground, and the whole wealth of the continent, the whole labour of a century, vanish'd in air." He felt confident "that a day *will* come" when Britain and America "shall discriminate between our interests and our resentments." They would reunite "as brethren that have differed through the instigation of mischievous incendiaries," and would exchange an acknowledgment of error by the aggressor and the "dropping the curtain of oblivion" by the injured.

The Moderator admitted that he harbored no doubt that "nature must, at last, have its course, and a total separation take place, between the new and the old world." But he could not assent to any argument "*that the time is now come*, or as the author of *Common Sense* has emphatically expressed it, *that the time has found us.*" The Moderator despised "the doctrines of hereditary succession and divine right to rule, as inherent in *this* or *that* man," and he rejected from his "creed every ordinance that has not the happiness of the people for its ultimate object—but the grand questions are, *is a change necessary, and is this the time for it?*"

He asked the writer of *Common Sense* to prove to him that "the change will produce us more real happiness." If his long list of questions about religious liberty, property, finances, and other subjects could be answered to his satisfaction, "here's my hand, and here's my heart." The Moderator was "divested of all prejudices in favour of our old connection, except what are founded in a recollection of the blessings we once enjoyed, and in the belief of a possibility of a happy reunion." Ultimately, he could "discover no immediate necessity for coming to a decision on the point," because he thought that "every day adds strength to America, and England alone can suffer by the delay."[59] Once again, the question of American independence was ultimately a matter of timing.

The Conclusion of Cato

The independence controversy consumed the attention of the Philadelphia press for the entire spring of 1776. The May 27 issue of the *Pennsylvania Packet*, for instance, was John Dunlap's first paper in months without an essay on independence or reconciliation. But the independence controversy was not over. It had moved its primary theater of combat from the pages of Philadelphia's newspapers to the Pennsylvania State House. The May 27 issue of the *Pennsylvania Packet* may not have printed any opinion pieces treating independence, but it did include "The Protest of diverse of the inhabitants to the Representatives of the Province of Pennsylvania," a petition disputing the authority of the Pennsylvania Assembly to enact the May 15 resolve of the Continental Congress that each colony establish a new government.[60]

As the nature of the conflict shifted from the press to a grassroots campaign for political legitimacy, the influence of William Smith evaporated. He had been a formidable advocate for reconciliation, and it even appeared on May 1, 1776, that his arguments had won the day. But the rapid course of events in the meetings of the Continental Congress and in the artisan-crowded streets of Philadelphia made Smith's victory fleeting.

Cato's identity had been common knowledge among politically savvy Philadelphians the very same week he began publishing his letters.[61] From the middle of March through the remainder of the spring, Smith became *persona non grata* and was subjected to piercing glares and whispering threats by pro-independence artisans. He looked backward over both shoulders wherever he walked in the city and avoided traveling alone at night. By the beginning of June, Benjamin Rush wrote to his wife, "Poor Dr. Smith is half distracted. You would hardly know him." Rush continued, "The party that once protected him in his insolence and villainy are now in the situation that we are told the rocks and mountains will be in at the last day. They can no longer hide him from the impending wrath of an insulted people."[62]

The noise made by Pennsylvania's aristocracy during the spring of 1776 was, said Rush, "nothing but the *last* convulsion of expiring ambition and resentment." Like the devil, who "assaults good Christians most violently in their last moments," the clamorous Pennsylvania loyalists, said Rush, knew that this was their last chance to injure their opponents. As soon as the Pennsylvania Provincial Convention met on June 18, Rush predicted, he would "see the monster tyranny gnash his impotent teeth in the dust in the Province of Pennsylvania."[63]

Notes: Chapter 10

¹ WS to Revd. Mr. [Thomas] Barton, 3 July 1775. Memorandum Book, Smith Papers, UPA.
² Revd. Mr. [Thomas] Barton to WS, 10 July 1775. Memorandum Book, Smith Papers. UPA.
³ WS to the Bishop of London, 8 July 1775. Memorandum Book, Smith Papers. UPA; cf. WS to Revd. Dr. Hind, Secretary to the Society for Propagating the Gospel, 28 August 1775. Memorandum Book, Smith Papers. UPA.
⁴ Smith, *A General Idea of the College of Mirania*; see also, Margeson, "Defender of the Atlantic Empire."
⁵ "Constitution of the Public Academy in the City of Philadelphia."
⁶ Trustees of the University of Pennsylvania, "Minute Books."
⁷ Gegenheimer, *William Smith, Educator and Churchman*, 179-180.
⁸ Gegenheimer's is the best biography of Smith to date (laudatory, but attempting objectivity). Perhaps the most comprehensive biography, but sullied with a desire to create a good reputation for the author's great grandfather (to the extent that "Cato" is not listed in the index): Smith, *Life of Rev. William Smith, D.D.* Other biographies of Smith: Fletcher, *Cato's Mirania*; Jones, *A Pair of Lawn Sleeves*.
⁹ PL, February 17, 1776.
¹⁰ 25 January 1776. RS 2:496.
¹¹ William Smith's biographer and descendant, Horace Smith, speculated that the Continental Congress invited the provost to speak with the ulterior motive of making him commit to a line of policy, but this is unlikely. He was their second choice after Jacob Duché, and though the attitude of the congressional delegates toward independence was changing, there existed on January 25 no majority strong enough to carry out such a scheme. See Horace W. Smith, 1:543-545.
¹² 12 February 1776. RS 2:501.
¹³ PL, February 17, 1776.
¹⁴ PL, February 17, 1776; cf. 19 February 1776. *Robert Treat Paine Diaries.* MHS.
¹⁵ 19 February 1776. RS 2:503-504.
¹⁶ WS, *An Oration in Memory of General Montgomery.*
¹⁷ SA to Mrs. [Elizabeth] Adams. 26 February 1776. Cushing, *Writings of Samuel Adams*, 266.
¹⁸ 12 May 1776 and 26 May 1776, Bradford, "Memorandum Book," Bradford Papers. HSP.
¹⁹ John Dunlap, the printer of Smith's *Oration*, first advertised it in his paper on March 11, and in the same issue Dunlap printed Letter II, "To the People of Pennsylvania," the first appearance of any of Smith's letters by "Cato." Dunlap also printed an extract from Rittenhouse's 1775 *Oration*, newly published in pamphlet form, in the same issue. DPP, March 11, 1776.
²⁰ See "Proposed Alterations in William Smith's Oration on General Montgomery," [Before March 6, 1776]. Willcox, 22:376-377.
²¹ 21 February 1776. RS 2:505.
²² JA to AA, 28 April 1776. Butterfield, et al., *Book of Abigail and John*, 125-126.

[23] Ibid.
[24] WS, *Oration*.
[25] DPP, February 19, 1776.
[26] In the dialogue, Paine referenced more sources from early modern political theory, including Montesquieu, Sidney, and Hampden, as well as classical military heroes, including Epimanondas, Pericles, and Scipio. His reference to Rousseau in *The Forester's Letters* indicates that he was, in the spring of 1776, reading widely in political theory, perhaps to remedy his own insecurities about the precise structure of republican government.
[27] The William Smith Papers in the University of Pennsylvania Archives demonstrates one of the challenges for research on loyalism in early America. The Smith family withheld anything from the papers that might shed a bad light on Smith, so there are large gaps from the revolutionary period (because of Smith's loyalism) and the end of his life (because of Smith's alcoholism). Smith was an opportunist Tory who disguised himself as a Moderate. Smith and fellow Philadelphia loyalist, Benjamin Chew, only signed the oath of allegiance at the very last minute. Chew, for fear of losing everything he owned, laundered his money by selling his estate to a pro-independence "patriot" and keeping the proceeds in a Dutch bank account.
[28] WS to the Lord Bishop of London, July 1774. Smith Papers, UPA. The bishop's reply, in the same folder, is dated October 3, 1774.
[29] Chronology of the Principle Contributors to the Pennsylvania Newspaper Controversy of March-May 1776.
(The entries for the Philadelphia newspapers are complete. I have also included in brackets some additional newspapers, which are intended as a representative but not exhaustive catalogue of republication in other colonies.)

By Cassandra (James Cannon, 4 letters total)
Cassandra 1: "On Sending Commissioners..." PEP, March 2; PG, March 20; {*Essex Journal*, March 22;} DPP, March 25; {NYG, April 1.}
Cassandra 2: "Letter to Cato," DPP, March 25; PG, March 20.
Cassandra 3: "Number II. Cassandra to Cato." DPP, April 8; PL, April 13, 20; {NYG, April 15.}
Cassandra 4: "Cassandra to Cato. Number III." PL, April 27; DPP, April 29; PG, May 1.

By Cato (William Smith, 9 letters total)
Cato 1: PG, March 13; DPP, March 18.
Cato 2: DPP, March 11; PG, March 13; PEP, March 14; PL, March 16; {NYG, March 25.}
Cato 3: PG, March 20; PL, March 23; DPP, March 25; {NYG, April 1.}
Cato 3.5 [Intercalary Letter]: "Cato to Tiberius, Greeting." PL, March 23; DPP, March 25.
Cato 4 ["Alas, Poor Cato!]: DPP, March 25; PG, March 27; PL (*Supplement*), March 30; {NYG, April 8.}
Cato 5: PL, March 30; DPP, April 1; PG, April 3; {NYG, April 15.}
Cato 6: DPP, April 8; PG, April 10; PL, April 13; {NYG, April 22; *Norwich Packet*, May 13.}

Cato 7: PG, April 10; DPP, April 15; PL, April 20-27; {*Norwich Packet*, June 3.}
Cato 8: PG, April 24; PL, April 27; DPP, April 29; {NYG, May 6.}

By The Forester (Thomas Paine, 5 letters total)
The Forester 1: DPP, April 1; PJ, April 3; PG, April 3; PL, April 6; {*Norwich Packet*, May 6.}
The Forester 2: PJ, April 10; PG, April 10; DPP, April 15; {NYG, April 22, 29; *Norwich Packet*, May 20.}
The Forester 3: DPP, April 22; PJ, April 24; PG, April 24; {*Norwich Packet*, May 27; Address "To the People" excerpted in the *Essex Journal*, May 31.}
The Forester 3.5 [Intercalary Letter]: PEP, April 30.
The Forester 4: {NYG, May 6;} PJ, May 8; DPP, May 20.

[30] "On Sending COMMISSIONERS to treat with the CONGRESS," PEP, March 2, 1776.
[31] Cato, "To the People of Pensylvania. Letter II." DPP, March 11, 1776; PG, March 13, 1776.
[32] Cato, "To the People of Pennsylvania. Letter I." DPP, March 18, 1776; PG, March 13, 1776.
[33] WS to Lady Juliana Penn, 14 March 1776. Gegenheimer, 178-179.
[34] These were references to notorious traitors in Shakespeare's *Othello* and Addison's *Cato*, respectively.
[35] "Cassandra to Cato," DPP, March 25, 1776.
[36] Cato, "Letter III," PG, March 20, 1776.
[37] Cato, "Letter IV," DPP, Mach 25, 1776; PG, March 27, 1776.
[38] Cassandra, "Number II. Cassandra to Cato" [Cassandra 3], DPP, April 8, 1776.
[39] Cassandra, "Cassandra to Cato. Number III" [Cassandra 4], PL, April 27, 1776.
[40] Cato, "Cato to Tiberius, Greeting," PL, March 23, 1776.
[41] Cato, "To the People of Pennsylvania. Letter V," PL, March 30, 1776; DPP April 1, 1776.
[42] Cato, "To the People of Pennsylvania, Letter VI," DPP, April 8, 1776.
[43] The Forester, "Letter I," DPP, April 1, 1776.
[44] The Forester, "Letter II. To Cato," DPP, April 15, 1776.
[45] Cf. Ezekiel 35:3-6, quoted in Cato, "Letter V."
[46] Cato, "Letter VII," PL, April 20-27, 1776.
[47] The last clause is a biblical reference commonly employed in late colonial discourse from Habakkuk 2:2.
[48] Cato, "Letter VIII," PL, April 27, 1776.
[49] See 8 May 1776, Bradford, *Memorandum Book*. Bradford Papers, HSP. The fourth letter of The Forester was, curiously, the only essay to be published initially outside of Philadelphia. It first appeared in the *New York Gazette* on May 6 and in the *Pennsylvania Journal* on May 8. We know that Paine was in Philadelphia during this time, so he had probably finished the piece on May 3 or 4 and sent it by express to New York. If Paine had preferred, for whatever reason,

to publish his essay in the *Pennsylvania Journal* (a weekly publication) he had to wait until the first issue after the election.

[50] The Forester, "Letter IV," NYG, May 6, 1776; PJ, May 8, 1776.

[51] *Norwich Packet*, May 6, 1776.

[52] DPP, May 13, 1776.

[53] "Conversation between Cato and Plain Truth," DPP, March 25, 1776.

[54] "The FORESTER and the LION," PG, April 3, 1776.

[55] Quoted from Blackstone's *An Answer to the Question Stated* (1769) in reply to Meredith's pamphlet, *The Question Stated* (1769). Junius, among many others, weighed in on the constitutional questions surrounding John Wilkes's exclusion from Parliament in his *Letter XVIII*, addressed to Dr. William Blackstone (July 29, 1769).

[56] "R." [signature], PEP, April 18, 1776.

[57] "Eudoxus," "For the *Pennsylvania Packet*," *Postscript* to the DPP, April 22, 1776.

[58] "For the *PENNSYLVANIA EVENING POST*," PEP, June 1, 1776.

[59] "Moderator," PL, April 27, 1776.

[60] DPP, May 27, 1776.

[61] 15 March 1776, Marshall, *Diary*.

[62] BR to Mrs. [Julia Stockton] Rush, 1 June 1776. Butterfield, *Letters of Benjamin Rush*, 101-103. See also, "Tiberius to Cato," DPP, May 6, 1776.

[63] BR to Mrs. [Julia Stockton] Rush, 1 June 1776. Butterfield, *Letters of Benjamin Rush*, 101-103.

Chapter Eleven

Bicameral Philadelphia

You ask me why we hesitate in Congress. I'll tell you my friend, because we are heavily clogged with instructions from these shamefully interested Proprietary people, and this will continue until Virginia sets the example of taking up Government, and sending peremptory Orders to their delegates to pursue the most effectual measures for the Security of America. It is most certain that the people in these Proprietary Colonies will then force the same measure, after which Adieu to Proprietary influence and timid senseless politics.

Richard Henry Lee to General Charles Lee
April 1776

Governments arise, either *out* of the people, or *over* the people.

Thomas Paine
Rights of Man, Part the First
1791

PART ONE
JOHN ADAMS'S TWO HOUSES

John Adams and Common Sense

American students learn in their earliest civics lessons that the United States Congress is a bicameral body, comprised of a "popular" House of Representatives and an "elite" Senate. The bicameralism of the United States legislative branch can be traced back to the political theory of early modernity, but the individual most responsible for inculcating the necessity of a two-house legislature in American politics was John Adams. Adams's short pamphlet, *Thoughts on Government* (1776), was written as a series of "hints" on government, originally for the delegates to the Continental Congress from North Carolina who had requested his input on forming a new provincial government in the spring of 1776. Adams was pleased with the result, and he began to distribute copies of the letter to a handful of friends in Philadelphia and in the other colonies. Soon he decided to publish his *Thoughts* in pamphlet form to gain a wider circulation for his ideas.[1]

Adams, the persnickety Massachusetts delegate, had read *Common Sense* with emotions as mixed as the government structure he adored. Adams was a definitive figure in the congressional debate over independence, and he had been among the first of the delegates to broach the subjects of independence and republican government, if only in oblique ways, in late 1775. The young lawyer from Braintree, Massachusetts, was a firebrand in congressional circles, but he was at the time little known among the general American populace, especially when compared to his famous cousin and fellow delegate, Samuel Adams. In the closed-door deliberations of the Continental Congress, John Adams became a persistent proponent of independence during the spring and summer of 1776. Possessing an incisive mind and a sharp tongue, he had arrived at the propriety of a separation from Britain earlier than most of his fellow delegates, and he prodded colonial affairs in the direction of his *a priori* conclusions.

John Adams was quite a curmudgeon later in life, and his aged disdain for Thomas Paine pervaded his memory. He looked back on the last decades of the eighteenth century with a sneer and called them the "Age of Paine." Likewise, in the early nineteenth century, Adams referred to *Common Sense* as "a poor, ignorant, Malicious, short-sighted Crapulous Mass," but such a commentary represented Adams's retrospective partisan bias. In 1776, Adams was more even-handed in his evaluation of the pamphlet, and he even displayed a measured enthusiasm for the text.[2]

On his journey back to Philadelphia after spending the Christmas of 1775 with his family, Adams had stopped in New York to receive a briefing on military preparedness from General Charles Lee. While in New York, Adams first encountered the buzz created by a new pamphlet advocating independence, and he sent a copy of *Common Sense* to his wife, Abigail, expressing the hope that the pamphlet's "Doctrines" would soon become "the common Faith."[3] Shortly after his arrival in Philadelphia, Adams made it a point to find out and meet with the author of *Common Sense*. The two men met and exchanged compliments, and they discussed the military necessity of political independence. Together Adams and Paine lamented the loss of Quebec as a symptom of inadequate supplies and French ambivalence toward the colonial cause. Adams related his recent experience reviewing General Lee's troops in New York, and Paine wished aloud that he, too, could get a first-hand perspective on the Continental Army, while also seeing parts of his new country beyond the city of Philadelphia. Adams encouraged Paine's plan and agreed in mid-February to write a letter of introduction on Paine's behalf to General Lee. Adams described his new acquaintance as "a Citizen of the World to whom," he wrote with a wink, "a certain Heretical Pamphlet called *Common Sense* is imputed."[4]

Paine left for New York at the end of February, and during his absence from Philadelphia, Adams's approbation of *Common Sense* began to temper. Abigail had asked John, in one of her letters, to elaborate upon the response to *Common Sense* in Philadelphia. In mid-March, John replied, "Sensible Men think there are some Whims, some Sophisms, some artful Addresses to superstitious Notions, some keen attempts upon the Passions, in this Pamphlet. But all agree there is a great deal of good sense, delivered in a clear, simple, concise and nervous Style."[5] He continued, clarifying that the "Sentiments of the Abilities of America, and of the Difficulty of a Reconciliation" with Britain in *Common Sense* were "generally approved." Paine's "Notions and Plans of Continental Government," were, however, "not much applauded." Paine had, thought Adams, "a better Hand at pulling down than building." Adams had been flattered by rumors that he had written the pamphlet, and he admitted that he "could not have written any Thing in so manly and striking a style." On the other hand, he thought he would make "a more respectable Figure as an Architect, if I had undertaken such a Work," because Paine held "very inadequate Ideas of what is proper and necessary to be done, in order to form Constitutions for single Colonies, as well as a great Model of Union for the whole."[6]

Paine returned to Philadelphia at the end of March, and Adams again saw Paine as a key accomplice in the movement toward independence. In April, General Lee had written to Adams expressing appreciation for the introduction to Paine, a man whom Lee thought had "Genius in his Eyes."[7] In an April letter to Abigail, John Adams noted a "strong Aversion" in many of the southern "Patricians" toward

Common Sense, which he attributed to the gross "Inequality of Property" in their colonies that gave "an Aristocratical Turn to all their Proceedings." The "Spirit of these Barons," was, he noted smugly, "coming down" and they soon "must submit."[8]

Adams appreciated *Common Sense* as a catalyst for independence, but he had been alarmed by the avid reception of *Common Sense*'s populist "hints" favoring a unicameral legislature. As Adams paid more attention to the issue of provincial governance in late April and early May, he again began to sour on Paine and to see the Englishman as a mixed blessing. Writing to James Warren, Adams said, "It is the Fate of Men and things which do great good that they always do great Evil too. *Common Sense* by his crude, ignorant Notion of a Government by one assembly, will do more Mischief, in dividing the Friends of Liberty, than all the Tory Writings together. He is a keen Writer, but very ignorant of the Science of Government."[9]

John Adams and Bicameralism

Adams penned his *Thoughts on Government* as a corrective to what he considered the simplistic and corruptible unicameral plan of *Common Sense*. Moreover, Adams fretted about the immediate influence that Paine's pamphlet would have on the formation of new provincial governments. At the request of John Penn of North Carolina, Adams wrote *Thoughts on Government* as a handbook for setting up a new government.[10] He copied the letter by hand for a few of his friends and then decided to publish the version that he had sent to George Wythe of Virginia. This was a standard trajectory for the publication of an elite-oriented pamphlet, and Adams's ideas were also standard republican principles. He reminded his readers of the basic truisms of republican government from his readings of Sidney, Harrington, Locke, Milton, Nedham, Neville, Burnet, and Hoadly, adding that, in the company of dismissive Englishmen, "no small fortitude is necessary to confess that one has read" these republican writers.[11] Adams was a traditionalist republican, and he invoked the customary definition of a republic as "an empire of laws, and not of men."[12] Republicanism was appealing to Adams chiefly because of its ability to preserve *order*, while promoting *liberty* was for him a matter of secondary importance.

In *Thoughts on Government*, Adams was laying out the commonplace eighteenth century argument for republican government. Citing the Prohibitory Act as "the present exigency of American affairs" whereby "we are put out of the royal protection, and consequently discharged from our allegiance" to the Crown, Adams said, "it has become necessary to assume government for our immediate security."[13] Without government, Adams feared, personal property became susceptible to the whims of anarchy. *Some* kind of government was required without delay, but what form should the American colonies choose? He skirted the possibility of other forms of government besides a republic, because he was opposed to both monarchy and democracy. He followed a proto-utilitarian argument to justify his choice of the government structure most productive of "happiness" to "the greatest number of persons, and in the greatest degree." A republic, he concluded without much evidence, was "the form of government which is best contrived to secure an impartial and exact execution of the laws."[14]

Adams viewed a strong government as a necessary precondition for a vibrant society. For Adams, politics was "the Art of Securing human Happiness," and the "Prosperity of Societies depends upon the Constitution of Government under which they live."[15] The Massachusetts delegate to the Continental Congress recognized that the "Coincidence of Circumstances" that allowed "thirteen Colonies at once" to begin "Government anew from the Foundation and building as they choose" was "without Example." He asked, "How few have ever had any Thing more of Choice in Government, than in Climate?"[16]

Adams confided, "In order to determine which is the best Form of Government, it is necessary to determine what is the End of Government," to which he answered, "in this enlightened Age, there will be no dispute, in Speculation, that the Happiness of the People, the great End of Man, is the End of Government, and therefore, that Form of government, which will produce the greatest Quantity of Happiness, is the best."[17] The "Happiness of Mankind, as well as the real Dignity of human Nature," Adams insisted, was dependent upon virtue, and so the best form of government boasted "Virtue" as its "Principle and Foundation."[18]

Adams's crucial contribution to practical political theory in *Thoughts on Government* came in response to his question, "But shall the whole power of legislation rest in one assembly?" Following Montesquieu, Adams answered that "the legislative power ought to be more complex" to prevent collusion between the legislative and executive powers.[19] Adams had by no means invented the concept of bicameralism, but he translated it from the descriptive theory of Montesquieu into a normative political plan. The British Parliament was bicameral by necessity—to appease the competing demands of the aristocracy and the common people—but Adams thought the American governments should replicate the effects of this system even though its formal causes were absent on the western shore of the Atlantic. While *Common Sense* had collapsed the distinctions of traditional republican terminology and claimed that all government was, in fact, executive, Adams held fast to the sources, categories, and ideals of classical republicanism. A bicameral republican government, said Adams, would inspire such an "elevation of sentiment" that it would make "the common people brave and enterprising." He continued, "If you compare such a country with the regions of domination, whether monarchical or aristocratical, you will fancy yourself in Arcadia or Elysium." He took great satisfaction in being "sent into life at a time when the greatest lawgivers of antiquity would have wished to live," and he viewed his own political role in an unbroken connection with those ancient philosopher-statesmen.[20]

Adams gave several reasons for dispersing the powers of government between legislative, executive, and judicial branches, and, especially between two houses within the legislative branch. He was concerned that a single assembly would be "liable to all the Vices, Follies, and Frailties of an Individual—Subject to fits of Humour, Transports of Passion, Partialities of Prejudice." A unicameral legislature was prone to make "absurd Judgments" and "hasty Results," while it was likely to become "avaricious" and "ambitious." It would only be a matter of time, said Adams, before a unicameral legislature without "some controlling Power" would "vote itself perpetual."[21]

Adams had more trouble constituting his bicameral legislature than he did decrying potential excesses of a unicameral one. He urged the "Representative Body" of each colony to elect "from among themselves or their Constituents, or both, a distinct assembly, which we will call a Council." This Council "may consist of any Number you please, say twenty or thirty," and it should "be given a free and independent Exercise of its Judgment upon all Acts of Legislation, that it may be able to check and correct the errors of the other."[22]

In Adams's system, the bicameral legislature would select the officers of the executive branch and the Governor would—"not without the Advice and Consent of the Council"—appoint "all judges, justices, and all other officers civil and military." Only representatives to the popular house of the assembly and sheriffs for each county would be elected by the direct vote of freeholders. Adams stressed, "This Plan of a Government for a Colony you see is intended as a temporary Expedient under the present Pressure of affairs. The Government once formed, and having settled its authority will have Leisure enough to make any Alterations that Time and Experience, and more mature deliberation may dictate."[23] Even Adams's political certitude wavered in the face of setting up new provincial governments, and he found himself offering modest "hints" instead of ineffable laws.

Thoughts on Government was an important political essay in 1776, and it laid the practical foundation for legislative bicameralism that persists in America today. But John Adams's most noteworthy contribution to the movement for independence happened inside the Pennsylvania State House in mid-May. Adams pressed for the congressional resolution of May 10 that authorized each colony to set up a new government structure, and he drafted the resolution's subversive preamble that, when affirmed by the Continental Congress on May 15, sounded the death knell of royal authority in the American colonies.

We will devote ample attention to these two important textual events later in this chapter and in the next, but first we need to pay attention to another aspect of revolutionary politics that was equally essential for the independence movement.

Adams's theoretical bicameralism *did* matter in 1776, but its import was dwarfed that spring by Philadelphia's practical bicameralism. The Second Continental Congress and the Pennsylvania Assembly both met in the Pennsylvania State House in 1776, a fact that magnified the influence of the Pennsylvania legislature upon late colonial affairs. But the congress and the assembly were not *themselves* the "houses" that shaped the independence movement. In this chapter I want to focus on a more literal connotation of bicameralism—a political tension between two "houses"—that sealed the decision for independence. Those two "houses" were the Pennsylvania State House—the seat of Continental and Pennsylvania government—and the London Coffee House—the seat of popular politics and Philadelphia society. Independence was forged in the friction between these two centers of political activity during the spring of 1776.

PART TWO
PHILADELPHIA'S TWO HOUSES

Pennsylvania State House and Government

The Pennsylvania State House, now known as Independence Hall, is a dignified Georgian edifice occupying a full Philadelphia city block bordered on the north and south by Chestnut and Walnut Streets and on the east and west by Fifth and Sixth Streets. The building crouches in the posture of a sphinx, a thick-necked bell tower with solid brick shoulders laid in a Flemish bond pattern. The State House, the original home of the mythic "Liberty Bell," would play host to the bookend events of the American Revolution, the signing of the Declaration of Independence in 1776 and the Constitutional Convention of 1787, and it is memorialized as the birthplace of the United States.[24] But although the building is now a recognizable symbol of democracy and freedom, before July 1776, such was not the case.

The Pennsylvania State House was originally built in the 1730s by master carpenter Edmund Wooley under the supervision of Andrew Hamilton, the Speaker of the Pennsylvania Assembly.[25] During the 1750s, the building's original cupola was replaced with the belfry tower and steeple that we now associate with the iconic structure, and the State House solidified its status as "the greatest ornament in the town" of Philadelphia.[26] The west wing of the State House building had for several years housed upstairs "a valuable collection of books belonging to the Library Company of Philadelphia" that had been moved to Carpenters' Hall in 1773, while the lower floor of the wing contained an apartment for the "keeper of the house." The lower floor of the east wing held the "Rolls of the Province," while the second story contained the quarters where "the Indians make their abode when in town."

The first floor of the main structure included two large rooms, divided by a wide hallway. To the west of the hallway was the Supreme Court Room, where the highest court in the colony tried cases in the shadow of the Royal Arms hung above the judge's bench. Across the hall to the east, the Assembly Room, where the Pennsylvania Assembly met, was "finished in a neat but not an elegant manner." A door in the corner of the room led to a "very elegant apartment" that housed in glass cases the books "of all the laws of England made in these later years, and besides these history and poetry."

The Pennsylvania State House was primarily the domain of the Pennsylvania Assembly, a body controlled by the competing oligarchies of the proprietary family's minions and the ostensibly Quaker mercantile interest. The Assembly Room of the Pennsylvania State House was the arena where Pennsylvania elites, elected by others of ample landed estate, sparred for a larger slice of the colony's economic pie.

The members of the First Continental Congress in 1774 could have met in the Pennsylvania State House, but they declined an invitation to do so. The delegates decided to hold their meetings instead at the more plebian Carpenters' Hall, one block east of the State House, spurning the offer of Joseph Galloway, then-Speaker of the Pennsylvania Assembly and himself a loyalist delegate to the Congress. In 1775, with Galloway no longer occupying the Speaker's chair, the Second Continental Congress accepted the invitation of the Pennsylvania Assembly to utilize their Assembly Room on the east side of the main floor in the State House.[27]

The Pennsylvania Assembly wielded greater power in continental affairs than did its sister provincial assemblies, but this power had little to do with the colony's relative size, wealth, or respectability. Pennsylvanian politicians enjoyed a tremendous geographic advantage over their colleagues in other colonies. As we have seen, a journey by sea invited the prospect of naval siege, and an overland trip meant accepting the hard-swallow reality of primitive roads. Thus a state of war, on one hand, and a state of rustic disrepair, on the other, crimped the flow of intercolonial travel and communication. The South Carolina Provincial Congress, for example, could not manage to keep a full delegation in the Continental Congress in 1776 because of the colony's intimidating distance from Philadelphia. If one of South Carolina's congressional delegates fell ill—a commonplace occurrence among their notoriously frail representatives—two months might elapse before a replacement could arrive.[28] By contrast, the Pennsylvania Assembly met in the very same building as the Continental Congress.[29] Continental Congressmen and Pennsylvania Assemblymen mingled in the central hallway and on the front steps of the Pennsylvania State House morning, noon, and evening. Pennsylvanians who held dual membership in both bodies could even slip out of one meeting to deliver a message to the other.[30]

The neighboring Continental Congress and the Pennsylvania Assembly, like most legislative bodies, both operated at a snail's pace. Formalities of deliberative prudence dictated complex processes and circumlocutions. In the simultaneous sessions of the congress and the assembly, pronouncements, petitions, proclamations, and preambles were the heart of the business. These legislative bodies were the pinnacle of order, even as the streets outside pulsed with unrest. Inside the walls of the Pennsylvania State House, the rule of law was always manifest and lawyers shone in their element. Both bodies moved slowly and carefully because, behind their dignified veneers, they hid deep structural flaws. The Continental Congress held only obeisant power, and the Pennsylvania Assembly derived its strength from a "people" that were not wholly representative of the Pennsylvania population. The congress and the assembly were not unlike the clock at the top of the building where they met. The striking of the clock at the top of the State House steeple could, in theory at least, be heard anywhere in the city, but by 1774 the wooden steeple structure holding the clock and bell was "in such a ruinous condition that they are afraid to ring the bell, lest by so doing the steeple should fall down" over a hundred feet to the front steps on Chestnut Street.[31] As long as the political culture of the Pennsylvania State House governed American affairs, the colonists were not going to hear the bells peal that the time for independence had arrived.[32] For the Pennsylvania State House to become Independence Hall, another *house*—and another political culture—would have to intervene.

Coffee Houses in British Culture

Prior to the publication of *Common Sense*, Thomas Paine experienced America at the intersection of Front and Market streets in Philadelphia. He had arrived in the colonies as a perpetual outsider, but he stumbled upon an existence centered in the liveliest spot in the largest American city. Paine rented a room on the southeast corner of Front and Market streets, right next door to Robert Aitken's shop and just across from William and Thomas Bradford's London Coffee House. The public market from which Market Street took its name occupied another corner. It was here that Paine purchased the staples of his new American life and where he witnessed the buying and selling of goods and property of all kinds, from vegetables and spices to estates and human slaves.[33]

The London Coffee House held a pleasant familiarity for Paine amidst the newness of his surroundings. He had spent much time in the myriad coffee houses and clubs of London, where he had first brushed shoulders with the likes of Oliver Goldsmith and Benjamin Franklin. Paine's political views had matured in the vociferous debates of the Headstrong Club that met in the White Hart Inn in Lewes, and the sights, smells, and sounds of the Bradfords' London Coffee House stirred up fond memories of his life in England.

The first coffeehouse in England had been established at Oxford in 1650, and by the early decades of the eighteenth century, coffee had become an inexpensive commodity, and Londoners of every social stratum could choose from over 2000 coffee houses dotting the city. The coffee house quickly became much more than a place of refreshment: it was also a cultural institution, a business internet, and a social center.[34] For just a penny per cup, patrons could chat, argue, or joke with some of the greatest minds in England. Coffee houses became known as "penny universities," where a person of modest means could gain a liberal education for the price of a cup of coffee. Richard Steele had described in *The Spectator, No. 49*, the coffee house as "the Place of Rendezvous" where men could "transact Affairs or enjoy Conversation" about politics and philosophy without the drunken distractions of a tavern or the annoying "Assemblies of the fair Sex."[35]

By the late eighteenth century, coffee houses had a long-standing reputation in British culture as a subversive political space. As early as 1675, King Charles II had attempted to suppress coffee houses because they had become centers of republican resistance to his rule. The king ordered the following broadside proclamation to be posted on the doors of these dangerous establishments:

> Whereas it is most apparent, that the multitude of Coffee-houses set up and kept within this Kingdom...and the great resort of Idle and Disaffected persons to them, have produced very evil and dangerous effects; as well for that many Tradesmen and others, do therein misspend much of their time, which might and probably would be otherwise employed in and about their Lawful Callings and Affairs; but also, for that in such houses, and by occasion of the meetings of such persons therein, diverse false, Malicious and Scandalous Reports are devised and spread abroad, to the Defamation of his Majesty's Government, and to the Disturbance of the Peace and Quiet of the Realm; his Majesty hath thought it fit and necessary, that the said Coffee-houses be (for the future) put down and Suppressed, and doth (with the Advice of his Privy Council) by this Royal Proclamation, Strictly Charge and Command all manner of persons, that they or any of them do not presume from and after the tenth day of January next ensuing, to keep any public Coffee-house, or to utter or to sell by retail in his, her, or their house or houses (to be spent or consumed within the same) any Coffee, Chocolate, Sherbet or Tea, as they will answer the contrary at their utmost perils. ...God save the King.[36]

The prohibition by Charles II, of course, did not last, and coffee houses proliferated. The immense number of coffeehouses, taverns, and chocolate houses in London facilitated a specialized clientele that was not replicable in any other city or town in the British Empire. When Paine was an excise officer, for instance, he met with Oliver Goldsmith, George Lewis Scott, and his fellow officers at the Excise Coffee House in London, just as traders to the Baltic region met at the Baltic Coffee House, shipping insurers at Lloyd's, and stockbrokers at Jonathon's.[37] Scientists and popular educators, like James Ferguson and Benjamin Martin, lectured and demonstrated experiments and inventions in the public milieu of their favorite coffeehouses.

This specialization of coffee houses led to the establishment of "clubs" designed to promote particular activities and interests. While in London in the early 1770s, Benjamin Franklin had belonged to a philosophical "club" that met at St. Paul's Coffee House every other

Thursday. The club, according to James Boswell, another member, conducted itself in formal conversation "sometimes sensibly and sometimes furiously" while members drank wine, punch, porter, and beer and dined on Welsh rabbit and apple puffs.[38] Small tradesmen of London followed suit with more Spartan clubs like the "Robin Hood," a debating club that charged six pence for a pint of beer and a chance to address the club for five minutes only on any subject they chose.[39]

Coffee houses provided a space for deliberation, education, and exchange unencumbered by the restrictive formalities of official British society. Many of the Fellows of the Royal Society in London during the 1780s were concurrent members of the less formal Coffee House Philosophical Society, a regular meeting that men such as Joseph Priestley and Richard Price found more conducive to open discussion than the stiff proceedings of official scientific culture.[40] These intellectual forums were not restricted to only scientific subjects. Conversations bent easily between natural philosophy, theology, and politics. The spirit of these seamless exchanges was captured well in a famous passage from Joseph Priestley's *Experiments and Observations on Different Kinds of Air* (1774), a book that Paine had read and commented upon prior to composing *Common Sense*. Priestley extolled the "rapid progress of knowledge" as "the means, under God, of extirpating all error and prejudice, and putting an end to all undue and usurped authority in the business of religion, as well as of science." He declared that "all the efforts of the interested friends of corrupt establishments of all kinds" would be "ineffectual for their support in this enlightened age." Priestley extended the implications of diffuse knowledge into the political realm as well, warning "the English hierarchy" that it had good reason "to tremble even at an air-pump, or an electrical machine."[41] Priestley could have just as easily added "or a cup of coffee" to his list of unexpected mechanisms of subversion.

London Coffee House and Society

The walls of an early American coffee house, tacked full of notices and advertisements, echoed with conversation and masculine conviviality. Often located adjacent to docks and markets, the coffee house was a primary nexus for the business community. Shippers, merchants, planters, and men of all sorts clutched steaming cups of boiled coffee and puffed long-stem pipes as they transacted business.[42] British and American businessmen realized that beer was not conducive to shrewd dealing, and they latched onto coffee as a stimulating and prudent alternative. Other patrons gathered around in Windsor chairs to convey the latest gossip, to debate philosophical topics, or to entertain one another with stories, jokes, and political arguments.[43]

Samuel Carpenter had opened the first coffee house in Philadelphia on the northwest corner of Front and Walnut Streets in 1703. Carpenter also opened Philadelphia's first bakery, erected its first crane, and built its first wharves to accommodate ships. All kinds of business, including the selling of slaves, took place in Carpenter's coffee house, while its semiprivate meeting room hosted gatherings of the Common Council of the Philadelphia city government.[44] After five decades of thriving business, this inaugural coffee house closed, and the political and mercantile men of Philadelphia lamented its loss. In response to the entreaties of his friends, William Bradford, who had launched the *Pennsylvania Journal* in 1742, opened the London Coffee House on a subscription basis in 1754, around the same time that construction of the Pennsylvania State House was complete. Leading Philadelphia merchants received some control over the house rules in exchange for a regular fee. Bradford's amiable personality helped the London Coffee House to become, like its predecessor, a hub of Philadelphia society.

From the start, the London Coffee House served more than just coffee. "Some people may be desirous at times to be furnished with other liquors besides coffee," William Bradford had written on his application for a business license.[45] Bradford's establishment likewise sought from its inception to be more than a purveyor of food and drink. Bradford's establishment was, at its core, a public exchange of goods, property, information, and gossip. State House enmities became open secrets around the tables of the London Coffee House. In the words of one nineteenth century historian, the London Coffee House was among America's leading "social climacterics."[46]

The ground floor of the London Coffee House featured a traditional hissing coffee urn, and upstairs were committee rooms and a large hall for public meetings that had, until 1776, proudly displayed a portrait of King George III. Every day at noon Philadelphia merchants assembled on "high Change" to hear the latest commodity prices, the reports of ship captains, and a smattering of maritime and political news. While gathered, the traders transacted business and made appointments. Most members of the Continental Congress and other prominent visitors preferred to receive their correspondence at the London Coffee House rather than at the post office. The Bradfords sold writing materials and provided in-house complimentary copies of all colonial and many British newspapers, magazines, and public notices. Busy merchants might not visit the coffeehouse every day, but the public hall was packed on "post Days" when the "freshest Advices, both Foreign and Domestic" would be read to an eager audience.[47]

Unlike many other coffee houses, the London Coffee House did not offer lodging for travelers—which made it more of a local haunt than most inns or taverns—but it did serve meals and a wide variety of beverages—beer, wine, lemonade, chocolate, liquor, and coffee—

preferred by the colonists instead of water. One drink conspicuously absent from the coffee house menu was tea. When the British Parliament first imposed a duty on tea, the inhabitants of Boston protested by boycotting consumption of the beverage altogether. A group of students at Harvard College, for instance, resolved in 1768, "with a spirit becoming Americans, to use no more of that pernicious herb." Drinking tea thus became associated in the colonies with Toryism, and coffee provided an equally vivifying substitute.[48]

The London Coffee House had been a command center for Philadelphia opposition to the Stamp and Tea Acts. As publishers of the *Pennsylvania Journal*, almanacs, and pamphlets, William Bradford and his son, Thomas, had a business incentive to oppose mandatory stamps on all printed materials. The Bradfords took an even more prominent role in the opposition to the Tea Act. Many Americans viewed "the pernicious project" of the East India Company to send reduced-duty tea to America as a cunning scheme of the British ministry to tempt the colonies into accepting parliamentary taxation. But as early as 1773, many Philadelphians were experiencing town meeting-fatigue, and there was real concern that the resistance movement would be unable to collect a sufficient number of residents to make a "respectable and formidable" opposition to the anticipated landing of the tea. William Bradford took the lead in organizing a group of Philadelphians to draw up resolutions forbidding the tea from being landed, and those resolutions were approved by a public meeting also organized by Bradford. The Philadelphia resolves encouraged the resistance in Boston, where many residents had begun to acquiesce in receiving the tea because they thought their efforts would lack the support of the other colonies. Immediately following the Boston Tea Party in December 1773, the controversial tea ships were redirected to Philadelphia. When the first tea ship arrived in the Delaware River and anchored three miles below the city, the captain went directly to the London Coffee House to inquire of his chances to land the contraband cargo. At least eight thousand people gathered in the State House Yard to protest the landing, and public pressure against the Pennsylvania merchants who stood to benefit from a "commission to enslave your native Country" reached a fever pitch. Captain Ayres of the Tea-Ship *Polly* stayed in Philadelphia less than two days before being escorted, along with one of the tea merchants, "to the wharf by a concourse of people who wished them a good voyage."[49]

By 1775 and 1776, William Bradford had retired from the day-to-day affairs of the coffee house and publishing house to focus on his military duties.[50] His son, Thomas, was the primary caretaker of the family business, but the spirit of the Bradfords' enterprise remained unchanged. The London Coffee House was the center of the Philadelphia resistance to British military encroachment. The primary vehicle for this resistance was a meeting held nearly every day of 1776 upstairs in one of the coffee house's private rooms. The Committee of Inspection and Observation of the City and Liberties of Philadelphia—commonly referred to as the "Committee of Inspection"—met upstairs in a dedicated "Committee Room."[51]

The Philadelphia Committee of Inspection had been created in 1774 to implement the articles of association drafted by the First Continental Congress. It began with 43 members (of which William Smith was one), expanded later to 66 members, and by 1776 had an even hundred members. The Committee of Inspection's mandate was to execute the resolves of the Continental Congress, but under this guise the committee's members exercised wide-ranging authority. They regulated the price of goods, searched merchant ships for contraband, shuttered the shops of noncompliant businessmen, publicly chastised "Tory" Philadelphians, and even jailed those considered to be traitors.[52]

By 1776 the Committee of Inspection had become a magnet for aspiring politicos traditionally excluded from participation in the official Pennsylvania oligarchy. A secret January 1776 meeting of a handful of self-styled "friends of America" at the Fountain Tavern in Philadelphia illustrated the *modus operandi* of these ascendant popular politicians. James Cannon (a tutor at the College of Philadelphia), Timothy Matlack (a brewer), Christopher Marshall (a druggist), Thomas Young (an itinerant physician), and a few others met soon after learning of the disastrous loss at Quebec "in order to consult and consider of proper persons to be elected" to the Committee of Inspection.[53] They met away from the London Coffee House specifically to avoid the appearance of electoral subterfuge. This self-appointed subcommittee met one more time before settling on their pro-independence ticket. Among the new members of the committee, elected on February 16, 1776, was Benjamin Rush.[54]

Both sides of the independence question held numerous private meetings throughout the spring to accomplish their political agendas. Christopher Marshall was convinced that the Pennsylvania Moderate coalition—whom he described as "those who are for reconciliation with Great Britain upon the best terms she will give us, but by all means to be reconciled to or with her"—used "many" private meetings "to promote, to accept and adopt all such measures" as would ensure the election of their preferred candidates.[55]

The pro-independence Committee of Inspection benefited from the expert advice of the most accomplished popular mobilizer in the colonies: Samuel Adams. Marshall revealed in his diary repeated visits to the Philadelphia quarters of the Boston brewer and propagandist. For example, Marshall busied himself in early February writing an "Address to the Congress" to be approved by the Committee of Inspection at an evening meeting at the London Coffee House. After the committee meeting, Marshall paid a visit to Samuel Adams, with whom he conversed for several hours.[56] Marshall also spent much time with Thomas Paine during the spring of 1776. Paine was not formally a member of the Committee of Inspection, but his close association with the group made him its unofficial spokesman. On April 1, the day Paine's first Forester piece appeared in the Philadelphia press, Marshall and Paine spent five hours in conversation at James Cannon's house along with Thomas Young, James Wigdon, and Timothy Matlack.[57]

Coffee House Argument

Scholars often have questioned how Paine, the son of a rural staymaker, learned to write, but few have paid attention to how he learned to argue. Given the orality of Paine's prose style, I would contend that Paine's method of argument supersedes his method of composition as a key to the force of *Common Sense* and other of Paine's texts. We know that Paine's interest in politics was stoked in the fires of debate during his stint as an exciseman in Lewes, England. While in Lewes, Paine identified himself as a Whig, and he acquired a reputation among the locals for tenacity in argument and "bold, acute, and independent" opinions.[58] Paine was an active member of a debating society called the Headstrong Club that met regularly in a local tavern.[59] The Headstrong Club kept a record of its meetings called *The Headstrong Book, or Original Book of Obstinacy*. The book contained the following panegyric on Thomas Paine:

> Immortal PAINE, while mighty reasoners jar,
> We crown thee General of the Headstrong War;
> Thy logic vanquish'd error, and thy mind
> No bounds, but those of right and truth, confined.
> Thy soul of fire must sure ascend the sky,
> Immortal PAINE, thy fame can never die;
> For men like thee their names must ever save
> From the black edicts of the tyrant grave.[60]

Paine thrived in this culture and only left from the ironic necessity of unemployment, bankruptcy, and divorce. But Paine's tragic flaw of bitter contentiousness was also a key ingredient in his success as a political debater. He took offense to personal slights and aired his grievances in public, and, conversely, he was able to take complex public issues and make them intimate personal decisions.

It was Paine's rare ability to speak the language of statecraft with a beer-swilling swagger that made his prose unique. In this respect, the nearest stylistic precursor to *Common Sense* was *The Spectator* of Joseph Addison and Richard Steele from the early eighteenth century. The purpose of *The Spectator*, according to Addison, was to bring

"Philosophy out of Closets and Libraries, Schools and Colleges, to dwell in Clubs and Assemblies, at Tea-Tables and in Coffee-Houses."[61] Paine's reputation among the members of the Headstrong Club was not unlike Steele's description of "Beaver the Haberdasher," a fictitious friend who presided in his preferred coffee house over "a Levy of more undissembled Friends and Admirers, than most of the Courtiers or Generals of Great Britain." Steele was fictionalizing a common occurrence in London coffee houses of the eighteenth century. "Every Man about him has, perhaps, a News-Paper in his Hands; but none can pretend to guess what Step will be taken in any one Court of Europe, till Mr. Beaver has thrown down his Pipe, and declares what Measures the Allies must enter into upon this new Posture of Affairs."[62] The label "coffee house politician" carried in eighteenth century British vernacular the same connotation as "arm chair quarterback" or "backseat driver" does today.[63] Paine was a publishing coffee house politician, but in the American colonies of 1776, places where the structure of government was being flipped on its head, spectator-commentators like Paine and his readers found themselves clutching the steering wheel of political culture.

The line between a coffee house, an inn, and a tavern was blurry: all served alcoholic beverages and meals, and most provided accommodations to travelers. In colonial America, the distinction was, most often, simply a matter of location. A city like Philadelphia or New York had all three types of establishments, but outside of urban centers, inns were typically found at crossroads and along remote byways, while taverns were found in the center of towns. In fact, a tavern was the "first requisite" of a town in colonial America, followed by a mill, a blacksmith's shop, and a church.[64] Two roads crossed in a clearing, and an ambitious proprietor set up an inn to capitalize upon the presence of parched and weary travelers. And so other businesses and institutions followed suit until a town had sprung up around this intersection of demand and supply.[65]

Unless we understand early American tavern culture, we cannot grasp the resonance of Paine's prose with his colonial audience. *Common Sense* was a transcribed tavern debate, and as such, it resisted examination with the same logical scrutiny invited by a more formal treatise. Paine's "reason" was not cool logic, but warm feeling. Because *Common Sense* did not aim to be a technical proof of independence, we should not be surprised that it is riddled with logical gaps and inconsistencies. Indeed, one can find an example of almost every kind of logical fallacy in *Common Sense*. This is not to say that the pamphlet was irrational, but it was far from a water-tight argument. Like a spirited debate in a tavern or coffee house, however, *Common Sense* did not rely on dry precision but, instead, on clever bluster.

Paine's argumentational style is best illustrated by a tactical maneuver he employed with the greatest frequency: turning the tables, a form of concession-and-revocation. In its most basic form, this technique was a simple refutation camouflaged as a contingent argument.. For example, in the second section of *Common Sense*, Paine wrote, "The most plausible plea, which hath ever been offered in favor of hereditary succession, is, that it preserves a nation from civil wars; and were this true, it would be weighty." The subjunctive mood in the second sentence was a tip that Paine viewed this argument as a nonexistent precondition. He proceeded from his tiptoeing introduction to a wholesale refutation of the civil war argument as "the most barefaced falsity ever imposed upon mankind." He railed,

> The whole history of England disowns the fact. Thirty kings and two minors have reigned in that distracted kingdom since the conquest, in which time there have been (including the Revolution) no less than eight civil wars and nineteen rebellions. Wherefore instead of making for peace, it makes against it, and destroys the very foundation it seems to stand on.[66]

Often, Paine used this technique with more subtlety and sophistication. After spending multiple paragraphs demolishing the applicability of the parent-child metaphor to the relationship between Britain and America, Paine conceded a point that he had already annihilated, "But Britain is the parent country, say some." He then took this invalid conclusion as his new premise and twisted it to his advantage: "Then the more shame upon her conduct. Even brutes do not devour their young, nor savages make war upon their families; wherefore the assertion, if true, turns to her reproach."[67]

Again, after a scorching critique of the prospects of reconciliation, he continued, "But admitting that matters were now made up, what would be the event? I answer, the ruin of the continent," and he proceeded with "several reasons" for his secondary conclusion.[68] Time and again, Paine feigned giving the benefit of the doubt to his opponents, and in every instance, he turned their best case scenario into a nightmare.[69] In formal argument, the *pro* or *contra* side would engage in anticipatory refutation or reactionary rebuttal, but Paine's pet tactic did not fit into either of these categories. After flaying a topic, he used this concession-and-revocation technique as a twist of the knife to his enemies and a high-five to his friends.

Paine's approach to argumentation was unique insofar as it reflected his commitment to temporal disorientation. It was as if he had so completely dismantled an opposing position that he had erased all memory of both that position and of his refutation. Then, with a false charity, he pushed his opponents' views to their *ad absurdum* conclusions, effectively disproving the original position on its own merits. This technique allowed Paine, who was always concerned with prejudice, to destabilize the *premises* of arguments for reconciliation as effectively as he had countered his opponents' conclusions.

Paine's argumentation technique was unconventional and infelicitous. Simply put, it did not belong in the arena of formal political argument, but in bawdy coffee house harangues and tavern tussles. *Common Sense* was infecting staid colonial political discourse with a vernacular vocabulary and with the galloping cadences of raucous debate. This innovative approach to argument was the outworking not just of coffee house and tavern culture, but of Paine's philosophical commitment to parsing the fundamental concepts of government and society. The restrictive decorum and hierarchy of the Pennsylvania State House was a synecdoche for "government," and the freewheeling, organic exchange of the London Coffee House was Paine's picture of "society."

Part Three
THE LOCUS OF SOVEREIGNTY

Society and Government

Paine was by no means the first writer to propound a theory of society and government. A litany of philosophers and politicians from antiquity forward had weighed in on the subject before this working class Englishman arrived on the scene. Two of the most relevant British precursors to *Common Sense*'s treatment of the subject were published in the late 1760s. Adam Ferguson and Joseph Priestley, two celebrated members of the republic of letters, each composed a prominent treatise on the subject of the origins of society and government. Since these essays were the most immediate British forerunners on a central topic of *Common Sense*, it will be worthwhile to touch briefly upon their contents. My specific emphasis here is to demonstrate their respective approaches to the relationship between society and government.

Adam Ferguson's *Essay on the History of Civil Society* (1767) blended together an insightful analysis of state of nature narratives, a discussion of liberty and rights, and a theory of moral sentiment, but Ferguson abided in the functional conflation of society and government. Ferguson, a Scotsman, was no republican, and he identified "an aversion to control" as the common source of a "passion for independence" and the "love of dominion." Ferguson contended that the "leader of a faction would willingly become, in republican governments," what "the prince, under a pure or limited monarchy, is by the constitution of his country."[70]

Paine had likely not read Ferguson, but he would have been familiar with the political writing of Joseph Priestley, with whom he shared a strong ideological affinity. Priestley began his *Essay on the First Principles of Government* (1768) with a careful delineation of his terminology in order to gain "clear ideas on the subject." Priestley acknowledged that "almost all political writers" had postulated "a number of people existing, who experience the inconvenience of living independent and unconnected." He realized that "no society on earth was ever formed in the manner represented above" because all existing governments had been "in some measure, compulsory, tyrannical, and oppressive in their origin," but he justified the thought experiment as the outline of "the only equitable and fair method of forming a society." Like Paine in *Common Sense*, Priestley was not claiming historicity for his scenario, but rather, he was illustrating constitutional equity.

Priestley continued, "It must necessarily be understood, therefore, whether it be expressed or not, that all people live in society for their mutual advantage." Thus, Priestley equated the "public good" with the "general happiness of mankind." Priestley itemized three kinds of liberty: political, civil, and religious, and he looked to the American colonies for examples. He explained Pennsylvania's flourishing more "than any other of the English settlements in North America" as a "consequence of giving more liberty in matters of religion at its first establishment."

A crucial distinction between the systems of Priestley and of Paine was the former's lack of differentiation between society and government. Priestley said, "The great instrument in the hand of divine providence, of this progress of the species towards perfection, is society, and consequently government." Societies were progressing, argued Priestley, "towards a state of greater perfection," but their advance was "retarded by encroachments on civil and religious liberty." Government was, for Priestley, "the great instrument of this progress of the human species towards this glorious state," and he judged a "form of government based upon the degree to which it favored or precluded this forward march.[71]

Paine's most recent biographer, political theorist John Keane, points out that *Common Sense* was the first modern political essay to distinguish between civil society and the state. The ideas of civil society ("society") and the state ("government") were used in European and American political writing "without exception," says Keane, as "coterminous" and "interchangeable terms" prior to *Common Sense*.[72] One of the deep structural innovations of *Common Sense* was in redefining society as a separate and antecedent concept that existed in tension with government.

Paine later claimed to have arrived at his novel position in early 1775. As he recalled it in the *Rights of Man*, he had stumbled upon the distinction between society and government as an empirical reality in late colonial America:

> During the suspension of the old governments in America, both prior to and at the breaking out of hostilities, I was struck with the order and decorum with which everything was conducted; and impressed with the idea, that a little more than what society naturally performed, was all the government that was necessary, and that monarchy and aristocracy were frauds and impositions upon mankind.[73]

In an unheralded passage in the first section of *Common Sense*, Paine not only dissociated society and government, he made them antitheses. He opened the first full section of the pamphlet with the following line: "Some writers have so confounded society with government, as to leave little or no distinction between them; whereas they are not only different, but have different origins." Here is a schematic of the three sentences that follow:

Society	Government
Produced by our wants	Produced by our wickedness
Promotes our happiness positively	Promotes our happiness negatively
By uniting our affections	By restraining our vices
Encourages intercourse	Creates distinctions
Patron	Punisher
A bless	A necessary evil (or an intolerable evil)[74]

One contemporary critic of *Common Sense* called Paine's ideas about society and government "only introductory to his main View," adding that they laid "a very indifferent Foundation for a very indifferent Building."[75] This critic was missing the point entirely. Paine was building a Lockean political system wherein "society" represented a state of nature, and "government" represented its antithesis, a state of war. Likewise, "society" embodied natural liberty at one end of the political continuum, while "government" stood at the opposite end as the consummate representation of manufactured order.[76] "Government" was what was happening inside the Pennsylvania State House, while "society" could be found within the walls of the London Coffee House.

The Upheaval of Political Authority

Paine's seemingly pedestrian distinction between society and government harbored monumental implications for American political theory.[77] Paine was not an anarchist, and he realized that human affairs demanded a degree of government to supplement the natural structure of society. He acknowledged that the "defect of moral virtue" in humankind forced advanced societies to choose some form of government or to risk anarchy.[78] Thus the presence of government was a necessary response to an originary defect in society, as he wrote, "Government, like dress, is the badge of lost innocence; the palaces of kings are built on the ruins of the bowers of paradise."[79] The temporal virtue created by a crisis, Paine argued, momentarily compensated for the systemic defect in humanity and allowed the natural functioning of society to accommodate the immediate need for political order.

Paine knew that a formal governmental structure was a long-term necessity. Following the conventions of early modern political theory, he identified "security" as the "true design and end" of government, but then Paine's argument in *Common Sense* took an unexpected turn. Any answer to the age-old political question "What is the end of government?" presupposes an implicit antecedent: "What is the beginning of government?" Paine drove this implicit question to the surface of his pamphlet. He included a hypothetical narrative, discussed in detail in Chapter Three of this study, of "the first peopling of any country" for the purpose of gaining "a clear and just idea of the design and end of government." To clarify the *end*, Paine traversed to the *beginning*, and he determined that, in "this state of natural liberty," the "first thought" of any small population was "society."[80]

The question of the beginning of government is ultimately an exposition of sovereignty: what or where or who is the font of power and right? As Samuel Johnson had said in his royalist pamphlet, *Taxation no Tyranny* (1775), "In sovereignty there are no gradations. There may be limited royalty, there may be limited consulship; but there can be no limited government." In every society, said Johnson, there must be "some power or other from which there is no appeal, which admits no restrictions, which pervades the whole mass of the community." From this power "all legal rights are emanations, which, whether equitably or not, may be legally recalled. It is not infallible, for it may do wrong; but it is irresistible, for it can be resisted only by rebellion, by an act which makes it questionable what shall be thence-forward the supreme power."[81]

What was the source of legitimate political authority and power—in a word, of sovereignty—in the American colonies? The answer was so self-evident that it was rarely enunciated. The ultimate sovereign was God, whom the American colonists most often referred to as the "Creator" or the "Almighty," two appellations that stressed respectively God's role as originator and omnipotent actor. Very few persons living in the eighteenth century disputed tracing the origin of sovereignty to God. The point of contention for Western political culture in early modernity—as it had been for religious culture during the Reformation—was whom God had designated the earthly caretaker of his deputed sovereignty. The monarchial divine right of kings and Catholic papal primacy were both answers to the question of the origin of earthly sovereignty, and hereditary succession and apostolic succession were essentially vehicles for the efficient transfer of sovereign legitimacy. Because no human can possess innate omnipotence, a distributive system of divine sovereignty was a necessary ideological anchor for establishing practical political power. In absolute monarchies, divine sovereignty was concentrated in the person of the king, while in the British Crown-in-Parliament system, political sovereignty was distributed between the king and the British electorate.[82]

In colonial America, every exercise of political authority was justified according to the flow of royal sovereignty, since colonists had been excluded from the British electorate.[83] The British colonies in North America had been set up originally as royal land grants to companies or individuals, but by the late eighteenth century most of the colonies had transitioned to a more direct monarchical connection and were ruled by "royal" governments. Connecticut and Rhode Island were still governed by corporate charters, but in practice, their assemblies functioned in accord with most of the other provinces. Only Pennsylvania and Maryland held fast to their proprietary governments in early 1776. The descendants of William Penn in Pennsylvania and Lord Baltimore in Maryland possessed delegated sovereignty over their provincial territories and enjoyed some prerogative by being a step removed from the control of British government. In the two proprietary colonies, then, this extra degree of separation from royal authority clouded the fact that all political authority in America was essentially derived from the king.

The Prohibitory Act made it clear to many wavering Americans that they had been officially excluded from the protection of the Crown, and only then did officials in most royal colonial governments admit that their umbilical connection to sovereignty had been severed. The colonists were operating royal governments without royal sanction. Without an American king-in-waiting, the royal colonies had to find an immediate substitute for royal governmental authority.

English republicanism was here a crucial antecedent for the American politicians. As a result of the English Revolution and even the restoration of monarchy in the "Glorious Revolution," the English people—the "commons"—had become the theoretical embodiment of sovereign legitimacy. The problem of Hanoverian contractualism in the seventeenth and eighteenth centuries was the disconnect between theory and practice. The British Constitution did incorporate a popular House of Commons to "check" the power of the Crown and Lords, but the practical flow of power, as evidenced in the exclusion of John Wilkes from parliament, was still decidedly top-down. Political sovereignty in the British Constitution remained fundamentally deductive. Like the subversive revolutions in science and religion that we investigated in Chapters Three and Four, Paine was attempting to topple a system of deductive sovereignty and to replace it with a new inductive paradigm.[84] In his new system, "the people" had been designated by God as the exclusive trustees of political sovereignty.

The Causes and Necessity of Taking up Sovereignty

The legislative encroachment of the British Parliament had, for over a decade, drawn the ire of America's colonial assemblies, and as a result, sovereignty was at the forefront of late colonial discourse. Thomas Jefferson recounted in his *A Summary View of the Rights of British America* (1774) the outrage felt throughout the colonies when "one free and independent legislature," the British Parliament, took it "upon itself to suspend the powers of another," the New York Assembly, "free and independent as itself." Parliament, said Jefferson, was pretending to hold a power "unknown in nature, the creator and creature of its own power." Jefferson continued,

> Not only the principles of common sense, but the common feelings of human nature, must be surrendered up before his majesty's subjects here can be persuaded to believe that they hold their political existence at the will of a British parliament. Shall these governments be dissolved, their property annihilated, and their people reduced to a state of nature, at the imperious breath of a body of men, whom they never saw, in whom they never confided, and over whom they have no powers of punishment or removal, let their crimes against the American public be ever so great?[85]

Jefferson's 1774 argument instantiated the inherent contradiction in the American position. He recognized, on the one hand, that "From the nature of things, every society must at all times possess within itself the sovereign powers of legislation," and yet he laid the colonies' grievances "before his majesty." Jefferson did not apologize for what he considered to be an aggressive tone of address, since he had written "with that freedom of language and sentiment which becomes a free people claiming their rights, as derived from the laws of nature, and not as the gift of their chief magistrate."[86]

Jefferson was bold in 1774, but he was not yet revolutionary. He, along with many other American colonists, still needed to wrestle with the question of royal sovereignty that Paine would present in *Common Sense*: "How came the king by a power which the people are afraid to trust, and always obliged to check?" Paine concluded that "such a power" could neither "be from God," nor could it "be the gift of a wise people."[87] The general American populace had been attuned to tyranny, mobilized for action, and primed for revolution in over a decade of resistance to parliament, and they had acquired a political vocabulary to describe their collective situation. Paine did not, therefore, have to invent new arguments in *Common Sense*; he simply had to extend arguments against parliamentary sovereignty to the royal domain. When the strands of royal sovereignty finally came unraveled—*emotionally* through the king's proclamation, speech, and *Common Sense*, and *legally* through the Prohibitory Act—the "middling class" of each colony was by then sufficiently conversant in British politics to demand their participation in the formation of new governments.

The peaceful compliance of the American people during the interregnum period—when *society*, not *government*, preserved order—became empirical proof of the rectitude of popular sovereignty. On May 29, 1776, the Reverend Samuel West preached a special sermon in Massachusetts commemorating the first anniversary of that colony's executive council, a body that had been elected in the aftermath of Lexington and Concord. West directed most of his attention to encouraging his audience of Massachusetts politicians to uphold high standards of virtue and fortitude in the face of adversity. But he also commented upon the political situations of Massachusetts in particular and of the colonies in general. West's description of the political necessity for Massachusetts to form a government of its own was a telling commentary upon the growing American consensus about the connection between governors and governed. West spoke,

> Who could have thought, that when our charter was vacated, when we became destitute of any legislative authority, and when our courts of justice in many parts of the country were stop'd, so that we could neither make, nor execute laws upon offenders, who, I say, would have thought, that in such a situation, the people should behave so peaceably, and maintain such good order and harmony among themselves! This is a plain proof, that they, having not the civil law to regulate themselves by, became a law unto themselves; and by their conduct they have shewn, that they were regulated by the law of God written in their hearts.[88]

West's election sermon shared with *Common Sense*—a text the minister owned and had read—an underlying belief in the natural beneficence of the American populace, a chief precondition for the plausibility of democracy as a legitimate governmental system.[89] In *society*, both West and Paine were arguing, the American people possessed both goodness and sovereignty. By separating society and government, *Common Sense* was redirecting the flow of sovereignty and erasing the ancient distinction between rulers and ruled.

The People of America

When royal authority evaporated in America, "the people" were the only conceivable repository of sovereignty.[90] But "the people" were not a concrete reality; they were a political ideal. Even though all agreed that the people's sanction was required for the formation of new governments, demonstrating that sanction was a complex theoretical question. The composition of "the people" was hotly contested and subject to numerous political maneuvers. Colonial politicians had to answer multiple questions before they could proceed with any plan of government: Who qualified as a member of "the people?" How did "the people" speak, or whom had they designated to speak for them?

Many of the provincial assemblies argued that "the people" of their respective colonies had delegated the full measure of political authority to their elected representatives. This was a persuasive argument, and it held an appealing republican logic for many colonists, including many of the elite delegates in the Continental Congress. In the colonies where the governing assembly was perceived to be acting in alignment with the general will of the populace, little exception was taken to this mediated approach to reconstructing government. But in colonies like Pennsylvania, Maryland, and New York, where street-level opinion seemed to be running in the opposite direction of official legislative proclamations, the idea of delegating the task of state formation to representatives of the old system seemed grossly illogical.

The dispute was, in short, whether the "people of America" were best represented in the State House or the Coffee House. The former "house" represented in 1776 the elite establishment, while the latter—though frequented by elites as well as artisans—represented a wider swath of the population. A writer in the *Pennsylvania Packet* questioned the disproportionate political influence of the wealthiest merchants and lawyers, asking, "Do not mechanics and farmers constitute ninety-nine out of a hundred of the people of America?" In Philadelphia specifically, he said, "one half of the property in the city" was owned "by men who wear LEATHERN APRONS," and "the other half" of the property belonged "to men whose fathers and grandfathers wore LEATHERN APRONS."[91]

Common Philadelphians were infuriated with what they viewed as the suicidal cowardice of the Pennsylvania legislature. In late February and early March, the Philadelphia Committee of Inspection had reviewed "the proceedings of the late sessions of Assembly" alongside the "very vigorous measures" of the British administration "which the latest accounts assure us may every day be expected to take place." The discrepancy between the aggressive British Parliament and the passive Pennsylvania Assembly was striking. The committee also noted "the appearance of intrigue by the appointment of Commissioners" who "are invested only with an insulting power to pardon (perhaps to corrupt and divide)." After taking into consideration these developments, the committeemen testified that they "could not acquit themselves to their own consciences, to you, and to the American interest," without offering "an immediate opportunity of a conference" in which the inhabitants of Pennsylvania "might speak the unrestrained language of determined freemen" and to "act with the vigor which has ever been the characteristic of Pennsylvania when free from the influence of partial councils." The committee's authority, it reminded the public, rested upon the injunction "of the late Provincial Convention" that the committee should "call another Convention when they may judge it necessary."

The Philadelphia Committee of Inspection determined that a provincial conference was necessary to prevent the continuance of the Pennsylvania Assembly's reluctance to place the colony in a strong defensive posture. Since the force of this opposition "arises chiefly from the members representing the three interior counties," who themselves "constitute a majority of the House" in spite of their tiny populations, the "proceedings of the Assembly might more properly be said to be the proceedings of those three counties than of the province in general."

The Committee of Inspection thus identified "the present unequal representation" as "the ground of every other complaint" and passed a resolution to call a provincial convention. Before the call could be circulated to the other local committees, the leaders of the Philadelphia committee met "with several of the members of the House" and found "with great satisfaction" that "those gentlemen indulged themselves in the hopes that a full and equal representation would be obtained in consequence of petitions now before the Honorable House, from several of the counties." Therefore, the Committee of Inspection ordered their Committee of Correspondence "not to forward, for the present, their letters for calling the Convention."[92]

To avoid an embarrassing conflict with the Philadelphia Committee of Inspection, the Pennsylvania Assembly agreed to expand its membership in underrepresented counties and within the city of Philadelphia.[93] The committee agreed to the assembly's choice of May 1 as the date for a supplemental provincial election designed to enlarge the ranks of the assembly.[94] But the struggle for power within Pennsylvania politics was far from over. In Chapter Ten, I outlined the heated newspaper controversy over independence, and we saw that the debate was not primarily an exposition of the merits of independence or reconciliation. By the late spring of 1776, both the "Moderate" party and the "Independent" party were deeply entrenched in their respective positions, and there was little defection between camps. While the interlocutors in the Philadelphia newspaper controversy interlaced their essays with matter relating directly to independence, the combative discourse revealed another, more fundamental point of contention: the constitution of the American public.

Since neither ideological camp received the benefit of a mass exodus from the other party, both sides of the controversy realized the importance of how they chose to circumscribe the political arena. As a rule, the Moderates believed that they would prevail if the public sphere remained compact and elite, while the Independents wanted to expand the boundaries of the public sphere to include more of the American populace. The reading and circulation of *Common Sense* was, of course, a landmark in the expansive strategy of the Independents. Before Paine's affordable, accessible, and affective text began to stir the pot of American opinion, colonial politicians would never have guessed that the agrarian-artisanal majority would squarely favor independence. The inordinate sales of *Common Sense*, coupled with breast-beating public support for the pamphlet's doctrines, keyed pro-independence politicians into the fact that they were backed by a potential landslide majority of colonists. If Independents could expand the electorate, then independence was a foregone conclusion.

The independence controversy, therefore, became in the late spring progressively less concerned with its nominal point of contention. The Continental Congress did not possess within itself the authority to declare independence; only the amorphous American public could initiate a declaration of independence. But who was the American public? How, or through whom, did they speak? Without the deductive flow of royal sovereignty coming from England, every political body in America claimed its mandate on the basis of an inductive popular sovereignty. Thus both sides of the independence controversy worked furiously to constitute a public that aligned with their objectives. In the remaining sections of this chapter, I will demonstrate the dynamic creation of competing publics during the eventful months of May and June in Philadelphia. By observing the creative struggle in Pennsylvania politics in the final months of colonial culture, we will acquire a deeper understanding of the high-stakes game of defining and vocalizing the sovereign public.

PART FOUR
RECONCILIATION'S LAST GASP

An Unpopular Assembly

Ten of the 41 members of the Pennsylvania Assembly who took their seats for the legislative session that began on October 14, 1775, came from the vicinity of Philadelphia, but only two, Benjamin Franklin and David Rittenhouse, represented the *city* of Philadelphia.[95] The eight representatives from the *county* of Philadelphia were John Dickinson, Robert Morris, Michael Hillegas, George Gray, Thomas Potts, Samuel Miles, Joseph Parker, and Jonathon Roberts. The artisan-lined streets of the *city* of Philadelphia were modestly represented, while the *county* of Philadelphia, a wealthy and sparsely populated suburban district, alone controlled twenty percent of the colony's votes. Pennsylvania had, at the time, eleven counties, but all of the legislative power was concentrated in a triumvirate of Philadelphia County, Bucks County, and Chester County. These three counties—because of historical ties to the proprietary interest and not because of relative population—together controlled 24 of 41 votes, a standing majority, in the Pennsylvania Assembly. The other eight "back Counties" and the city of Philadelphia were merely political window dressing.

On November 4, 1775, the Pennsylvania Assembly chose its delegates to the Continental Congress: John Dickinson, Robert Morris, Charles Humphreys, John Morton, Thomas Willing, Andrew Allen, James Wilson, Benjamin Franklin, and Edward Biddle, a group called by nineteenth century historian Charles Stillé, "the very flower of the moneyed and intellectual aristocracy of the Province."[96] Five days after appointing these distinguished gentlemen as delegates, the assembly gave them their political marching orders. John Dickinson, the primary drafter of the assembly's instructions, attempted, along with his coalition of political moderates and loyalists, to buttress the *status quo* by prohibiting Pennsylvania's congressional delegation—including himself—from voting for independence or any change in government structure. The last paragraph of those 1775 instructions kept the Pennsylvania delegates far from independence for most of eight months:

> Though the oppressive Measures of the British Parliament and Administration have compelled us to resist their Violence by Force of Arms, yet we strictly enjoin you, that you, in Behalf of this Colony, dissent from, and utterly reject, any Propositions, should such be made, that may cause, or lead to, a Separation from our Mother Country, or a Change of the Form of this Government.[97]

Why were the delegates in congress *bound* to obey the instructions of the Pennsylvania Assembly? One answer is obvious: the delegates were chosen by and served at the pleasure of the Pennsylvania Assembly and, therefore, could be recalled or reprimanded for veering off of the prescribed path. But a second answer rests deeper in the circulation of sovereignty in colonial America. The Pennsylvania Assembly was, in 1775, the only "legitimate" expression of the will and voice of "the people." The Pennsylvania electorate, "the people" as qualified by franchise rights, had deputed their sovereignty at each local election to their respective assemblymen. Because "the people" only spoke during the election, they were dissolved as a functional body at the close of the voting. Their sovereignty had been transferred to the Pennsylvania Assembly, which now acted and spoke on their behalf. On every day of the year besides an election day, the assembly *was* "the people" of Pennsylvania. This point cannot be missed: the inhabitants and even the qualified electors of Pennsylvania busying themselves in fields, shops, and offices everyday were *not* "the people" in a technical sense. Only if they assembled and spoke, as it were, with one voice, did the residents of Pennsylvania become "the people" of Pennsylvania. Therefore, the Continental Congress had to obey the instructions of the Pennsylvania Assembly, not out of respect for the assembly *per se*, but as an act of obedience to "the people" for whom the assembly spoke.

The Pennsylvania Assembly's unequivocal November 1775 instructions were designed to squash the possibility of independence. The instructions caused no major kerfuffle at the time they were issued, but the movement of popular opinion in the wake of *Common Sense* and the stubborn stagnation of the assembly's position unveiled a widening chasm between the common people and elites in Pennsylvania. In other words, the people and "the people" were dividing upon the issue of independence.

The assembly's stance on independence remained virtually unchanged from November 1775 through June 1776, in spite of accumulating evidence against the likelihood of reconciliation. The assembly was trying to dam up Pennsylvania politics against the swelling current of events and opinion. As pressure against the assembly's conciliatory position continued to build in early 1776, what had been amenable to most Pennsylvanians the previous November was becoming insufferable.

The Pennsylvania Assembly was digging in its heels against what it perceived to be an assault on its political dogma. To see the assembly's intractable loyalty to royal culture, one need look no further than the title page of their proceedings as published by Hall and Sellers in the late spring of 1776:

Anno Regni Georgii III. Regis, Magnae Britanniae, Franciae Y Hiberniae, Decimo Sexto. At a General Assembly of the Province of Pennsylvania, begun and Holden at Philadelphia, the fourteenth day of October, *Anno Domin* 1775, in the sixteenth year of the reign of our sovereign Lord George III, by the Grace of God, of Great Britain, France and Ireland, King, Defender of the Faith, &c. And from thence continued by adjournments to the sixth of April, 1776.[98]

The Pennsylvania Independents, especially those clustered in the Philadelphia Committee of Inspection, found this medieval habit of address—and the deferential culture it symbolized—repulsive. Pro-independence political strategists, so concerned with the British naval blockade off the coast of America, began to realize that the Pennsylvania legislature was functioning as a British political blockade erected in the heart of colonial government.

Electoral Compromise

The first step to break through this political blockade was the Philadelphia Committee of Inspection's early 1776 call for a provincial convention. In the eighteenth century, conventions were the primary means for constituting "the people" outside of the existing constitutional infrastructure, and the Pennsylvania Assembly rightly took the call for a convention as a threat to its sovereign legitimacy. As we have seen, the committee and assembly reached a compromise that would redistribute power within the legislature by increasing the representation of populous districts. On May 1, a colony-wide election would designate 31 new members of the assembly, nearly doubling the size of the legislature without adding a single representative for the three dominant counties.[99] Four of the new assemblymen would be chosen by the electorate in the city of Philadelphia, where the stakes of an election had never been higher.

The atmosphere in Philadelphia in the days leading up to the election was tense. Caesar Rodney, a congressional delegate from Delaware, observed in a letter scrawled on the morning of May 1, "this day is likely to produce as warm, if not the warmest, Election that ever was held in this City. The Forms for the parties are Whig & Tory—dependence & Independence."[100] Another Delaware delegate, George Read, wrote the same morning to his wife, "This day is their election for additional members of Assembly. Great strife is expected. Their fixed candidates are not known."[101] As Rodney and Read observed, the May 1 election was not merely a reapportionment; it was a plebiscite on independence.[102]

One Philadelphia broadside published on the eve of the election revealed the seething enmity between the two sides. The author, "Old Trusty," provided "the Tories" with "a handfill" of requisite lies to use the following day, since "we know ye can't go on without some." He also suggested that the Tories address the electorate concerning their political platform: "We, the King's judges, King's attorneys, and King's Custom-House Officers, having had a long run in this city, grown rich from nothing at all, and engrossed every thing to ourselves, would now most willingly keep every thing to ourselves."[103]

The Philadelphia newspapers boiled with accusations and arguments on both sides of the election. In an unsigned letter "To the Electors and Freeholders of the City of Philadelphia" in the *Pennsylvania Gazette* of May 1, a contributor tried to focus attention before the election on "A question [that] has been lately started, which has greatly changed our political ground." According to the writer,

> [The question] is, whether united, as heretofore, we shall continue our resistance to an oppressive ministry, till we can bring vengeance on their heads, and open the door for renewing our happy connection with the people of Great-Britain, or whether, without waiting to know clearly whether this be possible or not, we shall by our own act shut the door against reconciliation, immediately declare ourselves a separate people—and run the risk of all the evils which may follow.

The pro-reconciliation bloc, said this essayist, was supported by "every declaration of the Continent," while the pro-independence bloc was driven by "the publications of nameless writers, setting themselves up in opposition to public bodies—striving to inflame the passions and lead us on to schemes of dangerous and uncertain event, wholly inconsistent with our original purposes." The "essential difference between a declaration of independence (as it hath been called) and the continuing our defense upon the present foundation" was that the former left "no room" for "a conviction of her error on the part of Great Britain that may restore peace and tranquility." The writer warned the Philadelphia electorate, "If violent men, who have predetermined this great question, should be our choice, the guilt of every rash measure into which we may be hurried will lie at our own door." The writer conveyed his perception of the centrality of the independence issue upon the election: "Upon this single consideration the matter now rests. All other distinctions are vain and trifling." He condemned an "An Elector" who had encouraged, in "a most daring publication" in the *Pennsylvania Packet*, the people of Pennsylvania "to trample the charter of this colony under their feet" and "to pay no regard to the legal qualification of voters." Expanding the franchise, argued the anonymous essayist, would be a "fatal stab to our liberties."[104]

Also in the May 1 issue of the *Pennsylvania Gazette*, "Civis" made a similar point. Civis decried those "innovators" who had been "attempting to bring about a revolution in the happy constitution of this province" and "now, by a bold stroke" were trying "to take the election of four members for this city out of the hands of the lawful electors." Civis "need not tell" his audience that he referred to the aforementioned essay by "An Elector," a piece "that contains treason—the worst of treason—treason against the constitution." Civis recognized that the strategy of An Elector was to deprive "every stickler for dependency on Great Britain" of a voice in the provincial government, and to replace that political bloc with "those only who have already fixed their sentiments in favour of independence, without regard to their age, condition, or their knowledge of our constitution." Civis was appalled at the thought of an electorate composed of "a great number of associators in this city," including "minors and apprentices," some "new men lately arrived among us," and those "who know not the happy form of the government of Pennsylvania."

Civis argued that "the opposers of independence, in every public body, from the Congress downwards, and in the mass of the people, are the true whigs, who are for preserving the constitution." These were "the men who first set on foot the present opposition," and these were the men, Civis opined, who ought to "bring it to a happy conclusion." An Elector had declared that "the idea of a crown is rendered detestable to the whole western world," but Civis countered, "What daring falsehood is this! when have the western world authorized you, Mr. Elector, thus to speak their sentiments?" Civis asked An Elector to point to "one colony whose representatives, either in Assembly or in Convention" had instructed "their Delegates to favour the whim of independence and a republic." Advocates for independence, said Civis, were "attempting to hurry you into a scene of Anarchy" and a "leap in the dark."[105]

An Elector did not respond to these dual attacks until May 15 in an essay titled significantly, "To the free and independent Electors of the City of Philadelphia." An Elector was "astonished at the hardiness of Civis and his fellow addresser" who had endeavored "to persuade the Electors that none but a handful of insignificants in Philadelphia favour *the whim of independence and a republic*," citing Adams's *Thoughts on Government* as proof that a republic was "the only rational government that ever was established among mankind." An Elector observed that "there is more opposition to independence in this Province, than in all the Continent besides." The Pennsylvania Moderates had been "lulling us asleep with the fallacious pretence of *reconciliation on constitutional terms*," and they were responsible for causing the colony "to let slip a season" they had been "warned to improve." After reading the parliamentary records on sending commissioners, said An Elector, "Every step taken in the business plainly sets forth their commission *to receive submissions, and grant pardons with proper exceptions*." According to An

Elector, These were the grounds for a reconciliation that Civis and Cato were "driving at you to accept."[106]

The First of May

We can gain a vicarious sense of the heady day of May 1, 1776, by following Independent activist Christopher Marshall around Philadelphia. Marshall awoke, ate breakfast, and walked to a friend's school room at nine in the morning to confer in private with his fellow pro-independence strategists. Marshall left the meeting and stopped by his son's house to make arrangements for a lunchtime visit. He went next to the London Coffee House and then returned home for a few minutes' reprieve before what he knew would be a long afternoon and evening. Marshall again put on his jacket and walked to the Pennsylvania State House, where the elections were being held. There he ran into Thomas Paine, who agreed to go with Marshall to his son's house for a late lunch. After finishing their meal, the two returned to the State House, where they lingered until five o'clock. They then walked with James Cannon back to his house to drink coffee. The trio returned to the State House and stayed until eight, when Marshall went home to eat supper. After supper he came back to the State House once again and stayed until past ten o'clock at night, when the Sheriff announced the closing of the polls.

The election, wrote Marshall in his diary, was "one of the sharpest contests" in many years, though it was conducted in a mostly "peaceable" manner. One man, Joseph Swift, had made "some unwarrantable expressions" toward the Germans "that except they were naturalized, they had no more right to a vote than a Negro or Indian," words that raised the hackles of the sizable "Pennsylvania Dutch" community. When the sheriff, "without any notice to the public," at six o'clock "closed the poll and adjourned till nine tomorrow and shut the doors," the people were "alarmed" and immediately "flew to the Sheriff and to the doors and obliged him again to open the doors and continue the poll till the time above prefixed." The sheriff's actions sparked rampant speculation among Independents that the election had been fixed, since the six o'clock closing of the polls seemed calculated to exclude the city's working class electors. Marshall noted that "the Quakers, Papists, Church, Allen family, with all the Proprietory [sic!] party, were never seemingly so happily united as at this election."

The results were posted at midnight at the State House. The "Tories and Moderates" elected three of their candidates, Samuel Howell, Andrew Allen, and Alexander Wilcox, while the "Whigs" elected only one, George Clymer.[107] This was a grave disappointment to Marshall and to the other Independents, but they took solace in the fact that they split the top eight positions in the election with a spread of only 51 votes separating the first from the eighth candidate.[108]

The Moderates had won the day, and men like William Smith raised their glasses the next evening in celebration of a hard fought victory. But the Moderates' success was fleeting. Philadelphian James Allen was elected on May 1 as a Moderate candidate from Northampton County—his country home. On May 15, Allen recorded in his diary that he was "now a political character," and boasted that he had only met with marginal opposition. But Allen saw clearly that the crafty Independents viewed the election as a setback rather than a defeat. Just two weeks after the contest, Allen frankly perceived that his election was fruitless. Although he was scheduled to assume his seat in the Pennsylvania Assembly on May 20, he anticipated that "we shall soon be dissolved."[109]

Part Five
CIRCUMVENTING THE CONSTITUTION

The Difference of Two Weeks

What happened between May 1 and May 15 to cause such a dramatic swing in Philadelphia politics? As I shall discuss in detail in the next chapter, the Continental Congress passed a resolution on May 10 and added to it a stronger preamble on May 15, which together urged the American colonies to establish new forms of government where the old forms were defunct. On the surface, this resolution was intended for those colonies whose royal governors had abdicated their positions or attempted to foment internal rebellion. But Pennsylvania Independent leaders saw in the congressional resolution an interpretive opening for dismantling their colony's proprietary government.

James Allen understood what was happening around him. The May resolve of the Continental Congress, recommending "to the different Colonies to establish new forms of Government, to get rid of oaths of allegiance &c." would be opposed, thought Allen, by the [Pennsylvania] assembly—a body with no inclination "to change their constitution." Allen predicted that a provincial convention would result from this impasse. He worried, "A Convention chosen by the people, will consist of the most fiery Independents; they will have the whole Executive & legislative authority in their hands." Allen recorded in his diary that on May 14, "the Resolve of Congress was read by [Thomas] Bradford at the Coffee House." As Allen observed the episode, the room was paralyzed by the announcement. He wrote, "One man only huzzaed; in general it was ill received. We stared at each other. My feelings of indignation were strong, but it was necessary to be mute." He believed that this "step of Congress, just at the time commissioners are expected to arrive, was purposely contrived to prevent overtures of peace." Allen continued, "Moderate men look blank," but he remained convinced—by the results of the May 1 election—that "the Majority of the City & province are of that stamp." Allen acknowledged that "Peace is at a great distance, & this will probably be a terrible Summer." With a hint of pride, he confessed, "I am very obnoxious to the independents; having openly declared my aversion to their principles & had one or two disputes at the coffee house with them." Still, Allen remained "determined to oppose them vehemently in Assembly, for if they prevail there; all may bid adieu to our old happy constitution & peace."[110]

A handful of pro-independence members of the Continental Congress clearly coordinated their efforts with those of the Pennsylvania Independents who used the Philadelphia Committee of Inspection as a base of operations. Between the congress's resolution on May 10 and its supplemental preamble on May 15, the Independent leaders sprang into action. On May 13, James Cannon hosted an evening gathering of Thomas Paine, Benjamin Rush, Timothy Matlack, Christopher Marshall, Benjamin Harbeson, and Paul Fooks.[111] The following evening, Paine, Marshall, and Fooks met with several others in "Burnside's school room" and "Agreed to draw up the heads of a Protest to be brought tomorrow night for approbation."[112] As this group of Philadelphia upstarts worked on their "Protest," events continued to move in their favor. The British warships *Roebuck* and *Liverpool* moved up the Delaware River toward Philadelphia, causing "Great numbers of families" to move out of the city, including most elite families in possession of secluded country estates.[113]

Protest and Remonstrance

The Philadelphia Committee of Inspection had sent several petitions to the Pennsylvania Assembly in late 1775 and early 1776, most of which were immediately tabled and later scuttled.[114] By late May, the Independents refused to petition a body they considered to be lacking sovereign legitimacy. The "Protest" that Paine and the other Independent leaders were composing was intended to express an alternative voice of "the people." The Independent cabal organized a May 20 gathering of Philadelphians in the State House yard condemning the Pennsylvania Assembly's restrictive instructions and demanding that the assembly cease functioning altogether. The "Protest" also called for a provincial conference of committees to elect a provincial convention in order to "carry the said Resolve of Congress into execution."

James Clitherall, a physician from Charleston then in Philadelphia to attend to the delegates from South Carolina, was fascinated by the partisan spirit in Pennsylvania. He observed that before the May 15 resolution of the Continental Congress, "the rage of the multitude" had "only vented itself in whisperings," but when the people heard from the congress "that those Colonies that did not find their present form of government sufficient for the exigency of the times [should] settle a form of government for themselves," then "the rage of the people burst out in a protest against their present Assembly, who had instructed their Delegates not to vote for Independency."

Out of curiosity, Clitherall attended the May 20 public meeting in the State House yard, and he was appalled at what he witnessed. The Independent leaders had drawn up a "Protest," which Daniel Roberdeau read aloud to receive the approval of the audience. Clitherall complained, "The people behaved in such a tyrannical manner that the least opposition was dangerous. They came seemingly with a determined resolution to comply strictly with the recommendations of the paper," since "Colonel Cadwalader, one of their favorites, was grossly insulted for proposing a different [wording], preserving at the same time the sense of the resolves." When the questions were put before the crowd, if a man "would not vote as they did," he would be "insulted and abused." Clitherall confessed, "I, therefore, thought it prudent to vote with the multitude, and we resolved that the present Assembly was incompetent to form a new constitution, which was absolutely necessary," and then the crowd proceeded to call "a conference of committees from each county to debate whether a convention should be held or a new Assembly chosen." Clitherall loathed the tactics used "to force men into Independency," but he clarified, "I do not mean by this that there was not a majority in their way of thinking, but to shew how unfair and partial their proceedings were."[115]

Paine and his associates took the resolves from the meeting and published them the next day in the *Pennsylvania Evening Post* as "The PROTEST of diverse of the Inhabitants of this province, in behalf of themselves and others," addressed to the Pennsylvania Assembly.[116] In response to—in fact, in concert with—the May 15 preamble of the Continental Congress that recommended forming new governments under the "AUTHORITY of the PEOPLE," the protesters pointed out that the "chartered power" of the Pennsylvania Assembly was "derived from our Mortal Enemy the King of Great-Britain, and the members thereof were elected by such persons only, as were, either in real or supposed allegiance to the said King." According to the protesters, the May 1 election had excluded "many worthy inhabitants whom the aforesaid resolve of Congress hath now rendered electors." The protesters decreed that the Pennsylvania Assembly "in its present state" was unfit to comply with the resolve of the Continental Congress. Because the Committee of Inspection had "on all occasions" supported "the rights of the people," the anonymous "inhabitants of this province" made "an application" for them to call a "conference of Committees of the several counties of this province." The "conference of Committees" would "issue out summonses for electing, by ballot, a Provincial Convention, consisting at least of one hundred members, for the purpose of carrying the said Resolve of Congress into execution."[117]

This group of pro-independence protesters was so angry with the loyalist actions of the Assembly that they published a separate address "To the Public in all Parts of the Province" in the same issue of the *Pennsylvania Evening Post*. In a chiasmus that only Paine could have written, the Independents informed their "Friends and Fellow Countrymen" that they would soon be "called upon to declare whether you will support the union of the colonies in opposition to the instructions of the House of Assembly, or whether you will support the Assembly against the Union of the Colonies." The Philadelphian authors of the address said, "The sense of this city hath been publicly taken, and we will not be belied by Tories." A crowd of 7,000 Philadelphians had met at the State House "and have sworn to support the Union."[118]

The Philadelphia Independents were positioning themselves and their semi-official seat of power, the Committee of Inspection, as a direct manifestation of "the people" of Pennsylvania. But the resistance of the Moderates was still vigorous. Directly beneath a reprint of the "Protest" in the May 22 issue of the *Pennsylvania Gazette*, readers encountered "The Address and Remonstrance of the Subscribers, Inhabitants of the City and Liberties of Philadelphia." The "Remonstrance" had been presented "to the Honourable the House of Assembly" as a petition signed by "a respectable number of the inhabitants of this city and liberties." According to the "Remonstrance," the purpose of the "Protest" was "to subvert and change the constitution of this government, upon sundry allegations which we cannot conceive to be well founded." The "charter and wise laws of Pennsylvania," argued the remonstrators, were a "birthright" either "consented to by ourselves or delivered down to us by our ancestors." The "Remonstrance" disputed the "Protest" on the grounds that it held up the "Resolve of the Congress, of the 15th instant, as an *absolute* injunction" to take up "*new governments* throughout all the united colonies, under the authority of the people." The congressional resolution was, instead, "only a conditional recommendation" addressed to the "respective Assemblies and Conventions of the United Colonies, where *no government sufficient to the exigencies of their affairs has been established.*" Wherever "*Assemblies* exist, and can meet as the ancient constitutional bodies in their respective colonies," argued the remonstrators, then

> the public business is to be carried on by *them*, and by *Conventions*, only in those urgent cases where arbitrary Governors, by prorogations and dissolutions, prevent the Representatives of the People from sitting, to deliberate on their own affairs, or have subverted the constitutions, by abdicating their offices, and levying war against these colonies.

The remonstrators accused the protestors of "setting on foot a measure which tends to disunion and must damp the zeal of multitudes of the good people of Pennsylvania in the common cause, who, having a high veneration for their civil and religious rights, as secured by their charter, never conceived" that, by participating in "the support of the charter rights" of Massachusetts, they "they would be called upon to make a sacrifice of their own charter." The "Remonstrance" urged that "whatever temporary alteration in *forms*" may be justified as expedient by "the urgency of affairs or the *authority* of the people" of Pennsylvania, "*that* authority is fully vested in our Representatives in Assembly freely and annually chosen."[119]

The Pennsylvania Proprietary Party aggressively circulated its "Remonstrance" in late May and June. Two members of the party, busily going door-to-door with the "Remonstrance" in Lancaster and York, had been detected by pro-independence militiamen. According to Benjamin Rush, the first remonstrator fled, and the second was "arrested by a county committee" and forced to leave "without gaining a single convert to toryism." The document had been burnt as "a treasonable libel upon the liberties of America" in Reading, said Rush, and "many hundred" who signed it in the vicinity of Philadelphia had "repented of their folly and scratched out their names." Rush recounted another story of the fate of the "Remonstrance" with glee. In the town of Oxford, "a spot watered with the tory dew of the Reverend Dr. Smith's ministry," one German accosted the man "who by a direct falsehood had prevailed upon him to sign the Remonstrance, and begged him to erase his name." When the proprietary man refused, the "German in a passion took the paper out of his hands and tore it into a thousand pieces," all the while calling him a damned liar.[120]

By the beginning of June, the principles set out in the "Remonstrance" had lost their political traction. "A Protestor" wrote in the *Pennsylvania Journal* that the Moderates' "Remonstrance" was "decent in point of language and innocent in appearance," but in fact it was "as insidious, as villainous and treasonable a paper as ever yet appeared in North-America." According to "A Protestor," the powers of government could not, after a "renunciation of allegiance to the Tyrant of Britain," fall into the hands of a "set of men who had jointly shared these powers with him." Since the powers of government "did in a whole and entire manner originate from the people at large," then they must, upon a "dissolution of government, return to the people at large again" in the "same whole and entire condition." The remonstrators tried, said "A Protestor," to "persuade the people and the House [of Assembly], that the House had a power the most dangerous that can be imagined, a power to frame a constitution to perpetuate themselves." Thus, said the writer, "the contrivers and knowing abettors of said remonstrance are treasonable subverters of the fundamental right of society: the right of disposing the powers of government in the manner they judge most for their happiness and security."[121]

Political theory became very practical in the spring of 1776. One writer in the May 22 *Pennsylvania Journal* asked a series of fifteen "Serious QUESTIONS proposed to all friends of the rights of mankind in Pennsylvania." The questions, beginning with "WHAT is government?," demonstrated the writer's concern over the legitimacy of political authority and representation in his colony. He held that a new government ought to be established, "When the old becomes impracticable, or dangerous to the rights of the people." He then asked, "Is that the present state of our government?" His answer:

Every officer of it is bound by oaths of allegiance and fidelity to our enemies. The chief magistrate is wholly independent of the people both in fortune and authority. The use of our constitution is impracticable in many instances, and dangerous in all, therefore, necessity says it ought to be laid aside.

The writer then asked "Who ought to form a new constitution of government?," and he answered, "The people." Any "public persons" ought "to derive their authority to govern" from "the people whom they are to govern," and the "object of the government" should be the "welfare of the governed."[122] In this anonymous contributor's comments, we see "the people" equated with "the governed," and here an important shift was taking place. "The people" were the beginning and the end of government, and property qualifications no longer held pride of place in defining the electorate. The *governed*, and not the *governors*, were now "the people."[123]

Evacuating Philadelphia

Numbers were currency in revolutionary Philadelphia. In an ironic twist of political events, the motivating January combination of *Common Sense* and the news of defeat in Quebec actually may have *slowed* the independence cause by about a month, because many of Philadelphia's most fervent supporters of independence marched for Canada with the city's First Battalion at the end of January, in spite of "severe cold weather for some days past."[124] Moderate and loyalist Philadelphians, of course, remained where they were, and thus cobbled together a slim majority on May 1.

But the same circumstantial skewing of the electorate would, one month later, bite back at the Moderates. The imminent threat of a British siege of Philadelphia sparked the evacuation of the city by wealthy families to the safety of their rural estates.[125] When this elite core of Moderate support absconded from their townhomes, the only residents left in Philadelphia were those who were prepared to fight for the only home they could afford. The *Declaration of Independence* was approved in Philadelphia by a unanimous and self-selected majority. After the *Declaration*, Benjamin Rush observed, "The tories are quiet—but very surly. Lord Howe's proclamation leaves them not a single filament of their cobweb doctrine of reconciliation." Rush added, "The proprietary gentry have retired to their country seats, and honest men have taken the seats they abused so much in the government of our state."[126]

James Allen, one of Rush's "surly" Tories, remained in Philadelphia longer than most of his elite peers because of his duties in the Pennsylvania Assembly. As early as March 6, 1776, Allen was preparing to leave the city. He recorded in his diary that day, "The plot thickens; peace is scarcely thought of—Independency predominant. Thinking people uneasy, irresolute & inactive. The Mobility triumphant." Allen complained, "Every article of life doubled. 26,000 troops coming over; The Congress in *æquilibris*: on the question, Independence or no? Wrapt in contemplation of these things I cry out—'*O! Rus quando ego te aspiciam &c.*,'" a line from Horace which translates as, "O! Rural home, when shall I behold you?"[127]

On June 16, Allen finally got his wish, and he "set off" with his family, his "Chariot," and two horses for his country estate in Northampton. Allen recorded in his diary that, from May 20 until that day, he had been "very active in opposing Independence & a change of Government" from his seat in the assembly. Allen conceded, "But the Tide is too strong, we could not prevent a change of instructions to our Delegates." The loyalist assemblyman noted, "The names of those 13 members, (of whom I was one) that voted against changing the instructions were put on the Coffee House books. We were undone by false friends in Assembly, who have since turned out warm independents, tho' they affected to oppose it then."[128]

James Allen, who considered the "madness of the multitude" but "one degree better than submission to the Tea-Act," came from a family of unwavering loyalists.[129] On September 3, 1776, "high words passed at the Coffee House" as William Allen, James's father, declared "that he would shed his blood in opposition to Independency," while Colonel John Bayard retorted that he would do the same "in the support of Independency."[130] William Allen's vehement behavior was, according to Christopher Marshall, censured following William Bradford's complaint to the Committee of Safety "of the abuse offered by Allen to the public."[131] Opposition to independence, only months earlier a hallmark of patriotism among the guardians of the old order, was now construed as abusive to a newly constituted public.

Part Six
DESTRUCTION OF THE INSTRUCTIONS

Declaration of Indecision

After May 15, 1776, the Pennsylvania Assembly was only a shadow of its former self. The anti-independence Moderate coalition had rejoiced in its success at the election of May 1, but the day scheduled for swearing in the new assemblymen, May 20, revealed how just transient was that success. The Moderates and Independents had hammered out a compromise after the election that erased the standard obligation of new assemblymen to swear allegiance to the King of England. With that concession, the Moderates expected the assembly to return to business-as-usual. But at the May 20 induction meeting of the Pennsylvania Assembly, only 27 of the 71 members were present.[132] Without the requisite quorum, the assembly adjourned to the next day. The records of the Pennsylvania Assembly indicate that, from that day until the proprietary legislature was officially dissolved, no official quorum ever materialized.[133]

In a position of manifest weakness, the Pennsylvania Assembly decided to revise its instructions to the colony's congressional delegation. This decision was not motivated by a change of heart on the matter of independence; it was a desperate attempt to affirm the assembly's authority. On June 8—the day *after* Richard Henry Lee had introduced the resolution for independence in the Continental Congress—a new set of instructions met with the Pennsylvania Assembly's dispassionate approval and then were laid aside for a transcription and a final vote. In the week between informal approval of the instructions and a formal vote, the shriveled Pennsylvania Assembly met briefly every morning and afternoon for a depressing headcount and then a routine adjournment due to the lack of a quorum.[134] Rather than admit defeat, the assembly decided to continue meeting and even to pass bills under the pretense of a quorum.

On June 12, the *Pennsylvania Gazette* published two divergent texts on the same page. Turning to the second page of Hall and Sellers's paper, readers encountered the Virginia Provincial Congress's *Declaration of Rights* and the Pennsylvania Assembly's new instructions to the colony's delegates in Continental Congress.[135] The revised instructions, written yet again by John Dickinson and approved by an unconstitutional minority in the assembly, kept the topic of independence at arm's length.[136] Even after unremitting public outrage forced the assembly to draw up new instructions for its delegates, those instructions included no apology for the restrictions of the prior November. "The situation of public affairs is since so greatly altered," admitted the assembly, "that we now think ourselves justifiable in removing the restrictions laid upon you by those instructions." The assembly acknowledged the change that had taken place within the colony in half a year, but their new instructions employed only the negative agency of *removal*, not the positive agency of *injunction*. The new instructions included several explanations for the political shift that merited lifting the November restrictions. The combined measures of the British government, the assembly said, "manifest such a determined and implacable resolution to effect the utter destruction of these Colonies, that all hopes of a reconciliation, on reasonable terms are extinguished." But rather than following this conclusion with a resounding call for independence, the assembly's instructions whimpered, "Nevertheless, it is our ardent desire that a civil war, with all its attending miseries, should be ended by a secure and honourable peace."

The Pennsylvania Assembly's new instructions authorized the province's delegates "to concur with the other Delegates in Congress" in the formation of further "compacts between the United Colonies" and in the conclusion of treaties with "foreign kingdoms and states." The assembly stressed that the delegates should adopt only "such other measures as shall be judged necessary for reserving to the people of this colony the sole and exclusive right of regulating the internal government and police of the same." No mention whatsoever was made of independence.

The assembly pathetically repeated, "The happiness of these colonies has, during the whole course of this fatal controversy, been our fist wish. Their reconciliation with Great-Britain our next. Ardently have we prayed for the accomplishment of both." The assembly's sighing instructions concluded with a blubbering, abstract pseudo-commitment:

> But if we must renounce the one or the other, we humbly trust the mercies of the Supreme Governor of the Universe, that we shall not stand condemned before his throne, if our choice is determined by that over-ruling law of self-preservation, which his divine wisdom has thought fit to implant in the hearts of his creatures.[137]

The moment called for a statement of impenetrable resolve, but the assembly offered only a cross-your-fingers apology. This vacuous statement sealed the case for the impudence and impotence of the Pennsylvania Assembly, and a cascading majority of Pennsylvanians had had enough. Exactly one week after the publication of the assembly's new instructions, a Provincial Conference of Committees commenced its meeting at Carpenters' Hall to draw up an alternative set of instructions that reflected the will of the people in Pennsylvania.

The Philadelphia Committee of Independence

The organized boycotts and nonimportation agreements of the previous decade had started the demolition of colonial dependence upon Great Britain, while the measures' enforcement by local committees erected the social scaffolding upon which America's independence would be built.[138] The Philadelphia Committee of Inspection and Observation had been dominated in its inception by merchants and Quakers. In May 1774 the committee included only one mechanic (or artisan) among its nineteen members, but by February 1776, mechanics comprised 40 of the 100 members.[139] By the late spring of 1776, the city of Philadelphia was being run by the Committee of Inspection, which, in turn, was being run by a band of ragamuffins, many of whom lacked the traditional qualifications for political leadership. At the core of the Pennsylvania resistance to British authority were a few dozen men, drawn first into local politics via their involvement in the militia and their outspokenness in the London Coffee House.

The Philadelphia Committee of Inspection, with Colonel Thomas McKean serving as chairman, conceived it "to be their duty, as it is their inclination, to exert their utmost endeavours for carrying into execution" the May 15 resolve of the Continental Congress, "as well as others of that honourable body." The committee was taking over political authority in Pennsylvania from the king's deputies. In early June the committee instructed the "worshipful Justices of his Majesty George the third, of his Courts of Quarter Sessions and Common Pleas" in the County of Philadelphia to "surcease the exercise of any authority in the present courts until a new government is framed, and all the powers thereof exerted under the authority of the people of this province."[140]

By the end of May, Benjamin Rush, a pivotal member of the committee, was "*constrained* to believe" by the success of the independence movement following the May 1 election, that he was acting "under the direction of providence." Rush said, "The hand of heaven is with us," as evidenced in the fact that "Our cause prospers in every county of the province." Reinforcing the role of the Committee of Inspection at the head of affairs, Rush wrote, "General Mifflin and all the delegates from the independent colonies rely chiefly upon Colonel McKean and a few more of us for the salvation of this province." Rush anticipated "the establishment of liberty and the return of peace to our country," which he knew could only be made permanent in independence. In Rush's imagined future, "freedom shall prevail without licentiousness, government without tyranny, and religion without superstition, bigotry, or enthusiasm." Rush effused, "Oh happy days! To have contributed even a mite to hasten or complete them is to rise above all the Caesars and Alexanders of the world."[141]

Rush's close social network consisted of key leaders of every level of Pennsylvania politics: from the militia, the Committee of Inspection, the Committee of Safety, the Pennsylvania Assembly, and the Continental Congress. Rush—whose wife was staying in the safe confines of her family estate in New Jersey—spent long evenings shoring up support for independence. He was particularly encouraged by his time with "five of the back county assemblymen—*all* firm independents," and with word from Maryland that 7,000 men had taken up arms "to compel their convention to declare independence."[142]

Rush and the rest of the Philadelphia Committee of Inspection effectively drove the issue of independence out of the Pennsylvania Assembly and into the hands of local committees and militia battalions. The Philadelphia Committee, capitalizing upon the political opening created by the hobbled assembly, circulated letters throughout Pennsylvania in June urging each county to send representatives to a Conference of Committees in Philadelphia.[143]

Battalion Resolutions

The local committees and militia battalions scattered across the hills and valleys of Pennsylvania were often identical in their membership. Most groups who received the correspondence of the Philadelphia Committee of Inspection were eager to send representatives to a provincial conference, but many of these local bodies included with their acceptance of the invitation an advance statement of their political opinions. In county after county, committees and associations of militiamen began to publish their own local declarations of independence specifically to vocalize what they denominated to be the prevailing public opinion within their communities.

On June 10, the first battalion of Chester County "unanimously agreed" to a series of resolutions and instructions pertaining to independence and the formation of a new government. The Chester associators were particularly harsh in their disapproval of the Pennsylvania Assembly, condemning "the instructions given by our Assembly last fall, and renewed in the spring," because they displayed "the most dangerous tendency" and had been "calculated to break an important middle link in the grand continental chain of union." The battalion agreed with the Philadelphia Committee of Inspection that the province's governmental structure needed to be changed "to suit the present exigency of affairs," and they likewise concurred that "the present House of Assembly" had been "chosen for the sole purpose of executing the old, not framing a new, constitution." Since the assembly had "no authority to make the necessary alterations," any attempt to do so would be tantamount to "assuming arbitrary power." The associators closed their litany of resolutions with a confirmation of their support for American any of resolutions with a confirmation of their support for American independence, "at all hazards, be the consequences what they may."[144]

Another militia battalion from the same county echoed the sentiments of their neighbors. The Elk battalion of Chester County, consisting of 660 men, resolved publicly,

> That we, from a full persuasion that all hopes of a reconciliation between Great-Britain and these colonies are at an end, do think ourselves bound, in conjunction with the other colonies, solemnly to declare ourselves independent of Great-Britain. And we are of opinion, that the whole power of these colonies ought to be exerted in support of the unalienable rights of freemen.

Consistent with the resolution of the other battalion from Chester County, these associators acknowledged that "some alterations in the constitution of this province are absolutely necessary," and "That no body of men, elected for the purpose of legislation only, have the least right to alter one iota of the constitution, without powers delegated from the people for that purpose."[145]

Another battalion from Lancaster County gathered about the same time and listened to one of their members read in succession the May 15 resolve of the Continental Congress, the November instructions of the Pennsylvania Assembly, "The Protest of Diverse of the Inhabitants of this Province" and a circular entitled *The Alarm* by the Committee of Privates in Philadelphia.[146] In response to these texts, the battalion agreed unanimously to a series of spirited resolutions. They condemned the assembly's November 1775 instructions as operating "against the honour, interest, and safety of this Colony," adding that the instructions were also "very injurious to the American cause in general." The battalion blamed "the influence of those instructions" for the fact "that many of the people have viewed their rights and liberties as inseparably blended with the present constitution." In reality, continued the militiamen's resolutions, "the liberties of Pennsylvania, while in the tenure of the present government, are only nominal and precarious." Pennsylvania required a government "competent to the exigencies of our affairs," and the Lancaster battalion recommended that such a government "be immediately framed by a Convention appointed for that purpose." At the end of the meeting—which, it was noted, had been "conducted with the greatest decorum"—the battalion "gave three cheers" as further "testimony of their hearty approbation of the measures adopted."[147]

Back in Philadelphia, the "Committee of Privates of the Military Association belonging to the city and Liberties of Philadelphia" issued one more "Protest" that ushered in the Pennsylvania Assembly's final demise. The Committee of Privates protested the assembly's appointment of two new brigadier generals for the Pennsylvania Militia, effectively announcing that they would not serve under any officer appointed by the assembly. The Committee of Privates pointed out that "many of the Associators have been excluded by this very House from voting for the Members now composing it," and, "therefore, they are not represented in this House." Also, "the Counties which have the greatest Number of Associators have not a proportional Representation," for which reason those counties also declined to accept the assembly's authority.

The Committee of Privates presented the recent abolition of oaths to the king—for both electors and elected—as further proof of the assembly's illegitimacy. Most members of the Pennsylvania Assembly had been "chosen by those only who were acknowledged the liege Subjects of George our Enemy and derived the sole Right of electing this House from that very Circumstance." When the assembly "undertook to set aside this Allegiance" to the king, "they, by that very Act, destroyed the only Principle on which they sat as Representatives, and, therefore, are not a House on the Principles on which they were elected." Since the assembly had "derived no new Authority from the People, freed from such Allegiance," the legislature was "a Representative Body on no one Principle whatever."

Immediately after the Committee of Privates' "Protest" was read to the reeling legislators, according to the minutes of the Pennsylvania Assembly, "The House adjourned to Monday, the Twenty-sixth Day of August at Four o'Clock in the Afternoon." By that time, their services would no longer be required by the people of Pennsylvania.[148]

Provincial Conference of Committees

The Pennsylvania Provincial Conference of Committees convened on June 18 at Carpenters' Hall in Philadelphia. At the first meeting, the "Deputies from the Counties of this Province" selected two militia colonels, Thomas McKean and Joseph Hart, as their chairman and vice-chairman.[149] At the outset of the conference, all delegates were required to take multiple test-oaths to prove that they were not bound by any oaths to George III.[150] In the give and take of sovereign legitimacy, the Pennsylvania Provincial Conference justified its existence "in consequence of the Resolution of the Continental Congress of the 15th of May." The Continental Congress, of course, justified its own existence as a consequence of each constituent colony's sovereign will. In Pennsylvania, that authority had been transmitted through the assembly's process of nominating and instructing delegates. But the authority of the Pennsylvania Assembly was bound up in British charter rights, which had been abolished in theory, if not in practice, by the Prohibitory Act. By June 1776, most Pennsylvanians agreed that they needed a new government, but their certainty descended into confusion when asked whether the revocation of the sitting assembly's political authority should be followed by a provincial convention or simply by the election of an entirely new assembly.

The Philadelphia Independents wanted a provincial convention, because they viewed the existing proprietary charter as a flawed foundation upon which to build a new independent state. The invitation to the Conference of Committees advertised that there would be substantive debate on whether or not to call a provincial convention, but in reality the conference only concerned itself with deciding the mode of electing delegates to a convention. The Pennsylvania Provincial Conference met "for the express purpose of forming a new government for this Province, on the authority of the people only," but this was a tall order within a colonial culture pervaded with the mechanisms of royal sovereignty. Local committees and militia battalions were the only quasi-political entities in Pennsylvania that had not been appointed by the proprietor or the assembly. The "unconstitutional" Philadelphia Committee of Inspection and its sister committees in other counties benefited from a mature communication network and organizational infrastructure, and they became the most plausible institutional candidates for effective resistance to the claims of the Pennsylvania Assembly.

The theoretical objective of the Pennsylvania Provincial Conference of Committees was to prepare for a provincial convention, but the delegates also had another, more concrete objective: to replace the assembly's limp instructions with a forceful affirmation of independence. On June 24, the Pennsylvania Provincial Conference thus approved a new set of instructions—this time called a "Declaration"—to the colony's delegates in the Continental Congress. After a long string of "WHEREAS" clauses implicating the king, parliament, and people of Great Britain as the joint oppressors of America, the Pennsylvania Provincial Conference issued its positive instructions:

> WE THE DEPUTIES of the people of Pennsylvania, assembled in FULL Provincial Conference for forming a plan for executing the resolve of Congress of the fifteenth of May last, for suppressing all authority in this province derived from the crown of Great-Britain, and for establishing a government upon the authority of the people only, DO in this public manner, in behalf of ourselves, and with the approbation, consent and authority of our constituents, UNANIMOUSLY declare our willingness to concur in a vote of the Congress declaring the United Colonies FREE and INDEPENDENT STATES.[151]

The provincial conference did not limit its instructions to the Pennsylvania delegates in the Continental Congress. The body also sent clarifying instructions to the Pennsylvania Militia in words that echoed *Common Sense,*

> We need not remind you that you are now furnished with new Motives to animate and support your courage. You are not about to contend against the Power of Great Britain in order to displace one set of Villains, to make room for another. Your Arms will not be enervated in the Day of Battle, with the Reflection that you are to risk your Lives, or shed your Blood for a British Tyrant, or that your Posterity will have your Work to do over again. You are about to contend for permanent Freedom, to be supported by a Government which will be derived from Yourselves, and which will have for its Object not the Emolument of one Man, or class of Men only, but the Safety, Liberty and Happiness of every Individual in the community.[152]

In the wake of these instructions and in response to the coming declaration of independence, Pennsylvanians grabbed their muskets, pouches, and powder horns in record numbers to meet the British in battle. Across Pennsylvania and New Jersey, militia battalions marched to the aid of New York. Along the dirt roads leading to New York, "The fields were deserted, and every man seemed prepared to defend his liberties."[153]

A House Undivided

The warm, clear day of July 8, 1776, saw in Philadelphia a jubilant people basking in their newfound independence. The July 8 issue of the *Pennsylvania Packet* had announced the day's big news in the largest font that John Dunlap could find: "THIS DAY at Twelve o'clock, the DECLARATION of INDEPENDENCE, will be PROCLAIMED at the STATE-HOUSE."[154] But amidst the celebrations and demonstrations, July 8 was also an election day. Eight members from the city of Philadelphia and eight from the county of Philadelphia "were elected very quietly at the State House" that day to serve in the forthcoming Pennsylvania Convention.[155]

Beneath the drumbeats and fanfare, the Philadelphia Independents were still working. The city of Philadelphia's eight delegates to the Provincial Convention that began on July 15, 1776, were Benjamin Franklin, David Rittenhouse, James Cannon, Owen Biddle, George Clymer, Timothy Matlack, Frederick Kuhl, and George Schlosser.[156] These men—most of whom had been at the helm of the independence movement—knew that their work was not finished. They had engineered the unanimous popular approval of independence in Pennsylvania, but they still had a state government to form. And so, upon the same foundations and logic that had built the independence movement, these eight delegates led the charge for Pennsylvania's first state constitution, the most inclusive and democratic founding text of the entire revolutionary era.[157]

Common Sense made the question of independence relevant and accessible to a public that had been traditionally excluded from the political process. As coopers, tallow chandlers, and herdsmen walked from their shops and fields to their favorite inn or coffee house to read Paine's pamphlet, for the first time abstract political concepts began to make sense. Beginning at Front and Market Streets in Philadelphia and spreading to every corner of the American colonies, men grasped cups of steaming coffee and mugs of frothy beer and debated their collective political future. Political texts had always spoken *for* the people; *Common Sense* spoke *to* the people, and the people were eager to respond.

Common Sense had decentralized and democratized print culture, and Paine's associates in the Philadelphia Committee of Inspection had accomplished the very same objective in their diffusion and redirection of political sovereignty.[158] The network of committees and battalions gave a unified—if, at times, coercive—voice to the simmering sentimental independence of the Pennsylvania populace. When royal authority lost its meaning in America, "the people" became the last bastion of legitimacy. Traditionally, "the people" had been no more than a moniker used by elites to hijack power, but Paine and the Pennsylvania Independents plucked the term out of its theoretical purgatory and began forging it into a political reality.

Before *Common Sense*, there was no such thing as an "American people." There were Pennsylvanians, Virginians, South Carolinians, and the like, but colonial governance required no functional "American people." In fact, British colonial policy discouraged such collectivist thinking. *Common Sense* carved out a shared identity and a unified purpose for a new American people who were in 1776 reading and discussing the same political text for the very first time. That spring, public opinion began erupting from local committees and town meetings up and down the Atlantic coast. The American people were calling for independence, but only one body could give official voice to that call: the Continental Congress.

Notes: Chapter 11

[1] Adams's *Thoughts on Government* was first advertised in the DPP on April 22, 1776. For the circumstances of its composition, see: Butterfield, *Diary and Autobiography of John Adams*, 3:331-333. Adams sent a copy to James Warren on April 20, two days before it was first advertised in the newspaper. See also, T. R. Adams, *American Independence*, 150-151.

[2] Adams made this comment to Thomas Jefferson when comparing *Common Sense* to the Mecklenburg (North Carolina) "Declaration of Independence," which Adams believed authentic. Jefferson and most subsequent historians have dismissed the text as spurious. JA to TJ, 22 June 1819. Cappon, *Adams-Jefferson Letters*, 542.

[3] JA to AA, 18 February 1776. Butterfield, et al., *Book of Abigail and John*, 115-116.

[4] JA to Charles Lee, 19 February 1776. LDC 3:277.

[5] JA to AA, 19 March 1776. LDC, 3:398-399.

[6] Ibid.

[7] JA to AA, 28 April 1776. LDC, 3:592-593.

[8] JA to AA, 14 April 1776. LDC, 3:519.

[9] JA to James Warren, 12 May 1776. LDC, 3:660-662.

[10] JA to John Penn, [19-27? March 1776]. LDC, 3:399-400.

[11] Hyneman and Lutz, 1:403.

[12] Ibid.

[13] Ibid., 1:405.

[14] Ibid., 1:402-403.

[15] JA to John Penn, [19-27? March 1776]. LDC, 3:400.

[16] Ibid.

[17] Ibid.

[18] Ibid.

[19] Hyneman and Lutz, 1:404-405.

[20] Ibid., 1:408.

[21] JA to John Penn, [19-27? March 1776]. LDC, 3:403.

[22] Ibid.

[23] Ibid., 3:405.

[24] Of course, the building provided the setting for the *Articles of Confederation*, and the State House complex also housed the first sessions of the United States Congress before the nation's capital moved to Washington, DC, at the turn of the nineteenth century.

[25] Hamilton was the first trained lawyer in Pennsylvania and is best remembered for his role in the defense of John Peter Zenger in a landmark trial concerning freedom of the press.

[26] Massey, *Two Centuries of Philadelphia Architectural Drawings*, 1; Mires, *Independence Hall in American Memory*, 1.

[27] Edward Biddle of Berks County assumed the role of Speaker for the session beginning on October 14, 1774, and John Morton of Chester County, who had taken the Speaker's chair when Biddle had fallen ill, remained Speaker for the session that began on October 14, 1775.

[28] Some former delegates even begged their colleagues in the South Carolina Provincial Congress not to appoint them again to the Continental Congress.

They were physically drained by the travel, and their emotional health suffered not just because of their absence from family and friends, but because a simple epistolary exchange on business matters or family safety could take months to complete. See South Carolina, *Journal of the Provincial Congress of South Carolina*.

[29] We know that the Continental Congress met in the Assembly Room at the Pennsylvania State House, but it is less clear where the displaced Pennsylvania Assembly met within the same building during their overlapping sessions. The only other room on the first floor large enough and private enough for the assembly to meet was the Supreme Court Room, but it was still being used by Chief Justice Benjamin Chew and his court. Upstairs, the Long Gallery afforded insufficient privacy for the assembly to meet, since it functioned like an open reception area for the other two upstairs rooms. That leaves only two possible rooms in which the assembly could have met: the Assembly Committee Room and the Council Chamber. The Pennsylvania Assembly's records from the October 1774 session and earlier indicate the governor's secretary bringing "down" messages to the Assembly Room whenever the governor requested a meeting with the assembly in the Council Chamber on the second floor. In 1775 and 1776, the records of the assembly include no such directional markers, but the Speaker of the House and the full Pennsylvania Assembly were regularly requested to attend the governor in the Council Chamber to finalize legislation. Here is an account, taken from the Pennsylvania Assembly's minutes from March 23, 1776, of one such exchange between Governor John Penn and the colonial legislature:

> The Governor is in the Council-Chamber and requires the Attendance of the Speaker and the House to enact into Laws the Bills that have been returned with his Assent. Mr. Speaker then, with the whole House, waited on the Governor, and being returned from the Council-Chamber, the Speaker resumed the Chair.

This description (and others like it from the same session) indicates that the assembly was *leaving* their regular meeting room and *going to* the governor, who waited for them in the Council Chamber. By a process of elimination, then, the Assembly Committee Room was the alternate meeting location of the full Pennsylvania Assembly while the Continental Congress was using their regular space. The minutes of the Pennsylvania Assembly indicate that they ordered eighteen Windsor chairs on October 18, 1775 (during the first week of their new session), which would indicate that they were supplementing an existing number of chairs to accommodate their 41 members. It is plausible that the Assembly Committee Room already had two dozen chairs in it for committee functions, and with the addition of the new chairs, that number would have seated the entire Assembly. See Pennsylvania, *Votes and Proceedings of the House of Representatives of the Province of Pennsylvania*, 698, 625.

[30] The Pennsylvania delegates were conscientious and typically did not try to play an active role in both bodies at the same time. Benjamin Franklin tried in February 1776 to resign his seat in both the assembly and the Committee of Safety, blaming his age for the decision. See Pennsylvania, *Votes and Proceedings*, 675. The records of the Pennsylvania Assembly do indicate that on one

occasion John Dickinson served as a direct intermediary between the Continental Congress and the assembly. See, Pennsylvania, *Votes and Proceedings*, 6:644.

[31] Jordan, "A Description of the State-House."

[32] David Rittenhouse became the keeper of the State House clock at the end of 1774. See Pennsylvania, *Votes and Proceedings*, 560-561.

[33] Boggs and Randolph, "Inns and Taverns of Old Philadelphia," 187-189. See also, Brenner, *List of Philadelphia Inns and Taverns*.

[34] Lillywhite, *London Coffee Houses*, 17; Picard, *Dr. Johnson's London*, 199-200.

[35] Steele and Addison, 286-288

[36] Charles II, *By the King. A Proclamation for the Suppression of Coffee-Houses*.

[37] This specialization facilitated the later establishment of stock and commodity exchanges. Lillywhite, 24-25.

[38] Picard, 199-200. "Welsh rabbit" was the original term for "Welsh rarebit," a cooked cheese spread.

[39] Picard, 130-131.

[40] Levere, "Natural Philosophers in a Coffee House," 142-143.

[41] Quoted in Levere, 133.

[42] The London Coffee House was succeeded progressively as the center of economic activity in Philadelphia by the City Tavern (sometimes called the Merchants' Coffee House), the Philadelphia Merchants' Exchange, and the Philadelphia Bourse. This was the lineage of the first stock exchanges in America.

[43] Davis, "The Colonial Coffeehouse," 26-29, 86.

[44] Ibid.

[45] Scharf and Westcott, *History of Philadelphia*, 1:279n-281n.

[46] Wallace, *An Old Philadelphian, Colonel William Bradford*, 337-348.

[47] Bridenbaugh, *Cities in Revolt*, 161-162.

[48] Davis, 26-29, 86.

[49] Stone, "How the Landing of Tea was Opposed in Philadelphia."

[50] William Bradford's diary in the HPS reveals that he spent a great deal of time reading and studying during this period, and his leisurely schedule frequently involved oversleeping.

[51] 1 November 1775. Marshall, *Diary*.

[52] Hawke, *Benjamin Rush*, 142-143.

[53] 20 January 1776. Marshall, *Diary*. Pauline Maier described Thomas Young as a penniless physician who "spent his medical career teaching that the greatest danger lay in hesitation, in delaying 'heroic' remedies which alone could save the patient." Maier also observed that Young's "revolutionary politics were influenced less by England's radical Whig tradition than by the Enlightenment in science." Maier, "Reason and Revolution: The Radicalism of Dr. Thomas Young," 243, 247. Marshall and Matlack were among those who would be disowned by the Philadelphia Society of Friends on account of their participation in the Revolutionary War. These men joined about a hundred others in forming in 1781 "The Monthly Meeting of Friends, called by some Free Quakers, distinguishing us from those of our bretheren who have disowned us." See Biddle, "Owen Biddle."

[54] See Marshall, *Diary*, and Hawke, *Benjamin Rush*, 142-143.

[55] 21 April 1776. Marshall, *Diary*.

⁵⁶ 2 February 1776. Marshall, *Diary*.
⁵⁷ 1 April 1776. Marshall, *Diary*; also, 26 March 1776, 5 April 1776. Matlack was a rich source of political information for the Committee of Inspection. He had been employed by the Continental Congress on May 15, 1775, as a clerk to Secretary Charles Thomson, and he was later placed in charge of the United Colonies' supply stores. *Journals of Congress. Containing the Proceedings from Sept. 5, 1774, to Jan. 1, 1776*, 1:100.
⁵⁸ Rickman, 38.
⁵⁹ Paine's friend and biographer was careful to note that, when the two had spent extended time together in 1792, Paine was "not in the habit of drinking to excess," while in 1802 Paine "did not drink spirits, and wine he took moderately." Rickman, 11.
⁶⁰ Rickman, 39.
⁶¹ *The Spectator, No. 10*, Steele and Addison, 210.
⁶² *The Spectator, No. 49*, Steele and Addison, 287.
⁶³ See, for example, WL to Ralph Izard, 14 August 1775. Ford, *Letters of William Lee*, 1:168-169.
⁶⁴ Freneau, "The Country Printer" (1791), from Pattee, *Poems of Philip Freneau*.
⁶⁵ On tavern culture in early America, see: Salinger, *Taverns and Drinking in Early America*; McNamara, *From Tavern to Courthouse: Architecture and Ritual in American Law*; Conroy, *In Public Houses: Drink and the Revolution of Authority in Colonial Massachusetts*; Hooker, "The American Revolution Seen Through A Wine Glass"; Kornfeld, *Creating an American Culture*; Lender and Martin, *Drinking in America: A History*; Rorabaugh, *The Alcoholic Republic: An American Tradition*; Shaw, *American Patriots and the Rituals of Revolution*; Thompson, *Rum Punch and Revolution: Taverngoing & Public Life in Eighteenth-Century Philadelphia*; Waldstreicher, *In the Midst of Perpetual Fetes: The Making of American Nationalism 1776-1820*; Waldstreicher, "Rites of Rebellion, Rites of Assent: Celebrations, Print Culture, and the Origins of American Nationalism."
⁶⁶ CS 2.18.
⁶⁷ CS 3.11.
⁶⁸ CS 3.33.
⁶⁹ See also, CS 3.8, 3.36, 3.47, A.7.
⁷⁰ Adam Ferguson, *An Essay on the History of Civil Society*; See also, Hill, *The Passionate Society: The Social, Political, and Moral Thought of Adam Ferguson*.
⁷¹ Priestley, *An Essay on the First Principles of Government; and on the Nature of Political, Civil, and Religious Liberty*.
⁷² Keane, *Tom Paine*, 116-117; see also, Keane, "Despotism and Democracy: The Origins and Development of the Distinction between Civil Society and the State, 1750-1850."
⁷³ RM 2, CW 1:406.
⁷⁴ CS 1.1-1.2.
⁷⁵ [Middleton,] *The True Merits of a Late Treatise*.
⁷⁶ Cf. CS 1.7.
⁷⁷ Paine held to this distinction throughout his career. In *Agrarian Justice*, one of last major works, he had begun to use the word "civilization" rather than "society, but the terms overlapped in his lexicon (as we see in the later hybrid,

"civil society"). Paine wrote, "A revolution in the state of civilization is the necessary companion of revolutions in the system of government. If a revolution in any country be from bad to good, or from good to bad, the state of what is called civilization in that country, must be made conformable thereto, to give that revolution effect." CW 1:621.

[78] CS 1.5.

[79] The "bowers of paradise" here referred to the garden-dwelling of Eden. CS 1.2.

[80] CS 1.3.

[81] Greene, *Samuel Johnson: Political Writings*, 10:423.

[82] Religious sovereignty in Britain was also divided between the King of England and the Archbishop of Canterbury.

[83] Some Americans were members of the British electorate, but this was by virtue of their British estates and titles, no by the imputation of a parliamentary franchise to American colonies.

[84] Since the Christianization of the late Roman Empire, political sovereignty in the West was delegated by God, the ultimate sovereign and font of all power, to his agents on earth: namely, emperors, popes, and kings. One of the manifold effects of the Protestant Reformation had been the displacement of religious and political sovereignty from the papacy and its local manifestations in the bishopric and priesthood. Sovereignty, long embedded in the traditions of the Catholic Church, was relocated to the translated text of the Bible, imputing *de facto* sovereignty to every person capable of scriptural interpretation via functional literacy in a vernacular language. The redirection of revelation away from the top-down, Latinate, exclusive order of papal authority and toward a bottom-up, vernacular, inclusive "priesthood of believers" enacted a cataclysmic redirection of religious sovereignty. The interpretation of God's will was no longer mediated by hierarchical authority; it was now mediated only by vernacular literacy. Protestants who followed this logic to its radical ends and who wanted to discern God's will, now possessed that will in transcription within one book, making obsolete any prerequisite reading of traditional interpretations and, by association, any formal religious education or knowledge of classical languages. In the English context, the extent to which Anglicanism retained formal hierarchical authority represents the degree to which the Church of England was a disaffiliated and repackaged Roman Catholic Church with a political sovereign, the King of England, substituting for the religious sovereignty of the papacy. There was a direct correlation between the republican English Revolution of the seventeenth century and the Protestant Dissenting theologies that fueled resentment of "papist" royal authority. Puritans, Congregationalists ("Independents"), Methodists, Baptists, Quakers, and Mennonites, were all by definition, if not always in practice, Dissenting Protestants. Some, like the Wesleyan Methodists with whom Paine had been affiliated during his 20s and early 30s, considered themselves reform movements *within* the Church of England, while others created an identity wholly separate from Anglican institutions.

[85] Jefferson. *A Summary View of the Rights of British America*.

[86] Ibid.

[87] CS 1.15.

[88] West, *A Sermon Preached before the Honorable Council, and the Honorable House of Representatives, of the colony of the Massachusetts-Bay.*
[89] Samuel West's inscribed copy of *Common Sense* is held by the MHS.
[90] See the "Virginia Constitution," PG, July 17, 1776. Likewise, on July 4, the Maryland Convention, meeting in Annapolis, resolved "that a new Convention be elected for the express purpose of forming a new government, by the authority of the people only." PG, July 10, 1776.
[91] DPP, March 18, 1776.
[92] PEP, March 9, 1776.
[93] See 8 March 1776 in Pennsylvania, *Votes and Proceedings*, 688.
[94] At first the assembly agreed on April 25, 1776, as the date of the election, but later pushed back the election date one week. Pennsylvania, *Votes and Proceedings*, March 13, 1776, p. 691.
[95] Thomas Mifflin had initially been elected to the assembly but requested that his election be "considered as void" because of his military duties. The assembly approved of Mifflin's recusal on November 24, 1775. David Rittenhouse won a by-election to fill Mifflin's seat on March 2, 1776 and assumed the seat on March 5, 1776. Franklin only attended sessions of the Continental Congress during this period, and so Rittenhouse was the city of Philadelphia's only *de facto* representative in the assembly See Pennsylvania, *Votes of Assembly*, 8:7301.
[96] Stillé, "Pennsylvania and the *Declaration of Independence*."
[97] "The Pennsylvania Assembly: Instructions to Its Delegates in Congress," November 9, 1775. Willcox, 22:251-252.
[98] *Pennsylvania. Anno Regni Georgii III. Regis, Magnae Britanniae, Franciae Y Hiberniae, Decimo Sexto. At a General Assembly of the Province of Pennsylvania, begun and Holden at Philadelphia, the fourteenth day of October, Anno Domin 1775, in the sixteenth year of the reign of our sovereign Lord George III, by the Grace of God, of Great Britain, France and Ireland, King, Defender of the Faith, &c. And from thence continued by adjournments to the sixth of April, 1776.* Philadelphia: Hall and Sellers, 1776.
[99] Pennsylvania. *Votes of Assembly.* 8:7301.
[100] Caesar Rodney to Thomas Rodney, 1 May 1776. LDC, 3:616.
[101] Read, *Life and Correspondence of George Read*, 157.
[102] Grundfest, *George Clymer*, 96.
[103] [Donaldson,] *To the Tories. Mind How Ye Fight [with] Your Lies Tomorrow, Gentlemen...[Signed,] Old Trusty.* Philadelphia: April 30, 1776.
[104] PG, May 1, 1776.
[105] Civis, "To the Freeholders and Elector of the City of Philadelphia," PG, May 1, 1776.
[106] "An Elector," "To the free and independent Electors of the City of Philadelphia," PG, May 15, 1776.
[107] Andrew Allen was the King's Attorney in Pennsylvania. His brother James was elected that day from Northampton County, and the two joined their father, William, in the Pennsylvania Assembly. This large Philadelphia family was noted for its unflinching loyalism to the Crown throughout the Revolutionary War.
[108] 1 May 1776. Marshall, *Diary*.

[109] 15 May 1776, "Diary of James Allen, Esq., of Philadelphia, Counsellor-at-Law, 1770-1778," 176.
[110] Ibid.
[111] 13 May 1776, Marshall, *Diary*.
[112] 14 May 1776, Marshall, *Diary*.
[113] Ibid.
[114] See Pennsylvania, *Votes and Proceedings*. On April 1, 1776, the Philadelphia Committee of Inspection published an address to the Pennsylvania Assembly openly requesting that the assembly's November instructions be rescinded. DPP, April 1, 1776.
[115] "Extracts from the Diary of Dr. James Clitherall, 1776."
[116] PEP, May 21, 1776. The Protest was also published in the DPP on May 27 and the PJ on May 22. I have taken my quotations from the PJ version.
[117] "THE PROTEST Of diverse of the Inhabitants of this Province, in behalf of themselves and others. To the Honorable the REPRESENTATIVES of the Province of PENNSYLVANIA," PJ, May 22, 1776, and PG, May 22, 1776.
[118] PEP May 21, 1776. Page 3 featured "The Protest," and Page 4 included an address "To the Public in all Parts of the Province."
[119] "The Address and Remonstrance of the Subscribers, Inhabitants of the City and Liberties of Philadelphia," PG May 22, 1776.
[120] BR to Mrs. [Julia Stockton] Rush, 1 June 1776. Butterfield, *Letters of Benjamin Rush*, 101-103.
[121] PJ, June 12, 1776.
[122] "Serious QUESTIONS proposed to all friends of the rights of mankind in Pennsylvania, with suitable ANSWERS," PJ, May 22, 1776.
[123] By June 1776, "A Watchman" could plausibly address a letter in the *Pennsylvania Packet* "To the Common People of PENNSYLVANIA" in which he rebuffed Tories and "pretended Moderates." DPP, June 10, 1776.
[124] 23 January 1776 and 28 January 1776, Marshall, *Diary*.
[125] The diary of James Clitherall of South Carolina is a revealing look at elite Pennsylvania culture in the spring of 1776. Clitherall arrived in Philadelphia on May 13, and he immediately tried to make contact with his "best friends" in the city, Jacob Duché and Benjamin West. Clitherall was disappointed that "the appearance of the King's Ships so far up the river made them hurry their families out of town." It did not take Clitherall long to perceive that "parties ran high" in Philadelphia, and he noted that "the body of the people were for Independency." The proprietary party and "most of the gentlemen of the city" attached to the proprietor's interest "were against it, lest the form of government should be changed, and [the inhabitants of Pennsylvania] would no more acknowledge the old officers of the government." The proprietary interest, observed Clitherall, believed that it was prudent to be "still in times of danger," but the people thought that such "inactivity in times when they were surrounded with as many dangers as the hairs of their heads" was "a base desertion." The proprietary interest "too late saw their behaviour had been too timourous and impolitic." Many of these loyal elites had, by mid-May, "retired into the country disgusted at the present proceedings, fearful of the people, and railing at men in office on account of their low birth and little fortune." "Extracts from the Diary of Dr. James Clitherall, 1776."

[126] BR to Charles Lee, 23 July 1776. Butterfield, *Letters of Benjamin Rush*, 103-105.
[127] Horace, *Satires* 2.6.
[128] 16 June 1776, "Diary of James Allen," 176.
[129] 6 March 1776, "Diary of James Allen," 176.
[130] William Allen, Jr., had been the Chief Justice of the Supreme Court in Pennsylvania. He was the father of Andrew Allen, King's Attorney in Pennsylvania and a delegate in the Second Continental Congress who resigned because of his opposition to independence. William's sons Andrew and James were both elected on May 1, 1776, to the Pennsylvania Assembly. The entire family remained loyalists before and after independence.
[131] 4 September 1776, Marshall, *Diary*.
[132] 20 May 1776, Pennsylvania, *Votes and Proceedings*, 726.
[133] The highest attendance figure recorded in the minutes of the assembly for this period was 36 out of 71, barely half of the total membership, but beneath the threshold used for a quorum by the assembly.
[134] Pennsylvania, *Votes and Proceedings*, 738-740.
[135] PG, June 12, 1776.
[136] The Pennsylvania Assembly appointed a draft committee on June 5, 1776 and formally approved of the new instructions on June 14, 1776.
[137] PG, June 12, 1776.
[138] Doerflinger, "Philadelphia Merchants and the Logic of Moderation," 213-214.
[139] Ryerson, "Political Mobilization and the American Revolution."
[140] "To the worshipful Justices of his Majesty George the third, of *his* Courts of Quarter Sessions and Common Pleas, for the county of Philadelphia. The Memorial of the Committee of Inspection and Observation for the City and Liberties of Philadelphia, &c.," PJ, June 12, 1776.
[141] BR to Mrs. [Julia Stockton] Rush, 29 May 1776. Butterfield, *Letters of Benjamin Rush*, 99-100.
[142] Ibid. In response to this popular pressure, the Maryland Provincial Convention resolved on July 4 that "a new Convention be elected for the express purpose of forming a new government, by the authority of the people only." PG, July 10, 1776.
[143] DPP, June 17, 1776.
[144] PG, June 12, 1776.
[145] PG, June 19, 1776.
[146] *The Alarm: or, an Address to the People of Pennsylvania on the Late Resolve of Congress, for Totally Suppressing all Power and Authority Derived from the Crown of Great-Britain*. Philadelphia: Henry [Henrich] Miller, 1776. Miller also printed *The Alarm* in German, and both versions began to be distributed in Philadelphia on Sunday, May 19, 1776.
[147] PG, June, 19, 1776.
[148] "The Protest of the Committee of Privates of the Military Association belonging to the city and Liberties of Philadelphia," 14 June 1776. Pennsylvania, *Votes and Proceedings*, 742-743.
[149] PG, June 19, 1776. McKean was also a delegate in the Continental Congress from Delaware. "The Lower Counties" of Delaware had long been a sepa-

rate colony from Pennsylvania, but they had traditionally shared some government functions and offices, which is why McKean represented both colonies in different capacities.

[150] PJ, June 26, 1776.

[151] PEP, June 25, 1776. "The DECLARATION of the Deputies of Pennsylvania met in PROVINCIAL CONFERENCE at Philadelphia, June 24, 1776." Also printed in the PG on June 26, 1776; PJ, June 26, 1776; *Postscript* to the DPP, July 1, 1776. See also, *Proceedings of the Provincial Conference of Committees, of the Province of Pennsylvania; held at the Carpenters' Hall, at Philadelphia. Began June 18th, and Continued by Adjournments to June 25, 1776.* Philadelphia: W. and T. Bradford, 1776; Broadside. *Proceedings of a public meeting in favor of Independence.* Philadelphia: W. and T. Bradford, 1776.

[152] Provincial Conference of Committees of the Province of Pennsylvania, "Instructions to Pennsylvania Militia from Pennsylvania Provincial Conference." *Pennsylvania Provincial Conference Minutes.*

[153] "Extracts from the Diary of Dr. James Clitherall, 1776."

[154] DPP, July 8, 1776.

[155] 8 July 1776, Marshall, *Diary.*

[156] PJ, July 10, 1776. See also, Biddle, "Owen Biddle."

[157] The new Pennsylvania Convention approved a unicameral legislative structure.

[158] For a similar dynamic in Virginia, see Isaac, "Dramatizing the Ideology of Revolution," 384-385.

Chapter Twelve

The American Mind

The Delegates of some Governments Clogs the necessary measures suggested by others; and thus the Chariot goes heavily on. That dam'd Idea of Reconciliation is continually damping and dividing the Assembly. I wish the Devil would fetch it out of Congress and them that holds it up to view.

General Nathanael Greene to Christopher Greene
June 7, 1776

This was the object of the *Declaration of Independence*. Not to find out new principles, or new arguments, never before thought of, not merely to say things which had never been said before; but to place before mankind the common sense of the subject, in terms so plain and firm as to command their assent, and to justify ourselves in the independent stand we are compelled to take. Neither aiming at originality of principle or sentiment, nor yet copied from any particular and previous writing, it was intended to be an expression of the American mind, and to give to that expression the proper tone and spirit called for by the occasion.

Thomas Jefferson to Henry Lee
1825

PART ONE
TEXTUALITY AND SOVEREIGNTY

A Journey from Philadelphia

As I approach the end of this study, many of the points I have tried to make in the preceding chapters are clarified by the juxtaposition of two journeys, each fraught with trouble and freighted with meaning. Paul Revere's "Midnight Ride" to Lexington and Concord in 1775 has been recounted in myriad books, poems, and songs as a defining journey in the history of the American Revolution, but two lesser-known journeys in 1776—one from January and another from July—played comparably significant roles in the movement toward independence. Both trips involved members of the Continental Congress, but the results of the trips could not have differed more. The stories of Christopher Gadsden of South Carolina *leaving* Philadelphia in January and Caesar Rodney of Delaware *returning* to Philadelphia in July illustrate the remarkable change in America during that span of time.

Christopher Gadsden, a delegate from South Carolina, left Philadelphia on January 18, 1776, to return to Charleston, where he also served as a colonel in the colonial militia and as a delegate in the South Carolina Provincial Congress. Gadsden had been pressing for weeks to be released from his duties in the Continental Congress, because he sensed the urgent need to return home to help his colony fortify against a threatened British attack. Gadsden also recognized that his colony would soon have to set up a government of its own, and he wanted to be present for the important act of framing that government. He knew well that the trip aboard a small pilot boat would be risky, since British naval vessels were patrolling the American coastline. If everything went well, the voyage would take four or five days, but everything did not go well. Gadsden's boat was run aground on the North Carolina shore by a British man-of-war, and Gadsden and the other passengers scrambled into the woods to escape capture. In the chaos of the pursuit, the frantic colonists abandoned the boat and most of their belongings. Gadsden sprinted through the sand clinging to only four items: a flag and three copies of *Common Sense*.[1]

The ragged party finished their journey overland, and three weeks after departing Philadelphia, Gadsden burst into the South Carolina Provincial Congress holding a bright yellow flag emblazoned with a coiled rattlesnake and inscribed with the slogan, "DON'T TREAD ON ME." Gadsden walked to the front of the room amidst an awkward smattering of cheers and presented the flag to William Henry Drayton, the President of the Provincial Congress, who ordered the flag to be displayed at the left side of his chair.

The next day, February 10, 1776, Drayton invited Gadsden to address the Provincial Congress. Gadsden walked to the front of the room and began reading aloud from his heavily underlined copy of *Common Sense*. After he finished reading selections from the pamphlet, he presented a second copy of the pamphlet to Drayton for the perusal of the Provincial Congress and mentioned that he had sent a copy to Georgia immediately upon his arrival in Charleston the day before. Gadsden stared at his assembled countrymen and proceeded to declare his support for an immediate declaration of American independence.

Gadsden's speech, said Drayton, fell upon the hall "like an explosion of thunder." John Rutledge hurled accusations of treason at Gadsden and insisted that he would ride day and night to Philadelphia to prevent such a separation from the mother country. Rawlins Lowndes openly cursed the author of *Common Sense*. Henry Laurens and others stood to express their adamant disagreement, and the mockery spilled into the Charleston press, where one loyalist observed that "Gadsden is as mad with [*Common Sense*], as ever he was without it."[2]

The South Carolina Provincial Congress balked at Gadsden's rambunctious enthusiasm, and they reacted against it. They chose John Rutledge and Henry Laurens, two vocal opponents of independence, as their new president and vice president. Their new constitution was composed with the vaguest of language, and the framework of government ensured the continuance of elite control in military and government affairs. In fact, the new constitution was declared to be in effect at the end of March by the order of the Provincial Congress without popular review or ratification.[3]

A Journey to Philadelphia

Caesar Rodney, a delegate to the Continental Congress from Delaware, spent the month of June 1776 in his home colony, where he presided over the Delaware Assembly's change of instructions regarding independence. After the close of the assembly session, Rodney had planned to return to the Continental Congress in Philadelphia, but his military obligations diverted his attention elsewhere. As a general in the Delaware militia, Rodney led a group of soldiers in late June on an expedition to Sussex County, in the southern part of the colony, to put down a loyalist uprising there. Rodney had just returned to his home outside of Dover, when his reprieve was interrupted by a letter.

The second crucial journey of 1776 was initiated by a deadlock in the Delaware delegation in the Continental Congress. The "Lower Counties" of Delaware had appointed the same three delegates to the First and Second Continental Congresses: Thomas McKean, George Read, and Caesar Rodney. On July 1, in the first vote on the resolution for independence, McKean voted for it and Read against it.

McKean scrawled a desperate letter to "press the attendance" of Caesar Rodney, and placed it in the hand of the fastest rider he could find with instructions to deliver it directly to Rodney at his residence. Without Rodney's vote, Delaware would not vote for independence.

Rodney, who suffered from chronic asthma and an embarrassing facial cancer, was already exhausted from his harried political and military circuit that month, and he looked forward to a restful few days before returning to Philadelphia. Two years earlier, John Adams had described Rodney as "the oddest looking Man in the World," tall, thin, and pale with a face "not bigger than a large Apple." Yet even then Adams had recognized the "Sense and Fire, Spirit, Wit and Humour in his Countenance."[4] Caesar Rodney's actions on the night of July 1, 1776, would make his "Sense and Fire" legendary. The express messenger arrived that evening with McKean's letter, and Rodney read it immediately. Thunder rumbled in the distance. Rodney put the letter down, drew a deep breath, and called for his horse to be saddled right away. Rodney left his home late that evening and galloped north toward Philadelphia, about eighty miles away.

Like Gadsden, Caesar Rodney did not benefit from optimal traveling conditions. A thunderstorm that night swelled rivers, spooked his horse, and turned the primitive dirt roads into mud slicks. He had hoped to arrive in Philadelphia in time to sleep for at least a couple of hours before a long day of debate, but the treacherous conditions slowed his progress. The Continental Congress was just convening on the morning of July 2 when Rodney entered the Assembly Room still wearing his boots and spurs. A little bleary-eyed, he arrived "time enough to give my voice in the matter of Independence," breaking the tie within the Delaware delegation and placing his colony in the independence column.[5]

The two journeys presented here, Gadsden's southward trip *from* Philadelphia and Rodney's northward *to* Philadelphia, did not acquire significance just because they involved Congressional delegates who endured hardship before arriving at their destinations. Travel in colonial America, as we have seen, was difficult for everyone, and war made it even worse. What these particular episodes illustrate is the dramatic change in the American colonies in the first half of 1776.

The messages of both Gadsden and Rodney were virtually identical—"America should declare independence now"—but their political effects were sharply divergent. The timing of Gadsden's announcement seemed premature, while Rodney's arrival was the epitome of punctuality. If Rodney had returned to the Delaware Assembly in February with Gadsden's fiery message, he would have been met with the same frosty reception, and in July, if Gadsden had traveled to Philadelphia ready to cast his vote, he would have drug the leaden South Carolina delegation sooner in favor of independence. The turn of of imperial events contributed to the difference between the two times, but no factor played a greater role in accelerating the pace of political discourse than *Common Sense* and the independence debate it initiated. Gadsden, it seemed, was tossed by the breakers of loyalism, while Rodney surfed atop the rolling waves of independence.

Also illustrated in the juxtaposition of these two journeys is the circulation of *texts* and *sovereignty* in the American colonies on the eve of independence. Texts flowed outward from Philadelphia, and sovereignty flowed inward toward Philadelphia. In this final chapter, we will witness the complex political exchange that authorized the Second Continental Congress—the official linchpin of the United Colonies—to declare independence. The congress's constantly shifting membership—superintended by constantly shifting instructions—was trying to respond to a rollercoaster of news coming from England. Depending upon the day of the week, the composition of each delegation, and the morning's news, the Continental Congress was at times attracted to, but often repulsed by, the prospect of independence, and their final decision on the matter was anything but a foregone conclusion. We will observe the procedural and philosophical moves that enabled a majority of congressional delegates to vote for and declare independence, but my objective here is not simply the historical explication of legislative coalition-building. A close look at the Continental Congress in the spring and summer of 1776 will afford us the opportunity to draw some important conclusions about the relationship between *textual* constitutions and *sovereign* publics.

Part Two
CONTINENTAL CONGRESS AT THE HELM

A New Source of Authority

The Continental Congress was a clearinghouse of information, but it had no binding authority over the individual colonies beyond its members' aggregate referent power. The congress issued informed suggestions and advice—not constitutional or statutory edicts—to each colony. It was a hybrid body, appointed by constitutional colonial legislatures to do unconstitutional continental work. The issue of constitutionality was a fundamental problem for the colonists. At the beginning of 1776, there was no continental constitution, and all constitutional authority in America emanated from the individual colonial charters which, in turn, inherited their legitimacy from the British Constitution. In legal terms, the *constitutional* authority of the individual colonies always trumped the *consensual* authority of the Continental Congress.[6] Although the Continental Congress had the respect and admiration of most American colonists, the quasi-constitutional delegates saw themselves as bound "in all cases whatsoever" by the instructions of their colonial assemblies.

As we witnessed in Chapter Eleven, in the spring of 1776, the problem of legitimate political authority eclipsed almost every other concern in the Continental Congress and in many of the colonial legislatures. The only topic that more thoroughly occupied the attention of American politicians that spring was the necessity of supplying and supporting the colonial military resistance. The evacuation of royal governors, the snide addresses of the British government, and the vindictive Prohibitory Act effectually severed the British constitutional artery in America, creating an irreparable vacuum of power. The legislative bodies of colonial America could not simply take up the mantle of abandoned authority, because they existed as intermediaries, negotiating between the rights of propertied Americans and the authority of the British Crown. Cut off from royal authority, the colonial legislatures became straw governments. The ascendant local committees of inspection—regarded by elites as "extra-legal" or "extra-constitutional" bodies—threatened to supplant the legitimacy of colonial legislatures for the very reason the committees had been much-maligned: because their sanctioning authority came directly from the people, unmediated by the British Constitution. Since all legitimate authority in colonial America was ultimately British authority, in the spring of 1776 "official" colonial legislators found themselves anchorless and adrift on a sea of undesired constitutional independence.

There was only one source of non-British sovereignty available to interregnum American politicians that spring: the American people.

We cannot forget, however, that prior to the publication of *Common Sense*, the American colonists were often regarded as "more British than the British." They had been the faithful subjects of King George III and the longsuffering inhabitants of the British Colonies in North America, but they were not, before January 1776, a distinct *American* people. The only way that the dappled settlements in North America could forge a shared identity was to *experience* together a text that transcended the vast distances and conflicting cultures that separated them. *Common Sense* was the first such text in American history, and the *Declaration of Independence* was the second. Paine's text convinced the colonists that they were, in fact, *American*, and not British, while Jefferson's text made that identity official.

Common Sense diagnosed the British Constitution as incurably septic, and events in the months following the pamphlet's publication confirmed Paine's position. But the text did more than seal the fate of the British Constitution; in large measure, *Common Sense* replaced it. In a complex society, the power of individuals lies in their ability to accumulate a critical mass, and the vibrant reading community activated by *Common Sense* forged the only viable alternative to the sovereignty of the British Constitution: *American public opinion*. The vernacular political culture created by *Common Sense* reversed the flow of political power in America and gave a nascent nation its first textual referent. The first half of 1776 saw in America the fitful replacement of top-down monarchial sovereignty with bottom-up democratic sovereignty. In other words, political medievalism began then to give way to political modernity.

Appealing to the Constitution

To place into context the wholesale change in the tenor of the Second Continental Congress during the first six months of 1776, there is no better starting point than December 6, 1775. On that day, "the delegates of the thirteen United Colonies in North-America" agreed upon a response to the "proclamation issued from the court of St. James's on the twenty-third day of August last." The Continental Congress was convinced that the ministry, not the king, had published the venomous proclamation of rebellion. The congress rationalized, "The name of Majesty is used to give it a sanction and influence," but, they implied, the king would never have made such a statement. The Continental Congress thought it necessary, above all, to respond to the accusation that the colonies had forgotten "the allegiance which we owe to the power that has protected and sustained us." The delegates asked, "What allegiance is it that we forget? Allegiance to parliament? We never owed—we never owned it," and they continued, "Allegiance to our king? Our words have ever avowed it, our conduct has ever been consistent with it." The Continental Congress explicitly affirmed the source of all things colonial: "By the British constitution, our best inheritance, rights, as well as duties, descend upon us." At this point in the text, the authorial fingerprints of John Dickinson became plain. On behalf of the congress, Dickinson reminded the British government that the colonists' actions were strictly constitutional: "We view [the king] as the constitution represents him. That tells us he can do no wrong. The cruel and illegal attacks, which we oppose, have no foundation in royal authority." Dickinson—the best constitutional lawyer in the colonies—proceeded to point out that "a rebellion" was "a term undefined and unknown in the law," and since a *proclamation*, "by the British constitution, has no other operation than merely that of enforcing what is already law," then the imputation of colonial rebellion in the August 23 proclamation had no "known legal basis to have rested upon."

Toward the close of its response, the Continental Congress lamented "this unhappy and unnatural controversy, in which Britons fight against Britons and the descendants of Britons." The congressional delegates hoped that the British Constitution would "prevail" on the behalf of the colonies, but they left open the possibility that they could be forced to "resort to arguments drawn from a very different source." This vague threat sounded at first like an appeal to arms, but the colonists had already advanced far down that road in their fight against "ministerial oppression." What the congressional counter-proclamation was referring to was an alternative source of authority. The Continental Congress acted and spoke "in the name of the people of these United Colonies, and by [the] authority, according to the purest maxims of representation, derived from them."[7] What John Dickinson and the rest of the delegates in congress did not realize in December 1775 was just how soon they would find themselves obligated to transact authority from the British Constitution to the American people.

Inching into Independence

Besides James Wilson's star-crossed resolution affirming the congress's commitment to reconciliation—an episode we have already looked at in detail—January 1776 was a month in which the Continental Congress devoted themselves to military affairs, especially after the alarming news from Norfolk and Quebec. But, at least within the congress, military resistance did not yet seem inconsistent with an aspiration for reconciliation. The British Constitution specified that the colonists owed the king allegiance in return for his protection, and as long as the Continental Congress construed the war as *ministerial* in origin, the delegates could claim, as a matter of British jurisprudence at least, that the king was still their "Protector." But news arriving in Philadelphia in February confirmed the delegates' worst fears: the entire British government was arrayed against them.

The Continental Congress's first official movement toward independence thus came in response to the Prohibitory Act—a piece of legislation written by the ministry, passed by the parliament, and receiving the consent of the king. Initially, the congressional delegates acted in response to a specific clause in the Prohibitory Act that authorized the seizure of American merchant ships by British pirates. Several delegates' predispositions in favor of reconciliation had been dislodged by the combined jolt in January of *Common Sense* and the royal addresses, but this clause escalated matters to a new level. The sanctioning of piracy—like the hiring of mercenaries, an early modern taboo—was evidence of malicious intent on the part of Britain to cripple American trade. In our twenty-first century parlance, it was as if the British had contracted with terrorists to bring the American economy to its knees. The congress was aghast. For the first time during a congressional debate, delegates began to discuss independence as a practical option on February 29—the bissextile day. During the course of the day's debate over the issue of commercial alliances with France and Spain, "much was said about declaring our Independency on G. Britain," but the delegates together realized "that 5 or 6 Colonies have instructed their Delegates not to agree to an Independency till they, the Principals, are consulted."[8]

February gave way to March, and outside the windows of the Pennsylvania State House, Philadelphia began to thaw. Inside the closed door meetings of the Continental Congress, the tone of the debate began to warm up as well. On March 1, a packet of letters from New Hampshire "about a Dispute there on their setting up an Independent Form of Government" was read in the Continental Congress.[9] On the following day, a subcommittee of the congress, the Committee of Secret Correspondence led by Benjamin Franklin, issued instructions to Silas Deane to begin negotiations with France for military assistance.[10] The Prohibitory Act had crystallized the opinion of many delegates that the colonies now *must* seek military alliances with Britain's avowed enemies, France and Spain. Those nations would never consider giving aid to the colonies as long as the Americans were fighting for reconciliation with Britain. Without the promise of American political independence, many congressional delegates realized, the British stranglehold on resupply would force the colonists into submission. In consequence of the British Prohibitory Act, American independence and European interdependence became reciprocal requirements for survival.

The Prohibitory Act also had profound domestic consequences. On Saturday, March 9, the Continental Congress wrestled with the necessity of setting up governments in those colonies where royal governors had dissolved the legislature. The Prohibitory Act convinced reluctant delegates that royal governance was, *de facto* and *de jure*, a thing of the past. Every delegate agreed that some sort of government was required to preserve order in the colonies, but there was great controversy in the Assembly Room surrounding the mode of establishing new governments. As the debate progressed, the delegates sought to clarify the permanence or transience of new governments. One member proposed that the congress recommend to the colonies that they "form a Constitution and Governm't for themselves without Limitation [of] Time." John Jay of New York and several other delegates objected that such a recommendation amounted to "an independence," and the remainder of the afternoon was consumed with "much Argum't on this Ground."[11] The point of contention, once again, was temporal. Were the new governments merely temporary, stop-gap measures to preserve order until a full reconciliation was accomplished, or were they part of a larger scheme to precipitate permanent independence from Great Britain?

The Continental Congress decided to sanction American pirateering as a face-saving reprisal against the Prohibitory Act. On March 22, George Wythe of Virginia read to the entire congress a preamble he had drafted to place the new pirateering resolution in its political context. Accompanied by the vocal support of Richard Henry Lee, Wythe's preamble amounted to "an Amend't wherein the King was made the Author of our Miseries instead of the Ministry." The congress resolved itself into a Committee of the Whole in order to debate the point. Wythe's preamble—and specifically the shifting attribution of culpability to the king— sparked scorching remarks on both sides of the question. According to the notes of New Jersey delegate Richard Smith, proponents of the "amendment" included Richard Henry Lee, Samuel Chase, Jonathon Dickinson Sergeant, and Benjamin Harrison, while John Jay, James Wilson, and Thomas Johnson opposed it most vehemently "on Supposition that this was effectually severing the King from Us forever." Both sides "ably debated" the point for four hours, until "Maryland interposed its Veto and put it off till Tomorrow."[12] On March 23, the congress formally authorized the equipment of American pirates—the first real reply to the Prohibitory Act—but they narrowly voted down the proposed preamble.[13] Wythe's incendiary statement did not pass, but the studious John Adams had observed its effect and began concocting his own response to the Prohibitory Act.

We find an unlikely window into the daily affairs of the secretive Continental Congress during this period in the diary of a distant observer, the Reverend Ezra Stiles of Connecticut. Stiles made thorough notes of an April 22 conversation he had had with Francis Dana of Massachusetts, a close friend of many congressional delegates, who stopped in Connecticut on his way home from Philadelphia. Stiles reported, "At Congress is a good Majority prepared for any Question, even Independency, if necessary." The Maryland delegates were "under Instructions and themselves not yet clear for Independency, tho' coming to it." Some of the delegates from Pennsylvania were "against Independency, but at the new Assembly will be released from Instructions, and then will vote for it." Franklin was "firm for Independency," while Dickinson, a man of undoubted patriotism, was also "timid to the last degree & for putting off [independence] till Commissioners come, tho' he has little Expectation from them, but then, he thinks, the way will be more clear." New York delegates Jay and James Duane were "Tories at heart" and "insist on waiting for Commissioners & doubt not their bringing honorable Terms for Pacification." South Carolina was "not represented in Congress at this Time" because Gadsden had gone home to assist in setting up the new government, Thomas Lynch was "seized with a paralytic shock," and John Rutledge, "tho' present *never acts*." The Virginia delegates were "firm & immoveable & ready for all Events." According to Dana, "The *Cities* of Philadelphia and N. York [are] each equally divided between *Liberty & Parliament*." Besides "some of the Delegates of [Pennsylvania and New York]," the "rest of the Members of Congress are at HEART true Friends to Liberty & their Country."[14] Stiles' literary diary entry read like the character descriptions at the start of a play. The Assembly Room in the Pennsylvania State House was the stage upon which the plot would unfold over the next few months. The once-staid deliberations of the Continental Congress were beginning to escalate into a spectacle of political theater.

Instructing the Instructors

The congressional debate in February and March over the American response to the Prohibitory Act was a breakthrough in the movement toward independence. Faces reddened, neck-veins popped, and party lines hardened as delegates grappled with each other on the fundamentals of British constitutionality and the prerogative of revolution. Also arising from those debates was a new clarity regarding the decisive role of each colony's instructions to its delegates. Even if a majority of individual members of congress had wanted to declare independence, enough colonies had expressly forbidden the step to make any overture to independence a moot point. The British Prohibitory Act had excluded the colonies from traditional constitutional protections, but the American prohibitory instructions prevented the colonies from protecting themselves under the umbrella of new, independent constitutions. The creative response of the Continental Congress to this dilemma was to whisper in the ear of their respective assemblies, congresses, or conventions, and thereby, to channel the sovereign voice of the people toward independence.

The correspondence between Massachusetts congressional delegates, Elbridge Gerry and John Adams, and their mutual friend, James Warren, is one of many examples of this fascinating political dynamic. Gerry wrote from Philadelphia on March 26 to Warren, who was then serving in the Massachusetts General Court, "I sincerely wish that You would originate Instructions expressed with decent Firmness (your natural Style) and give your Sentiments as a Court in Favour of Independency," adding, "since some timid Minds are terrified at the Word Independency It may be well to give the Thing another Name." Gerry was certain that positive instructions from the Massachusetts legislature "would turn many doubtful Minds and produce a Reversion of the contrary Instructions adopted by some assemblies." He observed, "To accomplish such a Reversion, the Committee of Inspection of this City have proffered to the Assembly a petition for that purpose."[15]

James Warren was elated with Gerry's suggestion. In a letter to John Adams written at the beginning of April, Warren reported the current political mood in Massachusetts, "I can't describe the sighing after independence; it is universal." Warren added, "Nothing remains of that prudence, moderation or timidity with which we have so long been plagued and embarrassed. All are united in this question."[16] On April 16, Adams censured his friend's immoderate enthusiasm: "You deal in the Marvelous like a Traveler." He asked, "As to the Sighs, what are they after? Independence? Have we not been independent these twelve Months, wanting three days?" referring to the approaching anniversary of the Battle of Lexington. Like Paine, Adams saw independence as a political fact, not a goal, but Adams stressed the importance of legislative maneuvers rather than Paine's focus on sentimental independence. Adams continued his diatribe on independence directed at Warren,

> Have you Seen the Privateering Resolves? Are not these Independence enough for my beloved Constituents? Have you seen the Resolves for opening our Ports to all Nations? Are these Independence enough? What more would you have? Why, Methinks I hear you say we want to complete our Form and Plan of Government. Why don't you petition Congress then for Leave to establish such a Form as shall be most conducive to the Happiness of the People?[17]

In the convoluted system of interregnum sovereignty, the Massachusetts General Court needed to petition the Continental Congress to receive permission to establish a new government, but the Continental Congress required a reciprocal permit from each provincial assembly to declare independence. Adams closed his letter with a sarcastic suggestion: "Why don't your Honours of the General Court, if you are so unanimous in this, give positive Instructions to your own Delegates, to promote Independency? Don't blame your Delegates until they have disobeyed your Instructions in favour of Independency."[18]

Less than a week later, on April 22 Adams again wrote to Warren, but this time in a less caustic and more urgent tone. Adams exhorted Warren that "now is the proper Time" for the Massachusetts Assembly to act upon their unanimity in favor of independence and "instruct your Delegates to that Effect." Because their colony had been perceived as radical, the measure "would have been productive of Jealousies, perhaps, and Animosities a few Months ago, but [it] would have a contrary Tendency now." As Adams put it, "The Colonies are all at this Moment turning their Eyes that Way." Adams admitted that he understood the Americans' reluctance toward independence. "All great Changes are irksome to the human Mind, especially those which are attended with great Dangers and uncertain Effects." Since no one "can foresee the Consequences of such a Measure," he said, it made sense to wait until "the Design of Providence by a Series of great Events had so plainly marked out the Necessity of it that he who runs might read."[19] For good measure, Adams enclosed in his packet addressed to Warren a copy of *Thoughts on Government*, published that day in Philadelphia.

John Adams spent the month of April focused on one subject above all others: the formation of new state governments. He spent hours singing the praises of republicanism to other delegates, and he returned to his quarters every evening to revise and transcribe the letter that he would publish as *Thoughts on Government*. While Adams was sitting in the congressional debates of March, it dawned on him that establishing new state governments was a fundamental and irresistible step toward American independence. On April 14, he had written to Abigail, using verbiage that he would redeploy two days later in a letter to James Warren, "As to Declarations of Independency, be patient. Read our Privateering Laws, and our Commercial Laws. What Signifies a Word?"[20] Like a good lawyer, John Adams was, slowly and methodically, building the case for independence.

While the Pennsylvania Independents suffered a setback on May 1, calls for independence from other colonies continued to gather steam. Major Joseph Hawley wrote to Elbridge Gerry on May 1, "The tories dread a declaration of independency and a course of conduct on that plan more than death." Speaking of independence, Hawley said, "My hand and heart is full of it. There will be no abiding union without it." He asked rhetorically, "Will a government stand on recommendations?" The zealous Army officer concluded with a typical fiery plea, "For God's sake, let there be a full revolution, or all's been done in vain. Independence and a well planned continental government will save us."[21]

Hawley's battle-worn perspective enabled him to see matters with a clarity that was difficult to achieve from within the fog of imperial politics. On May 10, however, the Continental Congress began to view the state of American affairs with frightful vividness. On that day, the assembled delegates received unquestioned evidence that 12,000 Hessians had already embarked for the American shore.[22] The room was instantly aflutter with calls for an appropriate response to this outrage. John Adams unfolded a piece of paper he had been keeping in his pocket for an occasion such as this.

Resolution and Preamble

Adams rose before the congress and introduced a motion that at first blush seemed an ill-fit response to news of mercenary soldiers. The motion did not call for larger enlistments or increased ammunition production; it called for new governments. Every delegate present realized that the dearth of political authority in many of the colonies multiplied their vulnerability to attack and insurrection. A first step in response to the threatened invasion was to secure intracolonial authority. Adams was clever and meticulous, and he had perfected a resolution that would be at once amenable to a majority of delegates and yet would crack the door to political revolution. That afternoon, the Continental Congress approved what seemed to be a straightforward solution to the widespread lack of intracolonial governance:

> *Resolved,*
> That it be recommended to the respective assemblies and conventions of the United Colonies, where no government sufficient to the exigencies of their affairs have been hitherto established, to adopt such government as shall, in the opinion of the representatives of the people, best conduce to the happiness and safety of their constituents in particular, and America in general.

Adams had honed every word and phrase of this resolution to appear innocuously factual, and yet he had left gaping openings for creative interpretation. The resolution was directed to both "assemblies and conventions" wherever "no government sufficient to the exigencies" of affairs had, "in the opinion of the representatives of the people," yet been established. In those phrases, Adams had furnished the Pennsylvania Independents with every loophole they needed.

After the Continental Congress approved of the resolution, it appointed a committee of three "to prepare a preamble to the foregoing resolution." It was not unusual for a legislative body to add a preamble after passing a resolution, especially if there was some concern that a resolution might be prone to misinterpretation. A preamble provided the reasoning behind a resolution, and it is likely that opponents of the resolution demanded an explanation that clarified the intent of congress. To keep the draft committee more balanced, the congress selected two members in support of the resolution, John Adams and Richard Henry Lee, and one opposed to it, Edward Rutledge.[23] The preamble, drafted primarily by John Adams, made it out of the draft committee by a two-to-one majority, with Adams and Lee grinning and Rutledge fuming. When Adams reported the preamble to the full congress, half of the room smiled while the other half of the room sat in stunned silence. The new preamble had an entirely different tone from that of the resolution five days earlier:

> *Whereas* his Britannic Majesty, in conjunction with the lords and commons of Great Britain, has, by a late act of Parliament, excluded the inhabitants of these United Colonies from the protection of his crown;
>
> And *whereas*, no answer, whatever, to the humble petitions of the colonies for redress of grievances and reconciliation with Great Britain, has been or is likely to be given; but, the whole force of that kingdom, aided by foreign mercenaries, is to be exerted for the destruction of the good people of these colonies;
>
> And *whereas*, it appears absolutely irreconcilable to reason and good Conscience, for the people of these colonies now to take the oaths and affirmations necessary for the support of any government under the crown of Great Britain, and it is necessary that the exercise of every kind of authority under the said crown should be totally suppressed, and all the powers of government exerted, under the authority of the people of the colonies, for the preservation of internal peace, virtue, and good order, as well as for the defense of their lives, liberties, and properties, against the hostile invasions and cruel depredations of their enemies; therefore, resolved, &c.[24]

After a spirited debate, Adams's aggressive preamble passed by a slim majority on May 15. From that date on, no one in the Continental Congress talked about reconciliation as a practical political option.[25] Moreover, the preamble flung open wide the door that had been cracked for the Pennsylvania Independents by the May 10 resolution. The entirety of the British government was now officially implicated in the oppression of America, and "the people of these colonies" were relieved of any obligation to "any government under the crown of Britain." Moreover, the people were charged with totally suppressing "every kind of authority under the said crown" and reestablishing all government under their authority alone.

For the first time, the Continental Congress began to sound like a band of revolutionaries, and as word spread of the congress's bold resolution, the people of America began to respond. In a profound convergence of events, also on May 15 the first Hessian troops set sail for

America and Virginia issued its call for independence. The succession of events made America electric with change. Near the end of May, Adams wrote to Warren, "Every Post and every Day rolls in upon Us: Independence like a Torrent."[26]

Part Three
THE DRAMA UNFOLDS

Casting the Die

By the end of May, news had arrived in Philadelphia of the Virginia Convention's May 15 resolve. Thomas Bradford received the packet at the London Coffee House and read it aloud to his patrons before handing it to his typesetters to include in the next *Pennsylvania Journal*. The Virginians expressed their collective opinion with unequivocal force:

> *RESOLVED Unanimously,*
> That the Delegates appointed to represent this colony in General Congress be instructed to propose to that respectable body TO DECLARE THE UNITED COLONIES FREE AND INDEPENDENT STATES, absolved from all allegiance to or dependence upon, the crown or parliament of Great-Britain; and that they give the assent of this colony to such declaration, and to whatever measures may be thought proper and necessary by the Congress for forming foreign alliances, and A CONFEDERATION OF THE COLONIES, at such time, and in the manner, as to them shall seem best. Provided, that the power of forming government for, and the regulations of the internal concerns of each colony, be left to the respective colonial legislatures.[27]

Responding to their convention's instructions, Virginia's congressional delegation gathered often in the evenings with their pro-independence colleagues to hammer out a resolution and a strategy for its passage. About a week and a half after the instructions arrived, the plan was set, and the Virginia delegates nodded in agreement that it was time to press the issue.

Richard Henry Lee waited until late in the afternoon on Friday, June 7, before he rose on behalf of the Virginia delegation and read the following motion:

> *Resolved,*
> That these United Colonies are, and of right ought to be, free and Independent states; that they are absolved from all allegiance to the British crown; and that all political connection between them and the state of Great-Britain is, and ought to be totally dissolved.[28]

The resolution was seconded, but as 7 o'clock neared, the congress chose to refer the motion until the next morning, resolving "that the members be enjoined to attend punctually at ten o'clock, in order to take the same into consideration."[29]

On Saturday morning, June 8, the congress resolved itself into a Committee of the Whole with Benjamin Harrison of Virginia taking the chair. According to Thomas Jefferson, the only delegate who kept detailed notes of the debate in Congress over the resolution for independence, the entire opposition to Lee's motion hinged upon the matter of timing. The most vocal spokesmen for this position were James Wilson, Robert R. Livingston, Edward Rutledge, and John Dickinson. These men claimed to be "friends to the measures themselves" and saw, they said, "the impossibility that we should ever again be united with Great Britain," but they were against adopting the measure "at that time." They recommended "the conduct we had formerly observed" as "wise & proper now," and urged the Congress to defer "any capital step" until "the voice of the people drove us into it." Because the people "were our power," they could not carry any declarations into effect without their express consent, and, in their opinion, the people of Maryland, Delaware, Pennsylvania, New Jersey, and New York "were not yet ripe for bidding adieu to British connection." The arguments for and against independence were always temporal. The opponents of independents dangled before the congress that the middle colonies were "fast ripening & in a short time would join the general voice of America," but they also cautioned against declaring independence before an official American ambassador was ready to sail for France.[30]

According to Jefferson's notes, John Adams, Richard Henry Lee, and George Wythe took the lead in advocating independence. They pointed out that none of the other gentlemen had argued "against the policy or the right of separation from Britain" but only opposed "its being now declared." The pro-independence contingent argued that a declaration of independence would not "make ourselves what we are not" but would "declare a fact which already exists." They argued that any obligation to parliament or allegiance to the king had been dissolved by Britain's hostile acts and by a despotic determination "to accept nothing less than a *carte blanche*." Restrictive instructions from some colonies, they argued, were indicative of the time in which they were given, not of the current opinion of the people. In particular, the "backwardness" of Pennsylvania and Maryland owed itself to "the influence of proprietary power & connections," to their "having not yet been attacked by the enemy," and to their remarkable partitioning of "the voice of the representatives" from "the voice of the people." The pro-independence bloc rued the time already lost in forging alliances and opening trade, and they advocated a proactive role for the Continental Congress. "The people," they said, "wait for us to lead the way."[31]

As 7 o'clock in the evening approached once again, the Committee of the Whole again did not come to a vote and agreed to continue the debate on Monday.[32] Three hours after Congress adjourned that evening, Edward Rutledge of South Carolina sat down to write his friend, John Jay, who was then in his home colony of New York. According to Rutledge, "The Sensible part of the House opposed the Motion." Rutledge and his anti-independence compatriots thought that articles of confederation should be first drafted, alliances formed second, and only as a final desperate measure should independence be declared. Rutledge and his associates saw "no Wisdom in a Declaration of Independence," and only "the Impudence of a New Englander" or "the Reason of every Madman" would propose such a measure "in our disjointed State." The question was postponed until the next Monday, at which time, Rutledge said, "I mean to move that it be postponed for 3 Weeks or a Month." Rutledge wished Jay had been present, since "The whole Argument was sustained on one side by R. Livingston, Wilson, Dickinson, and myself, and by the Power of all N. England, Virginia, and Georgia on the other."[33]

Rutledge executed his plan on the following Monday. After another round of tedious debate on June 10, Rutledge introduced a motion that was passed by the Committee of the Whole:

Resolved,
That the consideration of the first resolution be postponed to Monday the first day of July next; and in the mean while, that no time be lost, in case the Congress agree thereto, that a committee be appointed to prepare a declaration to the effect of the said first resolution.[34]

Rutledge had proposed the delay in secret hopes that he could, in the mean time, summon reinforcements for his "moderate" bloc in Congress. Rutledge reiterated the argument from the Saturday before that the middle colonies and, he added, *South Carolina* "were not yet matured for falling from the parent stem." Others chimed in "that they were fast advancing to that state," and the debate remained at an impasse. The three-week delay was thus a compromise between two sides who thought they would be proven right in the interim.

On Tuesday, June 11, the congress appointed Thomas Jefferson, John Adams, Benjamin Franklin, Roger Sherman, and Robert R. Livingston as "the committee for preparing the declaration." That same day, the congress also appointed a committee "to prepare and digest the form of a confederation to be entered into between these colonies" and another committee "to prepare a plan of treaties to be proposed to foreign powers."[35] Shortly after the Congress adjourned that evening, the newly-appointed draft committee met, and Jefferson was charged with the task of composition.

The Bustle of June

During the spring and summer of 1776, Daniel of St. Thomas Jenifer, the President of the Maryland Council of Safety, received regular updates on the proceedings in the Continental Congress from his colony's delegates. On June 16, he put the question of independence in stark temporal terms, with the four New England governments, Virginia, and Georgia "for independence immediately" and the other seven colonies "against its taking place immediately."[36]

John Adams clarified matters further in a letter to John Winthrop on June 23. Adams wrote, "It is now universally acknowledged that we are and must be independent. But still, objections are made to a declaration of it." Opponents of a declaration claimed it would "arouse and unite Great Britain," but Adams believed it would "throw the kingdom into confusion" and produce salutary effects across the colonies. Adams expected that the committee work of June, including the drafting of a declaration, would be completed "in a week or two, and then the last finishing strokes will be given to the politics of this revolution. Nothing after that will remain but war."[37]

The extant correspondence of the delegates in the Continental Congress—and in many of the provincial assemblies—indicates that June was a harried month for colonial politicians. After months of tedious meetings, extended separation from their families, and the mounting stresses of an uncertain future, most politicians were exhausted. One of the best descriptions of the frenetic pace of change and the unrelenting crush of work for a colonial politician during the month of June, came from Thomas Jones, a delegate in the North Carolina Provincial Congress. Jones described "the amazing fatigue of business" involved in framing a new government. He had thought himself a busy man before but had "never yet experienced one-fourth part of what I now am necessarily obliged to undertake—we have no rest, either night or day." First thing every morning, he prepared "every matter necessary for the day," and after a quick breakfast, he would attend the provincial congress from nine until three o'clock. There was "no sitting a minute after dinner, but to different committees; perhaps one person will be obliged to attend four of them between four o'clock and nine at night." After committee meetings, he ate supper just before midnight. "This has been the life I have led since my arrival here—in short, I never was so hurried."[38] Jones was framing a new government for North Carolina, but the delegates in the Continental Congress were equally busy, wrangling in their committees over the present and future of the United Colonies. Were they, and would they remain, the "British Colonies in North America," or were they instead the "Free and Independent States of America?" To answer this question, Thomas Jefferson stepped away from the anxious tussles and backroom brokering of committee work, and he focused solely the problem of enunciating the principles upon which a new nation would be brought forth.

Drafting Original Equality

As Jefferson sat quietly in his rented quarters on the fringe of town at the corner of Market and Seventh Streets, his concentration was disrupted by uninvited horseflies from the stable across the street. Jefferson shooed the nuisance flies back outside through the open windows of his second-story apartment. Standing at the window for a moment before returning to his writing desk, the young Virginian could faintly hear the ruckus of popular protest riding atop the June breeze. The tinder of public opinion, prepared by *Common Sense* and the public debate over independence, had by the end of June erupted into a full blaze on the cobblestone streets of Philadelphia. A few blocks east of Jefferson's room, the Pennsylvania Conference of Committees busied themselves changing instructions and forming a constitutional convention. Several battalions of the Pennsylvania Militia drilled on the city commons, ready at a call to fly to the aid of their neighboring provinces. Jefferson returned to his chair and contemplated the "patient sufferance of these colonies," and he affirmed that "governments long established should not be changed for light and transient causes." Humans, he thought, "are more disposed to suffer, while evils are sufferable, than to right themselves by abolishing the forms to which they are accustomed." The colonists had certainly grown accustomed to the Crown-in-Parliament British Constitution. Before January 1776, very few individuals and no public bodies in the American colonies imagined a different form of government.

The colonies, ruminated Jefferson, had endured a "long train of abuses and usurpations," but they had viewed their hardships as parliamentary and ministerial aggrandizement, irksome anomalies of an otherwise perfect constitution. Only when the colonists' observational vigilance, with Paine's interpretive guidance, began to connect imperial policy to the *Crown*, did isolated cases of governmental abuse seem to metastasize into a pattern of systemic, constitutional corruption. Jefferson had come to the conclusion, along with a majority of the population in the colonies, that imperial affairs under the personal direction of "the present King of Great Britain" evinced "a design to reduce" the colonies "under absolute despotism." Jefferson referred to the scattered residents of the American colonies as "one people" who faced "now the necessity" of dissolving "the political bands which have connected them with another," the British people. The sinister machinations of the British government made it "necessary" for the American people to "alter their former systems of government" and "to assume among the powers of the earth, the separate and equal station to which the laws of nature and of nature's God entitle them." With each stroke of Jefferson's pen, the rationale for independence was coming to life. A singular *American people*, something that did not exist prior to January 1776, were choosing *now*, out of *necessity*, to discard the entirety of the customary British Constitution and to replace it with a new system, founded in *natural rights*, and deriving its *sovereign* powers "from the consent of the governed." Neither Jefferson nor Paine invented the discrete political principles from which American independence was wrought, but before 1776, no one had ever assembled those principles into a coherent, practical political system.

The British Constitution held that "the king can do no wrong," but in the *Declaration of Independence*, Jefferson leveled eighteen distinct charges against the person and office of King George III. Students of Jefferson's text, in the wake of Abraham Lincoln's profound reinterpretation of the *Declaration*, usually divide it into two autonomous parts: a timeless, literary statement on rights and equality followed by a timely, rhetorical case against the king.[39] Jefferson and his contemporaries, however, viewed the text as a seamless argument containing only the essentials of American independence. The most famous clause in the *Declaration*, "all men are created equal," would become the cornerstone of universal human rights, but as the words spilled from Jefferson's quill, they were intended as an indictment of the monarchial system. To clarify this point, we need look no further than *Common Sense*. "MANKIND being originally equals in the order of creation," Paine postulated, "the equality could only be destroyed by some subsequent circumstance." Although most people experienced inequality in "the distinctions of rich and poor," Paine considered economic inequality as symptomatic of a more basic problem. He explained,

> But there is another and greater distinction for which no truly natural or religious reason can be assigned, and that is, the distinction of men into KINGS and SUBJECTS. Male and female are the distinctions of nature, good and bad the distinctions of heaven; but how a race of men came into the world so exalted above the rest, and distinguished like some new species, is worth enquiring into, and whether they are the means of happiness or of misery to mankind.[40]

The theory of divine right held that most men were created to be ruled and only a handful were created to be rulers. The concept of original equality targeted this fundamental tenet of the monarchial order and, thereby, unlocked the door for democracy.

The Vote for Independence

With the committee's approval, Jefferson reported his draft to the Continental Congress on Friday, June 28, three days earlier than it was expected. It was read and "ordered to lie on the table" until the following Monday.[41] The gale force of Jefferson's text caught some members of the congress off guard. On Saturday, June 29, a worried Edward Rutledge again wrote John Jay "for the express Purpose" of requesting his attendance in Congress "during the whole of the ensuing week." On Monday, the Congress would begin deliberation on a declaration of independence, a plan of confederation, and "a Scheme for a Treaty with foreign Powers." Rutledge said, "Whether we shall be able effectually to oppose the first, and infuse Wisdom into the others will depend in a great Measure upon the Exertions of the Honest and sensible part of the members." Jay's colony of New York, Rutledge said, suffered from a lack of representation. The New York delegates were "silent in general" and, lacking in abilities, "never quit their Chairs." Rutledge had been "much engaged lately" with John Dickinson on a plan of confederation, but "It has the Vice of all his Productions to a considerable Degree; I mean the Vice of Refining too much." Rutledge collaborated with Dickinson, though, because he so despised "the Plan now proposed" by New England and its "destroying all Provincial Distinctions and making every thing of the most minute kind bend to what they call the good of the whole." Rutledge held the force of New England's arms "exceeding Cheap," but he confessed a dread of "their over-ruling influence in Council," "their low Cunning," and "those leveling Principles which Men without Character and without Fortune in general Possess, which are so captivating to the lower Class of Mankind, and which will occasion such a fluctuation of Property as to introduce the greatest disorder."[42] Jay was unable to extricate himself from his obligations in New York, and Rutledge's plea went unheeded.

The Continental Congress resumed consideration of Richard Henry Lee's resolution for independence on Monday, July 1, 1776. At the end of a full day's debate, when both sides had exhausted their arguments, the congress resolved itself into a Committee of the Whole, and the chairman put the question up for a preliminary vote. That evening, the vote went nine colonies to two in favor of independence, with New York abstaining, Delaware deadlocked, and Pennsylvania and South Carolina opposed. The South Carolina delegates, who had been free all spring to vote their consciences, acknowledged that the measure would carry and told their colleagues from the other colonies that they would switch their vote the next day. Of the Pennsylvania delegation, John Morton, Benjamin Franklin, and James Wilson voted for independence. Wilson had long been a vocal opponent of independence, but his constituents had recently threatened to recall him unless he changed his stance. A shaken Wilson explained to the delegates in congress that he had finally sensed a change in sentiment among the people of Pennsylvania and could, therefore, acquiesce in a vote for the measure. Pennsylvania's other four delegates, John Dickinson, Robert Morris, Thomas Willing, and Charles Humphreys, voted against the resolution on July 1.[43] As we saw earlier in this chapter, the Delaware delegation had only two members present, Thomas McKean, who voted for independence and George Read, who voted against it. That evening, McKean wrote to Caesar Rodney, the third delegate from Delaware, urgently requesting his attendance.

On Tuesday morning, July 2, a heavy rainstorm drenched the delegates on their way to the State House. As rain streaked the windows of their chamber, John Hancock called the session to order. A mud-spattered Caesar Rodney burst through the doors and apologized for his tardiness, having raced on horseback from Delaware after receiving Thomas McKean's urgent call for his attendance. Secretary Charles Thomson once again read Richard Henry Lee's motion to the delegates. Thomson began the vote tally with Connecticut, and a chorus of "Aye's" filled the room. Delaware, after splitting on the question the day earlier, added Rodney's "Aye" and fell in favor of the measure. After Georgia voted for independence, Maryland—whose delegates had just been authorized the day before to assent to independence—registered its affirmation. Massachusetts, New Hampshire, and New Jersey each voted for independence. The secretary called upon New York, and a delegate replied, "Abstained." North Carolina's affirmative vote made the total to that point 8-0.

Thomson then presented the question to the delegates from Pennsylvania, whose number was noticeably smaller than the day before. John Dickinson and Robert Morris, both ardently opposed to the independence motion, absented themselves from Congress that day, as an act of silent recusal and sighing acceptance of the turn of affairs. James Wilson *did* attend that day, and though he had often spoken against independence, he had, the day before, admitted that he finally sensed a change in sentiment among the people of Pennsylvania and would acquiesce in a vote for the measure. Secretary Thomson called the roll, and Benjamin Franklin, John Morton, and James Wilson voted "Aye," while Thomas Willing and Charles Humphreys voted "Nay." Pennsylvania was now placed in the affirmative column.

Rhode Island likewise voted for independence, and the South Carolina delegates followed through on their promise. No one wondered what would be the vote of Virginia. Thomson closed the voting and announced the results. Twelve colonies for the motion, none opposed, and one abstained. The vote was unanimous, but every delegate present knew that the unanimity was more apparent than real. New York had abstained on the ground that it lacked instructions, but even in colonies that voted for the measure, especially Maryland, Delaware, both Carolinas, and Pennsylvania, the delegations had been bitterly divided on the issue.

The Vote for the Declaration

After the affirmative vote on independence on Tuesday morning, July 2, the Continental Congress began debating Jefferson's draft line-by-line, a process that continued through Thursday evening, July 4. As Jefferson put it, "The sentiments of men are known not only by what they receive, but what they reject also." Passages in Jefferson's draft censuring the people of England were struck, he said, because "the pusillanimous idea that we had friends in England worth keeping terms with, still haunted the minds of many." Also the clause "reprobating the enslaving the inhabitants of Africa" was deleted "in complaisance to South Carolina & Georgia, who had never attempted to restrain the importation of slaves, and who on the contrary still wished to continue it." Even some of the Northern delegates "felt a little tender under those censures" because "they had been pretty considerable carriers" of slaves to other colonies.[44]

As the sun descended toward the horizon on July 4, deliberation ended, and a vote was called. The Committee of the Whole formally reported the declaration to the house, and the delegates approved of the text by voice vote. The delegates grasped the moment's gravity. Abraham Clark of New Jersey had awoken early on July 4 to write to his friend in the New Jersey Militia, Colonel Elias Dayton. Clark assured his correspondent, "Our Congress is an August Assembly—and can they support the Declaration now on the Anvil, they will be the greatest Assembly on Earth." Clark understood that "We are now, Sir, embarked on a most Tempestuous Sea; Life very uncertain, seeming dangers scattered thick around us." Though Clark was prepared for the worst, he shrugged, "We can Die here but once. May all our Business, all our purposes and pursuits tend to fit us for that important event."

Writing again to Dayton on August 6, Clark wondered whether history would consider him "honourable or dishonourable," and acknowledged that "the issue of the war must settle it. Perhaps our Congress will be exalted on a high gallows." Clark compared the situation of America to the biblical parable of the three lepers: "If we continued in the state we were in, it was evident we must perish; if we declared Independence we might be saved—we could but perish." Clark said, "I assure you, sir, I see, I feel, the danger we are in. I am far from exulting in our imaginary happiness; nothing short of the almighty power of God can save us. It is not in our numbers, our union, our valour, I dare trust." He continued, "I think an interposing Providence hath been evident in all the events that necessarily led us to what we are—I mean independent States; but for what purpose, whether to make us a great empire or to make our ruin more complete, the issue can only determine."[45]

Subscribing their Lives

Sometimes the patriotic glare of "Founding Father"-language obscures our vision of what really happened in Philadelphia during 1776. Those present at the meetings of the Continental Congress had no reason to engage in hero worship, and their candid character sketches of the other delegates remind us that these were flesh-and-blood, imperfect men who managed to accomplish remarkable feats. Benjamin Rush, who joined the Continental Congress soon after the *Declaration of Independence*, was unimpressed with most of his fellow delegates. Rush called Robert Treat Paine of Massachusetts the "Objection-Maker," because he "opposed everything." Rush's father-in-law, Richard Stockton of New Jersey, displayed timidity "where bold measures were required." Samuel Chase of Maryland, in Rush's opinion, "possessed more learning than knowledge, and more of both than judgment." Chase's speeches in congress "were more oratorical than logical." The President of the Continental Congress, John Hancock of Massachusetts, was too fond of ceremonies for Rush's taste and also lacked "industry and punctuality in business." Hancock's "frequent attacks of the gout," said the Pennsylvania physician, gave "a hypochondriacal peevishness to his temper." Only John Adams received Rush's unqualified praise: "He saw the whole of a subject at a single glance, and by a happy union of the powers of reasoning and persuasion often succeeded in carrying measures which were at first sight of an unpopular nature."[46] When we take a close look at the members of the Second Continental Congress during the summer of 1776, we see a group of flawed, prejudiced, and nervous men, some of whom wandered onto the continental stage after the *Declaration* was approved. These men felt the adrenaline rush of the risk they were taking, but none of them could have predicted the enduring symbolism of their actions.

On August 2, 1776, the delegates who were then in attendance at the Continental Congress signed their names to the official parchment copy of the *Declaration of Independence*. The President of the Continental Congress, John Hancock of Massachusetts, was the first to engross the text with his now-famous florid and outsized signature. The rest of the delegates arose from their seats, colony by colony, one member at a time, and walked to the front of the room. Each in his turn lifted the quill pen from its stand, dipped it into the silver inkwell, and added his name to the list. Many of the delegates leaned forward over the sheet and gave their names a short puff of air to help the ink set. Each returned the pen to its stand and turned to resume his seat. Blank spaces were left for those delegates absent that day, many of whom had been recently elected by their new state governments.

Benjamin Rush, one of Pennsylvania's new delegates, was present on August 2, and he witnessed the signing ceremony with wide eyes. Rush recalled "the pensive and awful silence which pervaded the house when we were called up, one after another, to the table of the President of Congress to subscribe what was believed by many at that time to be our own death warrants." The tense silence was punctuated by the slow metrical clop—like a clock winding down—of each delegate's shoes against the floor as he walked the aisle from and to his chair. Only once during this grave moment did anyone speak. Benjamin Harrison, a boisterous and rotund Virginian, turned toward Massachusetts delegate Elbridge Gerry, while both awaited their turn at the front, and said, "I shall have a great advantage over you, Mr. Gerry, when we are all hung for what we are now doing. From the size and weight of my body I shall die in a few minutes, but from the lightness of your body you will dance in the air an hour or two before you are dead." Rush observed that this remark "procured a transient smile" from several of the delegates, but the updraft of mood "was soon succeeded by the solemnity with which the whole business was conducted."[47] In the months and years leading up to this moment, colonial elites had frequently declared their willingness to support the American cause with the "fullest measure" of their "blood and treasure," but now their promissory notes were coming due.

Part Four
PUBLIC OPINION AND *COMMON SENSE*

About Face

My objective in this study has been to reveal the internal mechanisms of public discourse during the American Revolution—specifically, how colonial public opinion turned 180 degrees during the first half of 1776. We have witnessed the wholesale commitment to reconciliation in January and the overwhelming embrace of independence in July. We have watched the transformation of public opinion and have seen that the *public* changed just as dramatically as did the *opinion*. On another level, we have seen that *American* public opinion—in the sense of a coherent national identity and unified popular will—did not exist prior to the publication of *Common Sense*.

I have done my best to avoid oversimplifying the necessary complexities of the public decision for independence. *Common Sense* was not a magic bullet that single-handedly effected American independence. At the same time, it is hard to overstate the importance of Paine's pamphlet as a catalyst for the larger independence movement. In coastal cities and inland towns throughout America, the independence movement—fueled by a chain reaction of public discourse and public events—was the cause of American independence. The only way the Americans could *become* independent was to decide and to declare together that they *were* independent.

But how could a scattered and remote people gather to make *any* decision, much less one as momentous as the creation of a new nation? Obviously, the colonists could not all shoe their horses, hitch their wagons, and abandon their farms to convene upon the Pennsylvania State House yard. Instead, they sent representatives to conventions and assemblies, which, in turn, sent delegates to the Continental Congress. Those representatives and delegates did not possess decisional autonomy, however; they were given explicit and binding instructions, and they were held accountable for voting in accordance with the published opinion of their electors.[48] We have seen that in 1776, the font of royal sovereignty was cut off and replaced by the deep well of popular sovereignty. When that great transference of sovereignty took place, the decision mechanisms in the colonies underwent a sea change as well. Public decisions were now, in both theory and practice, governed by the expression of public opinion. In royal culture, public opinion had been a nuisance, but in democratic culture, public opinion became a necessity.

In modern political speech, we sling around the term "public opinion" as if it were a self-evident truth, when, in fact, it one of the most problematic concepts in the study of politics. In this concluding section, I will devote some attention to the problem of public opinion in American political culture. By looking once more at *Common Sense* and the *Declaration of Independence* as bookends of the independence movement, we will see the dynamic relationship among public opinion, textual sovereignty, and constitutions that forms the core of American political culture.

Problem Opinion

There exist only three factories that can plausibly produce public opinion: elections, discourse, and our modern statistical fabrication, the opinion poll. Regardless of the mode of production, public opinion is naturally elusive and almost impossible to voice without equivocation. Free elections are the closest approximation to a public opinion event, and for this reason they are the unalterable core of every political scientist's definition of democracy. But periodic elections are very imperfect mechanisms for gauging public opinion, not just because of the potential for corruption or system malfunctions. Even when elections are "free," they do not necessarily reflect the collective opinion of a population. By refusing to vote, an elector may self-select out of the public, and conversely, franchise restrictions may systematically exclude members of the community as unready or unfit to vote as a member of the public. Issues must inevitably be framed in ballot measures, and voters often find themselves faced with a many-questions fallacy at the polls: they are forced in a single response to answer dozens of questions on candidates, issues, and policies.[49] In the act of voting for a particular candidate or proposition, my opinion may be aggregated with untold others who followed an entirely different rationale but arrived at the same apparent conclusion. Our selections may match even when our opinions do not.

In this study we have seen both the opportunity and challenge of public discourse as a means of registering public opinion. Discourse is the only form of opinion expression that holds open the possibility of a real-time change in the public's position on a question. But as public discourse flows toward public decision, it tends to take the path of least resistance. We see a tendency toward polarization in discourse, because of a human penchant for stress-avoidance: we would rather sacrifice decisional precision than subject ourselves to paralyzing complexity. It is simply less stressful to choose between two options instead of hundreds. Nonetheless, the chief danger inherent in polarized public discourse is its tendency to create disingenuous dichotomies that ultimately obfuscate real issues.[50] Separation and polarity are not necessarily bad: in fact, they are unavoidable traits embedded in the etymology of political *discourse*, the sense that two entities stand apart or have taken separate paths. The health of public discourse is not measured by whether it is shrill or blasé, but by its effectiveness in dissecting and exposing the underlying values that inform public decisions.

The third mechanism for approximating public opinion is the opinion poll. Designed to remedy the slow periodicity of actual elections, public opinion polls are virtual secret ballot referenda. Since the public acquires an opinion more often than the election cycle allows, pollsters use advanced statistical methods and communication technologies to aggregate representative samples of public opinion on particular questions. Opinion polls face the same issue-framing concerns inherent in actual elections, and they are subject to less ethical oversight. "Free" opinion polls are even less common than "free" elections. Moreover, the virtual electors only "gather" as data in a database, a phenomenon that neglects the correspondence among a community of opinions. In an atomistic modern culture, public opinion is treated as the sum of private opinions, but the notion that a pollster can take a cross-section of individual opinions and statistically extrapolate it into public opinion misses an important distinction between the two.[51] Well-conceived, well-executed opinion polls can replicate the conditions of an actual election and can sometimes predict outcomes, but they cannot solve the deeper theoretical relationship between elections and public opinion.[52]

I do not here aim to propound a full theory of public opinion, but only to show the difficulty of trapping the concept between the plates of a microscope slide.[53] We cannot, however, dismiss public opinion as an insuperable conundrum, because it is the cornerstone of American political culture. Historian Gordon Wood has written of the transformation of public opinion during the Revolutionary generation: "Nothing was more important in explaining and clarifying the democratization of the American mind." He added, "Public opinion is so much a part of our politics that it is surprising that we have not incorporated it into the Constitution."[54] Wood was not alone in his assessment of the importance of public opinion for American politics: he was preceded by the two most important figures in American constitutional law.

James Madison, considered by many the "Father of the Constitution," wrote in 1791, "Public opinion sets bounds to every government, and is the real sovereign in every free one."[55] Abraham Lincoln, the most important figure in American history outside of the American Revolution, agreed in an 1859 speech: "Public opinion in this country is everything."[56] Lincoln, who used "opinion" and "sentiment" interchangeably, recognized that, because "public sentiment is everything" in American government, its formation was of massive importance. As he observed in his first debate with Stephen Douglas, "With public sentiment, nothing can fail; without it nothing can succeed. Consequently, he who moulds public sentiment, goes deeper than he who enacts statutes or pronounces decisions. He makes statutes and decisions possible or impossible to be executed."[57] In another speech from 1856, Lincoln explained his pathbreaking view of the relationship between public opinion and the *Declaration of Independence*,

> Our government rests in public opinion. Whoever can change public opinion, can change the government, practically just so much. Public opinion, [on] any subject, always has a "central idea," from which all its minor thoughts radiate. That "central idea" in our political public opinion, at the beginning was, and until recently has continued to be, "the equality of men."[58]

Given the centrality of public opinion in American politics, it is, as Wood suggests, surprising that the *United States Constitution* would neglect it. What is more surprising still, however, is that it has been there all along.

Constitutional Criticism

The only "Constitution" that meant anything to the American colonists at the beginning of 1776 was the British Constitution. Thomas Paine, as we have seen, had no kind words in *Common Sense* for that customary framework of British law and government. Englishmen were unduly prejudiced, he said, "in favour of their own government by king, lords and commons," a warped perspective that "arises as much or more from national pride than reason."[59] Even this, one of Paine's more sedate statements, was inflammatory to a degree that is now too easily forgotten. In eighteenth century imperial culture, the British Constitution was regarded as the pinnacle of political perfection. It was sacrosanct; in fact, no one in America had a problem with it except Paine. How unlikely then was the success of *Common Sense*, the first half of which billed itself as an "inquiry into the *constitutional errors* in the English form of government"?[60] Moreover, Paine pummeled the "overbearing part in the English constitution," the Americans' cherished monarchy.[61] He was not telling his American audience what they wanted to hear, much less what they had been thinking all along. While the Americans detected no defect in the health of the British Constitution, Paine diagnosed the cause for its "sickly" state in opposition to every colonial assumption. The Americans had assumed that *this* parliament and *this* ministry were the problem, and that *this* king was the solution; whenever a governmental change might be required, it involved elected personnel, not constitutional structure. Paine, on the other hand, contended that America's problems could be traced to a root constitutional defect: that "monarchy hath poisoned the republic" and "the crown hath engrossed the commons."[62]

Paine carried through his distinction between government and society into his description of the British Constitution. Britain's relative security and prosperity had little to do with *"the constitution of the government"* but were *"wholly owing to the constitution of the people."*[63] Britain had not become great because of its constitution, he was saying, but rather in spite of it. In *Common Sense*, Paine loosened the white-knuckled grip of the British Constitution on colonial political culture by mooning the monarchy. And, lest his opinion of the British Constitution be missed, he used the most salacious metaphor he could conjure up: "And as a man, who is attached to a prostitute, is unfitted to choose or judge of a wife, so any prepossession in favor of a rotten constitution of government will disable us from discerning a good one."[64]

Paine wanted to see America "form the noblest, purest constitution on the face of the earth."[65] In Paine's political vocabulary, "an independent constitution" was a "settled form of government," founded in "our natural right" to self-government, formed "in a cool and deliberate manner," and given as a priceless gift to posterity.[66] The constitution should be encapsulated in a "continental, not provincial," written charter that would serve as "a bond of solemn obligation, which the whole enters into, to support the right of every separate part, whether of religion, personal freedom, or property."[67] Paine was more interested in natural rights than in civil liberties, because he had seen the latter so abused in the customary, common law system of British constitutionality. Therefore, he saw a vernacular textual constitution as an essential safeguard against elite attempts to bury the rights of common people under stacks of legal commentaries.

In Chapter Three, we looked at a passage that now deserves a second glance. In a paragraph rich with the ingredients of political revolution, Paine called for a day to be "solemnly set apart for proclaiming the charter" to the people. On this day, the people would participate in a coronation ceremony unlike any other. Coronation ceremonies were elaborate rituals of the transfer of legal sovereignty to a new monarch. The crown at the American ceremony, imagined Paine, would rest atop the new charter as a symbol "that in America, THE LAW IS KING." At the conclusion of Paine's epoch-making ceremony, the crown would "be demolished and scattered among the people whose right it is." In America, the new written constitution would be the formal monarch, the textual embodiment of an inclusive reading public which was, in turn, the sole repository of political sovereignty.[68]

Because of the actual course of American history, we now have a tendency to assume that constitutions necessarily follow declarations. But when we interrogate that teleological propensity, we see an important reason why the *Declaration of Independence* had to precede the *United States Constitution*. In the *Rights of Man, Part the Second*, Paine explained it this way: "A constitution is not the act of a government, but of a people constituting a government; and government without a constitution, is power without a right."[69] No nation can have a *constitution* until it first has a defined *people*. Independence was, said Paine in *Common Sense*, "the only BOND that can tie and keep us together." After independence was declared, he continued, "We shall then see our object, and our ears will be legally shut against the schemes of an intriguing, as well, as a cruel enemy."[70] In 1776, Paine and his compatriots were "men laboring to establish an Independent Constitution."[71] The "present condition" of America, he argued in *Common Sense*, was "Legislation without law; wisdom without a plan; a constitution without a name; and, what is strangely astonishing, perfect Independence contending for dependence."[72]

The Americans, Paine and John Adams tirelessly contended in 1776, did not need to *become* independent; they needed simply to declare the fact that they already *were* independent. Before January 1776, it is true, some colonists murmured about the need for America to become independent, but Paine first introduced the concept of a declaration of independence in *Common Sense*. He wrote,

> Were a manifesto to be published, and dispatched to foreign courts, setting forth the miseries we have endured, and the peaceable methods we have ineffectually used for redress; declaring, at the same time, that not being able, any longer to live happily or safely under the cruel disposition of the British court, we had been driven to the necessity of breaking off all connections with her; at the same time, assuring all such courts of our peaceable disposition towards them, and of our desire of entering into trade with them: Such a memorial would produce more good effects to this Continent, than if a ship were freighted with petitions to Britain.[73]

Jefferson wrote the *Declaration* like a closed-book essay response to this single exam question.

In the agenda, audience, style, and vocabulary of *Common Sense*, Paine was working to constitute an independent and sovereign American people. Paine always addressed an *American*, not a *Pennsylvanian* audience, because he recognized that the constitution of a sovereign public was the first step in the constitution of a sovereign nation. As he put it in 1783, "Sovereignty must have power to protect all the parts that compose and constitute it: and as UNITED STATES we are equal to the importance of the title, but otherwise we are not."[74] After the Revolutionary War, Paine supported the Federalist-driven *Constitution*, because he was committed to "the Sovereignty and Independence of the United States," rather than the Anti-Federalist position that sovereignty should be seated in each individual state.[75] In 1776, Paine's commitment to an encompassing national sovereignty required first that America cut its ties to Great Britain. Even if *Common Sense* had only accomplished this destructive separation, it would have been a monumental text, but Paine had a constructive agenda as well. He was asking a motley population of colonial British subjects to wager everything they possessed and everything they had ever known, in order to become a unified nation of republican American citizens.

If we work backward from the *United States Constitution*, we can see an unexpected connection to the *Declaration of Independence* and *Common Sense*. The two most celebrated political texts from 1776 are not autonomous patriotic treatises but instead form the core of the *Constitution*'s jurisprudential heritage. The *Constitution* established a government system spoken into existence by the direct, sovereign voice of "We the people of the United States." Where was that sovereign voice formed? In the *Declaration of Independence*. The "we" in the *Declaration* stood for "the representatives of the United States of America, in General Congress assembled." The *Declaration*'s "we" acted and spoke "in the name and by the authority of the good people of these colonies." How did the Continental Congress receive word that the people had lent their "name" and "authority" for such a decision? From *Common Sense* and the public debate over independence.

Common Sense tuned the cacophony of colonial discontent into a harmonious anthem for independence. Just as important, *Common Sense* formed the first *American* reading public. The *Declaration of Independence* took that reading public and transformed it into a sovereign voice. The *United States Constitution* took that sovereign voice and transformed it into the textual foundation of government.[76] More concisely, *Common Sense* constituted an American public, the *Declaration* constituted the American people, the *Constitution* constituted the American government. Even as Paine insisted in January 1776 on a written, national constitution, he was excavating the ruins of an unwritten, colonial constitution, and he was also beginning to set the foundation stones for modern politics. *Common Sense* contained all of the materials for the constitutional democracy that the United States would become. And even though the *Constitution* of 1787 was framed according to the dictates of republican political architecture, the entire edifice rested upon the basic principle of democracy: public opinion.

A Common Identity

During the fall of 1775, Thomas Paine, Benjamin Rush, and Thomas Pryor had crouched in the dank crawl spaces beneath houses and barns to collect the saltpeter that the colonies required to produce their own gunpowder. Paine recognized that the colonies could not muster an effective military resistance to Britain without ammunition, and he also cringed at the colonies' lack of political firepower. In *Common Sense*, Paine was collecting and publishing "the straggling thoughts of individuals" and improving them into "useful matter."[77] His pamphlet thus became a "manufactory" of public opinion, the political ammunition the colonies so desperately lacked.

On one level, "common sense" meant the same thing in eighteenth century America that it does today: usually, in its absence, *the ability to perceive the obvious*, and in its presence, *street-smarts*. On another level, however, "common sense" admitted of a meaning in the eighteenth century that corresponded closely to what we think of today as "public opinion." Early Americans used the word "sense" in much the same way we use "opinion"—a thoughtful perception of reality with the added component of emotional "feeling."[78] Likewise, "common" fell along the line of meaning ranging from "shared" to "popular" to "mundane." Samuel Johnson catalogued multiple definitions of both words in his 1776 dictionary, but those definitions included *Common (adj.)*, "Public; general; serving the use of all," and *Sense (n.s.)*, "Opinion; notion; judgment."[79] In early 1776, *Common Sense* became public opinion, and public opinion became common sense.

Public texts fuel public discourse, public discourse shapes public opinion, public opinion drives public decisions, and public decisions forge a public identity. So traveled the course of events in America during 1776, and the result was a continent of subjects transformed into a nation of citizens. James Warren wrote to John Adams on July 17, describing the arrival of the *Declaration of Independence* in Boston. "Every one of us feels more important than ever," he said, and "we now congratulate each other as Freemen."[80] The *Constitution* of the United States government was yet to be written, but 1776 marked a constitution of equal importance, the constitution of the American public.

Notes: Chapter 12

---

[1] Walsh, *Writings of Christopher Gadsden*, 111.
[2] Godbold and Woody. *Christopher Gadsden and the American Revolution*, 148-151. Gadsden's personal copy of *Common Sense* is held in the College of Charleston Library.
[3] Godbold, 151-152; McDonough, *Christopher Gadsden and Henry Laurens*, 173.
[4] 3 September 1774, *John Adams Diary* 21, MHS
[5] Thomas McKean to Messrs. William McKorkle and Son, 16 June 1817. Appended to Marshall, *Diary*; Caesar Rodney to Thomas Rodney, 4 July 1776, Ryden, *Letters to and from Caesar Rodney*, 94-95.
[6] In lineal terms, the Continental Congress was really a bastard grandchild of the British Constitution.
[7] 6 December 1775, "Proclamation," JCC(A), 282-284.
[8] 29 February 1776, RS 2:507.
[9] 1 March 1776, RS 2:507.
[10] The Committee of Secret Correspondence, composed of Franklin, Dickinson, Morris, Harrison, and Jay, gave Silas Deane credentials and instructions to go to France, and "there to transact such Business, commercial and political as we have committed to his Care, in Behalf and by Authority of the Congress of the thirteen united Colonies." Deane Papers 1:117-119, 123. NYHS. See also, Friedenwald, *Declaration of Independence*, 74-75; "The Committee of Secret Correspondence: Instructions to Silas Deane," 2 March 1776, Willcox, 22:369-374.
[11] 9 March 1776, RS 2:510.
[12] 22 March 1776, RS 2:514.
[13] The resolution authorizing American pirateering met with mixed success. Before the end of 1776, the American pirates had taken almost 350 British prizes, causing shipping insurance rates in London to rise to 25 percent. The booty was, in fact, so great that the rage for pirateering was often blamed for deficiencies in official military recruitment. Fridenwald, "The Continental Congress."
[14] 22 April 1776, Stiles, *Literary Diary*, 2:10-11.
[15] Elbridge Gerry to James Warren. 26 March 1776. Gardiner, *A Study in Dissent*, 12.
[16] James Warren to JA, 30 March/ 3 April 1776. *Warren-Adams Letters*, 1:219. The acerbic Adams picked apart Warren's enthusiasm, clarifying that he could "scarcely believe" that "Moderation and Timidity are at an End. How is this possible?" He then asked sarcastically if cunning, reserve, hinting, trimming, duplicity, and hypocrisy are "at an End too," punctuating his thoughts with the condescending line, "You deal in the Marvellous like a Traveller." Adams's sober Calvinist belief in human depravity did not permit such utopian thoughts, one reason Adams was so well fitted to a classical republican ethic of vigilance and order. JA to James Warren, 16 April 1776. *Warren-Adams Letters*, 1:227.
[17] "Privateering" was a common euphemism for "pirateering."
[18] JA to James Warren, 16 April 1776. *Warren-Adams Letters*, 1:227.
[19] JA to James Warren, 22 April 1776. *Warren-Adams Letters*, 1:233-234; cf. Habakkuk 2: 2-3.

[20] JA to AA, 14 April 1776. Butterfield, et al., *Book of Abigail and John*, 122.
[21] Quoted in Commager and Morris, 294-295.
[22] See, 10 May 1776, JCC(F), 4:341; for Thomas Cushing's letter conveying the intelligence, see Force, *American Archives*, 4th Ser., 5:1184.
[23] JCC(F), 4:342.
[24] PG, May 22, 1776. See also, 15 May 1776, JCC(F), 4:357-358.
[25] Even outside of the Continental Congress, calls for reconciliation became very rare after this point. On May 15, 1776, the Maryland Convention signaled its tenacious loyalism in a series of resolutions. One of the resolutions says, "*Resolved unanimously*, That as this Convention is firmly persuaded that a re-union with Great-Britain, on constitutional principles, would most effectually secure the rights and liberties, and increase the strength, and promote the happiness of the whole empire, objects which this province hath ever in view, the said Deputies are bound and directed to govern themselves by the instructions given to them by this Convention in its session of December last, in the same manner as if the said instructions were particularly repeated." PG, May 29, 1776.
[26] JA to James Warren, 20 May 1776. *Warren-Adams Letters*, 1:249.
[27] "Report from the Virginia Convention on May 15, 1776," PJ, May 29, 1776.
[28] Lee also introduced measures on confederation and treaties, but for the purposes of this study, we will focus on the resolution for independence.
[29] 7 June 1776, JCC(A), 204-205. See also, *Robert Treat Paine Diaries*, MHS.
[30] The "middle colonies" to which he was referring were Maryland, Delaware, Pennsylvania, New Jersey, and New York.
[31] Boyd, *Papers of Thomas Jefferson*, 1:298-299.
[32] 8 June 1776, JCC(A), 205.
[33] Edward Rutledge to John Jay, Saturday Evening 10 o'clock [8 June 1776]. Morris, *John Jay, The Making of a Revolutionary*, 1:275-276.
[34] Boyd, 1:309-315; 10 June 1776, JCC(A), 205-206.
[35] 11 June 1776. JCC(A), 206-207. The confederation committee consisted of one member from each colony except for New York: Bartlett, S. Adams, Hopkins, Sherman, R. R. Livingston, Dickinson, McKean, Stone, Nelson, Hewes, E. Rutledge, and Gwinnet. The members of the treaty committee were Dickinson, Franklin, J. Adams, Harrison, and R. Morris. 12 June 1776, JCC(A), 207-210.
[36] Daniel of St. Thomas Jenifer to CCA, 16 June 1776. Hoffman, *Papers of Charles Carroll of Carrollton*, 2:920-922.
[37] JA to John Winthrop, 23 June 1776. Quoted in Commager and Morris, 307-308.
[38] Thomas Jones to James Iredell, 28 April 1776. Quoted in Saunders, 1033.
[39] From this interpretive perspective, the natural break in the text occurs between "to alter their former systems of government," and "The history of the present King of Great Britain…"
[40] CS 2.1-2.2.
[41] Jefferson's "Notes of Proceedings in the Continental Congress," Boyd, 1:309-315.
[42] Edward Rutledge to John Jay, 29 June 1776. Morris, *John Jay*, 280-281.
[43] Charles Carroll of Carrollton received regular updates on the Continental Congress during June and early July—in between his stints as a delegate. Ac-

cording to Carroll, New York had been the only colony to abstain from voting for independence, since their delegates did not have, "as they conceived, any powers for that purpose." Carroll remarked that "the 3 lower counties" of Pennsylvania were divided on the question, and thus that colony voted against independence on Monday, July 1. The following day, Pennsylvania was "unanimous for the question," but, said Carroll, "how this happened I know not." CCC to CCA, 5 July 1776. Hoffman, 2:926-927.

[44] Boyd, 1:309-315.
[45] Buffett, "Abraham Clark."
[46] Hawke, *Benjamin Rush*, 165.
[47] Quoted in Hawke, *Benjamin Rush*, 164.
[48] Even those rare delegates, like the South Carolinians in the Continental Congress, who were free to "vote their consciences," were acting in obedience to the instructions of their originating body.
[49] The most famous example of the many-questions fallacy is "Are you still beating your wife?"
[50] From a strategic perspective, polarization simplifies the game of politics by narrowing the field of contingency; hardening the fringes of the electorate allows politicians to devote more money and attention to "swing voters" in the middle.
[51] According to Montaigne, "There never was in the world two opinions alike, no more than two hairs, or two grains; the most universal quality is diversity." *Essays*, "Of the Resemblance of Children to their Fathers."
[52] Though methods of *measuring* public opinion have grown exponentially more sophisticated over the last two-and-a-quarter centuries, it is remarkable that techniques for *directing* public opinion have hardly advanced an inch.
[53] We could further complicate the problem by attempting to delineate the relationship between the *opinion* of the people (what they think), the *voice* of the people (what they say), and the *will* of the people (what they want done), but for my purposes in this chapter, I am eliding those distinctions and treating public opinion as the sovereign sanction of public decisions.
[54] Wood, "The Democratization of Mind," 82-83.
[55] In an "extensive territory" such as the United States, thought Madison, it was "favorable to liberty" to practically contract the territorial limits by facilitating "a general intercourse of sentiments." In his thinking, this was best accomplished by means of "good roads, domestic commerce, a free press, and particularly a *circulation of newspapers through the entire body of the people*, and *Representatives going from, and returning among every part of them*." Madison, "Public Opinion," *National Gazette*, December 19, 1791. See, Rutland and Mason, *Papers of James Madison*, 14:170.
[56] Lincoln, "Speech at Columbus, Ohio," 16 September 1859. Basler, *Collected Works of Abraham Lincoln*, 3:424.
[57] Lincoln, "First Debate with Stephen A. Douglas at Ottawa, Illinois," 21 August 1858, Basler, 3:27. Lincoln often railed against what he called "Douglas Popular Sovereignty," but he made it clear that he viewed Douglas's spin of the concept as a counterfeit of the legitimate principle. He said, "I believe there is a genuine popular sovereignty....I understand that this government of the United States, under which we live, is based upon this principle, and I am misunder-

stood if it is supposed that I have any war to make upon that principle." "Speech at Columbus, Ohio," 16 September 1859. Basler, 3:405.

[58] Lincoln, "Speech at a Republican Banquet, Chicago," 10 December 1856. Basler, 2:385.

[59] CS 1.18.

[60] CS 1.20.

[61] CS 1.17.

[62] CS 2.23.

[63] CS 1.19.

[64] CS 1.20.

[65] CS A.16.

[66] CS 3.48, 4.5.

[67] CS 3.45, 4.22.

[68] CS 3.47.

[69] RM 2, CW 1:375.

[70] CS A.18.

[71] CS E.4.

[72] CS A.11.

[73] CS 4.26.

[74] AC, No. 13, CW 1:234.

[75] See, for example, Boudinot, *Journal of Events in the Revolution*, 4-5.

[76] The chief problem of the *Articles of Confederation*—and a lingering issue in American politics through the end of the Civil War—was bound up in its inability to resolve the locus of sovereignty. As early as November 17, 1777, the congress apologized for the awkwardness of the *Articles of Confederation*: "The articles can always be candidly reviewed under a sense of the difficulty of combining in one general system the various sentiments and interests of a continent divided into so many sovereign and independent communities, under a conviction of the absolute necessity of united all our councils and all our strength, to maintain and defend our common liberties." Until *de jure* sovereignty shifted from the Virginian people, the Pennsylvanian people, etc., to the *American* people (and from the state governments to the federal government) in 1789 and *de facto* sovereignty followed the same path in 1865, the nation was virtually impossible to govern. See 17 November 1777, JCC(F), 9:932-936.

[77] CS 3.41.

[78] Samuel Adams, for example, used this connotation of "Sense" in his description of the New Hampshire capital's early resistance to the idea of independence: "I hope however that the Town of Portsmouth doth not in this Instance speak the Sense of that Colony." SA to JA, 15 January 1776. Cushing, 258-261.

[79] Johnson, *Dictionary*.

[80] James Warren to JA, 17 July 1776. *Warren-Adams Letters*, 1:261.

Appendix

The Text of Common Sense

Included here is an edited and complete transcription of the text of *Common Sense* as it appeared in Philadelphia beginning on February 14, 1776. Because there are many reprint editions of *Common Sense* now available in bookstores and libraries, it is important that I explain my rationale for producing my own version. First, I must note that I am by no means dismissing all other editions of *Common Sense* as deficient or incorrect; they simply do not fit the analytical parameters of this study. In the case of this book, my goal is not modernized clarity or grammatical correctness; it is to make accessible to my readers the text *as it appeared in Philadelphia during the spring of 1776*.

The overarching objective of this study is to facilitate a deeper understanding of the American colonial experience of *Common Sense* and of the political mentality driving the decision for independence. Therefore, my argument requires that twenty-first century readers engage with essentially the same text as did eighteenth-century colonists. I have not concerned myself in this study with what *Common Sense* meant to audiences in 1792, 1809, or 2007; I want simply to elucidate what the text meant to American colonists in early 1776.

Although my primary historical focus is highly specific, my methodological focus lends itself toward more generalization. I have intended in this book to exemplify a method of rhetorical historiography that can be applied to other texts and contexts, and this appendix is part of that metacritical strategy. In basic terms, my reasons for appending a complete text of *Common Sense* to this book are threefold: convenience, integrity, and precision.

Convenience. The expository and dialogic nature of my argument requires that readers have ready access to the nuanced pamphlet text. I include it here as a tool for readers to quickly cross-reference my arguments and footnotes with the source material itself. Original copies of *Common Sense* are the least convenient option for readers, since most extant 1776 editions are cloistered in research libraries. Microfilmed or digitized images of the pamphlet are more widely available, but they too often lack optimal navigability or legibility. Most Paine scholars still prefer to fish for an increasingly rare 1945 hardcopy of Philip Foner's *Complete Writings of Thomas Paine*, but even if a reader obtains an edition of this venerable work, Foner's editorial practice is too loose for a close textual analysis of *Common Sense* (though I do cite several other Paine texts from this edition, when textual exactitude is less of a necessity).

Integrity. By appending an edited version of *Common Sense* to this book, I am also, in the spirit of academic research, "publishing my data." Humanistic inquiry does not typically strive for replicable "results" with the verve of scientific inquiry, but even humanists can benefit from keeping the object of study consistent across multiple investigations. Page citations from a smattering of versions—especially in the case of a proliferated text like *Common Sense*—can too easily become empty conventionalities of scholarly discourse. To analyze a complex text like *Common Sense*, authors and readers alike need to verify that we are all talking about the same thing. In order to focus the critical vision of my readers on the inner workings of *Common Sense*, I have formally partitioned the text into sections and paragraphs. This citation technique should prove helpful to readers of this book, and it will also enable scholars of *Common Sense* to discuss the text— regardless of the edition used—with a specificity traditionally reserved only for versified poetry, drama, and scripture. A textual taxonomy of *Common Sense*—as part of a broader critical methodology—will be of great service in furthering the conversation about this core text of the American Revolution.

Precision. Instead of attempting to "merge" dozens of different editions of *Common Sense* from 1776, I decided to focus upon a single imprint that best represents the copies of the pamphlet circulating in America during the spring of 1776. The original edition used for this transcription was printed by Benjamin Towne and published by William and Thomas Bradford in Philadelphia in February 1776. The extant copy I used as my source is held in the Charles Deering Library at Northwestern University. Following Richard Gimbel's citation guide in *Thomas Paine: A Bibliographical Check List of Common Sense*, this edition is CS-12. I have omitted only page numbers, printer's footers, and a half-title page (directly preceding the full-title page) that reads, "COMMON SENSE." This individual imprint is virtually identical to other imprints of *Common Sense* produced in 1776 by Towne, although the printer did make one minor edit in this impression: the correction of a misspelled word (he missed a few others).

I use the Bradford/Towne edition here for two primary reasons. First, I chose this edition because it contains all of Paine's additions to *Common Sense*, including the British naval figures, the "Appendix," and the "Epistle to the Quakers." These "large additions" were added with the advent of the Bradford edition and subsequently pirated by Robert Bell and most other American printers. The second reason for using this impression in particular is its location—both geographical and social—at the very heart of the independence movement. Calling this the "Bradford edition" is somewhat misleading; William Bradford was semi-retired and preoccupied with drilling the Pennsylvania militia, while his son, Thomas, then the main proprietor of the London Coffee House and the *Pennsylvania Journal*, is best regarded as the "authorized retailer" of the expanded edition. It was Thomas Paine himself who spearheaded this round of republication as author, editor, advertiser, print broker, financial agent, and circulation director. Paine worked closely with the two print shops producing his new edition, Benjamin Towne and the German-American printers, Melchior Steiner and Carl Cist. Paine was by mid-February 1776 no longer anonymous in Philadelphia, so he certainly dropped in on the printers periodically to inspect their work. Towne's *Pennsylvania Evening Post* was a significant flashpoint of the independence movement during the late winter and early spring, and so it is fitting that the text printed here comes from his press.

A word about editing and style: the text of *Common Sense* is here reproduced exactly as it appears in the extant pamphlet from which it is derived. Spelling, misspelling, and idiosyncratic spelling have been fully preserved and replicated. Punctuation, capitalization, and italicization are likewise identical to the source. In a couple of instances, I have inserted a missing letter in brackets, but only when a lacuna threatened to confuse the meaning. My editorial policy in this text of *Common Sense* has been to avoid textual intervention and to preserve the original typography (the exception to this being the modernized internal "s" rather than "f"). In the rest of this study, I have taken some editorial license to smooth punctuation or to make minor spelling modifications with the same intent: to minimize the glaring, pedantic "[sic]" that would litter the verbatim republication of any early modern text. In the late eighteenth century, spelling and punctuation were yet far from standardized, and printers and typesetters were often as responsible for "mistakes" as authors. Inasmuch as standard spellings did exist during the eighteenth century, I have sought to preserve in the body of this book most Anglicised (e.g., rather than "Anglicized") spellings as a subtle reminder that *American* English did not yet exist in 1776.

The citations used herein conform to the following basic system: the capital letter or numeral representing the section, a separating period, and then the paragraph number within that section. The section heading citations are:

F. The "Foreword" (Introduction) to *Common Sense*.
1. Section 1 on the origin and design of government.
2. Section 2 on monarchy and hereditary succession.
3. Section 3 on the present state of American affairs.
4. Section 4 on the present ability of America.
A. The "Appendix" to *Common Sense* added by Paine to the Bradford edition.
E. The "Epistle to the Quakers" added to the Bradford edition.

COMMON SENSE;
ADDRESSED TO THE
INHABITANTS
of
AMERICA,

On the following interesting
SUBJECTS.

I. Of the Origin and Design of Government in general, with concise Remarks on the English Constitution.
II. Of Monarchy and Hereditary Succession.
III. Thoughts on the present State of American Affairs.
IV. Of the present Ability of America, with some miscellaneous Reflections.

A NEW EDITION, with several Additions in the Body of the Work. To which is added an APPENDIX; together with an Address to the People called QUAKERS.
N. B. The New Addition here given increases the Work upwards of one Third.

Man knows no Master save creating HEAVEN,
Or those whom Choice and common Good ordain.
THOMSON.

PHILADELPHIA printed.
And sold by W. and T. BRADFORD.

INTRODUCTION.

F.1
PERHAPS the sentiments contained in the following pages, are not *yet* sufficiently fashionable to procure them general favor; a long habit of not thinking a thing *wrong*, gives it a superficial appearance of being *right*, and raises at first a formidable outcry in defence of custom. But the tumult soon subsides. Time makes more converts than reason.

F.2
As a long and violent abuse of power, is generally the Means of calling the right of it in question (and in Matters too which might never have been thought of, had not the Sufferers been aggravated into the inquiry) and as the King of England hath undertaken in his *own Right*, to support the Parliament in what he calls *Theirs*, and as the good people of this country are grievously oppressed by the combination, they have an undoubted privilege to inquire into the pretensions of both, and equally to reject the usurpations of either.

F.3
In the following sheets, the author hath studiously avoided every thing which is personal among ourselves. Compliments as well as censure to individuals make no part thereof. The wise, and the worthy, need not the triumph of a pamphlet; and those whose sentiments are injudicious, or unfriendly, will cease of themselves, unless too much pains are bestowed upon their conversion.

F.4
The cause of America is in a great measure, the cause of all mankind. Many circumstances hath, and will arise, which are not local, but universal, and through which the principles of all Lovers of Mankind are affected, and in the Event of which, their Affections are interested. The laying a Country desolate with Fire and Sword, declaring War against the natural rights of all Mankind, and extirpating the Defenders thereof from the Face of the Earth, is the Concern of every Man to whom Nature hath given the Power of feeling; of which Class, regardless of Party Censure, is the AUTHOR.

F.5
P. S. The Publication of this new Edition hath been delayed, with a View of taking notice (had it been necessary) of any Attempt to refute the Doctrine of Independance: As no Answer hath yet appeared, it is now presumed that none will, the Time needful for getting such a Performance ready for the Public being considerably past.

F.6
Who the Author of this Production is, is wholly unnecessary to the Public, as the Object for Attention is the *Doctrine itself*, not the *Man*. Yet it may not be unnecessary to say, That he is unconnected with any Party, and under no sort of Influence public or private, but the influence of reason and principle.

Philadelphia, February 14, 1776.

COMMON SENSE.

Of the origin and design of government in general. With concise remarks on the English constitution.

1.1
SOME writers have so confounded society with government, as to leave little or no distinction between them; whereas they are not only different, but have different origins. Society is produced by our wants, and government by our wickedness; the former promotes our happiness *positively* by uniting our affections, the latter *negatively* by restraining our vices. The one encourages intercourse, the other creates distinctions. The first is a patron, the last a punisher.

1.2
Society in every state is a blessing, but government even in its best state is but a necessary evil; in its worst state an intolerable one; for when we suffer, or are exposed to the same miseries *by a government*, which we might expect in a country *without government*, our calamity is heightened by reflecting that we furnish the means by which we suffer. Government, like dress, is the badge of lost innocence; the palaces of kings are built on the ruins of the bowers of paradise. For were the impulses of conscience clear, uniform, and irresistibly obeyed, man would need no other lawgiver; but that not being the case, he finds it necessary to surrender up a part of his property to furnish means for the protection of the rest; and this he is induced to do by the same prudence which in every other case advises him out of two evils to choose the least. *Wherefore*, security being the true design and end of government, it unanswerably follows that whatever *form* thereof appears most likely to ensure it to us, with the least expence and greatest benefit, is preferable to all others.

1.3
In order to gain a clear and just idea of the design and end of government, let us suppose a small number of persons settled in some sequestered part of the earth, unconnected with the rest, they will then represent the first peopling of any country, or of the world. In this state of natural liberty, society will be their first thought. A thousand motives will excite them thereto, the strength of one man is so unequal to his wants, and his mind so unfitted for perpetual solitude, that he is soon obliged to seek assistance and relief of another, who in his turn requires the same. Four or five united would be able to raise a tolerable dwelling in the midst of a wilderness, but *one* man might labor out the common period of life without accomplishing any thing; when he had felled his timber he could not remove it, nor erect it after it was removed; hunger in the mean time would urge him from his work, and

every different want call him a different way. Disease, nay even misfortune would be death, for though neither might be mortal, yet either would disable him from living, and reduce him to a state in which he might rather be said to perish than to die.

1.4
Thus necessity, like a gravitating power, would soon form our newly arrived emigrants into society, the reciprocal blessings of which, would supersede, and render the obligations of law and government unnecessary while they remained perfectly just to each other; but as nothing but heaven is impregnable to vice, it will unavoidably happen, that in proportion as they surmount the first difficulties of emigration, which bound them together in a common cause, they will begin to relax in their duty and attachment to each other; and this remissness, will point out the necessity, of establishing some form of government to supply the defect of moral virtue.

1.5
Some convenient tree will afford them a State-House, under the branches of which, the whole colony may assemble to deliberate on public matters. It is more than probable that their first laws will have the title only of REGULATIONS, and be enforced by no other penalty than public disesteem. In this first parliament every man, by natural right, will have a seat.

1.6
But as the colony increases, the public concerns will increase likewise, and the distance at which the members may be separated, will render it too inconvenient for all of them to meet on every occasion as at first, when their number was small, their habitations near, and the public concerns few and trifling. This will point out the convenience of their consenting to leave the legislative part to be managed by a select number chosen from the whole body, who are supposed to have the same concerns at stake which those have who appointed them, and who will act in the same manner as the whole body would act were they present. If the colony continue increasing, it will become necessary to augment the number of the representatives, and that the interest of every part of the colony may be attended to, it will be found best to divide the whole into convenient parts, each part sending its proper number; and that the *elected* might never form to themselves an interest separate from the *electors*, prudence will point out the propriety of having elections often; because as the *elected* might by that means return and mix again with the general body of the *electors* in a few months, their fidelity to the public will be secured by the prudent reflexion of not making a rod for themselves. And as this frequent interchange will

establish a common interest with every part of the community, they will mutually and naturally support each other, and on this (not on the unmeaning name of king) depends the *strength of government, and the happiness of the governed.*

1.7
Here then is the origin and rise of government; namely, a mode rendered necessary by the inability of moral virtue to govern the world; here too is the design and end of government, viz. freedom and security. And however our eyes may be dazzled with show, or our ears deceived by sound; however prejudice may warp our wills, or interest darken our understanding, the simple voice of nature and of reason will say, it is right.

1.8
I draw my idea of the form of government from a principle in nature, which no art can overturn, viz. that the more simple any thing is, the less liable it is to be disordered, and the easier repaired when disordered; and with this maxim in view, I offer a few remarks on the so much boasted constitution of England. That it was noble for the dark and slavish times in which it was erected, is granted. When the world was over-run with tyranny the least remove therefrom was a glorious rescue. But that it is imperfect, subject to convulsions, and incapable of producing what it seems to promise, is easily demonstrated.

1.9
Absolute governments (tho' the disgrace of human nature) have this advantage with them, that they are simple; if the people suffer, they know the head from which their suffering springs, know likewise the remedy, and are not bewildered by a variety of causes and cures. But the constitution of England is so exceedingly complex, that the nation may suffer for years together without being able to discover in which part the fault lies, some will say in one and some in another, and every political physician will advise a different medicine.

1.10
I know it is difficult to get over local or long standing prejudices, yet if we will suffer ourselves to examine the component parts of the English constitution, we shall find them to be the base remains of two ancient tyrannies, compounded with some new republican materials.
First. — The remains of monarchical tyranny in the person of the king.
Secondly. — The remains of aristocratical tyranny in the persons of the peers.

Thirdly. — The new republican materials, in the persons of the commons, on whose virtue depends the freedom of England.

The two first, by being hereditary, are independent of the people; wherefore in a *constitutional sense* they contribute nothing towards the freedom of the state.

1.11

To say that the constitution of England is a *union* of three powers reciprocally *checking* each other, is farcical, either the words have no meaning, or they are flat contradictions.

1.12

To say that the commons is a check upon the king, presupposes two things.

First. — That the king is not to be trusted without being looked after, or in other words, that a thirst for absolute power is the natural disease of monarchy.

Secondly. — That the commons, by being appointed for that purpose, are either wiser or more worthy of confidence than the crown.

1.13

But as the same constitution which gives the commons a power to check the king by withholding the supplies, gives afterwards the king a power to check the commons, by empowering him to reject their other bills; it again supposes that the king is wiser than those whom it has already supposed to be wiser than him. A mere absurdity!

1.14

There is something exceedingly ridiculous in the composition of monarchy; it first excludes a man from the means of information, yet empowers him to act in cases where the highest judgment is required. The state of a king shuts him from the world, yet the business of a king requires him to know it thoroughly; wherefore the different parts, by unnaturally opposing and destroying each other, prove the whole character to be absurd and useless.

1.15

Some writers have explained the English constitution thus; the king, say they, is one, the people another; the peers are an house in behalf of the king; the commons in behalf of the people; but this hath all the distinctions of an house divided against itself; and though the expressions be pleasantly arranged, yet when examined they appear idle and ambiguous; and it will always happen, that the nicest construction that words are capable of, when applied to the description of something which either cannot exist, or is too incomprehensible to be within the compass of description, will be words of sound only, and though they may amuse the ear, they cannot inform the mind, for this explanation includes a previous question, viz. *How came the king by a power which the people are afraid to trust, and always obliged to check?* Such a power could not be the gift of a wise people, neither can any power, *which needs checking*, be from God; yet the provision, which the constitution makes, supposes such a power to exist.

1.16
But the provision is unequal to the task; the means either cannot or will not accomplish the end, and the whole affair is a felo de se; for as the greater weight will always carry up the less, and as all the wheels of a machine are put in motion by one, it only remains to know which power in the constitution has the most weight, for that will govern; and though the others, or a part of them, may clog, or, as the phrase is, check the rapidity of its motion, yet so long as they cannot stop it, their endeavors will be ineffectual; the first moving power will at last have its way, and what it wants in speed is supplied by time.

1.17
That the crown is this overbearing part in the English constitution needs not be mentioned, and that it derives its whole consequence merely from being the giver of places pensions is self-evident, wherefore, though we have been wise enough to shut and lock a door against absolute monarchy, we at the same time have been foolish enough to put the crown in possession of the key.

1.18
The prejudice of Englishmen, in favour of their own government by king, lords and commons, arises as much or more from national pride than reason. Individuals are undoubtedly safer in England than in some other countries, but the *will* of the king is as much the *law* of the land in Britain as in France, with this difference, that instead of proceeding directly from his mouth, it is handed to the people under the more formidable shape of an act of parliament. For the fate of Charles the First hath only made kings more subtle — not more just.

1.19
Wherefore, laying aside all national pride and prejudice in favour of modes and forms, the plain truth is, that *it is wholly owing to the constitution of the people, and not to the constitution of the government* that the crown is not as oppressive in England as in Turkey.

1.20
An inquiry into the *constitutional errors* in the English form of government is at this time highly necessary; for as we are never in a proper condition of doing justice to others, while we continue under the influence of some leading partiality, so neither are we capable of doing it to ourselves while we remain fettered by any obstinate prejudice. And as a man, who is attached to a prostitute, is unfitted to choose or judge of a wife, so any prepossession in favor of a rotten constitution of government will disable us from discerning a good one.

Of monarchy and hereditary succession.

2.1
MANKIND being originally equals in the order of creation, the equality could only be destroyed by some subsequent circumstance; the distinctions of rich, and poor, may in a great measure be accounted for, and that without having recourse to the harsh ill sounding names of oppression and avarice. Oppression is often the *consequence*, but seldom or never the *means* of riches; and though avarice will preserve a man from being necessitously poor, it generally makes him too timorous to be wealthy.

2.2
But there is another and greater distinction for which no truly natural or religious reason can be assigned, and that is, the distinction of men into KINGS and SUBJECTS. Male and female are the distinctions of nature, good and bad the distinctions of heaven; but how a race of men came into the world so exalted above the rest, and distinguished like some new species, is worth enquiring into, and whether they are the means of happiness or of misery to mankind.

2.3
In the early ages of the world, according to the scripture chronology, there were no kings; the consequence of which was there were no wars; it is the pride of kings which throw mankind into confusion. Holland without a king hath enjoyed more peace for this last century than any of the monarchical governments in Europe. Antiquity favors the same remark; for the quiet and rural lives of the first patriarchs hath a happy something in them, which vanishes away when we come to the history of Jewish royalty.

2.4
Government by kings was first introduced into the world by the Heathens, from whom the children of Israel copied the custom. It was the most prosperous invention the Devil ever set on foot for the promotion of idolatry. The Heathens paid divine honors to their deceased kings, and the christian world hath improved on the plan by doing the same to their living ones. How impious is the title of sacred majesty applied to a worm, who in the midst of his splendor is crumbling into dust!

2.5
As the exalting one man so greatly above the rest cannot be justified on the equal rights of nature, so neither can it be defended on the

authority of scripture; for the will of the Almighty, as declared by Gideon and the prophet Samuel, expressly disapproves of government by kings. All anti-monarchical parts of scripture have been very smoothly glossed over in monarchial governments, but they undoubtedly merit the attention of countries which have their governments yet to form. *"Render unto Caesar the things which are Caesar's"* is the scripture doctrine of courts, yet it is no support of monarchical government, for the Jews at that time were without a king, and in a state of vassalage to the Romans.

2.6
Near three thousand years passed away from the Mosaic account of the creation, till the Jews under a national delusion requested a king. Till then their form of government (except in extraordinary cases, where the Almighty interposed) was a kind of republic administred by a judge and the elders of the tribes. Kings they had none, and it was held sinful to acknowledge any being under that title but the Lord of Hosts. And when a man seriously reflects on the idolatrous homage which is paid to the persons of Kings, he need not wonder, that the Almighty ever jealous of his honor, should disapprove of a form of government which so impiously invades the prerogative of heaven.

2.7
Monarchy is ranked in scripture as one of the sins of the Jews, for which a curse in reserve is denounced against them. The history of that transaction is worth attending to.

2.8
The children of Israel being oppressed by the Midianites, Gideon marched against them with a small army, and victory, thro' the divine interposition, decided in his favour. The Jews elate with success, and attributing it to the generalship of Gideon, proposed making him a king, saying, *Rule thou over us, thou and thy son and thy son's son.* Here was temptation in its fullest extent; not a kingdom only, but an hereditary one, but Gideon in the piety of his soul replied, *I will not rule over you, neither shall my son rule over you,* THE LORD SHALL RULE OVER YOU. Words need not be more explicit; Gideon doth not *decline* the honor, but denieth their right to give it; neither doth he compliment them with invented declarations of his thanks, but in the positive stile of a prophet charges them with disaffection to their proper Sovereign, the King of heaven.

2.9
About one hundred and thirty years after this, they fell again into the same error. The hankering which the Jews had for the idolatrous

customs of the Heathens, is something exceedingly unaccountable; but so it was, that laying hold of the misconduct of Samuel's two sons, who were entrusted with some secular concerns, they came in an abrupt and clamorous manner to Samuel, saying, *Behold thou art old, and thy sons walk not in thy ways, now make us a king to judge us like all the other nations.* And here we cannot but observe that their motives were bad, viz. that they might be *like* unto other nations, i.e. the Heathens, whereas their true glory laid in being as much *unlike* them as possible. *But the thing displeased Samuel when they said, Give us a king to judge us; and Samuel prayed unto the Lord, and the Lord said unto Samuel, Hearken unto the voice of the people in all that they say unto thee, for they have not rejected thee, but they have rejected me,* THAT I SHOULD NOT REIGN OVER THEM. *According to all the works which they have done since the day that I brought them up out of Egypt, even unto this day; wherewith they have forsaken me and served other Gods; so do they also unto thee. Now therefore hearken unto their voice, howbeit, protest solemnly unto them and shew them the manner of the king that shall reign over them,* i.e. not of any particular king, but the general manner of the kings of the earth, whom Israel was so eagerly copying after. And notwithstanding the great distance of time and difference of manners, the character is still in fashion, *And Samuel told all the words of the Lord unto the people, that asked of him a king. And he said, This shall be the manner of the king that shall reign over you; he will take your sons and appoint them for himself, for his chariots, and to be his horsemen, and some shall run before his chariots* (this description agrees with the present mode of impressing men) *and he will appoint him captains over thousands and captains over fifties, and will set them to ear his ground and to reap his harvest, and to make his instruments of war, and instruments of his chariots; and he will take your daughters to be confectionaries, and to be cooks and to be bakers* (this describes the expence and luxury as well as the oppression of kings) *and he will take your fields and your olive yards, even the best of them, and give them to his servants; and he will take the tenth of your seed, and of your vineyards, and give them to his officers and to his servants* (by which we see that bribery, corruption, and favoritism are the standing vices of kings) *and he will take the tenth of your men servants, and your maid servants, and your goodliest young men and your asses, and put them to his work; and he will take the tenth of your sheep, and ye shall be his servants, and ye shall cry out in that day because of your king which ye shall have chosen,* AND THE LORD WILL NOT HEAR YOU IN THAT DAY." This accounts for the continuation of monarchy; neither do the characters of the few good kings which have lived since, either sanctify the title, or blot out the sinfulness of the origin; the high encomium given of David takes no notice of him *officially as a king,* but only as a *man* after God's own heart. *Nevertheless the People refused to obey the voice of Samuel, and they said, Nay, but we will have a king over us, that we may be like all the nations, and that our king may judge us, and go out before us, and fight our battles.* Samuel continued to reason with them, but to no purpose; he set before them their ingratitude, but all would not avail; and seeing them fully bent on their folly, he cried out, *I will call unto the Lord, and he shall send thunder and rain* (which then was a punishment, being in the time of wheat harvest) *that ye may perceive and see that your wickedness is great which ye have done in the sight of the Lord,* IN ASKING YOU A KING. *So Samuel called unto the Lord, and the Lord sent thunder and rain that day, and all the people greatly feared the Lord and Samuel. And all the people said unto Samuel, Pray for thy servants unto the Lord thy God that we die not, for* WE HAVE ADDED UNTO OUR SINS THIS EVIL, TO ASK A KING. These portions of scripture are direct and positive. They admit of no equivocal construction. That the Almighty hath here entered his protest against monarchical government is true, or the scripture is false. And a man hath good reason to believe that there is as much of king-craft, as priest-craft, in withholding the scripture from the public in Popish countries. For monarchy in every instance is the Popery of government.

2.10
To the evil of monarchy we have added that of hereditary succession; and as the first is a degradation and lessening of ourselves, so the second, claimed as a matter of right, is an insult and an imposition on posterity. For all men being originally equals, no *one* by *birth* could have a right to set up his own family in perpetual preference to all others for ever, and though himself might deserve *some* decent degree of honors of his cotemporaries, yet his descendants might be far too unworthy to inherit them. One of the strongest *natural* proofs of the folly of hereditary right in kings, is, that nature disapproves it, otherwise she would not so frequently turn it into ridicule by giving mankind an *ass for a lion.*

2.11
Secondly, as no man at first could possess any other public honors than were bestowed upon him, so the givers of those honors could have no power to give away the right of posterity, and though they might say, "We choose you for *our* head," they could not, without manifest injustice to their children, say, "that your children and your childrens children shall reign over *ours* for ever. Because such an unwise, unjust, unnatural compact might (perhaps) in the next succession put them under the government of a rogue or a fool. Most wise men, in their private sentiments, have ever treated hereditary right with contempt; yet it is one of those evils, which when once established is not easily removed; many submit from fear, others from superstition, and the more powerful part shares with the king the plunder of the rest.

2.12
This is supposing the present race of kings in the world to have had an honorable origin; whereas it is more than probable, that could we take off the dark covering of antiquity, and trace them to their first rise, that we should find the first of them nothing better than the principal ruffian of some restless gang, whose savage manners or pre-eminence in subtility obtained him the title of chief among plunderers; and who by increasing in power, and extending his depredations, overawed the quiet and defenceless to purchase their safety by frequent contributions. Yet his electors could have no idea of giving hereditary right to his descendants, because such a perpetual exclusion of themselves was incompatible with the free and unrestrained principles they professed to live by. Wherefore, hereditary succession in the early ages of monarchy could not take place as a matter of claim, but as something casual or complimental; but as few or no records were extant in those days, and traditionary history stuffed with fables, it was very easy, after the lapse of a few generations, to trump up some superstitious tale, conveniently timed, Mahomet like, to cram hereditary right down the throats of the vulgar. Perhaps the disorders which threatened, or seemed to threaten, on the decease of a leader and the choice of a new one (for elections among ruffians could not be very orderly) induced many at first to favor hereditary pretensions; by which means it happened, as it hath happened since, that what at first was submitted to as a convenience, was afterwards claimed as a right.

2.13
England, since the conquest, hath known some few good monarchs, but groaned beneath a much larger number of bad ones; yet no man in his senses can say that their claim under William the Conqueror is a very honorable one. A French bastard landing with an armed banditti, and establishing himself king of England against the consent of the natives, is in plain terms a very paltry rascally original.—It certainly hath no divinity in it. However, it is needless to spend much time in exposing the folly of hereditary right, if there are any so weak as to believe it, let them promiscuously worship the ass and lion, and welcome. I shall neither copy their humility, nor disturb their devotion.

2.14
Yet I should be glad to ask how they suppose kings came at first? The question admits but of three answers, viz. either by lot, by election, or by usurpation. If the first king was taken by lot, it establishes a precedent for the next, which excludes hereditary succession. Saul was by lot, yet the succession was not hereditary, neither does it appear from that transaction there was any intention it ever should. If the first

king of any country was by election, that likewise establishes a precedent for the next; for to say, that the *right* of all future generations is taken away, by the act of the first electors, in their choice not only of a king, but of a family of kings for ever, hath no parrallel in or out of scripture but the doctrine of original sin, which supposes the free will of all men lost in Adam; and from such comparison, and it will admit of no other, hereditary succession can derive no glory. For as in Adam all sinned, and as in the first electors all men obeyed; as in the one all mankind were subjected to Satan, and in the other to Sovereignty; as our innocence was lost in the first, and our authority in the last; and as both disable us from reassuming some former state and privilege, it unanswerably follows that original sin and hereditary succession are parellels. Dishonorable rank! Inglorious connexion! Yet the most subtle sophist cannot produce a juster simile.

2.15
As to usurpation, no man will be so hardy as to defend it; and that William the Conqueror was an usurper is a fact not to be contradicted. The plain truth is, that the antiquity of English monarchy will not bear looking into.

2.16
But it is not so much the absurdity as the evil of hereditary succession which concerns mankind. Did it ensure a race of good and wise men it would have the seal of divine authority, but as it opens a door to the *foolish*, the *wicked*, and the *improper*, it hath in it the nature of oppression. Men who look upon themselves born to reign, and others to obey, soon grow insolent; selected from the rest of mankind their minds are early poisoned by importance; and the world they act in differs so materially from the world at large, that they have but little opportunity of knowing its true interests, and when they succeed to the government are frequently the most ignorant and unfit of any throughout the dominions.

2.17
Another evil which attends hereditary succession is, that the throne is subject to be possessed by a minor at any age; all which time the regency, acting under the cover of a king, have every opportunity and inducement to betray their trust. The same national misfortune happens, when a king worn out with age and infirmity, enters the last stage of human weakness. In both these cases the public becomes a prey to every miscreant, who can tamper successfully with the follies either of age or infancy.

2.18

The most plausible plea, which hath ever been offered in favor of hereditary succession, is, that it preserves a nation from civil wars; and were this true, it would be weighty; whereas, it is the most barefaced falsity ever imposed upon mankind. The whole history of England disowns the fact. Thirty kings and two minors have reigned in that distracted kingdom since the conquest, in which time there have been (including the Revolution) no less than eight civil wars and nineteen rebellions. Wherefore instead of making for peace, it makes against it, and destroys the very foundation it seems to stand on.

2.19

The contest for monarchy and succession, between the houses of York and Lancaster, laid England in a scene of blood for many years. Twelve pitched battles, besides skirmishes and sieges, were fought between Henry and Edward. Twice was Henry prisoner to Edward, who in his turn was prisoner to Henry. And so uncertain is the fate of war and the temper of a nation, when nothing but personal matters are the ground of a quarrel, that Henry was taken in triumph from a prison to a palace, and Edward obliged to fly from a palace to a foreign land; yet, as sudden transitions of temper are seldom lasting, Henry in his turn was driven from the throne, and Edward recalled to succeed him. The parliament always following the strongest side.

2.20

This contest began in the reign of Henry the Sixth, and was not entirely extinguished till Henry the Seventh, in whom the families were united. Including a period of 67 years, viz. from 1422 to 1489.

2.21

In short, monarchy and succession have laid (not this or that kingdom only) but the world in blood and ashes. 'Tis a form of government which the word of God bears testimony against, and blood will attend it.

2.22

If we inquire into the business of a king, we shall find that in some countries they have none; and after sauntering away their lives without pleasure to themselves or advantage to the nation, withdraw from the scene, and leave their successors to tread the same idle round. In absolute monarchies the whole weight of business, civil and military, lies on the king; the children of Israel in their request for a king, urged this plea "that he may judge us, and go out before us and fight our battles." But in countries where he is neither a judge nor a general, as in England, a man would be puzzled to know what *is* his business.

2.23
The nearer any government approaches to a republic, the less business there is for a king. It is somewhat difficult to find a proper name for the government of England. Sir William Meredith calls it a republic; but in its present state it is unworthy of the name, because the corrupt influence of the crown, by having all the places in its disposal, hath so effectually swallowed up the power, and eaten out the virtue of the house of commons (the republican part in the constitution) that the government of England is nearly as monarchical as that of France or Spain. Men fall out with names without understanding them. For it is the republican and not the monarchical part of the constitution of England which Englishmen glory in, viz. the liberty of choosing an house of commons from out of their own body—and it is easy to see that when the republican virtue fails, slavery ensues. Why is the constitution of England sickly, but because monarchy hath poisoned the republic, the crown hath engrossed the commons?

2.24
In England a king hath little more to do than to make war and give away places; which in plain terms, is to impoverish the nation and set it together by the ears. A pretty business indeed for a man to be allowed eight hundred thousand sterling a year for, and worshipped into the bargain! Of more worth is one honest man to society and in the sight of God, than all the crowned ruffians that ever lived.

Thoughts on the present state of American affairs.

3.1
IN the following pages I offer nothing more than simple facts, plain arguments, and common sense; and have no other preliminaries to settle with the reader, than that he will divest himself of prejudice and prepossession, and suffer his reason and his feelings to determine for themselves; that he will put *on*, or rather that he will not put *off*, the true character of a man, and generously enlarge his views beyond the present day.

3.2
Volumes have been written on the subject of the struggle between England and America. Men of all ranks have embarked in the controversy, from different motives, and with various designs; but all have been ineffectual, and the period of debate is closed. Arms, as the last resource, decide the contest; the appeal was the choice of the king, and the continent hath accepted the challenge.

3.3
It hath been reported of the late Mr. Pelham (who tho' an able minister was not without his faults) that on his being attacked in the house of commons, on the score, that his measures were only of a temporary kind, replied, *they will last my time.*" Should a thought so fatal and unmanly possess the colonies in the present contest, the name of ancestors will be remembered by future generations with detestation.

3.4
The sun never shined on a cause of greater worth. 'Tis not the affair of a city, a county, a province, or a kingdom, but of a continent—of at least one eighth part of the habitable globe. 'Tis not the concern of a day, a year, or an age; posterity are virtually involved in the contest, and will be more or less affected, even to the end of time, by the proceedings now. Now is the seed time of continental union, faith and honor. The least fracture now will be like a name engraved with the point of a pin on the tender rind of a young oak; the wound will enlarge with the tree, and posterity read it in full grown characters.

3.5
By referring the matter from argument to arms, a new æra for politics is struck; a new method of thinking hath arisen. All plans, proposals, &c. prior to the nineteenth of April, *i.e.* to the commencement of hostilities, are like the almanacks of the last year; which, though proper then, are superceded and useless now. Whatever was advanced by the

advocates on either side of the question then, terminated in one and the same point, viz. a union with Great-Britain; the only difference between the parties was the method of effecting it; the one proposing force, the other friendship; but it hath so far happened that the first hath failed, and the second hath withdrawn her influence.

3.6
As much hath been said of the advantages of reconciliation, which, like an agreeable dream, hath passed away and left us as we were, it is but right, that we should examine the contrary side of the argument, and inquire into some of the many material injuries which these colonies sustain, and always will sustain, by being connected with, and dependant on Great Britain. To examine that connexion and dependance, on the principles of nature and common sense, to see what we have to trust to, if separated, and what we are to expect, if dependant.

3.7
I have heard it asserted by some, that as America hath flourished under her former connexion with Great-Britain, that the same connexion is necessary towards her future happiness, and will always have the same effect. Nothing can be more fallacious than this kind of argument. We may as well assert that because a child has thrived upon milk, that it is never to have meat, or that the first twenty years of our lives is to become a precedent for the next twenty. But even this is admitting more than is true, for I answer roundly, that America would have flourished as much, and probably much more, had no European power had any thing to do with her. The commerce, by which she hath enriched herself are the necessaries of life, and will always have a market while eating is the custom of Europe.

3.8
But she has protected us, say some. That she hath engrossed us is true, and defended the continent at our expence as well as her own is admitted, and she would have defended Turkey from the same motive, viz. the sake of trade and dominion.

3.9
Alas, we have been long led away by ancient prejudices, and made large sacrifices to superstition. We have boasted the protection of Great-Britain, without considering, that her motive was *interest* not *attachment*; that she did not protect us from *our enemies* on *our account*, but from *her enemies* on *her own account*, from those who had no quarrel with us on any *other account*, and who will always be our enemies on the *same account*. Let Britain wave her pretensions to the continent, or the

continent throw off the dependance, and we should be at peace with France and Spain were they at war with Britain. The miseries of Hanover last war ought to warn us against connexions.

3.10
It hath lately been asserted in parliament, that the colonies have no relation to each other but through the parent country, *i.e.* that Pennsylvania and the Jerseys, and so on for the rest, are sister colonies by the way of England; this is certainly a very round-about way of proving relationship, but it is the nearest and only true way of proving enemyship, if I may so call it. France and Spain never were, nor perhaps ever will be our enemies as *Americans*, but as our being the *subjects of Great-Britain*.

3.11
But Britain is the parent country, say some. Then the more shame upon her conduct. Even brutes do not devour their young, nor savages make war upon their families; wherefore the assertion, if true, turns to her reproach; but it happens not to be true, or only partly so, and the phrase *parent* or *mother country* hath been jesuitically adopted by the king and his parasites, with a low papistical design of gaining an unfair bias on the credulous weakness of our minds. Europe, and not England, is the parent country of America. This new world hath been the asylum for the persecuted lovers of civil and religious liberty from *every part* of Europe. Hither have they fled, not from the tender embraces of the mother, but from the cruelty of the monster; and it is so far true of England, that the same tyranny which drove the first emigrants from home, pursues their descendants still.

3.12
In this extensive quarter of the globe, we forget the narrow limits of three hundred and sixty miles (the extent of England) and carry our friendship on a larger scale; we claim brotherhood with every European christian, and triumph in the generosity of the sentiment.

3.13
It is pleasant to observe by what regular gradations we surmount the force of local prejudice, as we enlarge our acquaintance with the world. A man born in any town in England divided into parishes, will naturally associate most with his fellow parishioners (because their interests in many cases will be common) and distinguish him by the name of *neighbour*; if he meet him but a few miles from home, he drops the narrow idea of a street, and salutes him by the name of *townsman*; if he travels out of the county, and meet him in any other, he forgets the minor divisions of street and town, and calls him *countryman*, i.e.,

county-man; but if in their foreign excursions they should associate in France or any other part of *Europe*, their local remembrance would be enlarged into that of *Englishmen*. And by a just parity of reasoning, all Europeans meeting in America, or any other quarter of the globe, are *countrymen*; for England, Holland, Germany, or Sweden, when compared with the whole, stand in the same places on the larger scale, which the divisions of street, town, and county do on the smaller ones; distinctions too limited for continental minds. Not one third of the inhabitants, even of this province, are of English descent. Wherefore, I reprobate the phrase of parent or mother country applied to England only, as being false, selfish, narrow and ungenerous.

3.14
But admitting, that we were all of English descent, what does it amount to? Nothing. Britain, being now an open enemy, extinguishes every other name and title: And to say that reconciliation is our duty, is truly farcical. The first king of England, of the present line (William the Conqueror) was a Frenchman, and half the Peers of England are descendants from the same country; wherefore by the same method of reasoning, England ought to be governed by France.

3.15
Much hath been said of the united strength of Britain and the colonies, that in conjunction they might bid defiance to the world. But this is mere presumption; the fate of war is uncertain, neither do the expressions mean any thing; for this continent would never suffer itself to be drained of inhabitants, to support the British arms in either Asia, Africa, or Europe.

3.16
Besides, what have we to do with setting the world at defiance? Our plan is commerce, and that, well attended to, will secure us the peace and friendship of all Europe; because, it is the interest of all Europe to have America a *free port*. Her trade will always be a protection, and her barrenness of gold and silver secure her from invaders.

3.17
I challenge the warmest advocate for reconciliation, to shew, a single advantage that this continent can reap, by being connected with Great Britain. I repeat the challenge, not a single advantage is derived. Our corn will fetch its price in any market in Europe, and our imported goods must be paid for buy them where we will.

3.18
But the injuries and disadvantages we sustain by that connection, are without number; and our duty to mankind at large, as well as to ourselves, instruct us to renounce the alliance: Because, any submission to, or dependance on Great-Britain, tends directly to involve this continent in European wars and quarrels; and sets us at variance with nations, who would otherwise seek our friendship, and against whom, we have neither anger nor complaint. As Europe is our market for trade, we ought to form no partial connection with any part of it. It is the true interest of America to steer clear of European contentions, which she never can do, while by her dependance on Britain, she is made the make-weight in the scale of British politics.

3.19
Europe is too thickly planted with kingdoms to be long at peace, and whenever a war breaks out between England and any foreign power, the trade of America goes to ruin, *because of her connection with Britain*. The next war may not turn out like the last, and should it not, the advocates for reconciliation now will be wishing for separation then, because, neutrality in that case, would be a safer convoy than a man of war. Every thing that is right or natural pleads for separation. The blood of the slain, the weeping voice of nature cries, 'TIS TIME TO PART. Even the distance at which the Almighty hath placed England and America, is a strong and natural proof, that the authority of the one, over the other, was never the design of Heaven. The time likewise at which the continent was discovered, adds weight to the argument, and the manner in which it was peopled encreases the force of it. The reformation was preceded by the discovery of America, as if the Almighty graciously meant to open a sanctuary to the persecuted in future years, when home should afford neither friendship nor safety.

3.20
The authority of Great-Britain over this continent, is a form of government, which sooner or later must have an end: And a serious mind can draw no true pleasure by looking forward, under the painful and positive conviction, that what he calls "the present constitution" is merely temporary. As parents, we can have no joy, knowing that *this government* is not sufficiently lasting to ensure any thing which we may bequeath to posterity: And by a plain method of argument, as we are running the next generation into debt, we ought to do the work of it, otherwise we use them meanly and pitifully. In order to discover the line of our duty rightly, we should take our children in our hand, and fix our station a few years farther into life; that eminence will present a prospect, which a few present fears and prejudices conceal from our sight.

3.21
Though I would carefully avoid giving unnecessary offence, yet I am inclined to believe, that all those who espouse the doctrine of reconciliation, may be included within the following descriptions. Interested men, who are not to be trusted; weak men, who *cannot* see; prejudiced men, who *will not* see; and a certain set of moderate men, who think better of the European world than it deserves; and this last class, by an ill-judged deliberation, will be the cause of more calamities to this continent, than all the other three.

3.22
It is the good fortune of many to live distant from the scene of sorrow; the evil is not sufficiently brought to *their* doors to make *them* feel the precariousness with which all American property is possessed. But let our imaginations transport us for a few moments to Boston, that seat of wretchedness will teach us wisdom, and instruct us for ever to renounce a power in whom we can have no trust. The inhabitants of that unfortunate city, who but a few months ago were in ease and affluence, have now, no other alternative than to stay and starve, or turn out to beg. Endangered by the fire of their friends if they continue within the city, and plundered by the soldiery if they leave it. In their present condition they are prisoners without the hope of redemption, and in a general attack for their relief, they would be exposed to the fury of both armies.

3.23
Men of passive tempers look somewhat lightly over the offences of Britain, and, still hoping for the best, are apt to call out, "*Come, come, we shall be friends again, for all this.*" But examine the passions and feelings of mankind, Bring the doctrine of reconciliation to the touchstone of nature, and then tell me, whether you can hereafter love, honour, and faithfully serve the power that hath carried fire and sword into your land? If you cannot do all these, then are you only deceiving yourselves, and by your delay bringing ruin upon posterity. Your future connection with Britain, whom you can neither love nor honour, will be forced and unnatural, and being formed only on the plan of present convenience, will in a little time fall into a relapse more wretched than the first. But if you say, you can still pass the violations over, then I ask, Hath your house been burnt? Hath you property been destroyed before your face? Are your wife and children destitute of a bed to lie on, or bread to live on? Have you lost a parent or a child by their hands, and yourself the ruined and wretched survivor? If you have not, then are you not a judge of those who have. But if you have, and still can shake hands with the murderers, then are you unworthy the name of

husband, father, friend, or lover, and whatever may be your rank or title in life, you have the heart of a coward, and the spirit of a sycophant.

3.24
This is not inflaming or exaggerating matters, but trying them by those feelings and affections which nature justifies, and without which, we should be incapable of discharging the social duties of life, or enjoying the felicities of it. I mean not to exhibit horror for the purpose of provoking revenge, but to awaken us from fatal and unmanly slumbers, that we may pursue determinately some fixed object. It is not in the power of Britain or of Europe to conquer America, if she do not conquer herself by *delay* and *timidity*. The present winter is worth an age if rightly employed, but if lost or neglected, the whole continent will partake of the misfortune; and there is no punishment which that man will not deserve, be he who, or what, or where he will, that may be the means of sacrificing a season so precious and useful.

3.25
It is repugnant to reason, to the universal order of things to all examples from former ages, to suppose, that this continent can longer remain subject to any external power. The most sanguine in Britain does not think so. The utmost stretch of human wisdom cannot, at this time, compass a plan short of separation, which can promise the continent even a year's security. Reconciliation is *now* a fallacious dream. Nature hath deserted the connexion, and Art cannot supply her place. For, as Milton wisely expresses, "never can true reconcilement grow where wounds of deadly hate have pierced so deep."

3.26
Every quiet method for peace hath been ineffectual. Our prayers have been rejected with disdain; and only tended to convince us, that nothing flatters vanity, or confirms obstinacy in Kings more than repeated petitioning—and nothing hath contributed more than that very measure to make the Kings of Europe absolute: Witness Denmark and Sweden. Wherefore, since nothing but blows will do, for God's sake, let us come to a final separation, and not leave the next generation to be cutting throats, under the violated unmeaning names of parent and child.

3.27
To say, they will never attempt it again is idle and visionary, we thought so at the repeal of the stamp-act, yet a year or two undeceived us; as well may we may suppose that nations, which have been once defeated, will never renew the quarrel.

3.28
As to government matters, it is not in the power of Britain to do this continent justice: The business of it will soon be too weighty, and intricate, to be managed with any tolerable degree of convenience, by a power, so distant from us, and so very ignorant of us; for if they cannot conquer us, they cannot govern us. To be always running three or four thousand miles with a tale or a petition, waiting four or five months for an answer, which when obtained requires five or six more to explain it in, will in a few years be looked upon as folly and childishness—There was a time when it was proper, and there is a proper time for it to cease.

3.29
Small islands not capable of protecting themselves, are the proper objects for kingdoms to take under their care; but there is something very absurd, in supposing a continent to be perpetually governed by an island. In no instance hath nature made the satellite larger than its primary planet, and as England and America, with respect to each other, reverses the common order of nature, it is evident they belong to different systems: England to Europe, America to itself.

3.30
I am not induced by motives of pride, party, or resentment to espouse the doctrine of separation and independence; I am clearly, positively, and conscientiously persuaded that it is the true interest of this continent to be so; that every thing short of *that* is mere patchwork, that it can afford no lasting felicity,—that it is leaving the sword to our children, and shrinking back at a time, when, a little more, a little farther, would have rendered this continent the glory of the earth.

3.31
As Britain hath not manifested the least inclination towards a compromise, we may be assured that no terms can be obtained worthy the acceptance of the continent, or any ways equal to the expence of blood and treasure we have been already put to.

3.32
The object, contended for, ought always to bear some just proportion to the expence. The removal of North, or the whole detestable junto, is a matter unworthy the millions we have expended. A temporary stoppage of trade, was an inconvenience, which would have sufficiently ballanced the repeal of all the acts complained of, had such repeals been obtained; but if the whole continent must take up arms, if every man must be a soldier, it is scarcely worth our while to fight against a contemptible ministry only. Dearly, dearly, do we pay for the repeal of the acts, if that is all we fight for; for in a just estimation, it is as great a

folly to pay a Bunker-hill price for law, as for land. As I have always considered the independancy of this continent, as an event, which sooner or later must arrive, so from the late rapid progress of the continent to maturity, the event could not be far of[f]. Wherefore, on the breaking out of hostilities, it was not worth the while to have disputed a matter, which time would have finally redressed, unless we meant to be in earnest; otherwise, it is like wasting an estate on a suit at law, to regulate the trespasses of a tenant, whose lease is just expiring. No man was a warmer wisher for reconciliation than myself, before the fatal nineteenth of April 1775*, but the moment the event of that day was made known, I rejected the hardened, sullen tempered Pharaoh of England for ever; and disdain the wretch, that with the pretended title of FATHER OF HIS PEOPLE can unfeelingly hear of their slaughter, and composedly sleep with their blood upon his soul.
[*Massacre at Lexington.]

3.33
But admitting that matters were now made up, what would be the event? I answer, the ruin of the continent. And that for several reasons. *First*. The powers of governing still remaining in the hands of the king, he will have a negative over the whole legislation of this continent. And as he hath shewn himself such an inveterate enemy to liberty, and discovered such a thirst for arbitrary power; is he, or is he not, a proper man to say to these colonies, "*You shall make no laws but what I please.*" And is there any inhabitant in America so ignorant, as not to know, that according to what is called the *present constitution*, that this continent can make no laws but what the king gives leave to; and is there any man so unwise, as not to see, that (considering what has happened) he will suffer no law to be made here, but such as suit *his* purpose. We may be as effectually enslaved by the want of laws in America, as by submitting to laws made for us in England. After matters are made up (as it is called) can there be any doubt, but the whole power of the crown will be exerted, to keep this continent as low and humble as possible? Instead of going forward we shall go backward, or be perpetually quarrelling or ridiculously petitioning.—We are already greater than the king wishes us to be, and will he not hereafter endeavour to make us less? To bring the matter to one point. Is the power who is jealous of our prosperity, a proper power to govern us? Whoever says *No* to this question is an *independant*, for independancy means no more, than, whether we shall make our own laws, or whether the king, the greatest enemy this continent hath, or can have, shall tell us, "*there shall be no laws but such as I like.*"

3.34

But the king you will say has a negative in England; the people there can make no laws without his consent. In point of right and good order, there is something very ridiculous, that a youth of twenty-one (which hath often happened) shall say to several millions of people, older and wiser than himself, I forbid this or that act of yours to be law. But in this place I decline this sort of reply, though I will never cease to expose the absurdity of it, and only answer, that England being the King's residence, and America not so, makes quite another case. The king's negative *here* is ten times more dangerous and fatal than it can be in England, for *there* he will scarcely refuse his consent to a bill for putting England into as strong a state of defence as possible, and in America he would never suffer such a bill to be passed.

3.35

America is only a secondary object in the system of British politics, England consults the good of *this* country, no farther than it answers her *own* purpose. Wherefore, her own interest leads her to suppress the growth of *ours* in every case which doth not promote her advantage, or in the least interfere with it. A pretty state we should soon be in under such a second-hand government, considering what has happened! Men do not change from enemies to friends by the alteration of a name: and in order to shew that reconciliation *now* is a dangerous doctrine, I affirm, *that it would be policy in the king at this time, to repeal the acts for the sake of reinstating himself in the government of the provinces*; in order, that HE MAY ACCOMPLISH BY CRAFT AND SUBTILTY, IN THE LONG RUN, WHAT HE CANNOT DO BY FORCE AND VIOLENCE IN THE SHORT ONE. Reconciliation and ruin are nearly related.

3.36

Secondly. That as even the best terms, which we can expect to obtain, can amount to no more than a temporary expedient, or a kind of government by guardianship, which can last no longer than till the colonies come of age, so the general face and state of things, in the interim, will be unsettled and unpromising. Emigrants of property will not choose to come to a country whose form of government hangs but by a thread, and who is every day tottering on the brink of commotion and disturbance; and numbers of the present inhabitants would lay hold of the interval, to dispose of their effects, and quit the continent.

3.37

But the most powerful of all arguments, is, that nothing but independance, i.e. a continental form of government, can keep the peace of the continent and preserve it inviolate from civil wars. I dread the event of a reconciliation with Britain now, as it is more than probable, that it will be followed by a revolt somewhere or other, the consequences of which may be far more fatal than all the malice of Britain.

3.38
Thousands are already ruined by British barbarity; (thousands more will probably suffer the same fate) Those men have other feelings than us who have nothing suffered. All they *now* possess is liberty, what they before enjoyed is sacrificed to its service, and having nothing more to lose, they disdain submission. Besides, the general temper of the colonies, towards a British government, will be like that of a youth, who is nearly out of his time; they will care very little about her. And a government which cannot preserve the peace, is no government at all, and in that case we pay our money for nothing; and pray what is it that Britain can do, whose power will be wholly on paper, should a civil tumult break out the very day after reconciliation? I have heard some men say, many of whom I believe spoke without thinking, that they dreaded an independance, fearing that it would produce civil wars. It is but seldom that our first thoughts are truly correct, and that is the case here; for there are ten times more to dread from a patched up connexion than from independance. I make the sufferers case my own, and I protest, that were I driven from house and home, my property destroyed, and my circumstances ruined, that as man, sensible of injuries, I could never relish the doctrine of reconciliation, or consider myself bound thereby.

3.39
The colonies have manifested such a spirit of good order and obedience to continental government, as is sufficient to make every reasonable person easy and happy on that head. No man can assign the least pretence for his fears, on any other grounds, than such as are truly childish and ridiculous, viz. that one colony will be striving for superiority over another.

3.40
Where there are no distinctions there can be no superiority, perfect equality affords no temptation. The republics of Europe are all (and we may say always) in peace. Holland and Swisserland are without wars, foreign or domestic: Monarchical governments, it is true, are never long at rest: the crown itself is a temptation to enterprizing ruffians at *home*; and that degree of pride and insolence ever attendant on regal authority, swells into a rupture with foreign powers, in instances, where

a republican government, by being formed on more natural principles, would negociate the mistake.

3.41
If there is any true cause of fear respecting independence, it is because no plan is yet laid down. Men do not see their way out—Wherefore, as an opening into that business, I offer the following hints; at the same time modestly affirming, that I have no other opinion of them myself, than that they may be the means of giving rise to something better. Could the straggling thoughts of individuals be collected, they would frequently form materials for wise and able men to improve to useful matter.

3.42
LET the assemblies be annual, with a President only. The representation more equal. Their business wholly domestic, and subject to the authority of a Continental Congress.

3.43
Let each colony be divided into six, eight, or ten, convenient districts, each district to send a proper number of delegates to Congress, so that each colony send at least thirty. The whole number in Congress will be at least 390. Each congress to sit. [....] and to choose a president by the following method. When the delegates are met, let a colony be taken from the whole thirteen colonies by lot, after which, let the whole Congress choose (by ballot) a president from out of the delegates of *that* province. In the next Congress, let a colony be taken by lot from twelve only, omitting that colony from which the president was taken in the former Congress, and so proceeding on till the whole thirteen shall have had their proper rotation. And in order that nothing may pass into a law but what is satisfactorily just, not less than three fifths of the Congress to be called a majority.—He that will promote discord, under a government so equally formed as this, would have joined Lucifer in his revolt.

3.44
But as there is a peculiar delicacy, from whom, or in what manner, this business must first arise, and as it seems most agreeable and consistent, that it should come from some intermediate body between the governed and the governors, that is, between the Congress and the people, let a CONTINENTAL CONFERENCE be held, in the following manner, and for the following purpose.
A committee of twenty-six members of Congress, viz. two for each colony. Two members for each House of Assembly, or Provincial Convention; and five representatives of the people at large, to be

chosen in the capital city or town of each province, for, and in behalf of the whole province, by as many qualified voters as shall think proper to attend from all parts of the province for that purpose; or, if more convenient, the representatives may be chosen in two or three of the most populous parts thereof. In this conference, thus assembled, will be united, the two grand principles of business, *knowledge* and *power*. The members of Congress, Assemblies, or Conventions, by having had experience in national concerns, will be able and useful counsellors, and the whole, being impowered by the people, will have a truly legal authority.

3.45

The conferring members being met, let their business be to frame a CONTINENTAL CHARTER, or Charter of the United Colonies; (answering to what is called the Magna Charta of England) fixing the number and manner of choosing members of Congress, members of Assembly, with their date of sitting, and drawing the line of business and jurisdiction between them: (Always remembering, that our strength is continental, not provincial:) Securing freedom and property to all men, and above all things, the free exercise of religion, according to the dictates of conscience; with such other matter as is necessary for a charter to contain. Immediately after which, the said Conference to dissolve, and the bodies which shall be chosen conformable to the said charter, to be the legislators and governors of this continent for the time being: Whose peace and happiness, may God preserve, Amen.

3.46

Should any body of men be hereafter delegated for this or some similar purpose, I offer them the following extracts from that wise observer on governments *Dragonetti*. "The science" says he "of the politician consists in fixing the true point of happiness and freedom. Those men would deserve the gratitude of ages, who should discover a mode of government that contained the greatest sum of individual happiness, with the least national expence." *Dragonetti on virtue and rewards."*

3.47

But where says some is the King of America? I'll tell you Friend, he reigns above, and doth not make havoc of mankind like the Royal Brute of Britain. Yet that we may not appear to be defective even in earthly honors, let a day be solemnly set apart for proclaiming the charter; let it be brought forth placed on the divine law, the word of God; let a crown be placed thereon, by which the world may know, that so far as we approve of monarchy, that in America THE LAW IS KING. For as in absolute governments the King is law, so in free countries the law *ought* to be King; and there ought to be no other. But lest any ill use should afterwards arise, let the crown at the conclusion of the ceremony be demolished, and scattered among the people whose right it is.

3.48
A government of our own is our natural right: And when a man seriously reflects on the precariousness of human affairs, he will become convinced, that it is infinitely wiser and safer, to form a constitution of our own in a cool deliberate manner, while we have it in our power, than to trust such an interesting event to time and chance. If we omit it now, some * Massenello may hereafter arise, who laying hold of popular disquietudes, may collect together the desperate and the discontented, and by assuming to themselves the powers of government, may sweep away the liberties of the continent like a deluge. Should the government of America return again into the hands of Britain, the tottering situation of things, will be a temptation for some desperate adventurer to try his fortune; and in such a case, what relief can Britain give? Ere she could hear the news the fatal business might be done, and ourselves suffering like the wretched Britons under the oppression of the Conqueror. Ye that oppose independance now, ye know not what ye do; ye are opening a door to eternal tyranny, by keeping vacant the seat of government. There are thousands, and tens of thousands, who would think it glorious to expel from the continent, that barbarous and hellish power, which hath stirred up the Indians and Negroes to destroy us, the cruelty hath a double guilt, it is dealing brutally by us, and treacherously by them.
[**Thomas Anello, otherwise Massenello, a fisherman of Naples, who after spiriting up his countrymen in the public market place, against the oppression of the Spaniards, to whom the place was then subject, prompted them to revolt, and in the space of a day became King.*]

3.49
To talk of friendship with those in whom our reason forbids us to have faith, and our affections wounded through a thousand pores instruct us to detest, is madness and folly. Every day wears out the little remains of kindred between us and them, and can there be any reason to hope, that as the relationship expires, the affection will increase, or that we shall agree better, when we have ten times more and greater concerns to quarrel over than ever?

3.50
Ye that tell us of harmony and reconciliation, can ye restore to us the time that is past? Can ye give to prostitution its former innocence? Neither can ye reconcile Britain and America. The last cord now is broken, the people of England are presenting addresses against us.

There are injuries which nature cannot forgive; she would cease to be nature if she did. As well can the lover forgive the ravisher of his mistress, as the continent forgive the murders of Britain. The Almighty hath implanted in us these unextinguishable feelings for good and wise purposes. They are the guardians of his image in our hearts. They distinguish us from the herd of common animals. The social compact would dissolve, and justice be extirpated the earth, of have only a casual existence were we callous to the touches of affection. The robber, and the murderer, would often escape unpunished, did not the injuries which our tempers sustain, provoke us into justice.

3.51
O ye that love mankind! Ye that dare oppose, not only the tyranny, but the tyrant, stand forth! Every spot of the old world is overrun with oppression. Freedom hath been hunted round the globe. Asia, and Africa, have long expelled her.—Europe regards her like a stranger, and England hath given her warning to depart. O! receive the fugitive, and prepare in time an asylum for mankind.

Of the present ABILITY *of* AMERICA, *with some miscellaneous* REFLEXIONS.

4.1
I Have never met with a man, either in England or America, who hath not confessed his opinion, that a separation between the countries, would take place one time or other: And there is no instance, in which we have shewn less judgment, than in endeavouring to describe, what we call, the ripeness or fitness of the Continent for independance.

4.2
As all men allow the measure, and vary only in their opinion of the time, let us, in order to remove mistakes, take a general survey of things and endeavour, if possible, to find out the *very* time. But we need not go far, the inquiry ceases at once, for, *the time hath found us.* The general concurrence, the glorious union of all things prove the fact.

4.3
It is not in numbers, but in unity, that our great strength lies; yet our present numbers are sufficient to repel the force of all the world. The Continent hath, at this time, the largest body of armed and disciplined men of any power under Heaven; and is just arrived at that pitch of strength, in which, no single colony is able to support itself, and the whole, when united, can accomplish the matter, and either more, or, less than this, might be fatal in its effects. Our land force is already sufficient, and as to naval affairs, we cannot be insensible, that Britain would never suffer an American man of war to be built, while the continent remained in her hands. Wherefore, we should be no forwarder an hundred years hence in that branch, than we are now; but the truth is, we should be less so, because the timber of the country is every day diminishing, and that, which will remain at last, will be far off and difficult to procure.

4.4
Were the continent crowded with inhabitants, her sufferings under the present circumstances would be intolerable. The more sea port towns we had, the more should we have both to defend and to loose. Our present numbers are so happily proportioned to our wants, that no man need be idle. The diminution of trade affords an army, and the necessities of an army create a new trade.

4.5
Debts we have none; and whatever we may contract on this account will serve as a glorious memento of our virtue. Can we but leave

posterity with a settled form of government, an independant constitution of it's own, the purchase at any price will be cheap. But to expend millions for the sake of getting a few vile acts repealed, and routing the present ministry only, is unworthy the charge, and is using posterity with the utmost cruelty; because it is leaving them the great work to do, and a debt upon their backs, from which, they derive no advantage. Such a thought is unworthy a man of honor, and is the true characteristic of a narrow heart and a pedling politician.

4.6

The debt we may contract doth not deserve our regard if the work be but accomplished. No nation ought to be without a debt. A national debt is a national bond; and when it bears no interest, is in no case a grievance. Britain is oppressed with a debt of upwards of one hundred and forty millions sterling, for which she pays upwards of four millions interest. And as a compensation for her debt, she has a large navy; America is without a debt, and without a navy; yet for the twentieth part of the English national debt, could have a navy as large again. The navy of England is not worth, at this time, more than three millions and an half sterling.

4.7

The first and second editions of this pamphlet were published without the following calculations, which are now given as a proof that the above estimation of the navy is a just one. *See Entic's naval history, intro. page 56.*
The charge of building a ship of each rate, and furnishing her with masts, yards, sails and rigging, together with a proportion of eight months boatswain's and carpenter's sea-stores, as calculated by Mr. Burchett, Secretary to the navy.

For a ship of 100 guns	£35,553
90	29,886
80	23,638
70	17,785
60	14,197
50	10,606
40	7,558
30	5,846
20	3,710

4.8
And from hence it is easy to sum up the value, or cost rather, of the whole British navy, which in the year 1757, when it was as its greatest glory consisted of the following ships and guns.

Ships.	Guns.	Cost of one.	Cost of all.
6	100	£35,533	£213,318
12	90	29,886	358,632
12	80	23,638	283,656
43	70	17,785	746,755
35	60	14,197	496,895
40	50	10,606	424,240
45	40	7,558	340,110
58	20	3,710	215,180
85	Sloops, bombs, and fireships, one another, at	2,000	170,000
Cost			3,266,786
Remains for guns,			233,214
[Total]			3,500,000

4.9
No country on the globe is so happily situated, or so internally capable of raising a fleet as America. Tar, timber, iron, and cordage are her natural produce. We need go abroad for nothing. Whereas the Dutch, who make large profits by hiring out their ships of war to the Spaniards and Portuguese, are obliged to import most of the materials they use. We ought to view the building a fleet as an article of commerce, it being the natural manufactory of this country. It is the best money we can lay out. A navy when finished is worth more than it cost. And is that nice point in national policy, in which commerce and protection are united. Let us build; if we want them not, we can sell; and by that means replace our paper currency with ready gold and silver.

4.10
In point of manning a fleet, people in general run into great errors; it is not necessary that one fourth part should be sailors. The Terrible privateer, Captain Death, stood the hottest engagement of any ship last war, yet had not twenty sailors on board, though her complement of men was upwards of two hundred. A few able and social sailors will soon instruct a sufficient number of active landmen in the common

work of a ship. Wherefore, we never can be more capable to begin on maritime matters than now, while our timber is standing, our fisheries blocked up, and our sailors and shipwrights out of employ. Men of war, of seventy and eighty guns were built forty years ago in New-England, and why not the same now? Ship-building is America's greatest pride, and in which, she will in time excel the whole world. The great empires of the east are mostly inland, and consequently excluded from the possibility of rivalling her. Africa is in a state of barbarism; and no power in Europe, hath either such an extent or coast, or such an internal supply of materials. Where nature hath given the one, she has withheld the other; to America only hath she been liberal of both. The vast empire of Russia is almost shut out from the sea; wherefore, her boundless forests, her tar, iron, and cordage are only articles of commerce.

4.11
In point of safety, ought we to be without a fleet? We are not the little people now, which we were sixty years ago; at that time we might have trusted our property in the streets, or fields rather; and slept securely without locks or bolts to our doors or windows. The case now is altered, and our methods of defence, ought to improve with our increase of property. A common pirate, twelve months ago, might have come up the Delaware, and laid the city of Philadelphia under instant contribution, for what sum he pleased; and the same might have happened to other places. Nay, any daring fellow, in a brig of fourteen or sixteen guns, might have robbed the whole Continent, and carried off half a million of money. These are circumstances which demand our attention, and point out the necessity of naval protection.

4.12
Some, perhaps, will say, that after we have made it up with Britain, she will protect us. Can we be so unwise as to mean, that she shall keep a navy in our harbors for that purpose? Common sense will tell us, that the power which hath endeavoured to subdue us, is of all others, the most improper to defend us. Conquest may be effected under the pretence of friendship; and ourselves, after a long and brave resistance, be at last cheated into slavery. And if her ships are not to be admitted into our harbours, I would ask, how is she to protect us? A navy three or four thousand miles off can be of little use, and on sudden emergencies, none at all. Wherefore, if we must hereafter protect ourselves, why not do it for ourselves? Why do it for another?

4.13
The English list of ships of war, is long and formidable, but not a tenth part of them are at any one time fit for service, numbers of them not in

being; yet their names are pompously continued in the list, if only a plank be left of the ship: and not a fifth part, of such as are fit for service, can be spared on any one station at one time. The East, and West Indies, Mediterranean, Africa, and other parts over which Britain extends her claim, make large demands upon her navy. From a mixture of prejudice and inattention, we have contracted a false notion respecting the navy of England, and have talked as if we should have the whole of it to encounter at once, and for that reason, supposed, that we must have one as large; which not being instantly practicable, have been made use of by a set of disguised Tories to discourage our beginning thereon. Nothing can be farther from truth than this; for if America had only a twentieth part of the naval force of Britain, she would be by far an over match for her; because, as we neither have, nor claim any foreign dominion, our whole force would be employed on our own coast, where we should, in the long run, have two to one the advantage of those who had three or four thousand miles to sail over, before they could attack us, and the same distance to return in order to refit and recruit. And although Britain by her fleet, hath a check over our trade to Europe, we have as large a one over her trade to the West Indies, which, by laying in the neighbourhood of the Continent, is entirely at its mercy.

4.14
Some method might be fallen on to keep up a naval force in time of peace, if we should not judge it necessary to support a constant navy. If premiums were to be given to merchants, to build and employ in their service, ships mounted with twenty, thirty, forty, or fifty guns, (the premiums to be in proportion to the loss of bulk to the merchants) fifty or sixty of those ships, with a few guard ships on constant duty, would keep up a sufficient navy, and that without burdening ourselves with the evil so loudly complained of in England, of suffering their fleet, in time of peace to lie rotting in the docks. To unite the sinews of commerce and defence is sound policy; for when our strength and our riches, play into each other's hand, we need fear no external enemy.

4.15
In almost every article of defence we abound. Hemp flourishes even to rankness, so that we need not want cordage. Our iron is superior to that of other countries. Our small arms equal to any in the world. Cannon we can cast at pleasure. Saltpetre and gunpowder we are every day producing. Our knowledge is hourly improving. Resolution is our inherent character, and courage hath never yet forsaken us. Wherefore, what is it that we want? Why is it that we hesitate? From Britain we can expect nothing but ruin. If she is once admitted to the government of America again, this Continent will not be worth living in. Jealousies

will be always arising; insurrections will be constantly happening; and who will go forth to quell them? Who will venture his life to reduce his own countrymen to a foreign obedience? The difference between Pennsylvania and Connecticut, respecting some unlocated lands, shews the insignificance of a British government, and fully proves, that nothing but Continental authority can regulate Continental matters.

4.16
Another reason why the present time is preferable to all others, is, that the fewer our numbers are, the more land there is yet unoccupied, which instead of being lavished by the king on his worthless dependants, may be hereafter applied, not only to the discharge of the present debt, but to the constant support of government. No nation under heaven hath such an advantage as this.

4.17
The infant state of the Colonies, as it is called, so far from being against, is an argument in favor of independance. We are sufficiently numerous, and were we more so, we might be less united. It is a matter worthy of observation, that the more a country is peopled, the smaller their armies are. In military numbers, the ancients far exceeded the moderns: and the reason is evident, for trade being the consequence of population, men become too much absorbed thereby to attend to anything else. Commerce diminishes the spirit, both of patriotism and military defence. And history sufficiently informs us, that the bravest achievements were always accomplished in the non-age of a nation. With the increase of commerce, England hath lost its spirit. The city of London, notwithstanding its numbers, submits to continued insults with the patience of a coward. The more men have to lose, the less willing are they to venture. The rich are in general slaves to fear, and submit to courtly power with the trembling duplicity of a Spaniel.

4.18
Youth is the seed time of good habits, as well in nations as in individuals. It might be difficult, if not impossible, to form the Continent into one government half a century hence. The vast variety of interests, occasioned by an increase of trade and population, would create confusion. Colony would be against colony. Each being able might scorn each other's assistance: and while the proud and foolish gloried in their little distinctions, the wise would lament, that the union had not been formed before. Wherefore, the *present time* is the *true time* for establishing it. The intimacy which is contracted in infancy, and the friendship which is formed in misfortune, are, of all others, the most lasting and unalterable. Our present union is marked with both these characters: we are young, and we have been distressed; but our concord

hath withstood our troubles, and fixes a memorable æra for posterity to glory in.

4.19
The present time, likewise, is that peculiar time, which never happens to a nation but once, *viz.* the time of forming itself into a government. Most nations have let slip the opportunity, and by that means have been compelled to receive laws from their conquerors, instead of making laws for themselves. First, they had a king, and then a form of government; whereas, the articles or charter of government, should be formed first, and men delegated to execute them afterward: but from the errors of other nations, let us learn wisdom, and lay hold of the present opportunity — —*To begin governvent at the right end.*

4.20
When William the Conqueror subdued England, he gave them law at the point of the sword; and until we consent, that the seat of government, in America, be legally and authoritatively occupied, we shall be in danger of having it filled by some fortunate ruffian, who may treat us in the same manner, and then, where will be our freedom? where our property?

4.21
As to religion, I hold it to be the indispensible duty of all government, to protect all conscientious professors thereof, and I know of no other business which government hath to do therewith, Let a man throw aside that narrowness of soul, that selfishness of principle, which the niggards of all professions are so unwilling to part with, and he will be at once delivered of his fears on that head. Suspicion is the companion of mean souls, and the bane of all good society. For myself, I fully and conscientiously believe, that it is the will of the Almighty, that there should be diversity of religious opinions among us: It affords a larger field for our Christian kindness. Were we all of one way of thinking, our religious dispositions would want matter for probation; and on this liberal principle, I look on the various denominations among us, to be like children of the same family, differing only, in what is called, their Christian names.

4.22
In page twenty-five, I threw out a few thoughts on the propriety of a Continental Charter, (for I only presume to offer hints, not plans) and in this place, I take the liberty of re-mentioning the subject, by observing, that a charter is to be understood as a bond of solemn obligation, which the whole enters into, to support the right of every

separate part, whether of religion, personal freedom, or property, A firm bargain and a right reckoning make long friends.

4.23

In a former page I likewise mentioned the necessity of a large and equal representation; and there is no political matter which more deserves our attention. A small number of electors, or a small number of representatives, are equally dangerous. But if the number of the representatives be not only small, but unequal, the danger is increased. As an instance of this, I mention the following; when the Associators petition was before the House of Assembly of Pennsylvania; twenty-eight members only were present, all the Bucks county members, being eight, voted against it, and had seven of the Chester members done the same, this whole province had been governed by two counties only, and this danger it is always exposed to. The unwarrantable stretch likewise, which that house made in their last sitting, to gain an undue authority over the Delegates of that province, ought to warn the people at large, how they trust power out of their own hands. A set of instructions for the Delegates were put together, which in point of sense and business would have dishonored a schoolboy, and after being approved by a *few*, a *very few* without doors, were carried into the House, and there passed *in behalf of the whole colony*; whereas, did the whole colony know, with what ill-will that House hath entered on some necessary public measures, they would not hesitate a moment to think them unworthy of such a trust.

4.24

Immediate necessity makes many things convenient, which if continued would grow into oppressions. Expedience and right are different things. When the calamities of America required a consultation, there was no method so ready, or at that time so proper, as to appoint persons from the several Houses of Assembly for that purpose; and the wisdom with which they have proceeded hath preserved this continent from ruin. But as it is more than probable that we shall never be without a CONGRESS, every well wisher to good order, must own, that the mode for choosing members of that body, deserves consideration. And I put it as a question to those, who make a study of mankind, whether *representation and election* is not too great a power for one and the same body of men to possess? When we are planning for posterity, we ought to remember, that virtue is not hereditary.

4.25

It is from our enemies that we often gain excellent maxims, and are frequently surprised into reason by their mistakes, M. Cornwall (one of the Lords of the Treasury) treated the petition of the New-York

Assembly with contempt, because *that* House, he said, consisted but of twenty-six members, which trifling number, he argued, could not with decency be put for the whole. We thank him for his involuntary honesty.*

[*Those who would fully understand of what great consequence a large and equal representation is to a state, should read Burgh's political Disquisitions.*]

4.26
To CONCLUDE, however strange it may appear to some, or however unwilling they may be to think so, matters not, but many strong and striking reasons may be given, to shew, that nothing can settle our affairs so expeditiously as an open and determined declaration for independence. Some of which are,

First.—It is the custom of nations, when any two are at war, for some other powers, not engaged in the quarrel, to step in as mediators, and bring about the preliminaries of a peace: but while America calls herself the Subject of Great Britain, no power, however well disposed she may be, can offer her mediation. Wherefore, in our present state we may quarrel on for ever.

Secondly.—It is unreasonable to suppose, that France or Spain will give us any kind of assistance, if we mean only, to make use of that assistance for the purpose of repairing the breach, and strengthening the connection between Britain and America; because, those powers would be sufferers by the consequences.

Thirdly.—While we profess ourselves the subjects of Britain, we must, in the eye of foreign nations, be considered as rebels. The precedent is somewhat dangerous to *their peace*, for men to be in arms under the name of subjects; we, on the spot, can solve the paradox: but to unite resistance and subjection, requires an idea much too refined for common understanding.

Fourthly.—Were a manifesto to be published, and despatched to foreign courts, setting forth the miseries we have endured, and the peaceable methods we have ineffectually used for redress; declaring, at the same time, that not being able, any longer to live happily or safely under the cruel disposition of the British court, we had been driven to the necessity of breaking off all connections with her; at the same time, assuring all such courts of our peaceable disposition towards them, and of our desire of entering into trade with them: Such a memorial would produce more good effects to this Continent, than if a ship were freighted with petitions to Britain.

4.27
Under our present denomination of British subjects we can neither be received nor heard abroad: The custom of all courts is against us, and will be so, until, by an independance, we take rank with other nations.

4.28
These proceedings may at first appear strange and difficult; but, like all other steps which we have already passed over, will in a little time become familiar and agreeable; and, until an independence is declared, the Continent will feel itself like a man who continues putting off some unpleasant business from day to day, yet knows it must be done, hates to set about it, wishes it over, and is continually haunted with the thoughts of its necessity.

APPENDIX.

A.1

SINCE the publication of the first edition of this pamphlet, or rather, on the same day on which it came out, the King's Speech made its appearance in this city. Had the spirit of prophecy directed the birth of this production, it could not have brought it forth, at a more seasonable juncture, or a more necessary time. The bloody mindedness of the one, shew the necessity of pursuing the doctrine of the other. Men read by way of revenge. And the Speech, instead of terrifying, prepared a way for the manly principles of Independance.

A.2

Ceremony, and even, silence, from whatever motive they may arise, have a hurtful tendency, when they give the least degree of countenance to base and wicked performances; wherefore, if this maxim be admitted, it naturally follows, that the King's Speech, as being a piece of finished villany, deserved, and still deserves, a general execration both by the Congress and the people. Yet, as the domestic tranquillity of a nation, depends greatly, on the *chastity* of what may properly be called NATIONAL MANNERS, it is often better, to pass some things over in silent disdain, than to make use of such new methods of dislike, as might introduce the least innovation, on that guardian of our peace and safety. And, perhaps, it is chiefly owing to this prudent delicacy, that the King's Speech, hath not, before now, suffered a public execution. The Speech if it may be called one, is nothing better than a wilful audacious libel against the truth, the common good, and the existence of mankind; and is a formal and pompous method of offering up human sacrifices to the pride of tyrants. But this general massacre of mankind, is one of the privileges, and the certain consequences of Kings; for as nature knows them *not*, they know *not her*, and although they are beings of our *own* creating, they know not *us*, and are become the gods of their creators. The Speech hath one good quality, which is, that it is not calculated to deceive, neither can we, even if we would, be deceived by it. Brutality and tyranny appear on the face of it. It leaves us at no loss: And every line convinces, even in the moment of reading, that He, who hunts the woods for prey, the naked and untutored Indian, is less a Savage than the King of Britain.

A.3

Sir John Dalrymple, the putative father of a whining jesuitical piece, fallaciously called, "*The address of the people of* ENGLAND *to the inhabitants of* AMERICA," hath, perhaps from a vain supposition, that the people *here* were to be frightened at the pomp and description of a king, given, (though very unwisely on his part) the real character of the present one: "But," says this writer, "if you are inclined to pay compliments to an administration, which we do not complain of," (meaning the Marquis of Rockingham's at the repeal of the Stamp Act) "it is very unfair in you to withhold them from that prince, *by whose* NOD ALONE *they were permitted to do any thing.*" This is toryism with a witness! Here is idolatry even without a mask: And he who can calmly hear, and digest such doctrine, hath forfeited his claim to rationality—an apostate from the order of manhood; and ought to be considered—as one, who hath, not only given up the proper dignity of man, but sunk himself beneath the rank of animals, and contemptibly crawl through the world like a worm.

A.4
However, it matters very little now, what the king of England either says or does; he hath wickedly broken through every moral and human obligation, trampled nature and conscience beneath his feet; and by a steady and constitutional spirit of insolence and cruelty, procured for himself an universal hatred. It is *now* the interest of America to provide for herself. She hath already a large and young family, whom it is more her duty to take care of, than to be granting away her property, to support a power who is become a reproach to the names of men and Christians—YE, whose office it is to watch over the morals of a nation, of whatsoever sect or denomination ye are of, as well as ye, who, are more immediately the guardians of the public liberty, if ye wish to preserve your native country uncontaminated by European corruption, ye must in secret wish a separation—But leaving the moral part to private reflection, I shall chiefly confine my farther remarks to the following heads.
First. That it is the interest of America to be separated from Britain.
Secondly. Which is the easiest and most practicable plan, RECONCILIATION or INDEPENDANCE? with some occasional remarks.

A.5
In support of the first, I could, if I judged it proper, produce the opinion of some of the ablest and most experienced men on this continent; and whose sentiments, on that head, are not yet publicly known. It is in reality a self-evident position: For no nation in a state of foreign dependance, limited in its commerce, and cramped and fettered in its legislative powers, can ever arrive at any material eminence. America doth not yet know what opulence is; and although the progress which she hath made stands unparalleled in the history of other nations, it is but childhood, compared with what she would be capable of arriving at, had she, as she ought to have, the legislative

powers in her own hands. England is, at this time, proudly coveting what would do her no good, were she to accomplish it; and the Continent hesitating on a matter, which will be her final ruin if neglected. It is the commerce and not the conquest of America, by which England is to be benefited, and that would in a great measure continue, were the countries as independant of each other as France and Spain; because in many articles, neither can go to a better market. But it is the independance of this country on Britain or any other, which is now the main and only object worthy of contention, and which, like all other truths discovered by necessity, will appear clearer and stronger every day.

First. Because it will come to that one time or other.

Secondly. Because the longer it is delayed the harder it will be to accomplish.

A.6

I have frequently amused myself both in public and private companies, with silently remarking, the specious errors of those who speak without reflecting. And among the many which I have heard, the following seems the most general, viz. that had this rupture happened forty or fifty years hence, instead of *now*, the Continent would have been more able to have shaken off the dependance. To which I reply, that our military ability, *at this time*, arises from the experience gained in the last war, and which in forty or fifty years time, would have been totally extinct. The Continent, would not, by that time, have had a General, or even a military officer left; and we, or those who may succeed us, would have been as ignorant of martial matters as the ancient Indians: And this single position, closely attended to, will unanswerably prove, that the present time is preferable to all others: The argument turns thus—at the conclusion of the last war, we had experience, but wanted numbers; and forty or fifty years hence, we should have numbers, without experience; wherefore, the proper point of time, must be some particular point between the two extremes, in which a sufficiency of the former remains, and a proper increase of the latter is obtained: And that point of time is the present time.

A.7

The reader will pardon this digression, as it does not properly come under the head I first set out with, and to which I again return by the following position, viz.

Should affairs be patched up with Britain, and she to remain the governing and sovereign power of America, (which, as matters are now circumstanced, is giving up the point intirely) we shall deprive ourselves of the very means of sinking the debt we have, or may contract. The value of the back lands which some of the provinces are clandestinely deprived of, by the unjust extension of the limits of Canada, valued only at five pounds sterling per hundred acres, amount to upwards of twenty-five millions, Pennsylvania currency; and the quit-rents at one penny sterling per acre, to two millions yearly.

A.8
It is by the sale of those lands that the debt may be sunk, without burden to any, and the quit-rent reserved thereon, will always lessen, and in time, will wholly support the yearly expence of government. It matters not how long the debt is in paying, so that the lands when sold be applied to the discharge of it, and for the execution of which, the Congress for the time being, will be the continental trustees.

A.9
I proceed now to the second head, viz. Which is the earliest and most practicable plan, RECONCILIATION or INDEPENDANCE; with some occasional remarks.

A.10
He who takes nature for his guide is not easily beaten out of his argument, and on that ground, I answer *generally—That* INDEPENDANCE *being a* SINGLE SIMPLE LINE, *contained within ourselves; and reconciliation, a matter exceedingly perplexed and complicated, and in which, a treacherous capricious court is to interfere, gives the answer without a doubt.*

A.11
The present state of America is truly alarming to every man who is capable of reflexion. Without law, without government, without any other mode of power than what is founded on, and granted by courtesy. Held together by an unexampled concurrence of sentiment, which, is nevertheless subject to change, and which, every secret enemy is endeavouring to dissolve. Our present condition, is, Legislation without law; wisdom without a plan; a constitution without a name; and, what is strangely astonishing, perfect Independance contending for dependance. The instance is without a precedent; the case never existed before; and who can tell what may be the event? The property of no man is secure in the present unbraced system of things. The mind of the multitude is left at random, and seeing no fixed object before them, they pursue such as fancy or opinion starts. Nothing is criminal; there is no such thing as treason; wherefore, every one thinks himself at liberty to act as he pleases. The Tories dared not to have assembled offensively, had they known that their lives, by that act, were forfeited to the laws of the state. A line of distinction should be drawn, between, English soldiers taken in battle, and inhabitants of America taken in

arms. The first are prisoners, but the latter traitors. The one forfeits his liberty, the other his head.

A.12
Notwithstanding our wisdom, there is a visible feebleness in some of our proceedings which gives encouragement to dissensions. The Continental Belt is too loosely buckled. And if something is not done in time, it will be too late to do any thing, and we shall fall into a state, in which, neither *Reconciliation* nor *Independance* will be practicable. The king and his worthless adherents are got at their old game of dividing the Continent, and there are not wanting among us, Printers, who will be busy in spreading specious falsehoods. The artful and hypocritical letter which appeared a few months ago in two of the New-York papers, and likewise in two others, is an evidence that there are men who want either judgment or honesty.

A.13
It is easy getting into holes and corners and talking of reconciliation: But do such men seriously consider, how difficult the task is, and how dangerous it may prove, should the Continent divide thereon. Do they take within their view, all the various orders of men whose situation and circumstances, as well as their own, are to be considered therein. Do they put themselves in the place of the sufferer whose *all* is *already* gone, and of the soldier, who hath quitted *all* for the defence of his country. If their ill judged moderation be suited to their own private situations *only*, regardless of others, the event will convince them, that "they are reckoning without their Host."

A.14
Put us, says some, on the footing we were in sixty-three: To which I answer, the request is not *now* in the power of Britain to comply with, neither will she propose it; but if it were, and even should be granted, I ask, as a reasonable question, By what means is such a corrupt and faithless court to be kept to its engagements? Another parliament, nay, even the present, may hereafter repeal the obligation, on the pretence of its being violently obtained, or unwisely granted; and in that case, Where is our redress?—No going to law with nations; cannon are the barristers of Crowns; and the sword, not of justice, but of war, decides the suit. To be on the footing of sixty-three, it is not sufficient, that the laws only be put on the same state, but, that our circumstances, likewise, be put on the same state; Our burnt and destroyed towns repaired or built up, our private losses made good, our public debts (contracted for defence) discharged; otherwise, we shall be millions worse than we were at that enviable period. Such a request, had it been

complied with a year ago, would have won the heart and soul of the Continent—but now it is too late, "The Rubicon is passed."

A.15
Besides, the taking up arms, merely to enforce the repeal of a pecuniary law, seems as unwarrantable by the divine law, and as repugnant to human feelings, as the taking up arms to enforce obedience thereto. The object, on either side, doth not justify the means; for the lives of men are too valuable to be cast away on such trifles. It is the violence which is done and threatened to our persons; the destruction of our property by an armed force; the invasion of our country by fire and sword, which conscientiously qualifies the use of arms: And the instant, in which such a mode of defence became necessary, all subjection to Britain ought to have ceased; and the independancy of America should have been considered, as dating its æra from, and published by, *the first musket that was fired against her*. This line is a line of consistency; neither drawn by caprice, nor extended by ambition; but produced by a chain of events, of which the colonies were not the authors.

A.16
I shall conclude these remarks, with the following timely and well intended hints. We ought to reflect, that there are three different ways, by which an independancy may hereafter be effected; and that *one* of those *three*, will one day or other, be the fate of America, viz. By the legal voice of the people in Congress; by a military power; or by a mob: It may not always happen that our soldiers are citizens, and the multitude a body of reasonable men; virtue, as I have already remarked, is not hereditary, neither is it perpetual. Should an independancy be brought about by the first of those means, we have every opportunity and every encouragement before us, to form the noblest purest constitution on the face of the earth. We have it in our power to begin the world over again. A situation, similar to the present, hath not happened since the days of Noah until now. The birthday of a new world is at hand, and a race of men, perhaps as numerous as all Europe contains, are to receive their portion of freedom from the event of a few months. The Reflexion is awful—and in this point of view, How trifling, how ridiculous, do the little, paltry cavellings, of a few weak or interested men appear, when weighed against the business of a world.

A.17
Should we neglect the present favorable and inviting period, and an Independance be hereafter effected by any other means, we must charge the consequence to ourselves, or to those rather, whose narrow and prejudiced souls, are habitually opposing the measure, without either inquiring or reflecting. There are reasons to be given in support of

Independance, which men should rather privately think of, than be publicly told of. We ought not now to be debating whether we shall be independant or not, but, anxious to accomplish it on a firm, secure, and honorable basis, and uneasy rather that it is not yet began upon. Every day convinces us of its necessity. Even the Tories (if such beings yet remain among us) should, of all men, be the most solicitous to promote it; for, as the appointment of committees at first, protected them from popular rage, so, a wise and well established form of government, will be the only certain means of continuing it securely to them. *Wherefore*, if they have not virtue enough to be WHIGS, they ought to have prudence enough to wish for Independance.

A.18
In short, Independance is the only BOND that can tye and keep us together. We shall then see our object, and our ears will be legally shut against the schemes of an intriguing, as well, as a cruel enemy. We shall then too, be on a proper footing, to treat with Britain; for there is reason to conclude, that the pride of that court, will be less hurt by treating with the American states for terms of peace, than with those, whom she denominates, "rebellious subjects," for terms of accommodation. It is our delaying it that encourages her to hope for conquest, and our backwardness tends only to prolong the war. As we have, without any good effect therefrom, withheld our trade to obtain a redress of our grievances, let us *now* try the alternative, by *independantly* redressing them ourselves, and then offering to open the trade. The mercantile and reasonable part in England, will be still with us; because, peace *with* trade, is preferable to war *without* it. And if this offer be not accepted, other courts may be applied to.

A.19
On these grounds I rest the matter. And as no offer hath yet been made to refute the doctrine contained in the former editions of this pamphlet, it is a negative proof, that either the doctrine cannot be refuted, or, that the party in favour of it are too numerous to be opposed. WHEREFORE, instead of gazing at each other with suspicious or doubtful curiosity, let each of us, hold out to his neighbour the hearty hand of friendship, and unite in drawing a line, which, like an act of oblivion shall bury in forgetfulness every former dissention. Let the names of Whig and Tory be extinct; and let none other be heard among us, than those of *a good citizen, an open and resolute friend, and a virtuous supporter of the* RIGHTS OF MANKIND *and of the* FREE AND INDEPENDANT STATES OF AMERICA.

To the Representatives of the Religious Society of the People called Quakers, or to so many of them as were concerned in publishing a late piece, entitled "The ANCIENT TESTIMONY and PRINCIPLES of the People called QUAKERS renewed, with Respect to the KING and GOVERNMENT, and touching the COMMOTIONS now prevailing in these and oter parts of AMERICA addressed to the PEOPLE IN GENERAL."

E.1
THE Writer of this, is one of those few, who never dishonors religion either by ridiculing, or cavilling at any denomination whatsoever. To God, and not to man, are all men accountable on the score of religion. Wherefore, this epistle is not so properly addressed to you as a religious, but as a political body, dabbling in matters, which the professed Quietude of your Principles instruct you not to meddle with.

E.2
As you have, without a proper authority for so doing, put yourselves in the place of the whole body of the Quakers, so, the writer of this, in order to be on an equal rank with yourselves, is under the necessity, of putting himself in the place of all those, who, approve the very writings and principles, against which, your testimony is directed: And he hath chosen this singular situation, in order, that you might discover in him that presumption of character which you cannot see in yourselves. For neither he nor you have any claim or title to *Political Representation*.

E.3
When men have departed from the right way, it is no wonder that they stumble and fall. And it is evident from the manner in which ye have managed your testimony, that politics, (as a religious body of men) is not your proper Walk; for however well adapted it might appear to you, it is, nevertheless, a jumble of good and bad put unwisely together, and the conclusion drawn therefrom, both unnatural and unjust.

E.4
The two first pages, (and the whole doth notmake four) we give you credit for, and expect the same civility from you, because the love and desire of peace is not confined to Quakerism, it is the *natural*, as well the religious wish of all denominations of men. And on this ground, as men laboring to establish an Independant Constitution of our own, do we exceed all others in our hope, end, and aim. *Our plan is peace for ever*. We are tired of contention with Britain, and can see no real end to it but in a final separation. We act consistently, because for the sake of introducing an endless and uninterrupted peace, do we bear the evils

and burthens of the present day. We are endeavoring, and will steadily continue to endeavor, to separate and dissolve a connexion which hath already filled our land with blood; and which, while the name of it remains, will be the fatal cause of future mischiefs to both countries.

E.5
We fight neither for revenge nor conquest; neither from pride nor passion; we are not insulting the world with our fleets and armies, nor ravaging the globe for plunder. Beneath the shade of our own vines are we attacked; in our own houses, and on our own lands, is the violence committed against us. We view our enemies in the characters of Highwaymen and Housebreakers, and having no defence for ourselves in the civil law; are obliged to punish them by the military one, and apply the sword, in the very case, where you have before now, applied the halter——Perhaps we feel for the ruined and insulted sufferers in all and every part of the continent, and with a degree of tenderness which hath not yet made its way into some of your bosoms. But be ye sure that ye mistake not the cause and ground of your Testimony. Call not coldness of soul, religion; nor put the *Bigot* in the place of the *Christian*.

E.6
O ye partial ministers of your own acknowledged principles. If the bearing arms be sinful, the first going to war must be more so, by all the difference between wilful attack and unavoidable defence. Wherefore, if ye really preach from conscience, and mean not to make a political hobby-horse of your religion, convince the world thereof, by proclaiming your doctrine to our enemies, *for they likewise bear* ARMS. Give us proof of your sincerity by publishing it at St. James's, to the commanders in chief at Boston, to the Admirals and Captains who are piratically ravaging our coasts, and to all the murdering miscreants who are acting in authority under HIM whom ye profess to serve. Had ye the honest soul of * *Barclay* ye would preach repentance to *your* king; Ye would tell the Royal Wretch his sins, and warn him of eternal ruin. Ye would not spend your partial invectives against the injured and the insulted only, but, like faithful ministers, would cry aloud and *spare none*. Say not that ye are persecuted, neither endeavour to make us the authors of that reproach, which, ye are bringing upon yourselves; for we testify unto all men, that we do not complain against you because ye are *Quakers*, but because ye pretend to *be* and are NOT Quakers.
[*"*Thou hast tasted of prosperity and adversity; thou knowest what it is to be banished thy native country, to be over-ruled as well as to rule, and set upon the throne; and being* oppressed *thou hast reason to know how* hateful *the* oppressor *is both to God and man. If after all these warnings and advertisements, thou dost not turn unto the Lord with all thy heart, but*

forget him who remembered thee in thy distress, and give up thyself to follow lust and vanity, surely great will be thy condemnation.—Against which snare, as well as the temptation of those who may or do feed thee, and prompt thee to evil, the most excellent and prevalent remedy will be, to apply thyself to that light of Christ which shineth in thy conscience, and which neither can, nor will flatter thee, nor suffer thee, to be at ease in thy sins." Barclay's Address to Charles II.]

E.7

Alas! it seems by the particular tendency of some part of your testimony, and other parts of your conduct, as if, all sin was reduced to, and comprehended in, *the act of bearing arms*, and that by the *people only*. Ye appear to us, to have mistaken party for conscience; because, the general tenor of your actions wants uniformity: And it is exceedingly difficult to us to give credit to many of your pretended scruples; because, we see them made by the same men, who, in the very instant that they are exclaiming against the mammon of this world, are nevertheless, hunting after it with a step as steady as Time, and an appetite as keen as Death.

E.8

The quotation which ye have made from Proverbs, in the third page of your testimony, that, "when a man's ways please the Lord, he maketh even his enemies to be at peace with him"; is very unwisely chosen on your part; because it amounts to a proof, that the king's ways (whom ye are so desirous of supporting) do *not* please the Lord, otherwise, his reign would be in peace.

E.9

I now proceed to the latter part of your testimony, and that, for which all the foregoing seems only an introduction, viz.
"It hath ever been our judgment and principle, since we were called to profess the light of Christ Jesus, manifested in our consciences unto this day, that the sitting up and putting down kings and governments, is God's peculiar prerogative; for causes best known to himself: And that it is not our business to have any hand or contrivance therein; nor to be busy bodies above our station, much less to plot and contrive the ruin, or overturn of any of them, but to pray for the king, and safety of our nation, and good of all men: That we may live a peaceable and quiet life, in all goodliness and honesty; *under the government which God is pleased to set over us."*—If these are *really* your principles why do ye not abide by them? Why do ye not leave that, which ye call God's work, to be managed by himself? These very principles instruct you to wait with patience and humility, for the event of all public measures, and to receive *that event* as the divine will towards you. *Wherefore*, what

occasion is there for your *political testimony* if you fully believe what it contains? And the very publishing it proves, that either, ye do not believe what ye profess, or have not virtue enough to practise what ye believe.

E.10
The principles of Quakerism have a direct tendency to make a man the quiet and inoffensive subject of any, and every government *which is set over him*. And if the setting up and putting down of kings and governments is God's peculiar prerogative, he most certainly will not be robbed thereof by us; wherefore, the principle itself leads you to approve of every thing, which ever happened, or may happen to kings as being his work. OLIVER CROMWELL thanks you. CHARLES, then, died not by the hands of man; and should the present Proud Imitator of him, come to the same untimely end, the writers and publishers of the Testimony, are bound, by the doctrine it contains, to applaud the fact. Kings are not taken away by miracles, neither are changes in governments brought about by any other means than such as are common and human; and such as we are now using. Even the dispersing of the Jews, though foretold by our Saviour, was effected by arms. Wherefore, as ye refuse to be the means on one side, ye ought not to be meddlers on the other; but to wait the issue in silence; and unless ye can produce divine authority, to prove, that the Almighty who hath created and placed this *new* world, at the greatest distance it could possibly stand, east and west, from every part of the old, doth, nevertheless, disapprove of its being independent of the corrupt and abandoned court of Britain, unless I say, ye can shew this, how can ye on the ground of your principles, justify the exciting and stirring up of the people "firmly to unite in the *abhorrence* of all such *writings*, and *measures*, as evidence a desire and design to break off the *happy* connexion we have hitherto enjoyed, with the kingdom of Great-Britain, and our just and necessary subordination to the king, and those who are lawfully placed in authority under him." What a slap in the face is here! the men, who in the very paragraph before, have quietly and passively resigned up the ordering, altering, and disposal of kings and governments, into the hands of God, are now, recalling their principles, and putting in for a share of the business. Is it possible, that the conclusion, which is here justly quoted, can any ways follow from the doctrine laid down? The inconsistency is too glaring not to be seen; the absurdity too great not to be laughed at; and such as could only have been made by those, whose understandings were darkened by the narrow and crabby spirit of a dispairing political party; for ye are not to be considered as the whole body of the Quakers but only as a factional and fractional part thereof.

E.11
Here ends the examination of your testimony; (which I call upon no man to abhor, as ye have done, but only to read and judge of fairly;) to which I subjoin the foll[o]wing remark; "That the setting up and putting down of kings," most certainly mean, the making him a king, who is yet not so, and the making him no king who is already one. And pray what hath this to do in the present case? We neither mean to *set up* nor to *put down*, neither to *make* nor to *unmake*, but to have nothing to *do* with them. Wherefore, your testimony in whatever light it is viewed serves only to dishonor your judgment, and for many other reasons had better have been let alone than published.

E.12
First, Because it tends to the decrease and reproach of all religion whatever, and is of the utmost [d]anger to society, to make it a party in political disputes.
Secondly, Because it exhibits a body of men, numbers of whom disavow the publishing political testimonies, as being concerned therein and approvers thereof.
Thirdly, Because it hath a tendency to undo that continental harmony and friendship which yourselves by your late liberal and charitable donations hath lent a hand to establish; and the preservation of which, is of the utmost consequence to us all.

E.13
And here without anger or resentment I bid you farewel. Sincerely wishing, that as men and christians, ye may always fully and uninterruptedly enjoy every civil and religious right; and be, in your turn, the means of securing it to others; but that the example which ye have unwisely set, of mingling religion with politics, *may be disavowed and reprobated by every inhabitant of* AMERICA.

FINIS.

Bibliography

Abbatt, William, ed. *Memoirs of Major-General William Heath*. New York: William Abbatt, 1901.
[Adams, John.] *Thoughts on Government: Applicable to the Present State of the American Colonies, in a Letter from a Gentleman to his Friend*. Philadelphia: John Dunlap; Boston: John Gill, 1776.
Adams, Thomas R. *The American Controversy: A Bibliographical Study of the British Pamphlets about the American Disputes, 1764-1783*.
    Volume I: 1764-1777. Providence, RI: Brown University Press, 1980.
———. *American Independence: The Growth of an Idea. A Bibliographical Study of the American Political Pamphlets Printed Between 1764 and 1776 Dealing with the Dispute Between Great Britain and Her Colonies*. Providence: Brown University Press, 1965.
———. "The Authorship and Printing of *Plain Truth* by Candidus," *The Papers of the Bibliographical Society of America* 49 (1955): 230-248.
Adams, W. Paul. "Republicanism in Political Rhetoric Before 1776." *Political Science Quarterly* 85 (1970): 398-404.
Aesop. *Fables*, 10th edition. Edited by George Fyler Townsend. 1880. Reprint, Charlottesville: University of Virginia Library, 1993.
Agnew, Jean-Christophe. *Worlds Apart: The Market and the Theater in Anglo-American Thought, 1550-1750*. Cambridge: Cambridge University Press, 1986.
Aitken, Robert. "Wastebook" (1771-1802). LCP.
The Alarm: or, an Address to the People of Pennsylvania on the Late Resolve of Congress, for Totally Suppressing all Power and Authority Derived from the Crown of Great-Britain. Philadelphia: Henry Miller, 1776.
Aldridge, A. O. *Thomas Paine's American Ideology*. Newark: University of Delaware Press; London: Associated University Presses, 1984.
———. *Man of Reason: The Life of Thomas Paine*. Philadelphia: Lippincott, 1959.
———. "Natural Religion and Deism in America before Ethan Allen and Thomas Paine." *William and Mary Quarterly* 54 (1997): 835-848.
———. "Some Writings of Thomas Paine in Pennsylvania Newspapers."

The American Historical Review 56 (1951): 832-838.
———. "Thomas Paine and the Classics." *Eighteenth-Century Studies* 1 (1968): 370-380.
Alexander, Edward P. *A Revolutionary Conservative: James Duane of New York*. New York: Columbia University Press, 1938.
Altick, R. D. *The English Common Reader: A Social History of the Mass Reading Public, 1800-1900*. Columbus: Ohio State University Press, 1998.
American Philosophical Society. *Proceedings of the American Philosophical Society: Minutes, 1743-1838*. Philadelphia: 1885.
———. *Transactions of the American Philosophical Society, held at Philadelphia for Promoting Useful Knowledge*, vol. 1 (1769-1770). Philadelphia: William and Thomas Bradford, at the London Coffee-House, 1771.
American Society. *Minutes of the American Society*. Philadelphia: 1768.
Anderson, Benedict. *Imagined Communities: Reflections on the Origin and Spread of Nationalism*. London: Verso, 1991.
Archer, Jules. *They made a revolution, 1776*. New York: St. Martin's Press, 1973.
Aristotle. *On Rhetoric: A Theory of Civic Discourse*. Edited by George Kennedy. New York: Oxford University Press, 1991.
Ashcraft, Richard. *Revolutionary Politics and Locke's "Two Treatises of Government."* Princeton, NJ: Princeton University Press, 1986.
Ashworth, William J. *Customs and Excise: Trade, Production, and Consumption in England 1640-1845*. Oxford: Oxford University Press, 2003.
Babb, M.J. "The Relation of David Rittenhouse and His Orrery to the University." *The General Magazine and Historical Chronicle*. Philadelphia: [University of Pennsylvania], n.d.
Bacon, Francis. *The Advancement of Learning*. New York: Modern Library, 2001 [1605].
Bailey, Chris H. *Two Hundred Years of American Clocks and Watches*. Englewood Cliffs, NJ: Rutledge, 1975.
Bailyn, Bernard. "Common Sense." *American Heritage* 25 (1973): 36-41, 91-93.
———. *Faces of Revolution: Personalities and Themes in the Struggle for American Independence*. New York: Vintage Books, 1992.
———. *The Ideological Origins of the American Revolution*. Cambridge, MA: Belknap Press of Harvard University Press, 1967.
———, ed. *Pamphlets of the American Revolution, 1750-1776*. Cambridge: Belknap Press of Harvard University Press, 1965.
———. *To Begin the World Anew: The Genius and Ambiguities of the American Founders*. New York: Knopf, 2003.
Bakhtin, Mikhail. *The Dialogic Imagination: Four Essays*. Austin: University of Texas Press, 1983.

Baldwin, Ernest H. "Joseph Galloway, The Loyalist Politician." *Pennsylvania Magazine of History and Biography* 26 (1902): 289-322.
———, ed. *Joseph Galloway: Selected Tracts*, Vol. 1. New York: Da Capo, 1974.
Ballagh, James Curtis, ed. *The Letters of Richard Henry Lee*. Volume 1, 1762-1778. New York: MacMillan, 1911.
Bangs, Isaac. *Journal of Lieutenant Isaac Bangs*. New York: Arno, 1968.
Barclay, Robert. *Barclay's Apology in Modern English, Edited by Dean Freiday*, Newburg, OR: Barclay Press, 1991.
Baskerville, Barnet. *The People's Voice: The Orator in American Society*. Lexington: University of Kentucky Press, 1979.
Basler, Roy P., ed. *Collected Works of Abraham Lincoln*. 9 vols. New Brunswick, NJ: Rutgers University Press, 1953-55.
Beiner, Ronald. *Political Judgment*. Chicago: University of Chicago Press, 1984.
Belknap, Jeremy. *The History of New-Hampshire*. Dover, NH: George Wadleigh, [1784-1792] 1862.
Bell, Robert. *Additions to Plain Truth*. Philadelphia: R. Bell, 1776.
———. Broadside for a Book Auction. January 17, 1774. HSP.
———. *A Catalogue of New and Old Books, which Will Be Exhibited by Auction, by Robert Bell, Bookseller and Auctionier*. Boston: 1770. LCP.
———. *OBSERVATIONS Relative to the Manufactures of Paper and Printed Books in the Province of PENNSYLVANIA*. January 25, 1773. LCP.
———. *PROPOSALS For Printing by Subscription, "A Dissent from the Church of England, Fully Justified."* Philadelphia: Bell, 1774. LCP.
Benton, William Allen. *Whig-Loyalism: An Aspect of Political Ideology in the American Revolutionary Era*. Rutherford, NJ: Fairleigh Dickinson University Press, 1969.
Bevis, John. "Observations of the Last Transit of Venus, and of the Eclipse of the Sun the Next Day; Made at the House of Joshua Kirby, Esquire, at Kew. By John Bevis, MD. FRS," 15 June 1769. *Philosophical Transactions*, Royal Society of London (1769): 189-191.
Biddle, Henry D. "Owen Biddle." *Pennsylvania Magazine of History and Biography* 16 (1892): 299-333.
Black, Edwin. *Rhetorical Criticism: A Study in Method*. Madison: University of Wisconsin Press, 1978.
Black, Eugene Charlton. *The Association: British Extraparliamentary Political Organization 1769-1793*. Cambridge, MA: Harvard University Press, 1963.
Blackstone, William. *Commentaries on the Laws of England*. 4 vols.

Dublin: John Exshaw, et al., 1769-70.
Blair, Hugh. *Lectures on Rhetoric and Belles Lettres.* 2 vols. London: W. Strahan and T. Cadell, 1783.
Boggs, Mary Emma and Benjamin Randolph. "Inns and Taverns of Old Philadelphia." Philadelphia, 1917.
Bohman, George V. "Rhetorical Practice in Colonial America." In *A History of Speech Education in America*, edited by Karl Wallace. New York: Appleton-Century-Crofts, 1954.
Borden, Morton, and Penn Borden, eds. *The American Tory.* Englewood Cliffs, NJ: Prentice-Hall, 1972.
Boorstin, Daniel J. *The Americans: The Colonial Experience.* New York: Random House, 1958.
Borges, Jorge Luis. *Labyrinths: Selected Stories and Other Writings.* New York: New Directions, 1964.
Boudinot, Elias. *Journal of Events in the Revolution.* New York: Arno, 1968.
Boudinot, J. J., ed. *The Life, Public Serives, Addresses, and Letters of Elias Boudinot.* New York: Da Capo, 1971.
Boulton, James T., ed. *Daniel Defoe.* New York: Schocken, 1965.
———. *The Language and Politics in the Age of Wilkes and Burke.* London: Routledge, 1963.
Boyd, Julian P. *The Declaration of Independence: The Evolution of the Text as Shown in Facsimiles of Various Drafts.* Princeton, NJ: Princeton University Press, 1945.
———, ed. *The Papers of Thomas Jefferson*, vol. 1. Princeton, NJ: Princeton University Press, 1950.
Bradford, William. *A Memorandum Book and Register for the Months of May and June, 1776.* Bradford Papers. HSP.
Bradley, James E. *Popular Politics and the American Revolution in England: Petitions, the Crown, and Public Opinion.* Macon, GA: Mercer University Press, 1986.
Braithwaite, W. C. *The Beginnings of Quakerism.* 2nd rev. ed. Cambridge: Cambridge University Press, 1970.
Brands, H. W. *The First American: The Life and Times of Benjamin Franklin.* New York: Doubleday, 2000.
Branham, Anne K. "Teaching the Enlightenment in American Literature: Shedding Light on Faith and Reason." *The English Journal* 87 (1998): 54-59.
[Braxton, Carter.] *An Address to the Convention of the Colony and Ancient Dominion of Virginia; on the Subject of Government in General, and Recommending a particular form to their consideration. By a Native of that Colony.* Philadelphia: John Dunlap, 1776.
Breen, T. H. "'Baubles of Britain'" The American and Consumer Revolutions of the Eighteenth Century." *Past and Present* 119 (1988): 73-104.

———. "Ideology and Nationalism on the Eve of the American
Revolution: Revisions Once More in Need of Revising."
Journal of American History 84 (1997): 13-39.
———. *The Lockean Moment: The Languages of Rights on the Eve of the
American Revolution.* New York: Oxford University Press,
2001.
———. *Marketplace of Revolution: How Consumer Politics Shaped American
Independence.* New York: Oxford University Press, 2004.
———. *Tobacco Culture: The Mentality of the Great Tidewater Planters on
the Eve of Revolution.* Princeton: Princeton University Press,
2001 [1985].
Brenner, Walter C. *A List of Philadelphia Inns and Taverns, 1680-1850*,
Philadelphia, 1928.
Bridenbaugh, Carl. *Cities in Revolt: Urban Life in America, 1743-1776.*
New York: Alfred A. Knopf, 1955.
Broadie, Alexander, ed. *The Cambridge Companion to the Scottish
Enlightenment.* New York: University of Cambridge Press,
2002.
Buel, Richard, Jr. "Democracy and the American Revolution: A Frame
of Reference." *William and Mary Quarterly*, 3rd ser., 21
(1964): 165-190.
———. "Freedom of the Press in Revolutionary America: The Evolution
of Libertarianism, 1760-1820." In *The Press and the American
Revolution*, edited by Bernard Bailyn and John B. Hench.
Boston: Northeastern University Press, 1981.
Buffett, E. P. "Abraham Clark." *Pennsylvania Magazine of History and
Biography* 1 (1877): 445-449.
Bumsted, J. M. "'Things in the Womb of Time:' Ideas of American
Independence, 1633 to 1763." *William and Mary Quarterly* 31
(1974): 533-564.
Bumsted, John M., and Charles E. Clark. "New England's Tom
Paine: John Allen and the Spirit of Liberty." *William and
Mary Quarterly*, 3rd ser., 21 (1964): 561-570.
Burgh, James. *The Art of Speaking.* Philadelphia: R. Aitken, 1775
[1761].
———. *Political Disquisitions.* 3 vols. Philadelphia: Bell and
Woodhouse, 1775 [1774-75].
Burke, Edmund. *Speeches and Letters on American Affairs.* London: J.
M. Dent & Sons, 1961.
Burke, Kenneth. *Grammar of Motives.* Berkeley: University of
California Press, 1969.
*The Burlington Almanack for the Year of our Lord 1776. Being Bissextile or
Leap-Year. And the 16th Year of His Majesty's Reign, after the
25th of October 1775.* By Timothy Trumean, Philom.
Burlington [NJ]: Isaac Collins, [1775].

Butterfield, L. H., ed. *The Adams Papers.* Cambridge: Belknap Press of Harvard University Press, 1961.

———, ed. *Diary and Autobiography of John Adams.* Cambridge: Belknap Press of Harvard University Press, 1962.

———, ed. *Letters of Benjamin Rush.* Princeton: Princeton University Press, 1951.

Butterfield, L. H., Marc Friedlaender, and Mary-Jo Kline, eds. *The Book of Abigail and John: Selected Letters of the Adams Family 1762-1784.* Boston: Northeastern University Press, 1975.

Calkin, Homer L. "Pamphlets and Public Opinion During the American Revolution." *Pennsylvania Magazine of History and Biography* 64 (1940): 38-40.

Campbell, George. *Philosophy of Rhetoric.* 2 vols. London: W. Strahan and T. Cadell, and Edinburgh: W. Creech, 1776 [1750].

Cannon, John, ed. *The Letters of Junius.* Oxford: Clarendon, 1978.

Cappon, Lester J., ed. *The Adams-Jefferson Letters.* Chapel Hill: University of North Carolina Press, 1987.

Carter, Landon. "Diary of Colonel Landon Carter." *William and Mary Quarterly* 16 (1908): 149-156, 257-268.

Cash, Arthur H. *John Wilkes: The Scandalous Father of Civil Liberty.* New Haven: Yale University Press, 2006.

[Chalmers, James.] *Plain Truth; Addressed to the Inhabitants of America, Containing, Remarks on a Late Pamphlet entitled Common Sense.* Philadelphia: Bell, 1776.

Charles II, *By the King. A Proclamation for the Suppression of Coffee-Houses.* London: John Bill and Christopher Barker, Printers to the Kings most Excellent Majesty, 1675.

Charvat, William. *Literary Publishing in America, 1790-1850.* Philadelphia: University of Pennsylvania Press, 1959.

Cheetham, James. *Life of Thomas Paine.* London, 1817.

Chesnutt, David R., ed. *The Papers of Henry Laurens.* Columbia, SC: University of South Carolina Press, 1985.

Christian, William. "The Moral Economics of Tom Paine." *Journal of the History of Ideas* 34 (1973): 367-380.

Christie, Ian R. *Wilkes, Wyvill, and Reform: The Parliamentary Reform Movement in British Politics, 1760-1785.* London: Ashgate, 1994.

Christie, Ian R. and Benjamin W. Labaree. *Empire or Independence, 1760-1776: A British-American dialogue on the coming of the American Revolution.* New York: W.W. Norton, 1976.

Civil Prudence, Recommended to the Thirteen United Colonies of North-America. A Discourse, Shewing That it is in the Power of Civil Prudence to prevent or cure State Distempers, and to make an industrious, wealthy, and flourishing People... Norwich: Judah P. Spooner, 1776.

Claeys, Gregory. *Thomas Paine: Social and Political Thought*. Unwin Hyman, 1989.
The Claim and Answer with the Subsequent Proceedings, in the Case of the Right Reverend Charles Inglis, against the United States; under the Sixth Article of the Treaty of Amity, Commerce and Navigation, between His Britannic Majesty and the United States of America. Philadelphia: R. Aitken, 1799.
Clark, Harry Hayden. "An Historical Interpretation of Thomas Paine's Religion." *University of California Chronicle* 35 (1933): 56-87.
———. "Thomas Paine's Theories of Rhetoric." *Transactions, Wisconsin Academy of Sciences, Arts and Letters* 28 (1933): 307-309.
———. "Toward a Reinterpretation of Thomas Paine." *American Literature* 5 (1933): 133-145.
Clark, J. C. D. "Religious Affiliation and Dynastic Allegiance in Eighteenth-Century England: Edmund Burke, Thomas Paine and Samuel Johnson." *English Literary History* 64 (1997): 1029-1067.
———. *The Language of Liberty 1660-1832: Political Discourse and Social Dynamics in the Anglo-American World*. Cambridge and New York: Cambridge University Press, 1994.
Cmiel, Kenneth. *Democratic Eloquence: The Fight over Popular Speech in Nineteenth-Century America*. New York: W. Morrow, 1990.
Cockin, William. *The Art of Delivering Written Language* (1775). Menston, UK: Scolar Press, 1969.
Cohen, I. Bernard, ed. *Companion to Newton*. Cambridge: Cambridge University Press, 2002.
———. *Science and the Founding Fathers*. New York: W.W. Norton, 1995.
Cohen, Murray. *Sensible Words: Linguistic Practice in England, 1640-1785*. Baltimore: Johns Hopkins University Press, 1977.
Collins, Paul. *The Trouble with Tom: The Strange Afterlife and Times of Thomas Paine*. New York: Bloomsbury, 2005.
Commager, Henry Steele. "Science, Learning, and the Claims of Nationalism." *American Heritage* 23 (April 1972): 80.
Commager, Henry Steele, and Richard B. Morris, eds. *The Spirit of Seventy-Six: The Story of the American Revolution as Told by Participants*. New York: Bonanza Books, 1983.
Committee of Safety of the Colony of New York. *Essays Upon the Making of Salt-Petre and Gun-Powder*. New York: Samuel Loudon, 1776.
Common Sense a Common Delusion. Or, The generally-received Notions of Natural Causes, Deity, Religion, Virtue, &c. As exhibited in Mr. Pope's Essay on Man, Proved Ridiculous, impious, and the Effect of Infatuation; and the chief Cause of the present formidable Growth of Vice among Christians, and the great Stumbling-block

in the Way of Infidels. Earnestly recommended to the Perusal of all Men of Good-Sense, and Lovers of Truth. By Almonides, a believing Heathen. London: printed for T. Reynolds, sold by R. Baldwin, W. Owen, R. Davis, etc., 1751.

Common Sense: In Nine Conferences between a British Merchant and a Candid Merchant of America, in Their Private Capacities as Friends. London: J. Dodsley, 1775.

Common Sense: or, the Englishman's Journal. Being A Collection of Letters, Political, Humorous, and Moral; Publish'd Weekly under That Title, For the First Year. London: J. Purser and G. Hawkins, 1738.

Conroy, David W. *In Public Houses: Drink and the Revolution of Authority in Colonial Massachusetts.* Chapel Hill: University of North Carolina Press, 1995.

Continental Congress. *Journals of Congress: Containing the Proceedings from Sept. 5, 1774, to Jan. 1, 1776, Volume I.* Philadelphia: R. Aitken, 1777.

———. *Journals of the Continental Congress. Containing the Proceedings in the Year, 1776.* Philadelphia: R. Aitken, 1777.

———. *Several Methods of Making Salt-Petre; Recommended to the Inhabitants of the United Colonies.* Watertown: Benjamin Edes, 1775.

Conway, Moncure D. *The Life of Thomas Paine.* New York: Putnam & Sons, 1892-1896.

———. *Writings of Thomas Paine.* 4 vols. New York: AMS Press, 1967.

Corner, George W., ed. *The Autobiography of Benjamin Rush: His Travels through Life Together with His Commonplace Book for 1789-1813.* Princeton: Princeton University Press, 1948.

Countryman, Edward. *The American Revolution.* New York: Hill & Wang, 1985.

Crane, Verner W. "The Club of Honest Whigs: Friends of Science and Liberty." *William and Mary Quarterly,* 3rd ser., 23 (1966): 210-233.

Cox, J. Robert. "The Die is Cast: Topical and Ontological Dimensions of the *Locus* of the Irreparable." *Quarterly Journal of Speech* 68 (1982): 227-239.

The Crisis, No. I [London], "To the People of England and America." In *The Crisis, Numbers I-XI.* New York, 1775. APS.

Cushing, Harry Alonzo. The *Writings of Samuel Adams.* 4 vols. New York: G. P. Putnam's Sons, 1904-1908.

Cuthbertson, Brian. *The First Bishop: A Biography of Charles Inglis.* Halifax, NS: Waegwoltic Press, 1987.

Dalrymple, John, Sir. *The Address of the People of Great-Britain to the Inhabitants of America.* London: T. Cadell, 1775.

Davidson, Cathy. *Revolution and the Word: The Rise of the American*

Novel. New York: Oxford University Press, 1986.
Davidson, Edward H., and William J. Scheik. *Paine, Scripture, and Authority: The Age of Reason as Religious and Political Ideal.* Bethlehem, PA: Lehigh University Press, 1994.
Davidson, Phillip. *Propaganda and the American Revolution, 1763-1783.* Chapel Hill, NC: University of North Carolina Press, 1941.
Davies, K. G., ed. *Documents of the American Revolution, 1770-1783*, Vol. XII. Dublin: Irish University Press, 1976.
Davis, David Brion. *The Problem of Slavery in the Age of Revolution, 1770-1823.* Ithaca, NY: Cornell University Press, 1975.
Davis, James M., Jr. "The Colonial Coffeehouse." *Early American Life* 9 (1978): 26-29, 86.
Deas, Anne Izard, ed. *Correspondence of Mr. Ralph Izard, of South Carolina*, Vol. 1. New York: Charles S. Francis, 1844.
Defoe, Daniel. *The Shortest Way with the Dissenters.* London, 1702.
———. *A Tour Thro' the Whole Island of Great Britain.* 2 vols. London, 1724-26.
———. *The True-Born Englishman.* London, 1701.
D'Elia, Donald. "The Republican Theology of Benjamin Rush," *Pennsylvania History* 33 (1966): 187-203.
"Diary of James Allen, Esq., of Philadelphia, Counsellor-at-Law, 1770-1778. *Pennsylvania Magazine of History and Biography* 9 (1885): 176-197.
Dickinson, John. *An Essay on the Constitutional Power of Great-Britain over the Colonies in America: with the Resolves of the Committee for the Province of Pennsylvania, and their Instructions to their Representatives in Assembly.* Philadelphia: William and Thomas Bradford, 1774; London: John Almon, 1774.
———. *Letters from a Farmer in Pennsylvania to the Inhabitants of the British Colonies.* Philadelphia: William and Thomas Bradford, 1767.
———. "To my Opponents in the late Elections of Councillor for the County of Philadelphia, and of President of the Supreme Executive Council of Pennsylvania." In *The Freeman's Journal: or, the North-American Intelligencer* (Philadelphia), January 1, 1783.
Dill, Alonzo Thomas. *Carter Braxton, Virginia Signer: A Conservative in Revolt.* Lanham, MD: University Press of America, 1983.
Doerflinger, Thomas M. "Philadelphia Merchants and the Logic of Moderation, 1760-1775." *William and Mary Quarterly*, 3rd ser., 40 (1983): 197-226.
[Donaldson, Arthur.] *To the Tories. Mind How Ye Fight [with] Your Lies Tomorrow, Gentlemen...[Signed,] Old Trusty.* Philadelphia: April 30, 1776.

Dorfman, Joseph. "The Economic Philosophy of Thomas Paine." *Political Science Quarterly* 53 (1938): 372-386.
Dragonetti, Giacinto, marchese. *A Treatise on Virtues and Rewards.* London: Johnson and Payne, and J. Almon, 1769.
Drayton, John. *Memoirs of the American Revolution*, 2 vols. Charleston, SC, 1821.
Durey, Michael. "Thomas Paine's Apostles: Radical Émigrés and the Triumph of Jeffersonian Republicanism." *William and Mary Quarterly* 44 (1987): 661-688.
Eckhardt, George H. *Pennsylvania Clocks and Clockmakers: An Epic of Early American Science, Industry, and Craftsmanship.* New York: Devin-Adair, 1955.
Ellicott, Andrew. "Astronomical and Thermometrical Observations, made on the Boundary between the United States and His Catholic Majesty." *Transactions of the American Philosophical Society* 5 (1802): 204-205.
———. "Observations for Determining the Latitude and Longitude of the Town of Natchez." *Transaction of the American Philosophical Society* 4 (1799): 447-450.
Evans, Charles. *American Bibliography*, vol. 5. Chicago: Hollister Press, 1909.
Experience Preferable to Theory. An Answer to Dr. Price's Observations on the Nature of Civil Liberty and the Justice and Policy of the War with America. London: T. Payne, 1776.
"Extracts from the Diary of Dr. James Clitherall, 1776." *Pennsylvania Magazine of History and Biography* 22 (1898): 468-475.
Father Abraham's Almanack, for the Year of our Lord 1775; Being the Third after Leap-Year. (The Fifteenth Year of the Reign of King George III.) ....That the Ingenious David Rittenhouse...Has Favored Us with the Astronomical Calculations for This Year.... Philadelphia, John Dunlap, [1774].
Father Abraham's Almanack, for the Year of Our Lord 1777 ... Fitted to the Latitude of Forty Degrees, and a Meridian of Near Five Hours West from London. By Abraham Weatherwise, Gent. ... Philadelphia: John Dunlap, [1776].
Father Abraham's Pocket Almanack for the Year 1776. Philadelphia: John Dunlap, [1775].
Father Abraham's Almanack, For the Year of our Lord 1778; Being the Second after Leap-Year. Containing, The Motions of the Sun and Moon; the True Places and Aspects of the Planets; the Rising and Setting of the Sun; and the Rising, Setting and Southing of the Moon. Also, The Lunations, Conjunctions, Eclipses, Judgment of the Weather, Rising and Setting of the Planets, Length of Days and Nights, &c. &c. Fitted to the Latitude of Forty Degrees, and a

meridian of near five Hours West from London. By Abraham Weatherwise, Gent. ... Philadelphia: John Dunlap [1777].

Fehrenbacher, Don E. "The Words of Lincoln." In *Abraham Lincoln and the American Political Tradition,* edited by John L. Thomas. Amherst: The University of Massachusetts, 1986.

Ferguson, Adam. *An Essay on the History of Civil Society.* Edinburgh: A. Kincaid and J. Bell, 1767.

Ferguson, James. *Analysis of a Course of Lectures, on Mechanics, Pneumatics, Hydrostatics, and Astronomy; Read by James Ferguson.* London: printed for the author, 1761.

——. *The Art of Drawing in Perspective Made Easy to Those Who Have No Previous Knowledge of the Mathematics.* London: W. Strahan and T. Cadell, 1775.

——. *Astronomical Tables and Precepts, for Calculating the True Times of New and Full Moons, and... Projecting Eclipses, from the Creation of the World to A.D. 7800. To which is Prefixed, a Short Theory of the Solar and Lunar Motions.* London: printed for the author, 1763.

——. *Astronomy Explained upon Sir Isaac Newton's Principles, and Made Easy to Those Who Have Not Studied Mathematics.* London: J. Ferguson, 1756.

——. *Astronomy Explained upon Sir Isaac Newton's Principles, and Made Easy to Those Who Have Not Studied Mathematics. To Which Are Added, A Plain Method of Finding the Distances of all the Planets from the Sun, by the Transit of Venus over the Sun's Disc, in the year 1761: An Account of Mr. Horrox's Observation of the Transit of Venus in the Year 1639: And of the Distances of All the Planets from the Sun, as Deduced from Observations of the Transit in the Year 1761.* London: J. Ferguson, 1756; Philadelphia, reprinted: M. Carey, 1806.

——. *A Brief Description of the Solar System. To Which is Subjoined, an Astronomical Account of the Year of Our Saviour's Crucifixion.* Norwich: W. Chase, 1753.

——. "A Delineation of the Transit of Venus Expected in the Year 1769," 10 February 1763. *Philosophical Transactions,* Royal Society of London, (1763): 30-40.

——. *The Description and Use of a New Machine, Called the Mechanical Paradox; Invented by James Ferguson.* London: A. Millar, 1764.

——. *A Dissertation upon the Phænomena of the Harvest Moon. Also, the Description and Use of a New Four-wheel'd Orrery, and an Essay upon the Moon's Turning Round Her Own Axis.* London: J. Nourse and S. Paterson, 1747.

——. *An Easy Introduction to Astronomy, for Young Gentlemen and Ladies.* Second Edition. London: T. Cadell, 1769.

——. *An Idea of the Material Universe, Deduced from a Survey of the Solar*

System. London: printed for the author, 1754.
———. *An Introduction to Electricity. In Six Sections*. London: W. Strahan, and T. Cadell, 1770.
———. *Lectures on Select Subjects in Mechanics, Hydrostatics, Pneumatics, and Optics*. London: A. Millar, 1760.
———. *A Plain Method of Determining the Parallax of Venus, by Her Transit over the Sun: and from Thence, by Analogy, the Parallax and Distance of the Sun, and of All the Rest of the Planets. Second Edition*. London: Millar: 1761.
———. *Select Mechanical Exercises: Shewing How to Construct Different Clocks, Orreries, and Sun-dials, on Plain and Easy Principles… To Which is Prefixed, a Short Account of the Life of the Author*. London: W. Strahan and T. Cadell, 1773.
———. *Syllabus of a Course of Lectures on the Most Interesting Parts of Hydrostatics, Hydraulics, Pneumatics, Electricity, and Astronomy*. London: 1770.
———. *Tables and Tracts, Relative to Several Arts and Sciences*. London: A. Millar and T. Cadell, 1767.
———. *The Use of a New Orrery, Made and Described by James Ferguson*. London: printed for the author, 1746.
———. *The Young Gentleman and Lady's Astronomy, Familiarly Explained in Ten Dialogues between Neander and Eudosia. To Which Is Added, The Description and Use of the Globes and Armillary Sphere*. Dublin: Boulter Grierson, 1768.
Ferling, John E. *The Loyalist Mind: Joseph Galloway and the American Revolution*. University Park: Pennsylvania State University Press, 1977.
Fish, Bruce and Becky Durost Fish. *Thomas Paine: Political Writer*. Philadelphia: Chelsea House Publishers, 2000.
Fitzpatrick, John C., ed. *The Writings of George Washington from the Original Manuscript Sources 1745-1799*, vol. 4. Washington, DC: United States Government Printing Office, 1931.
Flemming, Thomas. *1776: Year of Illusions*. New York: W.W. Norton & Company, 1975.
Fletcher, Charlotte Goldsborough. *Cato's Mirania: A Life of Provost Smith*. Lanham, MD: University Press of America, 2002.
Fliegelman, Jay. *Declaring Independence: Jefferson, Natural Language, & the Culture of Performance*. Stanford, CA: Stanford University Press, 1993.
———. *Prodigals and Pilgrims: The American Revolution Against Patriarchal Authority, 1750-1800*. Cambridge: Cambridge University Press, 1982.
Flower, Milton E. *John Dickinson, Conservative Revolutionary*. Charlottesville: University Press of Virginia, 1983.
Foner, Eric. *Tom Paine and Revolutionary America*. New York: Oxford

———, ed. *Thomas Paine: Collected Writings*. New York: Library of America, 1995.
Foner, Philip S., ed. *The Complete Writings of Thomas Paine*. 2 vols. New York: Citadel, 1945.
Foot, Michael, and Isaac Kramnick, eds. *The Thomas Paine Reader*. London: Penguin Books, 1987.
Force, Peter, ed. *American Archives*, 4th ser., 6 vols. New York: Johnson Reprint Corp., 1972.
Ford, Edward. *David Rittenhouse, Astronomer-Patriot*. Philadelphia: University of Pennsylvania Press, 1946.
Ford, Worthington Chauncey, ed. *Journals of the Continental Congress, 1774-1789*. 12 vols. Washington: Government Printing Office, 1906.
———, ed. *Letters of William Lee*, 3 vols. Brooklyn, NY: Historical Printing Club, 1891.
Fortescue, John, ed. *The Correspondence of King George the Third from 1760 to 1783, Vol. III*. London: Macmillan, 1928.
Four Letters on Interesting Subjects. Philadelphia: Styner & Cist, 1776.
[Franklin, Benjamin.] *Plain Truth; or, Serious Considerations on the Present State of the City of Philadelphia, and Province of Pennsylvania, by "a Tradesman of Philadelphia."* Philadelphia, 1747.
Friedenwald, Herbert. "The Continental Congress." *Pennsylvania Magazine of History and Biography* 19 (1895): 197-208.
———. *The Declaration of Independence: An Interpretation and an Analysis*. New York: Macmillan, 1904.
Friedman, Bernard. "The Shaping of Radical Consciousness in Provincial New York." *Journal of American History* 56 (1970): 781-801.
Fruchtman, Jack Jr. *Thomas Paine: Apostle of Freedom*. New York: Four Walls Eight Windows, 1994.
Gardiner, C. Harvey, ed. *A Study in Dissent: The Warren-Gerry Correspondence 1776-1792*. Carbondale: Southern Illinois University Press, 1968.
Gegenheimer, Albert Frank. *William Smith, Educator and Churchman 1727-1803*. Philadelphia: University of Pennsylvania Press, 1943.
Gibbs, F. W. "Itinerant Lecturers in Natural Philosophy." *Ambix* 8 (1960): 111-117.
Gilbert, Felix. "The English Background of American Isolationism in the Eighteenth Century." *William and Mary Quarterly* 1 (1944): 156-158.
Gimbel, Richard. *Thomas Paine: A Bibliographical Checklist of Common Sense*. New Haven: Yale University Press, 1956.

Godbold, E. Stanly, Jr., and Robert H. Woody. *Christopher Gadsden and the American Revolution*. Knoxville: University of Tennessee Press, 1982.

Golden, James, and Edward P. J. Corbett, *The Rhetoric of Blair, Campbell, and Whately*. New York: Holt, Rinehart and Winston, 1968.

Goldsmith, Oliver. *An History of the Earth, and Animated Nature. In Eight Volumes*. London: J. Nourse, 1774.

Gordon, William. *The History of the Rise, Progress, and Establishment of the Independence of the United States of America. In Four Volumes*. London: Dilly and Buckland, 1788.

Gould, David. *Life of Robert Morris, an Eminent Merchant of Philadelphia, a Signer of the Declaration of American Independence, and Superintendent of Finance for the United States, from 1781 to 1784*. Boston: L.W. Kimball, 1834.

Gravlee, Jack, and James R. Irvine, eds. *Pamphlets and the American Revolution: Rhetoric, Politics, Literature, and the Popular Press*. Delmar, NY: Scholars' Facsimiles & Reprints, 1976.

Green, Ashbel. *The Life of Ashbel Green*. New York: R. Carter & Bros., 1849.

Green, James N. "Author-Publisher Relations in America up to 1825." Unpublished essay, presented to the American Antiquarian Society Summer Seminar, 1994.

Greene, Donald J. *Samuel Johnson: Political Writings*, vol. 10. New Haven, CT: Yale University Press, 1977.

Greene, Jack P. *Peripheries and Center: Constitutional Development in the Extended Polities of the British Empire and the United States, 1607-1788*. New York: W.W. Norton, 1986.

Greenman, Jeremiah. *Diary of a Common Soldier in the American Revolution*. Dekalb: Northern Illinois University Press, 1978.

Gribbin, John. *The Scientists: A History of Science Told Through the Lives of Its Greatest Inventors*. New York: Random House, 2002.

Gross, Robert A. *The Minutemen and their World*. New York: Hill and Wang, 1976.

Grundfest, Jerry. *George Clymer: Philadelphia Revolutionary, 1739-1813*. New York: Arno, 1982.

Hall, John. *The Grounds and Reasons of Monarchy Considered..., in "The Oceana" and Other Works of James Harrington*. London, 1771.

Hans, Nicholas. *New Trends in Education in the Eighteenth Century*. New York: Routledge, 1999.

Hanson, Russell L. "'Commons' and 'Commonwealth' at the American Founding: Democratic Republicanism as the New American Hybrid." In *Conceptual Change and the Constitution*, edited by Terence Ball and J. G. A. Pocock. Lawrence: University Press of Kansas, 1989.

Hariman, Robert. *Political Style: The Artistry of Power*. Chicago: University of Chicago Press, 1995.
Haroutunian, Joseph. *Piety versus Morality: The Passing of the New England Theology*. New York: H. Holt and Co., 1932.
Harris, Reginald V. *Charles Inglis: Missionary, Loyalist, Bishop*. Toronto: General Board of Religious Education, 1937.
Harrison, A. W. "Why the Eighteenth Century Dreaded Methodist Enthusiasm." *Proceedings of the Wesley Historical Society* 18 (1931): 40-42.
Hart, Charles Henry. "Colonel John Nixon." *Pennsylvania Magazine of History and Biography* 1 (1877): 188-203.
Hawke, David Freeman. *Benjamin Rush: Revolutionary Gadfly*. New York: Bobbs-Merrill, 1971.
———. *In the Midst of a Revolution*. Philadelphia: University of Pennsylvania Press, 1961.
———. *Paine*. New York: W.W. Norton & Company, 1974.
Heard, Nigel. *Thetford Grammar School*. Burford, UK. 1972.
Hedges, William L. "Telling Off the King: Jefferson's *Summary View* as American Fantasy." *Early American Literature* 22 (1987): 166-175.
Henderson, Ebenezer. *Life of James Ferguson*. London, 1867.
Hibbert, Christopher. *George III: A Personal History*. New York: Basic Books, 1998.
Hill, Christopher. *Puritanism and Revolution*. London: Secker and Warburg, 1958.
Hill, Lisa. *The Passionate Society: The Social, Political, and Moral Thought of Adam Ferguson*. Dordrecht, The Netherlands: Springer, 2006.
Hindle, Brooke. *David Rittenhouse*. Princeton, NJ: Princeton University Press, 1964.
———. *The Pursuit of Science in Revolutionary America 1735-1789*. Chapel Hill: University of North Carolina Press, 1956.
Hobsbawm, E. J. *Primitive Rebels*. New York: W. W. Norton, 1965.
Hoffman, David C. "Paine and Prejudice: Rhetorical Leadership through Perceptual Framing in *Common Sense*." *Rhetoric & Public Affairs* 9 (Fall 2006): 373-410.
Hoffman, Ronald, ed. *Dear Papa, Dear Charley: The Papers of Charles Carroll of Carrollton, 1748-1882*. Chapel Hill: University of North Carolina Press, 2001.
Holmes, J. H. John *Wesley and the Methodist Revolt*. Toronto: Ryerson, 1923.
Hooker, Richard J. "The American Revolution Seen through a Wine Glass." *William and Mary Quarterly*, 3rd ser., 11 (1954): 52-77.
Howell, Wilbur Samuel. "The *Declaration of Independence* and

Eighteenth-Century Logic." *William and Mary Quarterly*, 3rd ser., 18 (1961): 463-484.

——. *Eighteenth-century British Logic and Rhetoric*. Princeton, NJ: Princeton University Press, 1971.

Hudak, Leona M. *Early American Women Printers and Publishers 1639-1820*. Metuchen, NJ: Scarecrow Press, 1978.

Hume, David. *Enquiries Concerning Human Understanding and the Principles of Morals*. Ed. L. A. Selby-Bigge. Oxford: Oxford University Press, 1978.

Hutcheson, Francis. *Essay on the Nature and Conduct of the Passions and Affections, with Illustrations of the Moral Sense*. Dublin, 1728.

——. *Inquiry into the Origins of our Ideas of Beauty and Virtue, in Two Treatises*. Dublin, 1725.

Hutchinson, Peter O. *Diary and Letters of Thomas Hutchinson*, Vol II. New York: Burt Franklin, 1971.

Hyneman, Charles S., and Donald S. Lutz, eds. *American Political Writing during the Founding Era: 1760–1805*. 2 vols. Indianapolis: Liberty Fund, 1983.

Ierley, Merritt. *The Year that Tried Men's Souls: The World of 1776*. South Brunswick: A. S. Barnes, 1977.

[Inglis, Charles.] *The Deceiver Unmasked; or, Loyalty and Interest United: in Answer to a Pamphlet entitled Common Sense, by a Loyal American*. [New York: Samuel Loudon,] 1776.

——. *The True Interest of America Impartially Stated, in Certain St[r]ictures on a Pamphlet Intitled Commons Sense, by 'An American'*. Philadelphia: [James Humphreys, Jr.,] 1776.

Isaac, Rhys. "Dramatizing the Ideology of Revolution: Popular Mobilization in Virginia, 1774-1776." *William and Mary Quarterly*, 3rd ser., 33 (1976): 357-385.

——. *The Transformation of Virginia, 1740-1790*. Chapel Hill: University of North Carolina Press, 1982.

Isaacson, Walter. *Benjamin Franklin: An American Life*. New York: Simon & Schuster, 2003.

Jacobson, David L. "John Dickinson's Fight Against Royal Government, 1764." *William and Mary Quarterly*, 3rd ser., 19 (1962): 64-85.

Jardine, Lisa, and Michael Silverthorne, eds. *Francis Bacon: The New Organon*. Cambridge: Cambridge University Press, 2000.

Jefferson, Thomas. *A Summary View of the Rights of British America. Set Forth in Some Resolutions Intended for the Inspection of the Present Delegates of the People of Virginia, Now in Convention*. Philadelphia: John Dunlap, 1774.

Jensen, Merrill. *The Founding of a Nation: A History of the American Revolution, 1763-1776*. New York: Oxford University Press, 1968.

———. *Tracts of the American Revolution, 1763-1776.* Indianapolis: Hackett, 2003.
Johnson, Samuel. *Dictionary of the English Language*, 4 vols. Whitefriars: Thomas Davidson, 1805 [1776].
Johnston, Henry P., ed. *The Correspondence and Public Papers of John Jay, 1763-1781.* Vol. 1. New York: Burt Franklin, [1890] 1970.
Jolly, Cyril. *The Spreading Flame: The Coming of Methodism to Norfolk 1751-1811.* Dereham, 1972.
Jones, Thomas Firth. *A Pair of Lawn Sleeves: A Biography of William Smith (1727-1803).* Philadelphia: Chilton, 1972.
Jordan, John W. "A Description of the State-House, Philadelphia, in 1774." *Pennsylvania Magazine of History and Biography* 23 (1899): 417-420.
Jordan, Winthrop D. "Familial Politics: Thomas Paine and the Killing of the King." *Journal of American History* 60 (1973): 294-308.
———. *White over Black: American Attitudes toward the Negro, 1550-1812.* Chapel Hill: University of North Carolina Press, 1968.
Kahn, Victoria. *Rhetoric, Prudence, and Skepticism in the Renaissance.* Ithaca, NY: Cornell University Press, 1985.
Kames, Henry Home, Lord. *Elements of Criticism.* 3 vols. London: A. Millar, and Edinburgh: A. Kincaid & J. Bell, 1762.
Kaplan, Sidney, and Emma Nogrady Kaplan. *The Black Presence in the Era of the American Revolution.* Amherst: University of Massachusetts Press, 1989.
Kates, Gary. "From Liberalism to Radicalism: Tom Paine's *Rights of Man.*" *Journal of the History of Ideas* 50 (1989): 569-587.
Kaye, Harvey. *Thomas Paine and the Promise of America.* New York: Hill and Wang, 2005.
Keane, John. "Despotism and Democracy: The Origins and Development of the Distinction between Civil Society and the State, 1750-1850." In *Civil Society and the State: New European Perspectives*, edited by John Keane, 35-71. London: Verso, 1988.
———. *Tom Paine: A Political Life.* New York: Grove, 1995.
Kerber, Linda K. *Women of the Republic: Intellect and Ideology in Revolutionary America.* Chapel Hill: University of North Carolina Press, 1980.
Ketchum, Richard M. *The Winter Soldiers.* New York: Henry Holt & Company, 1975.
King, Henry C., and John R. Millburn. *Geared to the Stars: The Evolution of Planetariums, Orreries, and Astronomical Clocks.* Toronto: University of Toronto Press, 1978.
Kistler, Mark O. "German-American Liberalism and Thomas Paine." *American Quarterly* 14 (1962): 81-91.

Klett, Guy. *Presbyterianism in Colonial Pennsylvania*. Philadelphia: University of Pennsylvania Press, 1937.

Kloppenberg, James T. "The Virtues of Liberalism: Christianity, Republicanism, and Ethics in Early American Political Discourse." *Journal of American History* 74 (1987): 9-33.

Kornfeld, Eve. *Creating an American Culture 1775-1800*. New York: Palgrave, 2001.

Kramer, Lloyd S., ed. *Paine and Jefferson on Liberty*. New York: Continuum, 1988.

Kramer, Michael P. *Imagining Language in America: From the Revolution to the Civil War*. Princeton, NJ: Princeton University Press, 1992.

Kramnick, Isaac, ed. *The Portable Enlightenment Reader*. New York: Penguin, 1995.

———. "Religion and Radicalism: English Political Theory in the Age of the Revolution." *Political Theory* 5 (1977): 505-534.

———. *Republicanism and Bourgeois Radicalism: Political Ideology in Late Eighteenth-Century England and America*. Ithaca: Cornell University Press, 1990.

———. "Republicanism Revisited: The Case of James Burgh." *Proceedings of the American Antiquarian Society* 102 (1992).

———. "Republican Revisionism Revisited." *American Historical Review* 87 (1982): 629-664.

———. "Tom Paine: Radical Democrat." *Democracy* 1 (1981): 127-138.

The Lancaster Almanack, for the Year of Our Lord, 1776; Being Bissextile; or Leap-Year. The Sixteenth Year of the Reign of K. George, III. ...by Anthony Sharp, Philom. Lancaster: Francis Bailey, [1775].

Land, Aubrey C., ed. *William Eddis' Letters from America*. Cambridge, MA: Belknap Press of Harvard University Press, 1969.

Landis, David Bachman. "Robert Bell: Printer." *Lancaster County Historical Society* 12 (1908): 195-202.

Langguth, A. J. *Patriots: The Men Who Started the American Revolution*. New York: Simon and Schuster, 1991.

Larkin, Edward. *Thomas Paine and the Literature of Revolution*. Cambridge: Cambridge University Press, 2005.

Lawton, George. "Matthew Bramble, Tom Paine and John Wesley." *Proceedings of the Wesley Historical Society* 33 (1961): 41-45.

The Lee Papers. 4 vols. New York: New York Historical Society, 1871.

Leeds, John. "Observation of the Transit of Venus, on June 3, 1769. In a Letter from John Leeds, Esquire, Surveyor General of the Province of Maryland, to John Bevis, MD, FRS," 17 June 1769. *Philosophical Transactions*, Royal Society of London (1769): 444-445.

Lender, Mark Edward, and James Kirby Martin. *Drinking in America:*

A History. New York: The Free Press, 1982.
Levere, Trevor H. "Natural Philosophers in a Coffee House: Dissent, Radical Reform and Pneumatic Chemistry." In *Science and Dissent in England, 1688-1945*, edited by Paul Wood, 147-166. Burlington, VT: Ashgate, 2004.
Liell, Scott. *46 Pages: Thomas Paine, Common Sense, and the Turning Point to American Independence.* Philadelphia: Running Press, 2003.
Lillywhite, Bryant. *London Coffee Houses.* London: George Allen and Unwin, 1963.
Lincoln, Anthony. *Some Political and Social Ideas of English Dissent, 1763-1800.* New York: Octagon Books, 1971 [1938].
Lipscomb, Andrew A., and Albert E. Bergh, eds. *The Writings of Thomas Jefferson.* Washington, DC: 1903-1904.
Locke, Jeff. "Construction Details of Rittenhouse Compasses." *Professional Surveyor* (December 2001): 28-34.
Locke, John. *An Essay Concerning Human Understanding.* London: Penguin, 1997 [1690].
———. *Two Treatises of Government and A Letter Concerning Toleration.* Edited by Ian Shapiro. New Haven: Yale University Press, 2003.
Lockridge, Kenneth A. *Literacy in Colonial New England: An Enquiry into the Social Context of Literacy in the Early Modern West.* New York: W.W. Norton, 1974.
Lokken, Roy N. "The Concept of Democracy in Colonial Political Thought." *William and Mary Quarterly* 16 (1959): 568-580.
Loughran, Trish. "Disseminating *Common Sense*: Thomas Paine and the Problem of the Early National Bestseller." *American Literature* 78 (2006): 1-28.
Lowance, Mason, and Georgia B. Bumgardner, eds. *Massachusetts Broadsides of the American Revolution.* Amherst: University of Massachusetts Press, 1976.
Lucas, Stephen E. "Justifying America: The *Declaration of Independence* as a Rhetorical Document." In *American Rhetoric: Context and Criticism*, edited by Thomas W. Benson. Carbondale: Southern Illinois University Press, 1989.
———. *Portents of Rebellion: Rhetoric and Revolution in Philadelphia, 1765-76.* Philadelphia: Temple University Press, 1976.
———. "The Rhetorical Ancestry of the *Declaration of Independence.*" *Rhetoric & Public Affairs* 1 (1998): 143-184.
———. "The Renaissance in American Public Address: Text and Context in Rhetorical Criticism." *Quarterly Journal of Speech* 74 (1988): 241-261.
———. "The Stylistic Artistry of the *Declaration of Independence.*" *Prologue: Quarterly of the National Archives* 22 (1990): 25-43.

Lutnick, Solomon. *The American Revolution and the British Press 1775-1783*. Columbia: University of Missouri Press, 1967.
Lydekker, John Wolfe. *The Life and Letters of Charles Inglis: His Ministry in America and Consecration as First Colonial Bishop, from 1759 to 1787*. London: Society for Promoting Christian Knowledge, 1936.
Lynd, Staughton. *Intellectual Origins of American Radicalism*. New York: Pantheon, 1968.
McCartin, Brian. *Thomas Paine: Common Sense and Revolutionary Pamphleteering*. New York: PowerPlus Books, 2002.
Maccoby, Simon. *English Radicalism, 1762-1785*. London: George Allen & Unwin, 1955.
McConnell, Francis John. *Evangelicals, Revolutionists, and Idealists; Six English Contributors to American Thought and Action*. Port Washington, NY: Kennikat Press, 1972.
McDonough, Daniel J. *Christopher Gadsden and Henry Laurens: The Parallel Lives of Two American Patriots*. Sellinsgrove, PA: Susquehanna University Press, 2000.
McFarland, Thomas. *Originality and Imagination*. Baltimore: Johns Hopkins University Press, 1985.
McLoughlin, William G. "The American Revolution as a Religious Revival: The 'Millennium in One Country.'" *New England Quarterly* 40 (1967): 99-110.
McLeese, Don. *Thomas Paine*. Vero Beach, FL: Rourke, 2004.
McNamara, Martha J. *From Tavern to Courthouse: Architecture and Ritual in American Law, 1658-1860*. Baltimore: The Johns Hopkins University Press, 2004.
Madison, James. "Public Opinion." *National Gazette*. December 19, 1791.
Maier, Pauline. *American Scripture*. New York: Knopf, 1997.
———. "The Beginnings of American Republicanism," in *Development of a Revolutionary Mentality*. Washington, DC: Library of Congress, 1972.
———. *From Resistance to Revolution*. New York: W.W. Norton, 1991.
———. *The Old Revolutionaries: Political Lives in the Age of Samuel Adams*. New York: Knopf, 1980.
———. "Reason and Revolution: The Radicalism of Dr. Thomas Young." *American Quarterly* 28 (1976): 229-249.
Main, Jackson Turner, ed. *Rebel versus Tory; the Crises of the Revolution, 1773-1776*. Chicago: Rand McNally, 1963.
———. *The Social Structure of Revolutionary America*. Princeton: Princeton University Press, 1965.
Margeson, Ian. "Defender of the Atlantic Empire: Reverend William Smith and His Miranian Vision." *Utopian Studies* 16 (2005): 365-392.

Marshall, Christopher. *The Diary of Christopher Marshall: 1774-1776.* Edited by William Duane, Jr. Philadelphia: James Crissy, 1839.

Martin, Benjamin. *An Appendix to the Description and Use of the Globes.* London: B. Martin, 1766.

———. *Bibliotheca Technologica: Or, a Philological Library of Literary Arts and Sciences.* London: John Noon, 1737.

———. *Biographia Philosophica, Being an Account of the Lives, Writings, and Inventions, of the most eminent Philosophers and Mathematicians.* London: W. Owen, 1764.

———. *A Course of Lectures in Natural and Experimental Philosophy, Geography and Astronomy: In Which the Properties, Affections, and Phaenomena of Natural Bodies, Hitherto Discover'd are Exhibited and Explain'd on the Principles of the Newtonian Philosophy.* Reading: J. Newbery et al., 1743.

———. *The Description and Use of both the Globes, the Armillary Sphere, and Orrery.* London: B. Martin, 1765.

———. *The Description and Use of a Case of Mathematical Instruments; Particularly of All the Lines Contained on the Plain Scale, the Sector, the Gunter, and the Proportional Compasses. With a Practical Application.* London: B. Martin, 1771.

———. *The Description and Use of a Graphical Perspective and Microscope, for Drawing All Kinds of Objects in True Perspective, and a Just Proportion of Their Parts, with Readiness and Ease. To Which is Added, a Short Account of an Opaque Solar Microscope.* London: B. Martin, 1771.

———. *The Description and Use of a New Invented Pocket Reflecting Microscope, with a Micrometer.* Chichester: William Lee, and London: John Noon, 1739.

———. *The Description and Use of a New, Portable, Table Air-pump and Condensing Engine. With a Select Variety of Capital Experiments, Which, Together With the Different Parts of the Apparatus and Glasses, Are Illustrated by Upwards of Forty Copper-plate Figures.* London: B. Martin, 1766.

———. *The Description and Use of an Opaque Solar Microscope. In Which All Opaque Bodies, ... Are Shewn in the Greatest Perfection, ... at the Same Time All Transparent Objects Are Also Shewn in a New Light, and in a Manner Peculiar to This Instrument.* London: B. Martin, 1774.

———. *The Description and Use of an Orrery of a New Construction, Representing in the various Parts of its Machinery all the Motions and Phaenomena of the Planetary System; To Which is Subjoin'd a Mathematical Theory for Calculating the Wheel-Work to the Greatest Degree of Exactness.* London: B. Martin, 1771.

———. *The Description and Use of a Proportional Camera Obscura, with a*

Solar Microscope Adapted Thereto. London: B. Martin, 1770.
———. *The Description and Use of a Table-clock upon a New Construction, Going by a Weight Eight Days*. London: B. Martin, 1770.
———. *The Description of a New Universal Microscope, Which Has All the Uses of the Single, Compound, Opaque, and Aquatic Microscopes*. London: B. Martin, 1765.
———. *A Description of the Nature, Construction, and Use of the Torricellian, or Simple Barometer... Also the Theory and Construction of the Compound Barometer*. London: B. Martin, 1766.
———. *Directions for the Use of a New Hydrostatic Balance*. London: B. Martin, 1775.
———. *An Essay on a New Construction, of the Reflecting Telescope, Which by Means of a Scale of Magnifying Powers, Is Made on Universal Perspective*. London: B. Martin, 1775.
———. *An Essay on Electricity: Being an Enquiry into the Nature, Cause and Properties thereof, on the Principles of Sir Isaac Newton's Theory of Vibrating Motion, Light and Fire; ...With Some Observations Relative to the Uses That May Be Made of This Wonderful Power of Nature*. Bath: Leake and Frederick, Gloucester: Raikes, Salisbury: Collins, London: Newbury, 1746.
———. *An Essay on the Nature and Superior Use of Globes, in Conveying the First Principles of Geography and Astronomy to the Minds of Youth; Also a Candid Examination of the Construction and Use of Planispheres, ...and the Nature and Use of the Globular Projection*. London: B. Martin, 1758.
———. *An Essay on the Nature and Wonderful Properties of Island Crystal, Respecting Its Manifold and Unusual Refraction of Light*. London: B. Martin, 1770.
———. *An Essay on Visual Glasses (Vulgarly Called Spectacles), Wherein It Is Shewn, ...That the Common Structure of Those Glasses is Contrary to the Rules of Art, to the Nature of Things, &c. and Very Prejudicial to the Eyes; the Nature of Vision in the Eye Explained, and Glasses of a New Construction Proposed*. London: B. Martin, 1756.
———. *An Explanation of a New Construction and Improvement of the Sea Octant and Sextant, Containing, a ... Method of Adjusting and Rectifying Those Instruments for Use Both at Sea and Land*. London: B. Martin, 1775.
———. *The General Magazine of Arts and Sciences, Philosophical, Philological, Mathematical, and Mechanical*. London: W. Owen, 1755-1765.
———. *Institutions of Astronomical Calculations: Containing, I. A New Set of Solar Tables ...II. A New Set of Lunar Tables, ...III. A General*

———. *Exposition ... of Astronomical Tables.* London: B. Martin, 1765.
———. *An Introduction to the English Language and Learning. In Three Parts.* London: W. Owen, 1754.
———. *Lingua Britannica Reformata: Or, a New Universal English Dictionary.* London: C. Hitch, et al. 1754.
———. *Logarithmologia: or the Whole Doctrine of Logarithms, Common and Logistical, in Theory and Practice. In Three Parts. Part I. The Theory of Logarithms; ...Part II. The Praxis of Logarithms; ...Part III. A Three-fold Canon of Logarithms.* London: J. Hodges, 1740.
———. *The Mariner's Mirror, Part [III.] Being a New and Compendious System of Logarithms.* London: B. Martin, 1772.
———. *The Method of Calculating the Magnifying Power of a Reflecting Telescope, Illustrated by Example. With a General Table.* London: B. Martin, 1771.
———. *Micrographia Nova: or, a New Treatise on the Microscope, and Microscopic Objects. Containing I. The Description and Use of Two Different Reflecting Microscopes, ...II. A Large and Particular Account of All Kinds of Microscopic Objects, ...To Which Is Added, an Account of the Camera Obscura, and the Solar Microscope.* Reading: J. Newbery and C. Micklewright, London: R. Ware and T. Cooper, Oxford: J. Fletcher, Cambridge: W. Thurlbourn, and Salisbury, B. Collins, 1742.
———. *The Natural History of England; or, a Description of Each Particular County, Illustrated by a Map of Each County.* London: W. Owen, 1759-1763.
———. *The New Art of Surveying by the Goniometer; Containing, I. A New Method of Measuring Angles by This New Instrument ... II. The Description and Use of a New Protractor, ... III. The Rationale of Reducing Any Mult[i]angular Figure to a Plain Triangle, ... IV. The Principles of Leveling.* London: B. Martin, 1766.
———. *A New and Compendious System of Optics.* London: James Hodges, 1740.
———. *A New Complete and Universal System or Body of Decimal Arithmetic, Containing, I. The Whole Doctrine of Decimal Numbers, ...V. An Exact and Accurate Canon of Logarithms.* London: J. Noon, 1735.
———. *New Elements of Optics; or, the Theory of the Aberrations, Dissipation, and Colours of Light: of the General and Specific Refractive Powers and Densities of Mediums; the Properties of Single and Compound Lenses: and ...Telescopes and Microscopes.* London: B. Martin, 1759.
———. *A Panegyrick on the Newtonian philosophy, Shewing the Nature and Dignity of the Science.* London: W. Owen, 1749.
———. *Pangeometria; or the Elements of all Geometry.* London: J. Noon,

1739.

———. *Physico-geology: or, a New system of Philosophical Geography. Containing a New and General Description of the Terraqueous Globe. ... The Natural History of the Products ... in Every Country, ... with a New and Accurate Set of Maps.* London: W. Owen, 1769.

———. *A Plain and Familiar Introduction to the Newtonian Experimental Philosophy, In Six Sections, Illustrated by Six Copper-Plates. Designed for the Use of such Gentlemen and Ladies as would acquire a Competent Knowledge of this Science, without Mathematical Learning; And More Especially Those Who Have, or May Attend the Author's Course of Lectures and Experiments on These Subject.* London: W. Owen 1751, 1765.

———. *A Supplement: Containing Remarks on a Rhapsody of Adventures of a Modern Knight-errant in Philosophy.* Bath: Martin, Leake, and Frederick, Gloucester: Raikes, Salisbury: Collins, London: Newbury, 1746.

———. *The Theory of Comets, Illustrated in Four Parts.* London: 1757.

———. *The Theory of Hadley's Quadrant Demonstrated; and from Thence Its Nature, Construction, and Uses Are Fully Shewn. With a Table of the Sun's Declination for Finding the Latitude of the Place. To Which Is Added, a New Construction of the Quadrant.* London: B. Martin at Hadley's Quadrant and Visual Glasses, 1760.

———. *Thermometrum Magnum: or, Grand Standard Thermometer. Expressing All Degrees of Heat and Cold, ...to Which are Adjusted the Celebrated Scales of Sir Isaac Newton, Fahrenheit, De L'Isle, and Reaumur, for Comparing Observations Made in Every Part of the Globe.* London: B. Martin, 1772.

———. *Typographia Naturalis: or, the Art of Printing, or Taking Impressions from Natural Subjects, by Means of Isinglass.* London: B. Martin, 1772.

———. *Venus in the Sun: Being an Explication of the Rationale of that Great Phenomenon; of the Several Methods used by Astronomers for Computing the Quantity and Phases thereof; And of the Manner of applying a Transit of Venus over the Solar Disk, for the Discovery of the Parallax of the Sun; Settling the Theory of that Planet's Motion, and Ascertaining the Dimensions of the Solar System.* London: W. Owen, 1761.

———. *The Young Gentleman and Lady's Philosophy, in a Continued Survey of the Works of Nature and Art; by Way of Dialogue. The Second Edition Corrected.* London: W. Owen, 1772.

———. *The Young Trigonometer's New Guide.* London: B. Martin, 1772.

Mason, Bernard, ed. *The American Colonial Crisis: The Daniel Leonard-John Adams Letters to the Press, 1774-1775.* New York: Harper and Row, 1972.

———. *The Road to Independence: The Revolutionary Movement in New York, 1773-1777.* Lexington: University of Kentucky Press, 1966.
Massey, James C., ed. *Two Centuries of Philadelphia Architectural Drawings.* Philadelphia: Society of Architectural Historians and the Philadelphia Museum of Art, 1964.
Matthews, Albert. "Thomas Paine and the Declaration of Independence." *Proceedings of the Massachusetts Historical Society* 43 (1910): 241-253.
The Mechanicks in Union, and their associates, are earnestly requested to attend the general committee of mechanicks in union, at Mechanick Hall, on Monday evening next, to consult with them on Business of Importance. By order of the committee. Nathaniel Tylee, Chairman. New-York, April 12, 1776. God and the Righteous agree that all the Good should be Free. Keep your watch light burning. Mechanicks. New York: 1776.
Meranze, Michael, ed. *Benjamin Rush: Essays Literary, Moral and Philosophical.* Schenectady: Union College Press, 1988.
Merriam, Charles E. "The Political Theories of Thomas Paine." *Political Science Quarterly* 14 (1899): 389-403.
Metzger, Charles H. *Catholics and the American Revolution, a Study in Religious Climate.* Chicago: Loyola University Press, 1962.
Mevers, Frank C., ed. *The Papers of Josiah Bartlett.* Hanover, NH: University Press of New England, 1979.
Middlekauff, Robert. *The Glorious Cause.* London: Oxford University Press, 1982.
[Middleton, Henry.] *The True Merits of a Late Treatise, Printed in America, Intitled, Common Sense, Clearly Pointed Out. Addressed to the inhabitants of America. By a late member of the Continental Congress, a native of a republican state.* London: W. Nicoll, 1776.
Millburn, John R. "Benjamin Martin and the Royal Society." *Notes and Records of the Royal Society of London* 28 (1973): 15-23.
———. "The London Evening Courses of Benjamin Martin and James Ferguson." *Annals of Science* 40 (1983): 437-455.
———. *Wheelwright of the Heavens: The Life and Work of James Ferguson, FRS.* London: Vade-Mecum, 1988.
Miller, John C. *Origins of the American Revolution.* Boston: Little Brown & Company, 1943.
———. *Sam Adams, Pioneer in Propaganda.* Stanford, CA: Stanford University Press, 1964.
Mires, Charlene. *Independence Hall in American Memory.* Philadelphia: University of Pennsylvania Press, 2002.
Mitchell, Samuel Alfred. "Astronomy during the Early Years of the American Philosophical Society." *Proceedings of the American*

Philosophical Society 86 (1942): 13-21.

Monaghan, E. Jennifer. *A Common Heritage: Noah Webster's Blue-Back Speller*. Hamden: Archon Books, 1983.

———. "Literacy Instruction and Gender in Colonial New England." In *Reading in America: Literature & Social History*, edited by Cathy N. Davidson, 53-80. Baltimore: Johns Hopkins University Press, 1989.

Moody, James. *Lieutenant James Moody's Narrative of his Exertions and Sufferings*. New York: Arno, 1968.

Morgan, David T. and William J. Schmidt, eds. *North Carolinians in the Continental Congress*. Winston-Salem, NC: John F. Blair, 1976.

Morgan, Edmund S. *Benjamin Franklin*. New Haven: Yale University Press, 2002.

———. *The Birth of the Republic, 1763-89*. Chicago: University of Chicago Press, 1992.

———. *Inventing the People: The Rise of Popular Sovereignty in England and America*. New York: Norton, 1989.

———. "The Puritan Ethic and the American Revolution." *William and Mary Quarterly*, 3rd ser., 24 (1967): 36-41.

Morgan, Edmund S., and Helen M. Morgan. *Stamp Act Crisis: Prologue to Revolution*. Chapel Hill: University of North Carolina Press, 1953.

Morris, Anne Cary, ed. *The Diary and Letters of Gouverneur Morris*. Vol. 1. New York: Charles Scribner's Sons, 1888.

Morris, Richard B., ed. *John Jay, The Making of a Revolutionary*. New York: Harper & Row, 1817.

Morton, A. Q. "Lectures on Natural Philosophy in London, 1750-1765: S. C. T. Demainbray (1710-1782) and the 'Inattention' of his Countrymen," *British Journal of the History of Science* 23 (1990): 411-434.

Nash, Gary B. "The Transformation of Urban Politics, 1700-1765." *Journal of American History* 60 (1973): 618-19.

Neeser, Robert Wilden, ed. *The Despatches of Molyneux Shuldham: Vice-Admiral of the Blue and Commander-in-Chief of his Britannic Majesty's Ships in North America*. New York: Naval History Society, 1913.

Nelson, Craig. *Thomas Paine: Enlightenment, Revolution, and the Birth of Modern Nations*. New York: Viking, 2006.

Newcomb, Benjamin H. *Franklin and Galloway: A Political Partnership*. New Haven, CT: Yale University Press, 1972.

Newton, Isaac, Sir. *Mathematical Principles of Natural Philosophy*. [By Sir Isaac Newton, ... Translated into English, and illustrated with a commentary, by Robert Thorp. Volume the first.] London: W. Strahan and T. Cadell, 1777.

———. *Opticks: or, a Treatise of the Reflections, Refractions, Inflections and Colours of Light. The fourth edition, corrected*. London: William Innys, 1730.
Niles, H. *Principles and Acts of the Revolution in America*. Baltimore: William Ogden Niles, 1822.
Oberholtzer, Ellis Paxson. *The Literary History of Philadelphia*. Philadelphia: G. W. Jacobs, 1906.
———. *Robert Morris: Patriot and Financier*. New York: Macmillan, 1903.
O'Gorman, Frank. "The Paine Burnings of 1792-1793." *Past & Present*, no. 193, (November 2006) 111-156.
Jacobson, David Louis. *John Dickinson and the Revolution in Pennsylvania, 1764-1776*. Berkeley: University of California Press, 1965.
Oldys, Francis [George Chalmers]. *The Life of Thomas Pain, The Author of Rights of Men* [sic], *with a Defence of His Writings*. London: John Stockdale, 1791.
Ong, Walter J. *Rhetoric, Romance, and Technology*. Ithaca, NY: Cornell University Press, 1971.
Order of Procession, in Honor of the Establishment of the Constitution of the United States. To parade precisely at eight o'clock in the morning, of Friday, the 4th of July, 1788. Philadelphia: Hall and Sellers, [1788]. HSP/LCP.
Paine, Thomas. *Common Sense*. Edited by Edward Larkin. Peterborough, ON: Broadview Press, 2004.
———. *Common Sense*. New York, NY: Bantam Dell, 2004.
———. *Common Sense and Other Writings*. Edited by Gordon S. Wood and George W. Boudreau. New York : Modern Library, 2003.
———. *Common Sense, Rights of Man, and Other Essential Writings of Thomas Paine*. New York: Signet Classic, 2003.
———. *Common Sense and Related Writings*. Edited by Thomas P. Slaughter. Boston: Bedford/St. Martin's, 2001.
———. *Common Sense; & The Rights of Man*. Edited by Tony Benn. London: Phoenix, 2000.
———. *Political Writings*. Edited by Bruce Kuklick. Cambridge and New York: Cambridge University Press, 2000.
———. *Rights of Man; Common Sense; and Other Political Writings*. Edited by Mark Philip. Oxford and New York: Oxford University Press, 1995.
———. *Selected Works: Common Sense; The American Crisis; The Age of Reason*. Edited by Moncure Daniel Conway. Franklin Center, PA: Franklin Library, 1979.
Palmer, R. R. *The Age of the Democratic Revolution*. 2 vols. Princeton, NJ: Princeton University Press, 1959-65.
———. "Notes on the Use of the Word 'Democracy,' 1789-1799."

Political Science Quarterly 68 (1953): 203-226.

Passmore, John. *The Perfectability of Man.* Indianapolis: Liberty Fund, 2000.

Pattee, Fred Lewis, ed. *Poems of Philip Freneau: Poet of the American Revolution*, vol. 3. Princeton, NJ: Princeton University Library, 1907.

Payne, Ernest A. "Tom Paine: Preacher." *The Times Literary Supplement*, May 31, 1947.

Peach, Bernard. *Richard Price and the Ethical Foundations of the American Revolution.* Durham, NC: Duke University Press, 1979.

Peek, George A., ed. *The Political Writings of John Adams: Representative Selections.* Indianapolis: Bobbs-Merrill, 1954.

Penniman, Howard. "Thomas Paine: Democrat," *American Political Science Review* 37 (1943): 244-262.

Pennsylvania. *Minutes of the Provincial Council of Pennsylvania, From the Organization to the Termination of the Proprietary Government.* 10. Harrisburg, PA: Theo. Fenn, 1852.

———. *Votes and Proceedings of the House of Representatives of the Province of Pennsylvania* (1767-1776). Philadelphia: R. Aitken, 1777.

———. *Votes and Proceedings of the House of Representatives of the Province of Pennsylvania. Beginning the Fourteenth Day of October, 1767. Volume the Sixth.* Philadelphia: Henry Miller, 1776.

Pennsylvania Assembly. *Anno Regni Georgii III. Regis, Magnae Britanniae, Franciae Y Hiberniae Decimo Sexto. At a General Assembly of the Province of Pennsylvania, begun and Holden at Philadelphia, the fourteenth day of October, Anno Domin 1775, in the sixteenth year of the reign of our sovereign Lord George III, by the Grace of God, of Great Britain, France and Ireland, King, Defender of the Faith, &c. And from thence continued by adjournments to the sixth of April, 1776.* Philadelphia: Hall and Sellers, 1776.

———. *Votes of Assembly.* Pennsylvania Archives, 8th ser., 8. Harrisburg, PA, 1935.

Perelman, Chaim, and L. Olbrechts-Tyteca. *The New Rhetoric: A Treatise on Argumentation.* Notre Dame, IN: Notre Dame University Press, 1969.

Persons, Stow. "The Cyclical Theory of History in Eighteenth-Century America." *American Quarterly* 6 (1954): 147-163.

Peterson, Merrill, D. *Thomas Jefferson: Writings.* New York: Library of America, 1984.

The Philadelphia Newest Almanack, for the Year of our Lord 1776, Being Leap Year.... By Timothy Telescope, Esq. Philadelphia: R. Aitken, [1775].

Picard, Liza. *Dr. Johnson's London: Coffee-Houses and Climbing Boys,*

Medicine, Toothpaste and Gin, Poverty and Press-Gangs, Freakshows and Female Education. New York: St. Martin's, 2000.

Pierce, Kara. "A Revolutionary Masquerade: The Chronicles of James Rivington." *Binghamton Journal of History* (Spring 2006). State University of New York at Binghamton.

Plomer, H. R., G. H. Bushnell, and E. R. McC. Dix. *A Dictionary of the Printers and Booksellers Who Were at Work in England, Scotland, and Ireland from 1726 to 1775.* London: The Bibliographical Society, 1968.

Plumb, J. H. *The Development of a Revolutionary Mentality.* Washington, DC: Library of Congress, 1972.

———. *In the Light of History.* Boston: Houghton Mifflin, 1973.

———. "The Public, Literature and the Arts in the Eighteenth Century," in *The Triumph of Culture: Eighteenth Century Perspectives*, edited by Paul Fritz and David Williams. Toronto: A. M. Hakkert, 1972.

Pocock, J. G. A. *The Machiavellian Moment: Florentine Political Thought and the Atlantic Republican Tradition.* Princeton, NJ: Princeton University Press, 1975.

———. *Politics, Language, and Time: Essays on Political Thought and History.* New York: Atheneum, 1971.

———, ed. *Three British Revolutions, 1641, 1688, 1776.* Princeton, NJ: Princeton University Press, 1980.

———. "Virtue and Commerce in the Eighteenth Century." *Journal of Interdisciplinary History* 3 (1972): 119-134.

Pollak, Michael. "The Performance of the Wooden Printing Press." *The Library Quarterly* 42 (1972): 218-64.

Poole, Steve. *The Politics of Regicide in England, 1760-1850.* Manchester, UK: Manchester University Press, 2000.

Poor Richard Improved: Being an Almanack and Ephemeris of the Motions of the Sun and Moon; the True Places and Aspects of the Planets; the Rising and Setting of the Sun, and the Rising, Setting, and Southing of the Moon, for the Year of our Lord 1776. Being Bissextile or Leap-Year ... Fitted to the Latitude of Forty Degrees, and a Meridian of Near Five Hours West from London; but May, without Sensible Error, Serve All the Northern Colonies. By Richard Saunders, philom. Philadelphia: Hall and Sellers, [1775].

Poor Will's Almanack, for the Year of Our Lord, 1776; Being Bissextile, or Leap-year, and 16th Year of the King's Reign, till October 26. Philadelphia: Joseph Crukshank, [1775].

Poulakos, *Sophistical Rhetoric in Classical Greece.* Columbia, SC: University of South Carolina Press, 1995.

Powell, J. H. "Speech of John Dickinson Opposing the *Declaration of*

Independence, 1 July, 1776." *Pennsylvania Magazine of History and Biography* 65 (1941): 458-481.
Price, Mary Bell and Lawrence M. Price. *The Publication of English Humaniora in Germany in the Eighteenth Century.* Berkeley and Los Angeles: University of California Press, 1955.
Price, Richard. "A Letter from Richard Price, DD, FRS, to Benjamin Franklin, LLD, FRS, on the Effect of the Aberration of Light on the Time of a Transit of Venus over the Sun," 20 December 1770. *Philosophical Transactions*, Royal Society of London, (1770): 536-540.
——. *Observations on the Nature of Civil Liberty, the Principles of Government, and the Justice and Policy of the War with America. To Which is added, an Appendix, containing a State of the National Debt, an Estimate of the Money Drawn from the Public by the Taxes, and an Account of the National Income and Expenditure since the Last War.* Philadelphia: John Dunlap; Boston: T. & J. Fleet; New-York: S. Loudon; Charleston: D. Bruce, 1776.
Priestley, Joseph. *A Course of Lectures on Oratory and Criticism.* London: J. Johnson, 1777 [1762].
——. *An Essay on the First Principles of Government; and on the Nature of Political, Civil, and Religious Liberty.* London: J. Dodsley, T. Cadell, and J. Johnson, 1768.
Pütz, Manfred. *A Concordance to Thomas Paine's Common Sense and the American Crisis.* New York: Garland, 1989.
Rakove, Jack N. *The Beginnings of National Politics: An Interpretive History of the Continental Congress.* New York: Knopf, 1979.
Ramsay, David. *The History of the American Revolution.* 2 vols. Philadelphia: R. Aitken & Son, 1789.
——. *The History of South-Carolina: From Its First Settlement in 1670, to the Year 1808.* 2 vols. Charleston: David Longworth, 1809.
——. *Memoirs of the Life of Martha Laurens Ramsay.* Boston: Crocker and Brewster, 1827.
Randolph, Edmund. *History of Virginia.* Edited by Arthur Shaffer. Charlottesville: University Press of Virginia, 1970.
Read, William T. *Life and Correspondence of George Read, a Signer of the Declaration of Independence.* Philadelphia: J. B. Lippincott & Co., 1870.
Reid, Thomas. *An Inquiry into the Human Mind on the Principles of Common Sense.* London and Edinburgh: Millar, Kincaid & Bell, 1764.
Rhodehamel, John, ed. *The American Revolution.* New York: The Library of America, 2001.
Rice, Howard C., Jr. *The Rittenhouse Orrery: Princeton's Eighteenth-Century Planetarium, 1767-1954.* Princeton, NJ: Princeton

University Library, 1954.
Rice, John. *An Introduction to the Art of Reading with Energy and Propriety* (1765). Menston, UK: Scolar Press, 1969.
Richards, I. A. *The Philosophy of Rhetoric*. New York: Oxford University Press, 1936.
Richardson, Lyon N. *A History of Early American Magazines, 1741-1789*. New York: Octagon, 1966.
Richetti, John J. *Philosophical Writing: Locke, Berkeley, Hume*. Cambridge, MA: Harvard University Press, 1983.
Richey, Russell E. "The Origins of British Radicalism: The Changing Rationale for Dissent." *Eighteenth-Century Studies* 7 (1973-74): 179-192.
Rickman, Thomas Clio. *The Life of Thomas Paine*. London: Rickman, 1819.
Ricord, Frederick W. and William Nelson, eds. *Documents Relating to the Colonial History of the State of New Jersey*. Newark, 1886.
Robson, David W. *Educating Republicans: The College in the Era of the American Revolution, 1750-1800*. Westport, CT: Greenwood Press, 1985.
Rogers, Alan, and Alan Lawson, eds. *From Revolution to Republic: A Documentary Reader*. Cambridge, MA: Schenkman, 1976.
Rorabaugh, W. J. *The Alcoholic Republic: An American Tradition*. New York: Oxford University Press, 1979.
Rosenfeld, Richard N. *American Aurora*. New York: St. Martin's Press, 1997.
Rothenberg, Molly Anne. "Parasiting America: The Radical Function of Heterogeneity in Thomas Paine's Early Writings." *Eighteenth-Century Studies* 25 (1992): 331-351.
Rothermund, Dietmar. *The Layman's Progress: Religious and Political Experience in Colonial Pennsylvania, 1740-1770*. Philadelphia: University of Pennsylvania Press, 1961.
Royster, Charles. *A Revolutionary People at War: The Continental Army and American Character, 1775-1783*. Chapel Hill: University of North Carolina Press, 1979.
Rudé, George. *The Crowd in History: A Study of Popular Disturbances in France and England, 1730-1848*. London: Lawrence and Wishart, 1981.
———. *Wilkes and Liberty: A Social Study of 1763 to 1774*. Oxford: Clarendon Press, 1962.
Rufus, W. Carl. "David Rittenhouse—Pioneer American Astronomer." *The Scientific Monthly* 26 (1928): 506-513.
Rush, Benjamin. *An Address to the Inhabitants of the British Settlements in America, upon Slave-keeping*. By a Pennsylvanian. Philadelphia: John Dunlap, 1773.
Rusticus. *Remarks on a Late Pamphlet Entitled Plain Truth*.

Philadelphia: John Dunlap, 1776.
Rutland, Robert A., ed. *The Papers of George Mason 1725-1792*. 3 vols. Chapel Hill: University of North Carolina Press, 1970.
Rutland, Robert A., and Thomas A. Mason, eds. *The Papers of James Madison*, vol. 14. Charlottesville: University Press of Virginia, 1983.
Ryden, George Herbert, ed. *Letters to and from Caesar Rodney 1756-1784*. Philadelphia: University of Pennsylvania Press, 1933.
Ryerson, R. A. "Political Mobilization and the American Revolution: The Resistance Movement in Philadelphia, 1765 to 1776." *William and Mary Quarterly*, 3rd ser., 31 (1974): 565-588.
Salinger, Sharon V. *Taverns and Drinking in Early America*. Baltimore: The Johns Hopkins University Press, 2002.
Saunders, Richard [pseud.]. *The English Apollo: or, Useful Companion: Assisting all Persons In the right Understanding the Science of Time, Past, Present, and to Come. Particularly Applied to this Present Year 1776; Being the Bissextile, or Leap-Year.* London: George Hawkins, 1776.
Saunders, William L., ed. *The Colonial Records of North Carolina, Vol. X*. Raleigh, NC: Josephus Daniels, 1890.
Scharf, J. Thomas. *History of Maryland from the Earliest Period to the Present Day*. 3 vols. Hatboro, PA: Tradition Press, 1967 [1879].
Scharf, J. Thomas, and Thompson Westcott. *History of Philadelphia*. 3 vols. Philadelphia: L.H. Everts, 1884.
Schiappa, Edward. *The Beginnings of Rhetorical Theory in Ancient Greece*. New Haven, CT: Yale University Press, 1999.
Schiff, Stacy. *A Great Improvisation: Franklin, France, and the Birth of America*. New York: Henry Holt, 2005.
Schlesinger, Arthur M. *Prelude to Independence: The Newspaper War on Britain, 1764-1776*. Boston: Northeastern University Press, 1980.
Schutz, John A. and Douglass Adair, eds. *The Spur of Fame: Dialogues of John Adams and Benjamin Rush, 1805-1813*. San Marino, CA: Huntington Library, 1966.
Scott, John Anthony. *Trumpet of a Prophecy: Revolutionary America 1763-1783*. New York: Alfred A. Knopf, 1969.
Scribner, Robert L. and Brent Tarter, eds. *Revolutionary Virginia: The Road to Independence, A Documentary Record*. Charlottesville: University Press of Virginia, 1979.
Seaman, John W. "Thomas Paine: Ransom, Civil Peace, and the Natural Right to Welfare." *Political Theory* 16 (1988): 120-142.
Selsam, J. Paul. *The Pennsylvania Constitution of 1776: A Study in Revolutionary Democracy*. Philadelphia: University of

Pennsylvania Press, 1936.
Semmel, Bernard. *The Methodist Revolution*. New York: Basic Books: 1973.
Seymour, David. "Thetford Grammar School: The First Eight Hundred Years." In *Thetford: Antiq Burg*. Thetford, UK: Leaf (1985): 25-27.
Shallhope, R. "Republicanism and Early American Historiography," *William and Mary Quarterly* 39 (1982): 334-356.
Sharman, Cecil W. *George Fox and the Quakers*. London: Friends United Press, 1991.
Shaw, Peter. *American Patriots and the Rituals of Revolution*. Cambridge, MA: Harvard University Press, 1981.
Shepherd, Thomas. *The Sincere Convert*. London, 1641.
Sheridan, Thomas. *A Course of Lectures on Elocution: Together with Two Dissertations on Language; and Some Other Tracts Relative to Those Subjects*. London: W. Strahan, 1762.
———. *Lectures of the Art of Reading*. London, 1775.
Sherwin, William. *Memoirs of the Life of Thomas Paine*. 1819.
Shipton, Clifford K. and James E. Mooney. *National Index of American Imprints through 1800: The Short Title Evans*. 2 vols. Worcester, MA: American Antiquarian Society, 1969.
Showman, Richard K., ed. *The Papers of General Nathanael Greene*. Vol. 1. Chapel Hill: University of North Carolina Press, 1976.
Shy, John W. *A People Numerous and Armed: Reflections on the Military Struggle for American Independence*. Ann Arbor: University of Michigan Press, 1990.
Silver, Rollo G. *The American Printer, 1787-1825*. Charlottesville: University Press of Virginia, 1967.
Silverman, Kenneth. *A Cultural History of the American Revolution*. New York: Crowell, 1976.
Simmons, R.C., and P.D.G. Thomas, eds. *Proceedings and Debates of the British Parliaments Respecting North America 1754-1783, Vol. VI*. White Plains, NY: Kraus International, 1987.
Simon, Grant Miles. "Houses and Early Life in Philadelphia," *Transactions, American Philosophical Society* 43 (1953): 280-288.
Simpson, David. *The Politics of American English, 1776-1850*. New York: Oxford University Press, 1986.
Skinner, Quentin. "Conventions and the Understanding of Speech Acts." *The Philosophical Quarterly* 20 (1970): 118-138.
———. "Hermeneutics and the Role of History." *New Literary History* 7 (1975): 209-232.
———. "History and Ideology in the English Revolution." *The Historical Journal* 8 (1965): 151-178.
———. "The Ideological Context of Hobbes's Political Thought." *The*

Historical Journal 9 (1966): 286-317.
———. "The Limits of Historical Explanations." *Philosophy* 41 (1966): 199-215.
———. "Meaning and Understanding in the History of Ideas." *History and Theory* 8 (1969): 3-53.
———. "Motives, Intentions and the Interpretation of Texts." *New Literary History* 3 (1972): 393-408.
———. "On Performing and Explaining Linguistic Actions." *The Philosophical Quarterly* 21(1971): 1-21.
———. "The Origins of the Calvinist Theory of Revolution." In *After the Reformation*, edited by Barbara Malament, 309-330. Philadelphia: University of Pennsylvania Press, 1980.
———. *Reason and Rhetoric in the Philosophy of Hobbes*. Cambridge: Cambridge University Press, 1997.
———. "Some Problems in the Analysis of Political Thought and Action." *Political Theory* 2 (1974): 277-303.
Smith, Adam. *Lectures on Rhetoric and Belles Lettres, delivered in the University of Glasgow by Adam Smith, Reported by a Student in 1762-3*. Edited by John M. Lothian. Carbondale: Southern Illinois Press, 1971.
———. *The Theory of Moral Sentiments*. Edited by D. D. Raphael and A. L. Macfie. Oxford: Clarendon Press, 1976.
Smith, Frank. "The Date of Thomas Paine's First Arrival in America." *American Literature* 3 (1931): 317-318.
———. "New Light on Thomas Paine's First Year in America, 1775." *American Literature* 1 (1930): 347-371.
Smith, Horace W. *Life of Rev. William Smith, D.D., First Provost of the College of Philadelphia*. Philadelphia: Ferguson Bros., 1880.
Smith, Jeffrey. *Printers and Press Freedom: The Ideology of Early American Journalism*. Oxford: Oxford University Press, 1988.
Smith, Page. *A New Age Now Begins*. New York: McGraw-Hill, 1976.
Smith, Paul H., ed. *Letters of Delegates to Congress 1774-1789*, 26 vols. Washington: Library of Congress, 1976-2000.
Smith, Richard. "Diary of Richard Smith in the Continental Congress, 1775-1776. Part I." *The American Historical Review* 1 (1896): 288-310.
———. "Diary of Richard Smith in the Continental Congress, 1775-1776. Part II." *The American Historical Review* 1 (1896): 493-516.
Smith, Verena, ed., "The Town Book of Lewes 1702-1837." *Sussex Record Society* 69 (1972).
Smith, William, et al. "Account of the Transit of Venus Over the Sun's Disk, as Observed at Norriton in the County of Philadelphia, and Provincee of Pennsylvania, June 3, 1769." *Philosophical Transactions* 59 (1769): 289-326.

Smith, William. *A General Idea of the College of Mirania; With a Sketch of the Method of Teaching Science and Religion, in the several Classes.* New York: J. Parker and W. Weyman, 1753.

———. *An Oration in Memory of General Montgomery, and of the Officers and Soldiers, Who Fell with Him, December 31, 1775, before Quebec; Drawn up (and Delivered February 19th, 1776.) at the Desire of the Honorable Continental Congress.* Philadelphia: John Dunlap; New York: John Anderson; Newport: Solomon Southwick; Norwich: Robertsons and John Trumbull, 1776.

Sollors, Werner, ed. *The Interesting Narrative of the Life of Olaudah Equiano, or Gustavus Vassa, the African, Written by Himself.* New York: W.W. Norton & Co., 2001.

South Carolina. *Journal of the Provincial Congress of South Carolina, 1776.* London: J. Almon, 1776.

Sparks, Jared. *The Life of Gouvernor Morris*, 3 vols. Boston: 1832.

Spawn, Willman and Carol. "R. Aitken: Colonial Printer of Philadelphia." *Graphic Arts Review* (January-February 1961).

Stahlman, William D. "Astrology in Colonial America: An Extended Query." *William and Mary Quarterly*, 3rd ser., 13 (1956): 551-563.

Steele, Richard, and Joseph Addison. *Selections from the Tatler and the Spectator.* New York: Penguin, 1982.

Steiner, Bernard C. *The Life and Correspondence of James McHenry.* Cleveland: Burrows Brothers, 1907.

Stephans, Hildegard, ed. *The Thomas Paine Collection of Richard Gimbel in the Library of the American Philosophical Society.* Wilmington, DE: Scholarly Resources, 1976.

Stevens, B. F., ed. *Facsimiles of Manuscripts in European Archives Relating to America, 1773-1783.* 25 vols. London, 1889-1898.

Stewart, Larry. "The Public Culture of Radical Philosophers in Eighteenth-Century London." In *Science and Dissent in England, 1688-1945*, edited by Paul Wood, 113-130. Burlington, VT: Ashgate, 2004.

———. *The Rise of Public Science: Rhetoric, Technology, and Natural Philosophy in Newtonian Britain, 1660-1750.* Cambridge: Cambridge University Press, 1992.

Stiles, Ezra. *The Literary Diary of Ezra Stiles.* 3 vols. New York: Charles Scribner's Sons, 1901.

Stillé, Charles J. "Pennsylvania and the *Declaration of Independence.*" *Pennsylvania Magazine of History and Biography* 13 (1889): 385-430.

Stillman, Samuel. *Death, the Last Enemy, Destroyed by Christ. A Sermon, Preached March 27, 1776, before the Honorable Continental Congress; on the Death of the HonorableSamuel Ward, Esq. One of the Delegates from the Colony of Rhode-Island, Who Died of the*

Small-pox, in This City. Philadelphia: Joseph Crukshank, 1776.

Stone, Frederick D. "How the Landing of Tea was Opposed in Philadelphia by Colonel William Bradford and Others in 1773." *Pennsylvania Magazine of History and Biography* 15 (1891): 385-394.

Stone, William L., ed. *Journal of Captain Pausch.* New York: Arno, 1971.

Stout, Harry S. "Religion, Communication, and the Ideological Origins of the American Revolution." *William and Mary Quarterly* 34 (1977): 519-41.

Stout, Neil R. *The Perfect Crisis: The Beginning of the Revolutionary War.* New York: NYU Press, 1976.

Stowell, Marion Barber. *Early American Almanacs: The Colonial Weekday Bible.* New York: Burt Franklin, 1977.

Swift, Jonathon. *A Modest Proposal.* London, 1729.

Syrett, Harold C., ed. *The Papers of Alexander Hamilton.* New York: Columbia University Press, 1961.

Tallmadge, Benjamin. *Memoir of Colonel Benjamin Tallmadge.* New York: Arno, 1968.

Taylor, Robert J., ed. *Papers of John Adams.* Cambridge, MA: Belknap Press of Harvard University Press, 1979.

Teets, Donald A. "Transits of Venus and the Astronomical Unit." *Mathematics Magazine* 76 (2003): 335-348.

Thayer, Theodore. *Pennsylvania Politics and the Growth of Democracy, 1740-1776.* Harrisburg: Pennsylvania Historical and Museum Commission, 1953.

Thomas, D. O. *Richard Price and America.* Aberystwyth: Thomas, 1975.

Thomas, Isaiah. *The History of Printing in America.* 2 vols. Worcester, MA: Isaiah Thomas, 1810.

The Thomas Paine Collection at Thetford: An Analytical Catalogue. Norwich, UK: Norfolk County Library, 1979.

Thompson, E. P. *The Making of the English Working Class.* Harmondsworth, UK: Penguin, 1968.

Thompson, Peter. *Rum Punch and Revolution: Taverngoing & Public Life in Eighteenth-Century Philadelphia.* Philadelphia: University of Pennsylvania Press, 1999.

Tilghman, Oswald, ed. *Memoir of Lieut. Col. Tench Tilghman.* Albany: J. Munsell, 1876.

Trustees of the University of Pennsylvania. *Minute Books of the College, Academy and Charitable School, and University of Pennsylvania,* Vol. 2 (1768-1779, 1789-1791).

Tucker, Josiah. *A Series of Answers to Certain Popular Objections, against Separating from the Rebellious Colonies, and Discarding Them*

Entirely. Gloucester, 1776.

———. *The True Interest of Great-Britain, Set Forth in Regard to the Colonies; and the Only Means of Living in Peace and Harmony with Them*. Philadelphia, 1776.

Tully, James, ed. *Meaning and Context: Quentin Skinner and his Critics*. Princeton, NJ: Princeton University Press, 1988.

Tuveson, Ernest Lee. *Redeemer Nation: The Idea of America's Millennial Role*. Chicago: University of Chicago Press, 1968.

Tyler, Moses Coit. *History of American Literature 1607-1765*. Ithaca, NY: Cornell University Press, 1949.

———. *The Literary History of the American Revolution 1763-1783*. Vol. I. New York: G.P. Putnam's Sons, 1898.

The Universal Almanack, for the Year of our Lord 1776; Being Bissextile or Leap-Year. (The Sixteenth Year of the Reign of King George III ... The ingenious D. Rittenhouse, A.M. has again favour'd us with the calculations. Fitted to the latitude of forty degrees north, and near five hours west from London. Philadelphia: James Humphreys, Jr., [1775].

Van der Weyde, William M. *Life and Works of Thomas Paine*. 10 vols. New Rochelle, NY: Thomas Paine National Historic Association, 1925.

Vail, John. *Thomas Paine*. New York: Chelsea House Publishers, 1990.

Vale, Gilbert. *The Life of Thomas Paine*. 1841.

Ver Steeg, Clarence L. *Robert Morris: Revolutionary Financier*. Philadelphia: University of Pennsylvania Press, 1954.

Vickers, Brian, ed. *English Science, Bacon to Newton*. Cambridge: Cambridge University Press, 1987.

———. *In Defense of Rhetoric*. Oxford: Clarendon Press, 1988.

Vickers, John A. *The Story of Canterbury Methodism (1750-1961)*. Harbledown, UK: St. Peter's Methodist Trust, 1961.

Vincent, Bernard. *Thomas Paine ou la religion de la liberte*. Paris: Aubier, 1987.

———. *The Transatlantic Republican: Thomas Paine and the Age of Revolutions*. Amsterdam: Rodopi, 2005.

Waldstreicher, David A., *In the Midst of Perpetual Fetes: The Making of American Nationalism 1776-1820*. Chapel Hill: University of North Carolina Press, 1997.

———. "Rites of Rebellion, Rites of Assent: Celebrations, Print Culture, and the Origins of American Nationalism." *The Journal of American History* 82 (1995): 37-61.

Wall, A. J. "The Burning of the Pamphlet 'The Deceiver Unmasked' in 1776." *The American Book Collector* 3 (1926): 106-111.

Wallace, John William. *An Old Philadelphian, Colonel William*

Bradford, *The Patriot Printer of 1776. Sketches of His Life*. Philadelphia: Sherman & Co., 1884.
Wallis, Ruth. "John Bevis, MD, FRS (1695-1771): Astronomer Loyal." *Notes and Records of the Royal Society of London*, 36 (1982): 211-225.
Walmsley, Peter. *Locke's Essay and the Rhetoric of Science*. Lewisburg, PA: Bucknell University Press, 2003.
Walsh, John D. "Methodism and the Mob in the Eighteenth Century." In *Popular Belief and Practice*, edited by G. J. Cuming and D. Baker. Cambridge: Cambridge University Press, 1972.
Walsh, Richard, ed. *The Writings of Christopher Gadsden*. Columbia: University of South Carolina Press, 1966.
Walzer, Arthur E. *George Campbell: Rhetoric in the Age of Enlightenment*. Albany: State University of New York Press, 2003.
Warner, Michael. *The Letters of the Republic: Publication and the Public Sphere in Eighteenth-century America*. Cambridge, MA: Harvard University Press, 1990.
———. *Publics and Counterpublics*. New York: Zone, 2002.
Warren-Adams Letters. 2 vols. Boston: Massachusetts Historical Society, 1917-25.
Weber, Donald. *Rhetoric and History in Revolutionary New England*. New York: Oxford University Press, 1988.
Weber, Max. *From Max Weber: Essays in Sociology*. New York: Oxford University Press, 1958.
Wecter, Dixon. "Thomas Paine and the Franklins." *American Literature* 12 (1940): 306-317.
Wesley, John. *Sermons on Several Occasions*. London, 1746.
West, E. G. "Tom Paine's Voucher Scheme for Public Education." *Southern Economic Journal* 33 (1967): 378-382.
West, Samuel. *A Sermon Preached before the Honorable Council, and the Honorable House of Representatives, of the Colony of the Massachusetts-Bay, in New-England. May 29th, 1776. Being the Anniversary for the Election of the Honorable Council for the Colony*. Boston: John Gill, 1776.
Wilkes, John. *The Speeches of Mr. Wilkes in the House of Commons*. London, 1786.
Willard, Margaret M., ed. *Letters on the American Revolution, 1774-1776*. Boston and New York: Houghton Mifflin, 1925.
Willcox, William B., ed. *The Papers of Benjamin Franklin*. Vols. 21-22. New Haven: Yale University Press, 1978.
Williams, Gwyn A. "Tom Paine." *New Society*, August 6, 1970.
Williamson, Audrey. *Thomas Paine: His Life, Work, and Times*. London: Allen & Unwin, 1973.
———. *Wilkes, A Friend to Liberty*. London: Allen & Unwin, 1974.

Wills, Garry. *Inventing America: Jefferson's Declaration of Independence.* Boston: Houghton Mifflin, 2002 [1978].
Wilson, David A. *Paine and Cobbett: The Transatlantic Connection.* Toronto: McGill-Queens University Press, 1988.
Witherspoon, John. *The Dominion of Providence over the Passions of Men. A Sermon, Preached at Princeton, on the 17th of May, 1776. ... To Which is Added, An Address to the Natives of Scotland, Residing in America.* The fourth edition [Belfast], 1777.
Wolfe, Edwin, II. *The Book Culture of a Colonial American City: Philadelphia Books, Bookmen, and Booksellers.* Oxford: Clarendon Press, 1988.
———. *John Dickinson, Forgotten Patriot.* Wilmington, DE: Friends of the John Dickinson Mansion, 1967.
Woll, Walter. *Thomas Paine: Motives for Rebellion.* New York: Peter Lang, 1992.
Wood, Gordon S. *The Americanization of Benjamin Franklin.* New York: Penguin, 2005.
———. *The American Revolution: A History.* New York: Random House, 2002.
———. "Conspiracy and the Paranoid Style: Causality and Deceit in the Eighteenth Century." *William and Mary Quarterly*, 3rd ser., 39 (1982): 401-441.
———. *The Creation of the American Republic, 1776-1787.* Chapel Hill: University of North Carolina Press, 1969.
———."The Democratization of Mind in the American Revolution," In *Leadership in the American Revolution*, 63-89. Washington, DC: Library of Congress, 1974.
———. *Radicalism of the American Revolution.* New York: Vintage Books, 1993.
———. *Revolutionary Characters: What Made the Founders Different.* New York: Penguin, 2006.
Woodward, William E. *Tom Paine: America's Godfather, 1737-1809.* Westport, CT: Greenwood, 1973.
Young, Eleanor. *Forgotten Patriot, Robert Morris.* New York: Macmillan, 1950.
Zall, Paul M. *Benjamin Franklin's Humor.* Lexington: The University Press of Kentucky, 2005.
Zarefsky, David. *Lincoln, Douglas, and Slavery: In the Crucible of Public Debate.* Chicago: University of Chicago Press, 1990.
Ziff, Larzer. *Writing in the New Nation: Prose, Print, and Politics in the Early United States.* New Haven, CT: Yale University Press, 1991.

Index

Adams, Abigail xxiii, 243, 456,

Adams, John xxiii, xxv, 4, 13-14, 17-18, 28-29, 32n, 46, 64, 76n, 115, 124n, 132, 162, 164n, 177, 207, 212, 222, 225-226, 235n, 260, 263, 275n, 278n, 290, 296, 299, 303, 319n, 321n, 325, 351, 368, 372-374, 396n, 406, 420, 455-460, 487, 506n, 518, 524, 526-530, 532-534, 540, 547, 549, 550n-551n, 553n

Adams, Samuel xxxiii, 64, 112, 132, 240-241, 243, 258, 261-263, 275n, 277n, 287, 303, 351, 405, 420, 450n, 455, 468-469, 551n, 553n

Aesop 84, 194-195, 233n, 442

"Aesop, Junior" 442

Age of Reason xxiii, 73, 81-82, 95, 226

Agreement (Non-Importation, Non-Exportation) xv, xvi, 54

Aitken, Robert xxiv, 39, 40, 41, 43, 67, 68, 73n, 76, 77, 135, 233n, 270, 277n, 279n, 322n, 463,

Allen, Andrew 483, 488, 511n

Allen, James 439-440, 488-490, 495-496, 511n-513n

Allen, John 9

Allen, William 488, 496, 511n

almanacs 8, 32, 44, 48, 50, 57, 58, 91, 187, 188, 189, 190, 192-196, 231-232, 467

Almon, John xx, 349, 36,

American Crisis xxiii, 109, 111, 153, 157, 193, 202, 214-216, 227-228, 237, 267, 268, 277n, 280, 427,

American Philosophical Society xxiii, 41, 127, 128, 130, 136, 164n, 197, 210, 230n, 299,

American Revolution xxix, xxx, 6, 7, 8, 9, 10, 13, 22, 26, 27, 32, 68, 74, 98, 120, 121, 122, 215, 234n, 240, 275n, 279n, 292, 294, 295, 296, 326, 327, 329, 332, 341, 362n, 396n, 397n, 461, 509n, 513n, 516, 542, 544, 550n, 555,

Anderson, Benedict xxix, 91

"Appeal to Heaven" 21, 22, 84, 116

argument (argumentation) xxx-xxxi, 9-10, 12, 17, 21-22, 30, 40, 42, 49-50, 53, 56, 59-60, 67, 69, 80-81, 83, 86-91, 101, 111, 114, 119, 140, 143, 145, 154, 156-157, 162-163, 167n, 172, 184-185, 190, 192, 200, 203-204, 215-220, 222-223, 242-243, 247-249, 251, 259, 261, 263, 266-267, 271, 273-274, 284, 286, 288-290, 305-306, 311-313, 316-318, 341, 348, 350-351, 353, 358, 370, 373, 379, 384, 386-388, 393, 407, 411, 415-419, 421, 424-426, 429-436, 441-444, 448-449, 457-458, 465, 469-472, 476, 478-479, 486, 515, 522, 532-533, 536-537, 554, 574-575, 578, 583, 594, 601-602

"Aristides" 306, 307, 311, 323n, 441, 442

aristocrat 291

Arnold, Benedict 268, 327

artisans 9, 27, 53, 132, 156, 251, 375, 449, 480

Atlantic xxvi, 3, 10, 11, 99, 106, 118, 128, 135, 177, 238, 308, 338, 348, 351, 369, 450n, 458, 505

Austin, John xxix

author xxxiii, 6, 9, 12, 14, 42, 44, 46, 53, 58, 61, 62, 63, 64, 65, 66, 67, 76n, 78, 84, 99, 102, 103, 112, 141, 145, 166, 205, 216, 232n, 241, 246, 248, 254, 255, 256, 258, 259, 260, 261, 276, 283, 284, 288, 289, 290, 291, 304, 305, 306, 307, 312, 315, 318, 319n, 339, 341, 348, 353

authority xxxii, 2, 3, 12, 15, 20, 24, 30, 56, 80-81, 83-85, 88-89, 97, 101, 105, 107-108, 110, 113, 117-119, 142-143, 146, 162, 171, 177, 184-185, 204, 232, 255, 262, 282, 294, 300, 305, 311, 327, 333-335, 345-347, 354, 358, 359, 369, 382, 402, 412, 414, 415, 418, 428, 433, 437, 438, 439, 448, 459, 465, 468, 475, 476, 477, 479, 480, 482, 490, 492-495, 497, 499, 500, 502-503, 505, 509n, 510n, 511n, 513n, 520, 522, 528-529, 548, 550, 567, 571, 578, 584, 585-586, 594, 596, 606-607, 609

Aylett, William 290

Ayres, Captain 467

Bache, Benjamin Franklin 32, 134-135, 164

Bailyn, Bernard 176, 397

Baltimore, Lord 477

Bartlett, Josiah 59, 75n, 257, 260, 277n-278n, 551n

Barton, Thomas (Reverend) 173, 199, 211, 234-235, 401, 450

battle xii, xv, xvii, xxvi, 2-3, 21-23, 34, 39, 51, 72-73, 79, 102, 111, 161, 223, 239-240, 256, 266-270, 272, 274, 316, 343, 367, 382, 390, 403, 424, 428, 504, 526, 528, 569, 572-573, 602

Belfast 349

Belknap, Jeremy (Reverend) xxxii, xxxiiin, 119, 237, 278n,

Bell, Robert viii, xvii-xviii, xix, 41, 43, 44, 46, 50-69, 75n-77n, 96, 110, 132, 245-247, 251, 254-257, 276n, 277n, 288, 305, 310-311, 322n,

Ben-Saddi, Nathan 51

Biddle, Edward 74n, 483, 506n

Biddle, Owen 38, 130, 136, 164n, 197, 504, 508n, 514n

bicameralism 455, 457-460

Black, Edwin xxix

Blackstone, William 51, 78, 142, 443, 453n

Bland, Richard 295

Bolingbroke, Lord 31, 138, 142

book viii, xxvii-xxx, 8, 10-11, 15, 26, 39-41, 45-47, 50-55, 57-61, 64, 66-69, 73n, 75n-77n, 81-84, 90-91, 132, 137, 140-145, 151, 156, 158, 175, 177, 187-188, 190, 230n, 241, 246-247, 254-256, 270, 279n, 284, 309, 315, 322n-323n, 339-340, 349, 351, 375, 380, 391, 396n-398n,

400-442, 450n, 452n, 457, 461, 465, 469, 496, 506n, 510n, 516, 547, 551n, 554-556

Boston xv, xviii, xxvi, 51, 70-71, 75n, 100, 121n, 132, 176, 190, 201, 204, 234n, 239-243, 252, 255, 261, 264, 268-269, 276n, 299, 308, 329, 335, 339, 380, 410, 467-468, 549, 579, 607

Boswell, James 465

Boudinot, Elias 358, 359, 362n, 553n

Boulton, James xxix, 122n-123n, 353, 362n

Bradford, Thomas xvii, 42, 59, 61, 63-65, 68, 164n, 245, 254, 256, 276n-277n, 291, 307-308, 313, 322n-323n, 359, 397n-398n, 405, 450n, 452, 463, 466-467, 490, 514n, 531, 555, 556, 557

Bradford, William xvii, 59, 63-65, 68, 245, 254, 256, 276n-277n, 291, 307-308, 313, 322n-323n, 359, 392, 397n-398n, 405, 450n, 452n, 463, 466-467, 490, 496, 508n, 514n, 531, 555-557

Braxton, Carter 295, 303, 321-322

British xvi-xviii, xxiv, xxv-xxviii, 2-6, 10-12, 15-16, 21-22, 24-25, 28-30, 33n, 37-39, 46, 48, 54-55, 57, 60, 63, 70, 71-72, 74n, 79-80, 86-88, 90, 92, 99-103, 105-108, 111-112, 114, 117, 123n-125n, 127, 133-134, 138, 141, 144-148, 150-151,154, 176-177, 180, 181-182, 184-186, 192-196, 204, 208, 220, 222, 225, 232n, 237-239, 247, 252-254, 262, 264, 267, 269, 272-274, 279n, 282, 288-289, 291, 293, 297-302, 304-305, 310, 312-314, 316, 318, 327, 329-354, 356-357, 362n, 364, 365, 369-370, 377, 379-380, 389, 391, 393-395, 397n, 402-403, 410, 412, 416, 422-423, 430, 434, 439, 440, 444, 446, 458, 463-467, 470, 473, 476-478, 480, 483, 485, 491, 495, 498-499, 502, 504-505, 510n, 516, 520-523, 525, 529, 531, 532, 534-536, 545-548, 550n, 555, 577-578, 583-584, 591, 594, 597

British Constitution xxviii, 10, 15, 22, 29, 86, 88, 90, 92, 99, 101-102, 105, 108, 146-148, 150, 154, 184-186, 225, 273, 291, 305, 312-313, 316, 332-333, 348, 354, 365, 380, 423, 477, 520-522, 525, 535-536, 545-546, 550n

broadsheets 45, 54

broadsides 2, 3, 8, 32n, 38, 45, 47, 49, 54, 57

Brunswick, Duke of 114, 395

Bunker Hill xv, 73n, 79, 159, 225, 404, 582

Burgh, James 10, 19-20, 33n, 41, 50-52, 62, 75n-76n, 141-143, 166, 339-340, 349, 351-352, 597

Burke, Edmund xxix, 11, 25, 107, 110, 123n, 224-225, 229, 322n, 343, 347-348, 361n

Cadwalader, Colonel 492

"Candidus" xviii, 55, 305-306, 312, 322n-323n

Cannon, James xviii, 122n, 411-412, 415, 420, 422, 451n, 468-469, 488, 491, 504,

Carpenter, Samuel 466

Carpenters' Hall 335, 461-462, 498, 502, 514n

Carroll, Charles, of Annapolis (father) xxiii, 331

Carroll, Charles, of Carrollton (son) xxiii, 122, 331-332, 360n, 551n-552n

Carter, Landon (Colonel) 261, 278n, 286, 290-291, 295, 301, 320n-323n

The Case of the Officers of Excise 4, 32, 163

"Cassandra" xii, xviii, 411-413, 415-417, 420, 422-423, 440, 446, 451n-452n,

Catholic 25, 81, 83, 86-87, 92, 121n-122n, 185, 194, 299, 331, 421, 439, 476, 510

"Cato" (William Smith) xviii-xix, 96, 276n, 301, 322n, 400-401, 411-436, 440-449, 450n-453n, 488

Cato's Letters (Trenchard and Gordon) 20-21, 34n, 56

causality (Cause or Causes) x, xii, xxx, 123n, 140, 147, 163, 175-176, 243, 281, 428

Chalmers, James xviii, 51, 74n, 305-307, 329, 351, 386

charter 29, 92, 117, 173, 220, 272, 298, 335, 402-403, 407, 414-417, 422, 428, 437-438, 476, 479, 486, 492-493, 502-503, 520, 546, 586, 595

Chase, Samuel 331, 524, 540

church 20, 25, 51, 75, 79, 81, 83-84, 86-87, 92-94, 105, 120, 129, 194, 250, 252, 326, 336, 385-386, 389-391, 398n, 401-402, 405, 410, 445, 450n, 470, 488, 510n

circulation xi, xxx, 32, 49, 54, 58, 59, 63, 76n, 84, 177, 247, 252-257, 260, 276n-277n, 282, 307-309, 352, 455, 481, 484, 519, 552, 556

Cist, Carl 65, 236n, 244, 255, 277n, 556

"Civis" 486-488, 511n

Clark, Abraham 539, 552n

class xii, 9, 11-12, 14-16, 38, 47, 49, 82, 127, 132, 134, 149, 166, 237, 286, 292, 295, 298, 315, 323n, 326, 328, 353, 360n, 374, 374-375, 388, 397n, 402, 419, 458, 473, 478, 488, 504, 510n, 537, 550n, 558, 579

clergy xii, 93, 128, 173, 188, 283-284, 336, 365, 385-386, 390-391, 395, 398n, 401-402

Clifford, Thomas, Jr. 376, 397

Clinton, Henry (General) 236, 291, 320n

Clitherall, James 491-492, 512n, 514n

clock 42, 127, 132, 144, 150, 169, 172, 173, 178, 180-181, 185, 190, 197-199, 209-210, 212, 214, 220, 223, 230n, 394, 463, 508n, 541

Clymer, George 322n, 439, 488, 504, 511n

coffee houses 32, 57, 144, 245, 249, 309, 463, 464-466, 470, 508

College of Philadelphia xvii, 38, 173-175, 197, 211, 385, 391, 395, 402, 411, 468

colonies xv, xvi, xxv-xxix, xxxi-xxxii, 2, 5-6, 11-12, 15, 23, 29, 37, 40, 44, 46-48, 51-52, 54-55, 70-72, 73n,

79, 83, 86-87, 91-92, 100, 103, 106-108, 111, 113-115, 116, 119, 128, 132, 149-150, 158, 162, 173-174, 176-178, 183, 185, 187, 190, 203, 207-208, 211, 215-216, 219-220, 222, 228-229, 233n, 238-240, 244-245, 251-256, 258-265, 269-270, 272-274, 275n, 279n, 281-284, 286, 288-296, 299, 301-302, 307-309, 311-313, 315-317, 325, 328-333, 337, 341-346, 348, 350-351, 354, 356-359, 360n, 365, 367-370, 372-376, 379-381, 383, 386-387, 393-394, 397n, 405, 407-408, 410, 412, 414, 419, 422-426, 428, 434, 437, 440-442, 444-445, 451n, 454-459, 462-463, 467-468, 470, 474, 476-480, 490-493, 498-499, 501, 503, 505, 509n-510n, 514n, 518-525, 527-529, 531-535, 537-539, 542, 548-549, 550n-551n, 574-577, 582-586, 594, 604

commissioners 110, 207, 293, 301, 330, 345, 347, 367, 376-377, 393-395, 400, 410, 412-413, 415-416, 428, 451n-452n, 480, 487, 490, 525

Committee of Inspection 257, 414-418, 468-469, 480-481, 485, 490-493, 499-500, 503, 505, 509n, 512n-513n, 526

Committee of Privates 501-502, 513n

Committee of Safety 37-38, 73n, 161, 257-258, 295, 496, 500, 507

committees 32n, 37, 161, 197, 229, 259, 302, 328, 358, 380, 395, 410, 414, 418, 432, 439, 481, 491-492, 498-500, 502-503, 505, 514n, 520, 534-535, 605

"A Common Man" 316

Common Sense xv-xvii, xix-xx, xxiii, xxv, xxvi-xxix, xxxi, xxxiii, 8-10, 13-14, 16-23, 25, 29-30, 32n-33n, 40-42, 44-46, 50-51, 53, 55-56, 58-69, 71-72, 73n-77n, 80-83, 85-93, 95-96, 99, 109-112, 114, 117-118, 122, 127, 131-134, 136-137, 141-143, 145-151, 153-154, 156-163, 164n, 168n, 172-173, 175-178, 181-185, 190-195, 200, 202-208, 214-218, 222-223, 225-226, 228-229, 230n-231n, 235n-236n, 238-264, 266-268, 270-274, 275n-277n, 280-284, 286-291, 294-295, 297, 301, 304-308, 310-318, 319n-323n, 325-326, 334, 336, 338, 341-342, 346-354, 356-357, 359, 362n, 367, 369-371, 375, 382, 384, 386-389, 391, 393, 395, 398n, 401, 407, 412-413, 416-418, 419-422, 424-427, 429-431, 434-435, 441-444, 446-448, 455-458, 463, 465, 469-475, 478-479, 481, 484, 495, 504-505, 506n, 511n, 515-517, 519, 521, 523, 535-536, 542-543, 545-549, 550n, 554-557, 559, 575, 592

composition xxvi, xxviii, xxix, 9, 37, 40, 42, 47, 59, 77n, 109, 116, 132, 136, 141, 146, 149, 245-246, 310-311, 321n, 340, 402, 469, 479, 506n, 519, 533, 563,

Congress, Continental xv-xviii, xx-xxi, xxiii-xxiv, xxvi-xxvii, xxxi-xxxii, 4, 13-14, 16, 36-38, 59, 73n, 76n, 107, 109-110, 115-116, 120, 149, 176-177, 206, 211, 222-223, 229, 242, 244, 252, 256-258, 262-264, 266, 271-272, 275n-277n, 284, 292-302, 304-305, 312, 322n, 325, 330-332, 334-335, 340-341, 345, 351, 357-359, 361n, 367-369, 376, 379-382, 385, 388, 391, 394-395, 396n, 404-407, 411-412, 418, 429, 448-449, 450n, 455, 458-460, 462, 466, 468, 479, 482-484, 490-492, 497, 499-503, 505, 506n-511n, 513n, 516-526, 528-529, 532-534, 536-537, 539-540, 542, 548, 550n-552n, 585

Congress, Provincial xix, xxi, xxxi-xxxii, 48, 109, 115, 242, 257, 260, 286-287, 293-294, 320n, 357-358, 367-368, 376, 462, 497, 506n-508n, 516-517, 534

Connecticut xx, 71, 124n, 211, 250, 255-256, 259, 265, 276n-277n, 281, 283, 284, 294, 318, 319n, 476, 524-525, 538

connection(s) 114, 183, 257, 266, 288, 304, 364, 384, 410, 420, 429, 532, 547, 597

constitution (general) xix, xxi, xxviii, xxxi-xxxii, 9-10, 13-16, 18, 22, 25-26, 28-30, 34n, 50, 86, 88, 90, 92, 98-105, 107-108, 110-111, 114, 117, 119, 146-148, 150, 154, 184-186, 192, 223, 225-226, 265, 273, 276n, 287, 291-292, 301, 305-306, 312-314, 316, 328-333, 337, 346, 348, 350, 354, 357-358, 365, 368, 379-381, 386, 388, 390, 397n, 413, 414-419, 422-428, 432-434, 437-438, 442, 444, 450n, 453n, 456, 458, 461, 473, 477, 481, 485-487, 490, 492-495, 497, 500-501, 503, 505, 511n, 517, 519-522, 524-525, 535-536, 543-549, 550n-551n, 557, 560, 562-565, 573, 578, 582, 587, 590, 600, 602, 604, 606

Constitution, British (English) xxviii, 10, 15, 18, 22, 25, 28-29, 86, 88, 90, 92, 99, 101-105, 108, 146-148, 150, 154, 184-186, 225-226, 273, 291-292, 305, 312-313, 316, 328, 332-333, 348, 350, 354, 365, 380, 388, 397n, 423, 426, 434, 437, 444, 477, 520-522, 525, 535-536, 545-546, 550n, 557, 560, 562-565, 573, 578, 582

Constitution (of the United States) 13-14, 16, 26, 28, 226, 273, 292, 544-546, 548

Continental Army xvii, 27, 37, 60, 71, 120, 192, 207, 239, 250, 257, 264, 267-272, 278n, 327, 413, 456

controversy xxvii-xxix, 9, 36, 48-50, 52, 60, 67, 77n, 99-101, 105, 107, 112, 123n, 127, 144, 216, 255, 257-259, 279n, 284, 304, 307, 310-311, 316-317, 329, 333, 335, 338-340, 343, 352, 360n-362n, 369, 372, 382, 395, 397n, 401, 408, 410-411, 413, 416, 422-423, 430, 436, 440-443, 446, 448, 451n, 481-482, 498, 522, 524, 574

convention xxi, xxxiiin, 70, 82, 144, 185, 208, 228, 249, 250, 290, 292, 296, 298, 301-302, 321n-323n, 330-332, 360n, 362n, 381, 395, 415, 417-418, 438, 449, 461, 475, 480-481, 485, 487, 490-493, 500-501, 503-504, 511n, 513n-514n, 526, 528, 531, 535, 542, 551n, 555, 585-586

Cromwell, Oliver 12, 14, 16, 98, 389, 436, 609

Crown xvi, xxvi, 15, 19, 28-29, 36, 63, 78, 80, 85, 90, 100, 103, 105-108, 110, 113, 117, 119, 123n, 146, 150, 166n, 171, 192, 229, 242, 273, 280, 294, 296, 302, 313, 327, 345, 350, 367, 411, 437-438, 443, 445, 447, 457, 469, 476-477, 487, 503, 511n, 513n, 520, 529, 531, 535, 545-546, 563-564, 573, 582, 584, 586-587, 603

culture xxvi, xxviii-xxxi, 3-4, 8, 10-13, 25, 30, 34n, 45-49, 58-59, 70, 79, 82, 84, 91, 100, 116, 118, 127, 128-130, 132, 137, 141, 143, 151, 164n, 166n, 178, 181, 184, 189, 191, 195, 211, 214, 225-226, 232n, 244-245, 247-249, 252, 282, 284, 295, 310, 315, 321n, 333-334, 337, 348, 352-354, 356, 374, 380, 382,

463-465, 469-470, 472, 476, 482, 484-485, 503, 505, 509n, 512n, 521, 542-546

Dana, Francis 524-525

Dartmouth, Earl of xvi, 113, 124n, 344-345

Dayton, Elias (Colonel) 539

Deane, Silas xviii, xxi, xxv, 226, 279n, 320n, 523, 550n

The Deceiver Unmasked xviii, xx, 301, 321n-322n, 373, 386-387, 391, 398n

Declaration (declaration) xvi, xx-xxi, xxv-xxvi, xxxi-xxxii, 14, 22, 76n, 106, 115-120, 161, 175, 177-178, 223, 231n, 237, 241-242, 249, 257, 262-264, 266-267, 269, 271, 281, 292, 293, 295-296, 298, 318, 330, 332, 335, 342, 345, 348, 351, 354, 368-369, 371, 377, 379, 381-384, 391, 394, 397n-399n, 406, 421, 423, 429, 461, 482, 486, 495, 497, 500, 503-504, 506n, 511n, 514n, 515, 517, 521, 527, 531-534, 536-537, 539-540, 543, 545-549, 550n, 567, 597

Delaware, 128, 164n, 467, 485, 491, 513n, 516-518, 532, 537-538, 551n, 592

delegate xvi, xx-xxvi, xviii-xxiv, xxvii, xxxi-xxxii, xxxiiin, 14, 37, 59, 73n, 78, 115-116, 132, 175, 177, 206, 211, 223, 228-229, 251-252, 257-260, 264, 266-267, 275n, 284, 290, 293-296, 299-303, 330-332, 335, 342, 357-358, 367-368, 376, 380-381, 385, 394-395, 405-408, 418, 434, 445, 450n, 454, 455, 458, 462, 477, 479, 483-485, 487, 491, 496-499, 501-504, 506n-507n, 510n-511n, 513n

democracy 14-15, 18, 26, 28, 31, 92, 150, 217, 262, 285, 389, 458, 461, 479, 509n, 539, 543, 548

diary 10, 33n, 44, 54, 75n-76n, 106, 169n, 189, 228, 235n, 251, 258, 276n-277n, 281, 299, 318, 319n-324n, 340-341, 351, 362n, 389, 405, 453n, 468, 488-490, 496, 506n, 508n-509n, 511n-514n, 524-525, 550n

Dickinson, John 14, 136, 164n, 178, 259, 305-306, 321n, 334, 360n, 379, 381, 397n-398n, 425, 483, 497, 508n, 522, 532, 537-538

dictionary 2, 25, 32n, 34n, 53, 75n, 77n, 168n, 216, 235n, 361n,-362n, 400, 549, 553n

discourse xxviii, xxix-xxx, 3, 13, 17, 21, 26, 49, 54, 57, 69, 74n, 100, 122n, 142, 149, 157, 173, 177-178, 186, 215-216, 218, 222, 224, 228, 244, 251, 254, 258, 263, 267, 272, 304, 307, 312, 322n, 332, 333-334, 336, 339, 362n, 375, 401, 436, 442, 452n, 472, 477, 481, 519, 542-543, 549, 555

division 14, 100, 232n, 275n, 322n, 377, 429, 434, 576-577

Dixon, Jeremiah 129

Doerflinger, Thomas 376, 397n, 513n

Douglas, Stephen 322n, 544, 552n

Doyle, William 351, 362n

Drayton, William Henry 364, 516-517

Duane, James 259, 406, 525

Duché, Jacob (Reverend) 77n, 391-392, 404, 450n, 512n

Dunlap, John xviii, xxiii, 42, 55, 187, 190, 231n-233n, 311, 413, 442, 448, 450n, 504

Dunmore, Lord (Royal Governor) xvi, 56, 58, 176, 268, 270, 289,

Eddis, William 329-330, 332, 360n

Edinburgh 10, 41, 51, 349, 351-352

election xix, 29, 34n, 47, 74, 99, 101-102, 104, 115, 195, 224, 237, 257, 398n, 414-416, 418, 436-440, 453n, 468, 479, 481, 484-490, 492, 497, 499, 503-504, 511n, 517, 543-544, 561, 570-571, 596

"An Elector" 486-488, 511n

elite 2-3, 9, 11-12, 14-15, 19, 30, 32n, 49, 57, 82, 85, 88, 118, 121n, 127-128, 132, 143, 150, 187, 193, 229, 244-245, 247-248, 292, 294-295, 304, 309, 330, 357, 368, 372, 402, 455, 457, 461, 479-481, 484, 491, 495, 505, 512, 517, 520, 541, 546

empire xxvii, 16-18, 60, 133-134, 216, 280, 329-331, 344, 347, 349, 364, 382-383, 388, 408-409, 411, 450n, 457, 464, 510n, 539, 551n, 592

Enlightenment 11, 33n, 72n 130, 133-134, 137, 144, 165n, 171, 212, 214, 230n, 244, 341, 374, 508n

equality 31, 314, 356, 374-375, 397n, 431, 438, 447, 457, 535-536, 545, 566, 584

Equiano, Olaudah (Gustavus Vassa) 247, 276n

"Eudoxus" 444, 453n

Evans, Charles 45, 74n, 75n

excise 2, 4-5, 32n, 39, 52, 104, 134, 163, 464, 469

Exeter (New Hampshire) xxxii-xxxiii, 308

experiment 5, 16, 38-39, 41, 60, 73n, 128-130, 132-133, 135, 139-140, 141, 145, 147-148, 152-153, 156, 167-168, 175, 181, 213, 298, 326, 383, 440, 444-445, 464-465, 473

Falmouth xvi, 176, 264

The Federalist 14

Federalist(s) 10, 14, 16, 26, 121n, 226, 403, 547

feeling xxv, 59, 69-70, 94, 112, 150, 155, 172, 211, 238, 242, 287, 430, 434, 470, 478, 549, 558, 574, 579-580, 582, 584, 588, 604

Ferguson, Adam 51, 69, 144, 473, 509n

Ferguson, James 136, 141, 144-147, 151-152, 157, 163, 165n-168n, 209, 464

Fooks, Paul 491

"The Forester" xix, 164n, 322n, 401, 411, 423-424, 427-433, 435-440, 442-444, 451n-453n, 469

Fox, Charles James 108, 110, 343, 352

France xxi, 38, 73n, 81, 86-87, 101, 129, 143, 164n, 185, 264, 266, 286, 291, 301, 320n, 361n, 383, 421,

424, 426, 431, 485, 511n, 523, 532, 550n, 564, 573, 576-577, 597, 601

Franklin, Benjamin xv, xxiii, xxxiiin, 5, 32n, 35n, 40, 47-48, 61, 64, 82, 89, 12, 132-134, 136, 158, 164n-165n, 187, 241, 260, 270, 275, 334, 339-340, 344, 347, 350, 354, 357, 364, 402, 406, 463-464, 483, 504, 507n, 523, 533, 537-538

Franklin, William (Governor) 357, 362n

"A Friend to Posterity and Mankind" 207, 336, 360n

Gadsden, Christopher xxv, 370, 516-519, 525, 550n

Gaine, Hugh 387, 398n

Galloway, Joseph 164, 334, 343, 360n, 462

gender 95, 151, 275n

Gerry, Elbridge 241-242, 261-262, 275n, 278n, 526-527, 541, 550n

gentry 12, 15, 295, 334, 374, 495

George III, King xv-xviiii, xxiii, xxvi-xxvii, xxxi, 2-4, 6, 10, 12, 15-16, 18, 43, 69, 71, 78-80, 85-88, 96-97, 99-106, 108-117, 119-120, 122n-123n, 147, 150, 154, 158, 166n, 176, 184-185, 194, 196, 220, 232n-233n, 237, 242, 259, 261, 265-266, 269, 273, 278n, 286, 290-291, 293, 305, 311, 316, 323n, 326, 330, 333, 337, 342-345, 347-349, 351, 354, 356, 361n, 364, 367-369, 371-372, 377, 380-381, 383, 385, 390-391, 395, 396n, 407, 412, 417, 421, 423, 426, 428, 430, 432, 437-438, 439, 445-446, 464, 466, 476-478, 485, 492, 497, 502-503, 508n, 510n-511n, 521-524, 532, 535-536, 545-546, 551n, 558, 562-564, 566-574, 576-577, 582-583, 586-587, 594-595, 599-600, 603, 606-610

Georgia 109, 118-119, 124n, 244, 325, 370, 396, 517, 533-534, 538-539

Germain, Lord George 335, 341, 357, 360n, 362n

Goldsmith, Oliver 32n, 40, 73n, 165n, 463-464

government xix, xxvi-xxvii, xxxi-xxxii, xxxiiin, 3-5, 8, 13-24, 26, 28-30, 36, 39, 46, 48, 56, 70-72, 83-87, 90-92, 96-101, 106-107, 110, 113-115, 118-119, 123n, 133, 136, 138, 143-144, 146, 149-150, 160, 171, 182, 184, 191, 194, 201, 203, 206-208, 220, 222-223, 228, 238, 240, 242, 257-258, 261-262, 267, 270, 273, 282-283, 289-290, 292-293, 296-298, 300-301, 303, 305, 307, 312, 314-317, 321n, 323n, 325, 328-337, 339, 342-346, 351, 353-354, 356, 360n, 363, 374-376, 379-380, 383, 389-390, 395, 396n, 407-408, 410, 412, 415, 417, 419, 423-424, 426-427, 431-433, 435-436, 438, 444-445, 448, 451n, 454-461, 466, 470, 472-479, 483, 485, 487, 490-496, 498, 500-501, 503-504, 506n, 509n-514n, 515-517, 520, 522-529, 531, 534-535, 540, 544-549, 551n-553n, 556-557, 560-562, 564-567, 569, 571-573, 578, 581, 583-587, 590, 593-595, 602, 605-606, 608-609

Grafton, Duke of xviii, 99, 122n, 345

Gray, George 483

Great Britain xxv-xxvi, xxxii, 3, 5, 37, 80, 99-112, 114-115, 117, 119, 124n, 147, 159-160, 173, 183, 192,

224, 229, 239, 242, 262, 264, 273-274, 282, 288, 290, 293-294, 296-297, 298, 301-302, 311-316, 330-331, 336-337, 342-343, 345-346, 348, 354, 357-358, 365, 368, 370-373, 376, 379-381, 383, 386, 388, 393, 397n, 402, 405-408, 411-413, 419, 421-425, 429, 435, 441-442, 447, 468, 470, 485-487, 492, 498-499, 501, 503-504, 511n, 513n, 524, 529, 531-532, 534-535, 547, 551n, 575-578, 597, 609

Greene, Christopher 278n, 515

Greene, Nathanael (General) xxiii, 73n, 162, 264, 267, 515

Gutenberg, Johannes 8, 47

Halifax Resolves xix, xx, 124, 260, 367-368

Hall, John 389

Hamilton, Alexander 14, 294, 320n, 365, 396n, 461, 506n

Hamilton, Andrew 461

Hanau, Count of 395

Hancock, John 33n, 115, 258, 277n, 351, 538, 540

Hanoverian Dynasty 114

Harbeson, Benjamin 491

Harrington, James 16, 142, 457

Harrison, Benjamin 524, 531, 541, 550n-551n

Hart, Joseph 502

Hartley, David 347, 361n

Harvard College xxiv, 209, 467

Havelock, Eric xxix

Hawley, Joseph (Major) 242, 527-528

The Headstrong Club 40, 142, 463, 469-470

hereditary succession 29, 88, 225, 359, 448, 471, 476, 556-557, 566, 569-572

Hesse-Cassell, Landgrave of 395

Hessians ix, xii, 113, 393, 446, 528

Henry, Patrick 14, 33n, 207n, 234n, 262, 278n, 300, 303, 321n-322n

Hewes, Joseph 16, 259-260, 278n, 367-368, 396n

Hichborn, Benjamin 325

Hillegas, Michael 483

history x, xxv, xxvii-xxx, xxxiiin, 6, 8, 10, 15, 23, 32n, 40-42, 51, 64, 69, 73n-74n, 81-83, 85, 88, 96, 118-119, 123n-124n, 130, 136, 139, 141-142, 151, 154, 156, 165n, 172, 175, 184-185, 193-195, 202, 204, 206, 208, 224, 225, 227, 230, 234n, 236, 237, 247, 263, 270, 275n-276n, 279n, 280, 302, 310, 313, 316, 319n, 326, 334, 349, 362n, 377, 383, 388, 399n, 408, 424, 432-434, 461, 471, 473, 508n-509n, 516, 521, 539, 544, 546, 551n, 566-567, 570, 572, 590, 594, 600

Hobbes, Thomas 224

Holt, John 287

House of Commons 28, 99, 101-102, 107, 273, 344, 346, 477, 573-574

House of Lords xviii, 28, 102-103, 273, 343-345

Howe, Lord xxviii 214

Howell, Samuel 439, 488

Hughes, Hugh 287, 319n

Hume, David 74n, 140, 142, 176, 230n, 305

Humphreys, Charles 483, 537-538

Humphreys, James 124, 233n, 387, 398n, 483, 537-538

Hutchinson, Thomas 10, 33n, 340, 351, 362n, 446

identity 5, 32n, 46, 59, 64, 69, 91, 93, 97, 134, 141, 205, 254, 258, 273, 304, 312, 314, 339, 402, 415, 420, 428, 449, 505, 510n, 521, 542, 548-549

ideology 13, 16, 26, 277n, 514n

Independence Movement 98, 102, 239, 251, 259, 270, 281-282, 297, 311, 326-328, 332, 344, 354, 359, 384, 386, 395, 401, 414, 427, 460, 499, 504, 542-543

inequality 375, 431, 457, 536

Inglis, Charles (Reverend) xx, 120,124n, 166, 373, 386-391, 398

interest xx, xxv, xxx, 5, 15, 19, 32n, 40, 48, 53, 93, 98, 128, 133, 136, 145, 149, 163, 173, 184-185, 188, 191, 206, 213, 224, 237, 248, 251, 261, 265, 267, 288, 292-293, 295, 297-298, 301, 316-317, 325, 330, 341, 358, 364, 371-374, 376-377, 379, 383, 385-389, 391, 396n, 398n, 408, 413, 416, 419, 421, 425, 428, 446, 461, 469, 480, 483, 501, 512n, 561, 562, 575, 577, 578, 581, 583, 590, 600

instructions xx-xxi, xxvii, xxxi, xxxiiin, 62, 115-116, 177, 228-229, 242, 290, 297, 300-302, 332, 341, 347, 359, 376, 380-381, 395, 406, 418, 438, 455, 483-484, 491-492, 496-501, 503-504, 511n-514n, 517-520, 523, 525-527, 531-532, 535, 538, 542, 550n-552n, 596

Izard, Ralph 349, 361n, 509n

Jay, John 14, 293-294, 320n, 365, 396n, 524, 532, 537, 551n

Johnson, Samuel 2, 19, 25, 32n, 34n, 75n, 235n, 299, 332, 351, 356, 360n, 362n, 476, 510n, 524, 549, 553n

Johnson, Thomas 524

Keane, John xxxiii, 121n, 215, 235n, 474, 509n

Kuhl, Frederick 504

Laurens, Henry xxiii, 151, 167n, 368-371, 396n, 517, 550n

law 2, 5, 18, 20, 50-51, 55, 66, 70, 76n, 99, 108, 110, 117, 134, 147, 149, 158-159, 173, 176, 184, 213-214, 238, 247, 335, 365, 402, 445, 462, 479, 498, 509n, 512n, 522, 540, 544-547, 561, 564, 582, 583, 585-586, 595, 602-604, 607

lawyer(s) 373, 379-381, 384, 455, 506n

Lee, Arthur xxiii, 73n, 164n, 299, 321n, 361n

Lee, Charles (General) 1, 59, 75n, 260, 278n, 295, 301-302, 321n-322n, 454, 456, 506n, 513n

Lee, Francis Lightfoot 261, 278n, 299, 321n-322n

Lee, John 290

Lee, Richard Henry xx, xxiii, 13, 37, 62, 115, 207, 225, 234n, 236n, 267, 288, 291, 294-304, 321n, 454, 497, 524, 529, 531-532

Lee, William xxiv, 299-300, 321n, 354, 362n, 509n

Leff, Michael xxix

legitimacy (political) xxviii, 88, 281, 328, 416, 449

letter xviii, 5, 39, 62, 64-65, 74n-75n, 96, 99-100, 103-104, 106, 108, 112-114, 133-135, 164n-165n, 211, 222, 225, 240, 242-244, 257-258, 261, 266, 278n-279n, 283, 287-291, 297, 299-300, 309, 311, 313-314, 319n-323n, 329, 331, 336-337, 340-342, 349, 351, 353, 357, 361n-362n, 367, 369, 372, 374, 376-377, 380, 386, 393, 396n-398n, 400, 402-403, 410-411, 413-415, 417-422, 424, 426-431, 433-434, 436-437, 440, 442, 444, 450n -453n, 455-457, 485-486, 512n, 517-518, 526-527, 534, 551n, 556, 603

Lewes (Sussex, England) 2, 4, 32n, 40, 101, 142, 164n, 463, 469

Lewis, Fielding 289

Lexington and Concord, Battle of xv, xxvi, 23, 39, 111

liberty xviii, xxxii, 3, 6, 10, 15, 18, 20, 22, 31, 33n-35n, 38, 42, 50, 55-56, 62, 72, 81, 86, 92, 99, 104, 123n, 126, 133, 143, 161, 214, 241, 262, 266, 279n, 284, 293-294, 296, 300, 305, 308, 314-316, 321n, 328, 335, 337, 339, 340-341, 351, 360-361, 364, 368, 379, 381, 386-387, 391, 404, 407-408, 411, 417, 422, 423-424, 441-442, 445-448, 457, 461, 473-476, 499, 504, 509n, 525, 552n, 560, 573, 576, 582, 584, 595, 600, 602-603

Lincoln, Abraham 33n, 122n, 166n, 276n, 322n, 536, 544-545, 552n-553n

literacy xxix, 30, 57, 244-245, 247, 249, 275n, 510n

literary xxx, 9-11, 39, 54, 65-66, 75n, 187, 201, 234n, 246-247, 249, 253, 275n, 279n, 319n, 323n-324n, 353, 409, 441, 525, 536, 550n

Livingston, Robert R. 532-533

Livingston, William 406, 532-533, 551n

Locke, John 20-25, 34n, 74n, 84, 116, 137, 140, 142, 155-157, 166n, 168n, 457, 475

London Coffee House 41, 61, 63, 165n, 308, 460, 463, 465-470, 472, 475, 488, 499, 508n, 531, 556

London Evening Post 345, 361n

London Packet xv, 5, 135

Loudon, Samuel xviii, 287, 319n, 386, 398n

Lowndes, Rawlins 517

loyalists xvii-xviii, 245, 326-327, 329, 335, 356, 373, 376, 440, 445-446, 449, 483, 496, 513n

McKean, Thomas (Colonel) 499, 502, 513n-514n, 517-518, 538, 550n-551n

McLuhan, Marshall xxix

McPhee, John xxix

Machiavellian 16, 22, 205-206, 224, 226, 234n

Madison, James 28, 276n, 544, 552n

magazines 32n, 38, 132, 142, 466

marketplace 32n, 173, 251

Marshall, Christopher 169n, 251, 276n, 305, 322n, 420, 453n, 468-469, 488, 491, 496, 508n-509n, 511n-514n, 550n

Martin, Benjamin 136, 141, 144-153, 156, 163, 164n-168n, 209-210, 464, 509n

Martin, Josiah (Royal Governor) 367

Maryland xxi, xxiii, 74n, 122n, 165n, 174, 228-229, 236n, 256, 260, 283, 300-305, 325, 328-332, 360n, 394n-395n, 399n, 403, 477, 480, 500, 511n, 513n, 524-525, 532-533, 538, 540, 551n

Mason, Charles 129

Mason, George xx, xxiii, 22, 295-298, 321n

Massachusetts xv, xxiv, 10, 27, 37, 40, 74n, 100, 116, 132, 164n, 171, 239-243, 245, 247, 255-256, 264-265, 268, 277n, 296, 319n, 340, 351, 372, 440, 455, 458, 478-479, 493, 509n, 511n, 526-527, 538, 540-541

Matlack, Timothy 468-469, 491, 504, 508n-509n

mechanics 80, 126-127, 137-138, 144-150, 153, 157, 163, 166n, 172-175, 178, 180, 214, 228, 320n, 335, 480, 499

mercenary (mercenaries) 10, 113, 176, 373, 394-395, 424, 523, 528-529

merchants 2, 9, 12, 27, 47, 49, 54, 74n, 95, 101, 106, 156, 176, 188, 239, 286, 288, 292, 295, 308-309, 326-327, 365, 376-377, 379, 397n, 465-468, 480, 499, 508n, 513n, 523, 593

Middle Colonies 260, 262, 301, 325, 356, 532-533, 551n

Middling Class 47, 49, 127, 132, 315, 326, 375, 478

Miles, Samuel 483

Miller, Henrich xxiii, 513n

Milton, John 16, 88, 121n, 435, 457, 580

ministry xxvii, 6, 12, 21, 39, 48, 71, 79, 99, 106, 108, 114, 122n, 134, 159, 176, 219, 237, 262, 265, 268, 273, 293, 297, 299-300, 312-313, 316, 331, 339-342, 347-348, 350, 354, 402, 408, 410, 428, 467, 486, 494, 521, 523-524, 545, 581, 590

mob 2, 14-15, 17, 56, 101, 105, 118, 120, 292, 294, 335, 391, 604

moderates 207, 218, 220, 293, 310, 316, 336, 365, 369, 376, 393-394, 412, 434, 436, 444, 481, 483, 487-489, 493-497, 512n

"The Moderator" 446-448, 453n

monarchy 9, 14-19, 23, 25, 28-29, 33n-34n, 79-82, 85-87, 91, 93, 111, 114-115, 117-119, 146, 154, 182,

184-185, 194, 202, 225, 262, 273, 280, 315-316, 350, 359, 375, 389, 404, 407-408, 426-427, 431, 446-447, 458, 473-474, 477, 545-546, 556-557, 563-564, 566-573, 586

Montesquieu 15, 142, 148, 305, 436, 451n, 458

Montgomery, Richard (General) xvii-xviii, 78, 259, 268, 303, 401, 404-408, 429, 450n

Monthly Review (London) 353

Moody, James 328, 360n,

Moore's Creek Bridge, Battle of xvii, 367, 428

Morning Post (London) 351-352, 362n

Morris, Charles xxix

Morris, Gouvernor 292, 320n

Morris, Robert 322n, 376, 379, 397n, 483, 537-538

Morton, John 483, 506n, 537-538

mother country xxv-xxvii, 3, 46, 79, 87, 106, 274, 282, 327, 329, 331, 343, 346, 350, 358, 371, 379-381, 386, 483, 517, 576-577

natural philosophy 25, 127, 132, 136-137, 139-142, 144-145, 147, 151-153, 156, 163, 165n, 167n, 175, 209, 214, 465

nature xxxi, 20, 22-26, 29, 40, 42, 59, 69, 73n, 77n, 85, 113, 130, 136, 138-140, 145, 147-148, 150, 153, 156-157, 159, 165n 167n-168n, 171, 182, 185, 191, 194-195, 202, 205-206, 227, 241, 246, 269, 291, 298, 321n, 339, 345, 353-354, 359,

360n, 374, 384, 391, 409, 429, 430-432, 434, 436-437, 448-449, 458, 473, 475, 477-478, 509n, 535-536, 540, 554, 558, 562, 566, 569, 571, 575, 578-581, 588, 592, 599-600, 602

negroes 27, 58, 446, 587

Nelson, Thomas, Jr. 259, 277n, 295, 551n

New Brunswick 357-358

Newcastle upon Tyne 352

New Hampshire xx, xxxi-xxxii, xxxiii, 59, 119, 124n, 223, 237, 257, 261, 265, 277n, 523, 538, 553n

New Jersey xxi, xxiii, xxix, 48, 76n, 96, 119, 188, 197, 210-212, 230n, 238, 258, 283, 303, 306, 311, 317, 323n, 328, 336, 356-359, 362n, 381, 405-406, 500, 504, 524, 532, 538-540, 551n

newspapers xix-xx, 2-3, 8, 32n 39, 42-44, 47-48, 55, 57-58, 60, 63, 77n, 80, 120, 142, 241, 243, 253, 261, 283, 307-311, 314, 319n, 323n, 350-351, 367, 395, 398n, 410-411, 416, 441, 446, 448, 451n, 466, 486, 552n

Newton, Isaac 5, 80, 127, 137, 139-141, 143-145, 147, 148-150, 153, 157, 163, 164n-168n, 171-172, 188, 209, 214

New York xvii-xviii, xxi, xxiii-xxiv, 27, 38, 67-68, 70, 73n, 76n, 79, 119-120, 190, 207, 210, 217, 230n, 235n, 252, 254-256, 258, 260-262, 267, 271, 282-282, 286-288, 291-295, 300-301, 308, 319n-321n, 326-328, 335, 339, 341-342, 361n, 365, 376, 383, 386-387, 389-391, 398n, 401, 440, 452, 455-456, 470,

477, 480, 504, 524-525, 532, 537-538, 551n-552n, 596, 603

The New York Gazette xxiii, 308, 386, 390, 452n,

The New-York Journal xxiii, 254, 286-287

Nicholas, Robert Carter 295

Nixon, John 38, 161-162, 169n

Noah 193, 202 284, 447, 604

North Carolina xvii, xix, 252, 259-260, 290, 300, 318, 325, 367-368, 371, 396n, 428, 440, 455, 457, 506n, 516, 534, 538

North, Lord xxiii, 79, 103, 106, 108-109, 114, 293, 337, 343, 408, 412

"Old Trusty" 400, 485, 511n

oligarchy 374, 468

"Olive Branch" Petition xvi, xxvi, 12, 106-107, 109, 115-116, 192, 299, 342, 344, 381, 385, 405

Ong, Walter xxix

oppression 3, 15, 71-72, 102, 119, 160, 219, 294, 314, 348, 522, 529, 566, 568, 571, 587-588, 596

oral culture 3, 248

oration xvii-xviii, 404-407, 428-429, 450n-451n

origin (origins) 8, 13, 22-28, 32-33, 45, 51, 58, 74n, 83-88, 94, 97, 99-100, 111, 114, 139, 142-143, 149, 155-156, 162, 184, 188, 194, 203, 209, 215-222, 226-227, 230n, 246, 249, 256, 276n-278n, 286, 298, 317, 319n, 328-329, 339, 349, 351-353, 359, 362, 370, 375, 397n, 402, 404, 406, 413, 417, 426, 436, 438, 455, 461, 469, 472-477, 486, 494, 508n-509n, 515, 522, 526, 535-536, 552n, 554-557, 560, 562, 566, 568-571

Page, John 288, 295

Paine, Robert Treat 37, 75n, 450n 540, 551n

Paine, Thomas xv-xvii, xix, xxiii, xxv, xxvii-xxviii, xxxi, xxxiiin, 1-2, 4-6, 8-10, 13-14, 17-23, 25-26, 28-31, 32n-35n, 45, 50, 52, 58-72, 73n-77n, 78-93, 95-99, 10, 104, 109-114, 116-118, 121n-124n, 127, 131-137, 141-163, 167n-168n, 172-173, 175-176, 178-186, 190-196, 200-208, 212, 214-229, 231n, 235n-236n, 237-239, 240, 242-249, 251, 253-255, 257-263, 267-268, 270, 272-274, 276n-279n, 280-281, 284, 286-287, 289, 294-295, 298, 302-305, 307-308, 310-314, 316, 318, 319n-323n, 324, 334, 336, 343, 346-348, 350-354, 356, 359, 362n, 365, 369, 371, 373-374, 384, 386, 388-389, 393, 395, 396n, 401, 404, 407-408, 411, 419-420, 422-424, 426-438, 446, 450n-452n, 454-457, 463-465, 469-479, 481, 488, 491-492, 505, 509-510, 521, 526, 535-536, 540, 542, 545-548, 551n, 555, 556

pamphlet xxv, xxvii-xxviii, xxxi, 2-4, 8-12, 14, 22, 30, 32n, 36, 43-49, 51, 54-55, 61, 64-69, 73n-76n, 82, 84, 88, 91-92, 107, 112, 132-133, 143, 148, 153-154, 157, 160, 172-173, 175, 178, 181-182, 185-186, 194, 200, 204-205, 215, 217, 222, 225, 227-228, 238, 240-241, 243-249, 251, 254-260, 263-264, 267, 270-271, 273-274, 275n-277n, 281-284, 286-291, 301, 303-312, 315, 319n, 321n-323n, 339-342, 347-352, 357,

370, 372-373, 386-391, 396n, 398n, 406, 419-420, 425-426, 441-443, 446-447, 450n, 453n, 455-457, 467, 470, 474-476, 481, 505, 517, 521, 542, 549, 554-556, 558, 590, 599, 605

paper 2-3, 8, 41, 44-48, 53-58, 62-63, 65, 173, 175-176, 190, 213, 246, 248, 254, 256, 277, 309, 494, 528

parent state xxxii, 111, 224, 242, 266, 281, 292, 307, 316, 330, 346, 380, 389-390, 419

Parker, Hyde (Captain) 291, 320n

Parker, Joseph 483

Parliament xv-xvii, xxv-xxvii, 2-3, 11, 15, 21, 23, 28, 32n, 41, 43-44, 48, 50, 60, 71, 78-80, 86, 90, 99-110, 124n, 139, 142-143, 150, 176, 195, 220, 229, 239, 261, 265-266, 273, 283-284, 293, 295-296, 300, 309, 312, 318, 329-330, 333-335, 342, 350, 354, 356, 367, 369, 385, 388, 394, 407-408, 410, 412, 416, 422, 428, 444, 446, 453n, 458, 467, 476-478, 480-483, 487, 503, 510n, 521, 523, 525, 529, 531-532, 535, 545, 558, 561, 564, 572, 576, 603

Pendleton, Edmund 295-296, 322n

Penn, John 33n, 259-260, 278n, 290, 367, 457, 506n-507n

Penn, Juliana 415, 452n

Penn, Richard xvi, 344, 385, 402

Penn, Thomas (Governor) 197, 415

Penn, William 95, 477

Pennsylvania Assembly xvi, xx, xxvii, xxxiii, 50, 53, 95, 197, 335, 381, 405-406, 414-418, 423, 433, 436, 438, 448, 460-462, 480-481, 483-485, 489-490, 491-492, 495, 497-498, 500-503, 507n, 511n-513n

"A Pennsylvania Countryman" 317-318, 323n

The Pennsylvania Evening Post xviii, xxiii, xxvi, 42, 55-56, 60-61, 63-65, 308, 310-311, 393-394, 400, 412, 418, 421, 443, 445, 453n, 492, 556

"A Pennsylvania Farmer" 14, 305, 379

The Pennsylvania Magazine xxiii, 39-40, 68, 79, 95, 132, 136, 158, 307

The Pennsylvania Gazette xxiii, 42, 51, 210, 309, 312, 315-316, 411, 415, 428, 434, 442, 486, 493, 497

The Pennsylvania Journal xxiii, 42, 61, 307-308, 313, 322n, 428, 452n-453n, 466-467, 494, 531, 556

The Pennsylvania Ledger xxiii, 42, 124, 311, 404, 424, 446

The Pennsylvania Packet xviii, xix, xxiii, xxxiii, 42, 55, 207, 276n, 311, 313, 316, 320n, 336, 375, 394, 407, 411, 413, 427, 431, 441-442, 448, 453n, 480, 486, 504, 512

Pennsylvanischer Staatsbote xxiii

Pennsylvania State House (Independence Hall) 22, 128, 161, 197, 335, 426, 448, 459-463, 466-467, 472, 475, 480, 488, 491, 493, 504, 506n-508n, 523, 525, 538, 542, 561

"the people" xviii, xxv, 3, 6, 12, 18-19, 36-37, 56, 59, 85, 92-93, 96-97, 99-100, 102, 106, 112-114, 116-119, 124n, 132, 134, 143, 150-151,

154, 172, 184, 191, 208, 224, 226, 228, 235n-236n, 238-239, 242-243, 257, 259-262, 265, 267, 286-292, 296-298, 301-302, 305, 312- 316, 323n, 328, 330, 333, 335-336, 346- 348, 356- 357, 359, 365-368, 370- 371, 375-376, 380, 383, 385-386, 390, 398n, 407, 410, 413-418, 422- 424, 427, 430, 432-433, 435, 439- 440, 443, 445, 448, 450n, 452n, 454, 458, 477-480, 484-488, 490- 495, 498-499, 501-505, 511n-513n, 520, 522, 526, 528-529, 532, 537- 539, 546-548, 552n, 557, 562-564, 568-569, 583, 585-588, 596, 599, 604, 606, 608-609

petition xvi, xviii, xx, xxv-xxvii, 2-3, 12, 60, 84, 91, 93, 101-109, 115- 117, 123n, 134, 176, 181, 192, 237, 261, 298-299, 305, 341, 347, 354, 364, 381, 385, 405-406, 448, 462, 481, 491, 493, 526, 529, 547, 580- 582, 596-597

Philadelphia xv-xxi, xxiv, xxvi, 5, 27, 37-44, 50-51, 53, 55-56, 60, 64, 67, 70, 73n-77n, 78, 80, 95, 98, 110- 111, 115, 124n, 127-130, 132, 135, 161, 171, 173-175, 180, 190, 197, 204, 207, 211, 214, 230, 232n-233n, 236n, 239-243, 245, 251-252, 254- 260, 267-268, 270-271, 276n-277n, 279n, 282, 283, 288-290, 293, 297, 300-302, 308-315, 322n-323n, 331- 332, 335, 339, 350, 352, 367-368, 375-376, 380-381, 385-387, 391, 395, 396n-398n, 402-403, 405, 407, 410-416, 418, 420, 423, 440-441, 448-449, 450n-453n, 454-505, 506n-514n, 516-519, 523, 525-527, 531, 535, 540, 554-557, 559, 592

Plain Truth xviii-xix, 14, 44, 51, 55- 56, 74n-75n, 256, 294, 305-307, 312, 321n-322n, 329, 350-352, 357, 362n, 386, 419, 441-442, 453n, 564, 571

planters 9, 12, 27, 42, 465

Pocock, John G. A. xxix, 34n, 224- 225, 234n, 236n

polls 488, 543-544

popery 85-87, 194, 569

Portsmouth (New Hampshire) xxxi- xxxii, xxxiii, 59, 257, 261, 553n

Potts, Joseph 178, 180-181, 230n

Potts, Thomas 483

prayers 99, 104, 106, 297, 386, 391, 580,

press xxvii, 3, 8, 10, 20, 44, 46-51, 54-57, 60-63, 74n, 76n, 83, 110, 133-135, 143, 148, 176, 207, 245- 246, 253-254, 288, 294, 308-309, 339, 350-352, 362n, 387, 395, 413, 418, 432, 438, 441, 448-449, 469, 506n, 552n, 556

Price, Richard 133-134, 136, 164n- 165n, 339-342, 352, 360n-361n, 465

Priestley, Joseph 33n, 51, 135-136, 339-341, 360n-361n, 465, 473-474, 509n

Princeton 207, 211, 213, 359

printers 2, 40, 42-50, 53, 55-56, 58, 62, 65-67, 74n-76n, 82-83, 127, 132, 134, 246, 249, 253-255, 257, 277n, 279n, 287-288, 306, 308-310, 339, 349-350, 361n, 375, 397n, 417, 441-442, 450n, 509n, 555-556, 603

printing 8, 44-53, 56-65, 73n, 75n- 76n, 83, 110, 134, 254-256, 260, 277n, 287-288, 306, 322n, 349-350, 352, 357, 362n proclamation xvi, xviii, 38, 43, 45, 107-108, 113-116, 176, 214, 257, 273, 281, 289, 299, 345, 371, 381, 394, 396n, 416, 428, 462, 464, 478, 480, 495, 508n, 521-522, 550n

production 8-9, 41-42, 49, 57, 59, 66-67, 73n, 107, 111, 175-176, 178, 180, 204-205, 257, 284, 349, 441, 446, 528, 537, 543, 559, 599

Prohibitory Act xvi-xviii, 110, 300, 342, 345, 428, 457, 477-478, 502, 520, 523-525

propaganda 56, 216, 311, 343, 390, 429

property 2, 12, 29, 70, 82, 89, 92, 136, 143, 148-149, 173, 183, 197, 201, 261, 266, 291, 294, 307, 315, 321n, 327-329, 331, 337, 357, 372, 374-375, 416, 418, 436, 439, 445, 448, 457, 463, 466, 478, 480, 495, 537, 546, 560, 579, 583-584, 586, 592, 595-596, 600, 602, 604

proprietary 95, 98, 128, 149, 224, 300-302, 325, 328, 334-335, 344, 375, 385, 415, 417, 437-439, 454, 461, 477, 483, 490, 494-495, 497, 503, 512n, 532

protest xxvi, xxxii, 2-3, 70, 86, 101-103, 106, 111, 377, 448, 467, 491-494, 501-502, 512n-513n, 535, 568-569, 584

Protestant 80-81, 83-84, 86, 92, 117, 127, 185, 219, 279n, 299, 411, 421, 510n-511n

"A Protestor" 494

Pryor, Thomas (Captain) 38-39, 41-42, 60-61, 63, 66, 73n-74n, 76n, 130, 132, 136, 164n, 175, 178, 180-181, 230n, 548

public opinion xxvii-xxviii, xxxii, 55, 115, 177-178, 204, 237, 253, 268, 314, 387, 500, 505, 521, 535, 542-545, 548-549, 552n

publishing xvi-xxi, xxv-xxvi, xxxii, 3, 8, 10-11, 21-22, 32n, 34n, 38-41, 43-63, 65, 67-68, 73n-77n, 79, 96, 99, 101, 103, 108, 110-112, 119, 124n, 130, 133, 141, 142, 145, 151, 162, 164, 175, 178,187-188, 192, 195, 204, 207, 210, 214, 216, 222-223, 230n, 234, 241, 243, 245, 254-259, 271, 275n-277n, 288-290, 294, 305-311, 313, 319n, 321n-323n, 330,-331, 339, 349-352, 360n-361n, 373, 387, 407, 411-415, 419, 422, 427-429, 431, 441, 449, 450n, 452n-453n, 455, 457, 467, 470, 473, 484-485, 492, 497, 500, 512n, 521, 527, 543, 547, 548, 555, 590, 597, 604, 606-607, 609-610

Purdie, Alexander 255, 288, 290, 319n-320n

Quakers (Society of Friends) 81, 89, 95-98, 128, 188, 255, 259, 311, 323n, 325, 336, 437, 439, 488, 499, 508n-510n, 555-558, 606 -609

Quebec xv, xvii, 25, 60, 63, 258, 268, 327, 331, 404, 439, 456, 468, 495, 522

Quebec Act xv, xxvi, 86, 279n,

Quincy, Josiah, Sr. 364,

race 95, 202, 265, 536, 566, 570-571, 604

radicalism 25-27, 95, 294, 508n

Ramsay, David (Doctor) xxv, 6, 32n, 167n

"Rationalis" 315-316, 361n

Read, George 485, 511n, 517, 538

reading xxix-xxx, 10-11, 18, 48, 57, 72, 81-84, 88, 91, 112, 127, 142-143, 145, 153, 188, 201, 204-205, 216-217, 223, 227-228, 241, 244-249, 257, 265, 269, 271, 281, 284, 286-287, 305, 307, 331, 341, 352, 368, 374, 417, 431, 446-447, 457, 481, 487, 505, 508, 510, 517, 521, 546, 548, 599,

reason 1, 21, 23-24, 29, 40, 52, 58-59, 69, 81-83, 86-87, 91, 97, 109, 126, 133, 139-142, 144, 146, 153, 155-157, 163, 173, 185, 195, 204, 237, 241, 266, 283-284, 289, 294, 303, 306, 313, 318, 336, 344-345, 347, 350, 364-365, 369-370, 374, 382, 384-385, 388-389, 394, 406, 408, 410, 417, 420, 426, 429, 433-434, 436-437, 442-443, 445, 447, 465, 469-471, 498, 508n, 528-529, 533, 536, 545-546, 558-559, 562, 564, 566, 569, 574, 577, 580, 584, 587, 593-594, 596-597, 603-605, 607, 610

rebellion xv-xvi, xxvii, 43, 103, 106, 108, 110-111, 113, 294, 327, 333, 344, 347-348, 351, 360n, 381, 394, 471, 476, 490, 509n, 521-522, 572

reconciliation xxv, xxxii, 6, 16-17, 70-72, 88-89, 107, 114, 146, 148, 158-160, 176-178, 183, 207, 217-220, 228, 237, 260, 262, 266-268, 270, 274, 281-282, 286, 288, 293-294, 298, 303-305, 313, 316, 329-331, 334, 337, 341, 344-347, 350-351, 356-359, 364-370, 377, 381, 385-386, 388, 394-395, 405, 411, 413, 415, 419, 421-425, 427-428, 432-433, 435, 441-442, 445-447, 449, 456, 468, 471-472, 481, 483-484, 486-488, 495, 498, 501, 522-524, 529, 542, 551n, 575, 577-580, 582-584, 587, 600

Reed, Joseph 377, 393

Reformation 78-83, 86, 92, 117, 127, 219, 476, 510n, 578

religion xxx, 47, 74n, 80-83, 86, 92, 95-96, 100, 140, 142, 144, 149, 195, 203, 238, 316, 331, 353, 365, 379, 408, 411, 417, 465, 474, 477, 499, 546, 586, 595-596, 606-607, 610

remonstrance 100, 102-104, 297, 491, 493-494, 512n

representation xxx, 2, 15, 18-21, 28-30, 92, 96, 99, 102, 105, 143, 150, 175, 204, 226, 248, 257, 306, 332, 354, 417, 424-425, 434, 436, 438, 446, 475, 481, 485, 494, 502, 522, 537, 585, 596-597, 606

republican (republicanism) xxvii, 1, 8, 12-16, 18-22, 25-31, 36, 42, 44, 55-56, 58, 66, 81, 92-93, 101, 103, 113, 121, 128, 142, 150, 176, 205-206, 223, 225-226, 235n, 263, 282, 291, 315, 333, 351, 357, 370, 372-374, 388-389, 396n-397n, 408, 414, 418, 431-432, 435, 444, 451n, 455, 457-458, 464, 473, 477, 479, 510n, 527, 548, 550n, 553n, 562-563, 573, 585

"Republicus" 394

resistance xxvi, 2, 14, 16, 20-21, 32n, 37, 48, 72, 89, 91, 98, 101, 107-108, 116, 158-160, 222, 254, 270, 279, 298, 307, 326, 328, 354, 379, 382, 385, 416, 425, 437, 464, 467-468, 478, 486, 493, 499, 503, 520, 522, 543, 548, 553n, 592, 597

Resolves, Virginia xx, 124n, 296-297

Revere, Paul 516

Revolution, American xxv, xxix-xxx, 5-16, 22, 26-27, 32n, 68, 74n, 98, 120, 121n-122n, 126, 215, 224, 231n, 234n, 240, 243, 275n, 279n, 281, 292, 294, 295-296, 318, 326-327, 329, 332, 341, 362n, 396n-397n, 461, 509n, 513n, 516, 542, 544, 550n, 555

Revolution, English 3, 81, 96, 100, 105, 379, 435, 471, 477, 510n, 572

Revolution, Glorious 105, 477

rhetoric xxviii-xxxi, 10-12, 17, 26, 31, 33n, 37, 71, 91, 117, 150, 156-159, 161, 167n-168n, 173, 175, 178, 200, 202, 205, 208, 217-218, 223, 227, 234n-235n, 238, 240, 249, 264, 270, 272, 276n, 334, 350, 352, 388, 527, 536, 554

Rhode Island 54, 246, 252, 255, 260, 264-266, 278n, 476, 538

rights xx, xxxii, 22, 35n, 38, 83, 85, 97, 99, 102-103, 105, 119, 122n, 143, 150, 184, 273, 295-296, 298, 313, 321n, 331, 333, 335, 344-345, 347-348, 370-372, 374, 380, 383, 386, 407, 423, 428, 432, 436, 473, 476, 477-478, 484, 492-494, 497, 501-502, 510n, 512n, 520, 522, 536, 546, 551n, 558, 566, 605

Rights of Man xxiii, 1, 10, 18, 23, 28-29, 81, 88, 126, 191, 352-353, 362n, 454, 474

Rittenhouse, David xxiii, 38, 42, 128, 130, 132, 136, 163, 164n, 170-174, 178-181, 185, 187-188, 197-199, 209-216, 228, 230n-235n, 408, 450n, 483, 504, 508n, 511n
Roberts, Jonathon 483

Rockingham, Marquis of 123n, 377, 600

Rodney, Caesar 485, 511n, 516-519, 538, 550n

Rotterdam 352, 362n

Rousseau, Jean-Jacques 22, 142, 305, 451n

Royal Society (British) 129, 134, 136, 138-139, 145, 156, 165n-166n, 339-340, 465

Rush, Benjamin xxiii, 1, 13-14, 33n, 38, 41-44, 50, 60-61, 63, 67, 73n-74n, 76n, 128, 132, 136, 152-153, 175, 203, 234n, 262, 267, 276n, 322n-323n, 336, 360n, 420, 449, 453, 468, 491, 494-495, 499-500, 508n, 512n-513n, 540-541, 548, 552n

Rush, Julia Stockton 43, 60, 234n, 453n, 512n-513n

"Rusticus" 306, 322n

Rutledge, Edward 406, 529, 532-533, 537, 551n

Rutledge, John 517, 525,

saltpeter (saltpetre) 37-38, 41-42, 54, 60, 73n, 75n, 175-176, 270, 431, 548, 593

"Salus Populi" 312-314, 323n

savage 25, 109, 112, 237, 428, 430, 445, 471, 570, 576, 599

Searle, John xxix

Sergeant, Jonathon Dickinson 207, 234n, 524

Schlosser, George 504

science xxx, 5, 25, 30, 41, 53, 69, 80-81, 126-128, 130, 132-134, 136-

137, 139, 141, 144, 146, 150-154, 156, 162, 164n-168n, 172, 189, 209-210, 230n, 232n, 244, 305, 315, 402, 457, 465, 477, 508n, 586

Scott, George Lewis 32n, 39, 41, 64, 109, 134, 136, 464

Scotland (also Scottish Enlightenment) 11, 74n, 144, 157, 236n, 367, 402

sentiment xxv, 1, 17, 36, 58, 62, 66, 69-72, 77n, 94, 96, 100, 157, 172-173, 201-207, 223, 237-238, 240,242, 258, 260, 263, 265, 267, 270, 274, 281, 284, 287, 289-290, 292, 297, 306, 315, 330, 334, 337, 339, 342, 348, 351, 358, 365-368, 371, 380, 383, 388, 394, 406, 413, 417-418, 425, 427-430, 434, 446, 456, 458, 473, 478, 487, 501, 505, 515, 526, 537-538, 544, 552n-553n, 558, 569, 576, 600, 602

separation xxv, xxvii, 71, 92-93, 96, 109, 110, 133, 148, 150, 159, 161, 167n, 183, 215, 217, 219, 222, 239, 261, 264, 281, 283, 287-288, 290, 293, 296, 317, 325-326, 335-336, 338, 341, 358, 365, 368, 370-371, 394, 421, 424, 447-448, 455, 477, 483, 517, 532, 534, 543, 548, 578, 580-581, 589, 600, 606

Shakespeare, William 206, 452

Sherman, Roger 406, 533, 551n

Shuldham, Molyneux (Vice Admiral) 291, 320n

Sidney, Algernon 16, 101, 142, 436, 451n, 457

Skinner, Quentin xxix

slavery 33n, 41, 74n, 112, 216, 241, 261, 266, 305-306, 313-314, 322n, 407-408, 422-423, 446, 573, 592

slaves xvi, 9, 33n, 41, 52, 58, 74n, 94, 112, 216, 241, 245, 247, 249, 261, 264, 266, 289, 300, 305-306, 309, 313-314, 318, 319n, 322n, 328, 407-408, 422-423, 446, 463, 466-467, 539, 573, 582, 592, 594

Smith, Adam 11, 33n

Smith, Richard 258-259, 277, 322, 524

Smith, William (Provost) xvii-xviii, xxiii-xxiv, 96, 130, 136, 164, 173-174, 197-199, 210-213, 233n-234n, 301, 385-386, 389, 392, 395, 398, 401-407, 410-420, 423-429, 431-436, 449, 450n-451n, 468, 489, 494

Smith, William P. (New Jersey) 358

society xxiv, 5m 11, 22-24, 26, 28, 32n-33n, 40-41, 51, 69, 70, 80, 95-97, 102, 127-130, 132, 134, 136, 138-139, 145, 156, 160, 164n-166n, 173-174, 184, 197, 210, 230n, 241, 245, 253, 281, 299-300, 304, 315, 321n, 330, 339-340, 352, 372, 375, 397n, 413, 426, 450n, 458, 460, 465-466, 469, 472-473, 475-476, 478-479, 494, 508n-510n, 521, 546, 560-561, 573, 595, 606, 610

Sons of Liberty xviii, 294, 308, 386-387, 391

South Carolina xix, xxv, 151, 223, 239, 245, 252, 273, 283, 290, 299, 349, 368, 370, 462, 491, 506n-507n, 512n, 516-518, 525, 532-533, 537-539

sovereign xxvii, 85, 100, 104, 106-107, 109, 116-117, 154, 305, 350, 359, 367, 388-389, 430, 476, 478,

482, 485, 491, 502-503, 510n-511n, 519, 526, 536, 544, 547-548, 552n-553n, 567, 601

sovereignty xxviii, xxxi, 20, 88, 105, 117, 143, 154, 258, 279n, 282, 298, 300, 346, 383, 445, 473, 476-482, 484, 503, 505, 510n, 516, 519-520, 526, 542-543, 546-547, 552-553, 571

Sparhawk, John 64, 270

The Spectator (Addison and Steele) 21, 34n, 45, 54, 74n-75n, 275n, 464, 469, 509n

speech xvi-xvii, xxix, 80, 90, 100-101, 110-112, 114, 124, 156, 160, 176, 184, 186, 204-205, 243, 251, 258-259, 265-266, 269, 278n, 281-283, 293, 300, 320n, 327, 330-331, 343-344, 346-347, 353, 358, 361n, 398, 404, 406, 429, 435, 478, 517, 540, 542, 544-545, 552n-553n, 599

St. Thomas Jenifer, Daniel of 533, 551n

Stamp Act xxvi, 2-3, 32n, 48-49, 89, 253, 276n, 335, 580, 600

state of nature 23-24, 59, 182, 473, 475, 478

state of war 23-24, 462, 475

Steiner, Melchior 65, 236n, 244, 255, 278n, 556

Stiles, Ezra 54, 75n, 281, 318, 319n, 524-526, 550n

Stillé, Charles 483, 511n

Stirling 349, 352
Stockton, Richard 76n, 540

Stone, Thomas 394, 551n

style xxxi, 10-11, 28, 30-31, 42, 44, 84-85, 97, 99-100, 122n, 137, 141-143, 153, 157-158, 168n, 175, 181, 189, 244, 248, 274, 283, 307, 310, 315, 327, 339, 351-353, 392, 428-429, 434, 442-443, 456, 468-469, 471, 526, 547, 556

Swift, Jonathon 141

Swift, Joseph 488

tavern 32n, 40, 48, 51, 57, 120, 245, 249, 283, 290, 308-309, 335, 391, 464, 466, 468-472, 508n-509n

tax 2-6, 32, 48, 89, 106, 113, 144, 216, 220, 239, 279n, 292, 299, 329, 333, 335, 385, 388, 467, 476

Taylor, Samuel 64

Tea Act xxvi, 467, 496

temporality xxx, 3, 22, 32n, 80, 141, 175, 178-179, 181-186, 190, 193, 196, 200-201, 204-205, 207, 215-218, 220, 223-229, 242, 248, 270, 310, 334, 387, 471, 475, 524, 532, 534

theory xxix, 9, 88, 105, 113, 126, 141, 143, 146-148, 154, 171, 176, 201, 214, 226, 234n-235n, 312, 328, 339, 353, 356, 360n, 388, 402, 451n, 455, 458, 473, 475, 477, 494, 536, 544

Thomson, Charles 115, 164n, 509n, 538

Thoughts on Government xix, 13, 17-18, 46, 303, 321, 455, 457-459, 487, 506n, 527

"Tiberius" 424, 451n-453n

Tilghman, Tench (Lieutenant) 292, 320n, 332

time xxv, 6, 23, 38, 80, 90-91, 144, 146, 161-163, 165n, 170-175, 178-229, 230n-236n, 242, 248-249, 253, 266, 289-290, 305, 310, 315, 320n, 332, 347, 369, 376, 377, 382, 384, 387-388, 393, 400-401, 407-408, 413, 415, 421, 423, 428, 430, 433-442, 448, 459, 463, 491, 527, 532-533, 543, 558, 562, 564-565, 568, 570-572, 574, 578, 580-599, 601-604, 608-609

Tories 9, 16-17, 34n, 108, 218, 230n, 237, 255, 283-284, 301, 313, 326, 333-334, 336-337, 354, 360n, 365, 369, 391, 400, 416, 428, 433, 439-440, 485-487, 493, 495, 511n-512n, 525, 527, 593, 602, 605

Towne, Benjamin 42, 55, 60, 65, 277n, 308, 310-312, 555-556

tracts (publication) 3, 13, 33n, 45, 47, 56, 74n, 142, 154, 194, 274, 295, 303, 349, 353, 360n-361n, 387, 414

trade (artisanal) 46-47, 53-54, 57, 74n, 127, 180, 313, 396n, 445, 464

trade (exchange) xix, 37, 106, 159, 252, 261, 264-265, 276n, 282, 283-284, 292, 301, 314, 326-328, 341, 364-365, 464-466, 523, 532, 547, 575, 577-578, 581, 589, 593-594, 597, 605

traitor xxvii, 50, 161, 327, 372, 390, 394, 433, 452n, 468, 603

transatlantic 5, 47, 181, 216, 235n, 239, 252, 254, 273, 292, 310, 325-326, 340, 352, 377

Transit of Venus 128-130, 136, 162, 164n-165n, 174, 178, 197, 210, 233n

The True Interest of America Impartially Stated xx, 373, 387-388, 391, 398n

Tyler, Moses Coit 253, 273

tyranny (tyrant) 15-16, 18, 32n, 72, 90, 109, 111-112, 119, 201, 203, 206, 216, 219, 228, 265, 294, 296, 299, 313-314, 318, 332, 335, 357, 404, 428, 432-433, 449, 469, 476, 478, 494, 499, 504, 562, 576, 587-588, 599

Virginia xvi, xix, xx, 27, 56, 62, 70, 119, 171, 230n, 239, 247, 257, 268-269, 276n, 281-282, 286, 288-290, 294-303, 309, 318, 319n-322n, 325, 327, 330-331, 368, 375, 454, 497, 505, 511n, 514n, 525, 530-531, 533-535, 538, 541, 551n, 553n

Virginia Resolves xx, 124n, 296-297

Voltaire 137, 315, 400

Walpole, Horace 353

Walpole, Sir Robert 353

Wander, Philip xxix

Warner, Michael xxix, 122n

Warren, James 234n, 240-242, 258, 275n, 277n-278n, 457, 506n, 526-527, 530, 549, 550n-551n, 553n

Warren, Joseph (General) 79-80, 121n, 404

Warren, Mercy Otis 14, 241-242, 275n

Washington, George (General) xxiii, 33n, 37, 59, 82, 171-172, 195, 226-227, 233n, 265, 268, 278n, 289, 292, 294-295, 327, 373, 403

West, Samuel (Reverend) 479, 511n

Whigs, Radical 16, 25-26, 108, 33-334, 350, 352, 508n

Wigdon, James 469

Wilcox, Alexander 488

Wilkes, John 28, 40, 99, 101-105, 122n, 123n, 144, 305, 333, 349-350, 443, 453n, 477

William the Conqueror 10, 87, 185, 570-571, 577, 587, 595

Williamsburg 56, 288, 291, 294-297, 302-303, 308, 335

Willing, Thomas 406, 483, 537-538

Wills, Garry xxviii-xxix, 164n

Wilson, James 258-259, 406, 483, 522, 524, 532-533, 537-538

Winthrop, John 534, 551n

Witherspoon, John 39, 211, 263, 278n, 358-359, 363n

Wittgenstein, Ludwig xxix

Wolcott, Oliver 211-212, 235n, 259-260, 277n-278n, 406

Wood, Gordon 11-13, 26, 32n-33n, 226, 236n, 397n, 544-545, 552n

Woodfall, William 350

Woodhouse, William 64, 76n

Wooley, Edmund 461

writing (style and process) 3, 10, 30, 84, 92, 132-133, 142-143, 156, 158, 163, 185, 204, 244-245, 310, 325, 341, 415, 419, 425, 429, 434, 466

Wythe, George 406, 457, 524, 532

Yorktown, Battle of 403

Young, Thomas 305, 420, 468-469, 508n

www.ingramcontent.com/pod-product-compliance
Lightning Source LLC
Chambersburg PA
CBHW031641170426
43195CB00035B/122